CAPITAL MOVEMENTS
AND ECONOMIC DEVELOPMENT

Other symposia published for the
International Economic Association

THE BUSINESS CYCLE IN THE POST-WAR WORLD
Edited by Erik Lundberg

THE ECONOMIC CONSEQUENCES OF THE SIZE OF NATIONS
Edited by E. A. G. Robinson

ECONOMIC DEVELOPMENT FOR LATIN AMERICA
Edited by Howard S. Ellis assisted by Henry C. Wallich

THE ECONOMICS OF INTERNATIONAL MIGRATION
Edited by Brinley Thomas

THE ECONOMICS OF TAKE-OFF INTO SUSTAINED GROWTH
Edited by W. W. Rostow

STABILITY AND PROGRESS IN THE WORLD ECONOMY
Edited by D. C. Hague

THE THEORY OF CAPITAL
Edited by F. A. Lutz and D. C. Hague

THE THEORY OF WAGE DETERMINATION
Edited by J. T. Dunlop

INTERNATIONAL TRADE THEORY IN A DEVELOPING WORLD
Edited by R. F. Harrod and D. C. Hague

PROBLEMS IN ECONOMIC DEVELOPMENT
Edited by E. A. G. Robinson

THE THEORY OF INTEREST RATES
Edited by F. H. Hahn and F. P. R. Brechling

ECONOMIC DEVELOPMENT WITH SPECIAL REFERENCE TO EAST ASIA
Edited by K. Berrill

ECONOMIC DEVELOPMENT FOR AFRICA SOUTH OF THE SAHARA
Edited by E. A. G. Robinson

THE ECONOMICS OF EDUCATION
Edited by E. A. G. Robinson and J. E. Vaizey

PRICE FORMATION IN VARIOUS ECONOMIES
Edited by D. C. Hague

ACTIVITY ANALYSIS IN THE THEORY OF GROWTH AND PLANNING
Edited by E. Malinvaud and M. O. L. Bacharach

ECONOMIC PROBLEMS OF HOUSING
Edited by Adela Nevitt

CAPITAL MOVEMENTS
AND
ECONOMIC DEVELOPMENT

Proceedings of a Conference
held by the International Economic Association

EDITED BY
JOHN H. ADLER
WITH THE ASSISTANCE OF
PAUL W. KUZNETS

59066
MACMILLAN
London · Melbourne · Toronto

ST MARTIN'S PRESS
New York
1967

MACMILLAN AND COMPANY LIMITED
Little Essex Street London WC2
also Bombay Calcutta Madras Melbourne

THE MACMILLAN COMPANY OF CANADA LIMITED
70 Bond Street Toronto 2

ST MARTIN'S PRESS INC
175 Fifth Avenue New York NY 10010

Library of Congress catalog card no. 67–13679

PRINTED IN GREAT BRITAIN

CONTENTS

PART I
THE HISTORICAL RECORD

PART II
THE RESOURCES ASPECTS

Capital Movements and Economic Development

PART III
THE MONETARY ASPECTS

ACKNOWLEDGEMENTS

THE International Economic Association wishes to thank the International Bank for Reconstruction and Development, the International Monetary Fund and the Inter-American Development Bank which provided financial support and assisted in the organization of the Conference. The preparations for the Conference was in the hands of a Programme Committee. Its members were: Professor Henry C. Wallich (Chairman), John H. Adler, John S. de Beers, D. J. Delivanis and Marcus Fleming.

LIST OF PARTICIPANTS

Dr. John H. Adler, Economic Development Institute, International Bank for Reconstruction and Development, Washington, D.C., U.S.A.

Dr. R. N. Andreasyan, Institute of World Economics and International Relations, Moscow, U.S.S.R.

Professor G. H. Borts, Brown University, Providence, Rhode Island, U.S.A.

Professor A. J. Brown, Leeds University, England

Professor Hollis B. Chenery, Harvard University, Cambridge, Massachusetts, U.S.A.

Dr. John S. de Beers, Inter-American Development Bank, Washington, D.C., U.S.A.

Professor D. J. Delivanis, University of Thessaloniki, Greece

Dr. Just Faaland, The Chr. Michelsen Institute, Bergen, Norway

Professor Aldo Ferrer, University of Buenos Aires, Argentina

Dr. Marcus Fleming, International Monetary Fund, Washington, D.C., U.S.A.

Dr. Ravi Gulhati, International Bank for Reconstruction and Development, Washington, D.C., U.S.A.

Dr. Mahbub ul Haq, Planning Commission, Karachi, Pakistan [1]

Dr. Branko Horvat, Yugoslav Institute of Economic Research, Belgrade, Yugoslavia

Professor Alexandre Kafka, University of Virginia, Charlottesville, Virginia, U.S.A.

Dr. Andrew M. Kamarck, International Bank for Reconstruction and Development, Washington, D.C., U.S.A.

Professor Paul W. Kuznets, University of Indiana, Bloomington, Indiana, U.S.A.

Professor Gaston Leduc, University of Paris, France

Dr. Javier Márquez, Center for Latin American Monetary Studies (CEMLA), Mexico

Dr. Jorge Marshall, Central Bank of Chile, Santiago, Chile

Professor R. A. Mundell, McGill University, Montreal, Canada

Dr. Saburo Okita, Japan Economic Research Center, Tokyo, Japan

Dr. H. M. A. Onitiri, Nigerian Institute of Social and Economic Research, University of Ibadan, Nigeria

[1]Contributed paper but was unable to attend.

Professor G. Ugo Papi, University of Rome, Italy

Dr. I. G. Patel, Ministry of Finance, New Delhi, India

Dr. Felipe Pazos, Committee of Nine (OAS), Washington, D.C., U.S.A.

Dr. Rudolf R. Rhomberg, International Monetary Fund, Washington, D.C., U.S.A.

Professor P. Rosenstein-Rodan, Massachusetts Institute of Technology, Cambridge, Massachusetts, U.S.A.

Professor Matthew Simon, Queens College, Flushing, New York, U.S.A.

Dr. Hans W. Singer, United Nations, New York, U.S.A.

Professor Wolfgang F. Stolper, University of Michigan, Ann Arbor, Michigan, U.S.A.

Professor Brinley Thomas, University College of Wales, Cardiff [1]

Dr. Henry C. Wallich, Yale University, New Haven, Connecticut, U.S.A.

Mrs. Ona B. Forrest (Observer), United Nations, New York, U.S.A.

[1] Contributed paper but was unable to attend.

INTRODUCTION

BY

JOHN H. ADLER

THE Round Table Conference on Capital Movements and Economic Development was organized because it was felt that a discussion of the subject would constitute an important addition to the series of conferences which the International Economic Association had held on various aspects of the process of economic development, a subject of major concern in recent years to economic theorists, 'political' economists and officials of governments and international organizations. Although interest in the role of international capital movements in the development of poor countries is worldwide, it was befitting that the Conference was held in Washington, the seat of the United States Government and of three important international organizations concerned with international capital movements — the World Bank, the International Monetary Fund and the Inter-American Development Bank — and therefore the point of origin of a large proportion of the flow of capital across national boundaries. This enhanced the importance of the Conference because it facilitated the participation of a large number of economists who as officials of the United States Government or of international organizations are concerned with the practical aspects of international capital movements. In addition, participants coming from countries which obtain resources from abroad had reasonable assurance that they were reaching an important audience through their contributions at the Conference.

The papers and comments prepared for the Conference and the discussions there brought out with clarity and considerable unanimity the fact that economic theory dealing with international capital movements was in need of reconsideration and re-evaluation. This subject has been considered an important part of economic theory standing somewhere between the theory of the transfer of real resources across national boundaries and the theory of international financial relations, and therefore monetary theory. The need for reconsideration arises because of the advent of capital movements from public sources which in recent years have accounted for more than half of total capital movements to developing countries and which have been motivated by considerations which only in a very loose sense can be called economic.

The papers submitted to the Conference, and even more their discussion, reflected not so much the view that the neoclassical theory of international capital movements is inappropriate to explain the flow of capital to developing countries, but the recognition that this theory is in need of extensions in several directions in order to deal with eminently practical and important contemporary problems and to help in finding solutions to them. The inadequacy of the neoclassical framework of analysis stems to a large extent from imperfections of the economic, social and institutional structures of the developing countries (such as rigidities, inefficient administrations and widespread illiteracy) and from the complexities of policy considerations, only in part economic, of the national and international bodies which provide capital. Such issues as tied versus untied lending and programme versus project financing, such concepts as a country's absorptive capacity for foreign capital, and the various attempts to determine in quantative terms the needs for foreign capital and to allocate the amounts of available capital among recipient countries are novel and therefore cannot be dealt with on the basis of established propositions of neoclassical theory.

The participants of the Conference did not propose to treat these new problems the easy way, by assuming away those imperfections and policy constraints. They did not question the general validity of economic reasoning with regard to the allocative functions of the price and market mechanism and the dynamic role of the mechanism of saving and investment. Rather, the submitted papers and the arguments developed in the discussion tended to find solutions within the conceptual framework of economic thought. What did emerge was not a set of new general propositions, but attempts to find ways of minimizing the effects of structural deficiencies and policy constraints in specific situations.

It was of course inevitable — and in some sense desirable — that a considerable divergency of views among the participants emerged, chiefly with respect to the general validity of specific examples cited in the discussion and to the feasibility of eliminating or curtailing the constraints imposed by political and other non-economic considerations on economic performance. But it is interesting and important to record that these disagreements did not develop along 'political' lines. The conflicts were not between participants from the East and the West or between those from advanced and developing countries. More often than not the more 'radical' views were held by participants coming from academic institutions while the practitioners of development finance were more prone to express moderate views.

In accordance with the programme design the contributions to the Conference have been grouped under three headings: The Historical Record, The Resources Aspects, and The Monetary Aspects. Since for practical reasons of organization the papers could not be discussed in such logical sequence and since the various participants of the Conference were more interested in some facets of the subject than in others, the discussion — as its abbreviated record shows — inevitably covered much broader ground than the paper under consideration.

The papers grouped under the heading of The Historical Record dealt extensively with private capital movements. The chief topics which were taken up in the discussion were the relevance of the experience with international capital movements before the First World War, the role of private direct investment and the policies with respect to private investment which developing countries should pursue. It was generally recognized that for an indefinite period in the future the development efforts of the world's poor countries will depend on support by capital from public as well as private sources. Much attention was given to the cost of private capital and the distribution of the benefits of private investment between capital export and capital import countries. The contribution of private capital movements to development was generally recognized, but it was also argued that much of the benefit which developing countries derived in the past from imports of direct investment could now be obtained through arrangements under which managerial talent and technical competence would be imported, with capital resources made available in the form of loans from public and private sources. Many discussants expressed the view that a new code governing the behaviour of private investment and the policies of host countries toward private investors would be desirable while others voiced serious reservations about such arrangements. Some doubts were also expressed regarding the majority view that the cost of private investment to recipient countries was necessarily higher than the cost of foreign loans.

The papers grouped in Part II of this volume (The Resources

Aspects) dealt with a variety of conceptual, analytic and policy problems which continuously emerge in present-day development finance. There was remarkable unanimity that the total flow of financial resources to developing countries will have to be increased if the growth potential of these countries is to be realized. The papers and the discussion concerned themselves extensively with such new problems as the relation of capital inflows to domestic planning, capital movements and the trade of primary producing countries. They covered also the attempts to measure with some degree of accuracy the requirements of foreign resources and the absorptive and debt servicing capacity of developing countries. It became clear that many of the problems of contemporary development finance (including the flow of grants and loans on concessionary terms) require for their solution an extension of generally accepted theoretical propositions. Some participants argued that many of the problems of development finance were to a considerable extent the result of deficiencies in the economic policies pursued by developing countries and of non-economic considerations applied by countries providing development finance. But it was generally accepted that even if these man-made constraints on the pursuit of rational policies were eliminated, there would still remain important policy issues which deserve and require the economist's attention.

The discussion of the papers on The Monetary Aspects in Part III covered problems of price and exchange stability of developing countries and focused especially on one important characteristic of the economies of developing countries : limitations on factor mobility which adversely affect the balance of payments equilibrium. (Balance of payments constraints were also an important subject of discussion of the papers dealing with the Resources Aspects.) Although the close relation between balance of payments problems and resources problems — and the contribution which capital imports can make to the solution of both — was recognized, it was generally felt that issues of price stability and exchange adjustments deserve special attention. The discussion of the paper on financial integration led to a more general discussion of the subject of regional integration schemes. The Conference did not, however, concern itself with the various proposals to modify the international payments system, nor did it consider international capital movements among advanced countries.

One important aspect of the Conference which is not reflected in the papers or in the record of the discussions is the mood of intellectual integrity and professional modesty which prevailed throughout. Although the participants presented their views frankly and firmly they did not insist on their positions or plead the causes of special interest to them. To the contrary, there was widespread recognition that much work remains to be done to increase our factual knowledge of the complex process of development and the contribution of capital movements to it and to harness factual knowledge for systematic analysis, which in turn can serve as a basis for new solutions. In that sense this volume constitutes not only a contribution to the economist's knowledge of problems of worldwide importance, but also, it is hoped, a stimulus for further scientific inquiry.

INAUGURAL MEETING OF CONFERENCE

OPENING REMARKS

PIERRE-PAUL SCHWEITZER
Managing Director, International Monetary Fund

As Managing Director of one of the three international agencies associated with this Round Table of the International Economic Association on Capital Movements and Economic Development, it gives me great pleasure to join with my friends from the IBRD and the IDB in welcoming you to Washington.

Several of the Fund's staff have participated in previous Round Tables of the Association, and individual Executive Directors and members of the staff have also participated in meetings of other economic societies and in special international study conferences. The Fund has also been associated with the IBRD and the IDB as hosts for two informal meetings of Latin American Professors of Economics. However, this is the first time that the Fund has participated in sponsoring a fully international discussion conference such as this. I hope that it will not be the last time that we will have such an opportunity. I might say that it gives me a feeling of satisfaction that not only is one of the papers to be discussed by you to be presented by a member of the Fund's staff and that one of your discussants is a staff member, but that you have chosen so many of our 'alumni' to participate.

This Round Table deals with a set of problems of great interest to all the three sponsoring institutions. I hope that the attendance by a number of the Fund's Directors and staff at your discussions may help us to obtain new light on some of the problems and policies which concern us.

You will recognize that our interest in these questions is somewhat different from that of the two development banks. They have as a primary object the promotion of long-term capital flows to the developing countries. The Fund is not a development institution in the sense of being a provider of long-term capital resources for development. We tend, therefore, to look at the array of problems on your agenda with a slightly different outlook from that of our co-sponsors. We are equally interested in fostering the development of our member countries, but we approach this by a different route, stressing rather the maintenance of a healthy international financial climate in which the natural flow of capital can proceed without hindrance, and of a healthy domestic financial climate in which countries receiving long-term capital and aid will use it efficiently. You will understand, therefore, if I stress a little this particular section of your agenda rather than that more obviously and directly concerned with long-term development.

One of the basic beliefs which underlay the Bretton Woods conference was the conviction that the disorderly exchange markets of the 1930's discouraged the flow of long-term capital from the more developed to the less developed countries, as well as having other undesirable consequences. The experience of the Fund in the past 18 years has fully borne out this conviction. It has strengthened our belief that the objectives given to us by our founders — 'To promote exchange stability, to maintain orderly exchange arrangements among members, and to avoid competitive exchange depreciation' — do indeed contribute to the ultimate objective of 'the development of the productive resources of all members . . .'. And our experience has thereby strengthened our efforts to attain these objectives.

We realize, of course, that there are degrees of rectitude, in this as in so many matters. Nobody wishes to see repeated the situation of the 1930's. But equally it is impracticable to expect the immediate attainment of a system in which every country has and maintains a single exchange rate exactly appropriate for balance of payments equilibrium. Your discussions will, I am sure, touch on the exact significance of the exchange rate for capital movements and — no less important — of capital movements for the exchange rate. I would only leave with you the notion, borne of our experience, that the world has not yet attained perfection, and that where the circumstances of some countries make this necessary, a period of freely fluctuating rates, and even multiple exchange rates, may be a justifiable step on the way.

A related issue is that of exchange restrictions. The Fund's authority to approve or disapprove of restrictions extends, broadly speaking, only to those exchange restrictions relating to payments and transfers for current transactions. These are defined, however, to include certain payments which might otherwise be regarded as capital transfers, namely moderate amounts for amortization of loans and for depreciation of direct investments. We do therefore have considerable opportunities in this way to limit the hindrance of exchange restrictions to capital flows, and we are concerned with and have opportunities to express our views on other impediments to capital flows. I am confident that our efforts in this respect will have your full support. It was, of course, one of the unique features of the Fund, for which our founding fathers deserve the utmost credit, that they endowed us with resources to enable us to help countries through the trying times they might meet when moving towards a more liberal system of trade and payments.

More recently a great deal of attention has been devoted, in UNCTAD and elsewhere, to the very real difficulties which developing countries encounter when there is a sudden drop in their export receipts. We can help, and indeed have long been helping in this problem, under our general policies, but two or three years ago we established a special policy on compensatory financing of export fluctuations to enable us to help even more in this particular difficulty. But the shortfall which primary-exporting countries may experience in their receipts can be very substantial in relation to the kind of help which, by our constitution, we can provide. We have therefore been watching with a benevolent eye, and have been ready to collaborate in the studies of this problem which are being made in several quarters. Some of your papers will provide an opportunity to talk about this subject — and I look forward to the contribution which I am sure you can make to the current discussions.

Coming now more directly to the subject of your Round Table, I should like to comment on two aspects of the flow of capital which impinge closely on our work. The first is the problem of short-term capital movements. While one tends to think of this as a European, or at any rate a trans-Atlantic phenomenon, it is by no means always so. Many of the less developed countries have also had to cope with such transfers, and their effects on the economies concerned have been no less troublesome. There are, perhaps, two ways of tackling this kind of problem, and we have had some experience with both. On the one hand, it might be possible to diminish the loss of reserves by obtaining financial assistance from abroad, for example by means of a drawing on the Fund. On the other, it might be possible so to reinforce, prospectively, the resources at the disposal of the member that speculators would become convinced that the exchange rate would not be forced down. This reinforcement might come from a stand-by arrangement with the

Fund. Under such an arrangement, and subject to such conditions as may be included in it, a member is assured that it may use the Fund's resources up to an agreed amount during a specified period of time. I would draw your attention to the fact that this can be doubly beneficial to the member. On the one hand, as I have just said, it reinforces its available resources. On the other, the fact that the arrangement contains conditions that are designed to strengthen the member's efforts to combat inflationary or other adverse circumstances, helps to reassure the member's friends abroad — including prospective capital investors — that its problems are being tackled. But there may well be other answers to the problem of short-term capital movements, and I look forward to your advice on them.

The second type of problem with which we have recently had to cope is that of a country whose obligations on its external debts have come to assume alarming proportions — alarming, that is, in relation to its export earnings. You are aware that in recent years a number of developing countries, finding themselves in this position, have had to negotiate with their creditors to spread out their obligations over longer periods. Most of these countries are our members, and we have naturally been brought into the discussions. Once a country's international indebtedness gets out of hand, a rearrangement with its creditors, to spread out maturities, may be essential; but this is not a happy situation, and it is much better if it can be prevented from arising.

How is this to be done? We all know that in so far as external financing enables a country to build up its capital stock it is the very basis of development. All is well so long as the debt service payments keep within the limits set by the balance of payments — that is, so long as the product of the capital improves the balance of payments more than the debt service weakens it. Even with reasonable coincidence between debt maturities and investment productivity, there may be problems of international transfers, and in any event, policies with regard to foreign borrowing must be shaped with a country's eventual capacity to repay constantly in mind. The responsibility for setting the right limit must primarily be that of the borrowing countries, though some of them — with some justice — call for the capital-exporting countries to show greater concern for their problems before it is too late.

So to guide international capital movements that they maximize the benefit to developing countries is the very heart of the problem that you have met to discuss. I do not need to point out its complexities. Suppliers' credits which may be thought of as fairly long-term by manufacturing firms (for example, up to five years) may be unduly short for the needs of those purchasing the equipment, who are dependent upon its productivity to finance the purchase. One aspect, therefore, of the general issue is the relationship of export guarantees (and the limits they impose on the duration of credit) to the real needs of capital importing countries. But there are many others, and I have mentioned this only because it is one with which we in the Fund have recently been much in contact. The whole question is one on which I look forward to the results of your deliberations.

These points which I have mentioned relate to only a small part of your agenda. There are many other aspects of your wider subject which are of interest to us. While we are looking forward with special interest to your discussions of questions which relate directly to some of our day-to-day problems, we are also looking forward to your discussions of more general questions. It is with these expectations before us that I most sincerely welcome you.

Finally, I might say that it gives me great pleasure to welcome a number of old acquaintances personally, and I look forward to making new acquaintances in the next few days. I shall be seeing you all again this evening, and I hope you will find our society as enjoyable as your discussions will be stimulating.

FELIPE HERRERA
President, Inter-American Development Bank

I F this Conference had been held only two years earlier, I would have welcomed you on behalf of the youngest of the multinational development organizations. Although for a financial institution youth is not necessarily an asset, we may say that we have lost this status since the emergence of the African Development Bank and the prospects for establishment of an Asian Development Bank.

Thus in the last few years we have been witnessing a new development that bears closely on the subject of this gathering : the emergence of multilateral regional bodies designed not only to stimulate investment, in volume and quality, but also to utilize the process of association among developing economies as an effective means of overcoming the economic, political and technical causes of their backwardness. The Geneva Conference on Trade and Development made special recognition of the role of regionalism as a means of promoting economic growth.

For this reason we in the Inter-American Bank have welcomed this opportunity to join with the World Bank and the International Monetary Fund in the Round Table Conference of the International Economic Association on 'Capital Movements and Economic Development'. As an organization still in its formative stage, we have much to learn from the new ideas and the review of established concepts that a group such as yours can devise. It is interesting to note the variety of background of the experts in economic development here present, and the breadth and diversity of the geographic areas and nationalities they represent. For we can never forget the words with which Per Jacobsson welcomed the founding of the Inter-American Bank : 'Regional institutions may only be great, if they are really internationally minded'.

In slightly over four years of operations, the Inter-American Development Bank has acquired a wealth of experience in capital movements and economic development, not only through the 283 projects we have financed, close to U.S.$1·3 billion, with aggregate disbursements of half a billion dollars, but also through the new approaches and techniques we have developed in the conduct of our regional activities. It might be useful on this occasion to mention a few of these elements.

In the first place, with reference to the formation of our resources, a substantial portion has been supplied by contributions paid in or committed for the immediate future from the treasuries of our member countries, either as subscriptions to the Bank's capital or resources entrusted to our administration. The Bank's funds from this source add up to more than two billion dollars, three quarters of which has been put up by the United States, with the Latin American share supplied in gold and dollars, and in local currencies. In the former category, Latin America has placed one hundred and fifty million dollars at the disposal of our organization.

Of equal importance for the financing of what may be termed the Bank's 'hard' window, has been the additional 1·4 billion dollars in callable capital, which has enabled the Bank up to the present time to obtain 286 million dollars in the international capital markets.

The Bank has made a systematic effort to attract funds from non-member capital-exporting countries. More than 100 million dollars has been raised in the form of bond issues, loans or funds in administration, sales of participations or other arrangements, chiefly in Italy, Germany, England, Spain and Canada.

Negotiations with non-member countries have naturally been affected by the fact that those nations do not participate in the Bank's administration. While it is true that the growing interest of many capital-exporting countries in Latin America has helped to strengthen their financial relation with the areas, the policies of many of these nations still centre around the promotion of their exports, while the foreign aid programmes of others maintain a preference for bilateral arrangements.

These are the circumstances that have led us on several occasions to suggest that a multilateral 'European Investment Fund' for Latin America be set up under the administration of the Inter-American Development Bank. In the case of the European Common Market countries, this could take the form of an arrangement between the European Investment Bank and the Inter-American Bank; however, there is nothing to prevent such an agreement from including countries outside the European Economic Community.

Second, we would like to point out how development thinking has dynamically influenced the Bank's operations. We might well say that we are currently a 'four-dimensional' bank. The principal operating criterion for the drafting of our Charter was the financing of specific economic development projects. Later, through the administration of the Social Progress Trust Fund, our terms of reference were broadened to meet with soft lending demands not covered by other sources of international financing, such as land settlement and agrarian reform, water supply and sanitation, advanced education and support for housing policies directed towards low-income groups. A third dimension has emerged through the growing emphasis in Latin American countries on over-all programmes as a framework for specific projects. Lastly, a widespread interest in accelerating the economic integration of Latin America is leading us to attach increasing priority to the study and financing of projects that further that process. This is why our Bank in its role as 'The Latin American Integration Bank' — among other activities — has initiated the financing of exports of capital goods in the region and has assisted in the creation of a special Central American financial institution designed to strengthen the common market of that area.

Third, I would like to stress our efforts to achieve the most efficient utilization of our loans and the parallel mobilization of domestic resources, on which subjects various papers have been submitted to this Round Table.

It has been said that in Latin America, as in other developing areas, the problem is sometimes not so much one of investment resources as of the lack of projects and suitable institutional and managerial conditions. Like so many other dogmatic assertions, this is only a half truth. It has been our experience that the preparation of development projects cannot be encouraged if there are no assurances that financial resources will be available. The fact that an organization such as ours is offering our countries financing for projects in fields for which funds were previously unattainable is generating a surge of unsuspected national energies. This has been our experience in the establishment and strengthening of public and private development banks as well as authorities to implement rural development, housing, water supply and sanitation programmes.

There is a significant disparity between countries in Latin America in respect of their capacity to absorb foreign resources, owing to the diversity of their educational, technical, administrative and managerial levels and of their capacity to mobilize internal resources. We have tried to improve conditions in these fields through our pre-investment activities. This is borne out by the fact that in four years of activity we have made loans and grants amounting to U.S.$30 million for the carrying out of surveys, preparation of projects, training personnel, organizing public authorities and preparing national programmes. This work cannot be handled exclusively by a regional financing agency, since in its broader context it relates to the basic modernization of national structures, which is the responsibility of the interested governments ; furthermore, various other international agencies collaborate in this field.

The 'catalytic' action of our organization has permitted the mobilization of the equivalent of U.S.$2 in local funds for every dollar we have lent. This mobilization, however, is sometimes even more difficult than obtaining external loans, owing to a variety of circumstances. One of these, of course, is inflation which makes it difficult to mobilize the real value committed in local currencies for the execution of given projects. The Latin American experience has shown that inflation not only conspires against the formation of domestic savings, but also heavily handicaps the absorption of international resources and the proper servicing of contracted obligations. Nor should we forget that inflationary pressures drastically distort the financing of private enterprises and the fiscal system designed to finance public commitments.

It is essential that we view the work of the Inter-American Bank within the context of the total flow of external resources contributing to the capital formation in the region, and in relation to the prevailing trends in international trade. When the Bank was created the doubt was felt in some quarters that we might merely substitute for other sources of financing. The result however has been the opposite. Since 1960 the public external financing of Latin America has increased considerably. During 1950–60 for example loans authorized for the region by U.S. and international organizations averaged some U.S.$318 million a year, whereas during the period 1961–64, which coincides with the activity of the Inter-American Bank, the public external capital authorized for the region has averaged U.S.$987 million.

While this increase is impressive, it has been argued that it only compensates for the deterioration in the regional terms of trade and the failure of the value of Latin American exports to increase in proportion to the needs of the region. It is becoming increasingly apparent that until Latin American exports are able to generate sufficient foreign exchange earnings to cover these needs, particularly of capital goods, the area will have to supplement its own savings with a large and increasing flow of public and private funds from abroad.

It is no concidence that during periods of weakness in our foreign sector we have had to resort to international borrowing, often on unfavourable terms and conditions. This has been the source of many of the problems currently besetting some of our countries.

During the past year, the Inter-American Committee on the Alliance for Progress, after a thorough review of country-by-country estimates, concluded that regional balance-of-payments deficits on current account in 1965 and 1966 would amount to 1·1 billion and 1·4 billion dollars, respectively. If to these figures we add the value of service on the foreign public debt and the necessary minor increases in international monetary reserves, our gross foreign financing requirements would climb to 3·2 billion dollars for 1965 and to 2·9 billion for 1966.

These requirements should be met by additional public funds, direct private investment, suppliers' and banking credits. However, although disbursements on loans already contracted are estimated for 1965, for example, at 1·3 billion dollars, in addition to an annual private investment of 200 million and substantial refinancing of short-term indebtedness in several countries, the gap remaining in our foreign financing points up the need for further broad expansion of public and private financing from abroad.

It can be fairly argued that though the injection of new funds, particularly in the form of credits, may in itself afford an immediate solution, it also may tend to prolong imbalances into the future, with the concurrent disadvantages now being experienced by some of our countries. All of these factors confirm the criterion maintained by the Bank's Board of Governors and Board of Executive Directors during the last few years : Not only does Latin America need foreign credit, but such financing must be provided on conditions that will not excessively burden the balance of payments over a reasonable period. This is why an organization such as ours, if it is to function properly, must have funds that can be loaned on soft or flexible conditions in reference to term or to the currency of payment for principal and interest. It was for us a source of great satisfaction to learn that similar concepts were incorporated into a recent study published by the United States Agency for International Development (AID).

A few figures will suffice to support these views. Between 1956 and 1964, the region's external long-term public debt payable in hard currencies increased 147 per cent, from 4·3 to 10·6 billion dollars. During the same period, payments of principal and interest virtually tripled, from 455 million to 1·36 billion dollars a year. The foreign debt servicing burden rose from 5·5 per cent of balance of payments receipts on current account in 1956 to 15·4 per cent in 1964. In the latter year, this level stood at more than 20 per cent for four Latin American countries. More than 50 per cent of current foreign indebtedness will have to be repaid within the next five years, while only 28 per cent will mature in more than 10 years.

In addition to dealing with this external problem, it is imperative that our countries adopt sound domestic financing policies which, without restricting economic growth, can prevent the inflationary pressures that conspire to unbalance our foreign sector. We must strengthen the process of regional economic integration as a tool for the promotion of industrial and agricultural growth, which by expanding exports and replacing imports, can be the key sectors for greater progress and stability.

Latin America is in a position to deal with this problem, but we must have an understanding approach by the capital-exporting countries to the problem of service on past obligations and the need for an adequate flow of resources to the region. We must also have co-operation, on the international level, to prevent a deterioration in our terms of trade. From 1962 to the first half of 1964, according to country indexes, Latin America's export prices rose by about five per cent, which was only partly offset by a two-point rise in its import index. In the last twelve months, however, price weaknesses affecting foodstuffs, in particular, have probably erased more than half of that gain, leaving the general terms of trade of the area little better than they were at the low point of 1962.

All this points up the need for a broad approach to the problems of financing regional economic development, in which capital movements, debt service and trade problems should be reviewed in proper perspective and with regard to the very close interrelationships involved.

I believe that we have effectively contributed, particularly through our sound administration of available soft resources, to creating the internal conditions required for growth without excessively burdening balances of payment in our member countries. Actually, more than 50 per cent of our loans are repayable in local currency. However, it is obvious that our organization alone cannot resolve the complex problems of regional financing. In this respect, it is worthy of mention the close institutional coordination among the three financial organizations sponsoring this meeting and their basic common technical approach to the development problems of the region.

Gentlemen : These thoughts which I have wished to convey to you at the initiation of your highly significant discussions express the views of the President of an institution whose task is to assist in the efforts of more than 200 million Latin Americans who are striving for a prosperous and stable community of nations with real significance in the contemporary world. Few groups can realize better than you the rewarding aspects of this absorbing task, in which by multiplying the endeavours of our fellow men, we are sharing with them the fashioning of their own destiny.

IRVING S. FRIEDMAN
The Economic Adviser to the President, International Bank for
Reconstruction and Development

I am indeed happy to have the opportunity to join in welcoming the participants of this International Economic Association Round Table.

The World Bank is happy that it is able to offer facilities for this Conference and we do hope that they prove to be adequate.

I would like to begin by expressing the regrets of President George Woods; urgent business in Europe made it impossible for him to welcome you personally this morning. He has asked me to convey to you his warmest greetings and hope for a successful ten days. He feels, as all of us do in the Bank, that the subject matter which you are going to discuss is close to the centre of the difficulties which are now being faced by the world economy.

I have read with great interest the agenda for the Conference and have noted the names of those who are presenting papers and otherwise participating in the Conference. I am pleased to be able to say that many of them are friends of very long standing, and that I know from personal experience that this Conference is bound to be a most valuable and exciting one.

I also know from personal experience that many here have been drawn into the field of economic development from a great variety of backgrounds in the more general field of economics and finance. As someone who has travelled the same road, perhaps I can say for all of us, that we have come to this common area of activity because of the conviction that development is probably the most critical economic problem facing the world today. It is, at the same time, a field in which the need for the further application of economic science is very great. It is, therefore, not surprising to find that so many of our participants at this Conference are people who in their day-to-day lives find themselves in the dual occupation of decision-making on practical problems and responsibility for further research and thought on how to sharpen analytical techniques and improve the quality of data in this field. We in the World Bank are similarly engaged and we are, of course, pleased to participate fully in this Conference.

I do not wish to take much of your time from your important deliberations, but I would like to draw your attention to two points in development finance. The first is with respect to the size of the contribution of the developed countries to the total availability of resources to the developing countries for development purposes. The second is about the rising burden of indebtedness of developing countries. Both these points are closely related to the subject of your deliberations and I hope that they will receive your attention not only during the period of this Conference but also in your work elsewhere.

Over the post-war period, underdeveloped countries have been trying hard to increase their incomes, and some of their efforts are already beginning to bear fruit. Some of them have experienced growth rates which are equal to or greater than the Development Decade target of 5 per cent per year. The rate of increase of production in the industrial sector has averaged over 7 per cent per annum. This has demonstrated an increasing capacity to mobilize domestic resources and to absorb capital efficiently on a large scale. Agricultural production for the domestic market, particularly foodstuffs, has grown much slower, but agricultural production of export crops has risen markedly in many countries. The marginal rate of saving in a few of these countries has been as high as 25 to 30 per cent — this undoubtedly is an exceptional figure, but it is a fair generalization that underdeveloped countries have been trying, and in most cases succeeding, to save more and more of their incomes.

However, we simply cannot escape from the basic fact, with which we are all familiar, namely, that most of the less developed countries are starting from a level of income which in human terms is simply unbelievable. We have become so accustomed to the use of figures like $50 *per capita*, or $100 *per capita*, or $150 *per capita*, that we frequently forget the severe limitations that these actualities place on what can be done in the field of development. I believe that we would all agree that an average savings rate of 25 per cent would not only be high but probably simply unreal in most of the countries with which we are concerned. Yet, an average savings rate of 25 per cent for a country with a *per capita* national income of $60 a year implies annual savings of $15 *per capita*. If we then consider what are the calls in the modern world on these savings, it becomes more than obvious how difficult it is for the development process to be carried on. We are, of course, on very familiar territory and for this group I need not spell out the other difficulties, such as problems of export fluctuations, terms of trade, rapid population growth, etc., with which developing countries have to cope. As policy-makers we also know that many of our difficulties flow from the inadequacy of governmental policies or the unwillingness and inability of governments in both the developed and developing countries to follow economic policies best designed to encourage the development process.

But, the fundamental problem, I am sure we will all agree, is the shortage of available resources — human and material — for investment. I do not underestimate the complexity of the problem and there are a great many things that the underdeveloped countries have to do for themselves in order to obtain more resources domestically, but one of the critical needs is for external capital which not only supplements available savings, but performs other valuable functions.

Since the fifties, the developed countries have been extending assistance through loans and grants, which has been of considerable importance to the developing countries. But what has been the extent of this contribution in terms of the availability of resources for development purposes?

The figure for net financial flows from the developed into the developing countries that one carries in one's head is about $9 billion per year, including assistance from the Sino-Soviet countries. We do not have reliable data of investment in developing countries. However, if one takes 15 per cent of the gross product of these countries as the share of investment, which is probably not too far off, some $30 billion is indicated as an approximate order of magnitude for all the less developed countries taken together. And if one related the figure for total investment to the figure for the flow of foreign assistance, one might be tempted to say that approximately one-third of the investment resources of the underdeveloped have come from the developed countries.

However, the flow of traffic in resources has not been one way — in addition to amortization, developing countries themselves have been paying substantial amounts to the developed countries on account of interest, dividends and profits on past investments. Such payments amounted to about $3 to $3·5 billion in 1964. If we may take the liberty of allowing for these payments in the $9 billion figure, we get a figure in the order of magnitude of $5·5 billion to $6 billion as a measure of the actual contribution from the developed to the developing countries. As you all know, the gross national product of the developed countries is increasing each year by about $40 billion and now totals well over $1,000 billion.

The figures I have been giving are essentially looking at the problem from the donor or creditor end ; if we look at figures from the receiving end, that is from the point of view of the balance of payments of the developing countries, we come across an interesting fact. One would expect to see this $6 billion indentified somewhere in their balance of payments — either in the form of a merchandise import surplus or in an increase in reserves or in the form of a deficit on invisibles account (excluding, of course, payments for interest, dividends and profits which we have already accounted for).

But no such thing; we can only identify about half of this $6 billion, as follows : The trade deficit of developing countries in 1964, as in 1963, stood at only $1·3 billion. The level of monetary reserves of the developing countries in 1963 and 1964 increased by about $1 billion. The $9 billion figure of net assistance also includes a substantial amount of aid in the form of technical assistance, which is not likely to be fully reflected in the balance of payments data of developing countries. A full breakdown of the invisibles account is not yet available. However, the developing countries did show a sizeable deficit on freight and insurance account. On the other hand, these outpayments have been offset by a large inflow on military and governmental services account and some surplus on tourism.

Thus, judging the net availability of resources for investment from an examination of the balance of payments of the developing countries, we have about $3 billion that we can't identify. I will not suggest to what extent this is due to capital movements from developing countries — recorded and unrecorded, or underestimation of current account deficits in the developing countries, or perhaps some overestimation of the magnitude of capital flows from industrial countries, as we all are aware of the statistical gaps in such items as amortization.

In addition to these remarks on the flow of resources, I would like to speak briefly on another major problem in development finance, namely, the magnitude of the rising indebtedness in the developing countries. We at the World Bank have been much concerned about this problem. It is a dramatic fact full of many implications, that for a group of 37 developing countries for which we have been compiling data and which account for nearly three-fifths of the total exports of all developing countries (excluding Sino-Soviet countries), the external public and publicly guaranteed debt increased at an annual rate of 15 per cent during 1955–62 ; from $7 billion to $18·2 billion ; while over the two years 1963 and 1964, the annual increase was 17 per cent. For the developing countries as a whole, it is roughly estimated that outstanding public and publicly-guaranteed indebtedness with a maturity of one year or over may have amounted to some $33 billion at the end of 1964. This corresponds to nearly 15 per cent of the combined national product of these countries. This $33 billion, moreover, is not an all-inclusive estimate ; the debt of private parties not guaranteed by governments in developing countries is excluded and so are the obligations arising from commercial arrears.

It is very difficult to generalize on what constitutes a tolerable level of foreign indebtedness. It is easier to be more certain about the impact of debt servicing charges. The debt servicing charges (amortization and interest payments, but excluding dividends and payments on non-publicly guaranteed debt) are rising to worrisome levels. For the 37 countries that I mentioned, debt service charge increased from $680 million in 1956 to $2·5 billion in 1964 — almost a fourfold increase. For all the developing countries debt service on the external public debt alone is estimated to have amounted to $3·5 billion in 1964. If an allowance is made for the liquidation of commercial arrears and similar short-term obligations, aggregate debt service obligations may have easily amounted, in 1964, to well over $4 billion. This corresponds to about 12 per cent of the total export earnings of the developing countries ; for some individual countries the proportions are much higher.

I do not have to dwell on the gravity of this problem of rising indebtedness. It is rising when the flow of capital to the developing countries is more or less on a plateau. In the short-run there is little that can be done to reduce the burden of indebtedness, except by rescheduling operations or increasing the flow of capital. However, unless there are drastic changes in the terms on which capital is made available, the problem will grow geometrically. Large-scale rescheduling of the existing debt — in any case painful — would, of course, help technically. I cannot comment on its feasibility, but it clearly would not be a solution to the problem. My own view is that the solution to the problem of indebtedness in the longer run lies in reducing the weighted average rate of interest on which credits and loans are made and in lengthening the grace and amortization periods of these loans and credits.

The process of capital accumulation involves an ever-mounting level of indebtedness. This is sensible, but only so long as the result is an accumulation of worthwhile assets capable, among other things, of providing the income basis for the servicing of the debt as well as a surplus of savings for new investments. The subject of the efficient employment of available resources is a major preoccupation of the Bank and I note will figure importantly in your Round Table discussions.

The flows of financial resources from industrial countries into developing countries, the external indebtedness of developing countries and their debt-servicing obligations, the current account deficits of developing countries with industrial countries are all relevant to consideration of policy questions in regard to the provision of development finance to developing countries. I have attempted to bring together the available global data. It would appear that the actual role played by resources contributed by developed countries to the developing countries' development programmes is significantly smaller than the official aid data taken by themselves would indicate. However, it is difficult to be precise on the magnitudes involved. Inter-country comparisons are even more difficult than global estimates. Accurate global and country data are badly needed.

A number of international institutions are striving to develop data which could be the basis for an accurate assessment of the transfer of resources. The data on the flow of resources are published by OECD. The debt data are obtained by the World Bank from individual debtor countries; the balance of payments data are compiled and published by the IMF. A main element of uncertainty relates to what are generally termed suppliers' credits and the servicing burden they impose. Yet another discrepancy arises in respect to the allowances made in gross totals for amortization amounts. Again, as we are aware, the extent of reverse capital flows from developing countries is largely a guess. It is in these and other respects that the statistics should continue to be refined. If, as a result of current co-operative efforts by OECD, the IMF and the IBRD, it should become possible to reconcile the various sets of figures and minimize the discrepancies, it would help policy formulation in this most difficult but crucial field of development finance. Statistical refinement and reconciliation can only proceed on the basis of conceptual clarity. It is, therefore, most appropriate that the international institutions engaged in this work seek the advice of individual scholars and research institutions.

May I conclude by expressing the hope that the emphasis in these discussions will be to analyze rather than advocate. I believe that the great need is for a solid factual and analytical basis for our policy conclusions or findings in the field of development finance. Only then can we hope that these conclusions will be regarded as a necessary basis for policy making. It is indeed most difficult not to be carried away by our emotional concern, but as economists and technicians, it may safely be said that our contribution to the solution of these problems lies in providing a correct understanding of what

B

are the realities and what are the implications of different policy measures.

May I once again convey the wishes of Mr. Woods and all the members of the staff for a successful conference and express my own pleasure of having had the opportunity of addressing you and sharing the platform with Professor Papi, Mr. Schweitzer and Mr. Herrera.

PART I

THE HISTORICAL RECORD

Chapter 1

THE HISTORICAL RECORD OF INTERNATIONAL CAPITAL MOVEMENTS TO 1913

BY

BRINLEY THOMAS
University of Wales

I. PROBLEMS OF MEASUREMENT

United Kingdom

IT is now half a century since the appearance of C. K. Hobson's pioneering study, *The Export of Capital*.[1] Published in the year when the First World War broke out, the book did not attract the attention it deserved until well into the inter-war period. Hobson's was the first systematic attempt to produce annual estimates of British capital exports for the period 1870–1912. The fact that later research has thrown doubt on some of his figures does not detract from the magnitude of what he achieved. It is convenient to take this work as our starting-point in considering the quality of the sources and the extent to which the main problems of measurement have been overcome.

It is illuminating to compare Hobson's results for the period 1870–1912 with those presented by Imlah in his authoritative work published in 1958.[2] According to Hobson, the aggregate of the annual net outflows of British capital for this period amounted to £2,332·8 million, whereas Imlah estimated this aggregate as £3,073·0 million. Cairncross, paying special attention to shipping earnings and the yield of investments abroad, arrived at a total of £2,220 million, even lower than Hobson's.[3] This is a serious divergence, even though it does not materially affect the timeshape

---

[1] C. K. Hobson, *The Export of Capital*, London, Constable & Co., 1914. Reissued in 1963, with a Preface by Sir Roy Harrod.

[2] Albert H. Imlah, *Economic Elements in the Pax Britannica*, Harvard University Press, Cambridge, Mass., 1958, chap. 3.

[3] A. K. Cairncross, *Home and Foreign Investment*, Cambridge University Press, 1954, pp. 170–186.

of the series. There can be no doubt that Hobson over-estimated the size of Britain's creditor position in the 1870's by adopting A. L. Bowley's estimate of £1,400 million as Britain's foreign investment in 1875, a figure which must be rejected as too high.[1] A careful calculation by Giffen in 1878 showed that the income on British capital invested abroad was about £65·5 million in the fiscal year 1874–75.[2] By capitalising at appropriate rates, he estimated the value of the stock of investments at £1,048·3 million. When this figure is adjusted to make it comparable with Imlah's estimates, it becomes £1,038 million, which is very near to Imlah's figure of £1,013·8 million for the end of 1874. A detailed examination of Hobson's estimates for the various components of the balance of payments indicates that he erred on the low side in regard to interest and dividends, earnings of shipping, and commissions, insurance and banking charges. The main reason was his failure to take into account the profits on foreign trade.[3]

A major item in the invisible balance was the net earnings from shipping, including the outlays of foreign and colonial ships in British ports; up to the 1870's it was bigger than income from foreign investments. Much depends on the margin of error in calculating this item. Fortunately this problem attracted the attention of Robert Giffen when he was head of the Statistical Department of the Board of Trade, and his pioneering study has had a profound effect on subsequent work in this field.[4] His method was based on samples of freight earnings and of outlays abroad from a number of shipping firms at selected years, e.g. 1880 and 1898. Hobson followed his example in some respects but added a great deal that was original, especially his 'increasing efficiency factor', which led him to allow 4 per cent per annum for increased earning capacity due to technical progress between 1870 and 1912. Imlah went over the ground thoroughly and produced annual estimates of net credits from shipping from 1816 to 1913. In doing so he admits that he had to resort to the dubious expedient of using an import price index which is of necessity '. . . only a crude measure of the ups and downs of freight rates'.[5] Douglass North and Alan

[1] A. L. Bowley, *England's Foreign Trade in the Nineteenth Century*, London, 1905, pp. 76–77.
[2] Robert Giffen, 'On Recent Accumulations of Capital in the United Kingdom', *Journal of the Royal Statistical Society*, 1878, 41, pp. 1–39.
[3] See Imlah, *op. cit.*, pp. 76–78.
[4] Robert Giffen, 'The Use of Import and Export Statistics', *Journal of the Statistical Society*, 1882, 45, pp. 206–223, 259–270.
[5] Imlah, *op. cit.*, p. 53.

Heston, in a penetrating review of the whole subject, have shown that many difficulties still remain unsolved.[1] Given the primary data available, it is an open question whether a more accurate series can be attained.

As we go back through the nineteenth century from 1870 the difficulties of statistical estimation becomes more numerous. An outstanding work on British capital exports in that period is that of Leland H. Jenks, whose profound researches threw a flood of light on the subject.[2] Basing himself on the work of Giffen, Newmarch and others, Jenks constructed a table of Great Britain's international accounts for the period 1854–80.[3] The calculation indicated an aggregate net export of capital from 1854 to 1874 inclusive amounting to £332 million. Jenks paid particular attention to the problem of estimating the stock of British foreign investment at 1854, and came to the conclusion that Bowley's estimate of £550 million[4] was far too high ; he substituted for it a total of £195 to £235 million of British holdings of foreign publicly-issued securities. This was distributed as follows :[5]

	£ million
United States	50–60
French, Belgian, Dutch and Russian government securities	45–55
Spain and Portugal	35–45
Latin America	35–40
French railways	25–30
Belgian railways	5
	195–230

This estimate is the best available for mid-century, and it is reasonably consistent with the equally trustworthy one made by Giffen for the mid-1870's.

By his original research into the actual security issues Jenks drew a big question-mark over the ideas current about the extent of British capital exports in the first half of the nineteenth century. It was Imlah, through his notable work on Britain's trade statistics, who finally demonstrated how wildly inflated were the estimates of foreign lending in the decades after the Napoleonic wars. To quote his words, 'For the first part of the century, the size of British credit

---

[1] See Douglass North and Alan Heston, 'The Estimation of Shipping Earnings in Historical Studies of the Balance of Payment', *Canadian Journal of Economics and Political Science*, 1960, xxvi, pp. 265–276.
[2] Leland H. Jenks, *The Migration of British Capital to 1875*, London, Jonathan Cape, 1927, revised 1938.
[3] Jenks, *op. cit.*, p. 414.   [4] Bowley, *op. cit.*, p. 76.   [5] Jenks, *op. cit.*, p. 413.

balances and of the amount of capital export have generally been exaggerated, partly because of the assumption, which the "official" valuations of merchandise trade seemed to confirm, that British factories produced huge export surpluses at this time. Even when the merchandise trade statistics had greatly improved, after 1853, the uncertainty concerning the "invisibles" which offset the huge trade deficits left room for some very large errors. It is possible to be much more definite in these matters. By drawing on the findings and procedures of investigators who have worked on various facets of the problem by extending them over a longer period, and by filling in the remaining gaps on the basis of more or less guided assumptions and conjectures, one can construct annual balance-of-payments statements for the United Kingdom beginning with the year 1816 with some assurance that the main items are measured fairly closely, and that other items are adequately allowed for. The balances so constructed measure the growing volume of foreign investment which, in turn, can be checked at certain points with the more credible results achieved by other investigators who have made different approaches to the problem.[1] Economists and historians are deeply indebted to Imlah for providing this indispensable groundwork. Errors in some components are likely to be cancelled by compensating errors in others ; and, even if there may be doubts about the figures for some individual years, there is every reason to rely on the long-term movement and the long cycles.

A final check on the validity of Imlah's methods may be made by referring to Sir George Paish's well-known estimates for the end of the period, i.e. 1907–13. According to Paish, the amount of British capital placed abroad in publicly-issued securities at the end of 1907 was £2,693·7 million.[2] In addition, it was calculated that private placings, e.g. investment in unincorporated businesses and deposits in foreign and colonial banks, came to about £500 million. Of the interest and dividends assessed to income tax in 1906–7 about 10 per cent was paid out to foreigners ; accordingly Paish inferred that one-tenth of the publicly-issued securities was foreign-owned. To establish Britain's net creditor position in 1907 it is necessary to subtract from the gross total of British foreign investment an amount to cover holdings of British assets by foreigners ; there is reason to think that this deduction should be about 10 per

---

[1] Imlah, *op. cit.*, pp. 42–43.
[2] See Sir George Paish, 'Great Britain's Capital Investment in Other Lands', *Journal of the Royal Statistical Society*, 1909, 72, pp. 456–480, and discussion, pp. 481–495.

cent. In this way the Paish estimates give the size of Britain's net creditor position at 1907 as £2,874 million which is not very different from the accumulating balance of credit abroad of £2,913·7 million arrived at by Imlah.

Paish's estimates for the end of 1913 brought out the striking fact that in six hectic years the aggregate of British holdings of publicly-issued foreign securities had grown by over £1,000 million to £3,714·7 million.[1] Even this figure, according to Herbert Feis, was an under-estimate, in that too little had been allowed for Russian and Turkish loans; he raised Paish's estimate for investments in Russia from £66·7 million to £110·0 million and in Turkey from £18·7 million to £24·0 million.[2] When Imlah, at the conclusion of his exhaustive statistical exercise, compared his estimate of Britain's net creditor position on the eve of the First World War with that of Paish, as amended by Feis, he had ample reason to be satisfied. The latter, based on a survey at a point of time, yielded a figure of £4,014 million as against his own estimate of £3,989·6 million, resulting from an assessment of the component series over time; the disparity was merely 0·6 per cent.[3]

The United States, Canada and Australia

The difficulties raised by the unknown degree of error in the merchandise trade figures and the main components of the invisible account in the nineteenth century are as serious, if not more so, in the United States as in the United Kingdom. The section on the international transactions of the United States for 1821–41 and 1850–1918 in the authoritative abstract of historical statistics[4] issued by the Department of Commerce reproduces the well-known estimates of C. J. Bullock, J. H. Williams and R. S. Tucker published in 1919.[5] The text contains a warning that '. . . the data for the period prior to 1914 are admittedly far less satisfactory than the data for the later period because, with the possible exception of

[1] Sir George Paish in *The Statist*, Supplement, 14 February 1914, v–vi.
[2] Herbert Feis, *Europe: The World's Banker, 1870–1914*, New Haven, Yale University Press, 1930, pp. 23–24.
[3] Imlah, *op. cit.*, p. 80.
For a re-examination of the original data in *The Investor's Monthly Manual* see Harvey H. Segal and Matthew Simon, 'British Foreign Capital Issues, 1865–1894', *Journal of Economic History*, December 1961, pp. 566–581.
[4] *Historical Statistics of the United States, 1789–1945*, Washington, Department of Commerce, Bureau of the Census, 1949, pp. 242–243.
[5] C. J. Bullock, J. H. Williams and R. S. Tucker, 'The Balance of Trade of the United States', *Review of Economic Statistics*, July 1919, pp. 215–266.

merchandise trade, very few data are available for this early period to provide a basis for estimating international transactions'.[1]

Fortunately the situation has changed in recent years as a result of new researches on original sources and the application of more refined methods. Thanks to the enterprise of Douglass North and Matthew Simon, we now possess a detailed quantitative record of the balance of payments of the United States from 1790 to 1900.[2] These two studies are the first systematic attempt to apply the residual method to American data; these new annual estimates are an indispensable counterpart to the corresponding estimates for the United Kingdom by Imlah.

In introducing his results for the period 1790–1860, North is careful to emphasize the limitations of the data. 'The relative neutrality of the errors and omissions requires both confidence in the accuracy of the trade and invisible items and an intimate knowledge of the period and of the country's international economic relations. Reliable contemporary direct estimates of the individual items and particularly of the total debt (or credit) position of the economy provide the best indication of the degree to which errors and omissions are counterbalancing. But anyone who has calculated historical balance of payments is aware of the way small changes in the interest charge or in the initial debt figure become large changes over time. Even when the data are very good, it would be ridiculous to assert that the absolute figures are always accurate.'[3] According to North's calculations, there were marked long cycles in the inflow of capital with peaks in 1816, 1836 and 1853, and these were accompanied by similar swings in immigration, building, land sales, and transport and incorporations. The cumulative balance of indebtedness rose from \$86·7 million in 1820 to \$379·2 million in 1860.

In his exhaustive analysis of the period 1861–1900, Matthew Simon found much to criticize in previous estimates. He indicates his own approach in the following words: 'Since the international economic transactions of the United States during the late nineteenth century developed an extraordinary complexity, it is necessary to overcome the limitations of the fragmentary approaches to balance

[1] *Historical Statistics of the United States, 1789–1945*, p. 237.
[2] Douglass C. North, 'The United States Balance of Payments, 1790–1860' and Matthew Simon, 'The United States Balance of Payments, 1861–1900', in *Trends in the American Economy in the Nineteenth Century*, Studies in Income and Wealth, vol. 24, Princeton University Press, 1960, pp. 573–715.
[3] Douglass C. North, *op. cit.*, pp. 574–575.

of payments estimation by employing an alternative method. Scientific procedure requires that each of the many components be properly identified and distinguished from other parts of the balance of payments. The best possible series must be constructed to mirror the impact of the secular, cyclical and extra-economic pressures operating on the magnitude of the particular economic variable over the forty-year span. This does not permit lumping two or more items together or into a "miscellaneous category" or assuming that one or more items on the credit side can exactly offset specific items on the debit side for one or for forty years'.[1] He has shown that it is possible to construct series for nearly all the distinct items in the balance of payments on current account. Among the outstanding contributions to knowledge resulting from the work of North and Simon are the carefully calculated annual estimates of shipping earnings, and immigrants' funds, remittances and tourist expenditures. From what is established about the time-shape of Britain's capital outflow, it is not surprising, in view of the large proportion of it which went to the United States, to see the long swings firmly confirmed in Simon's figures, with peaks in 1872 and 1888. The net accumulating balance of indebtedness of the United States is estimated to have grown from $483·6 million in 1861 to $3338·0 million in 1896 and $2490·9 million in 1900.

The annual estimates of net international capital movements for the United States over the period 1820–1913 can be checked in various ways. The task has been well carried out by Jeffrey G. Williamson who found, over the long swing, '. . . general conformity in direction, timing and amplitude between available indirect and direct estimates of net capital movements, and general conformity among *all* independent estimates published in recent years'.[2] The conclusion is corroborated after a critical look at the merchandise trade and service balances and the net gold movements.

We must briefly refer to recent research on two other important capital-importing countries, Canada and Australia. Annual estimates of the Canadian balance of payments for 1868–99 have been produced by Penelope Hartland;[3] thus, with estimates previously available from 1900 onward, we now have an unbroken series covering almost

---

[1] Matthew Simon, *op. cit.*, p. 630.
[2] See Jeffrey G. Williamson, *American Growth and the Balance of Payments, 1820–1913*, University of North Carolina Press, Chapel Hill, 1964, Appendix A, pp. 234–254.
[3] Penelope Hartland, 'Canadian Balance of Payments since 1868', *Trends in the American Economy in the Nineteenth Century*, 1960, pp. 717–753.

a century. The gross inflow of capital accounted for 26 per cent of gross domestic investment in 1900–5 and 38 per cent in 1906–10. For Australia in the period 1861–1900, N. G. Butlin has presented annual estimates of British investment as well as the net proceeds of government loan raisings overseas, by colony. Butlin's comprehensive researches have added greatly to our understanding of the relation between capital movements and Australian economic development.[1]

II. THE WORLD INVESTMENT PICTURE IN 1913

The great era of accumulation and international lending which ended in 1913[2] had created a world sharply divided into creditor and debtor nations, as shown in Table 1.

TABLE 1

MAIN CREDITOR AND DEBTOR COUNTRIES, 1913

	Gross Credits			Gross Debts	
	$000 mn.	%		$000 mn.	%
United Kingdom	18·0	40·9	Europe	12·0	27·3
France	9·0	20·4	Latin America	8·5	19·3
Germany	5·8	13·2	United States	6·8	15·5
Belgium, Netherlands and Switzerland	5·5	12·5	Canada	3·7	8·4
United States	3·5	8·0	Asia	6·0	13·6
Other countries	2·2	5·0	Africa	4·7	10·7
			Oceania	2·3	5·2
	44·0	100·0		44·0	100·0

Source: United Nations, *International Capital Movements in the Inter-War Period*, Lake Success, 1949.

Britain's gross creditor position in 1913 amounted to $18 billion, or 41 per cent of the world total of $44 billion. This mirrored the

[1] See N. G. Butlin, *Australian Domestic Product, Investment and Foreign Borrowing, 1861–1938/9*, Cambridge University Press, 1962, pp. 405–444; and *Investment in Australian Economic Development, 1861–1900*, Cambridge University Press, 1964, pp. 334–351.

[2] The analysis in this paper is restricted to long-term capital. No account is taken of short-term capital movements.

prominent part played by British long-term lending in the nineteenth century. At first glance it is remarkable that the five continental creditor nations, France, Germany, Belgium, the Netherlands and Switzerland, had between them built up a creditor position of $20·3 billion, over $2 billion larger than that of Britain; even France by herself seemed to be half as important as Britain. This simple comparison, however, is misleading. There were profound differences between continental and British outflows of capital, in terms of quality, motivation and consequences. Private enterprise subject to the mildest of British government regulation was the mainspring in England, whereas in France and Germany foreign investment was an instrument for the attainment of national objectives.

French long-term foreign lending increased threefold between 1880 and 1914 when the aggregate reached 45 billion francs. The geographical distribution is set out in Table 2.

TABLE 2

GEOGRAPHICAL DISTRIBUTION OF FRENCH FOREIGN
LONG-TERM INVESTMENT, 1900 and 1914

(Billion francs)

Country	1900	1914
Russia	7·0	11·3
Turkey (in Asia and Europe)	2·0	3·3
Spain and Portugal	4·5	3·9
Austria-Hungary	2·5	2·2
Balkan States	0·7	2·5
Italy	1·4	1·3
Switzerland, Belgium and Netherlands	1·0	1·5
Rest of Europe	0·8	1·5
Europe	19·9	27·5
French Colonies	1·5	4·0
Egypt, Suez and South Africa	3·0	3·3
United States and Canada	0·8	2·0
Latin America	2·0	6·0
Asia	0·8	2·2
Outside Europe	8·1	17·5
GRAND TOTAL	28·0	45·0

Source: Herbert Feis, *op. cit.*, p. 51.

The political designs of the French Government resulted in the equivalent of £500 million being invested in Russian bonds, and the Russian Government was spending half the proceeds on armaments. Similar ill-fated loans were made to Turkey, Austria-Hungary, the Balkan States and Latin America. The yield was lower than that on domestic securities, and the borrowing countries did not increase their demand for French exports. Nearly all the loans were ultimately repudiated. It is estimated that French investors lost no less than two-thirds of the capital placed in foreign bonds, an amount equal to six times the German indemnity of 1870.

Germany experienced rapid economic expansion in the period 1871–1913. The domestic rate of interest was higher than in Britain and France, and the Government was determined that foreign investment should be subordinated to the needs of the German economy. The priorities to be observed were described by a contemporary writer as follows :

(a) The issue of foreign securities in the domestic market, like the establishment of branches of domestic enterprises and participations abroad, is permissible only after the domestic demand for capital has been fully satisfied, since the first duty of the banks is to use the available funds of the nation for increasing the national production and purchasing power and for strengthening the home market.

(b) International commercial dealings as well as international flotations ought to be but the means for attaining national ends and must be placed in the service of national labour.

(c) Even when the two foregoing conditions have been fulfilled, the greatest care will have to be used in selecting the securities to be floated.[1]

In interpreting the national interest the German banks had an important influence on the volume of foreign investment, and there is evidence that, particularly up to 1900, they were to a large extent engaged in 'borrowing short' in London and Paris and 'lending long' in foreign countries. Germany's foreign lending was much greater than the surplus in her trade and services account. On the eve of the First World War a little over half of the total of $5·8 billion of foreign investment was in Europe, partly inspired by the desire to increase the military effectiveness of her allies. The flow of

---

[1] J. Reisser, *The German Great Banks and their Concentration*, p. 384, quoted in Feis, *op. cit.*, p. 162.

TABLE 3

BRITISH OVERSEA INVESTMENTS IN PUBLICLY-ISSUED SECURITIES,
DECEMBER 1913, BY COUNTRY

	£ Mn.	%
Canada and Newfoundland	514·9	13·7
Australia and New Zealand	416·4	11·1
South Africa	370·2	9·8
West Africa	37·3	1·0
India and Ceylon	378·8	10·0
Straits Settlements	27·3	0·7
British North Borneo	5·8	0·2
Hong Kong	3·1	0·1
Other British Colonies	26·2	0·7
British Empire	1,780·0	47·3
United States	754·6	20·0
Argentina	319·6	8·5
Brazil	148·0	3·9
Mexico	99·0	2·6
Chile	61·0	1·6
Uruguay	36·1	1·0
Peru	34·2	0·9
Cuba	33·2	0·9
Other Latin American States	25·5	0·7
Latin America	756·6	20·1
Russia	110·0	2·9
Spain	19·0	0·5
Italy	12·5	0·3
Portugal	8·1	0·2
France	8·0	0·2
Germany	6·4	0·2
Austria	8·0	0·2
Denmark	11·0	0·3
Balkan States	17·0	0·5
Rest of Europe	18·6	0·5
Europe	218·6	5·8
Egypt	44·9	1·2
Turkey	24·0	0·6
China	43·9	1·2
Japan	62·8	1·7
Other countries	77·9	2·1
All foreign countries	1,983·3	52·7
GRAND TOTAL	3,763·3	100·0

Source : Feis, *op. cit.*, p. 27. Investments in shipping are excluded.

13

TABLE 4

BRITISH OVERSEA INVESTMENTS IN PUBLICLY-ISSUED SECURITIES,
DECEMBER 1913, BY CATEGORY

	£ Mn.	%
Dominion and colonial governments	675·5	17·9
Foreign governments	297·0	7·9
Overseas municipalities	152·5	4·1
Government and municipal	1,125·0	29·9
Dominion and colonial railways	306·4	8·1
Indian railways	140·8	3·7
United States railways	616·6	16·4
Other foreign railways	467·2	12·4
Railways	1,531·0	40·6
Electric light and power	27·3	0·7
Gas and waterworks	29·2	0·8
Canals and docks	7·1	0·2
Tramways	77·8	2·1
Telegraphs and telephones	43·7	1·2
Other public utilities	185·1	5·0
Coal, iron and steel	35·2	0·9
Breweries	18·0	0·5
Other commercial and industrial	155·3	41·0
Commerce and industry	208·5	5·5
Mines	272·8	7·2
Nitrates	11·7	0·3
Oil	40·6	1·1
Rubber	41·0	1·1
Tea and coffee	22·4	0·6
Raw materials	388·5	10·3
Banks	72·9	1·9
Financial, land and investment	244·2	6·5
Banks and finance	317·1	8·4
Miscellaneous	8·1	0·3
TOTAL	3,763·3	100·0

Source : Feis, *op. cit.*, p. 27. Investments in shipping are excluded.

capital to her colonies was very small ; nearly a third of her total
foreign assets was in North and South America.[1]

We may thus conclude that the State-controlled lending activities
of France and Germany in the forty years before the First World

[1] For an excellent summary of the influence of government policy on foreign
lending in France and Germany up to 1914, see Feis, *op. cit.*, pp. 118–188.

War, although considerable in scale, had a negligible effect on the growth of the international economy. The dominant influence was the flow of long-term capital from Great Britain.

The distribution of Britain's oversea investments in publicly-issued securities, by country and by category, is shown in Tables 3 and 4.

In the early phase Britain lent a great deal to governments; it is estimated that of the £1,150 million of foreign assets in 1880 nearly a half (£500 million) was in foreign government loans and guarantees, and about a fifth (£240 million) in railways in Europe, the United States and South America. British entrepreneurs like Thomas Brassey had been responsible for a large-scale direct investment in railway-building on the continent of Europe. In 1913 the aggregate of investments in publicly-issued securities amounting to £3,763·3 million was distributed geographically as follows: 47 per cent in the British Empire, 20 per cent in the United States, 20 per cent in Latin America, and 6 per cent in Europe. The large part played by investment in railways is clearly brought out in Table 4; it amounted to no less than £1,531 million, or 40 per cent of the total. Government and municipal securities at £1,125 million accounted for 30 per cent. Of the £1,780 million invested in Empire countries, 47 per cent comprised holdings of government and municipal bonds, and 25 per cent were in railway securities. The net income from foreign investments had grown from £58 million in 1875 to £200 million in 1913.

The great era of British foreign lending had been unique. At the end of the period her capital exports were at the rate of 9 per cent of her national income. It had been largely portfolio rather than direct investment, and mainly in securities yielding a fixed return; the plantation type of investment associated with colonies did not occupy a prominent place. Most of the capital went to developing countries of new settlement, particularly the overseas descendants of Western Europe — the United States, Canada, Australia and New Zealand — which are now in the world's top income bracket. Much of their infra-structure was built up on the savings of the British private investor. The leading creditor country had a high propensity to import; and the growth of the Atlantic economy was marked by alternating phases in which Britain was putting her money back into world circulation either through a wave of lending or an upsurge of imports. Under this régime it was possible for the effects of differential productivity increases to be transmitted internationally without serious disequilibrium.

III. THE TIME-SHAPE OF CAPITAL MOVEMENTS

In the nineteenth century the international flow of capital fluctuated with a periodicity of about eighteen years from peak to peak. This long swing was quite clear in the series for 1870–1912 published by C. K. Hobson in 1914, but it was many years before its economic significance was appreciated. Recent work by Douglass North has filled in the gap for the United States in the first half of the century ;[1] it is now established beyond doubt that net capital inflow into the United States exhibits five prominent long swings between 1820 and 1913, with peaks in 1836, 1853, 1872, 1888 and 1910, and troughs in 1827, 1840, 1858, 1878 and 1900. The record can be summarized as follows :

TABLE 5

UNITED STATES NET CAPITAL MOVEMENTS *

	Year	$ Million
Trough	1827	− 10·0
Peak	1836	+62·2
Trough	1840	− 30·8
Peak	1853	+55·6
Trough	1858	− 23·1
Peak	1872	+224·8
Trough	1878	− 161·9
Peak	1888	+285·0
Trough	1900	− 296·4
Peak	1910	+51·1

* For sources see Jeffrey G. Williamson. *op. cit.*, pp. 255–257.

We shall follow the example of workers in this field by referring to this type of fluctuation as the Kuznets cycle, since it was Kuznets who first drew attention to its importance as a general feature of economic growth.[2] In a recent work he has presented a comprehensive analysis of long swings in population growth, capital formation and national product in the United States since 1870.[3]

[1] Douglass North, *op. cit.*
[2] See S. Kuznets, *Secular Movements in Production and Prices*, Boston and New York, Houghton Mifflin, 1930.
[3] S. Kuznets, *Capital in the American Economy: Its Formation and Financing*, Princeton University Press for the National Bureau of Economic Research, Oxford University Press, 1961, pp. 316–360.

Any attempt to explain the ebb and flow of international factor movements must concentrate on the process of interaction within the Atlantic economy.[1] This can be shown by referring to Schumpeter's monumental analysis of the capitalist process in the nineteenth century.[2] His method was to set up a model of economic growth in a closed system and then to seek verification in the economic time-series of each of his countries — England, the United States and Germany — taken separately. International factor movements were regarded as 'external' or exogenous influences, i.e. not inherent in the working of the economic organism itself. He argued cogently that, in the light of his statistical testing, the rhythm of economic evolution postulated in his model could be observed *simultaneously* in the history of the three countries. Unfortunately, there was one irritating exception and it could not be brushed aside as peripheral. Schumpeter conceded that 'England's economic history from 1897 to 1913 cannot, owing to the comparative weakness of the evolution (in our sense) of her domestic industries, be written in terms of our model — the only case of this kind within the epoch covered by our material'.[3] One cannot help wondering why perfidious Albion failed to toe the line in this period. Was it the exception which proved the Schumpeterian rule? There is a significant clue in Volume II of *Business Cycles* where the reader is reminded that 'the cyclical aspects of international relations . . . cannot receive due attention within this book'.[4] Then comes this important admission :

> Of all the limitations imposed by the plan and purpose of this book, this is the most serious one. Not only do cycles in different countries systematically affect each other, so much so that the history of hardly any one of them can be written without reference to simultaneous cyclical phases in other countries, but cycles really are, especially as regards the great innovations which produced the Kondratieffs, international phenomena. That is to say, such a process as the railroadization or the electrification of the world transcends the boundaries of individual countries in such a way as to be more truly described as one world-wide

[1] See my paper, 'The Rhythm of Growth in the Atlantic Economy', in Hugo Hegeland, ed., *Money, Growth and Methodology and Other Essays in Economics in Honor of Johan Åkerman, March 31, 1961*, CWK Gleerup, Lund, Sweden, 1961, pp. 39–48.
[2] J. Schumpeter, *Business Cycles: a Theoretical, Historical and Statistical Analysis of the Capitalist Process*, vols. i and ii, New York and London, McGraw-Hill, 1939.
[3] *Ibid.*, vol. i, p. 435.   [4] *Ibid.*, vol. ii, p. 666.

process than as the sum of distinct national ones. Capitalism itself is, both in the economic and the sociological sense, essentially one process, with the whole earth as its stage.[1]

This is a crucial point. If the phenomena under review were 'one world-wide process' and not 'the sum of distinct national ones', one would have thought that Schumpeter might at least have indicated that his mode of verification, based on the notion that the process *was* the sum of distinct national ones, was to be regarded as an interim judgment. Instead of that, he went on to say that —

> ... both reasons — interactions and supernational unity of fundamental processes — explain why in our historical survey the cycles in our three countries were found to be so much in step. The fact that they were is not more obvious than the mechanism that produced it and also — in principle, at least — the manner in which these relations affected the working of pre-war central banks and the pre-war gold standard.[2]

Schumpeter was bent on having it both ways.

What happens when the basic postulates are changed? First, let us regard international factor movements as endogenous and the countries concerned as an entity, the Atlantic economy. Secondly, let us transfer attention from the Kitchin, Juglar and Kondratieff fluctuations to the Kuznets cycle. In other words, we conceive the evolution of capitalism (as Schumpeter said we ought to) as a process transcending national boundaries, and we drop his three-cycle scheme.[3] As soon as we regard the individual nations as regions comprising an aggregate and we ask what are the conditions under which the rate of growth of income in this aggregate can be maximized over time, there is no reason to expect each of the parts to pass through identical and simultaneous phases according to a theory of a closed system. Secular growth entails internal shifts within the aggregate via international factor movements; the expansion of the whole is likely to express itself through disharmonious rates of growth in the parts. It is now generally agreed that this is what happened in the Atlantic economy between the middle of the nineteenth century and the First World War. There were four major outflows of population and capital from Europe — 1845–54, 1863–1872, 1881–90 and 1903–13, and there was an inverse relation

---

[1] J. Schumpeter, *Business Cycles: a Theoretical, Historical and Statistical Analysis of the Capitalist Process*, vol. ii, p. 666.　　　　　　　[2] *Ibid.*
[3] This was the starting-point of my *Migration and Economic Growth: A Study of Great Britain and the Atlantic Economy* (Cambridge University Press, 1954).

between the long swings in capital formation in the United Kingdom and in countries of new settlement overseas. A wave of home construction in the United Kingdom drew the rural surplus into urban employment at home ; a wave of foreign investment drew the rural surplus into urban employment abroad. International movements of labour and capital were a pivotal element in determining the time-shape of economic development in the sending and receiving countries. One may summarize the process as an inter-regional competition for factors of production within the Atlantic economy, with the Old World and the New World alternating in their intensive build-up of resources. This is the essential characteristic which distinguishes these long swings from short business cycles. Long swings are fluctuations in the rate at which resources are developed, whereas the short business cycles are fluctuations in short-term investment in producer durables and inventories. From this analysis it is clear that Schumpeter was not justified in claiming that 'interactions and supernational unity of fundamental processes' gave added support to his finding that the cycles of his three countries were in step. On the contrary, this particular approach uncovers the inverse long swings and leads to the conclusion that the United States economy had fluctuations of a greater amplitude than the United Kingdom because in the latter country movements in home investment were partly counterbalanced by opposite movements in foreign investment and this was not the case in the United States. There was a clear long swing in real income per head in Britain in the period 1870–1913, inverse to the more violent swing in real income per head in the United States.[1]

Some of the important statistical findings relating to the mechanism of this inverse relation, mainly over the period 1870–1913, may be briefly noted. The main series are plotted in Figure 1 on page 21.

United States

(a) Population-sensitive capital formation (non-farm residential construction and durable capital expenditure by railroads) display long swings coincident with (or lagging slightly behind) those in population additions, immigration and internal migration.[2]

(b) Between 1817 and 1917 there were five long swings in net capital inflow and merchandise imports, with an average span of

---

[1] See Brinley Thomas, *Migration and Economic Growth*, p. 111.
[2] See Kuznets, *Capital in the American Economy*, chapter 7.

about eighteen years. Deflated imports tend to lag behind domestic activity, and the rate of capital inflow tends to be synchronous with domestic activity at troughs and to lead by about a year at peaks.[1]

(c) From 1870 to 1914 between 55 and 60 per cent of the net foreign investment in the United States was contributed by Britain.[2]

(d) The gross volume of population-sensitive capital formation was over 40 per cent of total capital formation in the 1870's, and even in the first decade of the twentieth century it was still 25 per cent of the total.[3]

(e) Long swings in population-sensitive capital formation were inverse to those in other capital formation (i.e. net changes in inventories, foreign claims and producer durable equipment). This inverse relation ceases and becomes a positive association from the 1920's.[4]

United Kingdom[5]

(a) From 1870 to 1913 there were long swings in additions to population inverse to those in the United States.

(b) The long swings in British domestic capital formation were inverse to those of population-sensitive capital formation in the United States.

(c) Long swings in British capital exports and in British and European over-sea migration were coincident with the long swings in population-sensitive capital formation in the United States.

(d) Long swings in British imports at constant prices were positively related to swings in British domestic capital formation and in American 'other capital formation', and negatively related to swings in American population-sensitive capital formation.

(e) Swings in British internal migration were inverse to those in the United States.

A satisfactory interpretation of this complex set of interactions must await further research. We might suggest the following as the basis of a two-country model, A being capital-exporting and B capital-importing, and each divided into a domestic capital-formation and an export sector. The word 'period' refers to either the upward or downward phase of the Kuznets cycle.

---

[1] Jeffrey G. Williamson, *op. cit.*, pp. 75 and 96.
[2] *Ibid.*, p. 145.   [3] Kuznets, *op. cit.*, chapter 7.   [4] *Ibid.*
[5] See Brinley Thomas, *op. cit.*, and 'Long Swings in Internal Migration and Capital Formation', *Bulletin of the International Statistical Institute, Proceedings of the 34th Session*, vol. xl, Book 1, Toronto, 1964, pp. 398–412.

(1) A substantial part of domestic capital formation is population-sensitive, i.e. varies with the rate of population additions.

(2) The rate of population additions is due mainly to the rate of change in net migration.

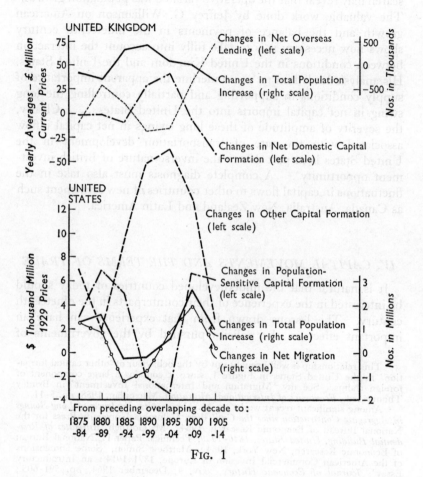

Fig. 1

(3) The expected growth of sales in the export sector in a given period depends on the marginal efficiency of investment in the domestic capital-formation sector of the other country in the same period.

(4) There is an inter-temporal relation between the output capacity of the export sector in a period and the rate of growth of investment

in the domestic capital-formation sector of that country in the previous period.[1]

A model based on these relationships can be tested in the light of the more abundant statistical data now available.[2] Deeper research may reveal that the operative variable was population growth.[3] The valuable work done by Jeffrey G. Williamson on American growth and the balance of payments in the nineteenth century shows how necessary it is to take fully into account the interaction between conditions in the United Kingdom and the United States. His analysis leads him to '. . . underline the apparent importance of supply conditions in supporting and partially controlling the long swing in net capital imports into the United States. . . . Clearly, the severity of amplitude of these long swings in net capital inflow associated with the rate of transportation development in the United States is in part due to the inverse nature of British investment opportunity'.[4] A complete diagnosis must also take in the fluctuations in capital flows to other countries of new settlement such as Canada, Australia, New Zealand and Latin America.

IV. CAPITAL MOVEMENTS AND THE TERMS OF TRADE

It is natural that the underdeveloped countries of today should be interested in the experience of their counterparts in the nineteenth century. The lessons drawn from that experience can have an important effect on the policies pursued by the governments of

---

[1] This relationship is well brought out by the behaviour of 'other capital formation' in the United States in Figure 1, since it contains a large component of foreign claims. See my 'Migration and International Investment' in Brinley Thomas, ed., *Economics of International Migration*, Macmillan, 1958, pp. 5–11.

[2] Among significant recent works are M. Abramovitz, *Evidences of Long Swings in Aggregate Construction since the Civil War*, Columbia University Press for the National Bureau of Economic Research, 1964; M. Gottlieb, *Estimates of Residential Building, United States, 1840–1939*, Technical Paper 17, National Bureau of Economic Research, New York, 1964; Matthew Simon, 'Some Dimensions of the American Commercial Invasion of Europe, 1871–1914 : an Introductory Essay', *Journal of Economic History*, xxiv, 4, December 1964, pp. 591–605; Richard A. Easterlin, 'Long Swings in U.S. Demographic and Economic Growth : Some Findings on the Historical Pattern' (a revised and shortened version of a report presented at the June 1964 meeting of the Population Association of America at San Francisco, mimeographed, 1964).

[3] It has been shown that damped Kuznets cycles are generated by the Klein-Goldberger econometric model of the United States, with population growth as an exogenous variable. See I. Adelman, 'Long Cycles : a Simulation Experiment', *Proceedings of a Conference on Simulation*, 1963. Further testing is required with population growth as an endogenous variable.

[4] Jeffrey G. Williamson, *op. cit.*, pp. 157–158.

countries which have passed from colonial to independent status. One of the ideas which has been fairly widely accepted is that the underdeveloped countries of the second half of the nineteenth century had the worst of both worlds, as consumers of manufactured goods and as producers of food and raw materials. If this proposition is true, one can hardly blame the peoples of the poorer countries for wishing to make certain that a similar fate will not befall them in the second half of the twentieth century.

The doctrine is based on a theoretical analysis of the distribution of gains between investing and borrowing countries. It is clearly set out in a well-known article by H. W. Singer.[1] There are two main strands which I shall call the lop-sided multiplier effect and the lop-sided terms of trade effect. The former is put by Singer in the following words :

> Could it not be that in many cases the productive facilities for export from underdeveloped countries, which were so largely a result of foreign investment, never became a part of the internal economic structure of those underdeveloped countries themselves, except in the purely geographical or physical sense? Economically speaking, they were really an outpost of the economies of the more developed investing countries. The main secondary multiplier effects, which the textbooks tell us to expect from investment, took place not where the investment was physically or geographically located but (to the extent that the results of these investments returned directly home) they took place where the investment came from.[2]

The argument on the terms of trade rests on the high income and price elasticity of demand for manufactured goods and the low income and price elasticity of demand for primary products. It is asserted that, because the rise in productivity was taken out in increased factor incomes in the investing countries, the latter took the lion's share of the fruits of technical progress at the expense of the primary-producing countries.

When pressed for a definition of 'underdeveloped', Singer simply said that he had in mind 'countries which are poor for reasons other than war destruction'; he did not mean 'countries which are not at present industrialized'. 'An underdeveloped country,' he added, 'is like a giraffe — difficult to describe, but you know one when you

[1] H. W. Singer, 'The Distribution of Gains between Investing and Borrowing Countries', *American Economic Review, Proceedings*, 1950.
[2] *Ibid.*, p. 475.

see one'.[1] I suggest that if Singer had been looking for giraffes round about 1860 he might well have picked on, say, Canada, Japan, Australia, Ireland and Denmark. He is being wise after the event when he assures us that he does *not* consider Saskatchewan, Iowa, Denmark or New Zealand to be 'underdeveloped'. His whole thesis is about the era of large-scale private foreign lending and he himself argues that '. . . ever since the seventies the trend of prices has been heavily against sellers of food and raw materials and in favour of the sellers of manufactured articles'.[2] To establish his case he must include all countries which would have been regarded as underdeveloped about the middle of the nineteenth century.

Let us first take the under-populated areas of new settlement, such as Canada, Australia and New Zealand. The rate of economic growth in these 'outposts' in the half-century before the First World War was much higher than in the creditor country. Real national product per head in Canada, for example, went up 24·7 per cent per decade as against 12·5 per cent in the United Kingdom.[3] It cannot be denied that the export of capital and labour from Britain to these countries had a cumulative effect on their productive capacity; they would never have grown as rapidly as they did if the secondary multiplier effects had been felt mainly in the investing country.

Careful work on the statistics of the terms of trade leaves room for serious doubt. Kindleberger concludes that

> . . . there is no long-run tendency for the terms of trade to move against primary products in favour of manufactures. On the contrary, if allowance is made for the unprovable but generally accepted fact that the improvement in the quality of manufactures over the past eighty years has been greater than that of primary products, the terms of trade may have turned against manufactures and in favour of raw materials per unit of equal quality, however that may be defined.[4]

Theodore W. Morgan also failed to find any conclusive evidence of a general worsening of the price position of primary producers;

---

[1] These quotations are from Dr. Singer's reply to Dr. A. N. McLeod's 'Trade and Investment in Underdeveloped Areas: a Comment', *American Economic Review*, vol. 41, 1951, pp. 419–421.

[2] *American Economic Review, Proceedings*, 1950, p. 477.

[3] S. Kuznets, 'Quantitative Aspects of the Growth of Nations, I, Levels and Variability of Rates of Growth', *Economic Development and Cultural Change*, University of Chicago, vol. v., no. 1, October 1956, p. 13.

[4] Charles P. Kindleberger, *The Terms of Trade: a European Case Study*, New York, John Wiley & Sons, 1956, p. 263.

he was impressed by the wide variety of experience of different nations.[1] It is dangerous to generalize from what has happened to particular countries. For example,

> . . . the rising terms of trade for agriculture in the Indian and New Zealand data, from the 1860's to the first decades of the twentieth century, suggest that falling world and local transport costs were then exerting a strong upward pull on farm prices in producing areas, and a downward push on manufactured prices in distant consuming areas. Increasing industrialization could weaken this effect later.[2]

The argument about factor incomes in relation to productivity in the investing country is not borne out by an analysis of the course of wage rates and export prices in the United Kingdom ; [3] there is no evidence that increases in the productivity of British industry were taken out to any marked extent in rising money wages.[4] The real issue is why some underdeveloped countries in the nineteenth century remained poor while others had a rapid increase in real product per head. Why did some of them plough back part of the yield of their export booms into an expansion of domestic manufacturing, while others did not? The average rate of increase per decade in real national product *per capita* in the forty or fifty years up to the First World War was 12·5 per cent in the United Kingdom compared with 17·9 per cent in Ireland, 19·3 per cent in Denmark, 24·7 per cent in Canada, and 33·7 per cent in Japan.[5] Why then did the 'backward export economies' of South-East Asia, West Africa and Latin America fare so much worse? Was it because of an 'export bias' forced on them by the rich industrial countries? The real reasons are to be found not in the process of international investment or in international division of labour but in the internal economic and social structure of these countries, and the colonial powers were partly responsible for the maintenance of these conditions. Perhaps the chief impediment was the cheap labour policy based on the fact that labour was available to the capitalist sector in perfectly elastic supply. In these conditions the wage became

[1] Theodore Morgan, 'The Long-run Terms of Trade between Agriculture and Manufacturing', *Economic Development and Cultural Change*, University of Chicago, viii, no. 1, October 1959, pp. 1–23.
[2] *Ibid.*, p. 17.
[3] G. M. Meier, 'Long-period Determinants of Britain's Terms of Trade, 1880–1913', *Review of Economic Studies*, xx (2), 52, 1952–53, pp. 122–125.
[4] E. H. Phelps-Brown, 'The Course of Wage Rates in Five Countries, 1860–1939', *Oxford Economic Papers*, ii, 2, 1950.
[5] S. Kuznets, *op. cit.*, p. 13.

frozen at the level needed for subsistence and the expansion of the capitalist sector raised the share of profits in the national income but not wages. The scarcity of entrepreneurs and skilled labour was often aggravated by non-competing groups and immigration. As Professor Myint has shown,

> ... in the latter half of the nineteenth century immigrant labour, particularly from India, may really be regarded as an international commodity having a uniform price rather than as a factor of production. Wherever it was imported, it decisively pulled down wages and incomes in the 'semi-empty' countries to the very low level appropriate to the over-populated countries instead of giving them a chance to rise a part of the way towards the high wage levels of the 'empty' continents of North America and Australia.[1]

There is plenty in this record to justify resentment on the part of the poorer countries, but the real culprit was not the system of international lending.[2]

Let us now pass from the long-run trend to fluctuations in the terms of trade. Was there a causal relationship between these fluctuations and those of capital movements? Cairncross, in his analysis of British experience between 1870 and 1913, concluded that '... it was upon the terms of trade that the distribution of investment between home and foreign, as well as the course of real wages, ultimately depended'.[3] On this reasoning, when the terms of trade moved against Britain and in favour of the countries supplying her with imports, British capital was attracted to these countries ; the downswing in capital exports would be brought about by a movement of the terms of trade against the oversea countries. In seeking to verify this thesis, Cairncross was troubled by the fact that the great upswing in foreign investment in the 1880's was accompanied by a movement of the terms of trade *in favour of* Britain, and he had to go to considerable pains to explain this away.[4] Since the same phenomenon is to be observed during part of the other two upswings in foreign investment, 1863–72 and 1902–13, it is necessary to examine these phases more closely. There may be an alternative explanation which better fits the facts.

[1] H. Myint, 'The Gains from International Trade and the Backward Countries', *Review of Economic Studies*, xxii (2), 58, 1954–55, p. 135.
[2] See my paper, 'The Alleged Exploitation of Underdeveloped Countries : a Review of the Evidence', *Proceedings of the Thirty-third Conference of the Western Economic Association*, 1958.
[3] A. K. Cairncross, *Home and Foreign Investment, 1870–1913*, Cambridge University Press, 1953, p. 208. [4] *Ibid.*, pp. 192–195.

There are serious objections to using the net barter terms of trade as an indicator of the distribution of gain between trading countries. What is significant is not so much the ratio between the average price of exports and the average price of imports as the quantities — factor movements, volumes of exports and imports, and rates of

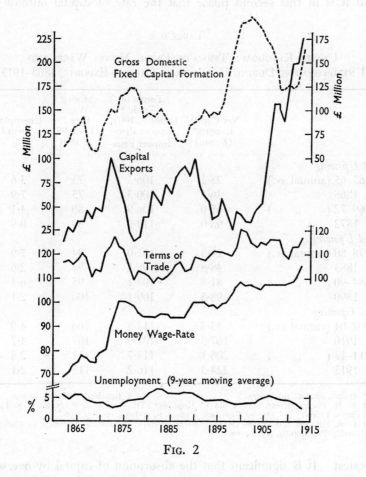

FIG. 2

productivity — lying behind the ratio. A glance at Figure 2 above shows that the three major upsurges in foreign investment between 1860 and 1913 shared one common feature ; in the second half of the boom when capital exports were at their heaviest and moving towards the peak, the terms of trade were moving sharply in favour of Britain, i.e. 1868–72, 1883–90, 1910–13. Further examination brings out other common elements shown in the data in Table 6 below.

In each upswing we note an initial phase during which the terms of trade move against Britain and there is a moderate revival in capital exports ; then the terms of trade turn in favour of Britain and it is in this second phase that the rate of capital outflow is

TABLE 6

UNITED KINGDOM : TERMS OF TRADE, MONEY WAGES AND
UNEMPLOYMENT DURING UPSWINGS IN CAPITAL EXPORTS, 1863–1913

	Net Capital Exports* (£ mn.)	Terms of Trade † (1880 = 100) Export Price ⁄ Import Price	Money Wage Rate ‡ (1890–99 = 100)	Unemployment § %
1st Upswing				
1863–65 (annual av.)	28·1	106·3	73	3·6
1868	36·5	100·3	75	7·9
1869–72 (,,)	65·0	106·9	80	4·1
1872	98·0	113·0	89	0·9
2nd Upswing				
1878–80 (annual av.)	29·3	101·0	94	7·9
1883	48·8	98·5	94	2·6
1884–90 (,,)	81·8	104·1	95	6·3
1890	98·5	109·1	100	2·1
3rd Upswing				
1902–04 (annual av.)	43·3	112·8	106	4·9
1910	167·3	107·9	107	4·7
1911–13 (,,)	206·1	113·7	111	2·8
1913	224·3	116·2	115	2·1

* Imlah, *op. cit.*, pp. 72–75.   † Imlah, *op. cit.*, pp. 96–98.
‡ E. H. Phelps-Brown and Sheila V. Hopkins, ' The Course of Wage-Rates in Five Countries, 1860–1939 ', *Oxford Economic Papers*, ii, 2, June 1950 p. 276.
§ B. R. Mitchell and Phyllis Deane, *Abstract of British Historical Statistics*, Cambridge University Press, 1962, pp. 64–65.

greatest. It is significant that the absorption of capital by oversea countries was at its height during years when the terms of trade were moving against them. Those who believe that the terms of trade played a decisive causal role will find it hard to explain this phenomenon. Perhaps an explanation can be found if we look behind the ratio. Given the inverse relation between home and foreign investment, the beginning of an upswing in foreign lending and exports is accompanied by a fall in the level of activity in domestic capital formation. Thus, during the first phase of a lending-export boom there is a high elasticity of supply of factors for the export sector due to the downturn in the construction sector. Unused labour and existing equipment are being re-absorbed in the export sector ; this entails a rise in productivity, and money wages and export prices are kept down. As the boom gathers momentum a turning-point is reached ; marginal costs rise sharply under the influence of bottlenecks at the higher level of employment in the export sector, while demand is running high in oversea construction activity ; productivity has now ceased to rise and may be falling, hence a steep rise in export prices relatively to import prices. Although the statistics at our disposal are inadequate for the measurement of productivity, the figures in Table 6 are a rough guide. In the 1863–72 upswing the first phase saw the terms of trade move against Britain (from 106·3 to 100·3), money wages rose only slightly, and unemployment was heavy. Then in the second phase, 1868–72, the terms of trade moved sharply in Britain's favour (from 100·3 to 113·0), wages rose by nearly 20 per cent, and unemployment fell to 0·9 per cent. A similar pattern is seen in the 1878–90 and 1902–13 upswings in capital exports. Between 1880 and 1887 British export prices fell by 30 per cent while money wages remained constant ; this is a strong suggestion of rising productivity in the export sector which did not lead to higher money wages. Then between 1887 and 1890 export prices rose by about 18 per cent and money wages went up by 8 per cent ; we may infer that in those years productivity declined. On this reading of the interaction between the terms of trade and the inverse swing in home and foreign investment, one is led to regard movements in the net barter terms of trade as a *consequence* of the fundamental forces at work rather than a causal factor determining the distribution of the flow of capital between home and foreign investment.

This is consistent with what was suggested in the previous section about the inverse relation between long swings in domestic capital formation in the lending and borrowing countries. In each country, the capacity of the export sector in the upswing phase is a function of the rate of home construction in that country in the previous phase. The export performance of the underdeveloped country in a given period is based upon the amount invested by the creditor country in its construction sector in the previous period ; and the ability of the industrialized country to expand its own construction in a given period is promoted by the increased flow of food and raw materials from the underdeveloped country. Given these inter-temporal relationships, there was a fundamental long-run com-munity of interest between lender and borrower which should not be overlooked.

V. THE EDWARDIAN CLIMAX

As the financial centre of the world, London had acquired an unrivalled expertise. *The Economist* proudly declared in 1909 that '... we enjoy at present an undisputed right to place our money where we will, for Government makes no attempt to twist the stream into a given channel, and every borrower — native, colonial and foreign — has an equal opportunity of satisfying his needs in London'.[1] The great upsurge in Britain's foreign lending in the years 1903–13, following the boom in home construction in the 1890's, was a continuation of the rhythm which had marked the country's growth over most of the nineteenth century. But this time there was a subtle difference. After the turn of the century there were ominous signs, though not yet perceived amid the pomp and glitter of the Edwardian age, that foreign investment was proving to be too much of a good thing.

Between 1907 and 1913 the outflow of British capital averaged £176 million a year as compared with average gross domestic fixed capital formation of £132 million a year. This was the climax of the age described by Keynes in 1919 as the 'economic Eldorado' in which the inhabitant of London

... could secure forthwith, if he wished it, cheap and comfortable means of transit to any country or climate without passport or other formality, could despatch his servant to the neighbouring office of a bank for such supply of the precious metals as might seem convenient, and could then proceed abroad to foreign quarters, without knowledge of their religion, language or customs, bearing coined wealth upon his person, and would consider him-self greatly aggrieved and much surprised at the least inter-ference. But, most important of all, he regarded this state of affairs as normal, certain, and permanent, except in the direction of further improvement, and any deviation from it as aberrant, scandalous, and avoidable.[2]

[1] *The Economist*, Commercial History and Review of 1908, 20 February 1909.
[2] J. M. Keynes, *The Economic Consequences of the Peace*, Macmillan, 1920, pp. 9–10.

Some statesmen were dimly aware that there was a serpent in this paradise ; Balfour and Joseph Chamberlain thought they recognized it in the shape of insular free trade. But there was no one who asked whether Britain, by investing so much abroad, was paying too high a price in terms of domestic productivity and employment.

The period 1897–1913 saw a wave of fundamental innovations in electricity, chemistry and the automobile industries. Countries such as the United States, Germany and Sweden took full advantage of this technological revolution ; their domestic investment and the physical productivity of their industries rose rapidly between 1900 and 1913. One cannot escape the conclusion that the technical efficiency of the British economy lagged behind in this period. It would be wrong to try to demonstrate this by analysing the preponderance of foreign issues on the London market. At the turn of the century the typical domestic entrepreneur was still a private company or a family business which had hardly any access to the new issue market. Cairncross has estimated that in 1907 the aggregate capital of manufacturing industry was about £1,000 million and net industrial investment about £50 million. If two-thirds of the latter came from profits, and only one-tenth from new issues, the remaining quarter must have come from other sources of borrowed capital.[1] The fact remains that adequate facilities for industries to avail themselves of the benefits of technical innovation were lacking. The domestic rate of interest rose from 2·76 in 1900 to 3·39 in 1913. There was a pronounced shift to profit and, unlike the 1880's, real wages were falling ; and there was bitter industrial warfare. The pursuit of private investment profits overseas had become inconsistent with the long-run social productivity of the British economy in a changed environment. The technical performance of British industry and the welfare of the wage-earners would have been improved if foreign lending had been on a smaller scale, with the domestic rate of interest reduced to the level consistent with full employment of home resources.

APPENDIX
DEFINITIONS AND SOURCES

Figure 1 (page 21)
 United Kingdom: Net overseas lending, population increase, and net

---

[1] A. K. Cairncross, 'The English Capital Market before 1913', *Economica*, xxv, 98, May 1958, p. 145.

domestic capital formation in current prices, in overlapping decades, 1870–79 to 1905–13.

James B. Jeffreys and Dorothy Walters, 'National Income and Expenditure of the United Kingdom, 1870–1952', International Association for Research in Income and Wealth, *Income and Wealth*, Series V, Bowes & Bowes, London, 1955, pp. 1–40.

United States: Net additions to total population; net migration; gross population-sensitive capital formation (i.e. non-farm residential construction plus railroad capital expenditures); other capital formation (i.e. net changes in inventories, foreign claims, and producer durable equipment); (all in overlapping decades, 1870–79 to 1905–13).

S. Kuznets, 'Long Swings in the Growth of Population and in Related Economic Variables', *Proceedings of the American Philosophical Society*, 102, 1 February 1958, pp. 25–52.

Figure 2 (page 27)
United Kingdom, 1862–1913, annual data.

Balance on current account, Albert H. Imlah, *Economic Elements in the Pax Britannica*, Harvard University Press, 1958, pp. 72–74.

Net barter terms of trade. (Export price index divided by import price index.) *Ibid.*, pp. 96–98.

Gross domestic fixed capital formation, in current prices. C. H. Feinstein, 'Income and Investment in the United Kingdom, 1856–1914', *Economic Journal*, lxxi, 282, June 1961, p. 374.

Money wage-rate (1890–99 = 100). E. H. Phelps-Brown with Sheila V. Hopkins, 'The Course of Wage-Rates in Five Countries', *Oxford Economic Papers* (New Series), June 1950, p. 276.

Unemployment. Nine-year moving average of the percentages of trade unionists recorded as unemployed. B. R. Mitchell & Phyllis Deane, *Abstract of British Historical Statistics*, Cambridge University Press, 1962, pp. 64–65.

THE PATTERN OF NEW BRITISH
PORTFOLIO FOREIGN INVESTMENT
1865-1914

BY

MATTHEW SIMON
Queens College, New York

IF in the next half century we are to create £5,000 or £6,000 millions more, what is to be the issue? [1]

Viewed from the vantage point of 1965 the international capital movements of the first half of the preceding century (1865–1914) exercised a unique, profound and long-run impact on the structure and the development of the world economy. The political and social repercussions of the pre-1914 foreign investments have, in turn, been a decisive factor in the world politics of the past five decades. As the leading creditor nation in the pre-1914 era, British international capital movements played a prominent and commanding role in these processes. At the very climax of this era, in 1914, C. K. Hobson initiated a systematic inquiry into the causes and effects of British foreign investment. To increase our understanding of this complex phenomenon he recognized the necessity to examine the reciprocal interplay between economic and political forces, apply the tools of economic analysis and contruct estimates of international capital movements and their components.

This paper, as the second phase of an investigation of the global aspects of international capital movements, presents a new comprehensive set of annual series of new British portfolio foreign investment for the half century ending in 1914.[2] Following in Hobson's tradition of analyzing cause and effect, we recognize the need to identify as accurately as possible the pattern of British capital exports. To learn more precisely who did the borrowing, in what form, and for what purposes, and in what amounts will serve this end.

The first part of the paper explains the nature and the development of the new statistics against the background of previous efforts of

[1] Robert Lucas Nash, *Fenn's Compendium of The English Foreign Funds* (London : Effingham Wilson, Royal Exchange, 9th Edition 1867), p. xi.
[2] Harvey H. Segal and Matthew Simon, 'British Foreign Capital Issues, 1865–1894', *Journal of Economic History*, December 1961, pp. 567–581.

estimating the capital account of the British balance of payments. This is followed by overall survey of what the new figures show for the entire fifty years. The third section identifies major trends and fluctuations in the pattern of pre-1914 British foreign investment. In the concluding section we compare the new data with related statistics and suggest some of the implications for further research and analysis.

I

The development of the quantitative record of pre-1914 British international capital movements has had a long history. The literature contains three types of statistical data: annual estimates of net international capital movements and of new overseas issues and estimates of the value of aggregate British holdings (and components thereof), of foreign and colonial securities for particular years.

These data are not mutually exclusive. Several writers, including Brinley Thomas in his comprehensive and provocative paper prepared for this Conference, have indicated and stressed the complementary nature of these statistics by employing them to validate the accuracy of particular estimates.[1] In addition, other students, notably A. G. Ford,[2] have utilized these statistics to provide an empirical basis for specific models they have constructed to explain the course of British foreign investment before 1914. It is, therefore, necessary to examine the characteristics and uses of each of these three types of statistics.

Annual estimates of the net international capital movements of Great Britain, calculated as the residuals of the balance of payments accounts, have been prepared for all or most of the half century before 1914 by Hobson, Cairncross and Imlah.[3] Although subject to various margins of error arising largely from the assumptions

[1] Brinley Thomas, 'The Historical Record of International Capital Movements to 1913' (Paper for International Economic Association Conference on Capital Movements and Economic Development, Washington, July 1965), pp. 1–7.

[2] A. G. Ford, 'The Transfer of British Foreign Lending 1870–1913', *Economic History Review*, December 1958, pp. 302–308; *The Gold Standard 1880–1914 Britain and Argentina* (Oxford: Clarendon Press, 1962) chap. iv, esp. pp. 52–57, 62–70; 'Bank Rate, The British Balance of Payments and the Burden of Adjustment, 1870–1914', *Oxford Economic Papers*, March 1964, pp. 24–39.

[3] C. K. Hobson, *The Export of Capital* (New York: The Macmillan Company, 1914), chap. vii; A. K. Cairncross, *Home and Foreign Investment, 1870–1913* (Cambridge: Cambridge University Press, 1958), chap. vi; A. H. Imlah, *Economic Elements in Pax Britannica* (Cambridge: Harvard University Press, 1958), chap. iii.

made in estimating current account invisible items, these figures serve two purposes. First, they facilitate the study of secular and cyclical changes in the relative importance of aggregate net foreign investment in the British economy and in the relationships between net international capital movements and various parts of the current account of the British balance of payments. Moreover, they provide benchmarks for the fruitful examination of independently derived estimates of individual components of the capital account.

Various contemporaries have employed a second method of estimating the value of the aggregate portfolio of foreign and colonial securities of British investors — with regional and industrial breakdowns — at particular points during the fifty-year span. George Paish, editor of *The Statist*, developed a set of such 'stock estimates for 1907 by capitalizing the yield from outstanding investments at an appropriate rate. He then used annual new issues to obtain similar figures for the end of 1913.[1] These statistics, to be sure, suffer from incompleteness of coverage. Moreover, they reflect secular, cyclical and random fluctuations in the market prices of the outstanding holdings of British investors. The latter changes clearly are not a product of capital account transactions of the balance of international payments. The stock statistics, nevertheless, provide a guide to the geographic distribution and industrial composition of British foreign investment.[2]

The third procedure has been the direct method of estimating individual components of the capital account. It has been impossible to develop annual measures of short-term capital movements or of long-term direct overseas investments.[3] Greater success has been obtained with statistics of portfolio foreign investment, which occupied a pre-eminent position in pre-1914 British long-term capital movements. Portfolio foreign investment can, in turn, be decomposed into total British purchases of new overseas issues,

---

[1] Sir George Paish, 'Great Britain's Investments in Other Lands', *Journal of The Royal Statistical Society*, lxxi (Sept. 1909), 456–480 ; 'Great Britain's Capital Investments in Individual Colonial and Foreign Countries,' *ibid.*, lxxxiv (Jan. 1911), 167–200 ; 'Export of Capital and The Cost of Living', *The Statist*, lxxix (Feb. 1914), Supplement ; Herbert Feis, *Europe The World's Banker 1870–1914* (New Haven : Yale University Press, 1930), pp. 17–32. Feis revised Paish's original estimates.

[2] For other sets of stock estimates see Cairncross, *Home and Foreign Investments*, pp. 183, 185 and A. R. Hall, *The London Capital Market and Australia 1870–1914* (Canberra : The Australian National University Press, 1963), pp. 9, 11, 13, 90, 161.

[3] Arthur I. Bloomfield, 'Short-Term Capital Movements Under the Pre-1914 Gold Standard' (Princeton, New Jersey : International Finance Section, Department of Economics, Princeton University 1963), pp. 49–50.

international movements in outstanding securities and redemptions of such British-held securities by foreign and colonial nations.[1]

Research has concentrated on the development and use of overseas new issue statistics. In his pioneering investigation of British foreign investment Leland H. Jenks developed estimates of new foreign capital issues.[2] *The Investor's Monthly Manual*, a supplement of *The London Economist*, has been regarded as the principal source of pre-1914 new issue statistics. Beginning in February 1865, this periodical regularly published monthly tables containing lists of publicly offered new securities, together with the amounts 'created' and 'called'. In their terms a capital creation 'includes only that part of the registered capital offered for immediate subscription by the public'. And excluded, where ascertainable, vendors' shares.[3] In listing specific creations, *The Investor's Monthly Manual* did not practise consistency. It would often record the gross total of the nominal amount offered, and on other occasions the actual market price at which the issue was disposed.

C. K. Hobson used *The Investor's Monthly Manual* creations data to develop annual estimates of new overseas issues offered in the British capital market between 1870 and 1913. He included both those issues floated exclusively in Great Britain ('the all-British issues') as well as those floated simultaneously in Great Britain and other places ('the partials'). Hobson assumed that one-half of the latter category in the aggregate was offered in Great Britain and added that amount to the 'all-British' component to obtain his series.[4]

The use of *The Investor's Monthly Manual* creation statistics as a measure of new British portfolio foreign investment and as an indicator of the net export of capital has been challenged on a variety of grounds. First, the amount offered for subscription may not be absorbed by the investing public. The issue may thus be totally or partially withdrawn by the responsible financial institution.

---

[1] Conceptually, net portfolio foreign investment is equal to total overseas issues — redemptions of outstanding issues — movements in outstanding securities. We neglect in this formulation as insignificant both British new issues floated in overseas markets and redemptions of outstanding British securities in the pre-1914 era.

[2] Leland H. Jenks, *The Migration of British Capital to 1875* (New York : Alfred A. Knopf, 1927), pp. 419–426.

[3] *The Investor's Monthly Manual*, December 1865, 374.

[4] C. K. Hobson, *The Export of Capital*, p. 219. It is misleading to suggest, as does Cairncross, that Hobson used money calls in his analysis of British foreign investment. Cf. A. K. Cairncross, 'The English Capital Market Before 1914', *Economics*, May 1958, p. 142.

The vendors also may have second thoughts and take a portion of the issue. Moreover, even if the entire issue is sold the amount of funds actually called from investors may represent only a fraction of the total.[1]

In 1961, Harvey Segal and I presented a paper that was designed in part to offset the limitations of the creation statistics. We realized the need for and the significance of accurate information on the money calls, the actual payments made by British investors in acquiring foreign and colonial issues. In a more fundamental sense it was necessary to examine each issue and the associated transactions in creation and calls in order to construct a complete universe of new overseas lending.

By focusing on the individual issue as the point of departure in the investigation, we could compile and develop valuable information on the geographic, political and economic characteristics of British overseas lending. To achieve this objective we established an elaborate numerical code that facilitated the classification of each issue by the following attributes of the borrower : (A) continent and country ; (B) political status ; (C) climatic-ethnic region ; (D) type of issuer ; (E) industry of issuer ; and (F) the kind of security issued. The code contains almost one hundred and eighty countries on seven continents, ninety industrial groups that have been consolidated into ten sectors and various combinations, and extensive subdivisions of the type of issuer and other classifications. With the assistance of contemporary sources such as the *Stock Exchange Year Book* and Burdett's *Stock Exchange Official Intelligence*, we proceeded to identify and code more than 9,100 foreign and colonial transactions from *The Investor's Monthly Manual*'s monthly listings of creations and calls for the period 1865–94. The data on each transaction was then punched on a card. The information on all the cards was placed on magnetic tape, and with the aid of a carefully prepared and elaborate programme, an IBM 704 computer generated a vast output of monthly and annual time series and matrices or cross-tabulations in less than an hour.[2] The paper we prepared summarized the salient features of the basic data which provided

---

[1] See the excellent discussions in C. K. Hobson, *The Export of Capital*, 209–211 ; N. G. Butlin, *Australian Domestic Product, Investment and Foreign Borrowing*, 1861–1938/39 (Cambridge, at The University Press, 1962), pp. 405–406 ; A. R. Hall, 'The English Capital Market Before 1914 — A Reply', *Economica*, November 1958, 342 ; and *The London Capital Market*, pp. 87–88, 203–206.

[2] At this point, I would like to acknowledge the innovating role of Harvey Segal in conceiving the 'grand design' of constructing an elaborate code and of employing the electronic computer to cope with this problem.

new insights into the geographic distribution and industrial composition of new British foreign investment. It also illustrated the possibilities and fruitfulness of data-processing techniques in illuminating the quantitative aspects of international capital movements.

The present paper employs the same basic procedure for the entire period 1865–1914. It, however, introduces several important innovations with the result that the new figures presented here are not comparable with the statistics contained in the 1961 paper. First, the earlier study confined its compilation to *The Investor's Monthly Manual* monthly lists, with a minimum of corrections. Subsequent research indicated that this source contained a variety of errors and omissions. Calls were not reported completely for many issues. In many instances, especially for small or private ventures, only the nominal initial payments accompanying the application for the issue were recorded. In other cases, particularly for government and railroad issues, the substantial payments made when the securities were allotted to the investor were omitted.[1] Besides, *The Investor's Monthly Manual* excluded private placements, omitted some offerings in the provinces and in foreign capital markets and even missed selected publicly offered issues in London throughout the entire period. In short, it was necessary to rely on a wide variety of sources that included Burdett's *Stock Exchange Official Intelligence*, *The Stock Exchange Yearbook*, *The Parliamentary Papers*, various financial journals, and above all, a vast mass of unpublished research material on British foreign capital issues that was provided by Leland Jenks ('The Jenks Files')[2] to compensate for the above deficiencies. We were then able to construct more complete creation and call estimates of new British portfolio foreign investments that included data on publicly offered issues in London, the Provinces, and non-British capital markets and private placements.

Second, in our first presentation, we followed the procedure of *The Investor's Monthly Manual* and differentiated between the 'all British' and 'partial' issues. Although series were compiled for both, our analysis of the data was confined to the former sector.

[1] This consistent bias towards under-reporting calls was corrected by analysis of the monthly lists of calls of *The Investor's Monthly Manual*, which contained a column 'already paid' that provided the basis for the correcting adjustment.

[2] The Jenks files refer to a massive parallel investigation that was conducted in England before 1940. It relied on the available abundant material in London and focused on assembling annual data on net capital subscribed.

In this paper, we eliminated the artificial distinction between the two types of issues by estimating the British share of the partials to obtain more complete statistics of total new British portfolio foreign investment. This objective was accomplished by rejecting C. K. Hobson's technique of assuming that the British component of the annual aggregate partial security flotations constituted 50 per cent of the total in favour of a thorough examination of each issue to determine as precisely as possible the amount of British capital subscribed.[1]

The final innovation involved the more systematic treatment of conversions. In our original presentation, the statistics derived from *The Investigator's Monthly Manual* compilations included some conversion issues. Conceptually, it is necessary to distinguish between two types of conversions: 'swap conversions' and 'export conversions'. A 'swap conversion' involved the exchange of a new issue for an old issue that was entirely in the hands of British investors. A variant would be the sale of a new flotation to a particular group of British investors to retire obligations possessed by another group of British security holders. In both cases, no new British long-term capital was forthcoming. 'Export conversions', on the other hand, required the sale of new issues to British investors to retire floating or short-term debt held either in Great Britain, the borrowing nation or third countries, or long-term debt that was held in either the borrowing nation or in third countries. In each instance, new long-term British capital would be mobilized for foreign investment.[2] It is therefore necessary to include the 'export conversions' as part of new British portfolio foreign investment. The Type of Issuer segment of the code was, consequently, modified to reflect this distinction and to facilitate the proper classification of each transaction.

The accomplishment of these three major operations for the entire period 1865–1914 required the accurate coding of more than 41,000 separate transactions (including more than 1,000 'swap conversions') and the punching of an equivalent number of cards. With a revised

[1] Commenting on C. K. Hobson's 50 per cent assumption, A. R. Hall states: 'This assumption appears to be generous for 1895–1899. It may lead to some understatement of total overseas issues in the last decade of the series.' A. R. Hall, 'A Note on The English Capital Market Before 1914', *Economica*, February 1957, p. 62.
[2] C. K. Hobson, *The Export of Capital*, p. 211. It should be noted that the flotation of security in Great Britain by a foreign borrower to retire short-term obligations held in Great Britain signifies that the United Kingdom is exporting long-term capital and importing short-term capital.

and more elaborate programme to provide additional matrices, an IBM 7094 computer in June 1965 — as a mark of technical progress — completed the operations in less than an hour !

II

We will first present the data on money calls in the form of fifty-year totals to obtain an overall view of the experience of the entire

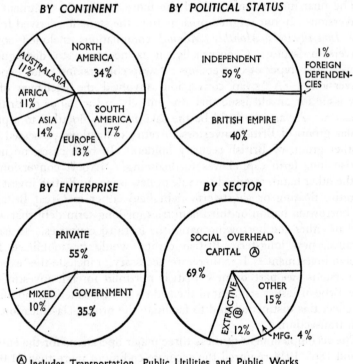

BY CONTINENT

BY POLITICAL STATUS

BY ENTERPRISE

BY SECTOR

Ⓐ Includes Transportation, Public Utilities and Public Works
Ⓑ Includes Agriculture and Mining

CHART I

half century. Aggregate new British portfolio foreign investment approximated £4,082,000,000 and occupied a pre-eminent position in total British capital exports.[1]

[1] If we subtract the 1914 figure of £203·0 million, the forty-nine-year total is £3,879·0 million, which can be compared, subject to the qualifications stated in the previous section, with Feis' adjustment of the Paish stock estimate of £4,014 million.

Chart I provides a breakdown of this total by four major classifications : continent, political status, industry, and type of enterprise of the issuer. A study of the pattern of pre-1914 British foreign investments shows a dual tendency towards concentration and proliferation. The latter feature, reflecting its almost cosmopolitan character and widespread involvement in diverse enterprises and industries, was especially evident in the last five years (1909–13) before the outbreak of the general war. In that short interval, almost 24 per cent of the total British capital called for the five decades was mobilized for overseas borrowers.

An examination of the chart presenting the continental breakdown shows that the New World received more than 51 per cent, or almost £2,100 million, of the total. North America, the leading continent, absorbed almost £1,400 million and far outstripped the other areas. Nevertheless, each of the remaining continents, illustrating the proliferation process, received at least ten per cent of new British long-term capital exports.

If the political status criterion is employed, we find that approximately 60 per cent of new British overseas lending went to independent countries and slightly less than 40 per cent to the Empire. The availability of abundant private ventures with attractive prospects for remuneration and appreciation and the expanding needs of various public authorities, especially in the independent countries of the New World and to a lesser degree in Europe and Asia, more than counterbalanced the real or 'alleged' advantages associated with the protection of the British flag.[1]

A fruitful method to study the composition of long-term capital exports is to determine its division among the major climatic-ethnic categories.

The great bulk of trans-European British investment — approximately 68 per cent, or £2,400 million — flowed to the temperate regions of recent settlement. Only 27 per cent, or less than £960 million, was absorbed by the tropics, and the remaining 5 per cent, or slightly over £180 million, was received by non-tropical Asia. The greatest capital-exporting nation of the pre-1914 world

---

[1] It should be noted that this 60 per cent–40 per cent division of new British foreign portfolio investment compares favourably with Paish's 52 per cent–48 per cent split of total British foreign security holdings. This disparity can, in part, be explained by the growing capacity of the independent developed nations of North America and of Europe to repurchase their own securities and to acquire foreign issues from the British.

was thus supplying an annual average of less than £20 million in new funds to those densely populated tropical regions which, by 1965 standards, are regarded as the most underdeveloped areas of the world.[1] The tropical section of the British Empire, including India, Egypt and Malaysia, received a total of £510 million, or slightly more than £10 million a year.

The Type of Issuers classification shows a diverse mix of enterprises obtaining new long-term funds in the British capital market. Private firms, with almost 55 per cent of the total, occupied the primary position. Colonial and foreign governmental bodies — national, provincial and local — received 35 per cent of the aggregate money calls for both additional requirements and export conversions. Mixed enterprises, distinguished by the contractual arrangements which they concluded with various public authorities providing for the guarantee of interest payments on their obligations, absorbed the remaining 10 per cent.

A study of the Economic Sector breakdown impressively demonstrates the significance of overseas lending for the purpose of building the social overhead capital of the borrowing nations. This category, which includes transportation, public utilities and other public works, received almost 70 per cent of new British foreign portfolio investment. Transportation, the largest industrial segment, obtained at least 46 per cent, and railroads, its major component, 41 per cent of the total.[2] By contrast, less than 12 per cent was invested in the extractive industries. The emphasis was thus placed on the development of those facilities which increased the capacity of primary producing nations to export marketable surpluses to Europe. Finally, it is abundantly clear that British funds did not directly foster the development of extensive overseas industrialization as less than 4 per cent of the total capital called was invested in manufacturing.

The use of our classification system provides some interesting insights into the industrial and regional concentration and spread of British foreign investment. Alan Hall attributes its geographical proliferation to the flexibility of British investors, who shifted their

[1] Ragnar Nurkse, 'The Problem of International Investment Today in The Light of Nineteenth-Century Experience', *Economic Journal*, lxiv (December 1954), p. 750.
[2] We say 'at least' because it is difficult to determine precisely these amounts owing to the variegated character of government expenditures on public works. In addition, it is likely that the 'miscellaneous' classification, consisting of almost 3 per cent of the total and represented almost exclusively by governmental bodies, contains some outlays for transportation and railways.

horizons in the wake of the appearance of new opportunities. He writes : 'This unevenness in the rate of lending to particular areas meant that the greater part of the investment outstanding in 1914 had occurred in relatively short periods of time. This certainly was the case with Australia and there is plenty of evidence that her experience was not exceptional.' [1]

Our data supports his contention strongly for Australasia, Southeast Asia, and possibly South Africa, areas in which one large spurt provided a significant portion of the total capital invested. It has substantial validity for Russia, Canada and Latin America. Hall's notion, however, is not relevant to the United States, which experienced an almost continuous influx of foreign capital, punctuated by sharp reversals in the late 1870's and the 1890's. In fact, it seems legitimate to infer from the data showing the fifty-year pattern contained in Chart I, that the single most important force accounting for the primacy of North America among the continents, independent countries in the Political Status categories, the regions of recent settlements among the climatic-ethnic groups, private enterprise in the type of issuers, and finally, social overhead capital among the economic sectors, was the huge demands for building and maintaining the 216,000 miles of the American rail net, constructed largely under private auspices in this epoch. Nor was it an accident that the largest department of the London Stock Exchange was American Railroads and the subtitle of Burdett's *Stock Exchange Official Intelligence* was 'A Precis of English, *American* and Foreign Securities'. Aggregate new British long-term portfolio investment in the United States, surpassing the amount placed in all of Latin America, exceeded £835 million and constituted almost 21 per cent of the total.

This phenomenon might appear paradoxical in view of the successful maturation of the American economy, which provided the basis of the rapid accumulation of capital throughout this period. Modern experience has shown that the largest volume of international trade takes place between developed or rapidly developing economies. The same point may be made for international capital movements. Just as post-1919 United States has had a low propensity to import but has remained the largest single importer in international trade due to its high level of economic activity, so the United States of 1865–1914, with a declining propensity to finance her total investment requirements by overseas borrowing, was the

[1] A. R. Hall, *The London Capital Market*, p. 189.

single most important foreign source of new security issues in the British capital market.[1]

In short, a nation, experiencing the largest absolute increments in national output and capital formation, may play a formidable role in foreign capital markets. The concentration and proliferation aspects of new British foreign portfolio investment was thus manifest in a spectrum extending from rapidly developing countries, especially the United States, to the tropics, colonial and non-colonial.

III

Our basic annual time series for total British portfolio foreign investment in money calls appear in Charts II through IV and the Appendix Table. They provide the basis for the following discussion of trends and fluctuations.

In Chart II, where the data on aggregate capital called for the entire world and particular continents have been plotted, we find no evidence of a persistent trend extending over the five decades. Each series (even North America) is subject to major reversals in direction, that reflect both changes in the volume of aggregate new British foreign portfolio investment and its periodic geographic redistribution.

Nor, despite the importance attached by some writers to the Empire, do we find evidence of a trend to invest in that area, at the expense of independent countries.[2] Others, notably John Hobson and various Marxists, have argued that the pressure to export capital arising within a developed capitalist economy in the United Kingdom was the principal force generating the overseas expansion of the British Empire, which, in turn led to a redirection of capital toward newly acquired territories.[3] An examination of the first

---

[1] S. B. Saul, *Studies in British Overseas Trade* (Liverpool : Liverpool University Press, 1960), p. 66. Foreign holdings of American securities on 30 June, 1914 aggregated $5,400,000,000. See United States Department of Commerce, *Historical Statistics of The United States, Colonial Times to 1957* (Washington, D.C.: Superintendent of Documents, U.S. Government Printing Office, 1960), p. 565 ; Matthew Simon, 'The United States Balance of Payments, 1861–1900', *Trends In the American Economy in The Nineteenth Century*, Studies in Income and Wealth, xxiv, pp. 629–711.

[2] For example, 'but from the mid-1870's onwards investment in Empire became more and more important', S. B. Saul, *Studies*, p. 67, and 'the long-term trend after 1873 was away from Europe to the primary producing countries and *especially* toward those within the Empire', A. R. Hall, *The London Capital Market*, p. 12.

[3] For a recent discussion, see D. K. Fieldhouse, 'Imperialism: An Historiographical Revision', *The Economic History Review*, xiv, no. 2, December 1961, pp. 187–209.

three panels in Chart III shows that, although substantial absolute
increases in the amount of new British foreign portfolio investment
occurred in both independent countries and the Empire, the Empire

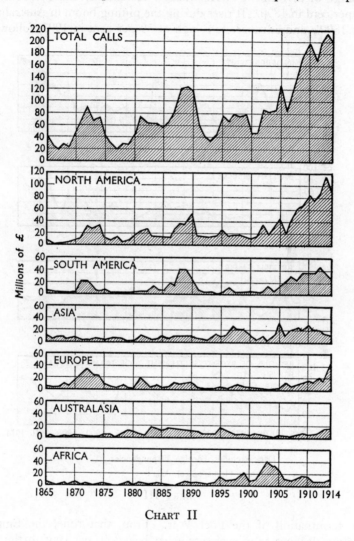

CHART II

portion displays no persistent trend. Those writers who emphasize
the shift from Europe to the Empire neglect the significance of pre-
1870 investments in Indian government and railroad securities and
over-estimate the importance of the pattern prevailing in the hectic

pre-1873 prosperous years and during the aftermath of the Franco-Prussian war. After reaching a peak in 1885 of 67 per cent following a surge of investment in Australasia, the Empire share declines to 25 per cent in 1890. It rises during the mining boom in Australia in the 1890's and advances to a high of 59 per cent in 1903, following

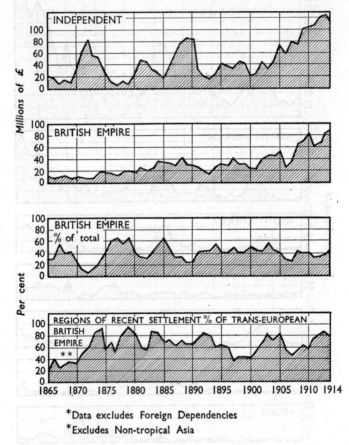

*Data excludes Foreign Dependencies
*Excludes Non-tropical Asia

CHART III

the termination of the Boer War. From that time, the Empire portion declines to a level somewhat below 40 per cent in the last three pre-war years.

With the exception of South Africa, most of the territory acquired by the British Empire in this period was located in the tropics. An examination of the last panel of Chart III indicates the absence of any tendency to invest an increasing share in the tropics, which included India, an area acquired before 1800. On the contrary, the great mass of British capital exported to the overseas Empire gravitated toward the regions of recent settlement. In the case of South Africa, new British portfolio foreign investment evolved through four stages : Advancing sharply from £1·5 million to £12·8 million in 1899, collapsing to an annual level of £2·4 million during the years of the Boer War (1900–1), reaching a new peak of £36·1 million in the immediate post-war aftermath in 1903, and declining to under

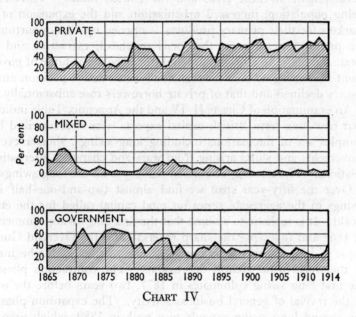

CHART IV

£5 million in the last three pre-war years. These statistics cast serious doubt about the crucial importance of the 'New Empire' as an outlet for British capital exports.

In the pre-1914 pattern, private enterprises acquired an increased importance among foreign and colonial flotations in the British capital market. Evidence of this trend can be found in Chart IV, where the data by type of issuer by shares of total calls is plotted.

The decline in the portion absorbed by mixed enterprises is attributable to two sets of factors, geographic shifts and the process of general development. Prior to 1875, British investors bought substantial quantities of the issues of the state guaranteed railroads

47

of India and Russia. The relative importance of these borrowers declined after that date. Of greater significance was the growth of such underdeveloped areas as Latin America, Canada and other parts of the Empire. This condition produced the revision of contractual arrangements between governments and railroads completed or in the process of contraction. Interest guarantee provisions were frequently eliminated. In other cases, new railroads and other public facilities were established without such support from government agencies. More fundamentally, the rapid, although uneven development of these areas and the United States — reflected in rising population, increased urbanization and the expansion of the markets for their primary products — opened up vast opportunities for private enterprise in the social overhead, extractive and real estate sectors. As a result, although the absolute volume of government borrowing advanced substantially, its relative position among issuers declined and that of private borrowers rose substantially.

An examination of Charts II–IV and the Appendix Table indicates that new long-term British capital exports were characterized by a complex set of fluctuations including long swings, shorter cyclical movements and shifts arising from wars and changing international relations. The ensuing discussion will focus on the long swings.

Over the fifty-year span we find almost two-and-one-half long swings in the aggregate series on total capital called for the entire world. It is realistic to assume that the first long swing commenced in 1862 and following the sharp reversal after the Overend Gurney panic of 1866, reaches a peak in 1872, one year before the beginning of the world-wide cyclical depression.[1] The contraction phase of the first long swing culminates in 1877, two years before the onset of the revival of general business activity. The expansion phase of the second long swing extends to a peak in 1889, which precedes the Baring Panic of the following year. The ensuing decline is especially pronounced in the early 1890's and reaches a bottom in 1893. Owing to the anaemic character of the recovery in the 1890's and the adverse impact of the Boer War on new overseas lending we place the trough of the second long swing in 1901.[2] The upswing

---

[1] The 1862 date is based on Imlah's data on net international capital movements. See Albert M. Imlah, *Economic Elements in the Pax Britannica* (Cambridge, Massachusetts : Harvard University, 1958), pp. 72–75, and the table and discussion in Jeffrey Williamson, *American Growth and The Balance of Payments 1820–1913* (Chapel Hill : The University of North Carolina Press, 1964), pp. 208–210.

[2] *Ibid.* Using Douglass' data, Brinley Thomas asserts : 'The years 1888 to 1901–2 saw a downswing in foreign lending', cf. Brinley Thomas, *Migration and Economic Growth* (Cambridge: at the University Press, 1954), p. 98.

TABLE 1

LONG-SWING DATING AND LEVELS FOR TURNING POINTS IN NEW
BRITISH PORTFOLIO FOREIGN INVESTMENT AND MAJOR
COMPONENTS, 1865–1914

(Millions of £ in Money Calls)

Series	First Peak	First Trough	Second Peak	Second Trough	Third Peak
World Total	93·9	19·4	122·9	49·5	217·4
	1872	1877	1889	1901	1913
Political Status					
Independent Countries	84·4	6·6	87·4	20·2	126·9
	1872	1877	1889	1900	1913
British Empire	20·9	13·3	42·2	24·0	90·9
	1874	1877	1888	1901	1914
Climatic-Ethnic					
Regions of Recent Settlement	40·9	8·5	86·4	24·7	148·0
	1874	1877	1890	1900	1913
Tropics	22·7	4·7	27·9	12·1	68·7
	1872	1879	1888	1901	1910
Continents and Country					
North America	33·1	4·3	52·8	10·7	116·9
	1874	1877	1890	1900	1913
South America	21·4	0·6	40·2	4·5	45·8
	1871	1877	1889	1902	1912
Europe	34·8	3·7	12·3	0·8	43·5
	1872	1877	1890	1904	1914
United States	25·4	1·6	44·8	5·5	53·9
	1872	1877	1890	1900	1913
Enterprise					
Private	41·4	4·4	86·6	29·3	152·4
	1872	1877	1890	1900	1912
Mixed		7·7	23·3	1·7	17·1
		1876	1887	1903	1914
Government	41·9	13·2	53·5	14·0	95·5
	1871	1877	1888	1901	1914
Industry and Sector					
Manufacturing	1·1	—	18·2	1·2	21·1
	1872	1879	1890	1900	1912
Railroad	34·2	7·1	57·6	14·9	88·6
	1872	1877	1890	1900	1913
Social Overhead Capital	66·2	15·2	89·8	31·9	176·4
	1872	1877	1888	1900	1914
Extractive	7·0	0·5	14·2	9·9	51·8
	1872	1879	1889	1900	1910

of the next long cycle then proceeds vigorously to reach a peak, one year before the outbreak of the First World War.

In Table 1, we have assembled the dates of the troughs and peaks of the long swings and the levels prevailing in those years for the major components of the principal classifications of the data. Observe the clustering of the turning points of various series around 1872, 1877, 1889, 1901 and 1913. An analysis of the data will show that the intensity of the swings, as reflected in per cent changes between peaks and troughs, for the following series — Independent Countries, Regions of Recent Settlement, North America, South America, Europe, the United States, Private Enterprise, Manufacturing, Railroads and Social Overhead Capital — are generally greater or almost equal to the comparable changes in the world total. By contrast, with the exception of the third long cycle, less pronounced swings can be found in the British Empire, Mixed Enterprise and Government Series. Moreover, little evidence can be found of the two-and-half cycle sequence in the Australian, African and Asian series. Africa experiences no major upswing prior to 1875, rises sharply between 1893 and 1903 — due to the mining boom and the aftermath of the Boer War — and trends downward to the war. Australia's behaviour is similarly perverse as it rises in the mid-1870's due to government borrowing for railroads and public works and peaks in 1886. In the mid-1890's it rises again due to the West Australian gold-mining boom and then declines in the early twentieth century until the immediate pre-war years.[1] Similarly, Asia shows no surge in the early 1870's, but does participate in the upswings of the second and third cycles.

The fluctuations in the volume of capital called for total new British portfolio foreign investment is largely, though not entirely, ascribable to the sharp fluctuations in the North American, the United States, Independent Nations and Regions of Recent Settlements Series.[2] In each of these areas, private enterprise played the principal and increasingly significant role. The flow of funds in the form of money calls to these private issuers was moulded by two sets of influences. The demand of foreign borrowers for new British capital was first determined by their changing appraisals of their profit prospects. The second force was the ability and willingness of the British investors to lend. Their actions were principally

---

[1] Alan R. Hall, *The London Capital Market*, pp. 189–191.
[2] See comparable discussion in Jeffrey Williamson, *American Growth*, pp. 212–216.

affected by their appraisal of profit prospects, including the risk factor in the borrowing nation, the state of the British money market and alternative opportunities in Great Britain and other foreign areas.

To contend, then, that the long swings in aggregate new British foreign investments were induced by the long swings in the capital called by the United States and other areas in the regions of recent settlements is to suggest the existence and persistence of a significant differential or the widening of the differential in bond yields and profit prospects, in favour of the borrowing nation over the expansion phase of the long cycle. The reverse condition, reflected in the diminution of capital called, would prevail in the contraction phase of the long swing.

These observations are preliminary and partial. They point up the statistical evidence for long swings in our data but do not attempt to provide a logical basis for their periodicity. Moreover, they omit an appraisal of the significant role of foreign public borrowing in affecting fluctuations in aggregate new overseas lending. An inspection of the data in the Appendix Table and Chart IV shows that the volume of capital called by foreign and colonial government displayed less volatility than private borrowing. In shorter cyclical contractions, the government share tended to rise and, on some occasions, notably 1907–8, the absolute magnitudes of calls experienced a substantial increase. On balance, the movements in aggregate volume of government borrowing conformed with the long swings in total new portfolio foreign investments. Further study of the data in disaggregated form may shed additional light on this problem.

IV

In this final section the basic aggregate series are compared with related statistics. In Table 2 (columns 1 and 4) we observe that Imlah's series on net international capital movements shows a close correspondence with the money calls series on total new British portfolio foreign investment. In both series are found the big surges of the early 1870's, the late 1880's and the decade 1904–13, and the depressed periods of the 1870's and the 1890's. Imlah's long swing turning points are 1872, 1877, 1890, 1898 and 1913. Whereas the corresponding peaks and troughs for portfolio foreign investment calls are 1872, 1877, 1889, 1901 and 1913. The two series moved

TABLE 2

NEW BRITISH PORTFOLIO FOREIGN INVESTMENT AND RELATED
STATISTICS, 1865–1914

(Millions of £)

	Imlah	Hobson	Brit. New Port. For. Inv.			Moniteur	
	Net. Int. Cap.	Creations	Creations	Calls	Calls	Creations	%
	Move. (1)	Total (2)	Total (3)	Total (4)	Gov't, RR., Ind. (5)	(6)	5/6 (7)
1865	34·9	—	59·0	42·5	24·3	—	—
1866	33·0	—	21·6	25·2	17·5	—	—
1867	42·2	—	26·5	18·4	15·5	—	—
1868	36·5	—	37·3	29·1	25·1	—	—
1869	46·7	—	17·8	21·9	16·2	—	—
1870	44·1	45·2	46·2	44·7	32·3	—	—
1871	71·3	84.3	77·5	70·2	60·9	618·6	9·8
1872	98·0	116·8	86·0	93·9	69·2	424·0	16·3
1873	81·3	54·9	79·1	69·3	50·4	363·5	13·9
1874	70·9	64·4	73·7	74·5	61·0	155·5	39·2
1875	51·3	35·2	44·2	46·1	37·0	50·2	73·7
1876	23·2	26·3	28·1	30·4	25·6	141·6	18·1
1877	13·1	13·7	22·9	19·4	16·6	292·8	5·7
1878	16·9	25·0	34·0	31·7	25·0	174·6	14·3
1879	35·5	27·0	34·5	30·5	23·5	278·7	8·4
1880	35·6	40·7	46·3	41·7	28·4	168·2	16·9
1881	65·7	60·0	89·9	74·2	52·5	233·7	22·5
1882	58·7	49·8	78·8	67·5	45·8	164·8	27·8
1883	48·8	45·5	71·9	61·2	55·9	148·5	37·6
1884	72·3	57·0	58·0	63·0	46·5	180·7	25·7
1885	62·3	55·9	52·7	55·3	46·6	124·7	37·4
1886	78·9	56·2	74·4	69·8	56·4	251·7	22·4
1887	87·7	65·8	83·7	84·4	62·6	190·0	32·9
1888	91·9	101·2	133·3	119·1	81·5	295·9	27·5
1889	80·9	107·1	138·5	122·9	74·9	501·9	14·9
1890	98·5	101·3	110·7	116·6	84·4	223·9	37·7
1891	69·4	51·2	51·8	57·6	37·1	225·5	16·5
1892	59·1	32·3	40·1	39·8	25·5	93·5	27·3
1893	53·0	25·2	31·5	32·1	23·3	134·7	17·3
1894	38·7	48·9	43·8	48·3	30·2	191·9	15·7
1895	40·0	57·6	74·2	77·7	34·3	179·5	19·1
1896	56·8	37·3	73·4	68·5	23·7	332·0	7·1
1897	41·6	36·7	77·3	78·4	40·7	318·6	12·8
1898	22·9	51·0	66·6	76·6	51·7	297·3	17·4
1899	42·4	45·9	82·3	78·2	42·8	362·7	11·8
1900	37·9	26·1	50·3	49·6	27·2	415·0	6·6

TABLE 2—(cont.)

	Imlah	Hobson	Brit. New Port. For. Inv.			Moniteur	
	Net. Int. Cap. Move. (1)	Creations Total (2)	Creations Total (3)	Calls Total (4)	Calls Gov't, RR., Ind. (5)	Creations (6)	% 5/6 (7)
1901	33·9	27·0	53·7	49·5	34·2	366·6	9·3
1902	33·3	62·2	88·3	89·3	63·1	371·0	18·4
1903	44·8	60·0	82·6	82·9	66·0	326·9	20·2
1904	51·7	64·6	87·9	88·0	65·7	446·7	14·7
1905	81·5	110·6	137·0	128·9	98·7	618·3	16·0
1906	117·5	73·0	87·8	85·0	50·2	553·0	9·8
1907	154·1	79·3	110·9	116·3	71·7	599·4	12·0
1908	154·7	117·9	154·7	147·4	110·4	773·9	14·3
1909	135·6	150·5	173·3	175·7	119·1	787·4	15·1
1910	167·3	179·8	203·2	198·0	99·1	801·4	12·4
1911	196·9	142·7	177·8	169·2	101·9	622·8	16·4
1912	197·1	144·6	206·5	200·7	115·6	642·6	18·0
1913	224·3	149·7	206·6	217·4	141·9	—	—
1914	—	—	192·6	203·2	137·2	—	—

(1) Albert M. Imlah, *Economic Elements in the Pax Britannica* (Cambridge, Massachusetts: Harvard University Press 1958), pp. 72–75.
(2) C. K. Hobson, *The Export of Capital* (London: Constable and Co. Ltd., 1914), p. 219.
(3), (4), (5) See discussion in Section I.
(6) Eugene Varga (Editor), *World Economic Crises*, vol. iii, *Monetary Crises* (1821–1938) (Moscow State Financial Press 1939), pp. 832–862. The data was expressed in Belgian francs and was converted at rate of 25·2 francs per £. See Arthur I. Bloomfield, *Short Term International Movements Under The Pre-*1914 *Gold Standard* (Princeton, New Jersey: International Finance Section, Department of Economics, Princeton University, 1963), p. 95.

together in 32 out of the 48 years, or 66·7 per cent of the time. The lack of greater congruence is not surprising since variations in new portfolio foreign investment may be offset in many years by movements in outstanding securities, redemptions and the short-term capital account.

A comparison of Hobson's creation statistics with our creation series (columns 2 and 3 of Table 2) shows they move together in 37 out of 40 years. It will be observed that Hobson's figures for 1871 and 1872 are substantially greater because his 50 per cent assumption for the partials is too high for the French war and indemnity loans. In most of the remaining years, our statistics are somewhat larger than Hobson's primarily due to the omissions of *The Investor's Monthly Manual* upon which his series is based. To a lesser degree, the 50 per cent assumption for partials actually leads to an under-estimation of the portion of these issues absorbed by the British in the pre-1914 years.

Our call series can also be compared with the annual new issues data compiled in the Belgian financial periodical, *Le Moniteur Des Interêts Materielles*, which was published by the De Lavelaye family in Brussels. They attempted to keep account of the total amount of new securities that were floated in all capital markets of the world including those of the borrowing nations. Since their coverage was not as complete as ours, we have confined the comparison to the data on aggregate government, railroad and manufacturing issues. In Table 2, columns 5, 6, 7, the data are presented and we have computed ratios which measure the share of new world capital issues in these sectors represented by new British portfolio foreign investment, for the period 1871–1912. It should be clear from inspecting column 7 that the British share experiences a secular decline. This trend reflects the more rapidly increasing capacity of the capital markets of the United States, France, Germany to absorb new issues.[1]

This introductory paper has concentrated on presenting and de-scribing the basic data in the new series. The fifty-year totals for our major components confirm the extent of the sharply unequal distribution of new British portfolio foreign investment. A relatively small portion was absorbed by the colonial and non-colonial tropics, while the regions of recent settlement — especially independent countries, such as the United States — received more substantial amounts to foster the growth of their social overhead capital. Examination of the annual time series shows the absence of any persistent trend toward particular regions or to the British Empire. Study of the enterprise data demonstrates the increasing importance of private foreign and colonial borrowers as the major source of new security issues in the British capital market. Finally, the statistics for the major series provide support for the existence of approximately two-and-half long swings as a principal form of fluctuation in the half century before 1914.

It now becomes necessary to combine further study with additional research on both general and specific questions in this area. In-tensive analysis of the vast body of output of the two-dimensional

---

[1] This conclusion could be altered in view of the heavy British absorption of private issues in the transportation sector and public utilities, agriculture and mining. Unfortunately, the *Moniteur* does not contain such data.

matrices and of monthly statistics will proceed. Study of the data on redemptions compiled from *The Investor's Monthly Manual* and processed by the same programme on the IBM-7094 will shed additional light on another item in the capital account and add to our understanding of the geographical shifts in pre-1914 British foreign investment. Of equal importance is the need to carry on external analysis by mobilizing related data on foreign trade, national income, public debts, security prices and yields in order to test the validity of variants of both the classical and the income approach to the theory international capital movements. In short, the agenda to continue the systematic exploration of the causes and effects of pre-1914 foreign investment including its relationship to economic development, more than a half century after the event, poses challenging possibilities.

APPENDIX TABLE

SELECTED COMPONENTS OF NEW BRITISH PORTFOLIO FOREIGN INVESTMENT (MONEY CALLS), 1865–1914

(Millions of £)

	(I) By Continents *						
Year	Europe (1)	North America (2)	South America (3)	Africa (4)	Asia (5)	Australasia (6)	Oceania (7)
1865	7·5	7·1	6·9	8·5	11·2	1·2	0·1
1866	4·5	4·4	4·6	4·1	4·5	3·2	—
1867	4·6	1·5	2·0	0·5	7·5	2·2	—
1868	11·7	3·5	1·5	1·5	8·1	2·8	—
1869	8·0	4·8	0·9	—	6·3	1·9	—
1870	18·6	10·0	4·1	2·2	7·1	2·5	0·3
1871	29·2	13·0	21·4	0·4	3·7	2·5	—
1872	34·9	30·8	21·4	1·9	2·2	2·8	—
1873	25·4	26·8	8·0	1·2	4·1	3·8	—
1874	24·7	33·1	5·7	0·5	5·9	4·6	—
1875	10·1	12·2	8·4	4·5	4·0	6·9	—
1876	5·0	9·3	1·5	2·1	5·1	7·4	—
1877	3·7	4·3	0·6	1·7	6·7	2·5	—
1878	6·1	6·2	1·9	3·2	5·0	9·3	—
1879	3·3	7·2	1·1	5·6	0·7	12·4	—
1880	2·7	18·3	3·1	2·7	3·2	11·7	—
1881	20·6	22·2	6·2	5·8	10·6	8·5	0·2
1882	12·1	28·6	7·6	4·5	9·4	5·3	—

55

Capital Movements and Economic Development

(I) By Continents *

Year	Europe (1)	North America (2)	South America (3)	Africa (4)	Asia (5)	Australasia (6)	Oceania (7)
1883	4·7	16·6	13·8	2·6	4·6	19·0	—
1884	7·3	15·1	9·7	6·7	5·8	18·5	—
1885	3·4	14·1	7·1	4·7	11·0	14·9	—
1886	5·0	14·0	19·3	2·5	9·6	19·4	0·1
1887	12·9	23·9	18·9	1·5	10·5	16·5	0·2
1888	10·1	37·2	40·3	4·2	10·7	15·7	0·9
1889	11·2	37·2	40·2	8·9	11·2	14·2	—
1890	12·3	52·8	23·3	4·6	10·8	12·8	—
1891	5·0	18·7	9·4	6·6	5·7	12·3	0·4
1892	2·7	14·9	5·4	3·3	4·1	9·2	0·2
1893	1·7	13·1	5·4	2·6	2·5	6·7	0·2
1894	1·8	17·0	1·7	5·2	13·1	9·4	0·1
1895	3·6	26·0	4·1	14·9	10·4	18·7	—
1896	2·7	13·2	11·8	9·6	15·4	15·4	0·4
1897	8·1	16·7	4·9	10·8	27·2	10·7	—
1898	10·1	19·8	6·0	11·6	21·1	7·9	—
1899	8·6	12·1	5·9	21·3	21·7	7·0	1·5
1900	6·9	10·7	6·9	7·2	11·9	6·0	0·2
1901	5·8	14·1	6·7	9·2	4·6	9·1	0·1
1902	5·2	37·3	4·5	24·7	10·8	6·9	—
1903	2·1	17·3	11·3	42·4	6·6	3·0	0·2
1904	0·8	31·3	7·1	32·0	15·2	1·7	—
1905	3·0	43·9	13·2	29·9	35·6	3·3	—
1906	14·7	19·1	21·7	10·5	15·8	3·1	0·1
1907	7·0	42·7	30·2	9·5	23·4	3·3	0·2
1908	10·4	62·7	24·6	13·9	29·6	6·1	0·1
1909	13·6	68·4	38·6	18·7	25·4	10·5	0·4
1910	18·8	82·5	39·6	16·3	32·9	6·9	1·1
1911	14·5	73·5	38·5	9·4	24·7	8·4	0·1
1912	22·8	89·9	45·8	9·8	21·5	10·8	0·1
1913	18·9	116·9	36·2	8·1	17·4	18·8	1·2
1914	43·5	82·5	28·2	12·9	16·4	19·4	0·5

	(II) By Political Status †		(III) By Climate and Ethnic Group		
Year	Independent (8)	British Empire (9)	Regions of Rec. Set (10)	Tropics (11)	Other ‡ (12)
1865	21·6	13·2	7·2	26·5	1·1
1866	17·0	8·1	7·7	12·8	0·2
1867	7·8	10·2	5·5	8·3	—
1868	16·9	12·2	6·6	10·8	—
1869	12·1	9·7	5·5	8·1	0·2
1870	33·9	9·9	12·1	12·5	1·5

APPENDIX TABLE—(*cont.*)

	(II) By Political Status †		(III) By Climate and Ethnic Group		
Year	Independent (8)	British Empire (9)	Regions of Rec. Set (10)	Tropics (11)	Other ‡ (12)
1871	62·0	7·8	20·9	19·8	0·2
1872	84·4	7·3	36·1	22·7	0·1
1873	58·3	9·9	35·4	5·5	2·8
1874	53·2	20·9	40·9	8·5	—
1875	27·2	18·6	21·3	14·6	—
1876	12·0	18·4	2·0	5·7	0·3
1877	6·2	13·2	8·5	6·9	0·4
1878	13·6	17·6	18·0	6·6	1·0
1879	9·6	20·8	22·4	4·7	—
1880	22·6	18·7	32·7	6·1	0·3
1881	47·0	25·8	36·1	16·5	0·3
1882	44·7	21·8	39·6	15·0	0·9
1883	33·9	26·1	42·5	11·4	1·8
1884	27·6	35·2	47·6	8·0	—
1885	17·3	35·1	35·2	12·4	4·2
1886	32·1	34·8	43·8	20·4	0·6
1887	55·9	27·9	55·2	15·7	0·6
1888	75·9	42·0	79·8	27·9	1·3
1889	87·4	30·6	83·1	26·4	2·5
1890	85·7	28·6	86·4	15·3	2·2
1891	30·4	25·9	42·3	7·1	2·9
1892	19·7	19·0	29·4	6·7	1·1
1893	15·6	15·9	21·9	8·0	0·3
1894	20·1	27·7	28·1	15·9	2·7
1895	43·8	33·4	54·0	14·7	5·4
1896	38·0	29·9	42·3	17·5	6·1
1897	35·8	42·0	33·4	31·1	5·9
1898	44·2	31·8	38·2	21·0	2·3
1899	40·9	34·0	31·8	26·0	11·8
1900	20·3	25·7	24·7	16·0	2·0
1901	24·7	24·0	31·0	12·1	0·7
1902	45·9	42·1	64·4	15·1	3·5
1903	32·5	49·6	64·1	12·5	4·1
1904	43·9	43·9	58·4	18·8	9·9
1905	74·0	54·3	74·1	23·6	28·2
1906	57·2	25·2	35·1	23·8	11·6
1907	80·3	33·2	71·6	30·4	6·9
1908	77·5	68·4	89·0	42·8	5·2
1909	99·8	71·1	109·7	42·7	8·8
1910	105·3	81·3	106·7	68·7	3·0
1911	107·9	57·4	97·1	44·2	12·4
1912	123·5	66·3	125·6	39·0	9·2
1913	126·9	82·9	148·0	41·1	8·4
1914	103·7	90·9	129·2	29·0	1·4

APPENDIX TABLE—(*cont.*)

	(IV) By Sector of Issuer §			(V) By Type of Issuer		
Year	Social Overhead ‖ (13)	Extractive ¶ (14)	Mfg. (15)	Private (16)	Mixed ** (17)	Gov't. (18)
1865	30·2	2·2	0·5	19·2	9·0	14·3
1866	15·4	1·1	0·1	10·5	5·1	9·8
1867	12·2	0·6	0·1	3·2	7·7	7·5
1868	26·3	0·9	0·1	4·5	13·5	11·2
1869	18·6	1·4	0·1	5·9	8·1	8·0
1870	29·9	5·6	—	14·7	6·5	23·5
1871	46·4	5·1	0·4	14·5	6·4	49·3
1872	66·2	7·0	1·1	41·4	4·5	47·9
1873	51·1	3·4	1·0	37·3	5·1	26·8
1874	65·0	3·8	0·7	28·7	7·8	38·0
1875	42·4	1·0	0·6	13·3	3·7	29·2
1876	27·1	0·6	0·3	9·2	0·8	20·6
1877	15·2	1·0	0·2	4·4	1·9	13·2
1878	22·7	0·8	0·6	9·8	2·3	19·6
1879	24·0	0·5	—	9·7	1·9	18·8
1880	33·9	4·6	0·2	26·3	2·0	13·4
1881	42·5	9·8	1·1	39·5	3·7	31·0
1882	45·5	4·4	1·7	35·5	13·0	19·0
1883	40·0	3·8	1·3	32·0	7·4	21·8
1884	41·6	6·3	0·7	23·9	9·2	29·8
1885	48·0	1·6	0·3	13·6	11·0	30·7
1886	59·4	6·1	0·6	19·5	12·8	37·5
1887	65·8	9·3	1·7	40·9	23·3	20·3
1888	89·8	8·9	2·7	48·5	17·1	53·5
1889	74·4	14·2	12·2	77·8	17·4	27·8
1890	70·2	8·4	18·2	86·6	9·1	20·8
1891	36·0	5·7	2·2	31·7	6·4	19·5
1892	28·7	4·2	2·9	20·7	3·5	15·6
1893	25·6	2·7	0·2	17·1	4·6	10·5
1894	35·2	5·3	0·9	19·1	6·1	23·1
1895	32·8	20·9	2·9	47·4	2·4	27·9
1896	31·2	23·9	1·6	41·0	8·7	18·8
1897	34·0	18·3	3·3	44·7	5·4	28·3
1898	43·7	15·4	5·7	45·3	5·4	25·9
1899	43·1	25·3	3·6	45·4	7·8	25·0
1900	31·9	9·9	1·2	29·3	4·0	16·2
1901	34·9	10·0	2·0	33·5	2·0	14·0
1902	68·1	13·7	2·1	62·0	3·8	23·4
1903	37·8	8·7	2·4	38·4	1·7	42·8
1904	55·5	8·5	1·6	46·0	3·7	38·3
1905	80·7	11·2	1·7	68·6	11·9	48·4
1906	43·7	14·1	2·9	54·7	5·5	24·7
1907	87·5	12·4	1·8	80·4	4·7	31·2
1908	122·4	9·1	4·6	76·1	13·7	57·6
1909	135·7	21·5	7·4	102·0	15·1	58·6

APPENDIX TABLE—(*cont.*)

	(IV) By Sector of Issuer §			(V) By Type of Issuer		
Year	Social Overhead ‖ (13)	Extractive ¶ (14)	Mfg. (15)	Private (16)	Mixed ** (17)	Gov't. (18)
1910	121·5	51·8	4·7	136·6	13·4	48·0
1911	116·7	28·8	7·1	116·6	16·3	36·2
1912	130·4	24·2	21·1	152·4	5·9	42·4
1913	170·6	17·0	6·3	139·4	16·2	61·9
1914	176·4	9·5	5·7	90·6	17·1	95·5

* The classification by continent presents data on seven continents but excludes figures on multi-national transactions that could not be allocated to continents or countries.
† The classification by political status presents data for independent nations and the British Empire. It omits the statistics for foreign dependencies.
‡ Refers to non-tropical Asia.
§ The classification by sector of issuer includes those groupings which are directly relevant to problems of economic development. The following categories are excluded : finance and real estate, trade, defence and miscellaneous.
‖ Refers to the sum of transportation, public utilities and other forms of public works.
¶ Refers to the sum of agriculture (including forestry) and mining.
** The 'mixed' category in the type of issuer classification is a heterogeneous group that includes issues by private enterprises that receive governmental assistance in the form of interest guarantees, etc.

ACKNOWLEDGEMENTS

The costs of machine time, programming, research assistance and key punching were financed by grants from The Social Science Research Council and The Graduate School of Business Administration of New York University.

The use of the IBM-7094 computer and auxiliary equipment on a liberal basis was authorized by Professor Eugene Isaacson of The Institute of Mathematical Sciences of New York University. I am very grateful to him, to Henry Mullish for arranging and to Roger Beyar for completing the operations on the electronic computer.

I am especially obligated to Emanuel Mehr of the Geo-Physics Laboratory of New York University for revising and elaborating the original computer programme and testing and 'de-bugging' the new one.

My debt to Professor Leland H. Jenks for providing his files on pre-1914 new British foreign investment and affording many concrete suggestions on the technical problems of estimation is very great. His resources and insights transformed the character of this investigation.

Harvey H. Segal, my collaborator in the earlier phase of the project, has been a constant source of encouragement and advice. Valuable suggestions were made by David E. Novack, Laura Randall, Babette Solon, Irving Stone and Brinley Thomas.

Professor Seymour Goodman of the Queens College Computer Center graciously authorized key-punching corrections, and the use of auxiliary equipment to prepare the data for final processing.

Lynn Alcosser prepared the charts. Research assistants, Leonard Mbogoa, Claire Pasternack, Martin Pollens and Marvin Sporn performed a variety of laborious tasks. I owe a personal debt to Hyman Pasternack for his help in the final phase of this project.

COMMENTS ON THE PAPERS BY BRINLEY THOMAS AND MATTHEW SIMON

COMMENT BY

GEORGE H. BORTS
Brown University

I HOPE that the undue length of these remarks will be taken as a tribute to the quality of the papers I am to discuss. Professors Thomas and Simon have made a first-rate contribution to the literature on international capital movements. These papers present and reflect two major issues. The first is the framework of analysis of capital movements, their causes and consequences. The second is the insight which can be utilized in the second half of the twentieth century from the experience of the preceding century.

1. FRAMEWORK OF ANALYSIS

Professors Thomas and Simon suggest a number of hypotheses to explain the pattern of capital movements in the nineteenth century. These fall into the wider net of what I would call an interregional growth model. Professor Thomas looks at the English-speaking world of the nineteenth century, perhaps properly so, in the same way that we would look at regions of a developed country today : he finds a fairly high degree of mobility of labour and capital ; well organized markets for transportable commodities, and a widespread although not uniform adherence to a system of fixed exchange rates. The last condition is probably more important for its historical similarity to the currency union that obtains among the regions of a given country, rather than as a pre-condition for the resource transfers which occurred. In this period there were substantial capital imports to the United States between 1865 and 1873, and to Argentina between 1884 and 1890, periods when both countries were operating freely fluctuating exchange rates.

The most important aspect of the balance of payments behaviour of the period seems to have been the ability of institutions and individuals in the peripheral countries to borrow large sums in the London money market at rates of interest one to two percentage points above those prevailing on domestic British securities. This means that balance of payments deficits and surpluses between the periphery and Britain were likely to be adjusted through the capital account rather than through gold movements. It also means that the conditions necessary to achieve a balance of payments equilibrium are related to the movements of the schedules of savings and investment in the peripheral areas. Formally then we have a structure very similar to that described by J. L. Ingram for Puerto Rico, and used by Jerome Stein and myself in our analysis of United States regions. These conditions explain the sensitivity of British exports to British overseas lending. They also explain why the balance of payments mechanism operated so smoothly during the period, in the sense that new capital issues were promptly accompanied by transfers of capital, through current account deficits in the periphery. The interaction worked both ways : from current account deficits to new capital issues ; and from new capital issues to current account deficits. In both instances there was a rise in investment in the periphery, with associated increases in the periphery's absorption of its domestic output, and in the periphery's borrowings in London.

The most important similarity between the English-speaking community of this period and the interregional economy of the United States lies in the movement of capital and labour from old to new areas and the resulting convergence of *per capita* incomes. Great Britain in this period sent capital and population to Canada, the United States, Australia and elsewhere. In this regard it played a role similar to that of the Northeastern quarter of the United States which has exported capital to the Southern and Western regions of the country. There is a second element of similarity suggested by the dependence of the periphery on capital imports from Britain. Observers have noted that in the nineteenth century, periods of tight money and central bank restriction in London sometimes led to temporary but sharp disturbances in the balance of payments of the periphery, as new capital issues fell off and the balance of borrowing became negative. (The balance of borrowing may be defined as new borrowing less interest payments.) The periphery in such periods were forced into a contraction of new investment projects, a rise in exports, weather willing, and a deterioration in export prices, domestic incomes and imports. Something of the same pattern may have been observed in times of financial panic in the United States, in the relations between the older capital exporting Northeast and the developing agricultural areas. Both the depressions of the 1870's and 1890's in the United States were marked by declines in railway construction in the West, and by sharp declines in agricultural income. The last of such occasions in the United States was the Great Depression of the 1930's, which witnessed sharp declines of capital values and money incomes in capital importing regions. It is noteworthy, however, that Great Britain escaped one aspect of this interregional pattern. The alternating cycles of British home and foreign investment noted by Cairncross and described by Thomas indicates that Britain was to some extent insulated from the sharp declines in aggregate demand experienced in the periphery. In this regard the experience is quite different from that of regions of the United States. A financial crisis in the United States would perhaps emanate in the centre, but the effects would then be shared by all regions. There is no evidence that investment in the Northeast alternated with that in other regions of the United States, in a manner similar to the British pattern of home and foreign investment. Information which we have on unemployment and labour unrest would suggest that the depressions of the 1870's and 1890's were felt in most major cities. The most that can be said is that in times of financial crisis capital values probably fell by a greater proportion in the capital importing regions. It would be useful to inquire why the pattern differs in view of the formal similarities which the two systems shared.

Having explained why Professor Thomas' analysis falls into the framework of an interregional model, I shall now turn to the explanations of the resource movements which occurred. Professor Thomas offers two major explanations : the first is an autonomous movement of population from the centre to the periphery. This would lead to a movement of capital for two reasons. Migrants take capital with them, and immigrants raise the demand for capital in the destination areas ; this is the explanation for population sensitive capital formation. Population movements are autonomous if they are caused by factors external to the economic relationships in view and if they are independent of other causes of capital movements. From this point of view, the Irish potato famine would be an autonomous factor. On the other hand, I suspect that the migration of British population from farm to city within Britain and then overseas is not autonomous. The hypothesis of autonomous population movements would be sufficient to explain much of the pattern of capital flow which occurred during the period. However, it could not explain the flow of capital to India or Egypt ; it could not explain the transport orientation of British foreign investment ; and it could not explain the cyclical pattern of the capital flow. For these reasons a second explanation is offered.

A second major explanation is the rise in the profitability of investment in the export sectors of the peripheral countries. In part this is due to the technological improvement in transportation and cultivation of agricultural commodities, and in part to a rise in the world demand for such commodities. Under this second hypothesis, the population movements could be regarded as induced by changes in the demand for labour in the periphery and in Britain. These are caused by the disturbances in the periphery and in Britain to the productivity of capital, to the real wage, and to the profitability of agriculture.

Presumably the statistical inquiries of negative covariation between the terms of trade and capital exports of Great Britain are designed to test the demand portion of the investment profitability hypothesis. Movements of British terms of trade are inversely related to the profitability of investment in the periphery, holding technology and the price of transport constant. British export prices measure the cost of capital goods imported by the periphery, while British import prices measure the price of periphery exports. A rise in British terms of trade would, therefore, lower the profitability of investment in the periphery. We may then write the following expression for m, the marginal efficiency of investment in the periphery :

$$m = \frac{(P_X - P_T)MP_K}{P_K + P_T}$$

where P_X is the price in Britain of the commodity exported by the periphery, P_T the price of transport, MP_K the marginal physical product of capital in the periphery's export sector, and P_K the price in Britain of capital goods exported to the periphery. Holding the technology and the price of transport constant, m varies inversely with P_K/P_X, the British terms of trade.

Professor Thomas attributes the cyclical behaviour of the terms of trade to the cyclical pattern of British exports and aggregate demand. When there is an expansion of exports and output in Britain, export industry prices rise with a lag. The profitability of home investment rises and the profitability of investment in the periphery declines. Under this explanation, the cycle of capital exports is caused by cyclical variation in British prices. This is an ingenious hypothesis, for it also explains the inverse relation between home and foreign investment. When British exports and output rise, the profitability of home investment rises as capacity utilization and domestic profit rates increase. Such an explanation while logical, is not wholly consistent with the data. The hypothesis puts great weight on rather narrow and sometimes inconsistent movements of the British terms of trade. In percentage terms, the terms of trade seem to swing about 13 points in Britain's favour during an upswing of capital exports (see Table VI, of Professor Thomas' paper). Swings of this magnitude are really too small to do the job, even taking into account the nature of the price indexes which are used to measure the terms of trade and the fact that many prices in the index will not move at all, or will move randomly. Furthermore, the terms of trade improve continually through one entire capital export cycle — after 20 years of improvement in British terms of trade ending in 1900, British capital exports begin an expansion, contrary to what we would expect. Thus as Professor Thomas recognizes, the terms of trade evidence is too slender to bear the burden of explanation. He notes, '... one is led to regard movements in the net barter terms of trade as a consequence of the fundamental forces at work rather than as a causal factor determining the distribution of the flow of capital between home and foreign investment'.

What alternative explanations are there? There is an alternative hypothesis suggested by the data, and I think it is worth examining.

The alternative hypothesis is very classical in that it assumes a given level of saving in Britain which is distributed among competing investment projects. The profitability of investment in the periphery (m) can vary as a consequence of cyclical variation in the productivity of capital. This could arise because transport facilities are generally built ahead of demand. A cycle of transport building could thus be self-generating. In addition, the profitability of prospective rail investment depends upon agricultural prices. A succession of years of low prices due to unusually good harvests could reduce the incentive to open new land through rail building. The cycle of capital export would occur in response to variations in the periphery's level of transport building. The alternating cycle of British home investment would occur as British savers found the volume of foreign issues falling off. They would turn to domestically generated securities and set off a wave of domestic investment. This pattern would be reinforced if British emigration simultaneously declined with a drop in capital formation in the periphery. Thus, population emigration is an induced phenomenon between countries. When emigration slows down, it acts to raise the demand for capital at home. This hypothesis is consistent with the behaviour of exports, the terms of trade, and wages, noted by Professor Thomas. As earlier it places the burden of explanation on cyclical disturbances to the profitability of investment in the periphery. However, the disturbance emanates in the periphery through a decline in the profitability of constructing new railways.

In concluding this section on explanatory hypotheses, I should point out that logically the pattern of interregional or international capital movements does not require a cycle to work itself out. The time paths of capital movements, induced population movements and export growth in the periphery could theoretically all occur at stable rates of change over time. That they do not do so, but instead display a cyclical pattern, provides an opportunity to test alternative explanations which might otherwise remain only informed conjectures.

2. THE LESSONS OF THE NINETEENTH CENTURY

I should like to turn now to the second issue which is raised in the papers by Professors Thomas and Simon. Is the nineteenth-century pattern worth while repeating or imitating today? It certainly brought great benefits to the periphery and is undoubtedly responsible for the great increases in income which they experienced. In addition, the returns to British foreign investment were far higher than at home. Cairncross is of the opinion that nineteenth-century foreign investment did pay, in terms of higher incomes to owners of capital, the development of British export industry and a reduction in the prices of imports.

There are three important differences between then and now which are of consequence to the question I have posed. Total capital exports from developed countries are less closely related to profitability because of foreign aid. Second, the developed countries are no longer exporting population to the underdeveloped world. Third, repudiation of foreign debt is harder to overcome today because of the socialized nature of foreign borrowing and domestic investment in the underdeveloped world.

I should like to comment on these points briefly. The movement of capital associated with foreign aid programmes is not really related to profitability calculations. The choice of countries in which to give aid and even the choice of projects are only dimly related to rates of return as the private investor would calculate them. While planners in various countries may endeavour to get the greatest return from the aid they receive, there really is no market test of their effectiveness as this was applied in the nineteenth century. The advantage to the planner is that he can include among his criteria of effectiveness concepts of externalities in the return of investment which would be alien to the railway developer of the nineteenth century. The disadvantage is, of course, that failure carries insufficient penalities and perhaps success insufficient rewards to drive the mass of undedicated souls who must operate the economy of any country. For this type of capital movement, therefore, the nineteenth-century pattern has only a negative moral.

What about private investment in today's world? Doesn't it operate much the same as in the nineteenth century? To some extent it does. Much of the capital exported from the United States is to develop sources of raw material for import into the United States and other developed countries. The raw material development in oil, iron ore, copper, bauxite, newsprint, lumber, is similar to the nineteenth-century pattern, with the important exception, of course, that we are not simultaneously exporting population to these overseas areas. In fact, the entire developed world — Europe, Australia, Japan, the United States and Canada — is not exporting population in contrast to the last century. This phenomena may be due to the slaughter of two great wars. The failure to export population means that today's periphery is more likely rather than less likely to experience a rise in *per capita* incomes as a result of continued importation of capital. An observer of United States regions will note that the greatest increase in *per capita* income has occurred in the Southeast, which has not imported population from the rest of the country.

It would seem that both the rates of return on investment and the real wage are generally higher in the developed world. This behaviour has been noted pessimistically by Myrdal and others to mean that a free world market in capital would not lead to converging incomes among nations. I think it has another meaning, which reflects political attitudes and changes in the undeveloped world. Rates of return on investment do not reflect the scarcity of capital in the underdeveloped world. The private foreign lender is discouraged rather than encouraged, for historical and political reasons which are too familiar to repeat. As long as this is true all an economist can do is point to the advantages of a free capital market from the point of view of both the lender and borrower.

In this regard the problem of repudiation of foreign debt is particularly vexing. When borrowers and lenders were private, repudiation could occur with far less damage to future loans than when borrowers and lenders are public. The British investor of 1870 could forget the history of re-pudiations of foreign debt in the United States by private companies, municipalities and even states in the 1830's. I don't think that repudiation is easily overcome or forgotten today when it is a matter of ideology and national government policy. As long as the foreign lender is looked upon as a parasite, private capital movements will be discouraged.

I think it is clear that private repudiation and bankruptcy does not discourage private foreign lending to the same degree as public repudiation, nationalization and socialization of private enterprise. The planners of the twentieth century, therefore, may be overlooking the advantages of private international borrowing. For when a private loan goes sour, it does not necessarily prejudice the ability of other individuals and firms in the country to borrow abroad.

DISCUSSION OF THE PAPERS BY PROFESSOR BRINLEY THOMAS AND PROFESSOR MATTHEW SIMON

THE discussion centred on the transfer problem and the roles of the United Kingdom and other leading creditor nations before World War I ; differences in the present role of the United States as the leading creditor nation ; and the evidence of relationships between changes in terms of trade, capital outflows and long swings in economic activity. Measurement problems were stressed throughout the discussion.

Dr. Ferrer said that England played a major role in integrating world trade before World War I. England was the major exporter of capital, source of population for countries of recent settlement, and also the largest importer of primary products. A large portion of British investment went to countries of recent settlement, and most of this went to infra-structure. England's large import coefficient and role as the major importer of primary products explains why the repayment capacity of debtor countries did not pose a serious problem before 1914. Today, with lower income elasticities of demand for primary products and protectionist policies in industrial countries, and dominance of finance and trade by the United States — a country with a specially low import coefficient — problems of repayment by debtor countries are much more serious. Argentina is a case in point. Deterioration of the country's terms of trade and the actual decline in demand for Argentina's exports in world markets both have reduced export earnings. This plus a drop in capital inflows touched off a bank crisis. Though there has been great long-run expansion, the economy is inherently unstable in the short-run because of this dependence on world markets.

Dr. Faaland was impressed by the fact that borrowing countries in the nineteenth century were countries of recent settlement with high rates of growth. They evidently also had flexible economies which could adjust to transfer problems and to balance-of-payments bottlenecks. If there is a lesson to be learned from this, it would seem to be that lending to poor countries can only be effective if the receiving country uses it in a broad range of activities. Professor Thomas stated in his paper that there were major differences between Britain and other creditor nations in terms, quality, motivation and consequences of lending. Private enterprise was the mainspring of English investment, whereas French and German foreign investment was an instrument of state policy. A much larger proportion of French and German than of British lending was in Europe, and, it is estimated, French investors lost two thirds of the capital placed in foreign bonds. Professor Thomas concluded that state-controlled activities of France and Germany before World War I had a negligible effect on the growth of the international economy. Most of the British overseas investments, Professor Simon noted, went to countries of recent settlement like the United States. The United States, especially during the era of railway expansion, was the single most important foreign source of new securities issued in the British capital market.

Professor Leduc said that even today there is no thoroughgoing study of French long-term foreign investment around the turn of the century. He speculated that the cost of French foreign investment to the French economy was very high. If French funds had been invested in France and her colonies instead of in Europe, France might have benefited greatly. He felt, however, that Professor Thomas's claim that French and German capital exports had little effect on the international economy is overdrawn. Czarist Russia certainly must have benefited from the trans-Siberian railway financed with French funds. *Dr. Kamarck* noted here that while Britain had a lending programme, France had a grant programme. *Professor Rosenstein-Rodan* added that if the role of French capital exports before 1914 had been underrated, this was because long-term and short-term capital markets had not been properly distinguished. While the French attempted to create a short-term acceptance market, they never succeeded as did London. As a result, short-term credit represented a much higher proportion of total credit in the London market than it did in the Paris market.

Professor Rosenstein-Rodan mentioned that the French case was not unique. He drew attention to the major increase in the scale of British overseas investment during the few decades before World War I, and added that if this capital had been invested in England, England would have been much stronger. The City of London and its financial institutions, he felt, were the greatest single threat to the prosperity of England. He would argue, however, that few inferences can be drawn from this experience. It represents a temporary abberation with no lessons for the future. He also wondered what the transfer burden for developing countries was prior to 1914. He noted that the burden was not adequately measured by adding amortization and interest figures shown in the United Kingdom balance of payments, since there was a lot of fund-switching from one country to another (i.e. repayments by country A to the United Kingdom were invested in country B) which was not recorded. Thus, since the total transfer burden of any one country is likely to be greater than is shown in its transfers to London, any study based solely on London's net receipts does not give a true picture of the transfer burden for individual debtor countries.

Dr. Singer did not agree that the pre-World War I burst of overseas investment by the United Kingdom was necessarily harmful. Foreign investments helped Britain to finance imports and pre-empt overseas supplies during both world wars. Also, British investment was coexistent with emigration from Britain. If we expand the geographical definition of the United Kingdom to include the Commonwealth countries, it is very difficult to show that overseas investment was in fact deleterious to the interests of the United Kingdom.

Professor Rosenstein-Rodan questioned next the extent to which import substitution or import-saving investments alleviated the transfer burden. The answer depends in part upon what role such investments play in the balance of payments, and in part how the investment affects the capital/output ratios in the country. A related question is : how much of foreign capital went into actual new investment and how much was merely a substitute for domestic investment which was then used for other purposes? If a foreign loan to finance an electric power project releases funds which are then used to build a night club, the impact is not the same as if the released funds were used to finance a railroad. In the first case the foreign lender is financing a night club, in the second case he is financing an addition to the borrowing country's infra-structure.

Professor Rosenstein-Rodan also observed that a larger proportion of total investment in developing countries is represented by domestic capital today than during the nineteenth century. In addition, a larger percentage of nineteenth century than of today's investment is not creditworthy by present standards. The security of today's investment is much greater than that of nineteenth-century investments ; this tends to offset partly today's more difficult transfer problems.

Dr. Singer also questioned the use in Professor Thomas's paper of his (Dr. Singer's) earlier work on the distribution of gains between investing and borrowing countries. Dr. Singer noted that his own analysis was done before Hirschman's studies of linkages, Arthur Lewis's growth model with unlimited supplies of labour, and Prebisch's work. His work is therefore relatively primitive. In asking why some countries developed successfully and others did not, Dr. Singer noted Professor Thomas's criticism of his (own) method. He added that while he may have argued with the benefit of hindsight, he had a lot of company in doing so. He also noted that Professor Thomas, in discussing the role of British capital export to the periphery, seems to have played down the skill content embodied in those who migrated to these areas. In this sense, nineteenth-century investment in countries of recent settlement was much larger than the capital flow figures would indicate.

Several discussants commented on the long swings discussed in Professor Simons' paper, and the inverse relationship between fluctuations in the United States and United Kingdom economies noted in Professor Thomas's paper. *Professor Brown* felt that Professor Thomas had over-emphasized the offsetting character of cycles in the centre and the periphery. He said that the direction of change in the two areas was still similar in one year of every three. Professor Brown noted the importance of this for Professor Thomas's analysis because Professor Thomas's theory of the terms of trade requires that the supply of United Kingdom exportable resources be high at the beginning of upswings in foreign lending. One does in fact see that large increases in foreign lending did begin during periods of high resource unemployment in the U.K. Professor Brown also pointed out that Professor Thomas's view — that movements in terms of trade are consequential, and that changes in capital outflows are mainly generated by changes in demand — seemed to be consistent with the evidence. The question still remains, however, of how booms in demand for capital all over the world are co-ordinated so as to result in such long swings. Professor Brown then cited Professor Simon's work to show that the booms were not very co-ordinated, but rather that the whole picture was dominated by demand for capital in North America.

Professor Rosenstein-Rodan said that he was an agnostic on whether long-term cycles existed or not. He cited the dangers of generalizing from scanty evidence in the case of very long cycles. *Professor Simon* replied that while he too was agnostic about the logic of long swings, he still felt that statistical evidence which supported the existence of long swings should be mentioned. He also agreed with Professor Brown that home and foreign investment did move in the same direction about one year out of three.

Capital Movements and Economic Development

Professor Wallich felt that there were a number of questions that had yet to be answered. For instance, do we know anything of terms of issue, such as the spread? What is the proportion of fixed-yield and equity issues? Are there any data on how market values of equities varied after issue? Is anything known of the quantitative importance of direct investment relative to portfolio stocks and bonds? *Professor Simon* replied that there is information on terms of issue, but it has not been systematically compiled. He felt that Professor Rosenstein-Rodan's off-the-cuff estimate that 65–70 per cent of new issues were represented by various types of stocks and bonds before 1914 was fairly accurate. He did not know what proportion direct investments represented of the total, but had the impression that this item represents a relatively small portion of British long-term holdings.

Chapter 2

THE FINANCIAL EXPERIENCE OF LENDERS AND INVESTORS [1]

BY

ANDREW M. KAMARCK

International Bank for Reconstruction and Development

IF you find any Island or maine land populous, and that the people hath no need of cloth then you are to devise what commodities they have to purchase the same withall.

If they be poore, then you are to consider the soile, and how by any possibilities the same may be made to enrich them, that hereafter they may have something to purchase the cloth withall.
— Instructions given by Richard Hakluyt to merchants of the Moscovie Company, 1580.

In the same era, Sir Francis Drake in commending colonial expansion to his countrymen remarked of the American Indians: 'their gain shall be the knowledge of our faith, and ours such riches as the country hath'.

Both of these widely different approaches towards development of a new area, frankly stated at the beginning of European expansion to the rest of the world, can be identified in the experience in Africa.

I. INTRODUCTION

The time period in which there has been substantial lending and investing from abroad in Africa is quite limited — for most of Africa, much less than the 60-odd years that it has had a significant economic contact with the rest of the world.

In evaluating the 'financial experience' of investors and lenders in Africa, I mean primarily, the financial return to foreign investors

---

[1] The help of Badri Rao and Dina Driva in assembling much of the material used in this paper is gratefully acknowledged. The paper as presented here is a revised version of the paper originally presented to the Conference. The revisions of the text are minor; some of the appended tables have been brought up-to-date.

and lenders on the particular investment concerned in Africa and not a financial appraisal of the whole activities of a particular individual or institution. This still is an unprecise term but a practical one. Let us see what it covers.

Let us consider first the financial return to lenders. This, formally, consists of interest and amortization. If we accept this as a working basis, the amortization is the repayment of the original capital, assuming the bond or the loan was made at par. The interest is, formally, the return on the capital. This last assumes, however, that there is no risk involved and that no risk premium is included in the interest. In foreign lending in the actual world, risk is always involved and the return to lenders must include not only a return on the capital but a differential payment for the particular risk undertaken. In addition, the lender usually will have certain costs of administration that have to be covered. For example, the make-up of the World Bank's interest rate was quite explicit until quite recently in this regard. It was made up, *grosso modo*, of the cost of money to the Bank — the interest rate being paid on its own borrowings at a particular time by the Bank — plus $\frac{1}{4}$ of 1 per cent for administrative expenses, and 1 per cent which went into a Special Reserve against losses. The result was a rate which combined explicitly a return on capital, administrative costs and risk premium. (In actual fact, the element of cost of money to the Bank was interpreted liberally in favour of the developing countries: it was raised only with a considerable time lag when the interest paid by the Bank on its borrowings was going up and lowered more rapidly when the interest paid by the Bank was going down and the administrative charge, $\frac{1}{4}$ of 1 per cent, did not fully cover the administrative costs of the Bank. On the other hand, as the Bank had no losses to charge to the Special Reserve, the risk premium seems to have been too high. The Bank now no longer sets its rate in this mechanical fashion but taking all of these factors and other policy considerations together sets a final rate without attempting to decompose it into the various elements as in the past.)

The 'return to investors' is even more complicated. 'Investors' I am defining as companies or people making direct investments abroad. The return to investors is a composite including some elements that are the same as in the return to lenders — a return on capital, payment for risk premium. It consists also of payment for the services of management and supervision and technicians of various kinds — engineers, accountants, salesmen, etc. — which are an important part of the direct investment. It can also consist of something much more — of profits in the Schumpeterian sense, that is to say, of profits made by the foreign entrepreneur from his importing knowledge and techniques from his own economy which are in advance of those available in the host country. This enables him to produce at lower cost than is true of the rest of the economy.

The direct investment undertaken by foreign entrepreneurs takes advantage of their access to know-how, the managerial techniques or capital equipment which is superior to the local entrepreneurs. This foreign-owned sector may expand quite rapidly and, if it has tariff protection or transport cost protection, it may keep most of the benefit of the high productivity for quite a time rather than pass it on to local consumers. In essence, this type of enterprise gains from exploiting a type of quasi-rent — which in some cases can last for a long while before the indigenous population can adopt similar techniques and methods or organization or before other foreign investors come in. The difference in level of development of technique represented by the foreign firm and that of the indigenous economy may determine how long it will take before this catching-up occurs and the quasi-rents are wiped out. In the case of Africa, this period could be a very long time — consequently the persistence of such profits may depend instead on how open the country is to imports and the entrance of additional foreign investors.

In a country like Australia the data appear to show that there is now no marked divergence in earning rates between foreign-owned companies in general and domestic companies. However, North American companies in Australia do appear to earn more than U.K. companies or the average of all overseas companies (Statistical Appendix, Table 2). This latter may be a real difference or it may be due to the uneven incidence of tax laws between the U.S. and other developed countries.

A somewhat similar type of quasi-rent arises from the exploitation of natural resources in an underdeveloped country. At the present stage of development in Africa, this is by far the more important. The greatest returns to investors in the developing countries very often come through investors providing the missing co-operating factors, such as transport, technical knowledge, management and the command over capital necessary to exploit a resource. Without these necessary co-operating factors, the value of many natural resources is zero or close to zero. This seems to be particularly true in Africa for mining development. The natural obstacles are usually so great that to get at and exploit most mineral resources takes such large capital and managerial and technical resources that the indigenous population cannot possibly mobilize. Where it is possible to buy resources at prices corresponding to their value in their present uses and turn them over to other more profitable uses which the rest of the economy is at the time in no position to exploit, large gains can be made. It is the attempt to secure such gains that provided and provides one of the main inducements to invest in much of Africa. One of the chief benefits of foreign investment in the development of Africa is that they make it possible to secure economic use for natural resources for which so far there have been none, and thus to convert objects without economic value into economic resources (Lachmann, pp. 698–713). This discussion so far has assumed that the return investors are searching for can be measured in terms of the money that can be directly made from an investment. But direct investment often is motivated by other reasons which are even less easily measurable. Much of the motive for investment in the development of the iron ore and bauxite resources of the African countries in recent years has been the desire of the iron and steel or aluminium producers in the developed countries to have a sure source of raw materials. At the other end of the process, a good part of the investment from abroad in manufacturing plants in Rhodesia, East Africa, and Nigeria, was touched off by the wish to get a foothold in a market which was likely to be (or was being) cut off from the foreign producers' exports by tariff barriers. Some direct investment by machinery manufacturers is also a result of their sales of machinery — as a partial return they take an equity in the factory. Then there are other motives also, for example, the 'empire building' instinct in corporate managers who want to have a far-flung corporation to run.

The philanthropic motive is not the least important in Africa. The Uganda Company, which has contributed a great deal to the development of Uganda, was organized around the turn of the century under the inspiration of the Church Missionary Society as a practical way of helping the people of Uganda. (*The Economic Development of Uganda*, p. 16.) A large part of the drive to accelerate the development of what is now Zambia and Rhodesia through intensified search for investment opportunities backed up with the money to put into them came from the desire of Sir Ernest Oppenheimer (Chairman of Anglo-American, de Beers, British South Africa Company, etc.) to make a personal contribution to the development of Southern Africa (Source : Conversations with the author in Johannesberg in 1955 and 1956).

In this paper, while the foregoing considerations affecting private investment in Africa need to be kept in mind, the emphasis is given to the financial returns.

II. RETURN TO INVESTORS IN AFRICA

Even so it has not been possible to make a comprehensive study of the returns on private foreign investment in Africa — much of the information is inaccessible or impossible to collect. However, it has been possible for me to get together some bits and pieces which I believe are fairly representative and do seem to present a fairly consistent story.

Slave Trade

Up to about 1860 in West Africa, and 1900 in East Africa, the bulk of the investment from abroad in Africa was devoted to the slave trade. Very little is known about the returns on this investment. Presumably it was very profitable, otherwise the large losses in men and ships would not have been borne for a period of some 400 years. It was an important part of the development of commerce in England, Western Europe and the new world. The Arab slave trade in the Indian Ocean must have also paid quite handsome returns to justify the continuance of the trade for so many centuries. The slave trade, however, is a field of activity which no longer is a subject for investment and has little relevance to us today.

Chartered Companies

Aside from South Africa, where the discovery of diamonds in 1867 and gold on the Rand in 1884 began the era of modern investment, in the rest of Africa South of Sahara up to around World War I the major investments that were made were in the form of the chartered companies. These were private companies or concessionaires who were given monopoly powers over large areas and were mostly organized in the period from the opening up of Africa in the 1880's to World War I. These companies were much like the companies and proprietors who had been given immense grants of

75

land in what is now the United States : the Virginia Company, Lord Baltimore's colony of Maryland, Carolina, New Jersey, Georgia, etc.). Among these African companies were the Imperial British East Africa Company for what is now Kenya and Uganda, the British South Africa Company for the former Rhodesias, the Royal Niger Company, the Portuguese Mozambique Company, the Compagnie du Congo pour le Commerce et l'Industrie, the Comité Spéciale du Katanga (CSK), Compagnie des Chemins de Fer du Congo Supérieur aux Grands Lacs Africains (CFL), Comité National du Kivu (CNKi), Société du Haut-Ogooné, the Deutsche Ostafrikanische Gesellschaft, etc. There were usually one or more per territory.

These companies in most of the areas where they were established followed Sir Francis Drake's approach and introduced a form of *Raubwirtschaft*. That is to say, the companies tried mainly to exploit the existing resources and to put as little as possible in the way of investment into the areas being exploited. There were, of course, some exceptions like the East Africa Company that was set up in order to reach Uganda and abolish the slave trade in East Africa. Most of these companies, however, simply went into an African territory and took out what could be easily taken out, such as the ivory, any gold that could be found, and any other natural riches that could be easily and quickly exploited. (See, in particular, Conrad, *Heart of Darkness* and Gide, *Voyage au Congo*).

But, as it happens, there was very little in the way of easily exploitable riches in Africa. And, one after another, nearly all of the companies went bankrupt or ran into such financial difficulties that the metropolitan governments had to take them over.

In most of the areas these chartered companies went out of existence by World War I. In French Equatorial Africa they remained in existence up to the 1930's. The British South Africa Company succeeded in surviving and still exists today having lost the last of its privileges, the mineral rights in what is now Zambia on the eve of Zambia's independence in October 1964. The three Belgian charter companies (CSK, CFL, CNKi) which were set up after the Congo ceased to be the personal property of King Leopold and most of the abuses of that period were abolished, remain in existence. By agreements between Belgium, the Democratic Republic of the Congo and the chartered companies, the Congolese Government took over the Portfolio of the former Belgian Congo consisting in part of shares in the chartered companies. The chartered companies lost their remaining concession granting privileges as well as their rights to royalties from the mines in their former territories (Kredietbank, *Weekly Bulletin*, Brussels, 24 April 1965).

The chartered companies that went out of existence before World War I or before World War II in no case gave a positive return on the capital that had been invested. In some cases, the investors were able to get a short-lived return while the territory was being initially exploited, but very soon in the case of most of these companies they found themselves unable to pay dividends. The British South Africa Company (BSA) which did succeed in surviving did not pay any substantial dividends until World War II although it was founded in 1887. This company, like the three Belgian concessionaires, differed from most of the other chartered companies in that it did put a substantial investment into permanent productive facilities. BSA built the railway from South Africa through Bechuanaland and the Rhodesias to the Congolese border as well as connected Southern Rhodesia with the Port of Beira in Mozambique. The CSK, CFL and CNKi through concessions secured the opening up and exploitation of the mines in the Katanga and plantations in the Kivu and built the rail connection between the Congo River at Stanleyville and later Tanganyika. The dividends that were paid in 1940 of £400,000 represented 5 per cent of the book value of the BSA at that date. As a return on the present value of the original investments the rate of return is derisory. Of the three Belgian chartered companies, the CSK with the rich mineral resources of the Katanga to exploit — and which were in part known before the CSK was organized — appears to have become quite profitable as early as the 20's. The other two did not enter a period of prosperity until after World War II.

South Africa

South Africa was an important exception to the frustrated hopes of foreign investors and remained an exception up until World War II. Like the investments in the CSK and in the BSA which finally began to pay off, the profitable investments in South Africa were in mining. In South Africa, the investment in mining did show fairly good returns — mostly in the range of 6 to 8 per cent — nothing particularly spectacular for most investors especially when it is remembered that this was the average return of the *successful* companies (Statistical Appendix, Table 2). The contrast between South

Africa and the rest of the continent is indicated by S. H. Frankel's classic study which showed that in 1936 the largest share of foreign direct investment in Africa South of the Sahara had taken place in South Africa.

Unilever

Outside of South Africa and mining the returns on other direct investment appear to have been very low before World War II. The experience of Lever Brothers or Unilever in Africa prior to World War II is instructive in this regard (Wilson, *Unilever*). Prior to the war, and still today, Unilever has had the biggest single foreign direct investment in Africa outside of mining. It is still the biggest foreign industrial interest outside of South Africa and the biggest trading, farming and transport complex in Africa.

By 1906, Lever Brothers had become the leading British soap-maker. Its growth had been of a fairly simple 'vertical' type, from raw material production, to output of soap. The imported vegetable oils required made William Lever particularly conscious of the importance of foreign supplies. He feared being 'squeezed' by the merchants and brokers who, he thought, were conspiring against the manufacturers and he also feared that other manufacturers might themselves take action to secure their own raw materials.

After failing to find land in West Africa, because of British colonial policy of refusing to alienate African land for establishment of plantations, in 1911 Lever established the Société Anonyme des Huileries du Congo Belge to buy wild palm oil from the Africans and grow oil palms in the Congo. This was intended to give him a secure raw material source. The Société was empowered to establish communications and other facilities which were to be made available also to others. The Société was also required to provide schooling and hospitals and to pay a guaranteed minimum wage to labour. The Société, in fact, like the chartered companies of the period, was almost more of a government than a business. The original concession covered 1·8 million acres leasehold of which eventually around one-half million acres became freehold.

The Huileries du Congo Belge was the greatest single enterprise that Lever had undertaken, and it ran into difficulties almost immediately. The available population was not large enough for the double task of collection of wild palm oil and construction of the new plantations. Costs were high and progress was slow.

Lever also acquired some six million acres from a French concessionnaire, la Compagnie Propriétaire du Kouilou Niari (CPKN) in the French Congo. But on closer investigation it turned out that only 10,000 acres of this were suitable for planting and this proved a total loss.

In British West Africa, the policy of the Colonial Office in refusing to allow plantations to be established led Lever to decide to acquire his palm oil by buying wild palm oil from the Africans. He consequently bought trading companies in Nigeria, Sierra Leone and Liberia. A second product of the oil palm is palm kernels and Lever decided to crush them on the spot for palm kernel oil to save on transport costs. But shipping the oil alone was found to be more expensive as the valuable by-product, the cake had no market in Africa. (This industry has still not shown itself economic in Africa.)

By 1914 about £1·5 million had been sunk in the African businesses. One of them — the CPKN — was a dead loss. The Belgian Congo showed no profit. The oil mills lost over £50,000 in 1913 alone.

The war years proved prosperous for Lever Brothers as a whole. Although separate figures are not available on the African investments, the indications are that they remained a burden on the rest of the business. Ordinary dividends were declared of 10 per cent in 1914, 15 per cent in 1917 and 17½ per cent in 1918.

The years 1919–29 were difficult years. Lever Brothers made them more difficult by taking on the Niger Company and merging it with the other Lever companies in Africa into the United Africa Company (UAC). In 1929 after the merger of the Margarine Unie with Lever Brothers into Unilever, UAC also acquired Margarine's West African trading companies.

UAC for years did not declare any dividends and was in severe financial trouble. Unilever's Congo plantations, now closely associated with the UAC, were producing palm oil at a cost higher than market price while this latter was a little more than a third of the value of palm oil when the original concession had been secured.

Because of its investments, Unilever felt compelled to continue to use African oils rather than other and possibly cheaper products. By the autumn of 1931 the banks and finance houses were pressing UAC to cut its commitments. But instead Unilever found £3 million of liquid capital which UAC required. The decision of Unilever to stay in Africa was reached by looking hopefully at Africa and her resources rather than at balance sheets.

79

Capital Movements and Economic Development

Better management and rising commodity prices served to improve the prospects of UAC between 1932 and 1936. But commodity prices broke again in 1937 bringing new trouble to UAC. Since World War II, UAC has done better. The following table shows, however, that while Unilever's rate of return since World War II is comparable to pre-war rates, the return on UAC investment is still smaller than on Unilever's investment as a whole. Unilever's policy over the last 7 or 8 years appears to have been to reduce the relative share of UAC in the total investment while reorienting the whole activity of UAC in such a way as to withdraw from sensitive areas such as the agricultural trade and to expand in manufacturing.

RETURN ON CAPITAL OF LEVER BROTHERS LTD.
AND OF UNILEVER

	Lever Bros.		Lever Bros. & Unilever	Unilever Ltd. & Unilever N.V.	
	1922	1927	1938	1955	1962
	£ millions				
Capital Employed*	64·4	68·1	100·5	425·0	690·0
(of which in Africa)	n.a.	n.a.	n.a.	(118·0)	(116·0)
Profits	4·6	5·4	9·9	42·3	54·3
(of which from Africa)	n.a.	n.a.	n.a.	(7·6)	(3·7)
	Percentages				
Rates of profits to capital employed	7·1	7·9	9·9	9·8	7·9
(of which from Africa)	n.a.	n.a.	n.a.	(6·5)	(3·2)

* *N.B.*—Figures for capital employed in 1922, 1927 and 1938 are based on data shown for aggregate liabilities and may not strictly conform to the definition of ' capital employed ' used in the later balance sheets.

Source : Data for 1922, 1927 and 1938 are from *Moody's Manual of Investments*, volumes dealing with 'Industrials' for the years 1928 and 1939. Figures for 1955 and 1962 are from *Unilever's Report and Accounts, 1962*.

U.S. Private Investment in Africa

Since World War II the returns on private direct investment in Africa appear no longer quite as bleak as in the past and there are indications that the opportunities for good returns on well-chosen investment are at least as favourable as in the rest of the world.

Using the U.S. Department of Commerce figures available on U.S. direct investments abroad, we have made some calculations of the rate of return shown. Obviously these are quite rough comparing as they do both value of investments and the annual earnings shown. Still, there is no particular reason to believe that the figures for Africa should not be comparable with those for other areas outside of the U.S. and, consequently, some conclusions can be drawn from these comparisons. (Statistical Appendix, Tables 3-6a-h.) The first point that comes out is that the average rates of return on the total U.S. direct investment in Africa over the period 1957–63 were, for five years out of the seven, below the average rates shown by U.S. direct investment in the world outside the United States as a whole. The rates of return in Africa fluctuated also a great deal more — from a high of 21 per cent to a low of 2·6 per cent, while for the world as a whole they remained within the range of 10·7 per cent to 13·2 per cent. Comparing the returns from Africa on the total of direct investment to those in other developing areas : generally both the Western Hemisphere and Asia paid better — Asia, in fact, much better. Europe too was a better paying area.

However, the figures for the average return on total investments are somewhat misleading. Figures on the return by sectors can only be calculated for the years 1958–63. What they show is that the returns on most types of U.S. direct investments in Africa tend to be higher than in other parts of the world : it is the petroleum investment in these years that dragged down the overall average. The return on manufacturing investment in Africa (and this is mostly in South Africa) is fairly consistently higher than in other parts of the world, ranging usually around 16 per cent but as high as 23 and 24 per cent in two years. Earnings on mining and smelting fluctuate considerably more — from 8·8 per cent to 24·7 per cent in these years — but again tend to be higher than earnings in other parts of the world — though not as consistently as in manufacturing.

Apparently, the return on U.S. direct investment, if the petroleum investments are excluded, for the years 1958–63, was higher from its African investments than the return secured by other investors. (In this comparison, different tax laws as between the U.S. and the other capital-providing countries may be in part at least responsible for this showing.) Using the available South African data on foreign direct investment in South Africa for the years 1956–63, the rough calculations on the return to foreign direct investment show a fairly consistent return of 4·6 to 6·2 per year. (Statistical Appendix, Table 8.) A consistently higher return for U.S. direct investment, it will be recalled, is also apparently true in Australia.

Congo

A number of comprehensive estimates have been made of private investment in the former Belgian Congo prior to World War II (Statistical Appendix, Table 9) but not of the returns on the investment. (Banque Centrale du Congo Belge et du Ruanda-Urundi, *Bulletin*, Août, 1955.) According to these, the total private investment in the Congo in 1939 was around the equivalent of about $800 million. For 1953, the estimate was almost $2 billion. Of this, half had come in from abroad and the other half was ploughed-back profits on the foreign investment. In a later study, the Congolese Central Bank calculated the dividends payable abroad by Congolese enterprises and found the total averaging from 11·68 to 13·10 per cent on their 'Moyens Propres' during the years 1951–56 (Statistical Appendix, Table 10). If one adds to this the 'allocations to reserves', total profits run at 30–35 per cent during these admittedly unusual years of high primary product prices. During these years, the conclusion of the Congolese Central Bank that firms in the Congo had a return much greater than that of firms in Belgium certainly appears justified. (Banque Centrale du Congo Belge et du Ruanda-Urundi, *Bulletin*, Janvier 1958.)

The Congolese Central Bank also made a comparison of the capital net domestic output ratio in Belgium (1950) and the Congo (1953), and with a total capital investment figure of $2·2 billion equivalent in the Congo, found a ratio of 3 to 1 and, to its surprise, found the same ratio in Belgium. The implication here is that the productivity of capital in the two countries must have been roughly the same.

III. EXPERIENCE OF LENDERS

Until World War II, the main lenders to Africa were private and institutional bond buyers in the capital markets of London and Paris and the main borrowers were the governments of Africa. Partly because information on the French record is less well known, and partly because France's policy-orientation as a result has led the way for other countries, the discussion on this point is concentrated on the French experience.

French-Speaking Territories

In the period up to World War II, the greater part of the funds needed for capital works in the French colonies in Africa was raised on the French market. The loans in almost all cases carried the guarantee of the French Government. A few loans were raised direct from government agencies, such as the Caisse des Dépôts et Consignations and the Caisse de Garantie des Assurances Sociales. In order to raise a loan on the market a colony first required a special Act of the French Parliament. The budgets of a colony which raised a guaranteed loan had to be submitted to the French Parliament for approval. From 1900 to World War I, the total of these loans amounted to some F315 million, all but F35 million of which went to two colonies — AOF (French West Africa) and Madagascar. This amount, F315 million, was equivalent to a little over $60 million at that time. Most of these loans were paid off after World War I at depreciated franc rates and the investors lost on an average from two-thirds to four-fifths of their original investment.

From 1919 to 1931, loans totalling only F510 million were raised, all by two colonies — AOF (French West Africa) and AEF (French East Africa). This in real terms was probably equivalent to $20–30 million of the period. During this period, too, the rates of interest went up, one tranche of the AEF loans being issued at an actual rate of more than 8 per cent. A large part of this loan was devoted to what was then a somewhat dubious project — the construction of the first railroad in AEF from Brazzaville to Pointe Noire which duplicated the existing Belgian line from Leopoldville to the sea.

In 1931, laws were passed authorizing new loans for public works in all the overseas territories. There was for the first time a general programme — The Maginot Programme for the development of the Colonies, but no direct financial aid was granted other than the usual guarantee. By the end of 1939 about F3 billion had been issued at rates of interest which rose steadily from 4 to $6\frac{1}{4}$ per cent. During World War II new authorizations of more than F1 billion were made to those colonies not adhering to Free France, these advances being made by the French Treasury in view of the unpropitious market conditions. These amounts totalled around $150 million at the exchange rates of the time. Again, of this capital the investors have lost from 80 to 90 per cent of the capital value. (Statistical Appendix, Tables 11–13.)

The total capital lent by French investors to Africa prior to World War II came thus to the equivalent of perhaps $200–250 million pre-World War II dollars. According to a calculation made by the French National Institute of Statistics, investment in bonds between 1914 and 1940 gave a negative yield of minus 3 to minus 7 per cent. (I.N.S.E.E., *Revue*, Octobre 1965.)

As one result, since World War II the bulk of the external capital provided to the public sector in the French-speaking areas in Africa has been provided by the French Government on a grant basis with a minor amount being extended in the form of loans, and these mostly soft loans. Since 1957, there has also been participation in this by the governments of the other European Economic Community members. The aid programme is discussed in more detail below.

Belgian Territories

From the beginning to 1920, a total of some 170 million francs (1914 francs), i.e. equivalent to around $35 million, was lent to the Belgian Congo Government by private investors, this increased by another $4 million by 1939. Again, as in the French case the bulk of the value of the loans was wiped out by the inflation connected with the war and the net return to investors was definitely negative. (Banque Nationale de Belgique, *Bulletin* d'information et de Documentation, Mars, 1952, pp. 174–181.)

The Belgian government found it necessary between the wars to finance the Congo directly. From 1921 to 1925, it advanced 17 million gold-francs equivalent. In principle, these were repayable but repayment was never demanded. Then, beginning during the depression, 1933 to 1940 when Belgium was over-run by the German army, it provided 104 million gold francs to meet the Congo budget deficits. Altogether from the beginning of the Congolese Free State to 1951, the Belgian Government had to pay net some 209 million gold francs (around $140 million foreign exchange equivalent as of 1965) as grants or non-reimbursed advances. (L'Institut Royal des Relations Internationales : La Belgique e L' aide économique aux pays sous-développés, p. 191.)

British Colonies

The British experience was less dramatic and the evolution followed by British policy was, consequently, behind that of the French. On the conclusion of World War II, the British Government began an expanded programme of grants to the colonies under the Colonial Development and Welfare Acts (CD & W), created the Colonial Development Corporation (CDC) to make direct investments in the colonies and the Overseas Food Corporation for investment in food production. The last organization passed out of existence after several disastrous investments. The CD & W also has become irrelevant to most of Africa as the countries become independent. The CDC, at first not allowed to operate in independent countries, has since been renamed the Commonwealth Development Corporation and allowed to function in its previous areas. The U.K. Government has also gradually been recreating a substitute for CD & W — first by setting up Commonwealth assistance loans with interest rates geared to the government's own borrowing costs ; then, by waiving interest charges on some loans for an initial 7-year period and latterly, in June 1965, announcing that the U.K. would make interest-free loans in appropriate cases.

Today, the vast bulk of the lending to the African as to the rest of the developing countries is done by governments or their official agencies or by the international development institutions. Of the public issues raised in the major capital markets of the world over the past 20 years by the developing countries, only the English-speaking African countries continued to be able to raise money in the foreign private capital markets until around 1960. Since then, both the black African and the southern African governments have not been able to secure any appreciable amounts in this way. The British Government like the French has had to replace the private capital market as the main source of external funds for the African governments. (Statistical Appendix, Table 14.)

In 1964, the total net flow of official long-term financial resources to the developing countries according to OECD estimates was $6 billion. Of this, $1¾ billion was lending (net of amortization). Meanwhile, the total amount of new issues (publicly issued) sold by all the developing countries in foreign capital markets was $97 million ; in 1963, this figure was $200 million. And these amounts are gross, since refunding or amortization is not deducted. None of this went to the African countries.

In Africa South of the Sahara the net flow of official capital has reached about $1 billion a year, with net official lending over $200 million a year.

Of the total financial resources made available to the developing countries by DAC countries on a bilateral basis, more than half are grants or grant-like contributions. In 1962, this percentage was 60 per cent ; in 1963, 56 per cent ; and in 1964, 54 per cent. In Africa South of the Sahara grants have been running at 70–75 per cent of the total. The loans themselves are made on quite favourable terms. The weighted average maturity of official loans has been increasing. It was 23·9 years in 1962, 24·6 years in 1963 and 27·6 years in 1964. The weighted average interest rate was 3·6 per cent in 1962, 3·4 per cent in 1963 and 3·5 per cent in 1964. These terms quite clearly are considerably below the cost of capital to the developed countries : they do not cover an economic return on capital, much less include any allowance for risk premium or costs of administration.

IV. AID PROGRAMMES IN AFRICA

Until after World War II, economic aid made available to the African countries was sporadic and not a part of the general policy line of any of the metropolitan or industrialized powers. After World War II both the British and French governments started grant aid programmes for their dependent territories as did the Portuguese at a much lower volume. Since independence has been won by the African countries, the aid programmes have been continued by the former metropolitan powers (without interruption by the French ; after a pause by the British). The United States came on to the African scene for a brief period during the Marshall Plan and after, mostly in connection with the use of local currency counterpart funds generated in the aid programmes in Europe. The amounts of the U.S. contribution are lost or obscured in the intricate accounting of the counterpart funds — particularly in France where a strict division was not maintained between the use of funds in France and overseas. In any case, somewhere around half a billion dollars of real resources that were made available to the European countries under the Marshall Plan were passed on to the African countries by France and the United Kingdom. Most of this went to North Africa but as much as a hundred million dollars of the French and British aid to Africa South of the Sahara might notionally at least be ascribed to the Marshall Plan. (Since during this period France and the U.K. were receiving aid from the U.S. and simultaneously extending aid and exporting capital to their currency areas, it is admittedly arbitrary to identify one final user as the 'recipient' of aid. The figure given here is essentially an accounting estimate of the amount of counterpart funds generated by Marshall aid that were made available to the African countries.

Economically, one could just as well argue that the aid given to the African countries by the U.K. and France during this period was the marginal use of resources and that if Marshall aid had not been received by the U.K. and France, aid to Africa would have been eliminated. On this basis, all of the French, British and Portuguese aid to their African territories during this period could be claimed as indirect U.S. aid.)

It was essentially after the independence of the African countries that the U.S. began directly making aid available to Africa. The U.S. programme although it extended at first to virtually every independent country is now concentrated on the English-speaking countries, the Congo (Leo), Ethiopia and Somalia. The Soviet Union and the other Eastern European countries also came in with independence but concentrated from the beginning on particular countries. Mainland China came on to the scene first in North Africa with help to the Algerian Nationalists and then in 1964, South of the Sahara with aid to Kenya and Tanzania. A number of other countries also have begun aid programmes in independent Africa ; among the most important of these are West Germany, in both capital and technical assistance, and Israel in technical assistance.

International and multilateral assistance is also important in Africa — about 10 per cent of the total flow of funds has come from the World Bank Group and the European Common Market's Economic Development Fund (FED).

The following table gives a summary picture of the main sources of the flow of funds to sub-Saharan Africa (excluding South Africa) over the last several years. The total has increased from a 1960 total of $650 million to around $900 million equivalent a year for 1962 and 1963, and over $1 billion in 1964.

The figures do not include Soviet and Eastern European or mainland Chinese aid. While no detailed reports are available on disbursements on these, from the information available on the aid agreements made by these countries and the exceptional slowness of disbursements under them, it is not likely that total disbursements exceeded $100 million from 1960 through 1962 with a maximum of $50 million in 1963. (Mainland China through 1963 for the whole of Africa — mainly Algeria — had made total commitments of $140 million ; in 1964, it made $90 million in commitments. Total disbursements are not likely to have exceeded 20 or 30 million dollars.)

The largest single programme has continued to be the bilateral programme of France to the former French colonies, supplemented

Capital Movements and Economic Development

since 1957 by the Economic Development Fund (FED) of the European Common Market. For these countries, the foreign aid

THE NET FLOW OF FINANCIAL RESOURCES FROM MULTILATERAL AGENCIES AND THE FLOW OF OFFICIAL BILATERAL NET CONTRIBUTIONS FROM INDIVIDUAL OECD MEMBER COUNTRIES TO AFRICA SOUTH OF THE SAHARA (EXCLUDING SOUTH AFRICA)

($ millions)

	1960	1961	1962	1963	1964 (Preliminary)
Multilateral Agencies					
World Bank Group	48·7	51·9	44·0	8·3	
Other UN Agencies *	16·0	39·9	29·5	36·0	
EEC	3·2	15·2	51·3	58·9	
Total multilateral	67·9	107·0	124·8	103·2	
Bilateral					
France	280·1 †	282·1 †	285·9 †	293·6 †	
U.K.	123·6	228·3	172·3	163·5	
U.S.	39·0	75·0	148·0	142·0	
Belgium	86·0	70·5	63·4	75·8	
Germany	5·3	13·4	59·2	54·1	
Portugal	36·6	32·4	40·7	51·1	
Italy	16·6	18·5	12·5	22·5	
Other ‡	0·5	2·9	3·5	4·3	
Total bilateral	587·7	723·1	785·5	806·9	
Total, Multilateral and OECD Bilateral	655·6	830·1	910·3	910·1	1,038

* Disbursements net of subscription payments for UNICEF, UNWRA, UN High Commissioner for Refugees, the UN Fund for the Congo, the UN Special Fund, and the UN Technical Assistance Programmes.
† Excluding aid to French overseas territories.
‡ Including funds from Austria, Canada, Denmark, Japan, Netherlands, Norway, Sweden and Switzerland.

Sources: Prepared from tables in OECD, *The Flow of Financial Resources to Less Developed Countries*, OECD, Paris, 1964; *Development Assistance Efforts and Policies, Report by Willard Thorp*, September 1965 (Paris).

received has amounted on the average to around 8 per cent of the countries' GNP's, with the range between 6 and 12 per cent. As gross investment in these countries averaged around 12 per cent of GNP during 1960, foreign aid was equivalent to about two-thirds

88

of this. Since 1960, aid to the French-speaking countries has increased by about one-quarter (mostly from the Common Market Investment Fund) or somewhat faster than the GNP and is probably around 9 per cent of total GNP ; with gross investment, perhaps, around 13 per cent of total GNP, on the average. The volume of aid *per capita* in the former French colonies is on the average around $9 equivalent.

In the rest of sub-Sahara Africa, aid has increased more rapidly than it has to the former French territories since independence — going up by some 70 per cent from 1960 through 1963, but it was still half the relative importance of French-speaking Africa — averaging over the whole area about $4 *per capita* in 1965. The aid funds for these countries amounted to around 5 per cent of their GNP, and were equivalent to about five-twelfths of their total investment.

Of course, the foregoing represents a rather heroic aggregation of a wide variety of programmes providing funds to the African countries. Not all of these amounts can appropriately be called 'economic aid', i.e. funds made available on a subsidized basis — below market cost — to a country designed to help its economic development. Certainly some of these funds were provided for political or military ends — to influence directly the political orientation of the recipient country, or to secure military bases. Also, some part of these funds were supplier or exporter credits, primarily designed to sell machinery or equipment — in some cases machinery that was basically unfitted or uneconomic to use in the country that it was sold to. Probably only the whole of the international and multilateral aid could be counted without reservation as being wholly 'economic aid'. But even capital that is made available for other ends can be helpful to economic development. Even aid to military forces can sometimes be helpful — through the army's construction of military roads which turn out to be generally useful, the training of soldiers which gives them useful skills or habits of mind, etc.

A substantial part of the aid provided to Africa has been in technical assistance : almost half of the French contribution is payment for technical assistance ; almost a third of the total official aid to Africa South of the Sahara consists of expenditures on and connected with technical assistance. In Africa, technical assistance in the form of trained key personnel is often even more important than additional capital. The ability of the African countries to absorb capital, in fact, in most cases depends upon the amount of technical assistance they have received. In general, Africa receives a greater volume of technical assistance in both relative and absolute terms than any other region of the world.

During 1963, there were 34,000 technical assistance personnel stationed in Africa South of the Sahara. This is 40 per cent of the total number provided to the developing countries by the OECD countries and the international agencies. (In North Africa, there is another 40 per cent.) Of this number, 8,000 were teachers and 23,000 were operational personnel and teachers. These figures are surely among the most significant for understanding the present position and prospects for development of Africa. Of these, 24,000 were provided by France at a cost of $136 million equivalent; 10,000 came from and were largely or partly financed by the United Kingdom at an annual cost to Britain of around $40 million equivalent; 3,000 by the U.S. (including Peace Corps); over 2,000 by Belgium; around 1,500 by the various U.N. agencies; and around 500 by Israel.

The distribution of French technical assistance personnel among the African countries aided varies considerably in intensity from country to country — it is seven times more intense per million of population in the Ivory Coast than in the Congo (Brazzaville), for example. In general, the higher the present *per capita* income, the greater the intensity so that Senegal and Ivory Coast each receive four times as much assistance as Upper Volta, for example, although Upper Volta's population is greater than either, while its *per capita* income is about a quarter or a fifth of that of the others. This certainly is not the basis on which the assistance is made available — the basis being rather the ability of a country to make good use of the assistance and its desire for assistance. The results, not entirely by coincidence, are that the more resources and the more developed a country already is, the more help it can usefully use to accelerate its growth further. Beyond a certain point in development a country obviously will be able to cut back on its need for technical assistance. But this point is not likely to come before the African countries have multiplied their present *per capita* income several times and are at least semi-industrialized.

Consideration of the French-speaking countries in this regard is particularly revealing since it does represent almost a controlled experiment. Because of the French government's generosity in paying liberally for the French technical assistance and in being willing to meet practically every reasonable request of the African country of this kind, the provision of French assistance is close to being the maximum amount that can be usefully employed. The finding that this assistance appears to vary directly with the level of development of a country is significant, therefore. It should be possible for a country as it develops to reduce its *use* of technical assistance — and this is what appears to have happened among the English-speaking countries in Africa — and still maintain a favourable rate of growth. But, if technical assistance were available on favourable terms and politically acceptable, it appears reasonable to assume that, as in the French-speaking countries, the capacity of a country to substitute its own nationals for prior technical assistance can also be used to absorb and make use of still more technical assistance and so secure an acceleration in the rate of growth.

Flow of Capital

Based on S. H. Frankel's figures, I have estimated that the total foreign capital invested in Africa South of the Sahara by World War II was around $6 billion; of this, about half was borrowed by the public sector of the African territories on the private capital markets, mostly in London and Paris, and the rest was private. From 1945 to 1960, probably another $6 billion, at current price, came in from private sources and around $10 billion of public funds. At varying dates since 1945, in much of Africa and certainly since 1960 for the whole of Africa South of the Sahara it has not been possible for the African public sector to secure an appreciable amount of funds from private lenders or investors at any reasonable range of return. The main reliance, therefore, has been placed on official sources abroad, that is, governments and the international development institutions to provide funds at concessional rates. Since 1960 through 1965 the net inflow of capital has been under $5 billion with the net inflow of private capital (including ploughed in profits) of around half a billion in Southern Africa, Nigeria, Ivory Coast and Liberia largely offset by capital flight or repatriation from other parts of the continent.

The indications are strong that except in mining the pre-war returns on private direct investment were very poor and not very exciting even in mining. Since the war, the situation seems to have improved : manufacturing, at least in South Africa, and mining appear to give very good returns. On the other hand, investment, other than mining, outside of South Africa does not appear particularly favourable.

Finally, one quite definite conclusion can be reached from this exercise — much more research is needed in this whole field of returns to foreign investment and much better statistics are needed on the flow of capital and the returns to capital. The World Bank, in co-operation with OECD and the IMF, is beginning a programme to improve the various data components on the flow of capital. We are also considering beginning research on the returns to capital.

SELECTIVE BIBLIOGRAPHY

Commonwealth of Australia Treasury, *Private Overseas Investment in Australia*, Supplement to the Treasury Information Bulletin, May 1965, Canberra, ACT.

Banque Centrale du Congo Belge et du Ruanda-Urundi, *Bulletin*, 4ᵉ Année, No. 8, Bruxelles, Léopoldville, Août 1955 ; *Bulletin*, 7ᵉ Année, No. 1, Janvier 1958.

Banque Nationale de Belgique, 'Les Investissements belges et étrangers au Congo', *Bulletin d'Information et de Documentation*, XXVII Année, vol. 1, No. 3, Mars 1952, pp. 174–181.

Belgium, Institut Royal des Relations Internationales, *La Belgique et l'aide économique aux pays sous-développés*, Martinus Nijhoff, La Haye, Bruxelles, 1959.

Joseph Conrad, *Heart of Darkness*, J. M. Dent & Sons, London (1902).

France, Ministère d'État Chargé de la Réforme Administrative, *La Politique de coopération avec les pays en voie de développement*, Rapport de la Commission d'Étude (Jeanneney), Paris, 1963.

S. H. Frankel, *Capital Investment in Africa*, OUP, London, New York, 1938.

André Gide, *Voyage au Congo*, Gallimard, (Paris, 1927).

Lord Hailey, *An African Survey*, Rev. *1956*, OUP, London, New York, 1957.

E. S. Mason, A. M. Kamarck, et al., *The Economic Development of Uganda*, Published for I.B.R.D. by Johns Hopkins Press, Baltimore (1962).

L. M. Lachmann, 'Investment Repercussions', QJE, vol. lxii, 1948, pp. 698–713.

OECD, *The Flow of Financial Resources to Less Developed Countries, 1956–1963*, Paris, 1964.

U.K., Secretary of State for the Colonies, *Colonial Development and Welfare Acts*, Cmd. 672, February 1959, London, H.M.S.O. (1959).

U.S. Department of Commerce, *Survey of Current Business*, various issues, various years, Washington, D.C.

Charles Wilson, *The History of Unilever*, 2 volumes, Cassell, London, 1954.

STATISTICAL APPENDIX

1 'Earning Rates' on North American, United Kingdom and Total Overseas Investment in Australia

2 Annual Yield to Capital Invested in Witwatersrand Gold Mining Companies, 1932

3a U.S. Direct Investments by Area

3b U.S. Direct Investments in Africa South of the Sahara, 1929–63

4 U.S. Direct Investments in Africa by Country, 1929–64

5 U.S. Foreign Direct Investment and Earnings by Area, 1956–63

6 U.S. Foreign Direct Investment and Earnings by Sector and Area :
   a. 1957
   b. 1958
   c. 1959
   d. 1960
   e. 1961
   f. 1962
   g. 1963
   h. 1964

7 South Africa : Foreign Direct Investment by Sector

8 Return on Foreign Direct Investments in South Africa

9 Former Belgian Congo : Capital investi dans le secteur privé, 1939

10 Dividend Returns on Investment in the Congo

11 Loans Issued by French African Colonies to 1930

12 The French Colonial Loan of 1931

13 The French Colonial Loan of 1931 : Expenditure in Major Colonies

14 Foreign Bonds Publicly Issued in Various Markets by Developing Countries

15 Distribution of Flow of Financial Resources from France to African Countries

16 Finance of Gross Fixed Capital Formation in French-Speaking Africa

17 British Financial Aid to Africa South of the Sahara

18 U.S. Official Economic Assistance to Africa South of the Sahara

19 World Bank Group Loans and Investments in Africa South of the Sahara

STATISTICAL APPENDIX — TABLE 1

COMPARISON OF 'EARNING RATES' ON NORTH AMERICAN, UNITED
KINGDOM AND TOTAL OVERSEAS INVESTMENT IN
COMPANIES IN AUSTRALIA

Income Payable as Percentage of Total Investment in Companies in Australia		
North America	United Kingdom	All Overseas Countries
%	%	%
1947–48	7·3	7·7	8·0
1948–49	6·9	5·6	6·3
1949–50	9·4	8·2	8·7
1950–51	13·9	8·5	9·5
1951–52	14·5	7·0	8·6
1952–53	11·7	6·6	7·6
1953–54	22·8	7·4	10·7
1954–55	18·7	7·6	10·1
1955–56	16·8	8·4	10·4
1956–57	14·8	7·7	9·5
1957–58	15·2	6·9	9·1
1958–59	17·3	7·3	10·0
1959–60	16·0	7·4	9·6
1960–61	12·8	5·8	8·0
1961–62	7·8	4·8	5·7
1962–63	8·2	6·3	6·8
1963–64	7·7	6·1	6·6

Source: Australia, Commonwealth Treasury, *Private Overseas Investment in Australia* (Canberra, 1965), p. 19.

STATISTICAL APPENDIX — TABLE 2

ANNUAL YIELD TO CAPITAL INVESTED IN WITWATERSRAND GOLD MINING COMPANIES
EXISTING AT THE END OF 1932

(Selected Years)

	Total 'Available' Profits £'000	Dividends £'000	Capital Invested Excluding Appropriations from Revenue £'000	Capital Invested *Plus* Cash Premiums *Plus* Appropriations from Revenue £'000	Percentage of Dividends to Capital Invested Excluding Appropriations from Revenue		Percentage of 'Available' Profits to Capital Invested Including Appropriations from Revenue and Cash Premiums %
					(A) %	(B) %	%
1888	261	251	2,585	2,596	38·0	9·7	10·0
1895	1,247	751	18,843	20,708	5·2	4·0	6·0
1900	121	115	38,537	43,504	0·2	0·3	0·3
1905	4,147	3,232	56,217	64,586	6·1	5·7	6·4
1910	7,435	6,016	67,882	84,139	9·4	8·9	8·8
1915	7,720	6,180	71,588	96,036	8·7	8·6	8·0
1920	9,071	7,842	78,356	110,969	10·2	10·0	8·2
1925	9,775	8,170	82,874	124,958	8·9	9·9	7·8
1930	10,258	8,930	90,630	138,904	10·0	9·9	7·4
1932	9,976	8,877	92,012	142,740	9·7	9·6	7·0

Source : Selected from Table 15, S. H. Frankel, *Capital Investment in Africa*, Oxford University Press, London, New York, Toronto 1938, pp. 96–97. Percentage figures under Column 'A' are from Frankel ; these seem to be in error. Figures 'B' have been computed from the data presented by Frankel.

STATISTICAL APPENDIX — TABLE 3a

U.S. DIRECT INVESTMENTS BY AREA

(Millions of dollars)

Year End	Total	Canada	Other Western Hemisphere	Europe	Africa	Asia	Other
1929	7,700	2,000	3,600	1,400	—	—	700*
1936	6,690	1,952	2,803	1,258	—	—	651†
1940	7,300	2,100	2,600	1,900	—	—	700*
1945	8,400	2,500	3,100	2,000	—	—	800*
1950	11,788	3,579	4,735	1,720	—	—	1,753†
1956	22,177	7,460	7,373	3,520‡	659	1,106§	2,059‖
1957	25,394	8,769	8,052	4,151	664	2,019	1,739
1958	27,255	9,338	8,447	4,573	746	2,178	1,974
1959	29,735	10,171	8,990	5,300	843	2,236	2,196
1960	32,778	11,198	9,271	6,681	925	2,291	2,412
1961	34,667	11,602	9,190	7,742	1,064	2,477	2,593
1962	37,226	12,133	9,474	8,930	1,271	2,500	2,918
1963	40,686	13,044	9,891	10,340	1,426	2,793	3,193
1964¶	44,343	13,820	10,318	12,067	1,629	3,062	3,447

* Including undistributed.   † Including Western European dependencies.
‡ Western Europe only.   § Middle East only.   ‖ Including the Far East.
¶ Preliminary.

Source: U.S. Department of Commerce; *Survey of Current Business*, 1929, 1940, 1945, November 1949 issue. 1936, December 1952 issue. 1950, November 1954 issue. For the years 1956 through 1964, figures are obtained from either August or September issues of each successive year.

STATISTICAL APPENDIX — TABLE 3B

U.S. DIRECT INVESTMENTS IN AFRICA SOUTH OF THE SAHARA FOR SELECTED YEARS, 1929–1963

(Millions of dollars)

1929	. . 92	1957	. . 558	1962	. . 880
1936	. . 83	1959	. . 695	1963	. . 1122
1943	. . 103	1960	. . 730	1964	. . 1247
1950	. . 231	1961	. . 810		

Sources: Department of Commerce; *U.S. Business Investments in Foreign Countries*, 1960, p. 92; and *Survey of Current Business*, August 1962, p. 22; August 1963, p. 18, August 1964, p. 10, and September 1965, p. 24.

STATISTICAL APPENDIX — TABLE 4

U.S. DIRECT INVESTMENTS IN AFRICA BY COUNTRY 1929–1964

(Millions of dollars)

Country and Area	1929	1936	1943	1950	1957	1959	1960	1961	1962	1963	1964
East Africa	—	—	4	12	30	43	46	56	—	—	—
Ethiopia	*	*	†	5	1	1	—	—	—	—	—
Fr. Eq. Africa }	1	*	3	4	9	8	—	—	—	—	—
Fr. West Africa }	—	*		11	34	76	—	—	—	—	—
Ghana	—	*	—	—	7	9	—	—	—	—	—
Liberia	5	*	18	16	72	115	139	160	184	197	187
Nigeria	—	—	5	11	15	16	—	—	—	—	—
Congo (L.)	†	1	4	8	19	17	—	—	—	—	—
Rhod. Nyasaland	—	—	18	26	59	72	82	85	83	—	—
South Africa	77	55	50	140	301	323	286	309	357	411	467
Total of foregoing	83	55	102	233	547	680	553	610	624	608	654
All other	19	38	27	54	117	163	372	454	647	818	975
Total Africa	102	93	129	287	664	843	925	1,064	1,271	1,426	1,629

* Not separately shown.   † Less than $500,000.

Source: Department of Commerce; *U.S. Business Investments in Foreign Countries*, 1960, p. 92. Survey of *Current Business*, August 1962, August 1963, August 1964 and September 1965.

97

STATISTICAL APPENDIX — TABLE 5

U.S. FOREIGN DIRECT INVESTMENT * AND EARNINGS † BY AREA, 1956–1963, AND PERCENTAGE OF EARNINGS ON TOTAL INVESTMENT

(Millions of dollars)

Year	Total Invest-ment (1)	Total Earn-ings (2)	Total % of 2 to 1 (3)	Africa Invest-ment (1)	Africa Earn-ings (2)	Africa % of 2 to 1 (3)	Canada Invest-ment (1)	Canada Earn-ings (2)	Canada % of 2 to 1 (3)	Other Western Hemisphere Invest-ment (1)	Other Western Hemisphere Earn-ings (2)	Other Western Hemisphere % of 2 to 1 (3)	Europe Invest-ment (1)	Europe Earn-ings (2)	Europe % of 2 to 1 (3)	Asia Invest-ment (1)	Asia Earn-ings (2)	Asia % of 2 to 1 (3)	Other Invest-ment (1)	Other Earn-ings (2)	Other % of 2 to 1 (3)
1956	22,177	3,135	14·1	659	—	—	7,460	701	9·4	7,373	1,052	14·3	3,520	485	13·8	1,106	—	—	2,059	897	43·6
1957	25,394	3,330	13·2	664	94	14·2	8,769	653	7·4	8,052	1,096	13·6	4,151	582	14·0	2,019	751	37·2	1,739	154	8·9
1958	27,256	2,954	10·8	746	51	6·8	9,338	569	6·1	8,447	760	9·0	4,573	582	12·7	2,178	800	36·7	1,974	192	9·7
1959	29,736	3,255	10·9	843	55	6·5	10,171	713	7·0	8,990	774	8·6	5,300	667	12·6	2,236	785	35·1	2,196	261	11·9
1960	32,778	3,545	10·8	925	33	3·6	11,198	718	6·4	9,271	829	8·9	6,681	762	11·4	2,291	901	39·3	2,412	302	12·5
1961	34,668	3,699	10·7	1,064	28	2·6	11,602	684	5·9	9,190	910	9·9	7,742	841	10·9	2,477	958	38·7	2,593	278	10·7
1962	37,226	4,245	11·4	1,271	81	6·4	12,133	825	6·8	9,474	1,010	10·7	8,930	844	9·5	2,500	1,040	41·6	2,918	445	15·3
1963	40,686	4,587	11·2	1,426	166	11·9	13,044	948	7·1	9,891	1,125	11·4	10,340	996	9·6	2,793	1,116	40·2	3,193	235	7·4
1964	44,343	5,118	11·5	1,629	343	21·1	13,820	1,104	8·0	10,318	1,253	12·1	12,067	1,112	9·2	3,062	1,067	34·8	3,447	239	7·0

* Position at the end of period.   † Per year.   Earnings is the sum of the U.S. share in the net earnings of subsidiaries and branch profits.

Source: U.S. Department of Commerce, *Survey of Current Business*, various issues. Earnings percentages calculated from U.S. Department of Commerce data.

STATISTICAL APPENDIX — TABLE 6a — 1957

U.S. FOREIGN DIRECT INVESTMENT * AND EARNINGS † BY SECTOR AND AREA AND PERCENTAGE OF EARNINGS ON TOTAL INVESTMENT IN 1957

(Millions of dollars)

	Total			Mining and Smelting			Petroleum			Manufacturing			Other		
	Invest-ment	Earn-ings	% of Earn-ings to Invest-ment	Invest-ment	Earn-ings	% of Earn-ings to Invest-ment	Invest-ment	Earn-ings	% of Earn-ings to Invest-ment	Invest-ment	Earn-ings	% of Earn-ings to Invest-ment	Invest-ment	Earn-ings	% of Earn-ings to Invest-ment
Total	25,252	3,330	13·2	2,634	281	10·7	8,981	1,623	18·1	7,918	852	10·8	5,718	574	10·0
Canada	8,332	641	7·7	996	71	7·1	2,154	95	4·4	3,512	348	9·9	1,670	127	7·6
Western Hemisphere‡	9,711	1,405	14·5	1,370	154	11·2	3,805	865	22·7	1,711	126	7·4	2,825	259	9·2
Europe	3,993	547	13·7	50	9	18·0	1,184	163	13·8	2,077	269	13·0	682	106	15·5
Other	3,216	737	22·9	218	47	21·6	1,839	499	27·1	618	109	17·6	540	82	15·2

* Position at the end of period.
† Per year. Earnings in the sum of the U.S. share in the net earnings of subsidiaries and branch profits.
‡ Including Western European dependencies.

Source: U.S. Department of Commerce, *Survey of Current Business*, September 1958. Earnings percentages calculated from U.S. Department of Commerce data.

STATISTICAL APPENDIX — TABLE 6b — 1958

U.S. FOREIGN DIRECT INVESTMENT * AND EARNINGS † BY SECTOR AND AREA PERCENTAGE OF EARNINGS ON TOTAL INVESTMENT IN 1958

(Millions of dollars)

	Total			Mining and Smelting			Petroleum			Manufacturing			Other		
	Invest-ment	Earn-ings	% of Earn-ings to Invest-ment	Invest-ment	Earn-ings	% of Earn-ings to Invest-ment	Invest-ment	Earn-ings	% of Earn-ings to Invest-ment	Invest-ment	Earn-ings	% of Earn-ings to Invest-ment	Invest-ment	Earn-ings	% of Earn-ings to Invest-ment
Total	27,075	2,954	10·9	2,856	219	7·7	9,681	1,307	13·5	8,485	873	10·3	6,053	555	9·2
Africa	789	69	8·7	234	37	15·8	276	−19	−6·9	139	23	16·5	140	28	20·0
Canada	8,929	568	6·4	1,083	42	3·9	2,410	66	2·7	3,696	337	9·1	1,740	123	7·1
Other Western Hemisphere	9,125	847	9·3	n.a.	n.a.	n.a.	3,211	404	12·6	1,759	107	6·1	n.a.	n.a.	n.a.
Europe	4,382	532	12·1	51	3	5·9	1,256	104	8·3	2,308	308	13·3	767	117	15·3
Middle East	1,315	648	4·9	n.a.	n.a.	n.a.	1,218	637	52·3	38	—	—	n.a.	n.a.	n.a.
Far East ‡	1,681	253	15·0	53	3	5·7	646	86	13·3	546	98	17·9	436	66	15·1
Other	854	37	4·3	1,435	134	9·3	664	30	4·5	—	—	—	2,970	221	7·4

* Position at the end of period.
† Per year. Earnings is the sum of the U.S. share in the net earnings of subsidiaries and branch profits.
‡ Including Australia and New Zealand.

Source: U.S. Department of Commerce, *Survey of Current Business*, August 1959. Earnings percentages calculated from U.S. Department of Commerce data.

STATISTICAL APPENDIX — TABLE 6c — 1959

U.S. FOREIGN DIRECT INVESTMENT* AND EARNINGS† BY SECTOR AND AREA AND PERCENTAGE OF EARNINGS ON TOTAL INVESTMENT IN 1959

(Millions of dollars)

	Total			Mining and Smelting			Petroleum			Manufacturing			Other		
	Invest-ment	Earn-ings	% of Earn-ings to Invest-ment	Invest-ment	Earn-ings	% of Earn-ings to Invest-ment	Invest-ment	Earn-ings	% of Earn-ings to Invest-ment	Invest-ment	Earn-ings	% of Earn-ings to Invest-ment	Invest-ment	Earn-ings	% of Earn-ings to Invest-ment
Total	29,735	3,255	10·9	2,858	315	11·0	10,423	1,185	11·4	9,692	1,129	11·6	6,762	626	9·3
Africa	843	56	6·6	255	38	14·9	338	−27	−8·0	120	17	14·2	130	28	21·5
Canada	10,171	713	7·0	1,090	67	6·1	2,465	74	3·0	4,558	438	9·6	2,058	134	6·5
Other Western Hemisphere ‡	8,990	869	9·7	1,416	192	13·6	3,312	340	10·3	1,426	121	8·5	2,837	216	7·6
Europe	5,300	709	13·4	50	10	20·0	1,453	114	7·8	2,927	444	15·2	870	142	16·3
Asia	2,236	757	33·9	20	3	15·0	1,662	663	39·9	248	37	14·9	305	55	18·0
Other	2,196	152	6·9	28	6	21·4	1,193	22	1·8	412	72	17·5	564	52	9·2

* Position at the end of period.
† Per year. Earnings is the sum of the U.S. share in the net earnings of subsidiaries and branch profits.
‡ Including European dependencies.

Source: U.S. Department of Commerce, *Survey of Current Business*, September 1960. Earnings percentages calculated from U.S. Department of Commerce data.

STATISTICAL APPENDIX — TABLE 6d — 1960

U.S. FOREIGN DIRECT INVESTMENT * AND EARNINGS † BY SECTOR AND AREA AND PERCENTAGE OF EARNINGS ON TOTAL INVESTMENT IN 1960

(Millions of dollars)

	Total			Mining and Smelting			Petroleum			Manufacturing			Other		
	Invest-ment	Earn-ings	% of Earn-ings to Invest-ment	Invest-ment	Earn-ings	% of Earn-ings to Invest-ment	Invest-ment	Earn-ings	% of Earn-ings to Invest-ment	Invest-ment	Earn-ings	% of Earn-ings to Invest-ment	Invest-ment	Earn-ings	% of Earn-ings to Invest-ment
Total	32,744	3,546	10·8	3,013	394	13·1	10,944	1,282	11·7	11,152	1,176	10·5	7,635	693	9·1
Africa	925	33	3·6	247	61	24·7	407	−77	−18·9	118	19	16·1	152	30	19·7
Canada	11,198	718	6·4	1,329	88	6·6	2,667	97	3·6	4,827	398	8·2	2,375	134	5·6
Other Western Hemisphere ‡	9,249	970	10·5	1,331	224	16·8	3,264	370	11·3	1,631	147	9·0	3,024	229	7·6
Europe	6,645	762	11·5	49	10	20·4	1,726	85	4·9	3,797	487	12·8	1,072	180	16·8
Asia	2,315	901	38·9	24	3	12·5	1,655	799	48·3	286	42	14·7	350	58	16·6
Other	2,412	162	6·7	33	8	24·2	1,223	9	0·7	494	82	16·6	662	63	9·5

* Position at the end of period.

† Per year. Earnings is the sum of the U.S. share in the net earnings of subsidiaries and branch profits.

‡ Including European dependencies.

Source: U.S. Department of Commerce, *Survey of Current Business*, August 1961. Earnings percentages calculated from U.S. Department of Commerce data.

Statistical Appendix — Table 6e — 1961

U.S. Foreign Direct Investment * and Earnings † by Sector and Area and Percentage of Earnings on Total Investment in 1961

(Millions of dollars)

	Total			Mining and Smelting			Petroleum			Manufacturing			Other		
	Invest-ment	Earn-ings	% of Earn-ings to Invest-ment	Invest-ment	Earn-ings	% of Earn-ings to Invest-ment	Invest-ment	Earn-ings	% of Earn-ings to Invest-ment	Invest-ment	Earn-ings	% of Earn-ings to Invest-ment	Invest-ment	Earn-ings	% of Earn-ings to Invest-ment
Total	34,684	3,700	10·7	3,061	359	11·7	12,151	1,449	11·9	11,936	1,180	9·9	7,536	711	9·4
Africa	1,070	28	2·6	285	44	15·4	491	−84	−17·1	113	19	16·8	180	50	27·8
Canada	11,804	684	5·8	1,380	90	6·5	2,841	121	4·3	5,093	360	7·1	2,490	113	4·5
Other Western Hemisphere ‡	9,108	1,032	11·3	1,284	205	15·7	3,648	465	12·7	1,678	152	9·1	2,497	209	8·4
Europe	7,655	841	11·0	48	8	16·7	2,131	84	3·9	4,212	532	12·6	1,264	217	17·2
Asia	2,482	958	38·6	27	4	14·8	1,750	840	48·0	321	50	15·6	384	64	16·7
Other §	2,564	156	6·1	36	8	22·2	1,289	24	1·9	518	66	12·7	721	58	8·0

* Position at the end of period.
† Per year. Earnings is the sum of the U.S. share in the net earnings of subsidiaries and branch profits.
‡ Including Western Hemisphere dependencies.   § Including Australia and New Zealand.

Source: U.S. Department of Commerce, *Survey of Current Business*, August 1962. Earnings percentages calculated from U.S. Department of Commerce data.

STATISTICAL APPENDIX — TABLE 6f — 1962

U.S. FOREIGN DIRECT INVESTMENT * AND EARNINGS † BY SECTOR AND AREA AND PERCENTAGE OF EARNINGS ON TOTAL INVESTMENT IN 1962

(Millions of dollars)

	Total			Mining and Smelting			Petroleum			Manufacturing			Other		
	Invest-ment	Earn-ings	% of Earn-ings to Invest-ment	Invest-ment	Earn-ings	% of Earn-ings to Invest-ment	Invest-ment	Earn-ings	% of Earn-ings to Invest-ment	Invest-ment	Earn-ings	% of Earn-ings to Invest-ment	Invest-ment	Earn-ings	% of Earn-ings to Invest-ment
Total	37,145	4,245	11·4	3,813	367	11·5	12,661	1,716	13·6	13,212	1,310	9·9	8,089	852	10·5
Africa	1,246	80	6·4	307	34	11·1	627	–6	–1·0	141	32	22·7	171	20	11·7
Canada	12,131	833	6·9	1,482	91	6·1	2,834	121	4·3	5,340	460	8·6	2,475	161	6·5
Other Western Hemisphere ‡	9,528	1,197	12·6	1,275	230	18·0	3,644	552	15·1	1,940	174	9·0	2,669	241	9·0
Europe	8,843	851	9·6	49	5	10·2	2,365	72	3·0	4,826	493	10·2	1,603	281	17·5
Asia	2,495	1,048	42·0	29	2	6·9	1,761	931	52·9	348	49	14·1	357	66	18·5
Other §	2,902	237	8·2	41	4	9·8	1,430	47	3·3	618	102	16·5	813	84	10·3

* Position at the end of period.
† Per year. Earnings is the sum of the U.S. share in the net earnings of subsidiaries and branch profits.
‡ Including 'Other Western Hemisphere'.   § Including Australia and New Zealand.

Source: U.S. Department of Commerce, *Survey of Current Business*, August 1963. Earnings percentages calculated from U.S. Department of Commerce data.

STATISTICAL APPENDIX — TABLE 6g — 1963

U.S. FOREIGN DIRECT INVESTMENT * AND EARNINGS † BY SECTOR AND AREA AND PERCENTAGE OF EARNINGS ON TOTAL INVESTMENT IN 1963

(Millions of dollars)

	Total			Mining and Smelting			Petroleum			Manufacturing			Other		
	Invest-ment	Earn-ings	% of Earn-ings to Invest-ment	Invest-ment	Earn-ings	% of Earn-ings to Invest-ment	Invest-ment	Earn-ings	% of Earn-ings to Invest-ment	Invest-ment	Earn-ings	% of Earn-ings to Invest-ment	Invest-ment	Earn-ings	% of Earn-ings to Invest-ment
Total	40,686	4,572	11·2	3,369	359	10·7	13,652	1,828	13·3	14,937	1,529	10·3	8,727	856	9·8
Africa	1,426	170	11·9	349	31	8·8	702	65	9·3	177	43	24·4	198	31	15·9
Canada	13,044	930	7·1	1,549	94	6·1	3,134	150	4·8	5,761	544	9·5	2,600	142	5·5
Other Western Hemisphere	9,891	1,125	11·4	1,303	219	16·8	3,636	532	14·7	2,203	171	7·7	2,739	203	7·4
Europe	10,340	992	9·6	55	4	7·3	2,776	67	2·4	5,634	605	10·8	1,876	317	17·1
Asia	2,793	1,120	40·2	32	2	6·5	1,920	1,001	52·0	430	52	12·4	410	66	16·2
Other	3,193	235	7·3	82	8	11·4	1,484	14	0·9	723	115	15·8	903	98	10·7

* Position at the end of period.
† Per year. Earnings is the sum of the U.S. share in the net earnings of subsidiaries and branch profits.

Source : U.S. Department of Commerce, *Survey of Current Business*, August 1964 (Earnings) and September 1965 (Investments). Earnings percentages calculated from U.S. Department of Commerce data.

STATISTICAL APPENDIX — TABLE 6h — 1964

U.S. FOREIGN DIRECT INVESTMENT * AND EARNINGS † BY SECTOR AND AREA, AND PERCENTAGE OF EARNINGS ON TOTAL INVESTMENT IN 1964

(Millions of dollars)

	Total			Mining and Smelting			Petroleum			Manufacturing			Other		
	Invest-ment	Earn-ings	% of Earn-ings to Invest-ment	Invest-ment	Earn-ings	% of Earn-ings to Invest-ment	Invest-ment	Earn-ings	% of Earn-ings to Invest-ment	Invest-ment	Earn-ings	% of Earn-ings to Invest-ment	Invest-ment	Earn-ings	% of Earn-ings to Invest-ment
Total	44,343	5,118	11·54	3,564	505	14·17	14,350	1,860	12·96	16,861	1,816	10·77	9,567	936	9·78
Canada	13,820	1,104	7·99	1,671	191	11·43	3,228	170	5·27	6,191	565	9·13	2,730	177	6·48
Western Hemisphere	10,318	1,253	12·14	1,348	260	19·29	3,711	544	14·66	2,506	246	9·82	2,752	203	7·38
Europe	12,067	1,112	9·22	56	3	5·36	3,086	8	0·26	6,547	754	11·52	2,379	348	14·63
Africa	1,629	343	21·05	356	38	10·67	830	227	27·35	225	43	19·11	217	35	16·13
Asia	3,062	1,067	34·85	34	3	8·82	2,014	912	45·28	535	82	15·33	479	70	14·61
Other	3,447	239	6·93	100	10	10·00	1,482	−6	−0·40	856	126	14·72	1,009	104	10·31

* Position at the end of period.
† Per year. Earnings is the sum of the U.S. share in the net earnings of subsidiaries and branch profits.

Source : U.S. Department of Commerce, *Survey of Current Business*, September 1965 issue.

STATISTICAL APPENDIX — TABLE 7

SOUTH AFRICA: FOREIGN DIRECT INVESTMENT BY SECTOR OF INVESTMENT

(SOUTH AFRICAN DIRECT INVESTMENTS ABROAD)

(£ million)

	Grand Total 1963	Grand Total 1956	Official Sector 1963	Official Sector 1956	Private Sector Total 1963	Private Sector Total 1956	Mining 1956	Manufacturing 1956	Trade 1956	Insurance 1956	Other Financial Organizations 1956	All Others 1956
U.K.	670·5 (54·0)	556·1 (14·0)	40·0 (1·0)	32·3	630·5 (53·0)	523·8	164·0 (1·9)	186·6 (1·8)	74·9 (1·9)	17·0	47·5	33·8 (4·6)
U.S.A.	120·5 (3·5)	126·3 (2·5)	2·0	1·1	118·5 (3·5)	125·2	54·0 (0·1)	36·2 (0·3)	28·7 (0·8)	0·6 (3·4)	1·2	4·4 (0·2)
France	40·5 (0·5)	24·2 (0·2)	2·5	2·4	38·0 (0·5)	21·8	12·2	1·4	5·0	0·6 (1·1)	1·5	1·1
Switzerland	28·5 (1·0)	17·0 (0·1)	0·5	0·2	28·0 (1·0)	16·8	4·3	8·4	1·0	0·6	1·7	0·9
Rhodesia/Nyasaland	23·0 (154·5)	13·0 (94·8)	3·0	3·1	20·0 (154·5)	9·9	2·0 (24·3)	1·7 (28·6)	1·0 (16·9)	3·2 (12·2)	1·3	0·7 (12·4)
Netherlands	n.a.	9·9 (0·1)	n.a.	2·3	n.a.	7·6	0·3	5·6	0·5	0·5	0·3	0·4
Canada	n.a.	9·8 (0·1)	n.a.	0·1	n.a.	9·7	0·4	6·0	2·6	0·5	0·3	0·5
Grand Total including countries other than those identified above	985·0 (242·5)	809·0 (122·2)	56·0 (1·0)	46·9	929·5 (241·5)	762·1	242·5 (26·4)	265·7 (34·6)	119·1 (22·8)	28·4 (14·8)	61·2	45·0 (22·6)

N.B.—As the 1956 data are in South African Pounds (S.A.£ = $2·8), the 1963 data are *also* shown in pounds although the figures published are in Rand. Figures shown within brackets indicate South African direct investments abroad. There is a small discrepancy of £1 million in the figures for South African investments abroad in 1963 which is probably the amount of direct investments in foreign public sector enterprises.

Source: Data for 1956 are from the Final Results of the 1956 Census of The Foreign Liabilities and Assets of the Union of South Africa, published as a supplement to the December 1958 issue of the South African Reserve Bank's *Quarterly Bulletin of Statistics*. Figures for 1963 are from the December 1964 issue of the South African Reserve Bank's *Quarterly Bulletin of Statistics*.

107

STATISTICAL APPENDIX — TABLE 8

RETURN ON FOREIGN DIRECT INVESTMENTS IN SOUTH AFRICA

Year	Total Value of Direct Investment (Rand Million) (a)	Cumulative Total of Undistributed Profits (Rand Million) (b)	Undistributed Profits Invested During the Year (Rand Million) (c)	Transferred Profits and Dividends During the Year (Rand Million) (d)	Total of Undistributed Profits and Transferred Earnings (c+d) (Rand Million) (e)	% of Total Undistributed Profits and Transferred Profits and Dividends (e) to Value of Direct Investment (a) and Cumulative Total of Undistributed Profits (b)
1956	1618	558		105		
1957	1670	599	41	93	134	6·2
1958	1809	663	64	91	115	5·1
1959	1855	687	24	90	114	4·6
1960	1873	716	29	100	129	5·1
1961	1861	728	12	123	135	5·2
1962	1917	787	59	103	162	6·2
1963	1970	848	61	108	169	6·2

Source : Data for columns (a), (b) and (c) are from Statement I on 'Total Foreign Liabilities of South Africa, 1956–1963', from the *Quarterly Bulletin of Statistics* of the South African Reserve Bank for December 1964.   Data for column (e) are from Table XXXIIIA on Balance of Payments — Services and Transfers from the same publication.   Figures in column (c) are derived by reference to data for (b) for any year to the preceding year's figure.

STATISTICAL APPENDIX — TABLE 9

FORMER BELGIAN CONGO : ESTIMATES OF CAPITAL INVESTED IN THE
PRIVATE SECTOR AT END — 1939

(Millions of gold francs)

Author		
Van de Velde :		
Total end — 1935, including capitalized reserves	2,245	
Addition 1935–39, as estimated by Banque	76	
Nationale		
		2,321
Frankel :		
Total end — 1935	2,462	
Addition 1935–39, as estimated by Banque	76	
Nationale		
		2,538
Verriest :		2,350
Banque Nationale de Belgique (excluding reserves)		1,460
Ministry of Colonies :		
Total 1887–1953 in francs of 1953	61,341	
Less investments 1948–53 (revalued in accordance	23,696	
with fiscal coefficients)		
investments 1940–47 (as estimated by	2,522	
Banque Nationale and revalued in		
accordance with fiscal co-efficients)		
Total investments 1887–1939	35,123	
Equivalent in gold francs (in accordance		2,150
with fiscal coefficients)		

Note.—Despite minor differences, it can be seen that the various estimates quoted yield very similar results, placing the total of capital invested in the private sector of the Congo Belge at about 2,350 million gold francs at end–1939. The estimate of the Banque Nationale, which departs most appreciably from this figure is confined to the capital actually imported from a foreign source.

Source : Banque Centrale du Congo Belge et du Ruanda-Urundi, *Bulletin*, 4ᵉ Année, No. 8, Août 1955, p. 292.

STATISTICAL APPENDIX — TABLE 10

DIVIDEND RETURNS ON INVESTMENT IN THE CONGO

			Distributions of Profits of Congolese Enterprises				
Year	Average Dividend %	Amor- tisation Funds	Direct Taxation	Reserves	Dividends Interest and Royalties	Total	Dividend Paid Abroad
1950		1,860	1,230	4,760	3,200	11,050	1,540
1951	12·09	2,260	1,310	6,770	3,660	14,000	2,020
1952	12·45	2,910	1,420	7,180	3,710	15,220	2,600
1953	12·02	3,870	2,040	4,840	4,070	14,820	2,610
1954	11·98	4,470	2,170	4,200	5,010	15,850	3,480
1955	11·68	4,930	2,250	3,730	6,200	17,100	4,700
1956	13·10	5,350	2,240	4,450	6,360	18,400	—

Source : Banque du Congo Belge et du Ruanda-Urundi, *Bulletin*, Janvier 1958, p. 15.

STATISTICAL APPENDIX — TABLE 11

LOANS ISSUED BY FRENCH AFRICAN COLONIES TO 1930*

(Million francs)

	Issued before 1900	Issued 1900–14	Issued 1919–30
A.O.F.	—	204	102
Togo	—	—	—
Cameroons	—	—	—
A.E.F.	—	21	408
Madagascar	26	75	—
Somaliland	—	—	—
Reunion	79	—	—
Total	105	300	510

* Figures given are amounts realized, *not* nominal value of issue.

Sources : Compiled by B. B. King from *Annuaire statistique des possessions françaises, années antérieures à la guerre*, 1944, Min. de la France d'Outre-Mer.

STATISTICAL APPENDIX — TABLE 12

THE FRENCH COLONIAL LOAN OF 1931

(Million francs)

	Original Author- ization	Issued up to 1939	Subsequent Author- ization	Total Author- ization	Total issued or advanced by 1946
A.O.F.	1,690	734	1,430	3,120	2,630
Togo	73	73	—	73	73
Cameroons	57	46	—	57	55
A.E.F.	1,513	1,104	—	1,513	1,513
Madagascar	735	709	100	835	764
Somaliland	44	41	—	44	37
Reunion	63	45	13	136	68
Total	4,175	2,752	1,543	5,778	5,140

Note.—Figures given are amounts realized, not nominal value of issue.

Sources : Compiled by B. B. King from *Annuaire statistique des possessions françaises, années antérieures à la guerre*, 1944, Min. de la France d'Outre-Mer. *Inventaire de la situation financière (1913–1946)*, 1946, Min. des Finances. *The Colonial Problem*, 1937, R.I.I.A.

STATISTICAL APPENDIX — TABLE 13

THE FRENCH COLONIAL LOAN OF 1931 : EXPENDITURE 1931–38 IN MAJOR COLONIES

(Million francs)

	A.O.F.	A.E.F.	Madagascar	Total
Railroads	179	719	272	1,170
Roads and bridges	33	—	57	90
Ports and rivers	171	179	176	526
Irrigation	207	—	—	207
Production	57	51	—	108
Social services	75	65	78	218
Miscellaneous	29	32	108	169
	751	1,046	691	2,488

Note.—(i) Expenses given cover only actual projects ; loan issue expenses, etc. are excluded. The categories are quite possibly not comparable in some instances. (ii) The three colonies tabulated account for some 8o per cent of the expenditure during the period 1931–38 (Indo-China excluded).

Source : Compiled by B. B. King from *Annuaire statistique des possessions françaises, années antérieures à la guerre*, 1944, Min. de la France d'Outre-Mer.

STATISTICAL APPENDIX — TABLE 14

FOREIGN BONDS PUBLICLY-ISSUED IN VARIOUS MARKETS BY DEVELOPING COUNTRIES 1946–64

(Nominal amounts in millions U.S. dollars)

Country	Total	Capital Markets								
		Belgium	Canada	Germany	Luxem-bourg	Nether-lands	Switzer-land	United Kingdom	United States	Various †
		Bonds of, or Guaranteed by, Governments and Political Subdivisions								
Argentina	10·4			3·0			7·4			
1961	10·4			3·0			7·4			
Congo (Belgian)	70·7						55·7		15·0	
1950	14·0						14·0			
1952	13·7						13·7			
1953	14·0						14·0			
1956	14·0						14·0			
1958	15·0								15·0	
Ceylon	14·0							14·0		
1954	14·0							14·0		
Fed. Rhodesia and Nyasaland*	347·0							341·0	6·0	
1947	129·0							129·0		
1948	20·2							20·2		
1950	16·8							16·8		
1951	14·0							14·0		
1952	21·0							21·0		
1953	28·0							28·0		
1954	28·0							28·0		
1955	28·0							28·0		
1958	34·0							28·0	6·0	
1959	28·0							28·0		
Iceland	10·8							10·8		
1949	5·2							5·2		
1962	5·6							5·6		

See footnotes at end of table.

Capital Markets

Bonds of, or Guaranteed by, Governments and Political Subdivisions

Country		Total	Belgium	Canada	Germany	Luxem-bourg	Nether-lands	Switzer-land	United Kingdom	United States	Various †
Ireland	1951	*15·4*	—	—	—	—	—	—	*15·4*	—	—
	1951	15·4	—	—	—	—	—	—	15·4	—	—
Israel	1951	*665·6*	—	*29·0*	—	—	—	—	—	*636·6*	—
	1951	50·0	—	—	—	—	—	—	—	50·0	—
	1952	41·0	—	—	—	—	—	—	—	41·0	—
	1953	41·0	—	4·0	—	—	—	—	—	37·0	—
	1954	38·0	—	3·0	—	—	—	—	—	35·0	—
	1955	38·0	—	3·0	—	—	—	—	—	35·0	—
	1956	48·0	—	4·0	—	—	—	—	—	44·0	—
	1957	46·0	—	4·0	—	—	—	—	—	42·0	—
	1958	41·0	—	4·0	—	—	—	—	—	37·0	—
	1959	45·0	—	3·0	—	—	—	—	—	42·0	—
	1960	46·0	—	4·0	—	—	—	—	—	42·0	—
	1961	58·2	—	—	—	—	—	—	—	58·2	—
	1962	46·4	—	—	—	—	—	—	—	46·4	—
	1963	34·0	—	—	—	—	—	—	—	34·0	—
	1964	93·0	—	—	—	—	—	—	—	93·0	—
Jamaica	1959	*25·7*	—	—	—	—	—	—	*13·2*	*12·5*	—
	1963	12·5	—	—	—	—	—	—	—	12·5	—
	1963	4·2	—	—	—	—	—	—	4·2	—	—
	1964	9·0	—	—	—	—	—	—	9·0	—	—
Malaya	1963	*14·0*	—	—	—	—	—	—	*14·0*	—	—
	1963	14·0	—	—	—	—	—	—	14·0	—	—
Mexico	1963	*100·0*	—	—	—	—	—	—	—	*100·0*	—
	1963	40·0	—	—	—	—	—	—	—	40·0	—
	1964	60·0	—	—	—	—	—	—	—	60·0	—
Panama	1958	*16·8*	—	—	—	—	—	—	—	*16·8*	—
	1958	16·8	—	—	—	—	—	—	—	16·8	—

See footnotes at end of table.

STATISTICAL APPENDIX — TABLE 14 (cont.)

Country	Total	Belgium	Canada	Germany	Luxembourg	Netherlands	Switzerland	United Kingdom	United States	Various †
				Capital Markets						
			Bonds of, or Guaranteed by, Governments and Political Subdivisions							
Portugal	20·0	—	—	—	—	—	—	—	—	20·0
1964	20·0	—	—	—	—	—	—	—	—	20·0
South Africa	194·2	—	—	—	—	13·2	39·3	76·7	65·0	—
1949	28·0	—	—	—	—	—	—	28·0	—	—
1950	16·8	—	—	—	—	—	—	16·8	—	—
1952	16·5	—	—	—	—	—	13·7	2·8	—	—
1953	8·4	—	—	—	—	—	—	8·4	—	—
1954	16·2	—	—	—	—	—	14·0	2·2	—	—
1955	38·2	—	—	—	—	13·2	—	—	25·0	—
1958	44·5	—	—	—	—	—	—	4·5	40·0	—
1959	25·6	—	—	—	—	—	11·6	14·0	—	—
Total issues	1,504·6	—	29·0	3·0	—	13·2	102·4	485·1	851·9	20·0
1947	129·0	—	—	—	—	—	—	129·0	—	—
1948	20·2	—	—	—	—	—	—	20·2	—	—
1949	33·2	—	—	—	—	—	—	33·2	—	—
1950	47·6	—	—	—	—	—	14·0	33·6	—	—
1951	79·4	—	—	—	—	—	—	29·4	50·0	—
1952	92·2	—	—	—	—	—	27·4	23·8	41·0	—
1953	91·4	—	4·0	—	—	—	14·0	36·4	37·0	—
1954	96·2	—	3·0	—	—	—	14·0	44·2	35·0	—
1955	104·2	—	3·0	—	—	13·2	14·0	28·0	60·0	—
1956	62·0	—	4·0	—	—	—	14·0	—	44·0	—
1957	46·0	—	4·0	—	—	—	—	—	42·0	—
1958	151·3	—	4·0	—	—	—	—	32·5	114·8	—
1959	111·1	—	3·0	—	—	—	11·6	42·0	54·5	—
1960	46·0	—	4·0	—	—	—	—	—	42·0	—
1961	68·6	—	—	3·0	—	—	7·4	—	58·2	—
1962	52·0	—	—	—	—	—	—	5·6	46·4	—
1963	92·2	—	—	—	—	—	—	18·2	74·0	—
1964	182·0	—	—	—	—	—	—	9·0	153·0	20·0

114

See footnotes at end of table.

Capital Markets

Country	Total	Belgium	Canada	Germany	Luxembourg	Netherlands	Switzerland	United Kingdom	United States	Various †
						Bonds of Private Companies				
Fed. Rhodesia and Nyasaland										
1955	7·1	0·1	—	—	—	7·0	—	—	—	—
1958	7·0	—	—	—	—	7·0	—	—	—	—
Ireland										
1950	0·8	—	—	—	—	—	—	0·8	—	—
Israel										
1950	10·1	—	—	—	—	—	—	—	5·1	5·0
1957	2·5	—	—	—	—	—	—	—	2·5	—
1958	0·6	—	—	—	—	—	—	—	0·6	—
1961	2·0	—	—	—	—	—	—	—	2·0	—
1964	5·0	—	—	—	—	—	—	—	—	5·0
Mexico										
1964	8·0	—	—	—	—	—	—	—	8·0	—
Peru										
1952	3·5	—	—	—	—	—	3·5	—	—	—
1953	0·5	—	—	—	—	—	0·5	—	—	—
1954	1·3	—	—	—	—	—	1·3	—	—	—
1955	1·7	—	—	—	—	—	1·7	—	—	—
Portugal										
1961	10·0	2·0	—	0·3	1·2	0·5	1·0	—	—	5·0
1962	5·0	2·0	—	0·3	1·2	0·5	1·0	—	—	—
Spain										
1962	9·2	—	—	—	—	—	9·2	—	—	—
1963	4·6	—	—	—	—	—	4·6	—	—	—
1964	4·6	—	—	—	—	—	4·6	—	—	—
South Africa										
1950	68·8	—	—	11·9	—	—	42·9	14·0	—	—
1952	17·2	—	—	—	—	—	11·6	5·6	—	—
1954	5·7	—	—	—	—	—	5·7	—	—	—
1955	5·8	—	—	—	—	—	5·8	—	—	—
1956	8·2	—	—	—	—	—	8·2	—	—	—

See footnotes at end of table.

115

STATISTICAL APPENDIX — TABLE 14 (cont.)

| | | Capital Markets | | | | | | | | |
Country	Total	Belgium	Canada	Germany	Luxem-bourg	Nether-lands	Switzer-land	United Kingdom	United States	Various †
				Bonds of Private Companies						
South Africa (cont.)										
1957	8·4	—	—	—	—	—	—	8·4	—	—
1958	11·9	—	—	11·9	—	—	—	—	—	—
1962	11·6	—	—	—	—	—	11·6	—	—	—
Total Issues	117·5	2·1	—	12·2	1·2	7·5	56·6	14·8	13·1	10·1
1947	—	—	—	—	—	—	—	—	—	—
1948	—	—	—	—	—	—	—	—	—	—
1949	—	—	—	—	—	—	—	—	—	—
1950	18·0	—	—	—	—	—	11·6	6·4	—	—
1951	—	—	—	—	—	—	—	—	—	—
1952	6·2	—	—	—	—	—	6·2	—	—	—
1953	1·3	—	—	—	—	—	1·3	—	—	—
1954	5·8	—	—	—	—	—	5·8	—	—	—
1955	16·9	—	—	—	—	7·0	9·9	—	—	—
1956	—	—	—	—	—	—	—	—	—	—
1957	10·9	—	—	—	—	—	—	8·4	2·5	—
1958	12·6	0·1	—	11·9	—	—	—	—	0·6	—
1959	—	—	—	—	—	—	—	—	—	—
1960	—	—	—	—	—	—	—	—	—	—
1961	7·0	2·0	—	0·3	1·2	0·5	1·0	—	2·0	—
1962	16·6	—	—	—	—	—	11·6	—	—	5·0
1963	4·6	—	—	—	—	—	4·6	—	—	—
1964	17·6	—	—	—	—	—	4·6	—	8·0	5·0

See footnotes at end of table.

116

Year	Total	Belgium	Canada	Germany	Luxembourg	Netherlands	Switzerland	United Kingdom	United States	Various †
	Total Issues of Bonds Guaranteed by Governments or Political Subdivisions and Bonds Issued by Private Companies									
	1,622·1	2·1	29·0	15·2	1·2	20·7	159·0	499·9	865·0	30·0
1947	129·0							129·0		
1948	20·2							20·2		
1949	33·2							33·2		
1950	65·6						25·6	40·0		
1951	79·4							29·4	50·0	
1952	98·4						33·6	23·8	41·0	
1953	92·7		4·0				15·3	36·4	37·0	
1954	102·0		3·0				19·8	44·2	35·0	
1955	121·1		3·0			20·2	9·9	28·0	60·0	
1956	62·0		4·0				14·0		44·0	
1957	56·9		4·0					8·4	44·5	
1958	163·9	0·1	4·0	11·9				32·5	115·4	
1959	111·1		3·0				11·6	42·0	54·5	
1960	46·0		4·0						42·0	
1961	75·6	2·0		3·3			8·4		60·2	
1962	68·6				1·2	0·5	11·6	5·6	46·4	5·0
1963	96·8						4·6	18·2	74·0	
1964	199·6						4·6	9·0	161·0	25·0

Note.—Where country names have changed, the issues are shown under the name of the country at the time of issue (except in the case of Southern Rhodesia which is shown under the Federation).

* Bonds issued from 1947 to 1953 were issued by Southern Rhodesia, subsequent issues by the Federation.

† Amounts shown in this column are those bonds which are issued simultaneously in more than one market. The breakdown of amounts issued in specific markets is not available.

Source : Statistics Division IBRD-Economics Department July 19, 1965.

STATISTICAL APPENDIX — TABLE 15

DISTRIBUTION OF FLOW OF FINANCIAL RESOURCES FROM FRANCE
(DISBURSEMENTS EST.) TO AFRICAN MALAGASY STATES

(Millions of U.S. dollars)

Bilateral Official Assistance	1962	1963
A. Grants		
1. Capital expenditure	63·7	63·3
2. Technical assistance	132·2	136·4
3. Other	67·9	65·5
Total A	263·8	265·2
B. Loans (net)	22·1	28·4
Total bilateral official assistance	285·9	293·6
Private direct investment and other long-term capital	71·7	51·6

Source: *OECD, The Flow of Financial Resources to Less-Developed Countries, 1956–1963*, Paris, 1964, pp. 75, 76.

STATISTICAL APPENDIX — TABLE 16

GROSS FIXED CAPITAL FORMATION IN FRENCH-SPEAKING AFRICA
FINANCED BY LOCAL PUBLIC FUNDS AND BY FRANCE 1946–1960
(Millions of U.S. dollars)

Country	Local Funds	France	Total
I. Former A.O.F. States			
Senegal	209	276	485
Mali	76	156	232
Mauritania	21	38	59
Ivory Coast	179	197	376
Upper Volta	46	63	109
Guinea	70	130	200
Dahomey	46	69	115
Niger	46	40	87
Not classified by country	69	171	240
Total Former A.O.F. States	762	1,139	1,901
II. Togo	19	45	64
III. Former A.E.F. States			
Congo	37	110	146
Gabon	19	159	178
Chad	33	83	116
Central African Republic	25	59	84
Not classified by country	17	74	91
Total Former A.E.F. States	130	485	615
IV. Cameroun	106	355	461
V. Madagascar	216	312	528
Not classified, Africa and Madagascar	—	281	281
Grand total	1,233	2,616	3,850

Source : Calculated from tables in Institut d'Étude du Développement Économique et Social, Université de Paris, *Les Investissements publics d'origine locale et d'origine extérieure dans les pays francophones d'Afrique Tropicale, 1946–1960*, vol. ii, *Tableaux statistiques*, Paris, 1964.

Capital Movements and Economic Development

BRITISH FINANCIAL AID TO AFRICA, SOUTH OF THE SAHARA. PUBLIC
BILATERAL DISBURSEMENTS (GROSS) BY COUNTRY : FINANCIAL YEARS
(Thousands of £ sterling)

	1963/64			1964/65		
	Grants	Loans	Total	Grants	Loans	Total
Basutoland	1,788	40	1,828	2,098	—	2,098
Bechuanaland	2,055	—	2,055	2,765	410	3,175
Cameroons	—	—	—	24	—	24
Congo (Léopoldville)	—	—	—	538	—	538
East Africa (Common Services)	89	1,524	1,613	260	2,831	3,091
Federation of Rhodesia and Nyasaland*	—	2,163	2,163	960	—	960
Gambia	1,217	33	1,250	874	65	939
Ghana	6	737	743	—	1,855	1,855
Kenya	4,171	7,147	11,318	4,554	10,239	14,793
Malawi	5,241	2,966	8,207	7,448	1,485	8,933
Mauritania	21	—	21	4	—	4
Mauritius	524	954	1,478	480	143	623
Niger	9	—	9	—	—	—
Nigeria	161	1,084	1,245	125	4,290	4,415
Rhodesia	1	3,855	3,856	2,250	—	2,250
Seychelles	222	—	222	291	—	291
Sierra Leone	500	2,060	2,560	—	830	830
Somalia	15	—	15	—	—	—
St. Helena and Tristan da Cunha	172	—	172	238	2	240
Sudan	—	285	285	—	1,315	1,315
Swaziland	1,122	331	1,453	2,409	1,851	4,260
Tanzania	1,547	3,396	4,943	1,350	3,058	4,408
Uganda	1,200	2,458	3,658	262	1,947	2,209
Zambia	112	2,952	3,064	3,682	800	4,482
Unallocated †	—	—	—	49	—	49
Grand total	20,173	31,985	52,158	30,661	31,121	61,782

* Contributions to individual members of the former Federation of Rhodesia and Nyasaland are not identifiable.
† Includes grants to Basutoland, Bechuanaland and Swaziland which cannot be identified by individual recipient.

Source : Overseas Development : the work of the New Ministry ; Ministry of Overseas Development ; Cmnd. 2736 of August 1965.

U.S. OFFICIAL ECONOMIC ASSISTANCE TO LESS DEVELOPED COUNTRIES IN AFRICA SOUTH OF THE SAHARA

(Millions of U.S. dollars)

	Total Fiscal Years 1946/60					
	Net Obligations Grants		Loan Authorizations			Disbursements under For. Ass. Programme
Countries	PL 480	Other	PL 480	Other	Total	
Burundi	—	—	—	—	—	—
Cameroon	0·1	—	—	—	0·1	—
Cen. African Rep.	—	—	—	—	—	—
Chad	—	—	—	—	—	—
Congo (Brazz.)	—	—	—	—	—	—
Congo (Léop.)	—	—	—	—	—	*
Dahomey	0·1	—	—	—	0·1	—
Ethiopia	5·8	38·6	—	13·0	57·4	29·3
Gabon	—	—	—	—	—	—
Gambia	—	—	—	—	—	—
Ghana	1·3	2·7	—	—	4·0	2·0
Guinea	1·7	2·1	—	—	3·8	—
Ivory Coast	—	—	—	—	—	—
Kenya	0·5	4·6	—	—	5·1	4·1
Liberia	0·6	20·7	—	43·8	65·1	14·7
Malagasy Rep.	—	—	—	—	—	—
Malawi	—	—	—	—	—	—
Mali	—	—	—	—	—	—
Mauritania	0·1	—	—	1·4	1·5	1·4
Niger	—	—	—	—	—	—
Nigeria	0·2	5·0	—	1·0	6·2	2·0
Rhodesia and Nyasaland	*	0·2	—	32·4	32·6	10·0
Rwanda	—	—	—	—	—	—
Senegal	—	—	—	—	—	—
Sierra Leone	0·2	0·3	—	—	0·5	—
Somali Rep.	0·3	6·8	—	2·0	9·1	4·4
Sudan	*	34·1	—	10·0	44·1	20·2
Tanzania	0·1	0·1	—	—	0·2	—
Togo	0·5	—	—	—	0·5	—
Uganda	0·2	0·8	—	—	1·0	0·3
Upper Volta	—	—	—	—	—	—
Zambia	—	—	—	—	—	—
Africa Regl.	0·5	7·3	—	23·2	31·0	7·0
Grand total	12·2	123·3	—	126·8	262·3	95·4

See Sources at end of table.

	Fiscal Year 1960/61					
	Net Obligations Grants		Loan Authorizations			Disbursements under For. Ass. Programme
Countries	PL 480	Other	PL 480	Other	Total	
Burundi	—	—	—	—	—	—
Cameroon	0·1	2·0	—	—	2·1	*
Cen. African Rep.	—	*	—	—	*	—
Chad	*	0·1	—	—	0·1	—
Congo (Brazz.)	—	0·1	—	—	0·1	—
Congo (Léop.)	—	—	8·2	67·3	75·5	45·5
Dahomey	1·0	2·0	—	—	3·0	1·0
Ethiopia	3·0	9·3	—	29·1	41·4	9·0
Gabon	—	0·1	—	—	0·1	—
Gambia	—	—	—	—	—	—
Ghana	1·0	1·4	—	20·0	22·4	1·0
Guinea	—	0·2	—	—	0·2	1·4
Ivory Coast	—	2·1	—	—	2·1	1·1
Kenya	1·5	0·3	—	—	1·8	0·4
Liberia	0·4	6·2	—	40·8	47·4	3·5
Malagasy Rep.	—	0·5	—	—	0·5	*
Malawi	—	—	—	—	—	—
Mali	—	2·5	—	—	2·5	0·2
Mauritania	0·1	—	—	—	0·1	—
Niger	*	2·0	—	—	2·0	1·0
Nigeria	0·1	10·0	—	4·3	14·4	5·6
Rhodesia and Nyasaland	—	0·6	—	—	0·6	0·4
Rwanda	—	—	—	—	—	—
Senegal	—	3·6	—	—	3·6	—
Sierra Leone	0·1	0·5	—	—	0·6	0·2
Somali Rep.	*	4·1	—	—	4·1	4·1
Sudan	—	7·0	—	—	7·0	14·6
Tanzania	1·7	0·6	—	1·9	4·2	0·4
Togo	0·3	1·1	—	—	1·4	0·3
Uganda	0·1	*	—	—	0·1	0·2
Upper Volta	*	2·0	—	—	2·0	1·1
Zambia	—	—	—	—	—	—
Africa Regl.	0·3	3·7	—	− 10·7	− 6·7	1·4
Grand total	9·7	62·0	8·2	152·7	232·6	92·4

See Sources at end of table.

STATISTICAL APPENDIX — TABLE 18 (*cont.*)

Countries	Fiscal Year 1961/62					
	Net Obligations Grants		Loan Authorizations			Disbursements under For. Ass. Programme
	PL 480	Other	PL 480	Other	Total	
Burundi	3·5	—	—	—	3·5	—
Cameroon	0·1	3·7	9·2	—	13·0	0·6
Cen. African Rep.	—	0·2	—	—	0·2	*
Chad	*	0·3	—	—	0·3	*
Congo (Brazz.)	—	1·2	—	—	1·2	0·1
Congo (Léop.)	16·5	67·0	—	—	83·5	74·7
Dahomey	1·6	0·7	—	—	2·3	0·4
Ethiopia	2·0	6·8	—	—	8·8	17·6
Gabon	—	0·4	—	—	0·4	0·1
Gambia	—	—	—	—	—	—
Ghana	0·7	2·4	—	127·0	130·1	1·0
Guinea	4·3	6·1	—	—	10·4	0·4
Ivory Coast	—	2·5	—	—	2·5	0·7
Kenya	6·7	3·2	—	—	9·9	1·4
Liberia	0·1	11·1	2·9	—	14·1	5·4
Malagasy Rep.	*	0·6	—	—	0·6	0·2
Malawi	—	—	—	—	—	—
Mali	—	2·5	—	—	2·5	2·3
Mauritania	0·1	—	—	—	0·1	*
Niger	*	1·2	—	—	1·2	0·6
Nigeria	0·2	22·8	—	2·0	25·0	6·4
Rhodesia and Nyasaland	—	2·8	—	—	2·8	0·4
Rwanda	—	0·8	—	—	0·8	—
Senegal	0·4	3·0	—	—	3·4	3·6
Sierra Leone	0·2	2·3	—	—	2·5	0·2
Somali Rep.	2·9	11·9	—	—	14·8	3·3
Sudan	1·2	7·8	2·3	2·0	13·3	11·0
Tanzania	9·3	2·8	—	*	12·1	0·7
Togo	2·5	1·3	—	—	3·8	0·5
Uganda	0·6	3·6	—	—	4·2	0·2
Upper Volta	0·1	0·9	—	—	1·0	0·9
Zambia	—	—	—	—	—	—
Africa Regl.	0·2	8·2	—	—	8·4	2·4
Grand total	53·2	178·1	14·4	131·0	376·7	135·1

See Sources at end of table.

STATISTICAL APPENDIX — TABLE 18 (*cont.*)

Countries	Net Obligations Grants		Loan Authorizations			Disbursements under For. Ass. Programme
	PL 480	Other	PL 480	Other	Total	
Burundi	1·5	—	—	—	1·5	*
Cameroon	*	1·4	—	—	1·4	1·8
Cen. African Rep.	*	0·7	—	—	0·7	0·1
Chad	0·1	1·0	—	—	1·1	*
Congo (Brazz.)	—	0·4	0·2	—	0·6	0·8
Congo (Léop.)	37·2	37·8	—	—	75·0	22·5
Dahomey	0·3	0·7	—	—	1·0	0·2
Ethiopia	0·9	7·9	2·1	3·8	14·8	18·5
Gabon	—	1·1	—	—	1·1	0·2
Gambia	—	—	—	—	—	—
Ghana	0·6	2·3	—	—	2·9	3·5
Guinea	—	9·4	3·6	3·1	16·1	3·5
Ivory Coast	—	0·9	—	6·3	7·2	0·6
Kenya	0·8	2·6	—	2·2	5·6	1·7
Liberia	0·2	9·4	2·8	32·9	45·3	6·8
Malagasy Rep.	0·5	0·4	—	—	0·9	0·8
Malawi	—	—	—	—	—	—
Mali	—	1·7	—	2·1	3·8	1·0
Mauritania	0·1	0·1	—	—	0·2	*
Niger	—	0·7	—	0·5	1·2	0·6
Nigeria	0·3	17·2	—	12·0	29·4	9·3
Rhodesia and Nyasaland	*	2·1	—	—	2·1	0·7
Rwanda	*	—	—	—	*	—
Senegal	0·6	0·8	—	0·3	1·7	2·0
Sierra Leone	0·5	3·4	—	—	3·9	0·8
Somali Rep.	1·1	3·6	—	3·6	8·3	6·7
Sudan	1·5	1·6	3·0	3·8	9·9	5·7
Tanzania	3·1	2·1	—	6·9	12·1	1·9
Togo	0·2	0·8	—	—	1·0	0·6
Uganda	0·1	2·5	—	4·4	7·0	2·9
Upper Volta	0·5	0·4	—	—	0·9	0·7
Zambia	—	—	—	—	—	—
Africa Regl.	0·3	9·1	—	—	9·4	4·3
Grand total	50·4	122·1	11·7	81·9	265·1	98·2

Fiscal Years 1962/63

See Sources at end of table.

STATISTICAL APPENDIX — TABLE 18 (*cont.*)

	Fiscal Years 1963/64					
	Net Obligations Grants		Loan Authoriza-tions			Disburse-ments under For. Ass. Programme
Countries	PL 480	Other	PL 480	Other	Total	
Burundi	0·5	0·5	—	—	1·0	0·1
Cameroon	*	2·3	—	—	2·3	2·5
Cen. African Rep.	*	1·1	—	—	1·1	0·4
Chad	*	0·6	—	—	0·6	0·6
Congo (Brazz.)	—	0·2	—	2·7	2·9	0·3
Congo (Léop.)	21·8	19·8	—	—	41·6	15·6
Dahomey	0·7	0·5	—	—	1·2	1·0
Ethiopia	0·6	7·2	—	0·7	8·5	8·1
Gabon	—	1·7	—	—	1·7	0·6
Gambia	—	—	—	—	—	—
Ghana	2·2	1·3	—	—	3·5	5·2
Guinea	—	10·0	9·3	-2·4	16·9	9·5
Ivory Coast	0·1	2·0	2·5	5·0	9·6	1·0
Kenya	0·4	3·3	—	—	3·7	1·9
Liberia	0·4	7·0	2·9	7·4	17·7	8·8
Malagasy Rep.	0·6	0·7	—	—	1·3	0·7
Malawi	—	—	—	—	—	—
Mali	—	1·8	—	1·1	2·9	1·7
Mauritania	0·7	0·2	—	—	0·9	*
Niger	0·2	0·6	—	1·8	2·6	0·8
Nigeria	0·6	18·4	—	31·4	50·4	14·1
Rhodesia and Nyasaland	—	2·9	—	—	2·9	1·4
Rwanda	—	0·5	—	—	0·5	—
Senegal	1·0	1·4	2·6	1·3	6·3	0·8
Sierra Leone	1·0	2·6	—	10·2	13·0	1·3
Somali Rep.	—	3·4	—	—	3·4	3·8
Sudan	1·7	1·9	3·3	*	6·9	4·0
Tanzania	1·7	3·6	—	3·9	9·2	1·6
Togo	0·7	1·2	—	—	1·9	1·1
Uganda	0·2	2·1	—	0·4	2·7	1·8
Upper Volta	0·5	0·3	—	—	0·8	1·1
Zambia	—	—	—	—	—	—
Africa Regl.	0·4	11·5	—	1·5	13·4	6·2
Grand total	36·0	110·6	20·6	65·0	232·2	96·0

See Sources at end of table.

STATISTICAL APPENDIX — TABLE 18 (*cont.*)

	Fiscal Year 1964/65 (Preliminary)				
	Net Obligations Grants		Loan Authorizations		
Countries	PL 480	Other	PL 480	Other	Total
Burundi	1·0	0·1	—	—	1·1
Cameroon	*	2·3	—	3·2	5·5
Cen. African Rep.	*	0·7	—	—	0·7
Chad	1·1	1·0	—	—	2·1
Congo (Brazz.)	0·2	0·1	—	− 2·7	− 2·4
Congo (Léop.)	5·2	0·9	4·4	15·0	25·5
Dahomey	0·3	0·6	0·2	—	1·1
Ethiopia	0·5	8·0	—	10·3	18·8
Gabon	—	1·1	—	—	1·1
Gambia	—	0·1	—	—	0·1
Ghana	0·9	1·4	—	—	2·3
Guinea	0·3	8·8	7·9	4·8	21·7
Ivory Coast	—	0·3	4·0	—	4·3
Kenya	0·9	3·9	3·8	0·6	9·2
Liberia	0·3	8·6	—	32·4	41·3
Malagasy Rep.	1·5	1·1	—	2·7	5·3
Malawi	0·1	3·1	—	—	3·2
Mali	0·9	0·9	*	*	1·8
Mauritania	*	*	—	—	*
Niger	—	1·4	—	—	1·4
Nigeria	1·4	18·1	—	13·8	33·3
Rhodesia and Nyasaland	—	*	—	—	*
Rwanda	0·1	0·1	—	—	0·2
Senegal	0·9	0·6	—	—	1·5
Sierra Leone	1·1	2·7	1·8	—	5·6
Somali Rep.	3·0	4·2	—	0·6	7·8
Sudan	1·4	2·9	3·3	—	7·6
Tanzania	2·6	4·1	—	0·2	6·9
Togo	0·4	1·0	—	—	1·4
Uganda	0·4	2·1	—	—	2·5
Upper Volta	0·5	0·5	—	—	1·0
Zambia	0·1	0·9	—	—	1·0
Africa Regl.	0·8	11·7	—	—	12·5
Grand total	25·9	93·3	25·4	80·9	225·4

See Sources at end of table.

Sources: Figures in the first five columns for each time period on net obligations in respect of PL 480 and other grants and data for loan authorizations under PL 480 and 'other' are from the Special Report prepared by the U.S. Agency for International Development for the House Foreign Affairs Committee of the U.S. Congress entitled 'U.S. Overseas Loans and Grants and Assistance from International Organizations; Obligations and Loan Authorizations, July 1, 1945–June 30, 1964'.

Figures for Fiscal 1964/65 are from a preliminary tabular report prepared by the Statistics and Reports Division of the Agency for International Development entitled 'Trend of U.S. Overseas Economic Loans and Grants, by Region — Net Obligations and Loan Authorizations, FY 1946–1965'.

The above data for net obligations in respect of grants and loan authorizations relate only to U.S. bilateral assistance under Foreign Assistance Programmes administered by the Agency for International Development plus assistance under the Food for Peace and the Peace Corps programmes besides Export-Import Bank loans.

Authorizations data for Export-Import Bank loans, according to the source publication cited above, are for loans of five years or more maturity including loans by private financial institutions if guaranteed by the Export-Import Bank.

A minus figure under 'net obligations' indicates deobligations or deobligations exceeding new obligations; a minus figure under authorizations indicates cancellations or cancellations exceeding new authorizations.

An asterisk mark is for amounts of less than $50,000.

Disbursements data are from a report published by the U.S. Agency for International Development entitled 'U.S. Economic Assistance Programs administered by the A.I.D. and predecessor agencies, June 30, 1964'. Data for Fiscal 1964/65 are not yet available. Disbursements data given in this source, it must be noted, relate *only to programmes administered by the Agency for International Development* under the U.S. Foreign Economic Assistance Acts.

STATISTICAL APPENDIX — TABLE 19

WORLD BANK GROUP OPERATIONS IN AFRICA THROUGH
31 OCTOBER 1965

(Millions of dollars)

	No. Bank Loans	Bank Loans Net Amounts*	No. IDA Credits	Amount IDA Credits*
Bechuanaland	—	—	1	3·6
Burundi	1	4·8	—	—
Congo, Democratic Republic of the	5	91·6	—	—
Ethiopia	7	51·9	1	13·5
Gabon	2	47·0	—	—
Ghana	1	47·0	—	—
Ivory Coast^a	1	7·1	—	—
Kenya^b	3	52·0	3	10·3
Liberia	2	4·3	—	—
Mali^a	—	—	—	—
Mauritania	1	66·0	1	6·7
Mauritius	1	7·0	—	—
Niger	—	—	1	1·5
Nigeria	6	185·5	2	35·5
Rhodesia^c	3	87·0	—	—
Senegal^a	—	—	—	—
Sierra Leone	1	3·8	—	—
Somalia	—	—	1	6·2
South Africa	10	221·8	—	—
Sudan	3	74·0	1	13·0
Swaziland	1	4·2	1	2·8
Tanzania^b	1	24·0	2	18·6
Uganda^b	1	8·4	—	—
Upper Volta^a	—	—	—	—
Zambia	3	67·4	—	—
Total	53	1,054·8	14	111·7

* Net of cancellations, refundings and termination.

Loans shared with other countries marked ^a.
„   „   „   ^b.
„   „   „   ^c.

COMMENTS ON DR. KAMARCK'S PAPER

BY

HENRY C. WALLICH
Yale University

IT is probably no accident that the paper by Andrew Kamarck on 'The Financial Experience of Lenders and Investors', as well as those by Brinley Thomas and Matthew Simon dealing with the historical record of capital exports generally, have chosen the same selective approach. Thomas and Simon have limited their field to the history of British capital exports before World War I. Kamarck has focused his analysis upon Africa. The fact is that a comprehensive approach, covering all important countries in modern times, would require an enormous mass of factual material and might nevertheless, or perhaps precisely because of this wealth of data, not be analytically interesting within the confines of a paper suitable for this conference. The experience of investors in African countries is varied enough — portfolio investment, direct investment, foreign aid — to illustrate much of the experience that foreign investors have been heirs to. In these comments I shall raise a few points related to foreign investor experience generally, as well as to Mr. Kamarck's African subject.

MEASURING THE RATE OF RETURN

Even when the data are good, as in the case of the pre-1914 British material, the rate of return to the investor is rarely measured by the bond coupon. That the issue price must be taken into account is of course a truism. But in the nineteenth century, new issue discounts were not of the order of a few percentage points, as they are today. Discounts of 20, 30, 40 per cent were not unusual. In addition to the substantially higher yields resulting, such discounts may have been speculatively profitable for the underwriters and other insiders. To mention just one example, the great fortune of the Rothschilds certainly was not built by underwriting bonds with a 2 or 3 per cent spread.

Defaults have affected returns in various ways. There have been total losses, such as some United States local securities of the nineteenth and twentieth century, and the Russian and Eastern European bonds of more recent vintage. Usually defaults have ended with a more or less severe reorganization. For some low-income countries, such as the Dominican Republic, the history of successive defaults has been that an originally small debt was built up to a multiple through capitalization of unpaid interest. Some fortunate or skilful investors thus had large capital gains, though relatively little interest, while the borrower received very little cash from a sizeable indebtedness.

Inflation and devaluation of the creditor currency has been a source of loss to investors, just as inflation and devaluation in debtor countries has sometimes been a cause of default. Securities are typically denominated in the currency of the creditor country. Where, as in France, inflation was substantial, debtors have been virtually relieved of their obligations, for gold clauses in bond indentures have rarely stood up. The reduction in dollar debts that the continental countries experienced as a result of the 1933 devaluation of the dollar was a factor, albeit of dubious rationality, that contributed to their decision to delay devaluation.

For individual investors, the yield from a bond investment may differ substantially, of course, from the general experience of holders. Investors who sold Latin American or German dollar bonds during the 1930's lost much more than if they had held, with the buyers often making large profits.

INCENTIVES TO LENDING

It is not to be supposed that the return from investment has been the sole or even the principal motivating force. Other and more immediate although less visible incentives have played an important role. One such incentive has been the profit to be made by underwriting securities. While today the underwriting spreads on bonds may be of the order of a very few percent or percentage points, during the nineteenth century underwriting spreads often were substantially larger, as pointed out before. Bonds issued at 80, 70, 60, and even less, allowed very large earnings to the underwriter and made it worth his while to put forth great efforts to find buyers. These buyers, in turn, may have been attracted more by a quick speculative gain than by the yield to maturity. For bonds of well-established borrowers, of course, such incentives were not required.

Another incentive to the sale of bonds has been the profit to be made from the construction and sales being financed. Construction companies benefited enormously from the building of railways all over the world. Land speculators gained from the land grants often made to new railroads. In such cases, it was not the demand for securities that brought forth the supply, nor perhaps even the needs for the particular investment that was being financed. It was the collateral profits to be made that motivated the ingenuity of bankers in finding buyers for their securities.

At the national level, foreign investment produced benefits that usually were not relevant to entrepreneurial calculations. The creation of new sources of raw materials, the establishment of markets for exports, the promotion of political support, the creation of financial reserves that proved useful in wartime — all these were externalities to the issuance of securities.

EXPERIENCE OF BOND HOLDERS

All holders of foreign bonds have suffered from inflation in the same measure as holders of domestic obligations. Where in lending countries that suffered extreme inflation of their currency, such as France, the effect, as pointed out, was virtually to wipe out the bond holder.

Very sizeable losses were suffered by bond holders in connection with loans of a political character. Again, the French experience with loans to Russia before World War I and to Eastern Europe before World War II serves as an example. The assets of German foreign creditors were completely wiped out, partly by political changes, partly by the action of the Allied nations after World War I and World War II. On the other hand, the defaults experienced by American and British bond holders on their loans to Latin America and other developing countries were usually remedied at least in part.

It is interesting to speculate what part of these losses may have been covered by the risk premium usually included in foreign bonds. These risk premia frequently were high. With rates on domestic government securities at 3 or 4 per cent, foreign bonds often yielded 6 per cent or better. Losses could be limited by suitable portfolio diversification. Perhaps the relevant question to ask is not how well foreign bond holders fared in an absolute sense, but how they fared relative to holders of similar domestic securities. In view of the revival of the international bond market, better information on past performance might not be without interest.

PORTFOLIO INVESTMENT IN EQUITIES

Here the record has been for the most part good, sometimes spectacularly so. The bulk of international equity investment has been in industrial countries, the developing countries offering relatively few opportunities of this kind. Thus, losses on railroads and utility shares in Latin America and elsewhere must have been far overcompensated by profits particularly of European investors in American and Canadian stocks. Even here, however, diversification or else fortunate selection were essential to success. American railroad stocks have done little for their European holders in the last thirty-odd years.

During the 1950's and early 1960's, and until the imposition of the Interest Equalization Tax, American investors began to take an interest in European securities. Those who acted early so far can probably regard their investments as successful.

INTERNATIONALIZATION OF PORTFOLIO INVESTMENT IN EQUITIES

I would like to suggest that to purchase equities in foreign countries is an action likely to benefit the investor by risk reduction, even if it does not increase his yield. For that reason, one may expect it to grow provided currencies remain convertible. Risk is reduced, other things equal, because the investor already has substantial risk exposure in his home country where he has his job, his home, and undoubtedly good part of his assets. It makes sense for him not further to concentrate his risks by putting his remaining eggs into the same basket. This means that countries preventing the outflow of equity funds are interfering with the process of optimization on the part of the investor. There is no good economic reason why investors of country A should be compelled to invest in country A, any more than there is reason why investors living in Connecticut should invest in Connecticut securities. An essential condition for this happy state of affairs to come about is, of course, that country B and all others permit their citizens to invest in country A, much as the citizens of the remaining States of the Union are free to invest in Connecticut.

DIRECT INVESTMENT

Here we come to deal with what today is the great bulk of international equity investment. Mr. Kamarck's African examples are in part at least less than fully representative because some of the chartered companies emanating from the United Kingdom have been quite successful, the East India Company being a prime example. Today direct foreign investment occurs principally in the industrial countries, where inevitably it is market-oriented. This type of investment has proved profitable for many reasons. Very often, the investing company has created a market for its products by earlier exports. In any event, the company probably has engaged in similar activities elsewhere and knows how to proceed. If the company is large, its name is automatically well known. American companies have the advantage of substantial financial resources, although these have sometimes been overrated.

At the same time as these large international investors have acquired a highly successful foreign investment experience, they have been running into new difficulties. Local hostility has been growing, particularly in industrial countries. Friction has developed with local stockholders, who usually want quick dividends, whereas the parent company does not seek dividends. This has frustrated efforts to secure local participation which for protective reasons would otherwise be desirable.

Direct foreign investment in developing countries has been predominantly resource-oriented, although more recently capital has also moved into manufacturing, principally for import substitution. Results of investment in primary production usually have been profitable, except where the search for mineral resources has brought no results. In a few cases, foreign corporations have suffered expropriation. It is doubtful if these have greatly affected the overall results of their investments. Nevertheless, they have had the undesirable consequence of compelling companies to seek higher profits in other countries in order to maintain their average return. In this way, Venezuela has paid for the oil companies' confiscations suffered in Mexico, for instance. In contrast to trends in industrial countries, there has been observable in some developing countries at least, a tendency to take a more pragmatic view of direct foreign investment. Perhaps this reflects no more than a partial reversal of an earlier pronounced hostility. But it is a development worth noting.

EXPERIENCE OF SMALL INVESTORS

It is important to contrast the favourable experience of large direct investors with that of small investors whose operations are on the border-line between portfolio and direct investors. A small number of foreign investment companies have come into existence in the United States and elsewhere in the hope of taking advantage of favourable investment opportunities particularly in developing countries. Typically, these ventures do not involve management control, but rely on the management of an existing or new enterprise. From what is known, the experience of these small foreign investment companies has been extraordinarily adverse. They have encountered surprising difficulty in finding invest-ment opportunities. Such commitments as they have made have very often been disappointing. Their experience may suggest that this par-ticular form of foreign investment is not promising. It also may imply, however, that the risks of foreign investment are greater than appears on the surface and require a substantial risk premium.

TAX BENEFITS TO HOST COUNTRIES

In conclusion, it needs to be pointed out that the prevailing system of taxing foreign investment gives a substantial advantage to the govern-ment of countries where foreign direct investments are located. The United States, as the world's leading foreign investor, has concluded tax treaties with most industrial and a number of developing countries. The principal purpose of these treaties is to avoid double taxation, which would militate against optimal allocation of capital. This objective could be achieved by allowing either the host country or the parent country priority in taxing the income of the foreign investor. According to common practice, it is the host government that has the first right to tax. If the income of an American subsidiary is taxed abroad at the rate prevailing in the United States, at present 48 per cent outside the Western Hemisphere, the U.S. Treasury collects no tax even after the income has been transferred from the subsidiary to the American parent. If the foreign tax is below 48 per cent, the U.S. Treasury levies a tax equal to the difference between the foreign rate and 48 per cent, at the time the income is transferred. From an overall American point of view, this means that foreign investment may yield substantially less to the American economy than domestic investment : domestic investment yields a return to the investor and, via the tax mechanism, to the U.S. Treasury. Foreign investment yields a return primarily to the investor, with the U.S. Treasury receiving only what the foreign government does not choose to pre-empt. It follows that foreign countries can raise their corporate tax rate to the U.S. level without reducing the net return to the American investor. They would simply obtain a transfer from the U.S. Treasury.

DISCUSSION OF DR. KAMARCK'S PAPER

IN the discussion of Dr. Kamarck's paper the relevance of the financial experience of lenders and investors in Africa for lenders and investors elsewhere was questioned. Difficulties in measuring the returns on investment were also considered, and reasons for the apparently poor lender experience in Africa examined. Other topics discussed were the reasons for the apparently above-average profitability of American private foreign investment, and the nature of French assistance in Africa.

THE RELEVANCE OF AFRICAN FINANCIAL EXPERIENCE

Dr. Onitiri felt that the financial experience of foreign investors in Africa during the colonial period was not representative either of their experience elsewhere or of their experience in Africa at other times. In making his point, Dr. Onitiri distinguished between three stages of foreign investment in Africa. The first is the colonial stage, in which investment is solely profit-motivated, foreign enterprises are not integrated with the rest of the economy, and the typical investment is an economic enclave type. The second or present stage is one in which the young African governments are trying to reverse the former situation. Attempts are made to base investment decisions on factors other than profits, and foreign enterprise is encouraged to integrate with the rest of the economy. The third phase, yet to come, should be one in which foreign investment is treated much as it is in the present developed countries. During the colonial stage, profits cannot be considered independently of the relationship between foreign companies and their home government. In return for protection by the home government, the foreign companies usually perform services for the government. Also, since sales by foreign subsidiaries to the home companies are not made at market prices, it is hard to determine profits — especially when there are no world markets for the product. In addition, Dr. Onitiri saw South

Africa as a unique case in which profits are determined mainly by the lag of wages behind labour productivity. *Dr. Kamarck* agreed that it was difficult to measure returns on foreign investment, but noted that in his main example — the Unilever case — returns were unfavourable no matter how they are measured.

Dr. de Beers felt that the African experience is different from that of regions such as Latin America. For example, while tropical Africa was a colonial area, Latin America was not colonial — at least politically. *Dr. Marquez* agreed. Unlike the African cases cited in Dr. Kamarck's paper, foreign companies in Latin America — such as the business companies in Central America and tin mining companies of Bolivia — have received high rates of return for many years. *Dr. Andreasyan* added that the financial experience in South Africa and that in the rest of Africa South of the Sahara should be considered separately. He thought the high rates of return to capital shown in Table 6h of Dr. Kamarck's paper originated mainly in South Africa. *Dr. Kamarck* replied that the only available data combine figures for South Africa and the rest of Africa South of the Sahara. Also, since most of Africa South of the Sahara except South Africa is still mainly agricultural, possibilities for direct investment there are still quite small.

Problems of Measuring Financial Experience

In discussing the relevance of African financial experience, *Dr. Onitiri* pointed out that services performed by foreign companies for colonial governments and intra-firm sales at other than market prices tend to obscure profit calculations. *Dr. Singer* agreed that measuring profits of foreign investors was a problem. He noted that there is a difference between the return to private lenders and the return to the investor's home country. The return to private investors cannot be separated from the return to the trading system of which the particular foreign investment is a part. In this connection he noted that while the opening of countries to international trade results — according to the principles of comparative advantage — in a once-and-for-all increase in the standard of living for both the developed and the underdeveloped country, the long-term effect may be a deterioration in the terms of trade and more limited prospects for growth in the developing country. *Dr. de Beers* agreed and added that the time dimension had been neglected in Dr. Kamarck's paper. He felt that it is necessary to take this into account when examining the profitability of both direct and indirect investment.

Professor Rosenstein-Rodan suggested that in analyzing returns to foreign investors, we should note the difference between the viewpoint of lawyers and economists. He asserted that guarantees are often important for economic success, so that investment decisions become a function of government decisions. For this reason, the real incentives are not always the apparent market incentives. For instance, much railway investment was profitable for contractors and land speculators but not for bondholders of the railways.

Professor Wallich agreed with Drs. Onitiri and Singer that profit measures tended to be arbitrary, but he did not see that there is any bias in favour of showing either high or low profits by foreign subsidiaries. If there is such bias, it is a matter of tax incentives. Professor Wallich also argued that rates of return should be calculated on the replacement cost of capital. Since capital is usually valued at original cost, older companies usually show considerably higher returns than younger companies during periods of inflation. The picture is further complicated because profit estimates depend upon prior calculation of essentially arbitrary depreciation allowances.

WHY POOR INVESTOR EXPERIENCE IN AFRICA?

Professor Stolper said that profits in developing countries are low because absorptive capacity is low. He felt that Dr. Kamarck has given considerable evidence of this for Africa. *Dr. Singer* suggested that the African experience contradicts the usual text-book conclusion, which is that there must be a high rate of return on capital in a developing country since capital is a relatively scarce factor in such countries. Dr. Singer added that potential high-yield investment opportunities exist but are not easily attainable. This is why technical assistance in development of infra-structure is needed before advantage can be taken of such opportunities.

Dr. Adler felt that low returns to capital in developing countries are mostly due to misjudgment regarding the availability of co-operant factors. Profitability and absorptive capacity for foreign private investment are a function of the supply of co-operant factors. Low returns to capital may also result from misjudgment of the applicability of certain types of technology. In addition, much foreign investment in under-developed countries is of a defensive nature. This is investment to maintain the firm's market share and may not be profitable in the short run. *Professor Wallich* added that foreign capital often receives lower returns than local capital on the same types of investment because foreign investors are not as well acquainted with opportunities.

Professor Rosenstein-Rodan thought that low profits during early stages of development cannot be explained by referring to capital/output ratios. First, returns may be low because capital is below the minimum needed for efficient production. Second, it may be difficult to appropriate external economies. Internalization of profits may be difficult at low levels of development, and this might explain why productivity for the economy as a whole can be high while private investors lose money. The ability to internalize external economies should increase with the level of development. *Dr. Adler* disagreed with Professor Rosenstein-Rodan that profit rates are a function of the appropriability of external economies. Rather, profits are a function of correct anticipation of future changes in costs and demand when making the original investment decision. This might be why it has been found that private investors like government economic planning. It increases the likelihood that anticipations will be correct. *Dr. Patel* added that indirect effects of investment are often so hard to internalize that government investment and taxes are necessary to capture the gains. Further, some benefits of investment are so intangible that they cannot be appropriated at all. *Dr. Marquez* felt that the implication of the argument so far was that as countries develop investment becomes more profitable. He felt that this point could not be generalized.

Several of the discussants commented on the apparent increase in returns to foreign investment in Africa after World War II. *Professor Delivanis* wondered whether this might be due to a substantial rise in prices of the main African exports after 1939. *Dr. Faaland* was also struck by this increase in the rate of return. He felt that it might be explained by the increase in foreign private investment oriented toward the domestic market and the decline of the formerly predominant enclave type of investment. *Dr. Kamarck* agreed with Professor Delivanis that rising prices for African exports have increased the profitability of foreign investment. He added, however, that the increasing size of the market has probably been the one most important factor in raising the profitability of foreign investment during the postwar period. Both rising export prices and foreign aid programmes have served to expand domestic markets in Africa.

One of the points noted in the discussion of Dr. Kamarck's paper was that rates of return on American foreign investment seem to be higher than rates of return on foreign investment of other countries. *Dr. Singer* wondered if higher profitability of American investment might not be due to a different sectoral distribution of investment or possibly to different tax systems. *Dr. Faaland* suggested that greater profitability of U.S. investments might be a result of the increase in relative importance of investment in domestic markets as opposed to investment for raw-material exports. He observed that this trend has co-existed with a tendency toward increasing local participation in foreign private investment, especially investments of United States firms. *Dr. Kamarck* added that though the point made by Professor Wallich — that the present U.S. tax system subsidizes foreign investment — may in part explain the greater profitability of U.S. foreign investment, he thought that the greater success of American firms is due more to the greater drive of resident managers than to tax differences.

Professor Leduc pointed out that most French lending in Africa before World War II was not true investment, but rather what has been termed 'placement'. The loans went to colonial administrations that used them for public works. Professor Leduc also commented that in calculating French foreign investment in Africa, it should be noted that the flow of public capital from France to the colonies were offset by a return flow of private funds to France. The result is that the magnitude of the net flow is not known. Professor Leduc further indicated that French assistance after World War II was mainly technical assistance for educational purposes and because of that it is difficult to evaluate its economic impact.

Chapter 3

TREATMENT OF FOREIGN CAPITAL—
A CASE STUDY FOR JAPAN

BY

SABURO OKITA

AND

TAKEO MIKI

The Japan Economic Research Centre

I. PRE-WAR EXPERIENCE

1. Introduction

THERE is no doubt that foreign capital plays an important role in the process of economic development. When the economy of a nation rapidly develops, foreign capital performs a useful part in meeting the shortage of domestic resources ; in purchasing modern machinery and industrial technology from advanced nations and in supplying the shortage of foodstuffs caused temporarily by the rapid gravitation of farming population into industrial cities.

Consequently, proper management of foreign capital is highly important to each nation. In this connection a number of economists have pointed out that Japan succeeded in achieving the so-called 'take-off' by borrowing little overseas before the war. And Japan's achievement is expected to offer some helpful lessons to developing nations.

A more intensive study indicates that Japan induced foreign capital during those years under a world situation entirely different from today and under the influence of some accidental occurrences. When Japan ended its national isolation and opened its door to the outside world in the middle of the nineteenth century, Western powers were actively competing with one another in the acquisition of colonies. Twenty years later, the Civil War broke out in the United States and the Prussian War raged in Europe. A few years later Japan waged war against China and then against Russia.

A little over ten years after carrying out what Rostow calls the 'take-off', Japan participated in the First World War, and changed from a debtor to a creditor, from a borrower to a lender. Subsequently Japan started to establish and manage overseas colonies including Manchuria.

Today another world war could not be waged without risking the life of all mankind. On the other hand, the World Bank and various other organs for international co-operation have been formed. At the United Nations Trade and Development Conference held at Geneva in 1964, the former colonial powers were treated as culprits.

Thus there have been great changes during the past decades.

We should also recognize considerable difference between the internal situation in Japan in its early stage of economic development and the conditions now prevailing in less developed countries. For instance, most Japanese thought at that time foreigners and things foreign hardly acceptable. They held their own traditional culture in high esteem and despised foreign cultures. However, those Japanese who came into contact with foreigners had to admit their material superiority. Thereupon, the Japanese started avidly to import and absorb advanced foreign technology and systems so that Japan might catch up Western nations as quickly as possible. Nationalism which newly arose after the Meiji Restoration stimulated their efforts.

Today, however, modern technologies and industrial products are introduced to less developed nations and are familiar to their peoples. Their reactions against foreigners and things foreign are not so strong as the reaction of the Japanese. The resistance of developing nations to foreigners is now political but not economical. On the other hand, the gap between developing nations and advanced nations is incomparably wider than the gap that existed between Japan and the Western powers during those years. Developing nations must now primarily devote their energies to the elimination of what is left of colonial institutions, to political stabilization and unification. Japan smoothly started building up a modern state in the name of the Emperor by accomplishing the Meiji Restoration in 1868, and did not have to expel colonial rulers.

While there is a wide difference in the internal and international situation between Japan in its early stage of economic development and the less developed nations of today, both have many aspects in common. During those years 80 per cent of the population of Japan were farmers, the national income of the Japanese was exceedingly low, and Japan lacked domestic and foreign capital.

2. Foreign Capital Import Before the Sino-Japanese War (1894–95)

The students of Japan's foreign capital import often divide the history of Japan into 4 or 6 periods. But it can be clearly divided into the Pre-Sino-Japanese War period and the Post-Sino-Japanese War period in the study of Japan's policy or attitude towards borrowing overseas. Before the Sino-Japanese War, Japan was exceedingly conservative in including foreign capital, but after the war it became a very active borrower.

During the age of colonial domination by Western powers, it is natural that borrowing foreign capital should often be associated with foreign domination and that less developed nations should be cautious in borrowing from powerful countries. Great caution was already exercised against borrowing overseas during the last years of the Tokugawa Shogunate, the last feudal government of Japan which lasted until 1868.

When the Tokugawa Shogunate was going to borrow 6 million dollars from France, Yoshinaga Matsudara, the feudal lord of the province of Echizen, warned the government that unless the government was 100 per cent sure of being capable of repayment, it should not borrow the money. 'If the government should be unable to repay, it will lose the land offered as a security. This will lead to foreign invasion, as in the case of India.'[1]

Such a cautious attitude was carried over to the new Meiji Government. Thus in 1869 or the second year of Meiji, the new government restricted the floating of loans overseas by provincial governments; in 1870, it prohibited the import of ships and machinery by raising loans overseas. When provincial governments were replaced by prefectural governments, foreign loans which had been made by the Tokugawa Shogunate and provincial governments were all taken over and repaid by the Meiji Government.

In 1872, the government issued 'Mining Regulations' and prohibited mining by foreigners. At the same time, foreigners were prohibited from engaging in railway construction and city gas service.

On the other hand, the new government needed an enormous amount of capital with which to carry out various important programmes. For instance, it had to raise funds to cover military expenditures required for settling a series of rebellions; for recoinage which had been strongly demanded by foreign countries and

[1] Tokihiko Tanaka, *Political Situation during the Meiji Restoration and Railway Construction*, 1963, p. 184.

for clearing up borrowings by the Tokugawa and provincial governments from abroad.

In 1870, the Japanese Government issued bonds overseas to raise funds to support jobless Samurais. This was done reluctantly but apparently there was no alternative. There were many government leaders who believed that the floating of bonds on foreign markets would only disclose Japan's lack of capital and that heavy borrowing overseas would retard the economic development of Japan. While Japan felt the menace of foreign capital and was eager to attain economic self-sufficiency by accumulating its own capital, the new-born government had no alternative but to borrow foreign capital in order to carry out national programmes.

In 1877, the Seinan Rebellion broke out. The government issued a large amount of new bank notes and government notes, which later greatly affected Japan's fiscal operation. The floating of inconvertible notes adversely affected the Japanese economy, depreciated the currency and brought about inflation which caused a sharp rise in prices of rice and of imports. The Japanese currency was about to completely lose its value, and the economy of the nation was on the verge of collapse.

In an attempt to ameliorate the situation, Finance Minister Shigenobu Okuma proposed the flotation of bonds overseas amounting to 50 million dollars and reform in the currency system to redeem inconvertible paper money. But his proposal aroused keen opposition among government leaders who contended that heavy borrowing overseas would only lead to Japan's downfall. Government leaders split in two groups. Finally by the decision of the Emperor Meiji, his proposal was defeated and the government was told to follow a fiscal policy of retrenchment.[1]

By the imperial decision, Masayoshi Matsukata who succeeded Okuma as Finance Minister, adopted a strong deflationary policy which caused what is still known as the 'Matsukata Deflation'. During the period from 1881 to 1883, he took drastic tight money measures and substantially raised indirect taxes, notably those on tobacco and alcoholic beverages. He established the Bank of Japan as the central bank which was exclusively authorized to issue bank notes. The extreme retrenchment policy made money tight, caused a sharp decline in the price of rice and forced a great many farmers to leave their land to become factory workers. Matsukata not only re-established balance between specie and bank notes but also

[1] Ikujiro Watanabe, *A Biography of Shegenobu Okuma*, 1952, pp. 118–120.

believed that the currency could be stabilized only by raising the productive capacity to back the amount of currency in circulation. For this purpose he authorized the sale of government-owned factories to large private firms and thus helped the rise of Mitsui, Mitsubishi and other industrial capitalists. Matsukata also urged the nation to lead an austere life for some time and not to rely on borrowing overseas.

Regarding the floating of bonds overseas Matsukata stated as follows: 'To pay back a large amount of foreign debts, we must raise a large amount of capital. Since repayment is exclusively handled by the Toyo Bank, which is a foreign bank, it will come to control the finance of Japan and will cause not a small damage to this country.'[1]

In short, before the Sino-Japanese War, Japan was exceedingly sensitive to pressure from foreign countries. Resurgent nationalism urged the nation to resist pressure from outside and overtake advanced nations. In fact, during the 30 years' period from the Meiji Restoration to the Sino-Japanese War, Japan borrowed capital overseas only twice, totalling 16·6 million yen. And the total amount was repaid by the 30th year of the Meiji reign.

In this connection, it must also be admitted that Japan did not offer such an attractive market for foreign investors as China and India, and that since the gold standard had not been yet established in Japan, investment involved foreign exchange risks.

3. *After the Sino-Japanese War*

(A) *Period up to the Russo-Japanese War (1904–5)*. Indemnity payments amounting to 364 million yen which Japan received from China more than offset the war expenses totalling 200 million yen. Private companies started to develop actively industries in anticipation of capital inflows, the relaxation of the tight money policy and lower interest rates. But these expectations were not realized. The money market tightened, and interest rates went up, because the government redeemed only a small amount of government bonds and spent most of its money on military expansion and on other government programmes, thus causing a serious shortage of industrial funds.

---

[1] Yasuzo Horie, *Prospect and Retrospect of Foreign Capital Import*, 1950, p. 38, quoted in *Collection of Count Matsukata's Theses on Public Finance*, p. 288, vol. i, of *Data on the History of Finance and Economy in the Early Meiji Era*.

Before and after the war with China, the Japanese economy was rapidly growing. The textile industry was the most important of all the industries of Japan. In 1897, Japan started to export cotton yarns; six years later, in 1903, textile yarn exports accounted for 40 per cent of Japan's total export. During the period from 1895 to 1900, 95 railway companies were established. In 1901, it became possible to go by train from Aomori, at the northern end of Japan's main island to Nagasaki in Kyushu, Japan's southernmost island. Japanese industries rapidly expanded. Later, Prime Minister Hirobumi Itoh criticized: 'The Japanese economy excessively expanded after the Sino-Japanese War. As sufficient capital was not available at home, Japan could do nothing but borrow from other countries.'[1]

The problem was that while Japan did not have sufficient capital needed for the development of modern industries, it carried out at the same time a major armament programme. Imports of foreign capital became inevitable. Finally, the Japanese Government recognized the necessity of foreign capital imports and took steps to facilitate them.

In 1893, the government created the Currency System Research Committee and decided to adopt the gold standard. In 1897, Japan finally adopted the gold standard, using the war reparations received from China as a basis in order to stabilize the yen, to facilitate foreign capital inflows and to meet the shortage of domestic capital. With the latter objective in mind, the Industrial Bank of Japan was founded, primarily for the purpose of attracting foreign capital. It was difficult for individual private firms to raise foreign capital, and it was thought disadvantageous for individual firms to compete with one another in foreign capital market. The Industrial Bank of Japan functioned as the central organ handling the import of foreign capital on behalf of private firms.

In proposing the creation of the Industrial Bank of Japan, the following views were expressed:

'If foreign capital is allowed to flow in freely without passing through a central organ, foreigners will select Japanese enterprises in which they want to invest and will eventually take over the enterprises.

'As the Japanese manufacturing sector is now extremely depressed, it is thought most advisable not to allow individual firms to borrow capital overseas but to create a central organ which exclusively im-

[1] *History of Japan*, vol. ii, p. 139, published by the Yomiuri Shimbun.

ports foreign capital required for the development of Japanese industries.

'It is thought advisable to borrow foreign capital by making use of the credit of the nation and the government, without offering any tangible security, except for the intangible security of the national credit.'[1]

During those years, the Japanese economy expanded markedly, but both the government and industry keenly felt the shortage of capital. Gradually a positive attitude towards borrowing overseas developed. Japan was still exceedingly cautious, however, for fear of possible foreign domination. This was an important argument for the establishment of a central organ to engage exclusively in the import of foreign capital. It should also be noted in this connection that views opposing the Industrial Bank were also expressed.

'It is most proper and profitable for the government not to interfere with foreign capital imports by private firms but to allow private firms to raise the necessary capital freely from private investors overseas. The borrowed capital will directly help Japanese industries to develop. The profit which may be derived by foreign creditors will be only a small portion of what Japanese enterprises will gain by investing the borrowed foreign capital. If we gain profit, they will also gain ; if we lose, so will they. For this reason, the sale of stocks is the best way to attract foreign capital.'[2]

This view emphasizes that imported foreign capital should be directedly used for productive purposes. It seems also to raise the question as to how the debt should be paid if the borrowing enterprise did not show any profit. From a similar point of view, some opposed the import of foreign capital :

'(a) If imported foreign capital is not immediately "capitalized" (i.e. used productively), it will not help relax the financial situation. If imported capital is spent on importing warships or arms, it will never serve the purpose of lowering interest rates. Even if capital borrowed from foreigners is spent domestically, if it is used to pay salaries and wages or to buy merchandise, it will only bring about inflation and a rise in commodity prices.

'(b) Import of foreign capital will be welcomed only by speculators and will fan a speculative craze. It will not contribute to the development of the national economy.

[1] *The 50 Year History of the Industrial Bank of Japan*, 1957, pp. 23–24.
[2] Yasuzo Horie, *op. cit.*, pp. 61–62.

'(c) Even if foreign capital imports do not lead to foreign interference with the Japanese Government, if the loss caused by the payment of interest and the profit gained from production are not balanced, the nation will be the loser.

'(d) If foreign capital is imported, the prices of bonds and stocks will rise, and the financial circles will temporarily enjoy a boom. But if foreign creditors find more profitable markets and withdraw their invested capital from Japan, Japan will suffer a serious financial depression.' [1]

The main point of these views was that all circles in Japan except a few government leaders were opposed to the floating of bonds overseas to raise funds for armament or for other non-productive purposes. What the general public wanted was that if the government was to raise foreign capital by floating bonds, the imported capital should be used for purchasing domestic bonds and stocks by the fiscal authorities in order to furnish industrial and commercial funds to private business. However, the government felt it necessary to expand defence expenditures and to carry out various postwar programmes.

In 1899 the government decided to import foreign capital before the nation arrived at a consensus of opinion on this problem. However, in 1903, imported capital amounted only to 194 million yen, of which 97 per cent was raised by issuing government bonds. Although the import of foreign capital had been heatedly discussed among various sectors, not much capital was actually attracted. The reasons were that Japanese private enterprises had not yet achieved good credit standing overseas, that foreigners could not own land and that a war between Japan and Russia was thought imminent.

(B) *After the Russo-Japanese War.* With the outbreak of the Russo-Japanese War in 1904, Japan's import of foreign capital sharply rose. The foreign capital was mostly used for military purposes. Immediately after the war broke out, the government raised taxes, but it found it impossible to finance the war only with domestic resources. When the Japanese Government determined to wage war against Russia in 1903, Japan requested Great Britain, which was Japan's ally,[2] to furnish financial aid. When war was declared the following year, the government dispatched Korekiyo

---

[1] Yasuzo Horie, *op. cit.*, p. 56.
[2] Britain entered into an alliance with Japan to cope with the situation in China and to check Russia's advance to the Far East.

Takahashi, Vice-Governor of the Bank of Japan, to London, and he succeeded in selling 98 million yen worth of bonds there. As the war developed favourably for Japan, Japan issued bonds overseas a second and a third time. Japan's bond issue during the war totalled 800 million yen or nearly one half of her total war expenditure of 1,720 million yen.

While a great part of the foreign capital thus raised was spent for war purposes, as originally intended, a considerable portion was also allocated for reserves of the Bank of Japan to support the currency convertibility.[1] During the war, Japan's imports far exceeded its exports, reflecting heavy wartime demand, and the Japanese specie rapidly flowed out. At the same time, the bank-note issue sharply increased and the foundation of the gold standard was being undermined. In this critical situation, the imported foreign capital not only helped finance the war but also provided backing for the ever increasing bank-note issue by increasing the specie reserves.

TABLE 1

BALANCE OF PAYMENTS AND INFLOW OF FOREIGN CAPITAL BEFORE
AND AFTER THE RUSSO-JAPANESE WAR

(In millions of yen)

	Trade Balance	Balance of Invisible Transactions	Current Account Balance	Other Receipts	Foreign Borrowing
1903	− 13	37	23	15	(15)
1904	− 28	19	− 8	33	(33)
1905	− 78	− 78	− 156	101	(104)
1906	− 176	− 159	− 335	592	(529)
1907	− 3	− 26	− 30	131	(266)
1908	− 64	64	0	25	(177)

Source : Financial Monthly Statistics, compiled by the Finance Ministry.

Thus Japan became a major debtor in the international capital markets as a result of the Russo-Japanese War.

After the Russo-Japanese War, debt operations of the Japanese Government increased markedly because of increased expenditures on postwar programmes, increased payments overseas and rising

[1] Of total capital imports of 800 million yen, about 400 million yen are believed to have been paid to foreign countries.

prices. The government's total expenditure rose from 249 million yen in 1903 to 602 million yen in 1906 and 636 million yen in 1908, and one-third of government revenues had to be secured by the sale of bonds. But since all bonds could not be sold on the domestic market, the government had no alternative but to rely on foreign capital. Thus a large amount of foreign capital continued to flow in after the Russo-Japanese War. What deserves special attention is that sometimes the government issued foreign bonds for the purpose of replacing bonds issued at home bearing higher interest, and thereby relieving the financial burden of the government. But it should be noted that the real purpose of these measures was to return funds needed by industries to private enterprises. During the period from 1906 to 1911 more than 786 million yen worth of domestic bonds were redeemed.

The government's eagerness to secure funds for industry is shown by the following fact. When the government dispatched Korekiyo Takahashi, Vice-Governor of the Bank of Japan to London in 1905 to raise funds for financing the war, it ordered Takahashi —

(1) To explain that the Japanese Government would present a Railway Mortgage Bill, a Factory Mortgage Bill, a Mining Mortgage Bill, a Secured Debenture Trust Bill and a Mining Law to the current session of the Imperial Diet, that it would welcome and facilitate foreign investment in these sectors and that it guaranteed its safety.

(2) To explain that the Industrial Bank of Japan was organized by a special law for the purpose of handling the import of foreign capital, that it was protected and supervised by the government, that the Japanese Government strongly desired investors in Britain, the United States and other countries to become directors or auditors of the Bank and that it welcomed foreign investors to invest in Japanese industries through this bank, which can be easily supervised to assume the safety of foreign investment.[1]

On the other hand, however, 'the government instructed all prefectural governors in 1906 that (1) local governments must obtain the approval of the Finance Minister and the Home Minister when they want to raise foreign capital; (2) that of all municipalities only large cities would be authorized to raise foreign capital through the Industrial Bank of Japan; (3) that requests for small amounts must be combined and furnished by the Industrial Bank of Japan; and

[1] *The 50 Year History of the Industrial Bank of Japan*, p. 58.

(4) that debentures must be issued as much as possible through the Industrial Bank of Japan. In the same year, the Finance Minister instructed all Japanese ministers overseas to watch and prevent local governments and private firms from directly coming into contact with overseas capital markets.'[1]

Although Japan won the Russo-Japanese War, it received no indemnity from Russia. At the same time, Japan was bearing a heavy burden of foreign debts. Thus Japan's victory did not cause an industrial boom as its victory over China had done ten years before. But in due course an industrial boom started with the construction of hydroelectric power plants, which came to supply large amounts of electric energy at low cost and thereby laid the foundation of Japan's heavy industry.

In 1905, the first lathe was produced in Japan. Soon therefter a number of machine tool manufacturing companies were established in the country. After the Russo-Japanese War, the stable foreign exchange rate of the yen now on the gold standard, Japan's victory over Russia and its improved credit standing overseas, and the increased interest shown by foreigners in investment in Japan, caused a marked increase in direct foreign investment in Japan. By then Japan had developed into a considerably advanced capitalist country. Industrial capital which was scarce during the war was restored by the government policy of borrowing overseas. At that time the Japanese industry needed more advanced foreign technology rather than foreign capital. Thus, in most cases direct foreign investment took the form of joint ventures which were often supported by technical licensing agreements.

In 1910, Shibaura Seisakusho K.K. which later became Toshiba Co. Ltd. concluded a technical co-operation agreement with the General Electric Corporation of the United States. Mr. Otaguro, director of Shibaura, stated as follows :

'It is not difficult to raise funds necessary for expanding an enterprise in Japan. But what we really want is industrial technology rather than capital. Western nations are more advanced than our country, and they are making progress at a greater pace. They have better equipment and many things to study. Japan's industrial technology should be developed on a world-wide basis. We never can hope to reach great engineering achievements if we confine ourselves in our own country. We should promote technological interchange with Western countries. For instance, as it is very dry

[1] *The 50 Year History of the Industrial Bank of Japan*, p. 98.

in the United States, little precautions are exercised against moisture in manufacturing electrical machinery in that country. As it is very humid in Japan, American-made electrical machines often are out of order. We should exchange information on this point between the two nations.' [1]

Technical co-operation with foreign manufacturing firms greatly promoted the development of Japan's heavy industry. Enterprises that imported industrial technologies from abroad belonged for the most part to the Zaibatsu families. For instance, Shibaura Seisakusho belonged to the Mitsui Zaibatsu. In fact, to be in Zaibatsu families made it easier to contract technical tie-up agreements with foreign firms. Among the largest Japanese manufacturing companies, the following companies signed technical co-operation agreements during those years : Mitsubishi Electrical Machinery Co. with Westinghouse Electric International of the United States in 1923 ; Fuji Electrical Machinery Co. which was organized jointly by Furukawa Zaibatsu capital and Siemens of Germany in 1923 ; and Sumitomo Aluminium Co. which was jointly established by Sumitomo Metal Co. and Canada Aluminium Co. in 1931.

The development of the iron and steel industry played a leading part in the development of Japan's heavy industry. Yawata Iron Works which was established by the government in 1901 produced 59 per cent of the total pig iron consumption in Japan during the period from 1906 to 1910. By 1913, Japan produced all locomotives operated in the country. Between 1906–15, Japan built 60 per cent of all ships owned by Japanese shipping companies. Thus during the period from the end of the Russo-Japanese War to the outbreak of the First World War, Japan already produced a large percentage of various heavy industrial products which had been imported before.

As the Japanese economy expanded, the excess of Japan's imports over its exports gradually increased. During the nine years' period from 1905, when the Russo-Japanese War ended, to 1914, when the First World War broke out, Japan's imports exceeded its exports by 524 million yen in total. During the same period, the inflow of gold and silver exceeded their outflow by 44 million yen, reflecting heavy foreign capital imports. The trade deficit continued to rise, while the gold and silver outflow started to exceed their inflow in 1910. At the same time, Japan's payment of interest on foreign debts steadily increased. The figures for 1914 were as follows : [2]

[1] *The 65 Year History of Shibaura Seisakusho K.K.*, 1940, p. 53.
[2] Yasuzo Horie, *op. cit.*, p. 137.

Japan's credits :	Specie reserves	130 million yen
	Specie overseas	220 million yen
	Overseas investment	460 million yen
	Total	810 million yen
Japan's liabilities :		1,900 million yen

Net liabilities thus amounted to 1,100 million yen ; nonetheless Japan's imports continued to exceed exports. As a consequence, the Japanese economy was quite unstable and was approaching a serious crisis. When the war broke out, Japan's exports started to rise sharply. The large increase in exports during the war eliminated Japan's foreign exchange difficulties and made Japan a rich country. If the First World War had not broken out, Japan might have suffered from the aftermath of massive imports of foreign capital through large payments of principal and interest to foreign creditors, as many developing countries are now doing.

The great progress that had been made in industrial technology was an important factor enabling Japan to rise to the position of an important source of supplies during the First World War. If the Japanese economy had not been successful in raising its productivity, the inflow of foreign capital would have only caused inflation. Japan's export potential became effective as the war broke out.

(C) *After the First World War.* Although Japan's exports did not decline, a huge amount of foreign exchange, accumulated during the First World War, rapidly flowed out as Japan's imports sharply rose. To make matters worse, a great earthquake in 1923 shattered the Tokyo-Yokohama area and caused Japan's imports to increase further. As a result, Japan had to rely upon borrowing overseas again.

As compared with foreign capital imports before the First World War, the postwar foreign capital inflow was characterized by

(1) a marked decrease in the amount of national and local government bonds floated overseas ; and

(2) a substantial increase in industrial debentures, notably those floated by electric power companies.

Except for bonds floated overseas for emergency purposes for the reconstruction of the earthquake-torn area, virtually no government bonds were issued on foreign markets, partly because it had become possible to raise funds in the domestic market and partly because

TABLE 2

BALANCE OF PAYMENTS ON CURRENT ACCOUNTS, JAPANESE EMPIRE, 1881–1936

(SUMMARIZED BY PERIODS)

(¥ Millions, in current values)

	1881–95*	1896–1903*	1904–13†	1914–19†	1920–31†	1932–36†
Visible account: Balance of merchandise and specie (other than gold)‡	72·3	−354·5	−706·5	1,197·5	−4,517·8	−236·1
Invisible account						
Net interest and dividend payments	−8·1	−41·4	−636·9	−313·6	−756·4	−511·6
Net income on undertakings and service abroad	—	—	274·2	441·3	1,262·6	880·7
Net freight receipts	—	—	252·4	1,356·7	1,650·4	741·9
Net insurance payments	—	—	−17·9	9·8	83·7	66·9
Net tourist expenditures, etc.	—	—	23·5	66·5	133·1	93·9
Net government payments abroad	—	—	−329·7	165·5	−388·7	−615·9
Miscellaneous	—	—	−1·8	111·3	128·5	159·4
Balance of invisibles	—	—	−435·9	1,837·5	2,113·1	815·3
Specie movements‡	7·6	−62·3	59·7	−603·8	222·8	132·9
Balance on current account	—	—	−1,082·7	2,431·2	−2,181·9	712·1

* Adapted from H. G. Moulton, *Japan: An Economic and Financial Appraisal* (Washington, reprint ed., 1944), pp. 379–385; known items only.
† Adapted from E. B. Schumpeter, *et al.*, *Industrialization of Japan and Manchukuo*, 1930–40 (New York, 1940); end papers, Table III. Slight differences between balances and detail sums are due to rounding.
‡ For 1881–1903, the visible account refers to merchandise trade only, all specie movements being listed separately below. For 1904–36, specie other than gold is included in the visible account, while gold movements only are listed separately below.

Source: 'Foreign Capital and Domestic Development in Japan', by E. P. Reubens in *Economic Growth: Brazil, India, Japan*, S. Kuznets, editor, 1955, p. 188.

the government adopted a policy of restricting overseas borrowings as much as practicable towards the end of the Meiji Era.[1]

However, the floating of private bonds overseas helped to support Japan's specie reserves held abroad which had substantially decreased. The sharp increase in the amount of private debenture bonds floated overseas could be attributed to greater trust of foreign nations in Japanese industries and the greater ease of international capital transactions because of the return to the gold standard by various countries, along with the government's encouragement of private issues. But because the money market situation in Great Britain and the United States was very tight, the terms and conditions of borrowing operations were unfavourable.

The reason for the startling increase in the amount of debentures floated overseas by power companies was that the reconstruction of earthquake stricken areas stimulated the development of the power industry, that electric motors came to be extensively used in industry and that the construction of power plant facilities required long-term, low-interest foreign capital.

At the same time, a large volume of debentures was also issued overseas by the Oriental Development Company (Toyo Takushoku Kaisha), the South Manchurian Railway Company and the Taiwan Electric Power Company in order to promote the economic development of Japan's overseas territories.

In short, while the amount of national and local government bonds floated overseas declined, those issued by private firms increased. Japan continued to need foreign capital to promote the economic development of its metropolitan area and its overseas territories, and to maintain its economic prestige by increasing the amount of specie held overseas.

Japan continued to float bonds overseas until 1931. But the world crisis in 1929, a deep depression in Japan caused by the lifting of the gold embargo, Japan's foreign relations aggravated by the so-called Manchuria Incident and the re-embargo of gold shipments and the resulting fall in the foreign exchange rate of the yen made it exceedingly difficult for Japan to float bonds overseas. Thereupon, the Japanese Government took steps to reduce the amount of bonds outstanding on foreign markets, and purchased and redeemed the debenture bonds issued by the Japanese power companies.

---

[1] The Katsura Cabinet formed in 1908 adopted a policy to restrict the floating of national and local government bonds overseas and to encourage the floating of private bonds.

4. *Conclusion*

What lessons does this brief record of Japan's foreign capital imports provide? Above all, it points to the fact that the Japanese have always realized that 'borrowed foreign capital must be repaid sooner or later'. This is a matter of course. However, nations are often apt to rely on borrowing overseas to overcome acute difficulties the easy way, even though they know that borrowings must be paid some day. As mentioned already, this was exactly what Japan did during the period from the end of the Russo-Japanese War to the outbreak of the First World War. The Japanese Government chose the easy way of heavily depending upon foreign capital imports. As a result, the Japanese economy was seriously threatened. If the First World War had not broken out, the Japanese economy would have had severe balance of payments difficulties.

We can discern in the retrenchment policy to restrict foreign capital imports adopted by the Second Katsura Cabinet a spirit of self-discipline. Causes for Japan's borrowing so little overseas during the period from the Meiji Restoration to the Sino-Japanese War should be attributed in part to Japan's unpreparedness for receiving foreign loans, little interest shown by foreign capitalists in the investment in Japan and the undeveloped stage of Japanese industries which did not require much foreign capital. But the principal cause was to be sought in the fear as to what would happen if Japan was unable to pay back its foreign debts. It was for the same reason that even when the government and the people keenly felt the necessity of borrowing overseas after the Russo-Japanese War, most Japanese, except for a few government leaders, opposed the use of foreign capital for military and other unproductive purposes.

Another characteristic feature of the government policy towards borrowing overseas was that the government used the supply of foreign capital in order to relieve pressure on the domestic money market. For instance, government bonds floated in Japan during the Russo-Japanese War were later redeemed by raising funds overseas. This made it possible to keep the domestic capital market open for private enterprises.

At the same time, Japan established a commercial banking system at an early stage of the Meiji Era to gather and utilize effectively domestic savings and to protect the economy against the inflow of powerful foreign capital. If domestic savings had not been made available to industry, Japan would have to borrow more from foreign countries. In 1882, the Japanese Government formed the Bank of Japan as the central bank and for some time following the establishment the Bank even made loans to private firms on the security of stock in order to furnish funds to individual enterprises and to develop industries.

What deserves particular attention is the fact that Japan imported not only foreign capital but also industrial technology. As in the case of Shibaura Seisakusho, Japanese industrial firms actively absorbed advanced foreign technology. The Oji Paper Company periodically dispatched its engineers to Western countries to learn modern manufacturing methods. Mr. Jun Noguchi, founder of Nippon Chisso Hiryo K. K. (Japan Nitrogenous Fertilizer Co.) travelled in Europe and America and purchased production techniques from advanced nations. He imported ammonium sulphate manufacturing methods just developed by an Italian research institute and succeeded in employing it in a mass production process.

Many joint venture companies were formed. They helped improve not only production techniques but also business management. Rubens said that the greatest merit of direct foreign investments was the introduction of advanced technical know-how, and that it was fortunate for Japan that large foreign enterprises were not transplanted to Japan and did not nip Japanese industries in the bud and stop their development.[1]

Most foreign capital brought into the country by floating bonds overseas was handled by the Yokohama Specie Bank. It was resold to private Japanese firms and spent in importing commodities and technology. If restrictions had been imposed on the use of imported capital, the development of Japanese industries would have been retarded. Besides, it was fortunate for Japan to be able to obtain foreign capital from individual investors. This helped Japan to prevent powerful foreign capital from dominating Japanese industries.

Reubens stated that 'it was lucky for Japan that overseas money markets could supply Japan with the amount and the type of capital it desired. Unfortunately, less developed countries now find it difficult to borrow as much as they need and have either to depend upon financial aid from advanced nations or to cut back their development plans.'[2]

---

[1] E. P. Reubens, 'Foreign Capital and Domestic Development in Japan', in *Economic Growth: Brazil India, Japan*, S. Kuznets, editor, 1955.

[2] *Ibid.*, p. 221.

Finally, Japan's unblemished record of paying its foreign debts without a single default was an important factor enabling Japan to borrow as much foreign capital as it needed.

II. POSTWAR JAPAN'S ATTITUDE TOWARDS FOREIGN CAPITAL IMPORTS

1. Comparison with the Prewar System

From the viewpoint of foreign capital imports, one of the basic differences between the prewar and the postwar systems is the difference caused by the shift from the gold standard to a system of currency controls. Before the Second World War, the amount of foreign capital Japan needed was taken not as equivalent to the deficit on Japan's international accounts but as equivalent to an excess of the public expenditure over revenue or the shortage of funds in the domestic capital market. After the war, funds required for Japan's economic development were furnished by the central bank, and the amount of foreign capital Japan needs has been determined by the deficit on its external accounts.

Another difference is caused by the following fact : before the war, Japan carried out simultaneously armaments and economic development, making it impossible to balance the national budget and forcing the government to raise capital by issuing bonds overseas. Since the war, partly because defence expenditures were small, Japan has been able to maintain a balanced government budget, and this has helped to diminish the heavy reliance on foreign capital.

At the same time, a similarity to the prewar situation can be noticed : during the period from the end of the war to around 1955, Japan did not import much foreign capital on account of restrictions imposed by the Foreign Investment Law intended to maintain Japan's balance of payments equilibrium and to protect domestic industries. Since 1959 the Japanese economy has rapidly expanded ; foreign capital imports started to increase, notably in the form of loans, as restrictions imposed under the Foreign Investment Law began to be relaxed. This change in Japan's postwar foreign capital imports is similar to the change from Japan's small borrowing overseas during the earlier period of Meiji to its heavy dependence upon foreign capital in developing its heavy industries, during and after the Russo-Japanese War. Besides, just as excessive dependence upon foreign capital imports during the decade preceding the outbreak of the First World War was sharply criticized, so the easygoing way of borrowing overseas is now being critically re-examined.

Another important similarity between prewar and postwar policies can be found in Japan's active importation of advanced industrial technology. During and after the Pacific War, Japan lagged behind other nations in industrial technology, just as it was far behind Western nations in this field during the first years of Meiji. In order to make up the lag, Japanese entrepreneurs have actively imported foreign technology. Thus both in the prewar and postwar years, the import of technology and capital went side by side.

2. *Foreign Capital Imports until 1955*

As in the case of Japan's prewar foreign capital imports, we shall divide the postwar inflow of capital into Japan into the period ending 1955 when Japan was cautious in inducing foreign capital and the period after 1955 when Japan's foreign capital imports started to rise. Until 1955, Japan's economy was still in a state of disorganization and confusion. During this period, the Japanese Government severely restricted foreign capital imports because it feared that the subsequent outflow of the earnings of heavy foreign investment [1] would lead to a deterioration of Japan's balance of payments and weaken the Japanese economy. Japan was not alone in this respect, as many other countries followed a similar policy after the Second World War.

For this reason, a Foreign Investment Law was enacted in 1950 in order to check foreign capital inflow. However, Japan was in dire need of foreign capital. It was aid from the United States that supplied Japan's need during the early postwar years. During the five years from 1946 to 1950, the United States provided Japan with financial aids totalling 1·9 billion dollars, equivalent to 70 per cent of total imports during this period.

Despite great efforts, inflation became rampant immediately after the war. It was the so-called 'Dodge Line' that halted the progress of inflation. The Dodge Line was the policy formulated by J. M. Dodge, Chairman and Director of the Detroit Bank and Trust Co.,

---

[1] Foreign investments here include foreign investments by private companies and exclude financial aid from foreign governments or loans from the World Bank or IMF.

who came to Japan to serve as an economic adviser to General MacArthur, the Supreme Commander of the Allied Powers. The Dodge Line sought to attain (1) a balanced national budget, (2) disinflation and (3) economic self-support. By enforcing this policy, inflation was stopped and the exchange rate of the yen was set at ¥360 to the dollar. On this basis, domestic and international commodity prices were more or less brought into balance.

The enforcement of the 'Dodge Line' was as drastic a step as that of the deflationary policy adopted by Matsukata during the Meiji era. The successful enforcement of the Dodge Line laid the foundation for the subsequent development of the Japanese economy.

When the Korean War broke out in 1950, the economy, which had been slowed down by the Dodge Line, picked up. Although Japan's imports continued to exceed exports, its overall current transactions got back into the black in 1953 because of heavy procurement orders received from the U.S. forces. In the preceding year, Japan had joined the IMF and the World Bank, and in 1953 the World Bank extended a $40 million credit to Japan to assist in the construction of thermal power plants. This was the first sizeable foreign capital Japan imported since the end of the First World War.

Against the background of its prewar foreign capital imports, it is interesting to examine how Japan managed to raise industrial funds soon after the war, without relying on foreign capital imports. In 1947, the Rehabilitation Finance Corporation was formed for the purpose of supplying industrial funds badly needed by Japanese industries. The government supplied through this corporation funds necessary for the rehabilitation of industries accounting for 80 per cent of the total equipment investments in coal mining, power generation, fertilizer and steel industries. However, under the deflationary Dodge policy, the corporation ceased to operate. It was reorganized into the Japan Development Bank in April 1951 to engage in a more moderate financial business. Besides, the Bank became a channel through which Japan received credits from the World Bank. Although the operation of the Rehabilitation Finance Corporation was sometimes criticized as inflationary, it must be admitted that its provision of industrial funds played an important role in the postwar rehabilitation of Japan's industries.

In 1949, the Foreign Exchange and Foreign Trade Control Law was enacted and in 1950, the Foreign Investment Law was promulgated. When an investment is made in a foreign country, the ease with which the principal and profit can be remitted home is a decisive factor.

Under the Foreign Investment Law, the Japanese Government permitted the investment of foreign capital 'only when the foreign capital investment contributes to the attainment of self-sufficiency and the healthy development of the Japanese economy and also to the improvement of Japan's balance of payments situation'. The law guaranteed the remittance of the principal and profit overseas regardless of Japan's foreign exchange position, once the investment was permitted under the law. In other words, foreign investment had to satisfy two conditions: (1) it must contribute to the improvement of Japan's international accounts and to the development of its key industries and public utility services, and (2) it should not impede Japan's postwar economic rehabilitation and development, and the contract for foreign investment should not contain illegal or unfair clauses. Since at the beginning emphasis was laid on the first condition severe restrictions were imposed on foreign investment in Japan.

3. *After*

After 1955, technical know-how came to be actively imported especially in the field of the electrical appliances, synthetic fibres, petrochemical and automobile industries, and huge investments were started in plant modernization and rationalization. Since 1960, the government 'national income doubling plan' greatly stimulated the economic expansion of Japan. Japan's foreign exchange holdings have steadily increased, and the competitive power of Japanese industries in international trade has been substantially enhanced. As import liberalization made progress, the demand for the liberalization of foreign capital inflows has also become stronger. In order to meet these circumstances, the restrictions imposed under the Foreign Investment Law have been relaxed several times since 1959. In permitting foreign investment, emphasis is now laid on the condition that it does not adversely affect the Japanese economy rather than on its positive contribution to the development of the Japanese economy. Today, investment of foreign capital is usually permitted so long as (1) it does not put excessive pressure on small-sized industries, (2) it does not seriously disturb industrial order, and (3) it does not seriously impede the development of a new industrial technique which has been recently

TABLE 3

FOREIGN CAPITAL IMPORT

(Units: Import of Technology — Number of Contracts permitted, All others — Million Dollars.)

Fiscal Year	Imports of Technology	Shares Direct Investment	Shares Portfolio Investment	Shares Total	Yen Bond	Certificate of Investment Trusts	Medium and Long Term Loans	Bonds Issued Overseas	Grand Total
1950	27	2·6	0·6	3·2	—	—	—	—	3·2
1951	101	11·6	1·7	13·3	—	—	4·0	—	17·3
1952	133	7·2	3·0	10·1	0·0	0·1	34·5	—	44·8
1953	103	2·7	2·3	5·0	—	0·6	49·4	—	54·9
1954	82	2·5	1·5	4·0	—	0·0	15·3	—	19·3
1955	72	2·3	2·8	5·1	0·0	0·1	47·1	—	52·2
1956	144	5·4	4·2	9·5	0·0	0·1	93·7	—	103·3
1957	118	7·3	4·2	11·5	0·0	0·1	124·0	—	135·6
1958	90	3·7	7·6	11·4	0·0	0·1	231·5	30·0	273·6
1959	153	14·6	12·5	27·0	0·0	0·2	127·6	—	154·9
1960	327	31·6	42·6	74·2	0·0	0·6	127·1	9·8	211·7
1961	320	40·2	75·7	115·9	0·1	1·3	387·6	72·4	577·3
1962	328	22·6	142·1	164·7	0·1	0·7	358·4	155·0	678·8
1963	565	42·7	142·6	185·3	0·2	0·8	503·9	194·1	884·3
Total	2,563	196·8	443·5	640·3	0·5	4·7	2,104·0	461·3	3,210·8
Percentage		(30·7)	(69·3)	(100·0) 19·9	0	0·2	65·5	14·4	100·0

Source: *Foreign Capital Import Year-Book, 1964.*

160

commercialized or is about to be commercialized in Japan. When these conditions are satisfied, and a contract does not include a clause or clauses unfavourable for the Japanese party, the government does not instruct the parties to suspend or to change the contract.

In short, under the Foreign Investment Law, investment of foreign capital is now approved so long as it does not seriously affect the national economy. While the law formerly sought to encourage only desired types of foreign capital to flow into Japan, it now aims at alleviating shocks which may be caused by foreign capital import and at preventing or minimizing friction between domestic and imported capital.

Since direct foreign investments are more or less restricted, the rapidly expanding Japanese economy now requires more loans from abroad.

Just as investment bonds were the principal form of Japan's prewar foreign capital imports, so loans are now by far the most important form of its foreign capital inflow. Nearly 60 per cent of the total loans Japan raised overseas is furnished by the World Bank and the Export-Import Bank of the United States; the remaining 40 per cent is obtained from U.S. commercial banks. However, imported foreign capital now accounts only for 3 or 4 per cent of the total equipment investment in Japan. As the Japanese power and steel industries use more imported foreign capital in plant modernization and expansion, foreign capital accounts for nearly 10 per cent in their case.

Over the past several years, the periodic deficit on Japan's current account caused by a rapid expansion of the economy has been made up by the surplus on its capital transaction account. Against this background, some observers have warned against Japan's excessive dependence on foreign capital and particularly the large-scale reliance on short-term loans to finance industrial expansion.

Others contend that Japan is no longer an underdeveloped country and that it is quite natural that Japan should import foreign capital to finance its economic growth just as the United States did in the past. They maintain that Japan should continue its efforts to promote its economic growth while basic conditions are favourable for growth and that in the course of time Japan will eventually change from a debtor to a creditor country. They reason that to retard the nation's economic growth in order to save on foreign capital imports is unwise because it will unnecessarily reduce growth.

It may be recalled that similar discussions took place during the

Capital Movements and Economic Development

TABLE 4

BALANCE OF PAYMENTS

(In millions of dollars)

Fiscal Year	Current Account Balance (1)	Capital Account Balance (2) = (6)+(7)	Errors and Omissions (3)	Overall Balance (4) = (1)+(2)+(3)	Nominal GNP Growth Rate
1957	− 90	− 94	75	− 109	9·2
1958	500	− 35	− 120	345	2·4
1959	193	155	39	387	21·0
1960	− 69	677	28	636	16·6
1961	− 1,003	630	− 63	− 436	20·9
1962	66	326	90	302	8·9
1963	− 822	870	− 95	− 47	16·3
1964	50	157	−173	34	—

Source : Bank of Japan, Monthly Reports.

TABLE 5

CAPITAL TRANSACTION ACCOUNT

(In millions of dollars)

Fiscal Year	Long-term Receipts (5)	Long-term Balance (6)	Short-term Balance (7)
1957	− 43	− 10	− 84
1958	149	90	− 125
1959	132	− 27	182
1960	156	1	676
1961	384	174	456
1962	476	297	29
1963	787	474	396
1964	730	323	− 166

Source : Bank of Japan, Monthly Reports.

period from the Russo-Japanese War to the First World War. At that time, the government's heavy reliance upon foreign capital was severely criticized. But there were some who were of the opinion that if the government had not imported foreign capital, the shortage of domestic capital could not have been met.

During the period from 1906 to 1911, the government redeemed bonds issued in the domestic market totalling more than 700 million yen by floating bonds overseas and returned the funds which had been collected by the government for war purposes to the private sector. At that time Korekiyo Takahashi, a retired minister, commented on this step as follows :

'The present government as well as newspapers and magazines contend that the heavy foreign capital imports by the former government are now making the people "frivolous", and causing imports to exceed exports and that eventually the nation will go bankrupt. But the former government borrowed overseas simply to replace domestic war bonds by foreign bonds. This has made it possible for the government to supply funds for the development of private industry and commerce. Since the government could not return a sufficient amount of funds to the private sector, private firms sold debentures and cities floated municipal bonds overseas. As a result, Japan's foreign trade has been expanding, and its exports are increasing at a higher rate.'[1]

Along the same line, Reubens commented as follows :

'To curtail development in order to avoid further foreign borrowing, at a time when outside capital continued to be available, would have amounted to throwing out the industrialization "baby" in order to keep its bath water clean.'

The advocacy of increased foreign capital imports seems to have been persuasive. Large-scale investments in plant modernization and rationalization under the government's expansionary economic policy, supported by foreign capital imports, have enabled Japan to increase its exports by about 15 per cent each year since 1959. While proponents of this policy admit that foreign capital imports involve a risk, they maintain that Japanese industry has now adequate production techniques and managerial ability to take this risk, and that Japan cannot hope to achieve economic growth without taking such a risk. While supporting this basic principle, the majority now is inclined to take the view that Japan should reduce its dependence on foreign borrowings by carefully examining the continued availability of foreign capital and Japan's capacity for absorbing imported capital. And the Japanese Government is now (1965) modifying its policy along this line.

In connection with the liberalization of commodity imports and capital transactions which have taken place since 1960, the inflow of European and American capital into Japan on a large scale became

[1] Yasuzo Horie, *op. cit.*, p. 107–108.

the subject of serious discussions. Today, imports of technology often take the form of joint ventures, because (1) the export of industrial technology alone is not so profitable and, on the contrary, may strengthen the competitive power of the importing country; (2) exports of technology often take the form of the supply of know-how rather than on a patent royalty basis, and unless the exporter participates in the management of the importing firm, the benefits of the exporting firm are not guaranteed; and (3) the joint venture approach has the advantage in securing future markets in Japan. As a result, the participation of foreign firms in management of Japanese enterprises and the percentage of capital which foreign firms should be allowed to invest in a Japanese company became widely discussed

TABLE 6

JAPANESE EXPORTS : 1957–1964

Fiscal Year	Exports (in millions of dollars)	Change Over Previous Year (in per cent)
1957	2,951	—
1958	2,849	-3·5
1959	3,425	20·2
1960	3,920	14·5
1961	4,123	5·2
1962	4,874	18·2
1963	5,567	14·2
1964	7,036	26·5

topics. So far, the Japanese Government has approved, in principle, the formation of joint venture companies only when the share of investment held by foreigners is not more than 49 per cent and when the president of the joint venture is Japanese. The government has made it clear, however, that it will not approve the import of industrial technology for 'underdeveloped' or strategic domestic industries.

The question arises how Japan should tackle this problem if and when the Foreign Investment Law is repealed in the course of the continuing liberalization of capital transactions and if foreign capital in large amounts wants to come into the country. The entry of powerful U.S. corporations into France, West Germany and the United Kingdom, notably in the automobile industry, has become a serious problem to these European countries. It is natural that the Japanese industry should be apprehensive about the same problem.

Conflicts among national interests have often occurred, however. Moreover, it has never been so difficult as today to make a clear-cut distinction between politics and economics. It may be attributed to nationalism. But the prevention of the development of a country's infant industries or technologies by powerful foreign capital is as undesirable as the monopoly of industries by powerful domestic capital. It is most desirable that advanced foreign technologies be absorbed by a country and thus stimulate the development of the country's own industries. Needless to say, to perpetuate uneconomic industries by such measures should be avoided.

But all this may be true and relevant only for a nation which has already accomplished the so-called 'take-off' and which lies somewhere between the advanced and the developing nations. For nations just starting to develop it is necessary to induce foreign enterprises to promote their industrial development. By attracting foreign enterprises, developing nations can learn much about production techniques and business management; in addition, foreign investment sometimes saves social overhead cost. During the Meiji Era, Takashi Masuda, a powerful member of the management of the Mitsui Zaibatsu once said: 'I have told foreigners to come to Japan and start industries, and that there will be no better country than Japan to develop industries. I think Japan should develop industries, but we have neither sufficient capital nor enough brains. So let foreigners come and develop industries. It does not matter who will do it, foreigners or Japanese. In this way we can transplant industries into Japan.'[1] This was in 1907.

Imports of industrial technology have greatly helped to develop the Japanese economy. However, it cannot be denied that technology imports have implanted in the mind of the Japanese the idea that it is easier to import already developed foreign technology than to develop new technology at home. It is true that in a country like Japan where competition among enterprises is extremely keen, the earlier the import of new technology, the stronger becomes the enterprise. Thus, in fierce competition among Japanese manufacturers in the import of technical know-how for making polypropylene, they approached Montecatini of Italy so eagerly and so frequently that their efforts gave birth to a Japanese phrase 'Pilgrimage to the Montecatini Temple'. Likewise, in the case of a tetraethyl lead, while Japanese engineers had almost developed its manufacturing method, several Japanese companies competed in

[1] *The 65 Year History of Shibaura Seisakusho*, p. 54.

TABLE 7

IMPORTS OF TECHNOLOGY

(Unit: Number of Contracts Authorized)

Fiscal Year	1949–1951	'52	'53	'54	'55	'56	'57	'58	'59	'60	'61	'62	'63	Total
Electric Machinery	16	24	43	22	17	20	29	26	39	99	59	82	122	598
Transportation Machinery	7	8	8	7	8	12	2	6	6	17	24	17	4	124
Other Machinery	42	38	19	14	16	20	25	23	31	71	101	95	272	766
Metal	10	18	8	4	7	18	11	12	25	19	27	22	16	195
Chemical	31	16	14	22	7	46	30	11	33	77	59	82	93	532
Textile	4	5	7	8	1	12	7	3	8	8	23	3	16	104
Others	18	26	5	5	6	16	14	9	12	36	27	27	41	263
Total	128	133	103	82	72	144	118	90	153	327	320	328	564	2,562

Source: *Foreign Capital Import Year-Book, 1964.*

importing the same technique just to beat their rivals. Fortunately their efforts were stopped by the control exercised under the Foreign Investment Law. The fact that this control mechanism has been repeatedly employed as a powerful means of modifying investments in plant and equipment demonstrates how eager Japanese manufacturers have been to import foreign technology.

As Table 7 shows, imports of technology have been concentrated in such growing industries as electronics, machinery and chemicals.

TABLE 8

PAYMENTS ON CAPITAL IMPORTS

(Unit : Thousand Dollars)

Fiscal Year	Payment for Foreign Technology	Dividends, Interest and Repatriation on			Principal and Interest on Loans	Total
		Shares	Corporate Bonds	Total		
1951	5,343	734	—	734	24	6,101
1952	8,156	1,860	—	1,860	838	10,854
1953	11,467	2,899	8	2,907	3,564	17,938
1954	13,011	4,035	17	4,052	6,120	23,183
1955	17,963	4,435	22	4,457	8,313	30,733
1956	28,417	5,738	25	5,763	24,182	58,363
1957	39,439	6,556	39	6,596	18,765	64,799
1958	43,370	4,723	35	4,758	25,047	74,174
1959	54,196	6,039	43	6,083	42,121	102,401
1960	83,466	20,036	47	20,083	64,925	168,474
1961	98,228	17,067	85	17,152	82,884	198,264
1962	104,492	27,523	194	27,717	110,847	234,056
1963	123,929	54,118	134	54,252	154,154	332,335
Total	632,472	155,765	648	156,413	541,785	1,330,676

Source : *Foreign Capital Imports Year-Book, 1964.*

At the same time, there have been many cases where Japan had to import foreign know-how even though it developed the same technology domestically, because the foreign technology had been already patented. This type of imports accounted for about 40 per cent of total imports of know-how at the end of 1960.

Table 8 above shows that prices Japan has paid for its imports of foreign technology were almost as large as the total debt service payment during the same period. This fact gives a clear indication how technology imports are actively continued in Japan.

Foreign technology imports are now contributing much to keep out imports of similar products and to strengthen the competitive position of Japanese industries as well as to the effective use of foreign capital.

However, as in the case of foreign capital imports, Japan's heavy dependence upon technology imports is now being re-examined. The medium-term economic plan (1964–68) of the government emphasizes the necessity of expanding basic scientific research because the existing gap between Japan and foreign countries in the technological levels is being narrowed but the gap in the ability of developing original ideas and techniques is still large. So far Japan has been able to combine imported know-how and relatively cheap and abundant but efficient labour and thus develop a strong competitive position in international markets. Now that the wage levels are rising and labour supply is beginning to be scarce it has become all the more necessary for Japan to develop its own technology.

Japan's basic attitude towards foreign capital imports both before and after the Second World War is characterized by its intense and continuous consciousness that foreign debts and interest must be paid. Another distinctive feature is that foreign capital has always been treated within the framework of the government's policy for the development of domestic industries. At the same time, the success of Japan's imports of foreign capital must be attributed in a large measure to the readiness of Japanese entrepreneurs to take reasonable risks and their eagerness to learn new production and management techniques from their partners.

COMMENTS ON THE PAPER BY DR. OKITA AND DR. MIKI

BY

JOHN S. DE BEERS
Inter-American Development Bank

THE most interesting aspect of an essay in economic history and contemporary economic problems in a particular country is its applicability elsewhere. Can general principles be derived, or is the case unique in some way so that its lessons cannot be used elsewhere? Clearly neither end of the spectrum of possible answers to these questions is valid.

The authors are very restrained in treating their topic. They do not assert that other countries should follow Japan's example or even necessarily seek to avoid its mistakes. Perhaps our general discussion, being removed from the country under review, can be more free to speak of conclusions that might be drawn.

I. THE SPECIAL CHARACTERISTICS OF THE JAPANESE SITUATION

Based on this paper I would also stress the importance, in a growth context, of the strong Japanese traditions of self-discipline, loyalty, obedience and the willingness to put up with deprivations and austerity programmes.

Apparently the body of educated persons — at least around 1900 — was relatively larger than in many of the newer underdeveloped countries, and perhaps the Japanese educational background was a better background to business and productive activity than is that offered by the traditional curriculum elsewhere, if I may make a conjecture on which further discussion would be interesting.

The national character traits evidently had much to do with Japan's very high propensity to save and hence its extraordinary capacity to finance investment from internal resources. The national character also may explain 'Japan's proud record of non-default in paying its foreign debts' which the authors correctly cite as an important factor in opening up the possibilities of external borrowing.

It would be wrong of course to suggest that other poor countries do not share some of the characteristics of the Japan of 50 to 75 years ago. I conclude, however, that these were *special* characteristics, in degree if not in kind, and that they have affected the results obtained from foreign capital and the Japanese treatment of such capital.

II. INTERESTING ASPECTS OF JAPAN'S EXPERIENCE

A. *Virtual Rejection of Capital Inflow Before 1900.* The experience during the Meiji restoration (and earlier) seems to show that the policy in regard to receiving foreign capital was based not so much on purely economic considerations as on worries about international political risks. In the last thirty years of the nineteenth century, it seems that Japan could successfully achieve much economic development without foreign assistance — and without the benefit of a formal theory of economic development. Presumably the economic growth could have been more rapid with the aid of additional real resources from abroad channelled into investment. One might ask, however, whether there was absorptive capacity to utilize effectively additional investment, without too much of a drop in the yield schedule. Would the increased productivity of such additional investment have exceeded the service burden on the external capital?

B. *Emphasis on Bonds and Borrowing After 1900.* The reliance on bonds and loans rather than equities appears also to have been based primarily on political rather than economic considerations. We are told, however, that the Industrial Bank of Japan was used to attract an inflow of capital under more advantageous terms than individual firms would have been able to obtain, and the capital from abroad was needed to meet the shortage of domestic capital so economic considerations did enter into policy decisions. I find no reference here, however, to the theme frequently debated in recent years, that equity capital is more expensive because of heavy service payments and hence that loans are to be preferred.

One 'modern' aspect of the Japanese debate sixty years ago was the use of the Industrial Bank of Japan as a channel to direct foreign capital into the most desirable uses, both among the private firms and among the various governmental bodies. This reliance on a financial intermediary was apparently not only to interpose a higher standard of judgment than that of the market but also to take advantage of a better credit standing of the national institution and to reduce the danger of foreign intervention in Japanese industries.

The use of external borrowing to relieve the pressure on the domestic money market is also interesting in view of the prevalence of situations of inflation rather than of credit stringency. Another special difference of the Japanese economy is brought out here also : the fact that there was a capital market at all in the early 1900's. Most countries in a similar stage of development today probably do not have a capital market in the same sense.

C. *The Productive Use of Foreign Capital.* Some sixty years ago, the authors tell us, 'all circles in Japan except a few government leaders were opposed to the floating of bonds overseas to raise funds for armament or for other non-productive purposes'. A similar philosophy, this time with government sanction, was expressed in the Foreign Investment Law of 1950, and the authors seem to accept this common-sense view. Mr. Schweitzer and Mr. Friedman alluded in their remarks at the opening of this Conference to 'investment productivity' and the 'accumulation of worthwhile assets'.

These references and their implications bring us directly to one of the major issues of foreign capital in relation to economic development, namely the controversy on the project loan or directed use of foreign investment versus programme lending.

The main point I wish to make is that the analytical conclusion will depend almost entirely on one's assumptions as to the planning mechanism. If, as in Japan during the Russo-Japanese War, the government was determined to spend large sums on armaments, sacrificing many other objectives, then the external financing of an investment (economic or otherwise) with the very highest productivity and hence one that would have been carried out in any case, merely releases resources for some marginal use (military or otherwise) on the government's scale of priorities. Of course the government might assign some fraction of the additional marginal resources to industry as well as armaments but the presumption in war-time is that the military would get most of the benefit. It is as if one were to buy bread for an alcoholic who would then buy less bread and in effect convert most of the funds into liquid form.

Much the same analysis applies to a country with strong central planning, especially if it is intelligently operated. It would make little difference in economic analysis whether external capital went into productive or so-called non-productive uses, if one assumes that any inflow of foreign capital is subject to the review and control of the same planners who control the use of domestic investment resources.

We come to the controversial area, however, when we consider assumptions that correspond to the realities of most underdeveloped nations. The planning staff may consist of one or two dozen bureaucrats — or possibly several hundred — whose technical skill, general omniscience and power to enforce decisions may be limited in many ways. Under these conditions a different model should be constructed. In this case an international movement of capital may discover and develop an investment opportunity that was overlooked or incorrectly appraised, and the financing of a project may in fact change the structure of new investment. This is the 'leverage' of foreign capital. It may not always be welcomed — especially when it goes counter to political wishes — and in its turn may not always be 'correct' in its appraisals.

Probably this latter framework was what the authors of the 1950 Japanese Investment Law had in mind. They expected external capital to come in and choose certain fields, and the Law was intended to assure that the priorities assigned by the foreign investors were consistent with general guidelines of the government. Evidently the thought was that the planning process would not be complete or compelling, that foreign capital would have an influence, and hence that it was appropriate to control its influence in various ways.

DISCUSSION OF THE PAPER BY DR. OKITA AND DR. MIKI

THE discussion of the paper centred on : (1) Dr. Okita's proposal for an 'earnings fund', (2) inflation and (3) characteristics of different types of loans.

Capital Movements and Economic Development

I. The 'Okita Fund'

Dr. Okita proposed that enterprises in developing countries owned jointly by foreign companies and domestic investors might deposit earnings in a fund in local currency (e.g. pesos). The government of the foreign investor's home country would then pay the parent company its share of earnings in the currency of that country (e.g. dollars) and would either be reimbursed by transfer from the local fund in the host country or could use the fund for soft loans or grants in the developing country. The purpose would be to avoid accusations of exploitation associated with joint ventures, and to encourage entry of foreign technology and managerial skills. The main purpose of such a scheme would be to attract foreign managerial skills for the development of small and medium industries supplying the potential export markets.

Professor Singer noted that Dr. Okita's scheme may work adversely since foreign firms, formerly willing to re-invest earnings in the host country, might be unable to resist the new opportunities for repatriation. *Professor Wallich* indicated that a similar type of scheme using foreign holding companies had been proposed for the United States but had not been adopted. *Dr. Adler* suggested that, for tax reasons, there was the possibility of the Okita Fund being invested in a third country rather than in the host country. He also suggested that the scheme would be more acceptable if funds paid to the parent corporation by the parent government would have otherwise been given to the host country in the form of grants or aid. *Dr. Patel* observed that one disadvantage of the Okita Fund scheme would be the extra cost involved. On the other hand, he thought the scheme preserved the advantages of private capital movements while avoiding their disadvantages.

II. Inflation

A second issue discussed was the possibility that capital imports might cause inflation. *Professor Singer* suggested that capital inflows will not be inflationary where the recipient country changes its investment programme to provide for local investment costs and indirect costs of investment coming from abroad. In fact, there must be two development programmes, not one. One should reflect development patterns in the absence of capital inflow, and the other should take into account the presence of capital equipment brought in from abroad. They would be based on two different assumptions about the levels of available capital. *Professor Delivanis* pointed out that failure to use immediately capital imports for productive purposes is not a sufficient condition of inflation. Two additional assumptions are needed. These are: (a) the economy has reached full employment, and (b) supplementary demand is directed only to home-made products. Inflation will not necessarily result from capital inflow if it is possible to channel the supplementary demand into imported goods. *Professor Rosenstein-Rodan* concurred with Professor Singer, and noted that the danger of inflation arising from capital imports could be averted if such imports would cover not only the direct costs of projects, but also indirect costs (as those of working capital) and the increase in domestic demand resulting from the multiplier effects of the investment.

Professor Kafka asked whether concern for the inflationary effects of capital imports was primarily concern with absolute price level increases, or with changes in relative prices accompanying the inflation. In this connection, *Dr. Onitiri* suggested that an economy with an extensive subsistence sector needs a shift in relative prices in order to draw this sector into the local market. Since living standards in the subsistence sector lag behind those in the rest of the economy, some inflation and relative price shifts may draw the sector out. It is necessary, therefore, to look at the structure of the entire economy before assessing the inflationary effects of capital imports.

III. Characteristics of Different Types of Loans

Among the other topics discussed was that of project *v.* programme type loans. *Professor Singer* suggested that the tying of technical assistance to specific projects is an illusion. It is better to tie it to the total productivity of the economy. *Professor Rosenstein-Rodan* noted that programme loans are superior to project loans, but if programmes are non-existent, project loans are all right. *Dr. Patel* remarked that where a programme does not exist, the content of projects must be expanded to include indirect costs and effects.

Another issue raised was that of the relative merits of equity and loan capital. *Professor Kafka* observed that most people seem to think that equity finance was more expensive than loan finance in terms of its foreign exchange cost. Brazil's experience of a 3·2 per cent transferred return (in relation to the inflow of new foreign equity capital since 1947 excluding the reinvestment of retained profits) would raise doubts that equity finance is necessarily more expensive than loan finance. *Professor Rosenstein-Rodan* said that the short term balance of payments transfer burden poses a different problem from that of final repayment of long-term foreign capital. Equity capital may cost more in the long run though it may actually be worth more to the borrowing country. *Dr. Adler* added that in comparing imports of equity and loan capital, attention should be paid to the high foreign exchange cost of loans. On a 15-year, 5½ per cent loan, this might amount to 10 per cent of the loan principal annually. On the other hand, equity profits are generally ploughed back if profits are good.

Finally, *Professor Wallich* noted the importance of tax policies for

Capital Movements and Economic Development

capital imports. Countries do not seem aware of their implications. For instance, the capital importing country derives an advantage from current United States tax laws under which the host country gets the tax on the returns from American capital while the United States forgoes the tax on such returns if a tax has been imposed already. Further, the need for tax and administrative measures to encourage local participation in establishing local affiliates or subsidiaries of foreign firms is often not realized. Foreign promoters, for instance, may find it difficult to distribute shares locally because organized capital markets do not exist.

Chapter 4

PHILOSOPHY OF INTERNATIONAL INVESTMENT IN THE SECOND HALF OF THE TWENTIETH CENTURY[1]

BY

P. N. ROSENSTEIN-RODAN
Massachusetts Institute of Technology

I. A NEW PHILOSOPHY OF INTERNATIONAL INVESTMENT

A NEW analysis — new in the light of the changed economic structure and technology in our era — of the legitimate interests of both the investing or creditor, and the receiving or debtor countries is needed. The present spoken or unspoken rules of behaviour in the field of international investment are largely based on the economic structure of the past century. At that time they may have represented an area of common interest of both the creditor and debtor countries. Such an area undoubtedly still exists, but its configuration may well be different today. Let us find out what it is. The description of a newly established harmony of interests may help to avoid conflicts arising from misunderstanding and suggest guide-lines on conduct and policy with respect to future investments of both the developed and the underdeveloped countries.

An articulate up-to-date philosophy of international investment would influence thinking. It should deal with problem areas, not with norms; it should not deal with cases but with principles resulting from them. If the new philosophy of international investment clearly identified the area and the confines of a new harmony of interests it could have a moral power of persuasion which would gradually permeate the rules of conduct in this field.

---

[1] The problem area described in this memorandum will form the subject matter of an international inquiry organized by ICAP (Inter-American Committee of the Alliance for Progress).

Capital Movements and Economic Development

II. CHANGES IN ECONOMIC STRUCTURE AND IN THE
NATURE OF FOREIGN INVESTMENT

(1) *Changes in Economic Structure* since the nineteenth century will be described under three points : (i) different composition ('gearing' or 'leverage') of international investment today ; (ii) why the transfer problem is more difficult today ; and (iii) new forms of partnership (joint ventures, gradual national majority ownership, management contracts, etc.)

(2) *Different Composition of International Investment in Underdeveloped Countries.* (a) The foreign capital inflow in the nineteenth century was to the extent of two-thirds or three-fourths in bond form and only one-fourth or one-third in the form of equity. Today private international bond investment has shrunk to infinitesimal proportions and public credit or aid has taken its place. It is highly doubtful whether a substantial private international bond market for underdeveloped countries can be re-established. The overwhelming majority of what is today called 'private international investment' is in equity form.

(b) Remuneration of equity investment is in general between 15 and 24 per cent before taxes and 10–15 per cent after taxes. Bond credit, on the other hand, costs from 5–6 per cent. To those lower bond costs, additional costs for complementary technical assistance in some sectors would have to be added.

(c) In the nineteenth century equity investment was said to have the special advantage of being adjustable to cyclical fluctuations ; a zero dividend could be declared in a bad year. Bonds, on the other hand, carried the fixed annual charge whose burden was very much heavier in the years of crisis.

The ratio of benefits between equity and bond has changed markedly in our age. Cyclical fluctuations are nowadays much less intensive and of far shorter duration. The advantage of declaring a zero on low dividend has still some, but very much lower, weight than it used to have previously. In other words, bond credit had become relatively more attractive to underdeveloped countries than equity investment.

(d) Equity investment carries a higher remuneration and therefore a higher transfer burden. Since the transfer burden is heavier today (see (3) below) while the scarcity of technological knowledge is smaller, a change in the 'optimal' distribution of bond and equity among different sectors may be envisaged.

176

Equity investment brings with it not only capital but also know-how. One hundred years ago underdeveloped countries may have had to pay a high price for management and know-how they did not possess. Even a high profit for know-how to build railways, other public utilities, electric power stations, etc., may have been eminently worthwhile. Today the knowledge and the technology of how to build public utilities is well known and standardized. A lot of this knowledge is accessible to all and an experienced foreign engineer can be hired for 20,000 to 30,000 dollars annual salary. In those fields, therefore, foreign equity investment would seem to carry an excessive burden. On the other hand, in new industries know-how and management is not generally accessible and a high price to be paid for them may be eminently worthwhile. In between the standardized and the widely variegated technology in different sectors there may be some intermediate sectors (for instance steel mills, oil refineries, etc.) in which the plant's design and management is not completely standardized but in which the variety of design is limited. In those cases new forms of international investment may be appropriate (for instance, management contracts with or without a minority holding).

(3) *The Transfer Problem* today is more difficult and the need to economize on costs of foreign investment is greater than it was a hundred years ago for two or three reasons :

(*a*) The need to economize on the costs of foreign investment is very much greater than it was one hundred years ago for two reasons :

(i) In the nineteenth century the world economy functioned as an ' engine of growth ' ; an increase of 1 per cent in the GNP of the developed world led to an increase of the derived demand for the export of primary produce from underdeveloped countries of the same amount. Today, technological progress in developed countries, economizing in raw materials, producing substitutes and sometimes their own (competitive and non-competitive) primary produce, a 1 per cent increase in the GNP of the developed world only leads to an increase in derived demand for exports of underdeveloped countries of 0·5 per cent or 0·6 per cent. The ability of underdeveloped countries to transfer the debt service and profits is thus proportionately less than it was in the nineteenth century.

(ii) The rate of growth in the developed countries was moreover 2·5–3 per cent in the nineteenth century, while that of under-developed countries was lower. Today the target rate of growth in the underdeveloped countries is 5–5·5 per cent while the developed countries have a lower rate of growth (4 per cent).

(*b*) One institution, which acted as a safety valve for transfer of payment difficulties, i.e. bankruptcy, has practically vanished from the international scene. Defaults in international investment are not accepted anymore without much graver consequences for the defaulter.

(*c*) Partly due to the above two reasons — in addition to the urgency of achieving a high rate of growth, often without sufficient domestic savings — the convertibility of currencies is less firmly established and more difficult to achieve.

It follows from the above considerations that even from a strictly economic point of view the developing country can and should carefully distinguish between sectors in which foreign equity investment is more or less desirable. If two-thirds of the foreign capital inflow were in bond form at 5 per cent and one-third in equity form at the cost of 12 per cent (or say 8 or 9 per cent if 3 or 4 per cent were *always* reinvested in the country) then the combined cost of foreign capital would be 7·33 per cent (or 6 per cent if permanent plough-back of one-third of equity profits is assumed). If the bulk of foreign investment were in equity form, however, the cost of foreign capital would be very much higher ; too high probably to secure the transfer of dividends and occasional repatriation of capital.

(4) *New Forms of Partnership* are desirable in private foreign investment today. Apart from imported capital and know-how it should also promote local entrepreneurship by sponsored or induced imitation, education and participation. Even in those sectors in which foreign equity investment is more desirable a full or majority foreign ownership creates problems. In the longer run a spirit and a form of partnership and joint ventures serves best the interests of both parties. Foreign investors in the majority of cases should envisage to hold only a minority (up to 49 per cent) of equity. Even a minority holding can easily secure a decisive role in the management. In the initial phase foreign investors may hold a higher percentage of equity, but they should offer an option to national investors, or firmly announce their intention to sell some proportion of the shares to them in the future. Other forms of in advance *mutually agreed upon* ' nationalization ' (in the sense of gradual acquisition of a majority holding) should be studied.

Management contracts with or without a minority holding may be an important new form of private international investment in certain sectors (see 2 (*d*)). A foreign firm may construct and manage the plant and receive a management fee which is calculated as a percentage both of profits and of foreign exchange savings realized. At the same time the firm who holds the management contract offers a credit to the national firm (or parastatal agency) covering either the foreign exchange costs or 50 per cent of total investment costs of the project; the duration of this credit is to be equal to the duration of the management contract.

Finally a variety of forms of gearing in different sectors should be examined from the point of view of the economic advantage they bring to the receiving country. For instance, foreign minority holdings of, say, 49 per cent of equity is ' desirable ' if in sector *a* a long-term bond credit is provided in proportion of 1 : 1 per dollar of equity investment while in sectors *b*, *c*, *d* (with a less scarce know-how) this proportion might be 1·5 or 2 or 2·5 dollars per dollar of investment.

(5) *Transfer of Profits, Capital and Capital Gains.* The inquiry into international investment should also carefully consider the problem of transferring profits and the repatriation of capital and capital gains if the project were to be sold. With respect to transfer and repatriation, it may be useful to distinguish between the effectively imported foreign capital and reinvested profits earned thereon and the profits earned on that proportion of total assets which may be related to funds borrowed or otherwise raised locally. Such an analysis may provide useful guide-lines for transfer arrangements for new international investments.

(6) *Conclusion.* The arguments presented in section II lead to the conclusion that it may be in the common interest of developed and underdeveloped countries to aim at a certain proportion of foreign equity and bond investment. Since a high proportion of foreign capital inflow is desirable in bond form it is only natural that those sectors where technological managerial know-how is not so rare should be financed by this form of credit, while the more expensive equity investment should be preferred in those sectors where the complementary input of know-how is comparatively larger. Governments may therefore announce as a part of their development policy which are the more and the less desirable sectors for foreign equity investment. Different forms of gearing ('leverage') between foreign bond and equity may be listed as general conditions for investment in ' less desirable ' sectors. In addition to those functional economic considerations, governments may also declare and reserve

certain sectors as closed to foreign equity investment for political reasons.

III. RECONCILIATION OF MICRO- AND MACRO-ECONOMIC INTERESTS IN INTERNATIONAL INVESTMENT

While a certain proportion between bond and equity investment is desirable for the country as a whole, it naturally need not and cannot obtain in investment in specific sectors or projects. The over-all proportion can be realized for instance if some sectors are wholly financed by bond-credit (public utilities and infra-structures), some fully by equity investment while some may be financed by differently geared equity and bond capital.

The interest of the underdeveloped country to maintain a certain balance between equity and bond investment (as well as a certain proportion between short-, medium- and long-term credit) in her *over-all* foreign capital inflow does not correspond to the interests and motivations of investors in individual *single* projects. A foreign firm prepared to build and take equity in one factory does not know and cannot be expected to be responsible for the ' complementary ' bond credit which is necessary for the underdeveloped country, not in the majority of cases for the same project, if the over-all proportion is to be reached. Different economic units take (or do not take) such investment decisions. To make every one foreign investor's decision depend on decisions of his government or those of other investors from his country would put an unbearable burden on negotiation and hinder desirable international investment. Yet every foreign loan to (investment in) a project constitutes in reality *two* operations, or has two joint effects : (*a*) a loan to the project, (*b*) a contribution (sufficient or insufficient) to the balance of payments of the country. Private investors are only aware of the first of the two effects ; government should be aware of both. How to reconcile the two effects, without weakening private incentives is an important task of development policy.

COMMENTS ON THE PAPER BY PROFESSOR
ROSENSTEIN-RODAN

BY

PROFESSOR H. W. SINGER
Williams College

MY first difficulty arises at the very first footnote of Professor Rosenstein-Rodan's contribution, which he does not call a paper but a memorandum. A memorandum is defined by the dictionary as a short note written to remind someone to do something about a defined matter. I am not quite clear after repeated reading of this memorandum who is to be reminded to do what about what, but I know that Professor Rosenstein-Rodan can answer this question because this memorandum, prepared several months ago, presumably already has a history of action following it. As an innocent reader not being aware of the history and action behind it I was a little bit in the dark about its direct purpose, facing a slightly Kafkaesque situation — I do not refer to our colleague who is here with us now.

My second problem, also, on which I have a question is the term 'harmony of interests'. This term occurs twice on the first page. Now I can picture the existence of a basic harmony of interests between the governments of the richer countries and the governments of the poorer countries. That in fact is what we talk about when we talk about reasons for aid. I can picture a harmony of interest between the private entrepreneurs of an underdeveloped country and the government of an underdeveloped country. I find it more difficult to picture a basic harmony of interests between the private entrepreneurs of a foreign country and the government of an underdeveloped country, because in that case I would have to be told more precisely what we mean when we speak of 'the private investor'. Legally, the shareholder is the owner of a private firm. In other words, when we talk about du Pont de Nemours theoretically we speak about the widow of the executive living in Chicago who depends on dividends from her shares of du Pont de Nemours for her subsistence. Or we speak of the pension fund for retired university teachers which has invested in du Pont de Nemours. Now frankly in that sense the concept of harmony of interests is very remote. I do not think the widow of the executive in Chicago, or even the retired university teacher has a direct and strong community of interests or harmony of interests with the government of Peru, of Bolivia, or any other country in which du Pont de Nemours may be active. Hence presumably we do not mean the legal owner of the private firm — we must have in mind some other corporate interest — but whom do we really have in mind? I remember

181

in the early 1930's a much quoted statement by Lord Mond who at that time was Chairman of the Board of Directors of ICI, the British equivalent of du Pont de Nemours. When he was once reminded of what would your shareholders say he made a reply which at that time became quite classic 'The shareholders are the people who know nothing, do nothing and get nothing'. I don't know whether today it is still possible to argue like this.

There is a third point on which I follow along the lines of Professor Leduc. I find that Professor Rosenstein-Rodan's paper distinguishes between bond and equity investment but it does not distinguish between direct and portfolio investment. Now I take it in the paper equity really means direct equity investment. Bonds, you might think, are by definition portfolio investment, although even that is not quite clear because Professor Rosenstein-Rodan makes an interesting proposal, namely, of a management contract tied in with a credit to the new firm in the underdeveloped country which looks to me very much like a form of direct bond investment. The distinction between portfolio and direct investment cuts across the other distinction. Would it not be possible or desirable to, shall we say, develop portfolio equity investment in under-developed countries? Is that excluded? It seems to be excluded from our discussion.

One assumption of the paper is that cyclical fluctuations are nowadays much less intensive and for that reason it is assumed that the built-in waiver which is implied in equity financing is less important now than it used to be. I have a reservation here. Certainly cyclical fluctuations are less important than before 1914, but the statistics do not show that, shall we say, average fluctuations in export earnings of underdeveloped countries have become any less marked now than they were in the nineteenth century. In other words, there must have been some other new element that maintains these fluctuations. Since cyclical fluctuations in industrial countries are obviously less important now, there must have been some other compensating factors.

There is another basic assumption (found after paragraph 2(*d*)) that the lack of technological knowledge is smaller nowadays than it used to be and this in turn is supposed to remove some of the attraction from equity financing, and thus reduce the validity of the cost differential between equity and bonds in so far as this differential represents payment for technology or technical knowledge. Here also I find myself with a reservation. Certainly the stock of available technological knowledge has rapidly increased. This increase is presumably more or less a one-way street — but is this relevant? You could certainly argue, and many people are arguing today, that the present technology is much less useful in terms of technology adapted to the needs and factor proportions of the now underdeveloped countries. They have at their disposal a much lower percentage of the currently available technology as being suitable for them than was the situation 50 or 80 years ago, so there again the situation is not quite clear.

I also believe that Professor Rosenstein-Rodan has omitted from his philosophy, from his comparison of the two centuries, the very vital migration of people. This was obviously vital for the regions of recent settlement. This group of countries included in the nineteenth century, the United States, Canada, Australia, New Zealand, perhaps also Argentina, and so forth, where obviously the tremendous outpouring of people from Europe played a vital part in the transfer of technological knowledge. This transfer was found throughout neither on an equity basis nor on a bond basis, but it came as a free *gift* of technology incorporated in people. I think if we put these two things that I mentioned into the scale I am not too sure whether the emphasis on the greater availability of technology now compared with the nineteenth century is really valid. I am not even sure that the assumption is quite correct that by now the technology used in public utilities is well known and standardized. It obviously cannot be one hundred per cent true when you consider such possibilities as nuclear power plants, desalination of water, application of solar energy or geo-thermal energy for electricity production, new forms of transport like hovercraft or other possible new technologies especially fruitful for underdeveloped countries. Clearly in the field of public utilities there is a sector in which technology is by no means standardized and well known, so I would suggest on this aspect of the argument also a lot more detailed studies would be required. This is not a criticism of Professor Rosenstein-Rodan's paper because I gather it was exactly to get such inquiries started that he wrote his paper.

Now let me come to another point. Dr. Rosenstein-Rodan explains that in the nineteenth century a 1 per cent increase of the GNP of more developed countries produced a roughly 1 per cent increase in import demand for primary products from underdeveloped countries, while nowadays this has shrunk to 0·5 per cent or 0·6 per cent. But I would here also make this one reservation that in our analysis of the statistics of the postwar era we find that there has been no failure of the underdeveloped countries in terms of export volume. Export volume of exports from underdeveloped countries in the period 1950 to 1965 has increased at an average rate of about 5 per cent per annum which is higher than the growth rate of their GNP. Of course, I underline that this is export *volume*. Naturally, this is open to the counter argument that this volume was only saleable at falling prices so that in terms of export proceeds and capacity to import the contrast of the nineteenth and twentieth centuries seems perfectly valid and in that sense trade is no longer the engine of growth for the underdeveloped countries.

I would also raise a further question on the alleged greater transfer difficulty in the twentieth century. While this is certainly basically true, what we must also remember are the increased opportunities for import substitution. In other words, when we look at the question of transfer problems, import substitution is as good as export. The increase in volume of domestic output substituted for imports in underdeveloped countries is very striking and if we put the export volume plus import substitution together we get quite impressive figures.

Skipping some other points, I come to a question which looks to me very important. In Professor Rosenstein-Rodan's arithmetic, he states bonds are 5 to 6 per cent but if you think of underdeveloped countries they really are 6 per cent, since there are not many underdeveloped countries which can raise bond money at 5 per cent. I notice that 6 per cent is a figure which Mr. Gulhati and I believe several others used in their papers. So let us take 6 per cent as the cost of bond financing. For the lack of other information I accept Dr. Rosenstein-Rodan's figure of the cost of equity financing as 12 per cent or as low as 8 per cent if ploughing back of 4 per cent into domestic reinvestment in the underdeveloped countries is assumed. Now the difference between 6 per cent and 8 per cent is not strikingly high. Professor Rosenstein-Rodan's proposal of two-thirds bonds revalued at 6 per cent and one-third in equity valued at 8 per cent (assuming 4 per cent reinvestment), gives you an average cost to the underdeveloped countries of $6\frac{2}{3}$ per cent as against 8 per cent in 100 per cent equity financing. That is a margin of $1\frac{1}{3}$ per cent out of which technical assistance or managerial knowledge is supposed to come. With all due respect, this may be important, because anything that can be done to reduce the repayment burden is important, but it does not strike me as a revolutionary difference. Surely, if we argue quantitatively along those lines, there are a number of other things that are at least equally important and deserve our attention. For instance, if we consider that tying of aid whether to projects or to currency, or both, prevents underdeveloped countries from shopping around for the cheapest or most appropriate supplies, and if we assume that this results in a 20 per cent–25 per cent cost differential for them and that they have to pay 20 per cent–25 per cent more because of this tying, then that would strike me as a problem of a larger order of magnitude than the difference between $6\frac{2}{3}$ per cent cost of financing and 8 per cent.

I mention one other major point on which I think we must also be very careful. It is very fashionable now, and Dr. Rosenstein-Rodan also argues very strongly in the same direction, that we must create a spirit of 'partnership'. The word 'partnership', like 'harmony of interests', is a very emotive word in this respect. The picture of this partnership is usually that of a declining influence of the foreign investor. The foreign investor may be dominant at the beginning, but as quickly as possible he must train local people, he must raise money locally. That of course raises the problem that was so widely emphasized by Dr. Rosenstein-Rodan that, on the one hand, we want a private foreign firm to raise money locally in the name of the spirit of partnership but we certainly do not want the profits on this locally raised money transferred abroad because that certainly does not seem right and it certainly does not fit in with a low transfer capacity of underdeveloped countries.

But I would raise an even more important point. This whole picture of the foreign firm being dominant in the beginning and then gradually reducing its influence, selling shares to local people, training local people ; first having 100 per cent influence then perhaps 70 per cent then at an early point 49 per cent and then gradually petering out — basically this whole concept is not compatible with the other concepts that we used to emphasize more 10 or 15 years ago, i.e., that foreign enterprise must not remain an enclave in the country to which it goes ; that it must become part of the life of the country, and that it must have a continuing stimulating interest. In other words, if we tell private foreign investors that their job is to go in and pull out again as fast as possible, the worry in my mind is : in saying this to them do we not encourage a spirit of making hay while the sun shines, of engaging only in projects that are rapidly yielding? From a development point of view do not we encourage them to pull profit out at an early point when the project is not really viable? There is a latent conflict between the approach that we now adopt and what we originally wanted foreign enterprise in underdeveloped countries to do, and I believe that this latent conflict requires a little more thought ; there may be a lot of trouble if this latent conflict is not recognized and the signals are set to deal with it.

THE ROLE OF INTERNATIONAL MOVEMENTS OF PRIVATE CAPITAL IN PROMOTING DEVELOPMENT

BY

FELIPE PAZOS
Organization of American States

I. TYPES OF CAPITAL TRANSACTIONS

CAPITAL is transferred from savers to investors through different institutional channels and instruments that have different natures and perform different functions.[1] For this reason, a distinction is made in this paper between the different channels through which the international movements of private capital usually flow. A separate treatment is given to each.

The institutional forms involved are basically the same in national and international movements of capital. In both cases, savers may use their funds to finance : (*a*) the purchase or construction of production facilities that will be owned and operated by the savers themselves ; (*b*) the purchase of shares in the property of production facilities that will be operated by persons other than the savers ; (*c*) the acquisition of money claims against persons that are engaged in the construction or operation of production facilities ; and (*d*) the acquisition of money claims against financial intermediaries that will eventually purchase property shares or money claims from persons engaged in the construction or operation of production facilities.

The type of transaction described under (*a*) is generally known as direct investment, particularly when the transaction has an international character. Those described under (*b*), (*c*) and (*d*) are known as portfolio investment when the claims to property or to fixed money amounts are represented by transferable documents freely bought and sold in the market. They do not receive any special name when the claims are created through bilateral negotiations and are not incorporated in negotiable instruments ; for the sake of classification, we call these latter transactions ' contractual

---

[1] The author has profited from useful criticisms made by Walter Sedwitz and E. M. Bernstein to a previous draft of this paper and acknowledges the help received from Peter Jaszi in its preparation, but the opinions expressed are the author's exclusive responsibility.

investments'. Thus we can group capital transactions in three types: (i) direct, (ii) portfolio and (iii) contractual.

Capital transactions can also be classified as equity investments, covering transactions enumerated above under (*a*) and (*b*) or loans, covering those enumerated under (*c*) and (*d*). However, in the course of this paper we will use more frequently the direct-portfolio-contractual classification.

Nature of the Different Types of Capital Transaction

Direct investment is a financial transaction in the sense that it involves the transformation of savings into investment. But it transcends the purely financial sphere and belongs more to the real world of production: direct investment is the construction or enlargement of a plant, the opening or enlargement of a mine, the cultivation of a new field or the intensification of its cultivation. Direct investment is an act of entrepreneurship: it brings together the factors of production in order to produce additional goods and services.

Portfolio and contractual investments, on the other hand, are purely financial phenomena: they are transfers of claims to resources from savers to investors, direct or through financial intermediaries. In fact, it is confusing to give the name ' investment ' to these transactions; it would be much clearer to limit use of the term ' investment ' to the economic activity of expanding production capacity and use another term for the purchase of claims. Following Mrs. Robinson's terminology, we may call them ' placements '.

Direct investment does not involve any transfer of ownership of the resources utilized in the operation. Portfolio and contractual placements are essentially transfers of ownership of resources or claims to resources. In direct investment, the saver himself applies the liquid financial assets he has saved to purchase equipment and land and to pay for the construction of buildings and the installation of equipment. Neither the ownership nor the command of the resources saved changes hands. In portfolio and contractual placements, the saver transfers the ownership or, at least, the effective command of resources to the hands of an intermediary or of a real investor, in exchange for a financial claim.[1] Both types of

---

[1] More strictly, it should be said that the saver transfers the generic command over a certain value of unspecified resources which he has in the form of a non-interest-bearing sight claim against a commercial bank in exchange for an interest-bearing or dividend-yielding financial claim against a real investor or against a financial intermediary.

non-direct transactions are characterized by a change of ownership or command of resources.

Although direct investment does not imply a transfer in the ownership or command of resources, it may involve a transfer in space of such resources if the investment is made in a different area from that in which the income was earned and saved. If a corporation which does its main business in Illinois erects a new manufacturing plant in Los Angeles or in São Paulo, economic resources are transferred from one location to another. There is a transfer of resources through space, although not a transfer in ownership.

In the case of portfolio and contractual placements, there may be a transfer in both ownership and physical location of resources, if the securities acquired involve claims against wealth located in a different region of the country or in a foreign country.

II. ROLE OF FINANCIAL TRANSACTIONS

The function of financial transactions is to transfer resources from economic units having more savings than they need for investment in their own enterprise to economic units lacking the savings required for investment in their enterprise.

The function of financial transactions between regions or countries is to perform the above-mentioned transfer of resources between surplus and deficit savings units which reside in different geographic areas. The transfers may be — and frequently are — in crossed directions, since there are both types of units in each area and they may find it easier to match their compensating needs beyond the border. In fact, the general rule is to find capital movements in both directions between trading regions or countries, even in cases where there is a great difference of financial potential. But the general rule is also to find that the flow is larger in one direction and, in this sense, it may be said that one important function of interregional and international financial transactions is to transfer resources from regions or countries with more savings than they feel able to invest productively at home to regions or countries with less savings than they consider possible to invest productively within their boundaries.

The transfer may be made by means of portfolio placements, of contractual placements or of direct investments. Each mode for the transfer of funds has a specific use and satisfies a specific need, either of the source country or of the user country.

III. ROLE OF PORTFOLIO PLACEMENTS

In the case of portfolio placements, distinction has to be made between securities issued by governments and corporations of highly developed countries and securities issued by governments of countries that are not highly developed. Securities of the former countries are frequently floated in other highly developed countries responding to interest differentials and are customarily traded in other nations, highly developed or not, responding to speculative motives and/or to the desires of the buyers to place their funds abroad. In the case of new flotations and in the case of already issued securities purchased because of interest differentials, the movement may be said to have an equilibrating character (unless interest rates have been kept artificially low in the source country) but in the case of purchases intended to seek a safer currency or climate, the movements are in most cases of a disequilibrating rather than an equilibrating nature.

Securities of non-highly developed countries were floated and purchased in the past in the capital markets of highly developed countries, but this movement stopped after the depression of the 1930's. In the nineteenth century and first three decades of the twentieth, these portfolio placements served to finance public work programmes, military expenditures, ordinary government expenditures, consolidation of internal and external short-term debts and balance of payments deficits through the purchase of government bonds; and to finance railroads, power plants, telephone and telegraph systems, mining enterprises and plantations through the purchase of stocks or bonds of enterprises engaged in those businesses. As a general rule, these enterprises were promoted and controlled by residents of the capital source country and hence, these portfolio placements in corporate securities were, for all practical purposes, direct investments.

Before World War I, about four-fifths of the capital invested abroad by the United Kingdom was in the form of portfolio placements. It is estimated that in 1914, 77 per cent of the U.K.'s capital placed in Latin America was in the form of portfolio investment; 31 per cent in government bonds, 46 per cent in railway

TABLE 1

U.S. DIRECT AND PORTFOLIO INVESTMENT BY GEOGRAPHIC AREAS, 1908–1959

(Millions of U.S. dollars)

	1908	1914	1919	1924	1929	1935 *	1950	1959
Direct								
Europe	369	573	693	921	1,353	1,259	1,720	5,300
Canada and Newfoundland	405	618	814	1,080	2,010	1,952	3,579	10,171
Latin America	754	1,281	1,988	2,819	3,518	2,847	4,866	8,218
Africa	5	13	31	58	102	93	352	843
Asia	75	119	175	267	394	403	1,044	2,236
Oceania	10	17	53	117	149	91	226	876
Total direct	1,618	2,622	3,754	5,264	7,528	6,690	11,787	29,735
Long-Term Loans and Portfolio								
Europe	120	119	1,294	1,732	3,247	1,767	1,650	2,336
Canada and Newfoundland	292	249	729	1,552	1,650	1,706	3,618	5,435
Latin America	314	368	418	853	1,911	1,704	517	1,151
Africa	0	0	0	0	17	33	0	—
Asia	160	127	134	405	646	512	443 †	1,265 †
Oceania	0	0	1	24	254	322	—	—
Total portfolio	887	862	2,576	4,565	7,725	5,999	6,228	10,710

* Data for 1935 loans and portfolio investment was obtained by deducting 1936 direct investment (Office of Business Economics estimates) from 1935 total investment (Lewis). The discrepancy between direct investment items for 1935 and 1936 is approximately $45 million.
† This item represents a total of Africa, Asia and Oceania.

Sources: Cleona Lewis, *America's Stake in International Investments*, Brookings, 1938 ; U.S. Department of Commerce, Office of Business Economics, *Balance of Payments Statistical Supplement.*

securities. Portfolio placements formed a similar proportion of French overseas investment at that time.[1] This proportion corresponds roughly with that for capital inflows to the United States before World War I. In 1914, foreign investment in the United States amounted to US$6·7 billion of which US$1·3 billion was in the form of direct investment and US$5·4 billion was portfolio.[2] On the other hand, capital outflows from the United States have always tended to take the form of direct investment. In the heyday of portfolio investment, New York was not financially as important as London and Paris, the centres to which countries typically went to obtain loans or float securities. As may be seen in Table 1 it was only in the 1920's that portfolio placements began to weigh in the outflow of private capital from the United States.

Portfolio placements in securities of non-highly developed countries ceased during the Great Depression owing to the extended wave of defaults that took place, to the scandals provoked by the facts uncovered by Congressional investigations in the United States of the ways in which the funds had been used, and to the new regulations enacted in the United States on the flotation and sale of securities in the stock market. This cessation also owed to changes which occurred in the nature of direct investment, which came to be practised mostly by large corporations that usually do not need to raise funds in the market for their branches or subsidiaries abroad, and which, when they do, raise the funds in their own name and not in the name of the subsidiary. As shown in Table 1, from 1929 to 1950, long-term foreign loans outstanding and foreign portfolio assets of the United States diminished in every area except Canada and Newfoundland, the decrease being particularly marked in Latin America, where it fell from US$1,911 million in 1929 to US$517 million in 1950, and in Africa, Asia and Oceania, where it fell from US$917 million in 1929 to US$443 million in 1950. In the 1930's and 1940's, therefore, there was no net flow of loans and portfolio investments from the United States to underdeveloped countries, but a strong reverse flow of repayments.

The old direct channels of portfolio financing have been replaced in part by the new indirect channels provided by the World Bank and the Inter-American Development Bank. Instead of bonds issued by governments of developing countries, investors now buy bonds issued by these banks. The banks in turn lend the funds so

[1] United Nations, *Foreign Capital in Latin America*, 1954, p. 5.
[2] U.S. Bureau of the Census, *Historical Statistical Abstract of the United States*.

TABLE 2

FLOW OF FINANCIAL RESOURCES TO LESS DEVELOPED COUNTRIES, 1961–63*

(Million dollars; – indicates inflow)

	1961	1962	1963	Average 1961–63
FROM ALL OECD INDUSTRIAL COUNTRIES †				
Official	*6,134*	*6,013*	*6,048*	*6,065*
Grants and grant-like contributions	3,948	3,980	3,959	3,962
Bilateral loans	1,344	1,400	1,703	1,483
Contributions to multilateral agencies	842	633	386	620
Private	*3,086*	*2,462*	*2,437*	*2,662*
Direct investment including reinvested earnings	1,851	1,417	1,653	1,640
Loans and bilateral portfolio investment	631	250	249	377
Portfolio investment in securities of multilateral agencies	111	247	– 31	109
Guaranteed export credits	493	548	566	536
Total flow	*9,220*	*8,457*	*8,485*	*8,727*
FROM THE UNITED STATES				
Official	*3,488*	*3,573*	*3,721*	*3,594*
Grants and grant-like contributions	2,583	2,648	2,651	2,627
Bilateral loans	620	701	889	737
Contributions to multilateral agencies	285	224	181	230
Private	*1,099*	*818*	*818*	*912*
Direct investment including reinvested earnings	828	564	714	702
Loans and bilateral portfolio investment	273	45	69	129
Portfolio investment in securities of multilateral agencies	– 2	160	5	54
Guaranteed export credits	—	49	30	26
Total flow	*4,587*	*4,391*	*4,539*	*4,505*
FROM OTHER OECD INDUSTRIAL COUNTRIES				
Official	*2,646*	*2,441*	*2,327*	*2,471*
Grants and grant-like contributions	1,365	1,333	1,308	1,335
Bilateral loans	724	699	814	746
Contributions to multilateral agencies	557	409	205	390
Private	*1,987*	*1,644*	*1,619*	*1,750*
Direct investment including reinvested earnings	1,023	853	939	938
Loans and bilateral portfolio investment	358	205	180	248
Portfolio investment in securities of multilateral agencies	113	87	– 36	55
Guaranteed export credits	493	499	536	509
Total flow	*4,633*	*4,085*	*3,946*	*4,221*

* The figures represent actual net disbursements but do not coincide with receipts by the user countries owing to the differences between amounts received and amounts disbursed by the multilateral agencies.

† Austria, Belgium, Canada, Denmark, France, Germany, Italy, Japan, Netherlands, Norway, Portugal, Sweden, Switzerland, United Kingdom, United States.

Source: *The Flow of Financial Resources to Less Developed Countries, 1956-1963*, OECD, Paris, 1964 .Tables II-5, IV-1, IV-2, and IV-3.

acquired to the governments, for the most important of the purposes formerly financed through the direct sale of securities. According to Table 2, in 1961–63 4 per cent of the total flow of private funds from industrial countries to less developed nations moved through the purchase of these new portfolio securities.

In the last few years, some non-highly developed countries, for example, Venezuela and Mexico, have been able to float bond issues in the New York market. However, these issues have not been sufficiently large or frequent to indicate a significant reopening to underdeveloped countries of the old channels of portfolio financing.

IV. ROLE OF CONTRACTUAL PLACEMENTS

As explained above, the term ' contractual placements ' is used here to denote financial transactions that are not embodied in negotiable instruments and which do not give the supplier of the funds a controlling interest in the enterprise to which the resources are applied. In the international field, the two types of transaction originating in private sources that can be classified in this category and are currently being performed in substantial amounts are (*a*) medium-term credits to the importers of equipment, generally covered by the guarantee of the exporting country's government, and (*b*) commercial bank loans.

Medium-term suppliers' credits insured by a government agency of the exporting country is a new form of capital transaction, created after World War II, that has grown very rapidly and already has a significant volume. As shown in Table 2, in 1961–63 suppliers' credits accounted for 20 per cent of total net private capital movements from industrial countries to less developed nations.

Being specifically destined to finance the purchase of capital goods by public and private enterprises of developing nations, suppliers' credits play an obviously essential role in the promotion of development. They supplement domestic savings in financing the expanson and modernization of existing enterprises and the establishment of new ones ; and they frequently come accompanied by technical assistance supplied by the manufacturers of the equipment. In some instances, manufacturers design complete plants and make recommendations on the selection of technical personnel to help the local managers and engineers during the initial phase of operation of the new plant.

Table 3
Flows of Private Capital from the United States
(Millions of $US; − indicates inflow)

	1956	1957	1958	1959	1960	1961	1962	1963	1964
To Highly Developed Countries*									
Direct investment	1,114	957	626	952	1,479	1,065	1,349	1,537	1,798
New issues of foreign securities	398	337	599	553	281	395	774	1,146	735
Redemptions †	−111	−139	−55	−61	−137	−85	−116	−130	−122
Other long-term transactions (net)	221	217	241	150	240	446	153	567	953
Short-term transactions (net)	245	835	176	273	1,025	1,249	495	579	1,305
To Less Developed Countries‡									
Direct investment	797	1,361	482	287	203	425	231	412	522
New issues of foreign securities	55	73	−10	57	177	116	218	104	324
Redemptions §	−25	−24	−14	−15	−45	−45	−71	−53	−53
Other long-term transactions (net)	78	186	206	251	229	101	103	31	163
Short-term transactions (net)	239	206	137	54	323	307	49	206	807

* Europe (except Spain, Turkey and U.S. Office of Business Economics classification 'other countries'), Canada, Australia, New Zealand, South Africa, Japan.

† Data for redemptions includes Australia, New Zealand, South Africa, Japan with LDC's, excludes them from high developed. This discrepancy occurs because of the manner in which these figures are commonly itemized.

‡ All countries not listed in *.

§ Data for 1964 is not complete.

Sources: U.S. Department of Commerce: *Survey of Current Business*; *Balance of Payments Statistical Supplement*. U.S. Department of the Treasury: *Treasury Bulletin*. Board of Governors of the Federal Reserve System: *Supplement to Banking and Monetary Statistics, Section 15, International Finance*.

As currently provided, suppliers' credits are often criticized on the following grounds : (i) not having a long enough term, (ii) inducing and/or facilitating the initiation of low priority projects through pressure salesmanship, and (iii) shifting competition from considerations of quality and price to those of credit availability. As a consequence of these practices, suppliers' credits are considered to have a large responsibility for the heavy load of short-term debt that weighs upon many underdeveloped countries. There seems to be a great deal of truth in these criticisms, but they should not lead us to forget that suppliers' credits represent a substantial source of funds specifically devoted to cover a first priority need ; that these funds are obtainable through simple and easy procedures ; and that they come to strengthen local private enterprise, that does not have access to many other sources of medium- or long-term credit, either local or international. The policy objective should not be, therefore, to reduce the flow of these strategic credits, but to improve their mechanism and eliminate their shortcomings through the co-operative efforts of the guaranteeing agencies in the exporting countries and the planning offices in the importing nations.

The other important international capital movements under the heading of contractual placements are bank loans. Bank loans flow mainly between highly developed countries but move also to less developed nations. Traditionally, the principal field of international banking operations was the finance of foreign trade, but in recent years banks have been financing other activities beyond their borders, particularly working capital requirements, and even fixed capital needs, of the direct investment enterprises of their co-nationals. In the case of some countries — highly developed and non-highly developed — banks also lend to nationals of the country through the intermediation of local banks. Other frequent transactions are loans to central banks, generally guaranteed by their deposits.

OECD figures do not distinguish between loans and portfolio investments, which are grouped together in Table 2. United States statistics show the separate figures for each as can be seen in Table 3. But the distinction does not help our analysis in any substantial degree because in current practice there are no really meaningful differences between these two types of capital movements to under-developed countries. In most cases, security flotations are closer to bank loans than to authentic portfolio investments, owing to the fact that the securities are not freely traded in the market but kept by the underwriting banks. Under this broader definition, including among bank loans transactions classified as portfolio placements, bank loans accounted for 20 per cent of the total private flow of funds to less developed nations in 1961 and 10 per cent in 1962 and 1963, with an average of 14 per cent in the three years.

V. THE ROLE OF DIRECT INVESTMENT

As said before, direct investment is an entrepreneurial activity more than a financial transaction. Direct investment is generally carried out by large corporations which have all the facilities — organization, experience, technical and managerial skills, patents, trade marks, marketing channels, etc. — to establish new production units, and to expand existing ones, with a very high probability of success. Direct investment brings to a country what we might call ' prefabricated ' industries, ready for use and guaranteed to operate satisfactorily. Direct investment brings with it ready-made development in the particular field to which it belongs. Practically no effort is needed from the residents of the recipient country. There is no wait for training of technicians and managers, nor for try-outs and the gaining of experience. If it comes in adequate volume to the proper fields and is accompanied by the necessary amounts of loans to finance overhead capital facilities, direct investment is a short-cut to development.[1]

The main weakness of direct investment as a development agent is a consequence of the complete character of its contribution. As it brings enterprise, management and technology to the country, it may inhibit the emergence and formation of local personnel and local institutions to perform these essential functions. In so far as this happens, foreign investment does not help the country to advance towards self-sustaining development. But on the other hand, direct investment strengthens existing local enterprises and encourages the creation of new ones through its expanding effects on income, through its training of local personnel, through its direct purchases of parts, intermediate goods, raw materials and services from local enterprises (what Hirschman calls backward linkage effects) and/or its provision of cheaper and more abundant supplies of inputs to local enterprises (forward linkage effects).

In countries that are experiencing rapid development, foreign

---

[1] See 'Private Versus Public Foreign Investment in Underdeveloped Areas', *Economic Development for Latin America*, New York, St. Martin's Press, Inc., 1961.

investment probably induces the creation of more local enterprises than it potentially displaces. It certainly trains and employs many more administrators and technicians than it brings from abroad. But the effects, actual and potential, of foreign direct investment on local entrepreneurs, managers and technicians should be constantly borne in mind, not only for economic reasons, which are very important in themselves, but also on account of sociological and political considerations.

Direct investment increases production and income, expands employment, creates jobs of higher productivity, augments tax revenues and raises foreign exchange receipts or reduces foreign exchange payments. The country receives benefits, but not as a result of its own initiative and effort ; and the production facilities created do not belong to the country nor are they run by it. Direct foreign investment promotes development for the country, but not of the country or by the country.

For the above-mentioned reasons, direct foreign investment can be depended on to play an important role in development, but not the decisive one, that must be played by local entrepreneurs.

VI. QUANTITATIVE CONTRIBUTION OF FOREIGN PRIVATE CAPITAL

The contribution of foreign private capital to development might be measured quantitatively by comparing its annual net flow to the total volume of net investment during the year, but the figure would not have much meaning because it would express a mere arithmetic share without taking into consideration qualitative effects. The same can be said about an estimate of the proportion of total income, taxes or exports that originates in foreign-owned enterprises.

Since in spite of the reservations made above, these figures are of some interest, we may attempt to make some calculations. Choosing Latin America as a region where a rough estimate of this nature can be attempted, we may calculate that international private capital flow of all types (direct investment, reinvested earnings of subsidiaries, bank loans, portfolio investments and suppliers' credits) may have been financing around 8 per cent of total net investment in recent years (estimating the net flow of external private funds to the region in US$500 million to US$600 million and total net investment in all countries in US$7,000 million). With respect to

Capital Movements and Economic Development

TABLE 4

TOTAL NET FLOW OF PRIVATE CAPITAL FROM OECD INDUSTRIAL
COUNTRIES* TO LESS DEVELOPED COUNTRIES, 1956–63

	1956	1957	1958	1959	1960	1961	1962	1963
From the United States†	1,230	2,009	1,284	954	1,044	1,099	818	818
From other OECD countries†	1,743	1,651	1,603	1,797	1,999	1,987	1,693	1,650
Total net flow†	2,973	3,660	2,887	2,751	3,043	3,086	2,462	2,438

* Austria, Belgium, Canada, Denmark, France, the Federal Republic of Germany, Iceland, Italy, Japan, Luxembourg, the Netherlands, Norway, Portugal, Sweden, Switzerland, the United Kingdom and the United States.

† Includes direct investment including reinvested earnings, loans and bilateral portfolio investment, portfolio investment in securities of multilateral agencies and guaranteed export credits.

TABLE 5

FLOW OF DIRECT INVESTMENT FUNDS FROM THE UNITED STATES TO
LESS DEVELOPED COUNTRIES

(Millions of U.S. dollars ; – represents inflow)

	1956	1957	1958	1959	1960	1961	1962	1963	1964
Total	820	1,386	477	316	247	446	215	484	522
Petroleum	486	996	267	53	58	251	74	171	154
Manufacturing	107	110	77	66	134	84	157	179	178
Other	212	282	134	199	51	111	–16	134	190

Sources : U.S. Department of Commerce, Office of Business Economics. *The Flow of Financial Resources to Less Developed Countries — 1956–1963.* OECD, 1964.

TABLE 6

FLOW OF DIRECT INVESTMENT FUNDS FROM THE U.S. TO LATIN
AMERICAN REPUBLICS

(Millions of U.S. dollars ; – represents inflow)

	1956	1957	1958	1959	1960	1961	1962	1963	1964
Total	618	1,163	299	218	95	173	–32	69	156
Petroleum	363	862	147	24	–7	30	–111	–81	–3
Manufacturing	96	102	63	54	125	77	115	107	89
Other	159	244	113	140	–23	66	–36	43	70

Source : U.S. Department of Commerce, Office of Business Economics.

shares of income taxes and exports, the U.S. Department of Commerce estimates that U.S. direct investment enterprises in Latin America generated 10 per cent of total income, paid 20 per cent of total taxes and produced 30 per cent of total exports.[1]

Recent trends

In 1962 and 1963 international financial flows from private sources to less developed countries were about 33 per cent below their 1957 peak and about 20 per cent below their level in 1960 and 1961. A large part of the decline, although not all of it, is attributable to the extremely high level of petroleum investment in 1957 and its subsequent contraction. According to the OECD report from which the figures in Table 2 and 4 are taken, ' much of the year to year fluctuation in the level of recorded direct investment in the less developed countries is due to shifts in investment in the petroleum sector. Thus, in 1962, reduced investment in petroleum was a major factor in the overall investment decline of several countries, particularly the United States which reported net disinvestments in Venezuela alone of US$165 million.' [2]

Tables 5 and 6 show the large fluctuations in petroleum investment and confirm the above-quoted statement of the OECD. They also show substantial fluctuations in ' other industries ', the largest component of which is mining and smelting.

VII. POLICY CONSIDERATIONS

This paper is not supposed to enter into questions of policy, which will be covered by other participants of the Conference, but in some parts of the paper there are implicit policy considerations that should be made explicit for the sake of clarity.

The observations made on the weak aspects of direct investment contain implicit recommendations for strengthening them. If the shortcomings of this type of capital transaction is that it does not give the country an active enough role in the development process, the obvious remedy is to increase to the possible maximum extent the participation of the country in the initiative and effort to create

[1] U.S. Department of Commerce, *U.S. Business Investments in Foreign Countries*, Washington, D.C., 1960.
[2] Organization for Economic Co-operation and Development, *The Flow of Financial Resources to Less Developed Countries, 1959–1963* (Paris, 1964), p. 58.

the enterprises, in their ownership, in the adoption of basic policy decisions and in the day-to-day process of management and technical direction. In this respect, the recent arrangements made by the Government of Chile with the copper companies, and with the telephone and electric power concessionaries, may be cited as opening a new path.

Direct investment should not come to displace existing local enterprises by competition or purchase, but it should initiate operations in new fields and induce, through forward and backward linkage effects, the expansion of existing local enterprises and the creation of new ones. Direct investment should bring skills and technologies that are not already available in the country or easily hired abroad.

Direct investment is a powerful instrument that should continue to make a major contribution to world development, but in order to maximize its contribution and avoid unnecessary friction, we should study the nature of the obstacles it faces and find ways to overcome them. We must make our best effort to develop what in broadly coincident papers, yet unpublished, Victor L. Urquidi calls 'a new approach'[1] and Paul N. Rosenstein-Rodan, 'a new philosophy'.

COMMENTS ON DR. PAZOS' PAPER

BY

Professor GASTON LEDUC

University of Paris

I. THE TYPOLOGY OF INTERNATIONAL CAPITAL TRANSACTIONS :
INVESTMENTS AND 'PLACEMENTS'

THE first point of Dr. Pazos' paper on which some comment seems justified is the attempt to set up a kind of typology of international capital movements or transactions. It concerns only private capital — from the point of view of origin — and not public capital. So the classification which was proposed by the author in his communication to the IEA Conference held at Rio de Janeiro in 1957[2] is greatly simplified.

[1] 'Some Implications of Foreign Investment for Latin America', paper presented at the Seminar on Obstacles to Change in Latin America ; Royal Institute of International Affairs, Chatham House, London, 15–21 February, 1965.
[2] Filipe Pazos, 'Private versus Public Foreign Investment in Under-Developed Areas' in Howard S. Ellis, *Economic Development for Latin America* (London and New York, 1961), pp. 201–225.

Furthermore, the line of argument is here limited to the purely monetary terms, i.e. to the purely financial flows. We may agree with this kind of presentation, but on condition that we never forget that such flows are necessarily accompanied, or followed, by 'real' flows, i.e. by transfers of goods and services, even if they do not intend to bring them about immediately.

Nevertheless, with regard to the capital movements aimed at the financing of investment decisions in order to start or to sustain a process of development, the immediate purpose of these transfers is to set in motion 'real' international flows of goods and services, for an ultimate increase of the capital stock in the country of destination. Only in this sense may we agree with Nurkse's dictum : 'Capital is made at home'. The capital goods are, by necessity, utilized 'at home'. But they may be of external origin, in so far as the goods and services concerned are physically transportable.

Dr. Pazos' argument is in agreement with the distinction currently accepted in our days between *direct* investments, which consist in 'acquisitions or constructions of production facilities that will be owned and operated by the savers themselves' and other (why not *indirect?*) investments, called *portfolio* investments, which are represented by acquisitions of participations (*shares*) or *money claims*, the latter with or without an incorporation in negotiable instruments. For this second category, the author's proposal is to constitute a special group with the qualification of *contractual transfers*. So we have three categories of investments : direct, portfolio and contractual investments, with a further distinction for each of the two last types in *equities* and *loans*.

The operations of the first group (*direct investments*) are analysed as 'an act of entrepreneurship', involving the combination of the factors of production in order to produce (in the receiving country) additional goods and services. For the second group (*portfolio and contractual investments*), the process of operations consists, at first sight, in purely financial phenomena. From the saver's point of view, they are represented by '*placements*' according to the terminology proposed by Mrs. Robinson. (We note that the concept of 'placements' becomes somewhat more restricted than in the French meaning, and that it would be perfectly correct in the French use to apply the word 'placement' also to 'direct investments'.)

Of course, in the case of 'non-direct investments', implying 'transfers of claims to resources from savers to investors, directly or through financial intermediaries', it is the duty of the beneficiary of such transfers to act so as to convert the 'placements' into 'investments', that is to obtain an increase of the capital stocks and indeed to sustain the development of the economy. If the operation is successful it will produce the financial means necessary to pay dividends (on shares) and interest (on loans). But one must not forget that, in any case, interest on loans must be paid and that the eventual transfers of these sums in a foreign currency create for the debtor country a problem of international monetary relations.

II. THE ROLE OF PORTFOLIO 'PLACEMENTS'

Dr. Pazos puts forward a distinction between 'securities issued by governments and corporations of highly developed countries and securities issued by governments (why not by enterprises, too?) of countries that are not highly developed'. We presume that such a distinction is made as a matter of fact rather than on a conceptual distinction between the two groups of countries in regard to security issues. But where must the line be drawn?

We are told that the second category of 'placements' has in fact disappeared since the great Depression of the 1930's.

Dr. Pazos also points out that only a small proportion of the total transfers of private capital from industrialized countries to the less developed now passes through the channel of multilateral agencies —an average of 4 per cent for the three years 1961–63. But they are also passing through 'commercial bank loans', the amount of which is not negligible — 14 per cent of 'total net private flows of financial resources from the 15 industrial countries' for the same period — if we add to the 'loans' the 'bilateral portfolio investments', since statistically they cannot be distinguished.

III. THE PROS AND CONS OF 'SUPPLIERS CREDITS'

According to Dr. Pazos' own terms, the category of contractual placements includes the 'medium term credits to the importers of equipment, generally covered by the guarantee of the exporting country's Government'. It is worth noting that 'supplier credits' has a direct French equivalent in *'credits fournisseurs'*. This form of credit is nowadays rather widely used : 20 per cent of the total net private capital movements recorded by the OECD for the period 1961–63, with an annual average of US$536 million.

It has its supporters, but also many opponents. The case is still open to discussion. The doctrinal controversy is whether we may count such credits a form of aid to the debtor countries. Of course, whatever the doctrinal conclusion, the use of such credits is liable to abuses. But, if judiciously proportioned and employed, their use may facilitate the realization of true investment operations which would not be possible by other means or which otherwise would be more expensive.

We do personally believe that this is a problem of *cas d'espèce* — and that, on this point too, we are in agreement with the author himself. But it is well to put extra stress on the very great dangers attached to external debt on short and medium terms, of purely commercial nature, with very high rates of interest, which can lead to difficult problems of debt servicing.

IV. FOREIGN PRIVATE CAPITAL AND DEVELOPMENT

It is very difficult to determine the effects of external private capital contributions on the nature and the pace of economic growth in the recipient country. Should we consider the effects as being exactly proportionate to the importance of these private flows in the total of external financial resources, private as well as official? The relation is, for the time being, about one-fourth. Also, do we accept as a certainty that capital flows of external origin are exactly comparable to internal savings? We also have to notice carefully that, on the whole, the category of direct investments accounts for the most important part (about two-thirds of the total of private flows for the period 1961–63) and that it includes reinvested earnings, for which we do not have specific information.

The statistical figures relate to the *net* flows of financial resources. But it is necessary to point out that the methods of calculation of these net balances do not take into account interest on loans, nor dividends and profits distributed (and so perhaps indirectly re-invested). The differences between the net and the gross flows relate only to repayment of the loans themselves. We are told that inquiries are now being carried out, to determine the importance of the burden on debtor countries imposed by these other transfers of incomes. In the meantime, it seems to us quite impossible to give precise conclusions about the true nature and importance of the contribution of external resources to economic growth.

Another question calling for a complementary analysis is related to direct investments and Dr. Pazos' distinction between development *for* the (recipient) country and development *of* the country. Are we not entitled to say that in the long run, the development *of* one country concerned is, for the greatest part, a development *by* and so *for* the country itself? Of course, such a result would require an ever increasing participation of the internal (national) productive resources of the developing country in the general development effort.

Perhaps we may now, by way of conclusion, briefly comment on the implications on policy. The most important aid which external private savers are in a position to give to the less developed countries is to start investments, not in the nature of pure substitutions for local ones, but in addition to them, so as to promote or accelerate economic growth by putting into motion a variety of 'spread effects'. We think that, with some improvements, such a function is clearly possible for direct investments. Portfolio investments and contractual investments likewise are not to be considered as purely anachronistic categories. There remains, as Professor Rosenstein-Rodan has pointed out, an open question as to the optimal ratio between equity and loan 'placements'. Professor Rosenstein-Rodan's paper constitutes an appeal to the faculties of imagination for men of thought as well as for men of action. Our world is in great need of new formulations, ever more appropriate to the changing nature and the growing volume of the work to be done.

———

DISCUSSION OF THE PAPERS BY PROFESSOR ROSENSTEIN-RODAN AND DR. PAZOS

THE papers by Professor Rosenstein-Rodan and Dr. Pazos were discussed at the same time. The main topics of discussion were : changes in the composition of foreign investment and, related to this, the current role of direct private investment ; the need for a new code of international behaviour ; and the transfer problem. In addition, the increasing importance of suppliers' credits was considered.

I. CHANGES IN THE COMPOSITION OF FOREIGN INVESTMENT

Dr. Kamarck pointed out that in addition to the decline in the relative importance of bonds in favour of equity financing, there is another shift in the composition of private international capital flows that distinguishes nineteenth century from present capital movements. A large part of total capital flow today is directed towards tropical and semi-tropical countries where the state of technology and the level of ability to use the capital are lower than in the nineteenth century when capital was transferred from one temperate zone to another. *Dr. Adler* added that the big expansion of American private direct investment has not been in underdeveloped countries but in advanced countries in recent years, and this seems to be continuing. Private investors evidently prefer to go to Europe and Canada rather than to less developed countries. *Dr. Kamarck* suggested that this may in part be due to the fact that the demand for primary products is growing more slowly than income in industrialized countries. He noted that raw material producing countries may be able to escape from the terms of trade problem that this presents. Some mineral producers, for instance, have benefited from the shift in output of minerals from developed to developing countries.

II. A NEW CODE OF INTERNATIONAL BEHAVIOUR?

Professor Rosenstein-Rodan suggested in his paper that major changes in economic structure and technology require a new code of international behaviour to protect legitimate interests of both creditors and debtor countries, and urged his suggestion be implemented by forming new types of investor partnerships. The suggestion stimulated an extensive discussion of the virtues of direct private investment. *Professor Andreasian* indicated that direct private investment often does not reflect the real needs of developing countries. He cited the roles of the major international oil companies in the mid-East as cases in point. Here, excessively high returns on investments involved heavy losses for the developing countries. *Dr. Horvat* also cited Yugoslav experience with several international oil companies. Their price-setting, market-sharing and resource development behaviour was such that they could hardly be said to have helped the country. *Professor Kafka* replied that there are also many examples where both foreign enterprises and the modern developing companies prospered together. Dr. Horvat's example does not reflect a general tendency. *Professor Wallich* offered counter examples in which foreign companies were mistreated by developing countries. For a company operating in several countries to earn a competitive rate of return, he noted, it may be necessary to offset losses in one country with profits from another. The result is that the international company may take out more than the competitive rate of return from the first country.

Dr. Kamarck mentioned that new codes of behaviour and new institutions are already being developed. This is seen in World Bank policies which require that borrowers adhere to a code of reasonable economic behaviour. Secondly, a new centre for the settlement of investment disputes is being established. Thirdly, the OECD has recently proposed a scheme for multilateral investment guarantees.

Dr. Rhomberg found the concept of 'harmony of interest' intriguing, but also elusive and complicated. While foreign investment may help a country extract natural resources at low cost, the terms of trade may be affected adversely. Harmony of interest requires striking a balance between these two effects. The underdeveloped country may also serve as a market for industrial products of the advanced country, but here again, terms-of-trade effects have to be weighed if there is to be a harmony of interest.

Dr. Patel noted that the question is not whether private capital is good or bad, but what are the circumstances that affect the transfer problem and other aspects of capital movements? What is needed is a code for the developing countries which specifies the type of capital admitted and the terms for admitting capital. Here there is need for a dialogue between foreign private investors and the host countries.

Dr. Pazos felt that the need to form strong local entrepreneurship groups was ignored in the discussion of new codes of international behaviour. A workable capitalist system is one which is made up of local capitalists, not foreign capitalists and local workers. The latter obviously has adverse social implications.

Capital Movements and Economic Development

III. THE TRANSFER PROBLEM

Professor Rosenstein-Rodan emphasized in his paper that the transfer problem is more difficult today than it used to be. This is because the world economy today is no longer the 'engine of growth' it was during the nineteenth century. Growth in developed countries is no longer followed by increases in derived demand for primary products of developing countries as it once was. Moreover, the one institution which acted as a safety valve for transfer of payments difficulties — bankruptcy — has almost vanished today. The result is an increasingly difficult transfer problem. *Professor Delivanis* argued that bankruptcies and defaults have diminished only if Professor Rosenstein-Rodan refers to those which are settled in court. This may not be true if cases of devaluation, exchange control, and nationalization are considered a form of default. *Professor Rosenstein-Rodan* replied that even if nationalization is considered a form of default, defaults are fewer. In the nineteenth century investors had less contact with economists and tended to underestimate risks. Today investors are more sophisticated in evaluating risks.

Professor Mundell saw no reason in Professor Rosenstein-Rodan's argument why the transfer problem should be more difficult today, even if it may in fact be so. References to growth rates and income elasticities of demand imply nothing about transfer problems. The causes of transfer problems are more fundamental: countries have given up automatic balance of payments adjustments. They do not have flexible exchange rates, nor do they adhere to gold standards or fixed-exchange-rate principles. Rather, they operate through *ad hoc* monetary controls that appear to make the transfer problem more difficult than it really is. Further, changes in the role of the safety valve of bankruptcy are due mainly to differences between the political structure of the nineteenth century and that prevailing today. Gunboat diplomacy, which kept down the number of defaults in the nineteenth century, is no longer fashionable and a far more permissive attitude toward borrowing countries is now prevalent. This, plus the fact that there is no present equivalent to the gold standard, in large part explains the declining relative importance of loans in foreign investment. *Professor Rosenstein-Rodan* disagreed. Even with flexible exchange rates, the difference between the foreign-exchange gap and the resources gap would probably persist. He doubted that the various measures of monetary discipline mentioned by Professor Mundell would remove this difference.

Dr. Adler felt that the distinction between resource-oriented and market-oriented investments should be emphasized in analysing the transfer problem. The first type includes exploitation of oil and other mineral resources, the second or import-substitution type is becoming increasingly important. The two types lead to different results. Raw material, export-oriented investment helps ease the balance of payments problem while its contribution to spreading of skill and entrepreneurship is probably small. In contrast, investment in market-oriented industries does not increase exports but helps to breed entrepreneurship and managerial skills. *Professor Rosenstein-Rodan* added that in judging the value of resource-oriented as opposed to market-oriented investments, we need to establish the cost-benefit ratio of the investment for the receiving country, including external economies in the wider sense in the calculation.

Professor Rosenstein-Rodan's paper noted that the increasing importance of equity investment in the total investment mix aggravated the transfer problem. *Dr. Rhomberg* questioned whether the realized rate of return on equity capital is as high as the expected rate of return. His calculations for U.S. investments indicate that in Latin America, the realized rate of return is approximately 5 per cent to 8 per cent in some instances, compared with realized returns in Europe of from 15 per cent to 20 per cent. Also, in reading Professor Rosenstein-Rodan's proposals for new forms of investment partnership, Dr. Rhomberg did not see how profits attributable to imported capital can be separated from those attributable to domestic capital. There seems to be no economic basis for such a split, hence distribution could only be by some convention, not on economic grounds.

Professor Rosenstein-Rodan referred in the discussion to the problem of reducing the role of foreign investment in joint operations. He noted that the foreign-enclave problem could be minimized by rapid growth of the enclave sector, since converting from foreign to domestic ownership when there was rapid growth would not require a drop in absolute levels of foreign investment but only a decline in the relative share of total equity. Where growth is low, however, converting to domestic ownership can only result in the absolute reduction of foreign investment and exacerbates the transfer problem.

IV. Supplier Credits

Dr. Kamarck said that the recent increase in suppliers' credit has become an important component of the capital flow total. Suppliers' credit presents an enormous problem today because nobody knows how to handle it. *Dr. Pazos* suggested that a good German type of inflation in the United States and Europe would ease the problem. *Professor Rosenstein-Rodan* added that the problem is a two-fold one. First, how much credit should be contracted. The decision cannot be left to the recipients of suppliers' credits, financial management in many developing countries is frequently irresponsible. Second, and more important, is that suppliers' credits are used as a mechanism for tied assistance — a form of imperfection in international trade and a grave deviation from the international division of labour. Further, there is a danger of applying legal instead of economic criteria in examining such credits. Nominal interest rates may be much lower than real rates because suppliers often raise their prices when credit is tied to purchases from them.

PART II

THE RESOURCES ASPECTS

Chapter 5

ECONOMIC EFFECTS OF CAPITAL IMPORTS

BY

ALEXANDRE KAFKA

University of Virginia

I. INTRODUCTION

THE title of this session is, on the face of it, almost coterminous with that of the entire conference.[1] To attempt to say anything useful on a literal interpretation of this title, in the time allowed, seems impracticable. This paper, therefore, at the cost of being rather impressionistic, deals with a small number of fairly diverse issues whose only common characteristic is that they are all, at present, hotly debated in the developing countries. This is my justification for taking them up. There was unfortunately no time even to attempt the quantification of my conclusions.

Some of the issues selected concern the belief that capital imports may lead to retrogression rather than growth. This is not inconceivable, as every economist knows. I doubt if anybody has the information which would enable him to say with assurance how important in practice these cases of retrogression have been or are. Particularly if one feels — as I do — that they have been and are — on balance — quite unimportant, and that capital imports in all their forms have been and are a highly positive agent of progress in developing countries, it seems to me that it is not only an intellectually interesting but a practically useful, indeed important task for the economist to spell out and attempt to assess carefully these cases of retrogression: much hostility in developing countries — and in developed ones — towards capital flows does not stem from prejudice or defence of vested interests, but from the impression caused by isolated and by their nature rare instances of harmful effect.

[1] I am indebted for valuable suggestions of Professors Ronald Coase, P. N. Rosenstein-Rodan and Leland B. Yeager.

In order to show the latter, in my analysis, I have tried to present these cases in the strongest form I can conceive of.

The topical issues discussed concern mainly (i) the economic effects of the process of capital importation. But there are also some which concern the economic effects of (ii) the operation of assets installed and (iii) the liquidation of liabilities incurred as the result of capital imports. This threefold division obviously represents a considerable simplification. More numerous stages in the effects of a capital import should be distinguished, and it is also only a first approximation to assume, as is done here, that the effects of the various stages are additive rather than that their inter-action follows a more complicated pattern.

(i) In the part (II), which deals with (macro- and micro-economic effects of) the *process of capital importation*, five issues are discussed. Section A discusses the likelihood that (gross) capital flows to developing countries will not be transferred, but will end up as an accumulation of assets abroad. This possibility is found to be, on the whole, slight. Any building up of such balances is due to other factors than the presence or absence of (gross) capital imports and some mistakes are discussed in the measures taken to deal with those other factors. Section B discusses the possibility that effected net transfers (i.e. an increase in the current account deficit of the balance of payments) will not result in an increase in the absorption of goods and services by the capital importing country, but rather will result in a fall in output in the latter. Again, this possibility is found to be slight, except in the face of pronounced fluctuations of capital imports. Section C investigates the possibility that capital imports which are not available without discrimination to local entrepreneurs and to foreign entrepreneurs operating in the capital importing country may discourage the development of local private entrepreneurship. It finds the likelihood that this will happen to be slight, however, and discusses various measures which can be taken to reduce it further. Section D comments upon the effects of capital imports on the distribution of investment between various lives of activity. Section E examines the role of capital imports in stabilization programmes. It suggests that certain misconceptions have interfered with a wider use of capital flows in the crucial first years of recent stabilization programmes and that this fact has contributed to the failure of so many of these programmes.

(ii) The part (III) which deals briefly with the effects of the *operation* of the *additional capacity* installed with the help of capital imports, examines mainly the results of imperfections in the capital and product markets.

(iii) The final part (IV) discusses even more briefly the effects of various schemes for the liquidation of liabilities incurred to foreign countries by capital importing countries.

The 'model' of a capital importing country underlying most parts of the paper is more like Mexico than like a primitive village. The 'model' will be specified in detail, where necessary, as the argument proceeds.

Changes in capital imports are assumed, unless otherwise noted, to originate in policy decisions of official lenders or in changes in the view taken by private foreign lenders of prospects in and of the capital importing country, without any change in actual conditions there or elsewhere. It is remarkable how frequently such a model applies.

II. THE PROCESS OF CAPITAL IMPORTATION

A. *Transfer and 'Absorption'*

It is not customary to worry about the transfer of real resources into the developing countries of today, although there is much concern about the 'absorption' problem. The latter, however, refers not to the question whether or with what difficulties additional real resources supplied from abroad can be absorbed by developing economies. Nor is it concerned with the question whether an increase in the excess of absorption over output comes about without a fall in the latter, so that total absorption will change less than the change in the excess. Rather, the so-called 'absorption' problem refers to the question whether the excess of absorption over output can be employed by the recipient country in some way which the writer in question considers 'proper'. 'Proper absorption' may refer to the economy's ability to raise domestic investment, to transfer abroad any income deriving from the investment of the original resources absorbed by it, or to its ability to distribute the additional goods and services to the most 'deserving' groups, etc.

Generally, the customary attitude — of refusing to worry about the real transfers — makes a great deal of sense, as will become apparent. There can, nevertheless, exist, even in developing countries, not only a 'proper absorption problem', but also a transfer problem, because of which a capital import may end up as a mere switch of assets. If a capital import takes place in the legal sense, precautions can be taken that its impact effect should be an increase in consumption or investment somewhere in the capital importing country. There is, nevertheless, no guarantee at all that either increase will really result from the overall point of view.[1]

The IMF has recently tried to estimate the outflow of capital from developing countries. Though this is in its nature hard to do, it seemed to be satisfied that the outflow was by no means small. It seemed also to come mainly from Latin American countries.[2]

This paper returns later (Sections C and E) to some aspects of the connection between capital imports and capital exports by developing countries and finds that the correlation between rates (per unit of time) of capital inflow into and rates of capital outflow from a given country is likely to be positive, but the ' elasticity ' of the latter with respect to the former is not likely to be high in the long run.

Most capital outflows from developing countries, however, are not sparked by capital inflows. The rules under which many developing countries choose to operate are often quite sufficient to explain the capital exports which take place. Hence, the indignation felt in donor countries about the apparent waste to which their grants, loans and investments give rise may be somewhat misplaced : the outflows are a waste, at least from the developer's point of view, but since the inflows do not give rise to them one cannot say that the grants, loans and investments made to or in the developing countries are wasted.

What are these ' rules ' which give rise to capital exports from developing countries ? First, overvalued exchange rates will encourage capital exports in direct proportion to the extent of overvaluation of the exchange rate and in inverse proportion to the time for which it is expected to last. Second, even in the absence of overvaluation

---

[1] If the government of Ruritania, after many applications to the appropriate institutions, has received a foreign loan to erect a steel mill and has actually done so, there is no guarantee at all that the net result of the loan is not rather the accumulation of dollars in the Central Bank account or in the Swiss numbered accounts of Ruritanian citizens, who deposit abroad respectively the yield of export taxes which would otherwise have been spent on the mill, or the savings they would otherwise have invested in bonds which the government of Ruritania would have issued to finance the mill.

[2] One may, of course, doubt whether the apparently lower outflow from other developing regions reflects wholly the actual situation or in part results from the use of more sophisticated methods of capital export than those which have to be employed in Latin America.

expected to be short-lived, there are likely to be capital exports from developing countries, and not only for political reasons. They are due to institutional defects of the capital markets, especially under inflation. Current efforts to encourage capital imports or discourage capital exports by developing countries aim exclusively at raising the marginal efficiency of investment to the ultimate borrower. The ultimate borrower in developing countries is indeed often the ultimate lender if a local capital market or local financial intermediaries are totally absent. However, this is by no means invariably the case. Consequently it would make sense if the developing countries concerned themselves not only with raising the marginal efficiency of investment to the ultimate borrower, but also with creating inducements to the ultimate domestic lender to keep his money at home.

One way of doing so is to forbid capital exports. But this is not particularly easy to make effective. Another way, which has been a little more successful, has been the fragmentation of exchange markets : separate markets for financial and commercial transactions, etc. This fragmentation increases exchange rate fluctuations and the risks of holding foreign assets.

A better way is to address oneself to the root cause of steady capital outflows, which is interest rate control, particularly (but not only) in the face of inflation. Simply to free interest rates in the organized money markets (controls do not function anyway in the unorganized ones) after years of strong inflation may not be sufficient to enable medium term lending to take place, unless there is agreement on the future rate of inflation ; the ' indexing ' of bonds and bank deposits, or permission for local financial institutions to operate in foreign currency deposits and loans, is probably the correct procedure after and during really strong inflation. Equally useful is the stimulation of the domestic market in equities and of the establishment of financial intermediaries issuing them, i.e. investment trusts and so on.

B. *Effected Net Capital Transfers and Employment*

Will the capital import, if transferred, throw domestic factors out of employment ? This would generally be denied, on the grounds that the developing countries are either always in a state of excess demand, or that they are always happy to increase effective demand if available supply shows any sign of increasing without a concomitant rise in demand. There will, therefore, be no need for capital imports to be absorbed by means of appreciation of the exchange rate (relatively to domestic prices) which might cause employment problems.

By and large, this seems like a sensible model, but it will not operate, other things being equal, in the face of fluctuations in capital imports. While, surely, only pronounced fluctuations will lead to a serious misfunctioning of the model, there is evidence that misfunctioning can occur. Adaptation takes time, and, therefore, over a given longer period, capital imported in spurts will not be absorbed into given uses at a rate at which a similar steady rate of inflow would be absorbed. If the spurts are to be absorbed, special measures will have to be taken, like appreciating the exchange rate relatively to its long term trend or temporary removal of import restrictions ; or credit expansion. These special measures will interfere with the pattern of employment and *may* reduce its level. A rise in the rate of credit expansion will be inflationary, but the appreciation of the exchange rate or the removal of import restrictions not only will be deflationary but may mean that part of the transfer is frittered away in a rise in unemployment. There is some empirical evidence that such things have happened. One mechanism which has brought about an increase in absorption of capital imports along with the creation of unemployment in some developing countries has operated through a reduction in the share of construction in domestic investment. When import restrictions are relaxed or the exchange rate appreciates, investors' funds are channelled into equipment imports and employment in the construction industry is prejudiced.

Even capital flows whose fluctuations are compensatory of the fluctuations of export receipts may not be absorbable without special measures, and these may also be required in order to ensure the absorption of a given volume of capital flows where the *composition* of the flows fluctuates. The rest of the argument would run on similar lines as above.

So far, fluctuations of capital imports have been examined which are the results of spurts in the supply of such imports. Spurts in demand which provoke spurts in supply will not require special measures for their absorption. By bidding away certain factors from their accustomed uses they could, however, cause a fall in output through causing the unemployment of complementary factors.

Generally speaking, spurts in the commitment and disbursement of project loans and of private direct investment are unlikely to lead directly to unemployment. They could cause unemployment only among factors complementary to those which they bid away from their accustomed uses.

The above possibilities are not mentioned to add a few more illustrations of the well-known proposition that all change involves friction but to stress the advantages of smoothing fluctuations in capital flows, as far as possible. This is relevant because it is even true that on certain occasions official capital flows, instead of being invariant with respect to, or compensatory of, private capital flows, have shown a strange complementarity with them; i.e. official capital has flown, perhaps belatedly, only after private capital had, perhaps prematurely, become enthusiastic about a country.

This is not all which can be said about the relationship between capital transfer and employment. Some further remarks are made in the following section.

C. *Effected Net Capital Transfer and Domestic Investment*

The ' net outflow ' (not deducting investment in OECD countries by residents of developing countries) of long-term official and private capital, plus guaranteed export credits, from OECD to developing countries amounts to some 3–4 per cent of the latter countries' GDP (i.e. domestic production gross of (net) income payments to foreign residents). This ' net outflow ' is somewhat larger than the net transfer.

The ' net transfer ' probably represents over 25 per cent of gross domestic investment of the developing countries as a group (say about 14–15 per cent of GNP). If we deduct depreciation at about one-third of gross domestic investment, the net transfer represents nearly 40 per cent of net investment ; and, considering population growth of about 2·5 per cent per annum, and assuming a capital output ratio as favourable as 2 : 1, the net transfer represents about two-thirds of the net investment available for *per capita* growth of GDP. These, of course, are merely comparisons which say nothing about causation. But they do suggest a substantial contribution of the flows to the growth of average GDP, even without considering external terms of trade effects, or more generally, the problem of transforming savings into capital goods. It is interesting to note that Cairncross estimates the flows of capital to developing countries (excluding high income ones) to be much larger today, in terms of the recipients' GDP, than before the First World War. If one allows for grants and loans on concessional terms and is interested in GNP rather than GDP (as, of course, one should be) the potential contribution of today's total capital flow to the growth of the developing countries becomes even larger, relatively to its contribution at earlier times.

It is still necessary to inquire to what extent an increase in investment financed from abroad will be compensated by a reduction in investment financed domestically. This is, of course, one aspect of what I have called the 'proper absorption' problem. But it is one which seems to be rather neglected in discussions of the matter.

(i) The model which seems to underline most discussions of this matter and which is generally *not* explicitly spelled out is something like this :

Foreign capital is available for investment in a capital importing country at a certain cost or interest without distinction between (i) the capital importing countries' entrepreneurs, i.e. local entrepreneurs and (ii) foreign entrepreneurs operating in the capital importing country. Moreover, there is no distinction between lines of activity as to the availability of capital at a given cost.

To round out the model, one should also assume that the cost at which foreign capital becomes available is lower than the one prevailing so far in the capital importing country, though higher than the one prevailing in the capital exporting country. To simplify matters, one might also assume for the time being that all factors other than capital are accessible to local and foreign entrepreneurs operating in the capital importing country in whatever lines of activity and that, furthermore, local and foreign entrepreneurs have equal access to technology, managerial science and advertising skills.

Under these conditions one would expect an inflow of foreign capital for investment to lower the marginal efficiency of investment and this would presumably lower somewhat private domestic saving. Moreover (at least if the conditions of the model are relaxed slightly) domestic saving will now be directed into foreign assets to a larger extent than previously. Nevertheless, domestic investment will rise unless one makes extreme assumptions about the interest elasticity of supply of domestic saving or about the interest elasticity of demand for foreign assets.[1]

---

[1] It is, nevertheless, conceivable in this model that the incentive to invest for both local and foreign entrepreneurs might be lowered by the expectation that capital costs would in the future fall at a more rapid rate than was previously expected because a current of capital imports had started to flow.

(2) Some capital imports are, in fact, available indifferently to local — private and public — and to foreign entrepreneurs. It is, nevertheless, important to investigate what happens in a much more realistic family of models which is radically different from the one sketched above in that certain types of capital imports are reserved for certain types of borrowers.

In a first member of this family of models, foreign entrepreneurs have access to foreign capital and local entrepreneurs must rely on local capital. Local capital has so far received a higher interest rate than the one at which foreign capital becomes available, and it might seem that local entrepreneurs would have to continue to pay a higher interest rate for local capital than foreign entrepreneurs pay for foreign capital. This may indeed happen on extreme assumptions regarding the interest elasticity of supply of local capital, but it is most likely that the local interest rate will also fall when foreign capital-cum-entrepreneurship begins to flow in. For the interest rate differentiation would create a special risk for local entrepreneurs who would at all times be outcompeted by foreign entrepreneurs wherever they decided to move in. This special risk would lower the demand of local entrepreneurs for local capital and this would usually reduce the local interest rate.

(a) So far, the situation is no different from what it was in the first model. With lower domestic interest, the share of domestic investment which is financed from domestic savings will fall, as before. But so will — by contrast with the first model — the share of domestic investment which is locally *managed* (unless entrepreneurs are prepared to supply their services without regard to their remuneration net of risk). The effect on local entrepreneurship may seem to be merely of political importance except for the possibility that unemployment might be created among local entrepreneurs. There might, however, be cumulative effects through the discouragement of local entrepreneurship. It is *this* possibility which preoccupies the developing countries, particularly if foreign capital is selective and domestic entrepreneurship is thus discouraged mainly from the choice sectors which foreign capital prefers. (See below, Section D.)

(b) In so far as the local interest rate refuses to fall, a different pattern of results emerges. In the extreme case (which is hardly interesting, however) domestic investment ceases altogether. Such a result is less fanciful if considered to apply only to the sectors preferred by foreign capital, rather than to all sectors.

Having stated these possibilities, it is necessary to say something about the weight which should be attributed to them. In the first place, similar market imperfections exist inside countries and yet few people would suggest that every town should erect barriers to the entry of outsiders — e.g. the national chain store — in order to protect the investment incentives of actual (or potential) local grocers and their chance of remaining (or becoming) entrepreneurs. Secondly, there are, of course, many offsets to the fall in GNP or GDP which can be caused by the discouragement to local entrepreneurship, noted above, especially the fact that foreign entrepreneurship has more often than not probably ventured into precisely those sectors where local entrepreneurs have feared to tread.

Besides possible bias of foreign capital generally, in favour of foreign over domestic entrepreneurs, one must consider the possible bias of public foreign capital in favour of the government, or ' public entrepreneur ', of the capital importing country, over private entrepreneurs, both foreign and domestic, operating in the latter country. Such a bias may give rise to some similar situations as those sketched earlier in this section, *mutatis mutandis*.

The considerations made in this section illustrate the possible usefulness of measures which promote the unbiased functioning of the factor markets and equal access to technology, etc., but not — if the practical probabilities, rather than theoretical conceivabilities are considered — of measures which restrict capital imports. Local financial intermediaries financed from abroad are an example of the former type of measure. Another example are joint ventures and it may be worthwhile to note that joint ventures do not imply joint ownership. The *modus operandi* of — for instance — Sears and the automobile companies who subcontract with local suppliers makes them joint ventures in a very real sense.

D. *The Structure of Investment*

Since 1957, the net flow of long-term private capital (mostly direct) to developing countries has not exceeded 40 per cent of the total flow and has more recently been well below that proportion.[1] Since the official flow has gone largely to governments as ultimate

[1] See OECD *The Flow of Financial Resources to Less Developed Countries, 1956–63* (Paris, 1964) p. 19 ; OEEC, *The Flow of Financial Resources to Countries in Course of Economic Development, 1957–59* (Paris, 1961), p. 10 ; *The Economist*, 2 October 1965, p. 67.

borrowers (or to official enterprises), infra-structure and some large-scale industrial undertakings have benefited most from the official flow. Both had in the old days benefited from private capital flows. The private flow has gone into export development (national resources) as in the past and, increasingly, into import substitution.

But the official flow has also, most probably, affected the structure of private investment. In the absence of the official flow (or of any substitute for it), both foreign and local private investment would have been a good deal smaller in import substitution, while export development would have been hurt less. This is because foreign private investment in export development is more inclined to provide its own infra-structure than the local and foreign private investment in import substitution. In other words, the absence of official foreign investment would have reduced the share of infra-structure and of import substitution, the absence of private foreign investment would have had its main impact in reducing export development.

Within each of the two sectors (i.e. export development and import substitution), presumably those investments having large minimum sizes for efficient operation would have suffered most in the absence of private foreign investment. It is also obvious that within the import substitution sector foreign investment has made its main impact in those lines of activity where its superiority in access to cheap capital, technology, managerial and advertising skills counts most as well as those sectors where its length of past experience (if one can separate this factor conceptually from the others mentioned earlier) was particularly important. Thus, the natural inclination of foreign entrepreneurship and capital concentrates its effects on local entrepreneurship, noted in the previous section (C) on the most progressive sectors of the economy. This result has been accentuated by the fact that in all these lines foreign capital has often found the capital importing country's government eager to provide incentives. And they have, therefore, possibly, been overemphasized when a willing investor was prepared to be seduced by an eager government : e.g. the automobile industry.

It may be worth while recalling that the recent preponderance of official capital in international flows of capital to developing countries has probably not simply replaced flows of private bond capital but has presumably also responded to and encouraged the expansion of the public sectors of the developing countries. The latter expansion, because it has led primarily to the absorption of the most capital intensive sectors into the public sector limits the rise of private foreign direct investment in relation to the growth rate of the private sector and to the overall growth rate of the capital importing country, if outcries against foreign private economic domination are to be avoided. On the other hand such nationalism may result in a choice between lower growth of the private sector of the capital importing country of its increasing dependence upon finance obtained from or through its own government. The demands of nationalistic entrepreneurs in developing countries for easier and direct access to foreign official and private *lenders* are a reflection of this dilemma, quite apart from the role which the considerations made in section C above may play in such demands. The establishment in the developing countries of private financial intermediaries financed by private and official lenders in the capital exporting countries has been an increasingly important response to the demands noted.

E. *Capital Imports and Monetary Stability*

It is not at all clear whether the *long run* net effect of the process of capital importation of developing countries has been inflationary or deflationary. Correlation between rates of inflation and capital inflows relative to GNP proves nothing. Just as an example, countries with high rates of inflation have shown a remarkable ability to attract loans, even to the point of compensating for the denial of voluntary loans (which are made available to their more austere looking brethren) by attracting involuntary ones from private foreign suppliers. The countries run commercial arrears, are then bailed out by official lenders in the capital exporting countries, etc.

Spurts of capital imports have mostly been anti-inflationary. Where the spurts were not due to spurts in demand (which they helped to offset), the monetary authorities of the receiving country have mostly taken action so that these spurts could be largely absorbed (in the form of increased current deficits) *without* inflation, whether by temporary relief from import duties or other obstacles to imports or by allowing the exchange rate to appreciate relatively to its equilibrium value excluding the temporary excess of capital imports. Credit expansion has been, mostly, limited to the extent necessary to avoid absolute or substantial relative appreciation. Not the entire spurts of gross capital inflows have, of course, been absorbed by increases in current deficits. The temporary overvaluation of the exchange rate has probably encouraged the accumulation of foreign hoards in private hands. Whether these hoards have on balance been reduced when the spurts have ended, and with them the overvaluation — relative to trend — which had eased their absorption in the form of imports, is not clear. Whether, for example, penalties for capital exports have been more effective in deterring the original violation or the eventual repatriation is not at all clear.

But granting the fact that the effect of spurts of capital imports has been anti-inflationary, one may ask why more use has not been made of them in the numerous monetary stabilization programmes recently undertaken by developing countries, particularly in the crucial first year or so of such programmes. In fact, in recent stabilization programmes the first years have been characterized by a fall in current payments deficits and in imports. In one or two cases, this has been true perhaps even where large initial ' stabilization packages ' — over and above debt redemption and reserve reconstitution needs — were available. More frequently, the initial packages, while quite large in proportion to the recipients' GNP, have been small considering the absence of even a moral commitment to make available definite additional amounts, even conditional upon ' proper performance ' and the absence of a sufficient private inflow. Moreover, packages have contained, sometimes, a large proportion of project loans, which could not easily or quickly be used, even indirectly, to finance increased general imports.

This situation is largely the result of misconceptions concerning the role which capital imports can play at the start of stabilization programmes, including a confusion between two types of stabilization loans : the psychological and the absorption loan. This seems to be firstly the result of thinking of stabilization programmes in terms of the post-War I situation. Then, indeed, stabilization loans were often absent altogether or extremely small and, indeed, where available, were largely not used. Yet the programmes, as a League of Nations study once put it, worked with ' almost miraculous precision '. The fact is that in most of the stabilization programmes adopted after World War I, stabilization loans were needed mainly as one element among those which helped to create confidence that the government was, and had the means to be, serious about stabilization. For in most cases there had been extremely large capital exports before stabilization and their immediate cessation or reflux after the start of programmes made it possible rapidly to increase available goods and services without the use of large loans. Secondly, after World War II, the Marshall Plan of course was both a re-construction and a stabilization programme, but is regarded only as the former. This has obscured the very large amounts of capital imports which were transferred in the course of this particular stabilization programme. Thus, both postwar stabilization efforts enjoyed large increases in available goods and services through a rise in current payments deficits, although they financed them in different forms. In the recent stabilization programmes of the developing countries, such large increases in available goods and services have been not less but more necessary than after either war. Very briefly, stabilization today cannot count on as rapid a spon-taneous increase in civilian output as took place in the first years following World War II, and in some countries, following World War I ; none of the demand pressures are subject to spontaneous abate-ment today, as some of them were after the two wars (military, reconstruction, backlogs of consumer demand) ; the removal of distortions, an essential ingredient of all stabilization programmes, is harder today than it was then because the distortions serve more powerful political interests (organized urban labour, and entre-preneurs, the bureaucracy) while they hurt politically weak groups (the export sector, often composed of foreign enterprise, large land owners who are losing their grip, utilities which may also be foreign owned). An increase in available goods and services will not only offset inflationary pressures directly but will also mean that the changes in income distribution implied in the removal of distortions have less of an effect on the absolute real income of the ' victims ' of the stabilization programme. Even if the present real income of the latter suffers, the increased current deficit may permit a more rapid rise than would otherwise take place in investment and future real income and therefore a more rapid wiping out of the real income loss to the groups ' victimized ' by the removal of distortions. Thus, the opposition to the stabilization programmes can be held in check.

Although all this is widely realized it is also widely believed that the successful absorption of capital imports in the form of increased current deficits must sustain an ' overvaluation ' of the exchange rate which is not compatible with the programme's purpose of removing a distorted price structure. But overvaluation is harmful only in relation to the long-term trend. If, at the start of a pro-gramme, controls of various kinds are removed, which have hitherto bolstered an overvalued rate, the latter is quite likely to become undervalued from the long term point of view because short term elasticities of demand and supply are generally lower than long term ones. Consequently, even large increases in capital imports at the start of the programme need carry no necessary danger of over-valuation from the long term point of view. Furthermore, over-valuation can also be avoided by special action, like credit expansion or other methods of increasing demand (e.g. pending a fiscal reform, financing budgetary deficits from the counterpart of increased import surpluses rather than from higher taxes or import surcharges, etc.). Appropriately chosen, these measures need not negate the effects of eliminating exchange rate overvaluation on incentives for exports and import substitution. Nor need the absorption of loans to bolster a stabilization programme involve intolerable repayment obligations : by accelerating growth the loan may in fact improve the economy's ability to repay.

III. OPERATION

A. *Effects on GDP and GNP*

The general conditions which determine the extent to which additional capacity installed with the help of capital imports will affect the size of (*a*) GDP and (*b*) GNP require no repetition. The same goes for the general conditions which determine the effect upon income distribution of additional capacity installed with the help of capital imports, with or without imports of entrepreneurship and skills.

There are, nevertheless, certain particular cases which are of interest.

The preoccupation is sometimes expressed that the operation of additional capacity installed with the help of foreign capital can pre-empt local resources. One thinks of skilled manpower, managers, the resources of banks, etc. Two distinct problems are thought to arise. The first refers to the possibility that the markets for these resources function in a biased fashion to favour foreign investment. For example, the branches of foreign banks are sometimes said to prefer to lend to the subsidiaries of foreign corporations. This may be the reflection of the fact that the subsidiaries of foreign corporations prefer to deposit with the branches of foreign banks. But there is no question that such biases result in a less than optimal allocation of resources. The second problem is more subtle : in certain markets resources may be available both to domestic and to foreign investors at less than the value of their marginal product. This is often claimed to be the case for bank lending funds because of institutional restrictions on interest rates, a matter which is particularly important in countries with pronounced inflation. The point relevant to the treatment of foreign capital-cum-entrepreneurship is not the possible misallocation of the underpriced resources, but the fact that the foreign hiring factor may in this case get more than the value of its marginal product, because one of the local hired factors gets less. Of course, this is only one effect of the appearance of the foreign investment in the country and there is no reason to assume that its effect on balance must be to reduce GNP in absolute terms, though it will reduce it relatively to GDP.

A closely related problem concerns monopoly. It is frequently claimed in developing countries that their monopolistic market structure (quite apart from institutional restrictions on factor prices) insures the exploitation of the country by imported capital which functions as the hiring factor. This is necessarily true only in a technical sense. A monopoly pays hired factors less than the value of their marginal product. When a new employer enters the market, he will draw factors away from other employers and will 'exploit' the pre-existing group of employers and hired factors in the extent of the excess of the value of the marginal product of the latter over their cost to the new employer. This technical 'exploitation' may, of course, coexist with a rise in real income to the pre-existing group to the extent to which the appearance of the new employer and of any hired factors which he brings with him from abroad adds sufficiently more to output than the employer's 'normal profit' and the remuneration of the imported hired factors. The net of taxes and benefits (due to public expenditure) may also raise (or lower) real income to the pre-existing group.

Quite apart from these latter facts, there is a basic misconception underlying this analysis. It conceives of the typical developing country as being, in Mrs. Joan Robinson's words, 'a world of monopolies' when it would be more correct to see it as composed, at worst, of a monopolistic manufacturing and perhaps trading island in a sea of competition. In the sea of competition factor prices correspond to their marginal products (or more, if there is disguised unemployment). It is true that these factors work in the monopolistic sector for less than their marginal product in that sector. Moreover, their marginal product in the competitive sector is lowered — compared to what it would be under competition — because the monopolistic character of the manufacturing island restricts employment in that island.

Nevertheless, the presence of the sea of competition does change the terms of the problem. The appearance of a new foreign hiring factor will not draw resources from the monopolistic island if similar factors are available from the competitive sea. Consequently, no factor will be employed by the new entrepreneur whose marginal product exceeds its cost and there will be no ' exploitation ' even in a formal sense. (In fact, if there is disguised unemployment in the competitive sea the new entrepreneur — like the others — will pay hired factors drawn from that sea more than their marginal product.) GNP cannot possibly fall.

There is, however, an important proviso to be observed here. The impossibility of a fall in GNP applies only in so far as the new entrepreneur draws hired factors from the competitive sea. But there are always factors specific to the monopolistic island, if it exists. Restrictive legislation in developing countries on the importation by foreign entrepreneurs of skilled manpower may thus be particularly ill advised from the point of view of the economy as a whole. On the other hand, training programmes by foreign entrepreneurs for local labour may be an offset (at least if they are regarded as part of the overhead cost of the operation) to the possible harmful effects which may result from the drawing away from their former employment of factors specific to the manufacturing island, if the latter has a monopolistic structure.

B. *Effects on the Balance of Payments*

The general theory of the balance-of-payments effects resulting from the operation and presence of assets installed and liabilities created as the result of capital imports also requires no repetition. One matter which still seems to cause some difficulty refers to the relative cost of equity and bond finance. There is no question, of course, that equity investment carries a higher rate of remuneration than loans even if these are not granted at concessional terms. It is also agreed that the fluctuation of equity earnings in import substitution investments is not, like that in export industries, likely to compensate for fluctuation of current exchange receipts. What is relevant to the balance-of-payments problem, however, is not the difference between rates of remuneration, but the difference between rates of remittance. In some countries at least the reinvestment of earnings has been so high that remittances in relation not to total but to original equity (i.e. exclusive of reinvestments) have actually been lower than the remittances of interest on loans not issued on concessional terms, even after allowing for the remittance of earnings on equity investments disguised as royalties, etc.

IV. LIQUIDATION

The balance-of-payments problem of the liquidation of individual foreign liabilities offers no clear guide for the choice — in so far as such a choice may be practical — between equity and loan finance. It is a choice between small steady flows of amortization and uncertain flows of repatriation.

This latter problem is likely to become more burdensome if the present trend towards the ' nationalization ' of foreign subsidiaries continues. Even ' nationalization by growth ', i.e. obtaining local finance for part or all of the expansion of existing subsidiaries, is not a complete answer because it tends to reduce at least potentially the inflow of new foreign capital. Another method which has been used is that of nationalizing in one sector with the obligation upon the mother company of the nationalized subsidiary to reinvest the compensation in some other sector of the economy. Where this is used for nationalization of sectors with a particularly heavy foreign participation, e.g. utilities and export development, and where these sectors are large, it may run into a ' political saturation point ' in the sectors in which the compensation is invested. Still another method of ' nationalization ' is the conversion of equity into loan investment which has to some extent been used in the ' nationalization ' of utilities.

In the absence of arrangements for the reinvestment of the compensation for assets which are nationalized, repatriation or the amortization of loans by itself involves not only balance-of-payments (or terms of trade) problems but — irrespective of such problems — pressure on the capital importing country's savings potential. In some cases a solution to this problem has been found through the practice of charging for the goods or services produced with the help of assets installed by use of foreign loans and allowance not only for depreciation of the assets but for amortization of the loans as well. The effect of this is that the operation of these assets is automatically attended by an increase in domestic saving, at least in so far as the higher price or rate charged for the product does not lead to equal reduction in private saving on the part of the users. Whether a tax on users of the goods or services is advisable in order to raise additional saving is, of course, by no means certain. In fact, the objective of amortization enters into frequent conflict with the theory that many of these services should be subsidized rather than taxed and the latter theory generally carries the day, especially in countries with strong inflation.

COMMENTS ON PROFESSOR KAFKA'S PAPER

BY

BRANKO HORVAT

Yugoslav Institute of Economic Research

WHAT I propose to do is to extend Professor Kafka's analysis to the case of planned economies. I note in passing that it is a planned economy — and not the traditional perfect-competition idealization of an unplanned privately owned economy — which provides us with the basic theoretical model and standards of welfare comparisons. Perfect competition produces neither determined nor optimal solutions, however defined. Imperfect competition of the real world is then, of course, even less efficient.[1]

In order to be able to arrive at some specific results, I shall restrict the class of economies considered to one special category : planned underdeveloped economies with *per capita* income between $100 and $600. Only long-term capital movements are discussed. However, in certain respects the conclusions are more general than these restrictions might suggest.

THE NEED FOR LONG-TERM CAPITAL FLOWS FROM DEVELOPED TO UNDERDEVELOPED COUNTRIES

If within a country there are two regions whose levels of economic development are separated by a considerable gap and the market is left to operate on its own accord, the gap is likely to widen. By now this is no more a theoretical proposition ; it has been tested empirically many times :

[1] I have no possibility of proving these statements here. For that see my paper 'The Role of Accumulation in a Planned Economy' (Yugoslav Institute of Economic Research) and the references quoted there. One or two other theoretical points in these notes are also based on the paper mentioned.

Northern *vs.* Southern Italy, Northern *vs.* Southern Yugoslavia, etc. Quantitative studies of this phenomenon have contributed to our understanding of the underlying process. And since this process cannot be tolerated politically and since it is also economically detrimental in the longer run, something must be done to cope with the undesirable effects of the uncontrolled operations of the market mechanism.

What is true of regions within one country seems to be true of countries within one world. In the first half of the current century the gap between developed and undeveloped countries has been widened to an alarming degree and something had to be done about it. If the market cannot direct the flow of resources in desirable ways, this has to be done by planning. The need for a uni-directional flow of sources from developed to underdeveloped countries is usually substantiated by quoting the following three reasons :

(*a*) the lack of know-how in underdeveloped countries,

(*b*) the insufficiency of saving, and

(*c*) the import gap.

Let us discuss them in turn.

The lack of know-how is certainly a fact and an extremely serious obstacle to growth. But this obstacle cannot be eliminated by simply moving the capital into the country, nor is this the most efficient or most important way of dealing with the problem. Thus the discussion of this problem falls outside the scope of the present notes, and I shall restrict myself to only a few remarks later on.

The insufficiency of saving is a fake problem in a planned economy operating above the starvation level. Such an economy can always generate as much saving as is necessary for growth without ever reducing the living standard already achieved. An arithmetical example makes it clear. Suppose that the rate of saving s equals 15 per cent, and the capital coefficient k equals 3, then the rate of growth of output r is 5 per cent. Let net capital inflow represent 20 per cent of investment or 3 per cent of GNP. Then by suddenly eliminating all net capital inflow the expansion of consumption would be stopped for about seven months, to continue to grow at the traditional rate of 5 per cent thereafter without any capital import. If the rate of growth is about 10 per cent, the temporary stagnation of the living standard would last three months. But in the real world economy no sudden changes, like the one contemplated, need take place. Thus the 'insufficiency of saving' can be eliminated without the population having noticed any change at all. On the other hand all underdeveloped countries depend heavily on their agricultures, and crop fluctuations can affect GNP of the country as much as ± 20 per cent. A viable economy has to be adapted to such shocks. But they are several hundred per cent greater than the ones which would result from a sudden cessation of capital inflow.

Unlike the saving insufficiency, the import gap is a real problem.

230

Not, to be sure, because of its arithmetical significance. In this respect it is not different from the saving gap. What matters is its multiplying effect. The process of growth is a process of structural transformations. This cannot be done in a perfectly co-ordinated and balanced way. Rapid growth is always 'unbalanced'. While some sectors are pushing up, others are lagging behind. A backward economy is like an input-output table with most of the cells empty. The process of growth consists of filling the cells. But not all the cells can be filled simultaneously, even with very small quantities. On the contrary, only few of the cells will be filled by domestic output, while others will remain empty. Thus there will be a great discrepancy between the compositions of domestic demand and domestic output, too great a discrepancy to be repaired by imports arising from expanded exports.[1] The import surplus appears as a result.

Since structural transformation means a continuous creation and elimination of bottlenecks, an import surplus is not a financial phenomenon — like savings insufficiency — but a production function phenomenon. By eliminating bottlenecks an import surplus increases the efficiency of investment, shifts the entire production function and *increases the rate of growth beyond anything possible with domestic resources only*, no matter how great the rate of domestic saving. In other words, the expansion of trade in general and — since export cannot expand as fast as the needs for imports arise — import surplus in particular, increase the *absorptive capacity* of the economy thereby increasing the attainable rate of economic growth. At a later stage export gradually catches up with import and the country is able to balance its trade while preserving the high rate of growth. However, even in this stage a planned economy is vitally interested in the expansion of trade, and may find it advantageous to run an import surplus, as we shall see presently.

The duration of the structural transformation depends on the initial level of development and on the speed of growth. If a country starts with *per capita* income of, say, $150 and expands at a rate of 6 per cent, one may expect that it will need from 20 to 30 years to carry out the basic transformation. But long before it will have balanced its total trade, it will start exporting capital to countries which are even less developed. Thus capital, like water, will be flowing downwards all the time. But unlike water it will have to be pushed in this, seemingly natural, direction.

FORMS OF CAPITAL IMPORTS

The forms of capital imports are discussed in several papers and there is not much that I can add to this discussion in general. I shall therefore focus my attention on just one form of capital imports, whose merits I

---

[1] An instructive empirical analysis along these lines has been made for the Yugoslav economy expanding at a rate of about 10 per cent. Cf. L. Vukojević, *Structural Trends of the Yugoslav Economy in the Period 1952–1960*, Yugoslav Institute of Economic Research, Belgrade.

see in somewhat different light than most of the participants in the present conference. It is so-called direct investment or equity capital inflow. Elaborate schemes are designed and special policy measures undertaken to induce foreign firms to move into underdeveloped countries. It is often expected that they will make substantial contributions to the development, maybe even trigger the growth process. Are these policies commendable and expectations justified? There are at least five important aspects of the problem.

(1) It is said that equity capital has a stabilizing effect on the cycle and is therefore more desirable than, say, loan capital. The first part of the statement is probably true, but the conclusion does not necessarily follow. If we take into account that bonds earn 5 per cent to 6 per cent while net profits amount to from 10 per cent to 15 per cent, then it follows that the costs of the loan capital are two to three times smaller and the resulting saving may be used to counteract the cycle much more effectively. Besides, the repayments of loans may be stipulated in a very flexible way by tying them to the balance of payments position. Thus in this respect equity capital has no comparative advantage over loan capital and has a clear disadvantage in terms of costs.

(2) It is pointed out that although in the long run costs of equity capital are higher, in the short run they may be lower than the costs of loan capital since dividends may be smaller than interest plus amortization of the loan. Thus in the short run the balance of payments may be less adversely affected by equity capital. That is certainly true for the commercial interest rates and repayment periods shorter than about fifteen years. If interest rates are somewhat lower and/or amortization periods somewhat longer, the costs of a loan become lower even in the short run. However, other considerations have also to be taken into account. It is incomparably easier, faster and less costly initially to raise or float a loan than to attract equity capital when needed. Thus a loan may be partly repaid by another loan. As E. Domar[1] has shown, the ratio of amortization (A) and interest (I) to loans raised annually (L) settles after a while to

$$\frac{A+Y}{L} = \frac{a+i}{a+r}$$

(a = rate of amortization, i = interest rate, r = rate of expansion of loans). The analysis of the formula shows that even if the flow of loan capital fluctuates from year to year, this does not have too great an impact on the ratio. There is, of course, no guarantee that the flow of loan capital will be expanding at the rate higher than interest rate, but it might, and then there is always net capital inflow into the country.[2] At worst the

[1] E. D. Domar, 'Foreign Investment and Balance of Payments', *American Economic Review*, 1950, pp. 805–826.

[2] If on top of that the rate of loan expansion is lower than the rate of growth of GNP, the country may enjoy the benefits of the net capital import for an indefinite period of time, reducing the burden of debt outstanding all the time.

flow of loan capital will gradually diminish or fluctuate, but there is no need to assume that it will stop suddenly. And then the adverse effects on the balance of payments are moderate. One may add that in times of distress the conversion of loans may be negotiated and repayments postponed or a procedure along these lines may be stipulated in advance in the original contract.

(3) Professor Kafka argues in his paper that profits from the equity capital may be reinvested to such a high degree that remittances fall below interest paid on bonds. This is conceivable, but is highly unlikely in an underdeveloped country. The cases mentioned by Professor Kafka need a rather thorough statistical and accounting analysis before they can be taken as evidence.

(4) The import of know-how is perhaps the most positive and most important effect attributed to the import of equity capital. By moving into a less developed country a foreign firm brings along new technology, new managerial techniques, provides training for domestic workers and managerial staff, stimulates local entrepreneurship. There are some elements of truth in the above observation. But as far as it is true, the same effects may be achieved by joint ventures in otherwise domestically controlled firms. On the other hand, the impact tends to be rather limited. As Singer points out, foreign firms tend to remain an alien sector in the domestic economy. The more urgently the know-how is needed, the more rigid is the separation between the foreign and the domestic part of the economy because the greater is the cultural and economic gap between the two countries. It will be useful to draw the attention here to a paragraph in Mr. Okita's paper where he approvingly quotes Reubens saying about joint ventures in Japan '. . . that the greatest merit of direct foreign investments was the induction of advanced technical know-how, and that it was fortunate for Japan that large foreign enterprises were not transplanted to Japan and did not nip the Japanese industries in the bud and stop their development'.

(5) Unlike the four preceding aspects of the equity capital import, this one has only negative and none of the positive effects. Even when foreign capital is motivated by profit, it is the maximization of profit from the point of view of the foreign firms and not necessarily in the interest of the host country. However, since foreign businessmen are not only economic calculating machines, they will bring along their own cultural and political prejudices and they will tend to help, economically, politically and otherwise, their native countries regardless of legitimate interests of the host country.

(6) Finally, it may be useful to illustrate the five points made by at least one empirical example. In the prewar Yugoslavia about one-half of the non-peasant part of the economy was controlled by the foreign capital. From the point of view of the advocates of foreign capital this must have been an ideal situation, a great success for the Yugoslav

Government which was to be congratulated. However, the rate of growth was extremely low. After the war no foreign firm was left to operate in the country. Presumably know-how, entrepreneurship and other classical textbook effects of the foreign impact disappeared. But the rate of growth proved to be one of the highest in the world. What was wrong in the prewar situation may be illustrated by the case of oil industry.[1] Yugoslavia was created after World War I. Standard Oil of the United States and Shell Oil of Great Britain moved in the relatively empty market. After a few years of competition the market was divided and, together with two other foreign firms, a cartel was created, although that was illegal. In the booming decade of the twenties good profits were earned but not declared and, of course, taxes were not paid. It took more than a decade before the inexperienced administration of the new state could cope with this problem, and then one of the companies reacted by bribing government officials. The cartel, which later became legal, bought out domestic refineries and service stations. More obstinate domestic entrepreneurs were simply driven out of business. By the end of the 1920's the cartel reached the perfection of a textbook category: it controlled close to 100 per cent of output and trade of oil products. Instead of stimulating domestic entrepreneurs it, of course, annihilated them. Foreign firms acquired also concessions on prospective oil lands and never discovered any oil. The same area produces now about two million tons a year which covers the needs of the country. Once the cartel was perfected, investments were stopped. By the end of the second decade all capital imported into the country had already been repatriated and some 20 per cent to 50 per cent more exported out of the country in the form of interest and dividends. And after the war, on top of all that compensation had to be paid for nationalizing the firms.

The story just told does not imply that foreign capital is 'wicked' while governments are always good — the prewar Yugoslav government was certainly not a model government. Ethical categories like good and bad are irrelevant in this context. It implies, however, that by moving foreign firms in economically substantially less developed and culturally very different environment a social situation is created which is not favourable to growth and development.

We thus reach one of the rare clear-cut conclusions: the import of equity capital is neither desirable nor necessary. All good effects may be achieved in other ways avoiding at the same time bad consequences of direct foreign investment and control. This does not mean that a foreign firm should not be admitted to an underdeveloped country under any conditions. No dogmatism is profitable in the business of growth. But it is an illusion to expect a substantial contribution to growth from the

---

[1] Cf. B. Horvat, *Oil Industry in Yugoslavia*, three volumes, Yugoslav Institute of Economc Research, Belgrade.

import of the equity capital. Even more than that, too much of it taken with insufficient care may kill the patient.

Now, although equity capital import is undesirable and detrimental, practically all other forms of capital import—private as well as governmental — are highly desirable. Thus, for instance, the high rate of growth in postwar Yugoslavia may to a certain degree be explained by the high rate of capital import. The space does not allow me to describe these other forms of capital import which range from joint ventures to equipment credits to various loans agreements, private, governmental, and international, including various forms of economic aid.

MOTIVATION OF CAPITAL EXPORTING COUNTRIES

There are two main motives for capital export : profits and aid.

At least in economics, if not in ideology, unplanned private economies and planned non-private economies share a strong common interest. If, for instance, the marginal capital coefficient k is 3, the social marginal efficiency of investment is close to 33 per cent. But the interest rate on bonds in a private market is only 5 or 6 per cent. Thus the price for a loan settled somewhere between 6 per cent and less than 33 per cent will be advantageous for both parties.

Compared with unplanned economies, planned economies have a strong interest to import much more capital and for the following three reasons :

(1) They may take into account social marginal efficiency of investments which is much higher than the private marginal efficiency of investment.

(2) They have a higher absorptive capacity.

(3) Planning decreases risk of failures and fluctuations and so makes the burden of debt less onerous.

Thus, contrary to the frequent belief that planned economies are or should be autarchic, they have every reason to expand international trade in general, and capital movements in particular.

As to the aid motive, political, social and economic reasons for aid to less developed countries are similar to those for aid to a less developed region. Here I should like to make only one point : aid does not imply necessarily, even not primarily, free grants. Less developed countries are not beggars who do or should ask for charity, neither are donor countries bestowing alms upon them. Developed countries have an international obligation to help the less fortunate members of the world community, but not under any condition. First one should help oneself, and then God will help as well — as the biblical wisdom would put it. It would be cynical to apply this criterion to a country which, given certain conditions, just cannot help itself. Such a case should receive special attention ; but it is clearly exceptional. The criterion is applicable to countries in which aid is producing no visible effect on growth, and in particular to those which have what economists in their delightfully confusing jargon would call a transfer problem. In such a country aid is poured into the economy on the one side, but most of it, via corruption and mismanagement, quickly finds ways into the pockets of ministers, government officials and fraudulent contractors and after a short lag begins to flow out at the other side — to some interesting foreign country which was clearly not intended to be the primary beneficiary of the aid.

Since an increase in the rate of growth and not a substitution of domestic saving is the fundamental function of aid, repayable loans and not free grants are its main device. Grants are appropriate in exceptional circumstances — the first launching of a development programme, a sequence of bad harvests, exceptionally depressed export markets — and then the country in question has every right to expect them. But in normal circumstances it is loans we should concentrate upon. What seems to be needed today is much less international charity and much more an orderly functioning and an appropriate expansion of international capital markets. At first, to be sure, with various softening ingredients but with an aim to bring them gradually up to commercial standards.

DISCUSSION OF THE PAPER BY
PROFESSOR KAFKA

AMONG the main subjects considered in the discussion of Professor Kafka's paper were : (i) the definition of absorptive capacity ; (ii) the problem of capital transfer ; (iii) stabilization effects ; (iv) the impact of capital imports on domestic entrepreneurship ; and (v) questions of the need for and desirability of particular types of capital imports.

Professor Kafka distinguished between capital transfers, i.e. the absorption of additional real resources supplied from abroad, and 'proper absorption' defined in terms of ability to increase domestic investment, to transfer income, etc., abroad, and to redistribute income. *Professor Delivanis* noted the importance of foreign exchange reserves for Professor Kafka's definition of 'proper absorption'. If a country can increase its foreign exchange reserves, this should increase absorptive capacity and make planning much easier. He said that developing countries usually are short of foreign exchange, and added that the Greek experience during recent years illustrated the value of large reserves for avoiding payments problems. *Dr. Adler* objected that the problem of defining of absorption seems to be a semantic one, and that he could think of at least four meanings for the expression 'absorptive capacity'. The standard concept is defined in terms of mobilizing co-operant factors. Capacity limitations emerge in the form of under-utilization of capital assets when the supply of co-operant factors cannot be expanded. A second definition refers to the substitution of capital imports for domestic savings. In other words, domestic consumption can be increased by capital inflow even though investment remains constant. A third definition of absorptive capacity is needed when a capital inflow leads not to subsequent capital outflow, but to an accumulation of short-term assets by the receiving country. A fourth meaning refers to 'absorption' of domestic savings into investments. This comes close to Hirschman's concept of frustrated savings, or the disorganization of capital markets where a savings shortage and a drop in interest rates can occur simultaneously because nobody will accept savings at going rates.

A second problem discussed was that of the capital transfer, namely the association between capital inflows and outflows that is considered a major problem in lending to some of the less developed countries. *Professor Delivanis* argued that there may be not only an intrinsic connection but it must also be realized that an increase in foreign exchange reserves arising from capital inflows makes capital outflows easier. If the factors determining potential capital losses could be neutralized, it would be easier to reduce capital outflows from developing countries. As for index loans or index bonds as means of inducing people to keep money at home in the developing countries, he felt that experience showed these means were of limited value and their success a matter of maintaining confidence. *Professor Simon* noted here that interest-rate adjustments to avoid capital outflows when inflation was feared were unlikely to be successful. It might be better for purposes of analysis to distinguish between flight capital and outflows of speculative capital.

Professor Delivanis commented on the related point, raised by Professor Kafka, that capital inflows might conceivably have a negative influence on domestic savings. He suggested that if GNP increases as a consequence of the capital inflow, savings will also increase. An example to the contrary was noted by *Professor Wallich*. He mentioned the case of Puerto Rico in the mid-1950's, where easy access to the U.S. capital markets reduced domestic savings to nearly zero. Other cases were also listed by Professors Rosenstein-Rodan and Chenery. *Professor Chenery* noted further that since savings were a residual in the national accounts obtained by deducting the net foreign balance from investment, even though investment remains constant, if the net foreign balance increases, then savings by definition would be reduced.

Dr. Pazos agreed with Professor Kafka's point that increased imports could play an important role in implementing stabilization programmes. Dr. Pazos wondered, however, how a devaluation plan could be combined with an increase in exports and credit expansion. He could not see how all this could be achieved simultaneously. *Dr. Rhomberg* agreed that this raised problems of the proper timing of a stabilization programme. Should a country devalue first and stabilize later, or stabilize first and devalue later, or should both things be done simultaneously? *Professor Stolper* added, commenting on Dr. Pazos' and Dr. Rhomberg's points, that since most countries had exchange controls, the problem could be solved if the countries eliminated such controls.

Professor Singer pointed out that Professor Kafka minimizes the possibility that capital imports may have an adverse effect on local entrepreneurs. Though local entrepreneurs may send profits abroad while foreign enterprises may reinvest them in the country, local entrepreneurs deserve support if only because the balance generally works the other way round. Further, the need to encourage local entrepreneurship is of great importance with regard to savings. If savings are viewed as a result of investment rather than *vice versa*, the encouragement of local entrepreneurs — if it succeeds in bringing about more domestic investment — will also help to fill the savings gap in underdeveloped countries. *Professor Chenery* concurred with Professor Singer. If the government does not take any measures to expand total demand, he noted, any increase in the net foreign balance with investment fairly constant will result in a reduction of savings. This could explain the situation in a number of Latin American countries. Here *Dr. Pazos* questioned Professor Kafka's statement on a related point, in which he assumes that 'local and foreign entrepreneurs have equal access to technology'. Dr. Pazos thought that this is impossible by definition, since the basic difference between local and foreign entrepreneurs is that they did not have equal acess to modern technology.

In his discussion of Dr. Kafka's paper, *Dr. Horvat* argued that the reason for expanding long-term capital flows today is to bridge the widening gap between economic areas — a gap that has not been filled by the market mechanism. This is an argument against the theory of comparative advantage. Nor did Dr. Horvat find conventional arguments for equity capital as a source of technology and know-how in the borrowing country to be particularly convincing. Such capital is neither necessary nor desirable if accompanied by exploitation. *Professor Stolper* disagreed with Dr. Horvat. He indicated that the issue is not one of public versus private capital, nor of loans versus equity capital, but rather that the real issue is whether receiving countries are careful about what they get or not. He would also defend the doctrine of comparative advantage. Since a country cannot do everything it wants, the theory helps to indicate what should be done first. Despite its static character, the theory allows optimum allocation of resources now, so that a country will have more resources when facing the set of choices open in the next period. Professor Stolper also argued that the theory is intended to provide guidelines for any national economy to decide how to integrate within the framework of the world economy.

Dr. Rhomberg and *Dr. Adler* commented on Dr. Horvat's preference for equity to loan capital. They felt that he minimized the problem of repayment. *Dr. Adler* noted that the formulation underlying Dr. Horvat's position assumes continuity of capital inflows, and it is precisely the discontinuity of capital inflows that makes debt servicing a real problem. A similar point can be made with regard to his demonstration that the import cost of investment is very small if the rate of growth is reasonably high. This is only true when the import propensity is low, say 20 per cent, but in fact we are often dealing with countries where the import content of investment is not 20 per cent but 40 per cent or 60 per cent. Similarly the rate of growth of GNP is not always 10 per cent but often lower. Dr. Adler concluded that for the majority of countries, the relevant magnitudes are not as favourable as Dr. Horvat has indicated.

Chapter 6

THE 'NEED' FOR FOREIGN RESOURCES, ABSORPTIVE CAPACITY AND DEBT SERVICING CAPACITY

BY

RAVI I. GULHATI[1]
International Bank for Reconstruction and Development

I. INTRODUCTION

THE three phrases in the title of this article are used frequently by practitioners of foreign aid. Although this terminology has wide currency, the professional economist is aware of ambiguities in each concept. The Round Table Conference on Capital Movements and Economic Development is an appropriate forum at which to air these difficulties and to attempt more precise definitions. The object of this paper is to take up these three concepts in turn and to see how far we can go in this direction. Furthermore, we will try to examine the operational content of these concepts, i.e. the extent to which 'need' for foreign resources, absorptive capacity and debt servicing capacity can be measured. Finally, we will attempt to elucidate significant relationships among these concepts and draw some conclusions regarding the rationale and strategy of foreign aid decisions.

The concepts of 'need' and 'absorptive capacity' are discussed on the simplified hypothesis that foreign resources are a homogeneous category. No distinction is made between private investment, official capital on conventional terms and unrequited transfers. The question of the terms and conditions on which foreign capital

[1] The views expressed in this paper do not necessarily represent the official position of the World Bank, with whom the author is associated. The paper has profited from the comments of Messrs. Avramovic, van der Tak and Hussain, who were kind enough to read an earlier draft.

should be made available are discussed in the final section of the article.

The interpretation of the concept of 'need' depends on the attitude of the suppliers of foreign resources as well as the behaviour of recipient countries. In reality, there is little reason to expect that the motives of suppliers also inspire the actions of recipients. However, we have attempted to trace the logical implications of two schools of thought on the simplified hypothesis that in each case there exists a consensus regarding the mode of utilization of foreign and domestic resources.

To put it another way, the present paper does not discuss explicitly the concept of economic performance of developing countries. Foreign resource transfers are not viewed as a 'carrot and stick technique' to influence policy decisions of recipient countries. This is an important subject for another paper.

II. THE NEED FOR FOREIGN RESOURCES

The 'need' for foreign resources may be defined in terms of the desirability of reducing the gap between the standard of living of the prosperous societies of North America as well as Europe, and the poverty-stricken people of Africa, Asia and Latin America. Within the framework of static analysis, a transfer of resources from high-income to low-income countries can be justified on the grounds that such a redistribution enhances total welfare. This proposition is based on the idea that marginal utility of income diminishes as income increases.

The conceptual difficulties of applying this calculus on the global stage are formidable. The cardinal measurement of utility is controversial. Many economists challenge the propriety of making inter-personal comparisons of utility. High-income countries have pockets of poverty, just as low-income countries have their conspicuous rich families. Superimposed on these difficulties is the blatant political fact that the humanitarian impulse underlying such a definition of 'need' is too fragile to carry much weight. For it is reasonably clear that, if the rationale of foreign aid is increase of static welfare, then the present volume of resource transfers should be expanded enormously at once. Instead of the UNCTAD resolution, which urges industrialized countries to transfer 1 per cent of their GNP to developing countries, the policy prescription may be to raise this proportion steeply to, say, 10 per cent or more. On the assumption that all these transfers are channelled into consumption, the average *per capita* living standard of developing countries would rise instantaneously from about $138 to about $218. The gap between the standard of living of the developed countries and that of the developing countries would diminish by nearly 20 per cent.[1] However, even this raised standard of living of low-income countries would fall far short of the U.S. poverty line as defined by the Office of Economic Opportunity.[2]

Another interpretation of the concept of ' need ' for foreign resources is tied to a dynamic view of the growth process of developing countries. For example, Prof. Rosenstein-Rodan says :

> The purpose of (external) aid is to accelerate the economic development of these countries up to a point where a satisfactory rate of growth can be achieved on a self-sustaining basis. The overall aim of development aid is not to equalize incomes in different countries, but to provide every country with an opportunity to achieve steady growth.[3]

Foreign aid is viewed not as an instrument of income redistribution, but as a *catalytic agent* which can accelerate the progress of low-income countries on the path of self-sustained growth. Considerations of welfare now acquire a dynamic perspective. Foreign aid is not designed to raise living standards directly ; it supplements domestically generated resources which go into capital formation. By increasing the rate of investment, and thereby raising income growth, foreign aid permits recipient countries to raise progressively both the proportion of savings and the level of consumption expenditures. The total impact of foreign aid on the welfare of recipient countries depends not only on the volume of foreign aid, but also on the efficiency with which it is invested and on the proportion of the resulting income increment which is ploughed back into capital

---

[1] International comparisons of the standard of living in terms of *per capita* income, expressed in U.S. dollars at official exchange rates, are admittedly very crude.

[2] Families with an annual income of $3,000 p.a. or less are eligible to receive benefits under the new law. This implies a *per capita* consumption of about $700.

[3] 'Determining the Need for and Planning the Use of External Resources', *Organization, Planning and Programming for Economic Development*, U.S. Papers Prepared for the UN Conference on the Application of Science and Technology for the Benefit of the Less-Developed Areas, vol. viii, p. 69. U.S. Government Printing Office, Washington D.C. 1963.

formation. Benefits of foreign resource transfers should therefore be viewed as a flow over a fairly long time-span.

The accompanying chart illustrates the implications of these two doctrines concerning foreign capital for the time profile of consumption standards in developing countries treated as one group. If we assume that without foreign aid income rises at an annual rate of 3½ per cent, that the marginal rate of savings is equal to the average, and that population increases at 2 per cent p.a., then *per*

ALTERNATIVE TIME-PROFILES OF CONSUMPTION IN DEVELOPING COUNTRIES
(PER CAPITA CONSUMPTION — U.S. DOLLARS)

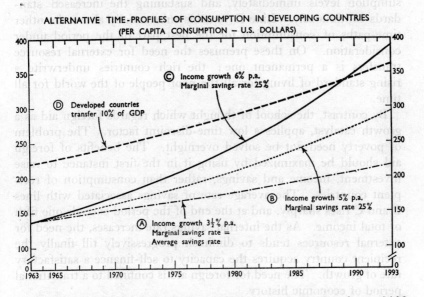

capita consumption of developing countries will rise from $138 to $216 during the next thirty years (see line A in chart). On the hypothesis that the maximum utilization of foreign aid as a growth catalyst accelerates income growth to 5 per cent p.a. and recipient countries raise the marginal savings rate to 25 per cent, *per capita* consumption at the end of three decades can reach a level of $295 (see line B in chart). A more optimistic assessment might place the potential growth rate in income at 6 per cent p.a., in which case the terminal value of *per capita* consumption will be $389 (see line C in chart).

If, on the other hand, 10 per cent of total income of developed countries is transferred every year as an equity measure, and the entire amount is channelled into consumption, then the *per capita* living standard will rise from $218 in the initial year to $361 in the final year (see line D in chart).[1] Line D is a composite of line A and the *per capita* resource transfer from abroad. In other words, the standard of living would improve in this fashion on the premise that low-income countries did not increase their rate of savings or investment.

Those who view foreign aid as a device for world income re-distribution, discount the future heavily; for them the problem of poverty is urgent and should be attacked frontally by raising consumption levels immediately, and sustaining the increased standards continuously. Line D remains substantially above the other time-paths of consumption for the best part of the period under consideration. On these premises the need for external resource transfers is a permanent one; the rich countries underwrite a rising standard of living for all the poor people of the world for all time.

By contrast, the school of thought which regards foreign aid as a growth catalyst, applies a low time-discount factor. The problem of poverty need not be solved overnight. The benefits of foreign aid should be maximized by using it in the first instance to raise investment, income and savings, rather than consumption of reci-pient countries. The average rate of savings associated with lines B and C rises sharply, and at the end of the period exceeds one fifth of total income. As the internal savings rate increases, the need for external resources tends to diminish progressively till finally the recipient country acquires the capacity to self-finance a satisfactory rate of growth. The need for foreign aid is confined to a transitional period of economic history.

It should be recognized that lines B and C on the one hand, and line D on the other, reflect not only differences in the attitudes of donors, but also different behaviour patterns of recipients. Both parties discount the future at a high rate in the case of D and at a lower rate in the case of B and C. Furthermore, we have deliberately over-drawn the contrast between foreign aid philosophies for analyti-cal purposes. The equity doctrine in its unadulterated form has few adherents today. Most practitioners of foreign aid base their decisions on an undefined blend of the two schools of thought. Even the most austere supporter of the growth-catalyst theory finds it difficult to resist pleas for equity in making judgments regarding absorptive capacity and debt servicing capacity.

Recently, many attempts have been made to calculate the 'need'

---

[1] GDP of developed countries is assumed to rise at 4 per cent p.a.

for foreign resource transfers within the framework of the growth catalyst theory.[1] These exercises are based on assumptions regarding absorptive capacity, which determines the speed at which investment should be raised, and hypotheses regarding the behaviour of savings in recipient economies. The 'need' for foreign resources is equal to the gap between the desirable level of investment and self-generated savings, or the gap between imports required to secure the target growth rate and the country's export earnings.

The plausibility and significance of these gap calculations are controversial issues in many quarters. Some authorities emphasize the weakness of available data on which these estimates rest. Admittedly, there are many among the 100 developing countries in which present information does not permit the derivation of the necessary quantitative relationships. Others challenge the gap calculations on the grounds that these estimates do no more than reflect the personal bias of the analyst. The value of the basic parameters cannot be derived solely from an objective examination of historical data ; to this must be added an assessment of the impact of future policy changes. The quality and operational significance of gap estimates depend on the extent to which policy-makers in developing countries concern themselves with long-run problems and the extent to which analysts have access to these policy-makers and enjoy their confidence.

III. ABSORPTIVE CAPACITY

If the function of foreign resource transfers is to accelerate economic growth by raising investment, then the speed at which capital formation can be increased assumes a critical importance in the determination of 'need'. The notion of an economy's absorptive capacity plays a crucial role at this stage of the argument. The idea is that at any point of time, or within a specified period of say five years, there exists a limit beyond which investment cannot be raised in recipient economies. This limit is set by the non-financial constraints to development, i.e. by the physical unavailability of

[1] B. Balassa, *Trade Prospects for Developing Countries*, Homewood, Illinois, 1964 ; H. B. Chenery and A. M. Strout, *Foreign Assistance and Economic Development*, AID Discussion Paper No. 7, Washington, 1965 ; P. Rosenstein-Rodan, 'International Aid for Underdeveloped Countries', *The Review of Economics and Statistics*, May 1961, pp. 107–138 ; United Nations, *Studies in Long-Term Economic Projections for the World Economy*, New York, 1964.

other factors of production necessary for further investment. Alternatively, the concept of absorptive capacity can be interpreted in terms of the familiar schedule relating the volume of investment to the expected rate of return at the margin.[1] In this context, absorptive capacity is defined as that volume of investment at which the marginal rate of return is equal to the 'socially acceptable discount rate'.[2] Before discussing which of these interpretations is the more relevant and more operational in the context of this essay, we will first explore the general nature of the concept of absorptive capacity.

Investment activity has three aspects or phases, and in each phase the determinants of absorptive capacity appear in a different light. In the *first phase*, development opportunities are identified, specific projects or programmes are formulated, their technical feasibility tested and their economic or financial merit assessed. In Schumpeterian language, this is the entrepreneurial function of innovation par excellence ; the exploitation of unused natural resources, the adaptation of unused technology to the local context and the discovery of new markets at home or abroad.[3] Schumpeter viewed this phenomenon of innovation in a rather romantic light ; the entrepreneurs, imbued with creativity and 'psychic freedom', were the heroes of early capitalism. In his later work, Schumpeter recognized the fact that the process of innovation was being reduced to a systematic routine.[4] Certainly one of the major objectives of national planning in developing countries is to establish a procedure for the preparation of a regularly rising volume of investment projects.

However, the historical record contains disappointingly few success stories on this score. Many developing countries have produced impressive plans based on econometrically tested models and internally consistent assumptions, but the operational content of most of these documents is rather low. The disaggregation of planned investment into specific projects and programmes for particular sectors and defined regions is seldom attempted. Apparently it is easier to think in terms of national accounting aggregates

---

[1] J. H. Adler, *Absorptive Capacity: The Concept and its Determinants*, Washington D.C., 1965.

[2] E. S. Mason, 'On the Appropriate Size of a Development Program', *Occasional Papers in International Affairs No. 8*, Cambridge, Mass., August 1964.

[3] *The Theory of Economic Development*, Cambridge, Mass., 1936, pp. 65–66.

[4] *Capitalism, Socialism, and Democracy*, New York, 1950, pp. 131–134.

than to identify concrete investment possibilities.

The failure of many countries to generate a sustained and expanding flow of well-prepared projects ready for execution may be traced to gaps in present knowledge — geology, soils, meteorology, hydrology, etc. The activities of the United Nations Special Fund and of other external sources of technical assistance are designed to narrow this information gap. Another factor inhibiting project preparation is the scarcity of professional skills — natural scientists, engineers, agronomists, financial analysts and economists. A physical shortage of professional skills is frequently accentuated by the sociological inability or unwillingness of developing countries to utilize national talent which is potentially available. Eminently qualified Egyptians, Indians or Filipinos have sought opportunities abroad (the brain-drain), while others remain unemployed at home. Unfortunately, the shortage of project analysts is not confined to developing countries; it is a global phenomenon. Consequently, the contribution of external technical assistance in this sphere is rather limited at present. Yet another constraint on the stream of prepared projects is the notable fact that decision-making is a painful and time-consuming process. Reluctance to take quick decisions in the sphere of projects may reflect a pre-occupation with non-developmental problems (military, language, party or tribal rivalry) or it may be caused by the unwillingness to accept the political implications of particular project choices. Discussing the basic causes of economic backwardness, Albert Hirschman says :

> Our diagnosis is simply that countries fail to take advantage of their development potential because, for reasons largely related to their image of change, they find it difficult to take the decisions needed for development in the required number and at the required speed.[1]

During the *second phase* of investment activity, projects or programmes are executed, physical structures take shape, and equipment is installed in place. The capacity of an economy to implement a development programme within a defined time period depends not only on its overall magnitude, but also on the internal balances of the chosen investment pattern and its consistency with the supply of co-operating factors of production. For example, Arthur Lewis

[1] *The Strategy of Economic Development*, New Haven, 1958, p. 25 (paperback edition).

cites the case of Ghana's First Development Plan which strained the bounds of absorptive capacity in this sense :

> The Government tried hard to complete the Plan in five years, and at all times had more than enough money to do so, but was unable to do so. At the beginning the physical limitation was the capacity of the building industry. Construction is normally about two-thirds of capital formation, and so a sudden attempt to increase capital formation is always frustrated by lack of trained construction workers, insufficiency of building firms, and difficulties of supervision. The result, as in Ghana, is that projects cost twice as much as they should, contractors make enormous profits, works are badly designed or badly built, and everything takes much longer to achieve than was expected.[1]

The elasticity of the Ghanaian building industry was grossly over-estimated, and the resulting bottleneck disrupted the implementation of the plan. Greater use of foreign building contractors might have alleviated the problem, but unless the bottleneck was anticipated in good time, delays would be unavoidable. In other instances, transport or power, services which are not normally imported, have proved to be the crucial bottleneck. Again there are cases in which a critical shortage of irrigation engineers prevents the achievement of planned targets while qualified road or railway engineers remain underemployed.

The capacity of external aid to offset the errors of planning and to compensate for the immobility (at least in the medium-term) of domestic personnel by financing the importation of foreign human resources is rather limited. Edward Mason says :

> Yet, in the course of supplementing domestic human-resource deficiencies by foreign skills, there are limits that do not apply in the case of substituting foreign exchange for domestic financial resources. Entirely apart from differences in language, custom, and technical procedures that may diminish the expatriates' efficiency, political and social considerations set limits to the number of foreigners a developing society can tolerate in advisory or supervisory positions . . . although the tolerance level for such imports varies considerably among less developed countries, it is fairly low in all.[2]

The *third phase* of investment activity begins as the second ends, and the newly constructed facility starts production. The ability

---

[1] 'On Assessing a Development Plan', *Economic Bulletin of the Economic Society of Ghana* (June–July 1959), pp. 2–11.   [2] *Op. cit.*, pp. 15–16.

of an economy to utilize fully its stock of capital is an important aspect of the notion of absorptive capacity. Finished projects require expert management, various grades of skilled labour, a regular flow of material inputs and markets of appropriate size to make their contribution to economic development. Departures from full capacity utilization, reflected in high capital-output ratios, can be the result of numerous causes — unavoidable indivisibility, unforeseen technological or other changes in world markets, unavailability of skills or material inputs, etc. In the present context, we are concerned only with those impediments which are relevant to the concept of absorptive capacity.

Excess industrial capacity, resulting from a chronic shortage of imported inputs, is a common phenomena in several developing countries. The underlying foreign exchange constraint may be caused by unrealistic policies (resource allocation, exchange rate) but it can be offset by the transfer of external resources. Such a foreign exchange constraint, therefore, is a symptom of unsatisfied absorptive capacity.

Other impediments to the satisfactory operation of existing capital assets are much more intractable. For example, many small countries have built ostentatious university buildings which cannot be justified in terms of the likely demand for higher education. Another instance is a steel mill which suffers repeated breakdowns because it lacks expert management or trained foremen. These are glaring illustrations of strained absorptive capacity; they represent uses of capital (whether internal or external) which are patently wasteful.

To recapitulate the argument, judgments regarding the absorptive capacity of an economy, within a specified time period, should be based on an assessment of the following factors :

(*a*) the state of knowledge regarding natural resources, etc. ;
(*b*) the stock of professional, managerial and medium-level manpower, its rate of utilization and mobility ;
(*c*) the national economy's tolerance for imports of foreign human resources ;
(*d*) the internal balances of the investment programme, and
(*e*) the ability of policy-makers to make developmental decisions.

Given this framework of analysis, should absorptive capacity be interpreted as a schedule relating the scale of investment to the rate of return, or as a fixed point without a determinate rate of return ?

From the theoretical point of view, the schedule is, of course, preferable. Absorptive capacity then becomes a matter of increasing or diminishing returns and not an absolute wall, which cannot be crossed under any circumstances. This approach is not only theoretically attractive, but the general idea of a schedule is confirmed by practical experience. A substantial increase in investment within a short period is almost always physically possible, provided the authorities are willing to tolerate higher costs, diminished durability of resulting assets, excess capacity or frequent breakdowns in operations.[1]

Ideally, absorptive capacity can be read off a schedule relating the scale of investment to the marginal rate of return. Alternatively, a range of investment programmes of various magnitudes may be plotted on the horizontal scale while the associated incremental capital-output ratios (ICOR) are shown on the vertical axis. Although serious difficulties are encountered in measuring and interpreting either the marginal rate of return or the ICOR, the latter is perhaps more operational at this stage of economic technique.

The marginal unit of investment is difficult to define without resorting to tortuous and arbitrary conventions. Projects have a certain minimum size beyond which they cannot be divided, and this indivisibility appears at different points in various parts of the economy. Many projects are closely inter-related — Hirschman's forward and backward linkages — and the rate of return on a project is dependent on other components of the investment programme. If the rate of return is derived by comparing costs and income over the whole life of the asset created by the investment, then the calculation rests on numerous explicit or implicit assumptions regarding the future behaviour of the economy. This procedure involves circular reasoning. We set out to discover the marginal rate of return in order to determine the appropriate size of total investment and the warranted rate of total income growth. However, the calculation of the marginal rate of return is itself based on assumptions regarding these macro-economic magnitudes. Also, a sizeable part of total investment — education, health, etc. — does not lend itself to rate of return calculations. Recent attempts to identify and then to measure the diffuse benefits flowing from expenditures on social projects are more heroic than convincing. Putting aside, for the

[1] As a limiting case, we can visualize situations in which the factor governing absorptive capacity is the ability of policy-makers to make developmental decisions (item *e* above) during a specified time period. In these contexts, the concept of a schedule loses its significance ; absorptive capacity may then be represented by a vertical line.

moment, the thorny question of whether the marginal rate of return of planned investment can be determined, it is even difficult to ascertain the historical marginal rate of return. Ex-post rates of return generally vary within a wide range — 50 per cent or higher in some branches of manufacturing or distribution, and very low or negative returns in other activities. In the light of these bewildering results, how should we identify what is happening at the margin ?

The concept of the ICOR evades many of these problems by measuring the overall productivity of alternative investment pro-programmes ; each treated as an indivisible unit. Also, the ICOR relates investment to value-added, which is a more appropriate measure of social productivity in the present context than the concept of profit. The ICOR is not simply a measure of the productivity of capital. It expresses the relationship between investment and output, taking account of changes in other factors of production — natural resources, labour skills, technology and management.[1] It should be recognized that the ICOR is not an unambiguous indicator of efficiency, particularly at the level of project or sector analysis. Capital assets with long gestation periods and long serviceable life show a high ICOR, but this does not necessarily mean that these investments are less productive than quickly maturing or less durable investments which show a relatively low ICOR. This implicit bias of the ICOR is an important drawback which reduces the value of this tool in appraising particular projects. Despite all its imperfections, the discounted rate of return must serve as an indicator of efficiency in the micro-economic sphere. However, judgments regarding absorptive capacity are concerned with the size of total investment programmes, consisting of projects with long and short gestation periods, as well as long and short productive lives. The implicit bias of the ICOR, therefore, tends to cancel out at this aggregative level of analysis. Nevertheless, in interpreting the level of the economy-wide ICOR allowance should be made for spectacular projects, such as the Volta Dam in Ghana or the Tarbela Dam in Pakistan. A relatively high ICOR, which is clearly attributable to a single overhead facility or an accidental bunching together of several projects with extraordinary gestation periods, should not be construed as a mark of inefficiency.

An illustrative schedule of absorptive capacity is presented in the

[1] See Harvey Leibenstein, *Economic Backwardness and Economic Growth*, New York, 1957, p. 178. Also, see W. B. Reddaway, *The Development of the Indian Economy*, London, 1962, pp. 207–208.

accompanying diagram. Policy makers are confronted with six alternatives (points *A*, *B*, *C*, *D*, *E*, *F*) from which to make the choice. Point *A* represents a modest expansion of investment (compared to the base period) and is associated with a modest growth rate in income (4 per cent p.a.). Point *B* represents a bigger investment associated with a lower ICOR, reminiscent of Rosenstein–Rodan's 'big push' theorem.[1] Further increase in the scale of investment is associated with rising values of ICOR, but right up to point *E* increase in investment is associated with an acceleration of GNP. Point *F* is clearly beyond the economy's absorptive capacity; the capital coefficient rises so rapidly between *E* and *F* that growth of GNP is adversely affected. Absorptive capacity is defined in the diagram by point *D* at which the calculated ICOR is equal to the cut-off criterion.

We should consider for a moment the nature of the judgment embodied in the cut-off criterion, which performs the same function as John Adler's 'minimum acceptable rate of return' and Edward Mason's 'socially acceptable discount rate'. Conceptually, these rates equate the future stream of benefits represented by extra production, with present sacrifices represented by the current savings effort. In the accompanying diagram, the cut-off criterion takes the form of the maximum acceptable ICOR. This ratio relates investment, financed by nationals and foreigners, to the increase in value added, possibly with a lag of one or two years. Providers of foreign resources will be concerned with the level of the cut-off criterion just as much as national planners. According to Branko Horvat, Yugoslav planners choose the cut-off criterion in such a way that growth in GNP is maximized [2] (point *E* in diagram). Planners in other developing countries have argued that attempts to maximize GNP would strain the economy's managerial resources, and the resulting conspicuous waste in development expenditures might undermine the political case for demanding continued austerity. Consequently, the optimum size of investment might be at points *C* or *D* in the diagram.

The cut-off criterion acceptable to suppliers of foreign aid depends on the urgency with which they view the problem of poverty. They might apply a less stringent standard to recipient economies at the

[1] 'Notes on the Theory of the "Big Push"', in Howard S. Ellis (Editor), *Economic Development for Latin America*, Proceedings of a Conference of the International Economic Association, New York, 1961.
[2] 'The Optimum Rate of Investment', *The Economic Journal*, December 1958, pp. 747–767.

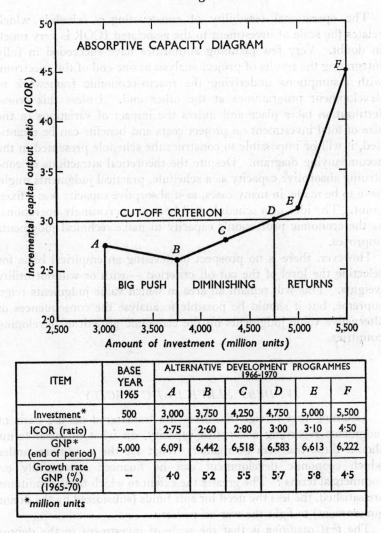

ABSORPTIVE CAPACITY DIAGRAM

CUT-OFF CRITERION

BIG PUSH   DIMINISHING   RETURNS

Amount of investment (million units)

Incremental capital output ratio (ICOR)

ITEM	BASE YEAR 1965	ALTERNATIVE DEVELOPMENT PROGRAMMES 1966-1970					
		A	*B*	*C*	*D*	*E*	*F*
Investment*	500	3,000	3,750	4,250	4,750	5,000	5,500
ICOR (ratio)	–	2·75	2·60	2·80	3·00	3·10	4·50
GNP* (end of period)	5,000	6,091	6,442	6,518	6,583	6,613	6,222
Growth rate GNP (%) (1965-70)	–	4·0	5·2	5·5	5·7	5·8	4·5
*million units							

bottom of the income scale than to developing countries at higher levels of *per capita* income. In other words, the cut-off criterion might be 'utility-weighted', to implement the value judgment that it is more desirable to raise income in poorer countries than in countries that are not so poor. The adoption of such a principle would synthesize to some extent the school of thought which regards foreign aid as an instrument of income redistribution with the school which views it as a growth catalyst (see Section II, above).

The operational feasibility of constructing a schedule which relates the scale of investment to the associated ICOR is very much in doubt. Very few planning authorities have succeeded in fully integrating the results of project analysis at one end of the spectrum, with assumptions underlying the macro-economic framework of development programmes at the other end. Unless this cross-fertilization takes place and unless the impact of variations in the size of total investment on project costs and benefits can be quantified, it will be impossible to construct the schedule presented in the accompanying diagram. Despite the theoretical attractions of construing absorptive capacity as a schedule, practical judgments might have to be made, in many cases, as if absorptive capacity was a fixed point. The idea of a schedule will become increasingly operational as the economic profession's capacity to make technical judgments improves.

However, there is no prospect of devising an empirical basis for selecting the level of the cut-off criterion — with or without utility weights. This will remain an area in which value judgments reign supreme, but it should be possible to analyse the consequences of alternative value judgments on the economic growth of developing countries.

IV. DEBT SERVICING CAPACITY

Assuming that foreign resources are transferred on the basis of judgments regarding absorptive capacity, on what financial terms should these transfers be made ? What are the conditions under which economic development can be financed successfully on commercial terms ? The greater the extent to which these conditions are satisfied, the less the need for soft funds (subsidized by the donor government) to fight the war on poverty.

The *first condition* is that the scale of investment in the debtor economy should be sufficient to secure regularly a perceptible rise in *per capita* GDP.[1] In other words, the determinants of absorptive capacity (and particularly the ability of policy makers to make developmental decisions) should not be so restrictive as to jeopardize the achievement of output growth faster than population increase.

[1] G. M. Alter, 'The Servicing of Foreign Capital Inflows by Under-developed Countries', in H. S. Ellis (Editor), *op. cit.*, p. 146. Cf. also Dragoslav Avramovic, assisted by Ravi Gulhati : *Debt Servicing Capacity and Postwar Growth in International Indebtedness*, Baltimore, 1958, p. 61.

If *per capita* product stagnates or declines, then there is low probability of the debtor economy extracting a surplus to service foreign capital. It is much more difficult to reconcile the competing claims of foreign creditors and national expenditures in the context of stagnating output than in the framework of an expanding economy.

The *second condition* is that the efficiency of investment, measured in terms of the marginal rates of return or the level of the ICOR, should remain above a critical minimum. If the pace of development is forced, notwithstanding steeply diminishing returns on investment, and if such development is financed by external loans on commercial terms, then the economy is likely to confront a viciously cumulative debt problem. Consequently, the cut-off criterion used to define absorptive capacity and the optimum level of investment has to satisfy a financial constraint. The minimum (although not sufficient) condition which must be satisfied to avoid an unmanageable debt problem can be derived from a formula developed by Messrs. Hayes, Wyss and Hussain : [1]

$$K = \frac{So}{r} + \frac{S' - So}{i}$$

where,

K = cut-off criterion defined in terms of the ceiling level of the incremental capital-output ratio ;

So = initial average gross domestic savings rate ;

S' = marginal gross domestic savings rate ;

r = annual rate of growth of gross domestic product ;

i = average effective interest rate on foreign debt.

Unless this equation is fulfilled, outstanding debt and debt service will grow faster than GDP, and thus absorb an ever-rising proportion of total product of the debtor country. Assuming that commercial loans carry an average interest rate of, say, 6 per cent, low-income countries which encounter rising capital-output coefficients can avoid unmanageable indebtedness only if they are prepared to accept rather low growth rates, or if they can generate extraordinary

[1] 'Long-Run Growth and Debt Servicing Problems : Projections of Debt Servicing Burdens and the Conditions of Debt Failure', Essay IV, in D. Avramovic and Associates, *Economic Growth and External Debt*, Baltimore, 1964. The original formula, based on a simple growth model, is as follows :

$$i = \frac{r(So - S')}{So - Kr} .$$

In this form, the equation defines the relationship among several variables which at some finite point in time will result in equiproportional growth of interest payments abroad and GDP. Consequently, an economy which satisfies this equation will experience a stabilization of the ratio of interest payments to total income.

marginal savings rates. For example, given an average savings rate of 5 per cent, marginal savings rate of 10 per cent, and ICOR of 3 : 1, the growth in output consistent with the above equation is only 2·3 per cent p.a. Under these circumstances, the debtor country must be content with barely maintaining *per capita* income. If we assume that income growth can be accelerated to 3·3 per cent p.a. by tolerating an ICOR of 4 : 1, then the debt problem will become unmanageable unless a marginal savings rate of 20 per cent can be achieved. Of course, these illustrations should not be taken literally; the underlying growth model is too mechanical and rigid to reflect reality. Nevertheless, these examples do demonstrate the limitations of commercial lending as an instrument of development finance.

The second condition does not have a time dimension. Debt servicing capacity is defined in terms of the prospect, no matter how distant, of stabilization in the ratio of service payments to GDP. Implicitly it is assumed that the international financial mechanism operates without frictions, that creditors have an unlimited time-horizon, and that the transfer of external resources takes place without interruption or impediment. In actual fact, of course, public sources of external capital (bilateral or multilateral) hesitate in accepting responsibility to supply funds in the future. Lenders are not organized to take a co-ordinated view of the financial needs of debtor economies, except in the few cases of consortia or consultative groups. Even these organizations do not make pledges for more than a year at a time. There is no ' invisible hand ' to integrate the actions of private investors scattered all over the world and guided by different sets of considerations.

While the international financial mechanism is in a state of disarray the developmental problems require an extended time-horizon for their solution. For example, Dragoslav Avramovic has argued that even the debt cycle of a developing country with a favourable constellation of macro-economic magnitudes ($r=5\%$ p.a., $So=10\%$, $S'=20\%$, $K=3 : 1$, $i=6\%$) spans 36 years; debt rises for 25 years and declines to zero in the following decade.[1]

The length of the debt cycle is related not merely to the financial gap between initial savings and desired investment, but also to deep-seated structural factors. If world demand conditions for the major export products of the borrower economy are unfavourable, then development will require a fundamental re-alignment of the

[1] *Op. cit.*, pp. 55–61.

productive factors. Such structural change is a time-consuming process even in mature industrialized economies. In the peculiar circumstances of highly specialized primary producers, the adjustment mechanism may take much longer. If traditional export industries are depressed, then it will be doubly difficult to secure a high marginal savings rate. If the pattern of investment emphasizes new import substitution industries, then the ICOR will tend to rise.

The required time-horizon is even greater in the case of countries with very low *per capita* incomes and very low initial saving rates, i.e. the 'long-haul cases'. The economic development of these countries may require a sustained transfer of foreign resources for half a century or more. Therefore, the *third condition* for the successful use of commercial loans in promoting economic development is the equivalence of the time-horizon of creditors, treated as one homogeneous group, and the gap (measured in years) separating the initial position of the debtor economy from the state of self-sustained growth.

The 'long-haul cases' also present another problem. They require a sustained net transfer of foreign resources (i.e. after allowing for debt service payments), frequently on a rising scale for a period embracing several decades. Lending on conventional terms in these circumstances is inefficient in the sense that a considerable share of gross disbursements leaks out of the debtor economy in the form of service payments.[1] The disbursement pump has to be worked with increasing frequency and vigour to effect the required net transfer, in spite of the demanding law of compound interest. Therefore, the *fourth condition* for the effectiveness of conventional lending is that the gross supply of foreign capital should be sufficiently elastic to accommodate the rapidly accelerating demand. In as much as bilateral creditors find it difficult to justify a sharply rising volume of gross capital outflows within the present budgetary and administrative frameworks, this condition will not be fulfilled in many cases.

The absorption of a sharply rising volume of gross foreign capital can also raise serious problems for the debtor economy under the existing rules of the game. On the one hand, the ratio of required gross capital inflow to domestic investment can rise to very high levels in 'long-haul cases'.[2] On the other, a large part, possibly

---

[1] Evsey Domar, 'The Effect of Foreign Investment on the Balance of Payments', *The American Economic Review*, September 1950, pp. 805–826.

[2] Even when the debt cycle spans only one generation, the ratio touches a peak of 36 per cent. See Avramovic and Associates . . . *op. cit.*, 1964, p. 62.

two-thirds, of the present flow of official foreign capital is tied to creditor currencies and a sizeable share (possibly one-third) is tied to specific projects. Bilateral and multilateral financial agencies frequently operate under serious constraints regarding the kinds of projects they will finance. There are few sources which will entertain requests for the financing of small-size projects and working capital, not to mention administratively complex schemes and projects which raise ideological issues. This rigidity poses a serious dilemma for a country which has to finance a large part of domestic investment through foreign borrowing. The country has to negotiate project loans for a gross amount considerably higher than what it will obtain net of service payments. Loan negotiations consume a lot of time and administrative skill. Since loan applications have to be tailored to the revealed preferences of creditor agencies, the task is even more difficult than it would otherwise be. Indeed, a rational solution to the problem of mobilizing the required volume of external funds from widely scattered sources, each subject to a medley of constraints, nuances and inhibitions, would require a complicated linear programming analysis.[1] Consequently, the *fifth condition* for the effectiveness of conventional finance is that the non-quantitative constraints on the supply of external capital should not be inconsistent with the peak ratio of required gross capital inflow to domestic investment.

So far, we have been concerned with debt servicing capacity in the context of long-term growth. This process of economic growth is marked by fluctuations arising from seasonal, cyclical or accidental factors. In developing countries, the impact of these short-run oscillations is concentrated on the balance of payments — exports, imports, foreign capital inflow and 'capital flight'. Temporary fluctuations in these variables may produce a liquidity crisis, although the economy is structurally sound. Therefore, an important aspect

[1] Mahbub ul Haq, chief economist of the Planning Commission of Pakistan, says: 'The desire to reduce foreign dependence originates not only from a desire to institutionalize growth rates but also because foreign dependence carries certain unpleasant economic choices, apart from its other political implications. Pakistan's development programme is, at present, entirely dependent on foreign assistance. This need not have worried the planners if foreign assistance was available in a flexible form. The difficulty is that most of the aid-giving agencies are now insisting on project-type assistance. This poses the possibility of a sharp conflict between planners' and aid-givers' ideas regarding national priorities. Since any project which is not aided has only a negligible chance of implementation, aid-givers are in an effective position to dictate national priorities. Again, since the aid-giving countries might themselves have widely divergent views about priorities, what projects are finally accepted for assistance may or may not fit into a logical whole.' Quoted from 'Problems of Formulating a Development Strategy in Pakistan', Studies in Development No. 1, *Development Plans and Programmes*, Development Centre of the OECD, Paris, 1964.

of the analysis of debt servicing capacity is concerned with the borrowing economy's liquidity position.[1]   Three questions have to be answered.   What is the degree of vulnerability of the borrower to temporary fluctuations ?   What is the strength of the flexible elements in the balance of payments — monetary reserves, external sources of compensatory finance, compressible imports — which can absorb the impact of fluctuations ?   And, finally, what is the importance of the rigid items in the balance of payments — contractually fixed debt service, minimum tolerable level of imports — which will strain the economy's financial position ?

The foreign financing of economic development on commercial terms leads to the gradual building up of a sizeable block of rigidity in the balance of payments of debtor countries.[2]   The movement of the ratio of debt service payments to external earnings describes a historical cycle.   This ratio is bound to rise sharply during the initial phases of growth, unless exports are a leading sector.   The level of the ratio tends to flatten out as the economy reduces its dependence on foreign capital, and finally the ratio can be expected to decline.   This is not an automatic or inevitable cycle, but it should materialize if economic development is successful.

The *sixth condition* for the effectiveness of foreign loans on commercial terms is that the unfavourable impact of high debt service ratios on the borrower's liquidity position should be offset by mitigating the severity of export fluctuations [3] and institutional innovations designed to improve the supply of compensatory finance. The widespread adoption of high employment policies in the industrialized countries has already reduced export fluctuations arising from short-term changes in fixed investment and output. However, further measures are necessary to offset the impact of the inventory cycle as well as other disturbances.   If these measures are difficult to improvise or to implement, then the burden falls on liberal provision of external compensatory finance.

We have formulated half a dozen conditions which must be satisfied for the successful financing of economic development on

[1] For an example of this kind of analysis, see Dragoslav Avramovic and Ravi Gulhati, *Debt Servicing Problems of Low-Income Countries 1956–58*, Baltimore, 1960.
[2] To the extent that development is financed by foreign equity capital, the element of rigidity is reduced.   If foreign capital is invested in the export sector, then profits and dividends tend to fluctuate in the same direction as export earnings. Also, foreign equity investment does not carry any pre-determined schedule of repatriation.
[3] Fluctuations in foreign capital inflow will be reduced as the result of fulfilling *condition three* (see page 257).

commercial terms. Countries which face formidable obstacles in expanding investment with a defined minimum of efficiency, which confront adverse demand conditions on the world market, and which start the development race from a position very far in the rear, are likely to prove risky debtors. The magnitude of these risks is magnified by the fact that the international capital market is disorganized, that lenders operate within short time-horizons, that the gross supply of funds is inelastic, and that there are many non-quantitative constraints on the transfer of resources. Finally, the riskiness of loan capital is further accentuated by the phenomenon of economic fluctuations which continues to plague the world, although to a lesser extent than heretofore.

The ' need ' for foreign resources, therefore, cannot be satisfied wholly by finance on commercial terms, even if the concept of 'need' is related to the growth catalyst theory. A rational strategy of foreign aid will blend hard and soft loans ; the precise mixture depending on a specific analysis of debt servicing capacity in the particular case. This is not to suggest that debt servicing capacity of an individual borrowing economy at a particular point in time is amenable to quantitative measurement. It is not. The impact of variations in the terms of lending on the borrower economy is spread over fairly long periods of time. The nature of this impact can be illustrated, within the framework of simple growth models, by using hypothetic values of the main parameters. However, our present ability to forecast the value of these parameters, within a reasonable margin of error, does not extend beyond a decade at the very maximum. Consequently, operational conclusions regarding debt servicing capacity, while they can be fortified by objective analysis up to a certain point, must finally rest on intuitive judgments.

These intuitive decisions need not be divorced from value judgments regarding the desirability of redistributing world income. The notion of equity can enter the scene through the backdoor and exercise an impact on the determination of the blend between hard loans and soft-aid. Very low-income countries can receive a higher component of soft-aid than debt burden considerations alone justify. The higher the proportion of soft-aid, the shorter will be the period, *ceteris paribus*, during which the target standard of living can be achieved. Just as the utility-weighting of the cut-off criterion can reconcile to some extent the principle of need and equity, so also the manipulation of the soft-aid component can synthesize partially these two schools of thought.

COMMENTS ON MR. GULHATI'S PAPER

BY

JUST FAALAND
The Chr. Michelsen Institute, Bergen (Norway)

MR. GULHATI makes many interesting points of a conceptual nature. He also offers some comments on quantitative aspects as well as on the operational significance of the three variables ; and finally he indicates some conclusions for development strategy. In this opening statement I shall confine my remarks to one or two points only, relating to each of the three main sections of Mr. Gulhati's report.

The concept of *the need for foreign resources* as defined and used by Mr. Gulhati refers to a large and very composite aggregate. In national accounts terms, the need for net inflow of foreign resources is equal to the difference between total imports and exports of goods and services ; this gap, as realized, is also equal to the difference between total domestic investment and savings. In projections and planning it is the size of this gap, or of these gaps, which constitutes the need for foreign resources. The need thus defined may, of course, be calculated or projected for individual countries or for groups of countries.

Mr. Gulhati has chosen to abstain from a discussion of the components of this need, the relative urgency of needs for the several components, the scope for substitution of one type of inflow of foreign resources for another, etc. This leaves out very important aspects of international resource flows in relation to development.

As for the concept itself, I find Mr. Gulhati's formulations a little unsatisfactory. The concept of the need for foreign resources, as I see it in this context, had to do with a quantity or a variable in a model of trade and growth, in which the amount of net inflow of foreign resources is determined by a set of other variables and parameters. Net inflow of resources is assumed — within the relevant ranges — to be independent of any single specific variable in the model and only determined by the interplay of all those other variables. Net inflow of resources, therefore, is not directly dependent on rates of growth of recipient or of donor countries, on past levels or changes in levels of transfer of resources, on savings ratios, or on any other such variable. The need for foreign resources is simply a quantity that would have to be made available for all the other assumptions of the model to be consistent with each other, consistent, that is, within the confines of the model adopted.

Differences of assumptions, of models and of data will of course give different values for the need for foreign resources, but there need be no difference as to the concept itself and the essential meaning of the concept. It can be very fruitful, however, to discuss choices between types of economic models, between alternative sets of assumptions, and between alternative values of parameters, including policy parameters.

This leads me to a few comments on the question of quantification. I for one believe that exercises in quantification in this area are highly important for a fuller understanding of the nature and the magnitude of the growth problem in less developed countries. But I also believe that the highest returns of research in this field are now to be found in less aggregative models, both geographically and sectorwise. Mr. Gulhati does not offer any comment on these aspects, perhaps because we may be expected to discuss such questions in relation to Mr. Chenery's paper tomorrow. In any case I feel it would be useful and interesting for us to know at some stage how Mr. Gulhati and his colleagues here in the Bank are dealing with this question of quantification.

As for the second topic of *absorptive capacity*, I would like to bring to the attention for possible discussion here two specific judgments of fact relating to absorptive capacity which have been presented to us.

(i) On page 247 of Mr. Gulhati's paper he explains that absorptive capacity is limited by the failure of many countries to generate a sustained and expanding flow of well-prepared projects ready for execution. This is a particularly important confirmation of a pretty widely held judgment of fact, coming as it does from a member of the Bank, where so much experience and information in this field have been accumulated. Such a judgment is also important, of course, for the views we may hold on the relative roles of project loans as compared to more general forms of assistance.

(ii) In this connection, Mr. Gulhati states that the contribution of external assistance in this area of project identification and formulation is rather limited at present. Moreover, the reasons he advances for this conclusion, some of which relate to conditions in developed as well as underdeveloped countries, indicate that there really is not much hope of greatly expanding external assistance in this area. If this is a fair interpretation of Mr. Gulhati's statement, I would like to question his conclusion. In my view we have not by a long way exhausted the potential flow of technical assistance to developing countries in the area of project formulation.

Finally, on this topic of absorptive capacity, I would like to make an observation to the diagram following page 253 in Mr. Gulhati's paper. He there postulates hypothetical values for six alternative levels of investment activity, each with given effects on GNP or the growth of GNP. The point of the diagram is to illustrate the changing values of ICOR for rising levels of development programmes. For each alternative he calculates the implied ICOR and shows that — with the values of GNP increases postulated — the magnitude of the ICOR first diminishes and then gets higher and higher. I suggest that his illustration would be more apt and more striking if he had also calculated the ICOR for the *increments* in development outlays required to move from one alternative development level to the next higher, not only the ICOR of each alternative relative to the base year level. Calculating what may perhaps be termed the differential incremental capital output ratios (DICOR), one finds that the *extra* capital required per unit of increase in GNP obtained by choosing alternative B rather than A is as low as 2·1. The DICOR for alternative C rather than B, however, is as high as 6·6, alternative D for C gives 7.7 and E for D, 8·3 and, finally, alternative F gives the negative DICOR of 1·3. Since, on Mr. Gulhati's own assumption, all six alternative levels of development programmes are open to the decision making authorities, the consequences of the choice between alternatives as revealed by these DICORs are more relevant to the decision makers, than the average ICORs given by Mr. Gulhati and discussed in his paper. If, indeed, we accept his asumption of a cut-off criterion of 3·0 as the maximum acceptable amount of development outlay per unit of output, the rational decision would be to choose development alternative B, not alternative D as stated by Mr. Gulhati.

The third section of Mr. Gulhati's paper deals with *debt servicing capacity* of developing countries. This is a question of particular interest and concern to the World Bank, and most of the data that we have and the analysis of data that has been made, are results of work done here. I shall only make one point in this connection, and this is to stress the importance of the first of the six conditions of adequate debt servicing capacity of capital importing developing countries, which Mr. Gulhati identifies, viz., the condition that the capital inflow has in fact been associated with perceptible and continuous increases in *per capita* GNP. It is my interpretation of the limited evidence available, that structural imbalances in an economy, bottlenecks in specific areas, deficiencies of savings or of exports, sluggishness in adjustment and adaptations to changes in the economic situation, are all much more difficult to deal with in a poor and stagnant economy than in one where backwardness has receded and where growth is rapid and continuous. As a poor country gets richer, as replacement investment and new additions to capital stock increase, as consumption as well as production patterns broaden and reach higher levels, etc., the economy gains in flexibility and responsiveness to policy manipulation. This flexibility, I submit, will also contribute to the correction — if need be — of insufficiency in the mobilization of savings, if that is the operative threat to foreign debt servicing ability, and to the expansion of exports and of import competing industries. My view, in other words, is that we are justified in being a good deal more optimistic than is now often the case with regard to the eventual debt servicing capacity of underdeveloped countries, provided the rates of growth associated with the capital inflows are high. My thesis, therefore, which I feel I can advance without being unduly lighthearted, is the following. The only really important test of a developing country's creditworthiness and debt servicing capacity is whether or not growth does in fact come about in association with the capital inflow. If that test is met, we can be reasonably confident that the country will also eventually develop — or at least, have the ability to develop — the necessary debt servicing capacity.

DISCUSSION OF PAPER BY DR. GULHATI

THE discussion of Dr. Gulhati's paper dealt principally with the main topics of the paper : (1) the need for foreign resources ; (2) absorptive capacity ; and (3) debt servicing capacity.

I. THE NEED FOR FOREIGN RESOURCES

Professor Singer suggested that there were motives for extending foreign aid other than the 'equity' and 'growth-catalyst' motives listed in the paper. Historical association or colonial responsibility are two such motives. Further, whether a capital transfer is called aid or not depends upon one's judgment of whether the country is underdeveloped. *Dr. Patel* added here that need is a moral issue and that this moral issue is the only relevant concept in discussing the question of how much aid rich countries should give. To place this issue in its proper context, Dr. Patel noted that there are three decisions involved in the field of aid : (1) how much aid should aid-giving countries provide ; (2) how much or in what way should this aid burden be distributed among the aid-giving countries ; and (3) how should aid be distributed among the receiving countries. According to Dr. Patel, Dr. Gulhati's distinction between need for foreign resources, absorptive capacity, and debt serving capacity applies only to the third of these decisions. *Professor Rosenstein-Rodan* added that we should distinguish between two moral judgments implied in the distinction between the equity and growth-catalyst motives for giving aid. Equity concerns the question of equality of income, while the growth-catalyst concept involves equality of opportunity.

II. ABSORPTIVE CAPACITY

Professor Chenery opened the discussion of absorptive capacity by arguing that absorptive capacity can be best defined in terms of what a country could do if it were offered a certain amount of foreign assistance. That is, how much might growth increase under given policies if a certain amount of foreign aid were granted for a given length of time. Even if net investment was zero, absorptive capacity might be high if external capital was employed to utilize excess capacity. In this sense, absorptive capacity is determined in part by utilization of existing capaital as well as by the building of new capital. It follows that identification of the function of resource transfer with investment is misleading. Also, since the productivity of foreign assistance rather than productivity of investment is at issue, indirect effects — such as effects upon savings — must be considered in assessing the effectiveness of aid utilization. The concept should not be limited to investment in the short run, therefore, since a country can grow just as much by generating savings as through efficient investment. Professor Chenery concluded that absorptive capacity cannot be properly measured with ICOR-type measures. *Professor Mundell* observed here that the capacity to absorb imported capital should be defined in the same way that the Keynesian concept of marginal efficiency of capital applies in a closed economy. Even in an open economy, the marginal efficiency of capital concept can be used by applying the going rate of interest as the cut-off point for investment. The rate of return — social rather than private — provides a more precise measure than ICOR in this instance.

Professor Singer felt that attempts to find criteria for absorptive capacity are made difficult by the circular nature of the concept. Absorptive capacity of a country depends upon the amount of aid that is available, on the terms on which it is available, and on the predictability of available aid. The ICOR cut-off point depends upon the terms of aid, for instance, while the terms of aid depend upon the ICOR cut-off point. *Dr. Patel* said that the problem of weighing need against absorptive capacity arises in answering the question of how to distribute aid to recipient countries. Should aid be given to countries on the basis of their absorptive capacity? The concept of absorptive capacity relates to the goal of making a country self-reliant, whereas need attaches to the standard of living. In determining absorptive capacity through the use of ICOR or marginal rates of return, it would be desirable to take into account the marginal utility of income to wage-earners in estimating returns. It is insufficient to look at the alternative cost side of the picture.

Dr. Okita noted that there is need to take into account the impact of foreign exchange earnings. This could affect both absorptive capacity and debt service capacity. *Professor Rosenstein-Rodan* agreed with Dr. Okita, and with Professor Chenery that absorptive capacity is the capacity to raise income. It has three components : (1) the capacity to organize and mobilize savings ; (2) the capacity to produce and to invest ; and (3) the capacity to influence the balance of payments or to mould foreign economic policy. These three components have to be properly distinguished.

Professor Rosenstein-Rodan also felt that while ICOR may be a good approximation of absorptive capacity for large investment programmes, it is hard to interpret when there is disguised unemployment or when the shadow price of labour is not unique, but made up of a number of shadow prices. What is the true ICOR in such cases? The results depend on what is included in value added. Where disguised unemployment exists, it may be desirable to use incentive shadow wages that lead to different ICORs than other shadow wages. *Professor Chenery* interjected at this point that since value added is the sum of profit plus wages, the use of different shadow wages would be irrelevant to the magnitude of value added. *Professor Rosenstein-Rodan* replied that ICOR depends not only on the value of a programme but on the composition of the programme and that this is where different shadow prices affect ICOR. Because of this, he believed the marginal rate of return to be better than ICOR in the case of total investment. Also, where differences in ICOR are due to excess capacity in social overhead capital or to bottlenecks in other areas, such differences — especially for relatively short periods as five years — do not reflect differences in absorptive capacity.

Professor Stolper defended ICOR as an indicator of profitability given the structural distribution of investments. ICOR may increase rapidly in certain cases because investment is increased but increases in output are not realized. Normally profitability and ICOR would be expected to move in opposite directions. This last point was made in reply to Dr. *Horvat*, who had argued that ICOR does not reflect profitability at all. The argument was resolved by Professor Rosenstein-Rodan in distinguishing between short periods (five years or so) in which differences in ICOR were of little relevance, and longer periods when ICOR might be said to reflect productivity better.

Dr. Andreasyan felt that while the problem of absorptive capacity is an actual problem, the main problem for developing countries is accumulation, which includes absorptive capacity. Internal factors such as social conditions effect both absorptive capacity and savings levels.

Professor Wallich noted that the concept of absorptive capacity had been extended by successive speakers from ICOR to need. In practice, we tend to separate welfare and productivity-raising programmes. In determining the optimum aid level or the optimal combination of direct foreign aid and lending, a cut-off basis like that used by Modigliani and Miller in assessing optimum combinations of loan and equity financing for private firms might be most appropriate.

Dr. Pazos agreed with Professor Rosenstein-Rodan that shadow wages are relevant for measuring the cost of public investment, but concurred with Professor Chenery that shadow wages do not make much difference in calculating value added. Dr. Pazos also agreed with Dr. Patel that the procedure for deciding how much aid a country should receive is unimportant and can be rationalized. He noted, however, that it makes a lot of difference in practice whether a country presents elaborate project proposals or not, especially if the funds are to be used in refinancing or amortizing part of existing debt. Failure to present elaborate proposals for new projects when in fact borrowing is largely to renew debt may give the impression that the country has less ability to prepare projects and less absorptive capacity than it actually has. Some device is needed in order to avoid this problem. *Dr. de Beers* felt that Dr. Pazos ignored the technical assistance content of project lending. It is only justified to ignore technical assistance if planning is well done. In general, technical assistance is necessary to ensure that the project is feasible and that the loan accomplishes its intended purpose.

III. DEBT SERVICING CAPACITY

Dr. Patel observed that debt repayment problems relate to commercial considerations. The capacity to service debt depends upon the terms of aid, but the terms of aid in turn depend upon the aid programme and prospects for repayment. Debt capacity concepts can be related to the need concepts when asking whether a recipient country which achieves self-reliance should start giving aid, should pay its debts or should just stop asking for aid.

Professor Rosenstein-Rodan questioned the existence of general principles for handling debt service problems. For instance, should those who are over-indebted have a claim to a certain proportion of their debt being converted, or should further distinctions be made to avoid the negative incentive principle of punishing those who are careful in their prior debt activities? On the other hand, these may be governments that are not responsible for the past carelessness of their colonial masters or predecessor governments. Should not extremely careful countries be allowed to sign debt agreements on the promise of debt reconversion later on? Essentially the problem is one of whether conventional or unconventional loans are justified in particular cases. Professor Rosenstein-Rodan also noted that while new aid has to pass through the legislatures of donor countries, provisions for extension of maturity dates or renewal of old loans do not, though the results are the same in each case.

Dr. Horvat commented on the effect of uncertainty on a country's debt servicing capacity. He felt that there might be some misunderstanding on the riskiness of soft loans. For planners in recipient countries the choice may be between a mix of soft and commercial loans with uncertainty on the one hand, and purely commercial loans and certainty on the other. In asking the question of how one chooses between commercial loans with certainty and a continued flow of soft loans with uncertainty, Dr. Horvat noted that there is a tendency for underdeveloped countries to act like beggars.

Chapter 7

FOREIGN ASSISTANCE AND
ECONOMIC DEVELOPMENT

BY

HOLLIS B. CHENERY
Harvard University

PROGRAMMES of public assistance to less developed countries have increased rapidly over the past decade in the United States and Western Europe. Since private investment has stagnated during this period, public grants and loans now provide over $6 billion of the total of about $9 billion of capital transferred. For most underdeveloped countries, foreign assistance is already a critical source of development finance and one of the main hopes for accelerated growth in the future.

Foreign aid programmes differ in their objectives, in the types and sources of resources furnished, and in the performance required of the recipient. At present, the resource flow from the members of the OECD to the underdeveloped world takes four principal forms : [1]

(1) grants, primarily for budgetary subsidies to ex-colonies and military allies (40 per cent) ;

(2) loans for capital projects (25 per cent) ;

(3) loans for general support of development (15 per cent) ;

(4) transfer of surplus agricultural commodities against loans repayable in local currency (15 per cent).

Only 15 per cent of this resource transfer is made by way of international institutions.

The evolution of these methods has been affected by many political and economic factors, such as the transformation of the colonial system, the extent of the public support for international institutions and the degree of success of the recipient countries in formulating and executing development programmes. On balance,

[1] A detailed accounting of the OECD assistance is given in OECD, *The Flow of Financial Resources to Less Developed Countries from 1956 to 1963*, Paris, 1964. The members of the OECD account for over 90 per cent of the public assistance to less developed countries ; most of the remainder comes from the Communist Bloc.

this complex of mechanisms has been shaped more by the desires and political requirements of the donor countries than by the needs and performance of the recipients.

The main thesis of this paper is that the system for administering public grants and loans can be greatly improved by tailoring it more specifically to the needs and performance of the aid recipients without sacrificing the legitimate interests of the donors. Before setting out proposals to this effect, it will be necessary to examine both the role of external resources in the development process and the systems of allocation and control currently in use.

I. THE ROLE OF EXTERNAL ASSISTANCE IN DEVELOPMENT [1]

From an economic standpoint, public and private capital flows perform very similar functions. They are distinguishable to the recipient primarily by the extent to which their allocation conforms to development priorities and by the terms of repayment. To the provider of capital, the differences are much greater. Public capital flows are designed primarily to promote the economic development of the recipient and can take a great variety of forms.

The following analysis of the role of assistance in development will form the basis for evaluating the effectiveness of public capital inflows and the ways in which they are controlled. With allowance for the difference in objectives and the transfer mechanism, much of this analysis is applicable to private foreign investment as well.

A. *Accelerating the Rate of Growth*

The transformation of a poor and slowly developing country into one capable of sustained growth at a fairly rapid rate is the core of the development problem. Its solution requires an improvement in the quality of human resources, a rapid increase in the capital stock, substantial changes in the composition of output and accompanying changes in attitudes and institutions. Without external assistance or private investment, a developing country would need to provide for all of these requirements from its own resources, including only such imports as can be financed by export earnings.

[1] The analysis summarized in this section is stated in more complete and formal terms in Chenery and Strout, *Foreign Assistance and Economic Development*, Agency for International Development, 1965.

A country's failure to develop is more often attributable to its inability to bring about these changes in a sufficiently co-ordinated way than to any single factor. The limits to development at any point in time are more likely to be bottlenecks in the supply of skills, of particular commodities or of productive capacity in particular sectors than general shortages of resources. This structural imbalance reflects the imperfect functioning of market mechanisms on a national basis, which is one of the distinguishing features of underdeveloped economies.

By relieving potential bottlenecks, external resources can make the requirements for co-ordinated changes in the economy less stringent and permit fuller use to be made of domestic resources. These contributions may be summarized under the headings of additional skills, importable commodities, and savings. The value of additional imports in a situation of bottlenecks and under-utilized capacity is increased by the fact that they can supplement whatever commodities are in short supply. For example, three dollars of additional imports may permit the production of ten dollars of additional GNP of a composition determined by consumer demand. In this case, an annual resource inflow costing one dollar will have a marginal productivity of 3·3 measured by the resulting increase in GNP.

While in many cases the main contribution of external resources is to offset the imbalance between the structure of supply and the structure of demand, in others their primary function is to finance additional investment. Since no incomes are generated by the receipt of external assistance, it should normally be possible to increase investment by the entire amount of the resource transfer, whatever the form of the additional commodities supplied.[1] The productivity of aid in these circumstances is equal to the marginal productivity of additional capital. It is typically lower than the productivity of assistance when there is a balance-of-payments bottleneck.

In order to present these ideas more systematically, it is useful to distinguish three 'phases' or types of situations, identified by the scarce factor that is more restrictive to growth :

[1] This is the assumption made in the conventional national accounts definition of savings as the difference between investment and the import surplus. In some cases, however, the additional resources take the form of income payments or agricultural commodities which are distributed in such a way as to increase consumption. In this case, the investment equivalent of the external aid is less than one.

(I) Skill-limited growth.
(II) Savings-limited growth.
(III) Import-limited growth.

While external capital — public or private — increases the supply of each of these scarce factors, the effect of additional resources will depend primarily on their effectiveness in offsetting the bottleneck which is most restrictive. If growth is limited mainly by lack of managerial talent and skilled labour, for example, a million dollars spent on adding to the supply of these factors will be more productive than an equal amount of additional capital goods or other commodities. A similar distinction can be made between the form of assistance that is appropriate when the principal need is to raise the level of investment and the appropriate form when there is a shortage of specific imports.

Assuming that external resources — accompanied by reallocation of other available foreign exchange — are provided in such a way as to increase the supply of the limiting factor, the short-run effects of aid can be measured by the contribution of that factor to additional output. This contribution is likely to be higher in the bottleneck situations of skill or import limitations than when aggregate savings and investment provide the limit to growth. In each case, however, it is the availability of under-utilized natural resources, labour, or physical plant which determines the productivity of the complementary resources supplied from abroad.

B. *Long-Term Effects of External Assistance*

In assessing the effectiveness of aid over a longer period, we must consider the alternative growth paths made possible by varying assistance streams rather than merely the effects of incremental resources at a given moment. The effect of aid on growth over a period of ten or twenty years will depend on the productive uses that are made of the increments it produces in GNP in addition to the short-term effects just described. The long-term productivity of aid can therefore be divided into two parts :

(i) the initial increments in GNP resulting directly from the additional resources provided ;

(ii) indirect effects on growth resulting from the productive use made of the initial increments in GNP.

The initial increments in GNP can be used to relax any or all of the three types of restrictions to further growth. Appropriate uses include labour training in the skill-limited phase; higher savings and taxes in the savings-limited phase; and import-substitution or additional exports in the import-limited phase. To measure the long-run productivity of assistance, we must specify the use to be made of the added production in promoting further growth.[1]

In studies of Israel [2] and Greece [3] my collaborators and I have calculated the long-term productivity of assistance by comparing alternative growth paths determined from economic models. From the analysis of Greek development over the period 1950–61, it was estimated that the marginal productivity of assistance — as measured by the ratio of the cumulative increment in GNP over the period to the corresponding increment in capital inflow — was of the order of 2·5. Similar estimates for Israel are nearly as high.

The relative importance of the indirect effects of assistance in determining the total outcome is illustrated by the case of Greece, where the savings limitation was estimated to have been predominant over the period studied. Of the total increase in GNP since 1950, 15 per cent would have been achieved without assistance at the estimated savings rate; 35 per cent respresented the direct effect of the assistance provided; and 50 per cent is attributable to the indirect effects of aid. As a result of the relatively high marginal savings rate of 22 per cent maintained by Greece, additional savings out of the aid-induced increase in GNP have financed a higher proportion of additional investment than the aid itself. If the marginal savings rate had been lower, the long-run effectiveness of aid would have been substantially less even if the direct short-run effects had been the same. Much the same conclusion can be drawn from the successful aid experiences of Israel, Taiwan and the Philippines.

To generalize from this experience, the productivity of external resources can be expressed as a function of the principal parameters in an aggregate growth model. The results for the cases of savings-limited and import-limited growth are as follows: [4]

[1] A similar point has been made by Eckstein in his analyis of the productivity of domestic investment. Cf. O. Eckstein, 'Investment Criteria for Economic Development and the Theory of Intertemporal Welfare Economics', *Quarterly Journal of Economics*, February 1957.

[2] H. B. Chenery and M. Bruno, 'Development Alternatives in an Open Economy: the Case of Israel', *The Economic Journal*, March 1962.

[3] Irma Adelman and H. B. Chenery, 'Foreign Assistance and Economic Development: the Case of Greece', *Review of Economics and Statistics*, February 1966.

[4] The formulae are given in Chenery and Strout *op. cit.*, p. 30. For a growth rate of 5 per cent, $\beta = 1\cdot8$ for five years, $3\cdot8$ for ten years, and $7\cdot0$ for twenty. Export growth is taken as given.

(i) *Savings limit*: $\dfrac{d\,Vn}{d(\Sigma F)_c} = \dfrac{1}{k - a'\beta}$

(ii) *Import limit*: $\dfrac{d\,Vn}{d(\Sigma F_c)} = \dfrac{1}{\mu^1\beta}$

where k is the marginal capital-output ratio

a' is the marginal propensity to save

μ^1 is the marginal ratio of required imports to increased GNP

Vn is the GNP at the end of the period

ΣF_c is the total capital inflow during the period

β is a constant which increases with the time period considered.

Over longer periods of time, the savings limit should predominate if good development policies are followed. In this phase, the importance of variation in the indirect effects of aid can be shown by assuming different values for the marginal savings rate, which represents a country's ability to channel additional income into investment by fiscal measures or otherwise. A variation in the marginal savings rate from ·10 to ·30 with marginal capital-output ratios of 3·0 or 4·0 produces the following variation in the marginal productivity of external assistance.[1]

PRODUCTIVITY OF EXTERNAL ASSISTANCE

Marginal Savings Rate	Over Ten Years		Over Twenty Years	
	$k=4{\cdot}0$	$k=3{\cdot}0$	$k=4{\cdot}0$	$k=3{\cdot}0$
·10	·28	·38	·30	·44
·20	·31	·45	·38	·63
·30	·35	·54	·53	1·11

From this example, it is clear that variation in the indirect effects of assistance is likely to be the dominant element in the total productivity of aid when a longer time period is considered. Differences in savings rates and balance-of-payments policies can easily outweigh substantial variations in the direct effects.[2] This fact is largely

[1] The median values of the parameters for the 31-country sample studied in Chenery and Strout, *op. cit.*, were : $k = 3{\cdot}7$, $a' = {\cdot}20$, $\mu^1 = {\cdot}21$, initial savings rate $(a^\circ) = {\cdot}12$.

[2] Variation in k represents the change in the productivity of all investment ; the effect of a change in the productivity of the aid-financed portion alone would be considerably less.

ignored in existing procedures for aid allocation and control, which are discussed in Section II.

C. *Achieving Self-sustaining Growth*

Virtually all recipients of aid are attempting to establish a process of growth which can continue in the future without further assistance. The possibilities for success depend on the country's ability to change its economic structure as it develops. Unless there is a rise in the savings rate or an improvement in the efficiency with which capital and human resources are used, the growth rate after aid has terminated will revert to the growth rate when it started, no matter how much aid and growth there has been in the intervening period. In other words, the prospects for achieving self-sustaining growth depend entirely on the indirect effects of assistance in changing the structure of the economy.

The structural changes that must be brought about in order to achieve self-sustaining growth at a given target rate may be summed up as follows :

(i) *Investment* must be raised until it equals the share of GNP required by the target growth rate ($\bar{r}$) and the capital-output ratio. For a 5 per cent growth target and a typical k of 3·0 to 4·0, investment must increase more rapidly than 5 per cent per year until it reaches the required share of 15–20 per cent of GNP.

(ii) *The marginal savings rate* (a') must exceed the required investment ratio ($k\bar{r}$) in order eventually to eliminate the need for external capital.

(iii) *Trade criteria.* If the ratio of imports to GNP is constant, exports must increase more rapidly than the target growth in GNP in order to close the trade gap. Cutting the marginal import ratio in half through import substitution lowers the required minimum export growth to 4 per cent to close the gap with a 5 per cent growth of GNP.[1]

The AID study [2] gives some estimates of the extent to which recent performance of aid-receiving countries meets these requirements of self-sustaining growth. Of the 26 countries for which these measures could be obtained for the period 1957–62, the performance of 11 satisfied all three criteria for ultimately attaining self-sustaining growth of 5 per cent or more. Five countries satis-

---

[1] Necessary conditions for closing the trade gap under other assumptions are given by the formula in Chenery and Strout, p. II–5. [2] *Ibid.*

fied neither the savings nor the trade criterion, and the remainder were deficient in at least one of the three.

Although experience with attempts to accelerate growth through aid is still limited, the comparative analysis that has been made throws considerable light on the relative difficulty of overcoming the several obstacles to further growth. Among the 50 countries for which data was analysed by AID, there were almost none which did not experience an annual rate of growth in investment of at least 8 per cent for a five-year period in the recent past. The median investment growth for the whole group for 1957–62 was over 10 per cent per year. These rates of increase in investment suggest that absorptive capacity may be less of an obstacle to raising the growth rate than is often supposed, except in the most primitive countries.[1] If past rates of increase are continued, investment can be raised to the levels required to sustain growth rates of 5–6 per cent in GNP in most countries within 10–15 years.

Of the several potential limits, the most serious obstacle to achieving self-sustaining growth at rates of 5 per cent or more is currently the balance of payments. It seems to be easier to increase the savings rate rapidly enough to prevent indefinite dependence on external aid than to follow trade policies that will eventually reduce the payments gap. Of the countries in which both savings and trade performance have been disappointing — most of which are in Latin America — there is strong evidence that a primary cause has been the sluggish performance of exports and the widening trade gap. The receipt of increased aid to fill the trade gap, unaccompanied by a rise in investment, leads to a diversion of potential savings into consumption because of inability to control inflation or lack of demand for investment. This seems to have happened in Bolivia, Brazil, Chile, Colombia, Costa Rica and other countries with falling savings rates.

The key role of exports in achieving progress toward self-sustaining growth is also demonstrated by an analysis of the countries which are currently succeeding in this effort. In almost all cases, the trade criterion has been met by an export expansion of 5 per cent or more. Although Brazil, Colombia, Turkey, India and a number of other countries have attempted to limit the need for external capital primarily through import substitution, none of them has succeeded in avoiding severe balance-of-payments difficulties in the long run.

[1] The 50-country sample covers 90 per cent of the GNP in underdeveloped countries, but it includes only 13 African countries and also omits the most primitive economies in other areas.

Projections for the future based on the experience of the recent past point to the increasing importance of structural deficits in the balance of payments as determinants of future aid requirements.[1] Aid is increasingly being provided not to accelerate investment and growth but to offset the growing imbalance between the structure of production and the structure of demand. Despite the success of a number of countries in raising rates of savings, investment and growth in GNP, an increase in capital inflow of 5 per cent per year will probably be required just to sustain past aggregate growth of GNP of slightly over 4 per cent. To raise the growth rate of the underdeveloped world to 5 per cent or more would probably require an annual increase in assistance of at least 10 per cent even with some improvement over past performance.[2] The difficulty of securing such increases in aid or private capital emphasizes the importance of making more effective use of the funds that are available.

The above discussion has omitted any explicit consideration of the effects of technological advance. Although studies of advanced countries usually attribute half of the increase in output to sources other than the increase in factor inputs, we do not yet have estimates of production functions in underdeveloped countries that would be useful in predicting the effects of future improvements. However, a considerable amount of technological improvement is implied by the demonstrated ability of some countries to raise investment rates substantially without a significant fall in the marginal productivity of capital.

It seems unlikely that in the next decade or so the less developed countries will be able to reduce the capital requirements for further growth even if there is much greater concentration on technical assistance. Although increasing the amount and effectiveness of technical assistance deserves the highest priority in aid efforts, it does not follow that external capital requirements are going to be reduced as a result.

II. THE ALLOCATION AND CONTROL OF ASSISTANCE

Unlike private capital, public assistance funds are allocated among countries in accordance with predetermined criteria. Any attempt

[1] See Chenery and Strout, p. II–17.
[2] A number of alternative projections of less developed countries' performance and corresponding assistance requirements are given in Chenery and Strout, Section II.

to evaluate the effects of public assistance must therefore examine the bases for its allocation and control. Starting from the objectives of assistance, a strong case can be made for a rapid increase in the amounts made available and for larger allocations to countries that perform well. From the working of the existing control system, however, it is often alleged that additional funds cannot be effectively absorbed under present criteria. The control system is therefore a key element in any discussion of future aid policy.

An ideal system of aid administration would include :
  (i) an explicit statement of objectives ;
  (ii) a set of criteria for allocating aid based on these objectives ;
  (iii) a mechanism for controlling the form and amount of resources to be transferred to each country.

Existing systems vary greatly in the relative emphasis given to these elements. In countries where it is politically important to secure an adequate flow of resources, the allocation tends to be made regardless of development objectives or controls which are normally applied in other cases. In the absence of this political urgency, the control aspect of the administrative mechanism tends to dominate ; allocation by country then tends to become a by-product of project review and other partial controls.

Most proposals for improving the present assistance mechanisms involve a clearer separation of the allocation and control elements in the system and greater attention to the incentive aspects of each. My proposals will be developed from an evaluation of the present aid mechanisms in the light of these functions.

A. *Objectives and Modes of Assistance*

Among recipients of economic assistance, there is a general consensus that its primary objective is long-term economic and social development, however defined. For the aid providers, the statement of objectives is more complicated : it involves both a choice among recipients and a balancing of benefits to the recipients against costs and secondary gains to the donor. The main purposes considered by donor countries and lending agencies include :
  (i) the long-term development of the recipients ;
  (ii) maintenance of minimum income levels and political stability in the recipients ;
  (iii) political advantages to the donor, including the strengthening of one recipient country instead of another ;
  (iv) economic advantages to the donor.

The first three donor objectives require a specific country allocation as part of the administrative process. This is particularly important in the less viable economies, which would have immediate
economic and political reactions to a reduction in aid. The allocative
aspect appears less important in some of the programmes designed
to produce development in the underdeveloped world as a whole,
such as IBRD project lending or the distribution of PL 480
commodities.

There are two types of country to which aid is currently allocated
in amounts designed to secure specific objectives :

(1) *Non-viable economies* — notably Korea, Vietnam, Laos, Jordan,
   the Congo and some other former colonies — which need a
   minimum of external support to prevent economic and
   political deterioration.

(2) *Countries with relatively effective development programmes* —
   such as India, Pakistan, Turkey, Chile, Nigeria, Tunisia —
   which have been judged capable of utilizing substantial
   amounts of assistance to increase their rates of growth.

For these two groups of countries, efforts are made by the principal
bilateral donor or by an international co-ordinating group to secure
a flow of assistance adequate to meet the primary objective.

Donor objectives are less well defined for countries which are
not at the top of the list in either political urgency or development
performance. Allocation in this large middle group tends to be
more the result of the piecemeal working of the control system than
of conscious decisions based on country performance and need.

B. *Efficiency Criteria*

Although it is impossible to set out unambiguous criteria for
evaluating an allocation system having multiple and ill-defined
objectives, the following partial tests can be deduced from the
assumption that long-term development is the primary reason for
the transfer of public capital. These tests are based to a large extent
on the preceding analysis of the role of assistance in the development
process.

(1) *The allocation system should be explicitly related to the principal
objective of long-term development.* In practice, this implies looking
more at indirect effects and considering longer time periods than
is usually done.

(2) *The allocation and control system should provide an incentive*

to improved performance by the recipient. Country allocation on the basis of development performance will tend to improve the use of total available resources, while country allocation on political criteria may actually reduce economic incentives and overall efficiency.

(3) *Maximizing growth should be preferred to avoidance of risk.* Many types of aid administration allocate funds to activities and countries primarily because the risk of failure is low. Examples are the preference of the IBRD and AID for power and transport projects. However, minimizing risk of individual projects may not be consistent with maximizing the prospects for development of the country as a whole. Use of this principle also distorts the allocation among countries.

(4) *Costs of secondary donor benefits.* Each condition attached to aid by the donor in order to secure some economic or political advantage is likely to have a cost to the recipient in comparison to an unrestricted loan or grant. These opportunity costs should be weighed against the gains to the donor and the attempt abandoned where the costs are excessive.

(5) *Effects on development strategy.* In addition to partial tests of efficiency, the combined effects of all controls on a country's choice of development strategy should be considered.

The significance of these criteria will be brought out in subsequent discussion of the alternative forms and conditions of aid.

C. *Project versus Programme Controls*

The most important difference among methods of aid administration lies in the choice between individual projects and overall programmes as the basis for allocating and controlling aid. The *project approach* takes a single plant or other unit of investment as the basis for analysis and aid decisions. The *programme approach* is based on the analysis and needs of the whole economy. While combinations of the two are possible, it is easier to compare them initially in a relatively pure form.

Under the project approach capital loans provide the imports required by individual investment projects. The commodities supplied are typically the investment goods to be used in executing the project, although an allowance may be made for the indirect imports needed elsewhere in the economy for producing investment goods or satisfying the increased consumer demand that results.

Control of disbursements of aid funds is related to the importation of the specific commodities used in the project and is typically spread over 3–5 years. The allocation of assistance among countries is largely a by-product in this system, although limits to the amounts of project aid going to any one country are often imposed by the lending agencies.

The programme approach is based on an assessment of the external resources needed to carry out a given set of development policies designed to achieve specified goals. These goals and the means to accomplish them are usually set out in a development programme prepared by the recipient government. The elements of country performance most commonly considered in determining aid requirements are its allocation of investment by sectors, its fiscal and balance of payments policies, and its recent experience in carrying out investment and mobilizing savings.

Under the programme approach, controls of aid can be applied on the basis of the end results — in increased investment, output, and use of income — more effectively than to the aid-financed imports. While it is customary to limit non-project assistance primarily to financing producer goods, this is a relatively meaningless form of control.

The benefits of the project system of aid administration to the recipient countries are limited to its impact on their own systems of budgetary review and control. While enforced emphasis on better project preparation is often beneficial, its opportunity cost may be very high. The system contains perverse incentives in both donors and recipients to select large projects with a high import content in order to minimize administrative effort and maximize the aid received. These criteria often conflict with the priorities of a well-conceived development programme if project aid is offered in any quantity.

In terms of the five criteria suggested above, the programme approach is likely to be superior on all counts in countries where sufficient stability and information exist to apply it.[1]

The main arguments in its favour are :

(i) The programme approach relates the amount and form of aid to the objectives and performance of the recipient country.

(ii) The programme approach can be more readily administered

[1] The two systems are compared in more detail in Agency for International Development, *Principles of Economic Assistance*, Washington, 1963.

so as to provide incentives to improved performance by the recipient.

(iii) Since the project approach focuses on individual projects and sectors, it gives less attention to overall development policies.

However, the programme approach requires a certain amount of continuity in policy and information for economic analysis, which only exist in a limited number of underdeveloped countries at the present time.

Apart from uncertainty and inadequate information, the main reasons for the persistence of the project approach lie in its suitability to other donor interests. Probably the most important of these is the fact that furnishing aid on a project by project basis allows the donor to remain uncommitted. Since project approval involves a complex of technical and economic judgments, it is quite feasible to increase or decrease aid for political reasons without appearing to do so. In the course of accepting a certain proportion of the projects received, a donor country can apply whatever additional political or economic criteria it chooses without being liable to a charge of discrimination. This is more difficult under the programme approach, where the conditions for qualifying for aid are more explicitly set out. The project approach also provides a convenient basis for limiting aid on the grounds that the recipient countries cannot prepare and submit a large number of acceptable projects.

The disadvantages of the project system can be mitigated by combining it with elements of country analysis and the programme approach. This trend is apparent in both the IBRD and AID procedures for project selection and review. Despite this trend, there are still relatively few countries than can rely on a continuing supply of assistance as a basis for development planning.

D. *Secondary Objectives and Donor Benefits*

A large proportion of the apparatus for controlling aid is designed to achieve trade or other benefits for the donors rather than to promote the interests of the recipients. For this purpose, aid is limited to commodities supplied by the donor, or even more narrowly to commodities for which the donor would like to establish export markets.

The costs of securing these donor benefits are of three types:

(i) overvaluation of the amount of aid ; (ii) reduction in the total assistance provided ; (iii) distortion of resource allocation of the recipient.

Aid is overvalued when commodities are exported at prices above the world market. This overvaluation occurs not only with PL 480 surpluses but also with steel, machinery, vehicles and other commodities when competition is reduced. Overvaluation is not of any great importance to the recipient in the case of grants or loans repayable in local currency (which covers the bulk of PL 480 commodities). For other loans, the extra cost due to tying must be absorbed by the purchaser and reduces the element of subsidy in the loan. Part of the popularity of the project approach among donors derives from the fact that it normally requires the procurement of the whole range of inputs for the project from the donor, regardless of relative prices.

Procurement and use of controls may lead to distortion of the recipient's allocation of resources when the choice of aid-financed commodities is too limited. The leading examples are agricultural surpluses and machinery tied to projects. To absorb this type of aid in substantial amounts may require the country to inhibit domestic production which would otherwise be economical if aid were not so restricted in form.

The cost of the resulting distortion in investment allocation can only be ascertained on a case by case basis. In the larger countries, such as India, Pakistan, Brazil and Turkey, where the development of machinery and metal-working industries is consistent with comparative advantage, excessive reliance on the project approach would force the country to inhibit the development of these sectors and limit the total aid.[1] The same is true of agricultural aid in other cases, where the distortion of resource allocation must be weighed against the value to the recipient of the additional assistance.

Considering the differences in opportunity cost to the donors, there may be more justification for tying aid to agricultural commodities than to machinery, since the political and economic problems of continuing excess capacity are more acute in the former. The cost of the present system would be clarified if all aid commodities were charged at competitive world prices, with a separate accounting for the subsidy to exporters such as now exists for PL 480 commodities.

---

[1] This reasoning has been accepted by the U.S. Government but not by most other donors.

E. *Effects of Multiple Controls*

The full effects of the present set of controls can only be seen when they are examined together as a system. Perhaps a quarter of all aid is supplied in a form that is sufficiently flexible to meet the general import needs of the country, and this type of assistance is limited to relatively few countries. The remainder is available in the form of certain commodities or for certain types of projects. Recipients must try to match up the portions of their development plans with the criteria of the various donors, while donors often have to search for suitable projects.

The most serious disadvantages of this system are :

(1) The incentives to aid recipients relate more to the technique of project preparation and good bookkeeping than to good development policy.

(2) The availability of unused funds for certain purposes gives a false impression of limited absorptive capacity, which in many cases is merely a product of the control system itself.

(3) Too much of the scarce administrative talent of the under-developed countries has to be devoted to making the system function rather than being available for more important tasks of development policy.

It is almost impossible to estimate the quantitative significance of these factors in any scientific way, but I would hazard the guess that the present volume of aid would contribute 40 to 50 per cent more to development if the control system were designed to operate entirely for the benefit of the recipient countries. If this order of magnitude is correct, it seems much too high a price to pay for the political support of special interest groups and the very limited real economic advantages gained by the donors. As with tariffs and export subsidies, aid tying and other restrictive measures become largely self-defeating when everybody adopts them.

III. INCREASING THE EFFECTIVENESS OF
ASSISTANCE

Three main conclusions emerge from the preceding analysis :

(1) Foreign assistance can be a powerful mechanism for securing rapid development when supplied in adequate amounts to

governments able to mobilize resources with reasonable effectiveness.

(2) The aid mechanism is operating far below its full potential because it is not sufficiently focused on the goal of development. The attempts by donors to secure secondary economic benefits for themselves involves a variety of controls that do not contribute to development and often inhibit it.

(3) Since the major donors compete for these secondary benefits, their efforts are largely offsetting. There is a substantial cost to the recipient in the system of source and use controls without any significant gain to the donors as a group.

Proposals for improving this situation must take account of the dominant position of the donor countries, their mixed motives in providing assistance, and the nature of existing international institutions. It is therefore not realistic to consider the abolition of all controls — nor would it be likely to yield as good results as a purposive combination of incentives and controls.

The following set of proposals is suggested as being both desirable for the aid recipients and within the realm of imaginative diplomacy for the aid providers.

(1) *Objectives of assistance.* There should be general agreement that long-term development of the recipient country is the overriding objective of economic assistance. It is not necessary to eliminate the variation in donor preferences for individual countries so long as the criteria for amounts and forms of aid are based on developmental considerations. International — or at least Free World — agreement on this subject would strengthen the hands of recipient governments interested in the welfare of their people and reduce the temptation to seek aid by playing off donors against each other.

(2) *Redesign of the control system.* With economic development established as the primary objective of public capital movements, a substantial redesign of the present system of conflicting and piecemeal controls should be possible. It should be aimed at improving the incentive aspects of the system as well as eliminating controls that hinder the efficient use of assistance.

(3) *Incentive programming.* Since the amount of aid required to achieve any given development objective depends largely on the use that a country makes of its added output, aid allocation should be designed to improve the indirect effects of growth and not concentrate only on the efficient use of aid-financed commodities. To vary aid

in accordance with performance, it is necessary to carry out an overall analysis of the economy. This procedure can be followed to some extent even when aid is being controlled on a project basis.

The potential effects of an incentive programming system can only be determined after the major donors have made it clear that better performance will lead to more aid when it is warranted rather than to cutting down assistance. While the United States has taken the first steps to establish this principle in its major support countries,[1] the correlation between changes in performance and variation in aid is not yet high enough to be very persuasive. Endorsement and use of this principle by the major bilateral and multilateral aid providers would make it much more effective.[2] The success of the IMF in securing acceptance of standards of balance of payments performance — even if one does not agree with all their applications — is suggestive of what could be accomplished in the aid field.

(4) *More purposive controls.* The control mechanism should be explicitly designed to promote the economic development of the recipient country. As information on performance improves, it should be possible to shift increasingly from project control to a programme-type of control. The greater economic validity and better incentives that result from programme controls have already been discussed.

With growing information, it should be possible to establish usable measures of savings, investment and balance of payments performance that would promote an adequate basis for control. For example, a country which had been performing well — investing at 18–20 per cent of GNP and saving 25 per cent of the resulting increase in income [3] — could safely be provided whatever assistance it needed to achieve growth rates of up to perhaps 7 per cent. So long as this performance was maintained, additional aid could only accelerate the rate of growth and reduce the total amount of assistance ultimately needed to attain self-sustaining growth.[4]

---

[1] See AID, *op. cit.*, and AID, *Proposed Mutual Defense and Development Programs for F.Y. 1966*, Washington, 1965, p. 7.

[2] The principle of allocating assistance against performance is implicit in the Charter of Punta del Este, but the agencies of the Alliance for Progress have only taken a few halting steps to apply it.

[3] These values of the savings and investment parameters represent performance in the upper quartile of performance, as shown in Chenery and Strout, *op. cit.*, Table 5. For countries starting from low investment levels, the rate of increase in investment would be a more appropriate measure.

[4] An upper limit to the growth rate to be supported is suggested to avoid the problem of a few exceptionally good performers receiving a high proportion of total aid, but this eventuality seems remote.

On tests such as this, the number of countries having access to international assistance without excessive controls might be increased from half a dozen to a dozen or more. The resulting incentive to others to try to achieve better performance should be substantial.

(5) *Redesign of the Project Approach.* To implement the preceding suggestions, the project approach should be redesigned to retain only the features which contribute effectively to development. Two changes are particularly needed : (*a*) consideration of projects in an overall framework of country analysis ; (*b*) weakening or abolishing the link between aid allocation and project approval, which tends to remove the incentive for better performance in other aspects of development policy.

(6) *Donor co-ordination.* To carry out the country programming approach outlined above, the donors need a common evaluation of recipient needs and performance. Here again the analogy of IMF reviews as a basis for agreed action comes to mind. Several organizations — the IBRD, the DAC, the OAS — have taken on some of the comparable aid co-ordinating functions, but a great deal more is needed.

The examples of countries where some of these conditions have been met — usually because of their political importance to particular donors — suggest that effective use of aid has not depended on detailed project-type controls. The most successful cases of the use of aid to transform underdeveloped economies in U.S. experience — Taiwan, Greece, the Philippines, Israel, Pakistan, etc. — have been supported largely by programme assistance. It is very doubtful that anything approaching the volume of resources transferred to these countries could have taken place under present project procedures. Furthermore, any estimate of absorptive capacity or development potential based on the project approach would have proven to be much too pessimistic.

With examples such as these in mind, I am very sceptical of the project approach to the analysis of absorptive capacity with its implied conclusion that aid levels cannot be substantially raised because additional aid cannot be effectively used. The ability to prepare projects is only one of the requirements for successful development, and probably not the most important. It would be equally logical to measure absorptive capacity by the external capital flow that could be absorbed without depressing the savings rate. The marginal savings rate and the marginal productivity of capital are of equal importance in determining the future rate of growth. If absorptive capacity is to have any operational meaning, it should be identified with the total productivity of assistance, not just one of its components.

The other aspect of recent experience which has great significance for future aid policy is the importance of achieving rapid growth. In countries which have 'graduated' from the category of aid dependents, one of the keys to success seems to have been the accomplishment of high levels of investment and growth of GNP. It is not at all clear that the marginal productivity of investment was particularly high in Greece, Taiwan or Israel in the early 1950's. What is clear is that the rapid growth of output has permitted the structural changes in savings rates, export growth and import requirements needed to make growth self-sustaining. In countries where conditions make it possible for additional aid to get growth started, it is likely to turn out to have been very productive in the long run even if the short-run returns seem low.

COMMENTS ON PROFESSOR CHENERY'S PAPER

BY

Professor D. I. DELIVANIS
University of Thessalonika (Greece)

MY comments are based not only on the paper itself but also on the background paper which both give a comprehensive treatment of the subject. I do not intend to summarize the paper but to stress those points where I cannot agree with Professor Chenery, maybe because I was not able to understand him and independently of my full agreement with him first about the importance of foreign assistance for development, second about the theoretical possibilities of increasing aid.

(1) Professor Chenery believes that growth may be limited by the lack of skills. I can accept this only if he means that the people available in the country cannot secure the quality and the quantity of output they would have provided if better equipped and if better trained. The propensity to give preference to foreign goods and to foreign services may be explained so. Of course, Professor Chenery is right when stressing the greater importance of the growth's limitation by foreign trade. This is the only bottleneck which cannot be removed by the country concerned without some collaboration of foreign countries. The latter very often

hampers exports of developing countries as it happens also in the case of those from Pakistan.

(2) Professor Chenery believes that foreign aid does not create supplementary incomes except if consumer goods are distributed free of charge. This happens, however, only in emergencies. May I add that foreign aid contributes to increased incomes by securing employment to those formerly unemployed, by increasing the employment of underemployed and also by making sometimes overtime work necessary.

(3) Import substitution by production at home and by conversion of unrealized savings in additional investment does not lead to the improvement of the balance of payments since supplementary nominal incomes and increased effective demand lead to increased imports, directly or indirectly. This is the reason of the failures not only in Brazil and India, but also in Turkey without, of course, omitting the contribution of inflation to these failures, particularly in Brazil. Developments have been similar in Greece after the achievement of self-sufficiency in wheat which up to the early fifties constituted the biggest import item of the country's trade balance.

(4) Professor Chenery is impressed by the results achieved by the development policies of Greece and Israel. He is perfectly right but in my opinion he does not seem to consider sufficiently first that these countries have long ago ceased to be underdeveloped, second that private capital transfers, a great percentage of them exclusively one way, have been and continue to be substantial, provided political, monetary and economic conditions are not particularly upset.

(5) Power and transport projects are favoured by the IBRD and AID not only because they have a small probability of failure, but also because real bottlenecks develop without inducing those responsible to undertake investments in these bottleneck sectors.

(6) I am afraid that Professor Chenery overestimates the perspicacity of foreign investors and of lenders whilst underestimating the importance of political factors when he expects them to refuse assuming more than 40 per cent of investments carried out in any country. The IBRD may be expected to act so and maybe is actually doing so by covering only expenses incurred outside the borrowing countries.

(7) Professor Chenery favours long-term development considerations. I do not think they may help a lot as too many unexpected things may happen as stressed by Lord Keynes and more recently by Mrs. Joan Robinson, in their preference for five-year maximum planning.

(8) When Professor Chenery favours variations of the growth rate in connection with substitution between two scarce factors, capital and foreign exchange, he does not consider the great importance in countries with past unorthodox monetary developments of fluctuations of foreign exchange reserves, of balance of payments deficits and of the accumulation of foreign debts.

(9) Professor Chenery is perfectly right when stressing the possibilities of improving the efficiency of foreign aid; but if the donor countries have to be deprived of their minor advantages, I am afraid that the taxpayers' opposition will lead to a substantial cut of foreign aid — at least when it comes from free countries.

(10) Professor Chenery refers to the replacement of grants by loans in Latin America. As however loans are often not repaid nor serviced, either by default or by agreement with the creditors involved, there is no change. I have to add that if the proceeds of loans are rationally invested, their servicing is no longer a problem.

Let me finish by stressing that my objections on the points raised did not reduce my appreciation of the work done by Professor Chenery in producing the two very important papers I have had the pleasure to comment on.

DISCUSSION OF PAPER BY PROFESSOR CHENERY

THE discussion of Professor Chenery's paper began with comments on the model building techniques exemplified in the paper. Among the main subjects considered in the subsequent discussion were the productivity of external assistance, objectives and modes of assistance, and the relative merits of programme and project approaches for controlling assistance.

I. THE USE OF MODELS IN ANALYSING FOREIGN ASSISTANCE

Professor Papi opened the discussion by stating that he doubted the value of the macro-economic model approach. He questioned the use of *ceteris paribus* assumptions of the continuity of past experience into the future, especially among the less developed countries where there are few data and the data that exist are poor. Extrapolation is dangerous especially when there is no detailed sectoral analysis, and when the purpose of the development process is to change the structure of the economy, not to continue it unchanged. In short, extrapolation neglects the very essence of economic development.

Professor Papi also argued that the problems of development are essentially qualitative, not quantitative. Ignoring this leads to an overemphasis on trade relations and to the neglect of basic structural problems. Deterioration in the terms of trade, for instance, is simply a reflection of the fact that the country cannot produce enough food. A preliminary identification of the main sectoral problems is needed to establish data and cost estimates for each country. During the first stages of development, it is especially necessary to improve the infra-structure or the 'human element'. Extrapolations tend to neglect this essential aspect of development.

Dr. Márquez agreed that Professor Chenery paid insufficient attention to the problem of social development. GNP *per se* was not a sufficient measure. Mr. Chenery seemed to assume that increases in GNP imply social development. *Dr. Faaland* added that the type of analysis used by Professor Chenery was inherently limited.

Professor Stolper said that Professor Chenery's model was not a development model nor an academic model, but rather a model designed to ask specific questions. He felt that some of the criticisms had missed this point and, further, had ignored the value of the model for deciding short-term aid allocation. *Professor Chenery* added that there was no inherent reason for being suspicious of model building. A model is no worse than its maker, and has the virtue that it requires consistent analysis.

II. THE ROLE OF EXTERNAL ASSISTANCE

Three phases marked by gaps or shortages of skills, savings and foreign exchange (exports) were distinguished in the analysis of the role of external assistance in Professor Chenery's paper. The distinction among phases seemed artificial to *Dr. Adler*, who felt that these three gaps were usually intermingled and did not necessarily occur in a sequential fashion. Particular scarcities of specific factors were the real problems limiting growth in particular instances ; capital and other inputs are not fungible. This converts the issue into a problem of absorptive capacity. *Dr. Horvat* agreed that there was no evident justification for the three phases of development suggested by Professor Chenery. *Professor Chenery* noted that the phases need not necessarily be viewed as sequential. *Dr. Horvat* replied that the analytical framework used did not explain the existence of the three different phases, sequential or not.

Dr. Horvat noted that since the difference between exports and imports is equal by definition to the difference between investment and saving, there is no reason for Professor Chenery's distinction between the export and savings gaps. Professor Chenery replied that while this may be true *ex ante*, the fact cannot be used to deny the value of the concept for analysis of the approach to equilibrium. Both gaps must be analysed to determine the possibility of their solution. Perhaps the gaps may be viewed better in linear-programming terms in which constraints would be set on the relationships between exports and imports, investments and savings. This has the added advantage that the problems need no longer be analysed in terms of phases.

Professor Chenery emphasized the importance of assessing the indirect effects of particular aid projects on the marginal rate of savings in the economy. He cited the case of Greece in which additional savings out of aid-induced increases in GNP have financed a higher proportion of additional investments than the aid itself. *Dr. Kamarck* questioned whether aid had such a large role in the subsequent economic growth of Greece.

Dr. Gulhati agreed that indirect effects were important, but thought that the productivity of capital of the ICOR should also be taken into account. Professor Chenery replied that using ICOR may be misleading. Is it better to invest in a country with a high marginal propensity to save and an ICOR of 5·0, or in a country with a low marginal propensity to save and an ICOR of 3·0 ?

In the discussion of the different phases of the growth process, *Professor Wallich* asked what raised the marginal rate of savings. Was it income redistribution, inflation, or price stability ? Second, why was balance of payments equilibrium assumed in the model ? The model deals with poor countries, who should be natural capital importers.

Dr. Onitiri disagreed with Professor Wallich's last point. He felt that Professor Chenery had not sufficiently stressed the importance of export possibilities. He said that changes in the economic structure of the developing countries should not be considered in isolation. They are interrelated with changes in the structure of developed countries and of world trade. He saw the need for a deliberate attempt by developed countries to alter their domestic economic structure and the structure of their trade to aid the less developed countries.

Dr. Onitiri also asked whether the success of Israel, Taiwan and the Philippines was not as much a matter of increasing exports as of raising savings rates. There seems to be a vicious circle here. Inability of the developing countries to increase foreign exchange earnings has led to an over-emphasis on import substitution, and this in turn leads to the development of high-cost protected industries. *Dr. Kafka* added here that countries which failed to meet Professor Chenery's savings criterion were also countries which have overvalued their exchange rates for long periods of time. Those countries with consistently sensible foreign exchange policies have begun to export manufactures. The key to increasing exports, then, appears to be a sensible foreign exchange policy. *Professor Chenery* agreed with Dr. Onitiri that he might have given more attention to export possibilities, but noted that the trade gap still reflects a structural problem.

III. OBJECTIVES AND MODES OF ASSISTANCE

Professor Chenery distinguished between 'nonviable' economies, in which a minimum of external support is needed to prevent economic and political deterioration, and 'viable' economies, which have been judged capable of utilizing substantial amounts of assistance to increase their rate of growth. *Dr. Horvat* felt that this distinction should be qualified to make clear that it is drawn from the viewpoint of the donor country, since many people in the 'nonviable' countries hold that the economic and political deterioration resulted from foreign intervention. *Dr. Kamarck* also objected to the use of terms like 'structural deficits', or 'nonviable' economies. He remembered predictions of unemployment in the United States after World War II, and the problem of 'structural unemployment' in Germany which was thought to be impossible to eliminate. He mentioned these cases because there seems to be a tendency to overlook the flexibility that an economy may have. *Professor Chenery*, in reply to Dr. Horvat's observation, noted that it was interesting to see in terms of the model why some countries remained viable and others did not.

IV. ALLOCATIONS AND CONTROL OF ASSISTANCE

Professor Chenery, in advocating the use of programme rather than project types of assistance, noted that more factors should be considered than can usually be considered in project grants. *Professor Kafka* thought that Professor Chenery's proposal was more radical than he might have imagined because it implies not only the replacement of project loans with programme loans, but the replacement of loans with outright grants. He added that in a sense the issue is purely semantic. Project loans are programme loans in the last instance, because when a project is evaluated, all the possible repercussions should be taken into account. Objections to project loans arise because the loans cover only the foreign exchange component of projects, not because the loans are made for specific projects. If loans covered the total cost of the projects, most difficulties associated with project lending would vanish.

Dr. Adler added that he agreed with a point made previously by Professor Rosenstein-Rodan that programme aid could not exist unless there was a programme. He would add that it is impossible to have a programme unless there are also projects. He felt that most aid-giving institutions have redefined 'projects' broadly enough to allow themselves to make lending decisions based on programme considerations. The selection of projects should be related to the internal rate of return — either private or social; the high marginal-savings ratio emphasized in Professor Chenery's paper would be assured by financing projects which yield high rates of return.

Dr. Ferrer agreed with Professor Chenery's proposals for programme instead of project lending, but argued that underdeveloped countries should be allowed to define their own development strategy with less interference from abroad. The Chenery proposal might conflict with this objective. *Professor Wallich* objected that project loans were an administrative device to protect the recipients from the misuse of resources made available through aid. If there was no danger of misuse, then programme lending would be more efficient than project lending. He thought that there were very few countries in which there was no danger of misuse.

Chapter 8

FOREIGN CAPITAL AND DOMESTIC PLANNING

BY

Dr. I. G. PATEL

Ministry of Finance, New Delhi

I. INTRODUCTORY

ACTORS in a joint production who have been assigned a part but are invited to write their own script are under strong temptation to steal each other's lines. In the hope of being able to avoid this temptation, I have defined the scope of this paper rather narrowly and have attempted to deal in the main with two questions. Assuming that a country has embarked on a course of planned economic development, what is the difference that will — and should — be made to its plans by the availability of foreign capital? And, if the absorption of foreign capital into a process of planned economic progress is to be as smooth and beneficial as possible, are there any conditions that the availability of foreign capital must satisfy? The focus clearly is on a poor country receiving capital from abroad both from private as well as public sources.

It would of course be a mistake to assume that the current emphasis on planning as a precondition for aid has already led to a situation where most developing countries have well-articulated plans which look sufficiently far into the future. Nor have we reached a stage where the commitment to assist the poorer nations has assumed a degree of firmness and continuity which makes it meaningful to relate it to well-considered long-term aims. The giving and receiving of aid at present, with a few exceptions, is essentially an *ad hoc* affair based on the presumption that when the needs of the poorer countries are so many and so urgent every little help will somehow go to add up to something worth while. It would nevertheless be useful to assume that an examination of how foreign capital might best be related to domestic planning will provide a few pointers to

293

a more rational policy towards foreign aid and private foreign investment.

II. PLANNING WITHOUT FOREIGN CAPITAL

The necessity for planning has been impressed of late on the rich and the poor alike. There is, however, an essential difference between the kinds of plans that the two sets of countries need and this difference relates to the appropriate time span or horizon for planning. We plan for a certain period ahead; and despite the blandishments of saints, philosophers and model-builders, we hesitate to take in our stride the entire period from here to eternity. But how far into the future is far enough? For a rich country whose task in ordering the use of its resources over time is of a marginal nature, a limited time horizon of four to five years at a time may well be sufficient. But for those left behind in the race for economic progress, there are a number of 'structural' problems which can be tackled only within a somewhat long-term perspective — of, say, twenty to twenty-five years. Problems remain in life at all levels of well-being; and there is no guarantee that those who have already established themselves at a base camp at the foot of Mount Everest will succeed in all the subsequent series of assaults. But there are major deficiencies in poor countries from the point of view of their ability to cope with the ceaseless struggle for 'higher' economic aims; and the removal of these basic weaknesses constitutes the first stage in domestic planning — a stage which unhappily must extend over a number of decades.

Without endeavouring to be exhaustive or to arrange things in the order of their importance, we might say that the end of stage I in domestic planning would be reached and the country would be reasonably free from 'structural' weaknesses when:

  (a) the bulk of its people have reached the standards of nutrition, clothing, shelter and health consistent with the requirements of efficiency;

  (b) the bulk of its working force has acquired education and technical training of the kind that makes it possible for them to respond to changing techniques and circumstances;

  (c) the rate of saving and investment is high enough — say 15 to 20 per cent — to permit a satisfactory rate of growth;

  (d) the community at large includes a sufficient number of people imbued with the spirit of enterprise — i.e. the desire to lead, manage, push, cajole and experiment ; and

(e) the structure of production and the available stock of capital and trained personnel are sufficiently diversified to permit a considerable degree of transferability of resources from one use to another without much loss.

There is of course no natural order in which the different ingredients of the necessary minimum of economic strength are bound to appear. Japan in all probability had achieved high enough standards of saving, training and entrepreneurship before achieving the standard of well-being consistent with economic efficiency ; and there are among less developed nations today some which enjoy fairly satisfactory living conditions without achieving high enough rates of saving or enterprise. But if the first task of domestic planning in a poor country is to arrive at a perspective of where it ought to go in the first instance, it should not be difficult to define the broad contours of this perspective — so much food and clothing and shelter must be available per person, so many hospitals, doctors, teachers of various kinds and a certain minimum rate of saving. Even entrepreneurs can be trained and encouraged, if not manufactured with absolute certainty. The 'goals' then are easy to define ; and the questions that remain in perspective planning are essentially two : how soon ought one to try to achieve these goals and what is the course along which the economy ought to be steered from year to year if it is to arrive at the goal at the appointed hour. The two questions, needless to say, are related and can be answered only simultaneously.

Artificial as it is, it might be instructive to inquire how these questions might be answered in a closed economy where both foreign trade and foreign capital are absent. At first sight, it might appear that the only relevant question for such a society is that of the pace at which the desired goals are to be achieved and that this in turn is a matter of the marginal rate of saving and investment to aim at. Since the goals are known and must be met from internal production, the marginal rate of saving will also uniquely determine the distribution of available investible resources between investment for the investment goods sector and investment for the consumer goods sector. One can further disaggregate this model to take account of the pattern of consumption at different levels of income and saving and derive a complete time-profile of the distribution of resources till the predetermined goals are reached in terms of the desirable rate of saving and desired levels of *per capita* consumption in essential directions. The period over which the objectives of the perspective plan would be reached would depend on the marginal rate of saving and the productivity of capital in different fields. While this way of setting out the planning problem has relevance and merit, it disregards at least four important aspects of the issue at hand.

The productivity of capital even within a given sector is not a fixed factor to be taken for granted. There is always a choice open for the method by which even a given basket of goods can be produced. Where savings are scarce and can be assumed to be determined independently by policy, it would make sense within each sector to choose the least capital-intensive method. But even this is not always a safe rule. Minor irrigation, for example (i.e. wells, tanks, etc.), may be capital-saving in relation to major irrigation schemes involving the training of rivers which is a time-consuming affair. But if the scope for minor irrigation is limited, it would become necessary to make a start with major irrigation sooner or later — and this will have to be done before the scope for minor irrigation is fully exhausted. Much the same is true of expansion of existing industrial complexes as distinct from the initiation of new ones. Investment — and its productivity — are almost always associated not only with labour but also with certain geographical or geophysical factors ; and the particular complex of investment which is most productive over time (even within a limited sector) cannot be determined with reference to simple criteria such as capital-intensity. But whatever the criteria for choice, the method of production to be chosen is an important area of planning as distinct from that of deciding on the rate of saving and investment.

Equally, if productivity is determined not only by investment but also by consumption and standards of training and enterprise, one has also to decide on the distribution of resources among all these productive uses. The normal national income accounting conventions which represent consumption as a withdrawal from the potential stock of productive assets and treat much of the expenditure on education, training, health, extension activities, marketing advice, etc., as expenditure on consumption are grossly misleading in the context of a developing society. A step-up in investment (e.g. irrigation facilities) unaccompanied by the necessary increase in training and entrepreneurship (e.g. spread of knowledge of better techniques and their demonstration) would be hardly productive, whereas a smaller increase in investment accompanied by efforts to stimulate or create the supply of complementary factors may be far more productive. There has been a good deal of discussion of late of what has been called the 'absorptive capacity' for capital. In reality, what needs to be emphasized is not some absolute measure of the capacity to absorb capital in general but the need for associating the growth of capital in different sectors with the growth of other productive forces so that the overall increase in productivity (per unit of capital) is sufficiently great. In this sense of the necessity for ensuring fuller realization of the productive potential of capital, the need for attention to 'absorptive capacity' is a continuing one and not something which has a relevance only to countries at the lowest stage of development. Any country can absorb any kind of capital within wide limits ; but the efficiency with which it can do so can also vary widely in accordance with the availability of complementary factors of skills, training and management. Domestic planning thus must pay as much attention to these factors as to the growth of capital.

Thirdly, planning is not simply an exercise in dividing the cake at each stage between consumption and investment leaving the distribution of consumption between different items to individual choice. The speed with which the goals of the perspective plan are achieved will also depend on conscious attempts to alter the pattern of consumption either by the use of the market mechanism or by direct restraint on (or stimulus for) the production of certain goods. Without undue elaboration, we might assert that consumption of the kind that leads to greater efficiency should be encouraged, whereas consumption (and production) of items which act as a spur to the demonstration effect without adding correspondingly to efficiency or effort should be discouraged. Similarly, consumption of items which require capacities (or other scarce resources) of the kind that are particularly required for enlarging the capacity to invest and train might be discouraged. Unfortunately, excessive emphasis on analytical aggregates such as consumption, investment, capital-output ratios and the like have tended to obscure the vital importance of a rational policy towards the pattern of consumption. But the difference between successful and not so successful efforts to develop are often the result of the degree of attention paid to this particular area of policy.

Lastly, a perspective plan without a conscious policy for distribution of income fails to come to grips with some of the most relevant aspects of the alternatives that are open to a society bent upon growth. Here again, the habit of thinking in terms of marginal rates of saving and the like distracts attention from vital issues. It is possible, for example, that the initial distribution of income — and property — in a society is capable of a radical adjustment leading to an immediate increase in the rate of saving and investment or/and to an advance towards more satisfactory levels of consumption for the poorest sections of the community. For subsequent periods also, the pattern of distribution one aims at will have a bearing on the supply of savings or entrepreneurship. Again, if a basic minimum standard for all consistent with requirements of efficiency is an essential objective of a perspective plan, one must at least inquire whether this is to be done with or without a change in the distribution of income. The quantitative significance of this consideration is so overwhelming that it is really surprising that so many plans in developing countries today can get by without being explicit on this point. Suppose, for example, that a country has an average *per capita* income of $60 per annum and that the minimum income consistent with efficiency is $180 per annum *per capita*. If, at one extreme, all incomes were equally divided all the time, one would need to increase total *per capita* income to only three times the present level. If, however, as is likely, the lowest 30 per cent of the population have only a 10 per cent share in total income to begin with, their *per capita* income would be only $20 per annum; and if they are to enjoy the basic minimum of $180 per person per year without any change in the distribution of income, *per capita* income for the community as a whole must rise to nine times the present level. In actual practice, the distribution of income cannot be changed at will without unfavourable repercussions. But one cannot plan for a certain perspective without any regard to this consideration.

Planning then, even in a closed economy, has to involve decisions on :

(*a*) the rate at which saving and investment are to be raised ;

(*b*) the choice of the method of production in different fields bearing in mind the relative availability of factors over time, including natural factors, and the time it takes to develop most resources ;

(*c*) growth of skills of various kinds and creation of an environment conducive to entrepreneurships by extension services, development of financial institutions, market facilities and the like ;

(*d*) the manner in which the pattern of consumption might be suitably modified by direct as well as indirect measures ; and

(*e*) the distribution of income between different classes at different times.

Whether all these questions are capable of simultaneous solution at one fell swoop on the basis of some theoretical model or whether they can be answered at best in a tentative or rough and ready way need not deter us here. But it cannot be too strongly emphasized that domestic planning is a matter of establishing the right interplay between technical factors and issues of policy involving institutional, social and psychological considerations.

The assumption so far of a closed economy was only intended to focus attention on some of the issues which would be equally relevant even if possibilities of trade (but not of capital inflow) existed. International division of labour generally relieves particular scarcities so that the possibility of trade enhances the productivity of capital and shortens the time span for reaching desired goals. The potential for taking advantage of international division of labour would vary from country to country and will have to be built up over time in much the same way as the potential for investing larger and larger amounts and for absorbing more and more productive techniques. Foreign trade would make no difference to the pattern of availability that a community ought to aim at in terms of the growth potential it seeks to establish at the end of the first stage of its domestic planning. But its structure of production need not coincide fully with the desired pattern of availability. In the nature of things, there has to be substantial overlap between the two. Many things like power, water and transport are rooted in the soil and under present conditions at any rate it is not possible to buy or hire skilled personnel from abroad to any significant extent. But in an open economy, the perspective plan will have to include some idea of the nature and extent of exports and imports at different stages of growth, bearing in mind the need for a balance between the two in the absence of capital movements. Apart from lending a measure of extra efficiency to the whole operation, the possibility of trade will not do away with the importance of the different aspects of planning that we have discussed earlier — in fact, it might well underscore them. Thus, a conscious policy towards the pattern of consumption becomes all the more necessary if export earnings are to be maximized and used in particular for obtaining those imports which have the most beneficial effect on growth potential.

III. PLANNING WITH FOREIGN CAPITAL

Assuming that a country is operating on the basis of some perspective plan of development, what is the difference that could be made by the availability of foreign capital ? The freedom to import foreign capital adds to the stream of resources ; it imposes also an obligation to respond to some extent to the interests and judgments or prejudices of those who provide the capital. Beyond this, many other problems flow from the terms on which such capital might be forthcoming. It might be useful first to take the simplest case of capital inflow where a country has at its command a given lump sum of foreign capital which can be used in any manner it likes without any obligation to repay. Ideally, one might wish that even the amount of foreign capital was left to be determined by the developing country. But this would be clearly unrealistic. For the present, we may assume that there is no uncertainty regarding the amount of capital available, no limitations on its use and no considerations to take care of about the conditions to be satisfied after the absorption of the capital at hand.

Under these conditions, foreign capital can either shorten the time-span for achieving the desired results or/and can permit a different course for the economy in the interim period. But the situation that must emerge ultimately, i.e. the pattern of production and foreign trade, must remain the same as before in so far as the stock of available foreign capital is limited and growth beyond the stage under consideration would require the same initial conditions. If foreign capital is absorbed in a manner which involves no gain of time, the entire difference it would make would be to the stream of consumption and the gain here may well be larger than what might be indicated by the purchasing power of the foreign capital. In ex-post national accounting terms, the inflow of foreign capital will represent a net addition to domestic savings ; but this does not mean that it is investment rather than consumption that would be necessarily larger than in the alternative case. And the gain to consumption — when all the gain is so taken — may well be larger than the value of foreign capital because, as a versatile resource, foreign capital could be used in substitution of particularly scarce tesources. Thus if a machine has to be imported and paid for by rhe export of foodgrains, it may well be that larger exports of foodgrains entail a deterioration in terms of trade. If the machine is imported by the use of foreign capital instead, the additional food-grains released for domestic consumption may well be larger than the amount of foodgrains that can be purchased at home by the local currency value of the machine at the current exchange rate. Generally speaking, the absorption of foreign capital has a sort of 'multiplier' effect because it makes it possible to avoid deterioration in terms of trade and to postpone difficult acts of investment till such time as the economy is better able to realize their full productive potential by the development of complementary factors.

It is perhaps as well to recognize that the gain from foreign capital might go primarily to consumption and that this might be desirable or inevitable in certain circumstances. The very fact that the gain to consumption may be a multiple of foreign capital offers a justification to this course from the welfare point of view. For a country with very low incomes and savings, some immediate gain in consumption may have a productive significance. If the only way out of the vicious circle of low incomes, low savings and stagnation in the absence of foreign capital is a revolutionary redistribution of incomes, such a revolution may be thoroughly impracticable or destructive in the short-run so that the injection of foreign capital initially may be required both for increasing consumption and investment. It may also be that in the absence of foreign capital, domestic planning may have to rely to a great extent on direct restraints on consumption of certain items (by import controls, licensing of production and the like) and some relaxation of these restraints on the basis of foreign capital may generate a better climate for expansion. But the dividing line between legitimate and other uses of foreign capital for assisting consumption is not easy to draw. Instances where the availability of foreign capital engenders undue complacency about redistributing incomes, or altering the pattern of consumption, or mobilizing domestic savings or exploiting avenues for fruitful international division of labour are not unknown ; and in many cases, such complacency is encouraged by the prejudices of the suppliers of capital. The case for assisting poor countries rests as much on the desire to put them on their feet as soon as possible as on the desire to help them avoid difficult social choices which might disrupt their political fabric. The very fact that there is this dual objective means that the claims of investment cannot have overriding significance over those of consumption. But the availability of foreign capital — even when it is on the generous terms we are postulating for the time being — cannot be allowed to supplant domestic discipline altogether.

.Given the extent to which it is legitimate to utilize foreign capital for reducing the rigours of domestic planning, the rest of the gain must be taken in shortening the time-horizon for achieving the goals of the perspective plan. If foreign capital were to represent a fully versatile resource which could be employed for any purpose whatsoever, there would be much to be said for absorbing it as rapidly as possible for enlarging investment. This would give the whole process of development a head start. But unfortunately, there are things which cannot be purchased with foreign capital (e.g. skills, managerial talent, etc.) and there are activities such as agriculture, small industry and the like where domestic productive agents cannot be replaced by foreigners. What is thus called lack of absorptive capacity can also be described as lack of capacity for absorption on the part of foreign capital. Whichever way one looks at it, there is clear need for migration of talent as well as for migration of capital. As it is, leaving private capital aside, foreign capital brings with it at best perfunctory advisory talent rather than a steady stream of talent for doing things ; and unless this can be remedied, we shall always be left with a bit of a dilemma in deciding on the absorption of a given amount of foreign capital. If it is absorbed early, its contribution will multiply over a longer period ; on the other hand, its initial contribution to higher productivity would be limited so that there would be greater temptation to embody it in higher consumption. The recent history of the liquidation of foreign exchange reserves accumulated during the war should provide an instructive illustration in this regard.

IV. UNCERTAINTY

The assumption so far that we were concerned with the utilization of a given lump sum of foreign capital was intended to do away with uncertainty regarding the availability of such capital. In real life, however, uncertainty presents one of the most baffling problems in relating foreign capital to domestic planning. A rational plan for development in a poor country must extend over a fairly long period of at least twenty to twenty-five years. Given the magnitudes of the tasks involved and the time it takes to remove some of the crucial shortages, a more limited time horizon will not give any assurance that future growth will not be held back by lack of timely action in a number of directions. Foreign aid, on the other hand, is voted and distributed from year to year ; and even the World Bank perhaps would react with consternation if not derision if it were asked for its plans and intentions over the next five years. In the nature of things, the flow of private investment must remain uncertain. What sense does it make then to speak of planning in the context of something which is so highly uncertain ?

It is perhaps useful to distinguish between two kinds of uncertainty relating to foreign aid : one, where a country could be reasonably sure of aid over a sufficiently long period while having to reckon with fluctuations in aid from year to year, and the other, where there is a real danger of aid disappearing altogether (or getting drastically reduced) at any time. The first kind of uncertainty is clearly more easy to live with and is in itself diminished by the increase in the number of countries and institutions from whom a poor country draws its aid. A fair share in the burden of aid by all also makes for greater certainty and efficiency in the use of aid. One might even argue that this kind of uncertainty is no different from that which every country dependent on foreign trade has to reckon with and must be dealt with, therefore, by the use of reserves and resort to short-term credit facilities from the International Monetary Fund. Unfortunately, poor countries are seldom able to have reserves adequate enough to meet normal fluctuations in trade and payments, and instances are not lacking where aid-giving countries and even international institutions show scant recognition of the importance of reserves to the poor countries.

The International Monetary Fund has recognized in practice that its accommodation is available for meeting payments difficulties arising from fluctuations in aid-flows. The IMF clearly cannot provide long-term development finance. But when there are sudden or unexpected variations in the flow of such finance from other sources, it is a legitimate use of the Fund's resources to provide short-term relief to the country concerned so that worthwhile long-term plans are not upset suddenly and are adjusted, where necessary, in an orderly manner. Useful as the IMF is as an insurance against uncertain (i.e. uneven) aid-flows, this usefulness is limited by the fact that accommodation from the IMF has to be repaid in a relatively short period. An alternative source of long-term but occasional finance for the developing countries is badly needed and the Horowitz plan for reactivating the international capital markets for the use of the developing countries can fill an important gap in this respect. Loans floated by the developing countries before the First World War in international capital markets had the great advantage that they could be used for any purpose — for buying more goods, for repaying old debts, for meeting sudden difficulties or even for adding to foreign exchange reserves. It would be too much to hope that even with interest subsidies this kind of foreign capital movement could now be revived on a large enough scale to meet a significant part of the need for long-term finance on the part of the poorer countries. But the Horowitz plan can be adopted for the more modest purpose of providing from time to time fully liquid resources repayable over a fairly long period to developing countries who find themselves in difficulties which cannot be overcome in the short run and for which other forms of long-term finance are not available at least for the time being. In short, the Horowitz plan could well be an adjunct to the Monetary Fund rather than to the World Bank and it could provide an answer to — or a reserve against — a part of the uncertainty that surrounds official capital movements to the developing world.

Where the uncertainty in question relates to the very existence of foreign aid, there is little that can be done to overcome it. Perhaps, the only thing useful one can say is that when faced with such uncertainty, the poorer countries would be best advised to utilize such aid as is currently available for speeding up the pace of their development rather than for reducing the rigours of domestic planning. In the ultimate analysis, the only safeguard against the sudden cessation of all aid is international public opinion or conventions and agreements. From this point of view, the efforts of the United Nations and others to define the long-term tasks of development and the responsibility of all nations in meeting these tasks deserve all encouragement as also the efforts to channel as much aid as possible through international agencies. The consortium techniques developed by the World Bank whereby the needs of a few countries over a five-year plan period are assessed in general terms and some tentative assurance of assistance for meeting these needs obtained is also a step in the right direction. More or less firm commitments under the auspices of the UN and other international agencies to devote as a minimum a certain proportion of national income to foreign aid would also serve to reduce the area of uncertainty. For the rest, uncertainty concerning aid will continue to encourage its utilization on an *ad hoc* and essentially unplanned basis.

V. LIMITATIONS ON USE

A country importing foreign capital is seldom free to utilize it as it likes in support of its plans. Private foreign investment is clearly available for specific purposes. Even official capital carries limitations on its use — much of it is tied to purchases within specific countries or to specific projects and purposes and often to specific methods of production. The conditions governing the use of aid sometimes extend even to the use of a country's own resources or to its general economic and social policies. Some of the issues involved here such as tied aid, aid tied to projects, etc., form the subject matter of other papers and we shall refer to them here only in so far as they have a bearing on domestic planning.

Much of developmental aid today is tied to purchases from the aid-giving countries. If aid did not have to be repaid, country-tying will present no real problem from the point of view of domestic planning. If costs in a particular country were high or if one had to buy in a certain market goods which could be bought cheaper elsewhere in order to utilize aid from that country fully, one would be simply making a mental note of the fact and reckoning that the flow was less than what appeared at first sight. Since there would be a number of countries giving aid, each insisting on the aid being used for buying goods produced in the country concerned, there would be a problem of deciding on how the purchases ought to be distributed between different countries. But this should not present insuperable difficulties. The real difficulty arises from the fact that although country-tying reduces the real value of aid, no allowance for this is made in the terms of aid including repayment. Thus a poor country might get only half or two-thirds of the value out of tied aid, but the debt is reckoned without taking this into account so that the real cost of aid is obscured. When foreign capital has to be repaid, an important planning problem that arises is that of determining how much capital at each of the terms available ought to be accepted from time to time ; and country-tying makes it difficult to adopt a rational approach to this problem. Equally, there is asymmetry in insisting that the use of aid should not put pressure on the balance of payments of the aid-giving country whereas no such safeguard must be provided in repayment terms for the country receiving aid. Sooner or later, tied aid will lead to a demand for tied repayments.

The desire to tied aid sometimes assumes more sophisticated and far-reaching proportions. It has been argued that even when aid is country-tied, an aid-receiving country could divert its use to third countries by reducing its normal commercial purchases from the first country and shifting them to another. Aid is thus sought to be tied to conditions regarding the total value of imports from the aid-giving country. Indeed, it is not entirely unknown for countries to take the position that they should assist poorer countries only to the extent that is necessary to balance their accounts with each of them as otherwise aid would put pressure on the balance of payments of the aid-giving countries. Thus, if a poor country increases its exports to a particular rich country, the latter would be entitled to reduce its aid unless the former chooses to increase its imports correspondingly! If all rich countries were committed to giving such amount of aid as was required to balance their accounts with each developing country, there would perhaps be no great disadvantage in complete bilateralization of aid. But as it is bilateralization is generally insisted upon only selectively to justify particular commercial interests or unwillingness to extend aid to particular countries to whom this argument fits. Domestic planning, in the context of such ferocious bilateralization of aid, is bound to become a hand to mouth and uncertain affair bedevilled by constant bargaining with a number of countries. The jig-saw puzzle of trying to maximize aid by constant diversion of purchases from one source to the other would take up energies which could be better devoted to domestic planning.

Apart from country-tying, aid is often tied to particular uses such as import of complete equipment or even a particular kind of equipment. This problem also is perhaps dealt with at some length elsewhere in this volume. But it may be noted that except in cases where available aid is small in relation to the needed imports of the categories eligible for aid, purpose-tying is likely to be wasteful. For one thing, when combined with country-tying, it adds to the wasteful use of aid in the sense that even within the country the eligible categories may not be the most competitive — or least disadvantageous — things to buy. Where an aid-receiving country has reached a stage where import of complete equipment is no longer all that necessary, purpose-tying may lead to inefficient or insufficient use of capacity already created. In general, limitation on the use of foreign capital would lead to wasteful use of such capital. Even without any conscious limitation, the tendency to import inappropriate techniques along with the import of foreign capital is a real one not only when the import concerned represents private foreign capital but also when it is sponsored by official or international agencies who often insist on the designing and the engineering of the projects being done by firms accustomed to deal with problems in more advanced countries. The tendency to over-import or to import inappropriate forms of capital does not always need encouragement from foreigners either. Domestic entre-preneurs or local governments also attach a certain snob value to doing things as they are done in the best of countries. And reper-cussions of foreign capital of this kind are difficult to regulate in any scheme of domestic planning unless it provides for a detailed scrutiny of each investment proposition — a remedy which can be worse than the disease.

Reference may be made here to one particular danger that arises from the fact that private foreign capital is necessarily available for only particular uses. In theory, it is easy to say that a country is free to decide which particular cases of private foreign capital to admit and which not ; and it might be argued that those particular lines of consumption which need to be discouraged should not be allowed to be developed even with the help of foreign capital. But in practice, the general desire to prove that one welcomes foreign capital or the pressure of domestic vested interests in league with foreign investors or the fact that investment propositions from abroad often come in a package (oil refining-cum-fertilizers-cum-synthetic fibres) leads to situations where foreign capital is allowed to set up industries where its contribution is essentially to the growth of inessential consumption based on a growing volume of imported raw materials and components. This danger is particularly great in the case of items whose imports are regulated on the ground of inessentiality but whose domestic (and often high-cost) production is not similarly discouraged. The general point that needs to be made is that in so far as foreign capital may be available only for specific uses, it might be advisable in some cases to reject it altogether.[1]

[1] A great deal of emphasis is being laid these days by international agencies and others on preparing a code for the treatment of private foreign capital. But a code for proper treatment of such capital is more likely to be adhered to if the same agencies urge a greater degree of caution and care in selecting the foreign invest-ments to be permitted in keeping with long-term goals. Perhaps it may also be noted in passing that an international code for the treatment of private foreign capital must also outline the obligations of such capital which are vital to the development process such as maximum training and employment of local per-sonnel and the fullest participation in the efforts of the country of domicile to increase exports and reduce the dependence on imports at least in certain areas.

It has been mentioned earlier that any society which relies on foreign capital must accept the fact that its domestic planning will have to respond to some extent to the wishes of those who supply the capital. This is true not only in respect of the particular use to which the foreign capital might be put but also of the general policies and plans of the aid-receiving country. Whether this particular aspect of the interaction between domestic planning and foreign capital represents a fruitful or healthy exercise in international economic co-operation is more than one can say on the basis of experience so far particularly when the use can turn so unpredictably on those irrational springs of action which still govern the conduct of nations as of individuals. We can only remind ourselves usefully that prejudice, irrationality and unwillingness to face facts and act upon them are not the special attributes of any particular group or nation, be it rich or poor; nor is any country or even an international agency likely to be altogether free from their hold.

VI. PROBLEMS OF REPAYMENT

We turn now to consider the fact that only a small part of foreign capital that is available today to the poorer countries is in the form of gifts. By far the larger part consists of loans and investments bearing a liability to pay interest or remit profits as well as to repay and repatriate. One could argue that this fact should make no difference to the purposes for which aid is utilized except perhaps that it heightens the importance of enhancing the pace of progress as distinct from reducing the rigours of development. But essentially, since the servicing of loans and the ability to live without aid require the acquisition of the same kind of balance of payments strength, there should not be any special use of foreign capital which would be dictated by the fact that it carries the burden of interest charges and repayment.

The question, however, that arises is that of the amount of foreign capital that it is prudent to borrow and on what terms. The two aspects are clearly related as more capital can be prudently and profitably employed at more favourable terms and the other way around. In an earlier volume in this series, Sir Roy Harrod has worked out a number of instructive examples to show how much foreign capital can be absorbed with assurance of being able to repay and on what terms and under what conditions.[1] Suffice to say here that given the terms on which foreign capital is available and the productivity of capital in general as well as the limitations on external markets and the minimum essential growth in consumption, it may not be possible for a country to service its debts without more and more external borrowing. Even where conditions are intrinsically favourable, repayment may pose a problem if aid or capital in necessary amounts is not forthcoming over a sufficiently long period. In this sense, there is generally a minimum amount of foreign capital that is necessary even for a successful case of 'assisted take-off' just as much as there might be cases where no reasonable amount of foreign capital might suffice for the purpose. In practice, it is rather unrealistic for a country to worry about whether it can afford to have foreign capital beyond a point because it can never be sure of how much capital it will ultimately receive over a number of years. Some projections over time of inflow of foreign capital and the feasibility of ultimately servicing it, however, would be useful both for creditors and debtors as long as the tendency to wishful thinking on either side is resisted. Such exercises could at least engender a realistic attitude towards what could be regarded as reasonable terms for assistance.

A great deal of attention has of late been devoted to this question of terms on which foreign capital ought to be made available if a crippling burden on the balance of payments of aid-receiving countries is to be avoided. Some improvement in this regard has also taken place. But much remains to be done. In a saner world, one might well advocate that whatever aid a country feels like giving should be by way of gifts and that this would make for a more rational aid policy as well as for more harmonious relations between aid-givers and aid-receivers even if it reduces the total flow of aid. But this is too much to aim at in the present circumstances. As it is, the desire to maximize aid flows in the short-run comes in the way of reducing or minimizing reliance on 'hard' loans from some quarters and this sets up a tendency for others to harden their terms as well. Indeed, there is also a certain asymmetry in the attitude of aid-giving countries and international agencies in this regard. The World Bank and several governments, for example, rightly insist on aid-receiving countries avoiding suppliers' credits and other

[1] Sir Roy Harrod, 'Desirable International Movements of Capital in Relation to Growth of Borrowers and Lenders and Growth of Markets', Roy Harrod and Douglas Hague (editors), *International Trade Theory in a Developing World*, London, 1963, pp. 113–14.

medium-term credits for development. At the same time, they encourage the maximum possible use of private foreign investment when it is abundantly clear that such investment imposes a very heavy burden of servicing charges on the balance of payments of the recipient countries. The truth, divorced from all ideological considerations, is that private foreign investment today makes sense in developing countries only when it comes for certain high-priority uses and when it forms in the aggregate only a small part of total foreign capital that is available by virtue of being accompanied by a much larger inflow of official capital on relatively 'soft' terms.

One important aspect of the burden of repayment is that it represents a first charge on the earnings of a country in good times as well as bad. Quite apart from anything else, the vital necessity of preserving the reputation as a good debtor makes it so. The inflow of foreign capital adds resources of the kind that would be particularly in short supply otherwise. But the reverse side of the medal is that repayment obligations take away the most valuable resource. Some mechanism of flexibility in respect of debt obligations is a vital need if the plans and programmes of developing countries are not to be thrown out of gear from time to time when they are faced with an additional temporary strain on their balance of payments. We have an excellent precedent here in the postwar Anglo-American and other loans where instalments of interest and repayments due in any year could be automatically deferred in the event of the debtor country being faced with a serious prospect of losing reserves. There is every justification for loans to developing countries, including those from international agencies, carrying a similar provision from the outset and laying down some definite procedure for the activation of the provision. This is a far better and more orderly course — generating more sense of confidence all round — than the practice of re-scheduling debts and of arranging emergency balance of payments assistance which is already becoming quite frequent.

Sooner or later, problems of repayment of foreign capital will bring to the fore the question of planned access to the markets of the aid-giving countries. The UN Conference on Trade and Development has already highlighted the connection between trade, aid and development. But if domestic planning in developing countries has to take account of foreign capital and its repayment, some sort of long-term planning on the part of the aid-giving countries to ensure an orderly and adequate absorption of the repayments is also urgently called for. Otherwise, the best that one can say about relating foreign capital to a plan of development in the poorer countries would be that such aid should be used for meeting situations that arise from year to year leaving the long-run to look after itself. From this point of view of planning the use as well as the return of foreign capital, the practice of allowing repayments at least in part in local currencies has much to recommend itself.

VII. SUMMING UP

The arguments in this paper, I am afraid, are generally suggestive and not conclusive so that it would be more appropriate to sum up the issues they raise for further discussion rather than to indicate the conclusions they point to. Among the questions that might be profitably discussed are the following:

(*a*) Can foreign capital be related to domestic planning in the absence of a long-term perspective plan?

(*b*) What are the ingredients of a perspective plan that deserve emphasis?

(*c*) In what circumstances would it be legitimate to employ foreign capital for reducing the rigours of domestic planning and when would it be more advisable to use it for shortening the time-horizon for achieving desired results?

(*d*) How useful is the concept of 'absorptive capacity' and what bearing does it have on the timing and extent of the use of foreign capital?

(*e*) Are there any ways in which the risks inherent in the uncertainty regarding the flow of foreign capital could be minimized?

(*f*) What are the special considerations that deserve emphasis in determining the nature and extent of private capital inflows?

(*g*) Among the possible conditions governing the use of aid, which are most harmful to rational planning at home and how can the legitimate interests of aid-giving countries in stipulating such conditions be safeguarded without the same harmful effects on aid-receiving countries?

(*h*) Is it possible to make an objective estimate of the amount of aid that a country can prudently and profitably absorb and on what terms?

Capital Movements and Economic Development

(*i*) How can we improve upon the prospects of repayment of foreign capital without an undue strain on the poorer countries?

COMMENTS ON DR. PATEL'S PAPER

BY

Professor ALDO FERRER

University of Buenos Aires

BEFORE making some brief comments on Mr. Patel's paper I would like to make two general observations. First, I found the paper excellent and most stimulating: as the author says, 'the giving and receiving of aid at present, with a few exceptions, is essentially an *ad hoc* affair', and this fact makes it very difficult to integrate the absorption of foreign capital in national development plans. Nevertheless, Dr. Patel has presented an ample discussion of the subject and given us the opportunity for a fruitful discussion of the problems involved.

My second general observation is that I do not find discrepancies with the author's point of view, which is why I prefer to concentrate my remarks on a further elaboration of two subjects mentioned in the paper rather than to make a comprehensive analysis of it. These are first, the importance of perspective planning and, second, the balance of payments short-run disequilibrium and its effects on monetary, financial and rate of exchange policies *vis-à-vis* national development plans and policies.

I. THE IMPORTANCE OF PERSPECTIVE PLANNING

As the author says, 'for those countries left behind in the race for economic progress, there are a number of "structural" problems which can be tackled only with a somewhat long-term perspective — of say, twenty to twenty-five years', and 'the removal of these basic weaknesses constitutes the first stage in domestic planning — a stage which unhappily must extend over a number of decades'.

I suggest that, besides these problems in countries with very low income levels, there are others which might present themselves in developing countries with relatively higher income levels and which also can be conveniently tackled within the framework of perspective plans or, at least, long-term projections. I would like to mention two specific problems in this connection.

The definition of industrialization and import substitution policies. Some developing countries have found, after having developed substantial industrial sectors, that they have concentrated too much attention on the

312

last stages of the industrial process without an adequate expansion of basic industries producing intermediate and capital goods. In these cases, increasing import needs arise to supply intermediate products for domestic industry and capital goods for the investment process in the economy as a whole. In the absence of a well balanced industrial structure, once the substitution process has been accomplished in the less complex industrial goods (i.e. durable consumer goods, textiles, etc.), the only way to increase the supply of intermediate and capital goods — to afford further industrial expansion — is the permanent increase of the import capacity. If this does not occur, as is typical in many developing nations, a serious bottleneck arises that might impair and distort the whole development process.

From this argument it follows that the important thing is not only the rate of industrial growth but also the composition of industrial production. For a number of reasons in free-enterprise or mixed economies the first stages of industrial growth tend to be concentrated in the less technological complex and capital-intensive manufactures. If we make an assumption concerning the expected income levels and import capacity within the framework of a perspective plan or long-term projection then it becomes possible to define to what extent the composition of industrial products demand should correspond to the structure of industrial production. A perspective plan could thus help to indicate when a country should launch the development of its basic industries to avoid future bottlenecks. A perspective plan will also help to define a policy of absorption of foreign resources into the industrial sector that will correspond to the long-term needs of the economy. It should also be pointed out that it is precisely in the basic industries where foreign capital and technology can play a more decisive role.

Regional integration. The second area of problems where perspective planning is particularly relevant is in regional integration. As a matter of fact, Report on the Latin American Common Market of the UN Economic Commission for Latin America, published some ten years ago, provided, on the basis of long-term projections, some of the most forceful arguments in favour of regional integration. On the basis of the expected behaviour of the region's traditional exports up to 1975 it showed how Latin America had to face either a reduction of its rate of growth or a sharp contraction of the imports/GNP coefficient which, in practice, meant an intolerable effort of import substitution which would compromise efficiency. In the case of the smaller countries, due to the restricted character of their domestic markets, the second alternative is very limited.

ECLA found that the way out was, of course, regional integration, and pointed out two favourable conditions to this end. First, the fact is that some countries in the region import from the rest of the world goods already produced by other Latin American countries at reasonably efficient levels. Therefore, the horizon of import substitution could be significantly expanded through formation of a regional market. Second, an increasing proportion of regional imports are and will be formed by intermediate products and capital goods produced by the basic industries. Consequently, a great development and integration effort was proposed for basic manufactures (capital goods, steel, heavy chemicals, etc.). The formation of a large regional market was to provide adequate conditions for obtaining full benefit of economies of scale in those activities.

A perspective regional plan or, at least, a long-term projection will help, therefore, to draw up the strategy of regional development and to reinforce the essential role of such integration in avoiding the increasing deterioration of the Latin American payments gap.

Finally, as pointed out in recent UN reports on the subject, not only national and regional perspective plans but also world economy projections are needed to give a sounder basis for national development efforts and to bring into light the responsibilities of the industrialized countries in a world that is becoming increasingly interdependent in all fields of human endeavour.

II. Short-term Policies *vis-à-vis* National Development Plans and Policies

Now let us come back from the world of tomorrow to the world of today. It is a typical problem in many developing countries that national development plans are not geared to the daily decisions taken by the financial and monetary authorities. In other words short-term policies have little to do with policies in the fields of investment, full employment (however one defines this concept in a developing economy), income distribution and sound stabilization policies.

To a large extent short-term policies are influenced nowadays in many developing countries by acute balance of payments disequilibria. It has been mentioned on several occasions at this conference, including the opening session, that foreign indebtedness is a grave problem in many developing countries and that debt service payments represent excessive proportions of their total export earnings. A position is being reached in some countries where the balance of payments on current account might not show a significant deficit but the balance of payments on capital account, due to heavy debt amortizations, presents an acute deficit. Argentina is today a typical case of this sort.

These balance of payments problems create the need to re-schedule debt payments and to adopt internal policies consistent with the objectives of reaching equilibrium in foreign transactions. But what are these policies? On more than one occasion they have been based on the simplest internal deflationary policies and on sharp devaluations which have created increased cost inflation, unemployment, regressive income redistribution and a contraction of capital formation.

314

Leaving aside consideration of the political elements behind short-term policies, it is clear that a stronger analytical effort is necessary in many developing countries to formulate monetary, financial and rate of exchange policies consistent with the economic and social objectives of national development plans and policies. At the same time a closer co-ordination is needed between the planning office and the economic and financial authorities.

To this end it is also essential to have in mind the foreign indebtedness problems mentioned above and to find some formulas which will avoid the already too frequent re-scheduling negotiations in order to provide some mechanisms which will allow national planners to draw up, on a sounder basis, long-term development policies. As Mr. Patel says: 'Some mechanism of flexibility in respect of debt obligations is a vital need if the plans and programmes of developing countries are not to be thrown out of gear from time to time when they are faced with an additional temporary strain on their balance of payments'. I draw your attention to the valuable suggestions contained in Mr. Patel's paper in this respect.

FURTHER COMMENTS ON DR. PATEL'S PAPER

BY

T. N. ANDREASYAN

Institute of World Economics and
International Relations, Moscow

IT was with great interest that I read Mr. I. G. Patel's paper on a subject so topical for the developing countries. The particular attraction of the paper lies in the fact that its author, coming from the largest of the developing countries, considers the matter of foreign capital from the viewpoint of these countries and in terms of domestic planning at that, which is of great importance for liberated countries. The paper by I. G. Patel contains some valuable ideas and highlights some issues which make one think and compare.

In my comments I should like to dwell on two basic questions: (1) the relationship between domestic planning and foreign aid, and (2) the role of private foreign capital.

I

I agree with Mr. Patel that the aim of planning is to help the developing countries reach the level of development of the industrial countries in respect of production pattern, consumption, education and the rate of accumulation (capital formation). Of course, the rate of economic development will depend on the rate of accumulation and the efficiency of investment in different branches of economy, on the 'absorption capacity' for the necessary capital. It seems, however, that for a high rate of growth to be attained neither the current rate of accumulation in the developing countries, 8 to 10 per cent, nor the goal set by the author, 15 to 20 per cent, will be sufficient. As the experience of the U.S.S.R. as well as of Japan and Italy indicate, for a rapid leap forward the rate of accumulation has to reach the 25 to 30 per cent level.

But how is such a high rate of accumulation to be attained ? What shall be the relation of foreign aid and the efforts of a developing country, of foreign aid and domestic planning ? The author himself in conclusion poses the questions as to what possible conditions governing the use of aid have the most harmful effect on rational planning in the developing countries ; how the legitimate interests of the aid-giving countries can be associated with conditions safeguarding the developing countries against the harmful effects of aid ; and how in the future the repayment of foreign aid can be improved upon so as not to impose an undue strain on the finances of the poorer countries.

The development of a country is evidently a matter of interest primarily to its people. Its progressive-minded thinkers realize that the struggle to do away with the bitter fruits of colonialism is not an easy one and calls for an immense effort and certain sacrifices on the part of the people, if the set goal is to be achieved in the shortest time possible. Foreign aid can only supplement — sometimes considerably — the effort of the people itself, but by no means replace it.

It seems to me that not only positive results of constructive aid but certain dark sides as well, should always be borne in mind. Indeed, the necessity of repayment leads to the origin and growth of a balance of payments deficit, and this cannot fail to affect adversely the whole economic structure which gets to be completely aid-oriented. There arises a tendency to develop only those industries which can secure foreign aid. All this, with incorrect utilization of aid, may slow down the independent development of an aid-receiving country.

This is why correct utilization of aid received is a matter of paramount importance. Dr. Patel repeatedly speaks of aid in terms of solving consumption problems. It would be absurd, of course, to deny the usefulness of obtaining relief — under emergency conditions — in the form of foodstuffs and other high-priority consumption goods. But if the aid is spent mainly on consumption it does not save a developing country from the deficiencies of its economy, and only drives the sickness deeper inside. If a country's economy is not developing, its agricultural and industrial production not rising, the need for such aid becomes permanent and its dark sides tend to stand out. The aid recipient turns into a sort of drug-fiend, unable to live another day without it. If this is not to happen, foreign aid should assist in the development of economy and in the change of the structure of colonial economies. Their growing output shall facilitate the repayment problem, shall minimize and eventually bring to zero requests for foreign aid, until the need for this method of developing an economy — which is, on the whole, an emergency and necessarily temporary one — becomes eliminated. Therefore, paradoxical as it may seem, the main ultimate goal of using foreign aid is for a developing country to eliminate the need for such aid. Common sense prompts that aid shall not and will not exist forever.

But in order to achieve such a result, it seems to me that foreign aid and domestic planning should be very thoroughly co-ordinated. This co-ordination should be both in the financial and in the material fields. At the beginning of his paper, Dr. Patel speaks on the material aspects of planning, but when he turns to the subject of aid he almost entirely concerns himself with currency and financial problems. The matter of aid application is, however, no less important. Would it not be more advisable before discussing the amount and financial terms of aid, to draw up a list of projects that require aid for their construction ? But a list of projects emerges during the planning process, when both financial and material balances are prepared, and a country's resources and needs are co-ordinated in perspective and short-term plans. It is in the material aspect of domestic planning that the tasks of development and the radical change of the backward economies of developing countries are most clearly manifest. It would be advisable that a definite structure of aid and private foreign investment projects should be incorporated in this material balance, since the market mechanism cannot adequately control capital investment spheres from the point of view of long-term plans for development.

In this context the Soviet Union's experience of economic relations with the developing countries will be of interest. The U.S.S.R. as a rule does not allocate as aid to this or that country any prearranged sum of credit. The government of a developing country approaches the Soviet Government with a request for economic and technical assistance in the construction of certain industrial, agricultural or infra-structure projects, which are parts of its plans for economic development. A list of projects having been agreed upon, the aggregate sum of credit can be determined. These credits are granted, as a rule, however, not in currency but in the form of specific equipment, machinery, various services, sending specialists on missions, and training of foreign students and experts in the U.S.S.R. This method makes it possible for aid to be turned into a highly efficient instrument for the development of the production and of the culture of a liberated country, and fits directly into the framework of its domestic plans for development. The Soviet Union thus provides an example of aid that is subordinated to the objectives of planning, and not the other way around.

Capital Movements and Economic Development

But these are not the only favourable terms that Soviet aid offers to the developing countries. Furthermore, there are the low rates of interest not exceeding 3 per cent ; favourable terms of repayment on commissioning an enterprise ; payments in domestic currency and traditional export commodities ; renouncement of any interest in the projects themselves ; non-interference in internal affairs or foreign policy, or imposing any political conditions or projects of its own. Soviet aid is disinterested and based on respect for the equality and independence of the developing countries. It has laid the foundation of an essentially new type of international relations. According to calculations of Soviet economists, the developing countries on servicing their credits and interest charges on a published sum of credit of $4·4 billion, will have paid the socialist countries by 1983 600 to 800 million dollars less than they would have paid Western powers, international banks and organizations, and private investors. Certainly, Soviet aid is not yet as big as the developing countries would want it to be, but it will be increased *pari passu* with the growth of the Soviet economies.

In the last years one may see a process of evolution of aid rendered by Western countries to the developing countries. It was only recently that the developing countries found themselves in a position to obtain credits and loans from the West for a 30- to 40-year period at a low rate of interest. It seems to me that this is the result of the impact of Soviet aid on the whole institution of aid. In fact, it was not long ago that the Western powers rendered aid on very hard terms — at a high rate of interest and short-term repayment in hard currency. Political strings were attached to aid, and its lion's share was allotted to member countries of CENTO and SEATO.

Accelerating the growth of an economy with the help of constructive Soviet aid results in the expansion of production and exports, including the growth and diversification of exports through an increased share of semi-finished products and finished industrial goods and the enlarging of the circle of trading partners. A boost in export activities, in turn, is instrumental in facilitating repayments and improving the balance of payments. It is growing increasingly evident that the best way — and a drastic one at that — of liquidating a balance of payments deficit is the development of exports and a reasonable restriction of imports, not emergency injections of aid. In the long run, it is trade and not aid that should become an effective method of solving the problem of accumulation. As to the problem of foreign trade, this is a special matter for discussion.

An important method of increasing the rate of accumulation domestically is the redistribution of income between the various sections of a society. I agree with Dr. Patel that no perspective plan should be drawn without giving consideration to this problem and without raising the standards of the poorer sections of a society, although the author believes that a ' revolutionary change in the distribution of income ' can be success-

318

ful only if foreign aid is rendered. As to the issue in question, the mobilization of all internal sources of accumulation makes it imperative that the means which are used to enrich already well-to-do sections of the community, remitted abroad, or invested in projects that are not advisable from the point of view of the national economy, should be used for common national goals. If the wealth saved up by the top members of a society is not to be used for economic development, any serious increase in the rate of accumulation and a rise in the standard of living of the poor social groups of a nation and hence an increase in the national income until it approaches the level of developed countries, will be out of the question. This is proved by the experience not only of the socialist countries, but also of a developing country like the UAR where a similar operation has had a beneficial effect on its economic development.

At the same time, I believe that the necessity of serious socio-economic reforms cannot be considered to be diminished by any aid. Social problems in the developing countries are so grave that even with a considerable expansion of aid no means can be found for their solution.

In this connection, Mr. Patel's thought that one of the aims of assistance to the developing countries is ' to avoid difficult social choices ' is very much to the point. This remark must be wholly attributed to the aid of the West. The many influential statesmen in the West fear that in the absence of aid many developing countries will be faced with the need of choosing a different social system, of embarking upon the road of building up socialism. It is common knowledge that in a number of countries in Asia and Africa serious socio-political transformations are under way already, and they are bound to lead to socialism. An even greater number of liberated countries have proclaimed socialism as their ideal.

II

Dr. Patel believes that private capital must play a secondary role to official capital and must be allotted for high priority uses only. I cannot but agree with this.

Such a cautious attitude toward private foreign capital is explained by the author in another place by the fact that its activities lead to the withdrawal from a country of its most valuable resources, while the import of private capital is characterized by total uncertainty, an inability to somehow plan its inflow. It is not without reason that Dr. Patel in conclusion offers for discussion the questions in what circumstances it would be legitimate to employ foreign capital for reducing the rigours of domestic planning and for shortening the time-horizon for achieving the desired goals ; how to minimize the risks inherent in foreign capital owing to the uncertainty of its flow ; and what are special considerations that deserve emphasis in determining the nature and extent of private foreign capital inflows.

Dr. Patel's misgivings as regards private foreign capital are quite sub-stantiated. The preservation of control over key sectors — sometimes the export branches — of the economy in the hands of private foreign capital is indeed one of the worst after-effects of the colonial era, a major reason for the economic dependence of the developing countries and for the reduction of an already low rate of accumulation. Direct foreign investments that used to be among the main economic bases of capitalism have turned now into the material basis of neo-colonialism. Terms of concessions, for instance, are as a rule inequitable and unjust. It can hardly be denied that the activity of foreign capital is determined by its owners and not infrequently runs counter to the interests of a developing country. The direct character of investments paves the way for foreign interference, serves as a source of international conflicts. The with-drawal of profits on foreign investments considerably exceeds the inflow of capital, and the volume of these losses is not less but evidently greater than that of the losses suffered by the developing countries on account of the ' scissors of price ' in foreign trade. Besides, ' repayment ' of private foreign investments in the shape of withdrawal of profits is prac-tically permanent, and the developing country becomes an eternal tribu-tary of a foreign company. Oil companies, for example, have for years been depriving Iran of 15 per cent, and Iraq of even 20 per cent of their respective national incomes. It is not surprising, therefore, that in the countries of Asia, Africa and Latin America a movement is spreading for nationalization of direct private investments, particularly of the concession type. Sooner or later they will become a thing of the past, as incompatible with economic independence and the goals of national planning.

While following the course of nationalization and restriction of private investment, the developing countries are striving to attract new foreign capital, especially in the form of portfolio investments, and of mixed companies, with domestic official or private capital participating. Private foreign investors are given an opportunity to derive normal profit on their investments. However, the developing countries offer terms that leave in their hands the control over activities and finances of the enterprises set up with the participation of foreign and private capital, and deprive the latter of a chance to derive abnormally high profits, prevent foreigners from interference into their internal affairs. It seems that if the govern-ment of a developing country pursues a firm and consistent policy of achieving economic independence, it may well draw private foreign capital and use it in patriotic interests. The U.A.R. and Ghana provide examples of such a policy. It is worthwhile recalling in this connection that the founder of the Soviet state, V. I. Lenin, considered it quite possible and even necessary that foreign companies should be given con-cessions for the exploitation of mineral resources of the young Soviet Russia.

However, to attract official foreign capital in the form of international and bilateral loans and credits is more beneficial to the developing countries than the import of private foreign capital. This form is not connected with acquisition of property. Servicing of loans and credits by a debtor country is made over a definite time period and by a definite amount. Furthermore, the developing countries can choose between donor countries. They can receive aid on favourable terms from the Soviet Union and other socialist countries.

————

DISCUSSION OF DR. PATEL'S PAPER

MAIN topics in the discussion of Dr. Patel's paper were : the effects of uncertainty on the planning and planning horizons of developing countries ; the relationship between lending terms and uses of loans ; and the relative merits of trade and aid. In the discussion of the last topic, the role of private investment and the terms of Soviet aid were also considered.

I. PLANNING AND UNCERTAINTY

Professor Chenery considered improvement of planning to be crucial. Planning serves to co-ordinate donors with the recipients and the donors among themselves, and to relate projects to the over-all programmes of the country. For countries with well-formulated plans, such as India and Pakistan, uncertainty in receiving aid was much less than in other countries. He agreed with a point raised by Dr. Ferrer that some countries might not be willing to discuss their plans, but noted that countries unwilling to discuss development strategy with donors tended to get less aid. An increasing amount of U.S. aid is based on an evaluation of development programmes of recipient countries. *Dr. Gulhati* suggested that a new category be added to those proposed by Professor Chenery. Co-ordination among recipients, possibly through the formation of common markets, is another form of co-ordination that would aid planning.

Dr. Singer and *Dr. Andreasyan* agreed that Dr. Patel had not faced the problem of what difference uncertainty should make to the actual contents of development plans. If uncertainty exists there probably should be several plans. In terms of projects, this may mean that one must choose different means to accomplish projects rather than choose among projects.

Dr. Faaland also commented on the problem of uncertainty. He agreed with Dr. Patel that the need for aid was of a long-run nature, but questioned whether the fact that aid was allocated on a year-to-year basis posed any special problems. He felt that aid fluctuated no more than other important elements in the development process. In fact, aid has been relatively stable. It might even be useful to allocate aid on a yearly basis as a compensatory device to offset other fluctuations.

Dr. Márquez said that co-ordination among donors might have disadvantages as well as advantages. If donors agreed to apply the most conservative procedures, co-ordination of donors would not necessarily guarantee the best flow of resources. Competition among donors can be healthy.

A point raised by Dr. Patel which provoked much discussion was the point that in developing countries, faced by a number of structural problems, planning horizons are necessarily longer than for developed countries. *Professor Wallich* was surprised by Dr. Patel's view. Considering the difference in the availability and reliability of statistical data between advanced and developing countries, he thought that it should be the other way around. He admitted on the other hand that as countries become richer, the necessity for planning should decrease. *Dr. Fleming* also questioned Dr. Patel's distinction between planning horizons. While the greater need for basic investment in developing countries provides a plausible reason for having a longer planning perspective, it is offset by greater future uncertainty. Also, when foreign trade is introduced with its increasing uncertainty, optimum planning periods for developing countries tend to be shortened. This was especially important because foreign exchange allows more feasibility in obtaining resources.

II. LENDING TERMS AND LOAN USES

Dr. Patel maintained in his paper that, ideally, uses of loans should not be influenced by the terms of lending. Where the problem is one of ability to pay, he would argue for increasing flexibility in repayment terms. *Dr. de Beers* noted that loan terms do in fact condition the way in which loans are used. He suggested that developing countries apply more severe standards to soft loans because this type of aid is more valuable. Also, lenders discriminate between types of loans according to the proposed use. For instance, in the field of social loans, the Inter-American Development Bank makes soft loans in areas where hard loans will not work. *Dr. Rhomberg* added that Dr. Patel's idea could be justified if the problem were purely a marginal one, i.e. if aid were allocated according to the cost of the marginal dollar of the loan. But if future payments must be considered there is reason to alter plan allocations according to type of aid. *Dr. Patel* replied that the interest rate question is irrelevant here. Even if project return is high in domestic terms, it is still necessary to repay the loan in foreign currency.

Dr. Okita said that soft loans should be avoided for industrial types of projects because they may encourage the use of too much capital. Also, in countries like Japan with high internal rates, to soften terms of lending may reduce the total amount lent. *Dr. Gulhati* noted here that arguments for borrowing on soft terms are weakened if the amount given may be less. The trade-off between the size of a loan and its terms must be known. He added that Dr. Patel's argument for increasing flexibility of debt servicing relates to the problem of uncertainty. Reducing uncertainty should be the objective, not increasing flexibility of repayment. *Professor Borts* felt that the repayment problem had been exaggerated. He noted that historically repayments had only been a problem in times of financial crises.

Dr. Singer also questioned the proposal by Dr. Patel for increasing flexibility of debt repayment. He said that this might jeopardize one of the great advantages of the present system ; that international organizations like the World Bank are able to finance loans through the issue of bonds to private investors in developed countries. The volume of aid for developing countries is greater and the terms are better than they would otherwise be, since the World Bank also makes loans to the developed countries and borrows on terms that are determined in part by the credit standing of these developed countries.

Dr. Patel answered that his argument for increasing flexibility of repayment was designed to handle the sort of short-term crises, especially those that could not be handled by the International Monetary Fund, which tend to shake confidence among lenders. There are strong arguments for arranging in advance flexibility of repayments to avoid such crises.

III. TRADE VERSUS AID

Dr. Andreasyan noted that aid is a temporary expedient. For development purposes, what is needed is trade, not aid. *Dr. Singer* disagreed. He thought that in some ways aid is much better than trade. If developed countries are to help developing countries, it is more logical that they should give aid in proportion to their ability to give aid, not in proportion to their imports. Proposals for trade instead of aid inevitably include a corollary that developed countries make trade concessions to underdeveloped countries. This leads to higher prices for products of underdeveloped countries, so those developed countries that are already large importers from developing countries will be the ones who pay most. This does not seem to be a rational means of allocating the aid burden among donor countries. *Dr. Andreasyan* replied that while he favoured both aid and trade, since aid cannot be eternal, it should be provided only until countries achieve self-sustained growth.

Dr. Kamarck thought Dr. Singer had gone too far in arguing that the trade approach would imply higher prices for the products of underdeveloped countries. He said that much could be done by merely eliminating barriers and discrimination in developed countries. *Dr. Onitiri* also disagreed with Dr. Singer because Dr. Singer had not defined what he considered to be aid, and because measures to raise prices for primary products of developing countries might be considered both as aid and as trade.

Capital Movements and Economic Development

Dr. Fleming felt that in considering the relative merits of trade and aid, the order of preference should be : (1) eliminate trade restrictions in developed countries, (2) provide direct transfers, and (3) give preferential treatment to exports from developing countries. Since the aid available is usually less than the optimum amount there is always room for preferential treatment of exports from underdeveloped countries. The answer to the trade versus aid debate is trade *and* aid from this viewpoint.

A point made in Dr. Patel's paper was that one of the functions of aid is to allow higher consumption during the development process than would otherwise be possible. *Professor Wallich* noted that though aid ultimately is consumed, the idea that aid should be directed toward consumption blurs the distinction between trade and aid. The marginal propensity to save and the growth process are no longer tied to the income generated by aid, as when aid is invested and not consumed. Further, in considering the savings generated by aid-financed investment projects, Professor Wallich warned that we should be careful to distinguish between net and gross savings. If growth is slow, heavy amortization may reduce net savings well below levels of gross savings. *Dr. Patel* replied that he did not advocate the use of aid for consumption, but that he was trying to show that much aid listed for consumption purposes is really investment, and that the need to raise consumption standards during the development process should not be ignored.

Dr. Kamarck thought that Dr. Patel had underrated the role of foreign private investment. While foreign private investment is not necessarily beneficial, foreign companies can sometimes play a vital role by ' shaking ' and ' awakening ' the economy to make it realize its potential, as they have done even in relatively developed countries like Australia and New Zealand. *Dr. Okita* added that he felt that Dr. Patel had also underrated the importance of 'know-how' associated with private investment, especially in export industries. He noted also that some of the developing countries like India should devote more effort to export promotion. The need for this is seen in the growth of non-competitive firms in the domestic market, protected by subsidies and tariff walls. *Professor Delivanis* agreed that foreign private investment was usually the only way of importing managerial skills. He felt this constitutes a strong case in favour of private foreign investment.

Dr. Patel pointed out that the desire to welcome foreign capital often leads in practice to uses of the capital in ways that do not fit in with goals of domestic planning. *Dr. de Beers* said that if this is so, it is the planners' fault, especially in an economy where imports are regulated. *Professor Borts* wanted to know how plans had been altered by the existence of private foreign investment. Dr. Patel seemed concerned by the fact that private foreign investment could disturb planning, but Professor Borts wondered if the relationship did not work the other way around. That is, did not planners impede foreign investment more than the investment disturbed the planners? *Professor Kafka* answered that foreign investors were often too enthusiastic about plans. He said that they liked the incentives offered by planning if not the restrictions, and that he thought foreign investors generally preferred the greater certainty held out in countries with development plans. *Dr. Patel* concluded that private foreign investment can be taken only in small doses. Planners in the developing countries must know how private investment will fit within the plan framework for plans to be effective.

In his comments on Dr. Patel's paper, *Dr. Andreasyan* emphasized the real or material aspects of domestic planning and aid, the Soviet policy of giving aid in the form of material balances, and the relatively favourable terms on which Soviet aid is offered to developing countries. *Dr. Singer* doubted that Russian aid had been given on more favourable terms than other kinds of aid. While competition between East and West is a healthy process, he thought that available evidence would not support the conclusion that either Soviet or Western aid was granted on more favourable terms. He felt that presently published aid figures are meaningless, and if properly recomputed would show that effective rates of interest on Western aid were lower than nominal rates. He also questioned the pricing of Russian commodities supplied to underdeveloped countries. He noted that this was especially important since all Russian aid is tied, and since this type of aid generally is worth less than its face value. *Dr. Andreasyan* replied that Soviet aid is priced according to world prices and quality standards for the particular commodities. He added that if the U.S.S.R. provides assistance in the form of exports rather than in free foreign exchange, this is due to the scarcity of free currency in the U.S.S.R., which in turn is a consequence of the small trade between the U.S.S.R. and the United States. If trade between the U.S. and the U.S.S.R. were increased, the U.S.S.R. would then be able to give more untied aid to developing countries.

Chapter 9

TIED CREDITS — A QUANTITATIVE
ANALYSIS

BY

Dr. MAHBUB ul HAQ

Planning Commission, Government of Pakistan

I. INTRODUCTORY

THE developing economies will do well to recognize that they have
to live with tied credits for a long time to come.[1] It is largely
academic at this stage to argue that the world would have been
better off if the credits were untied and if the pattern of foreign
assistance was more liberal and less restrictive. Tied credits, after
all, are merely a symptom of the basic maladjustments in the international balance of payments and the lack of any automatic mechanism
for the correction of these maladjustments. If world trade becomes
more genuinely multilateral in nature and some success is achieved
in devising an international system to take care of the recurrent
balance of payments crises in the developed countries, the problem
of tied credits will lose much of its current significance. But the
prospects for such favourable developments are hardly bright at
present. Nor would it be wise to count on them. A more realistic
course would be to explore carefully the adverse implications of tied
credits for the recipient countries and to devise concrete institutional arrangements to overcome or minimize these implications.
The intention of this paper is to offer a quantitative analysis of tied
credits from the experience of Pakistan so as to present the general
problem in a concrete and sharper focus.

Tied credits come in all sorts of packages — they are tied to the
country of origin, tied to individual projects, tied to specific end-
uses. In most cases, all the three forms of tying are applicable.
The most important form, however, is country-tying which makes

[1] Dr. Haq was unable to attend the conference. His paper was presented by
Dr. Adler.

326

it difficult for the recipient countries to take advantage of the competitive conditions in the international market. All forms of tying result, in one way or another, in higher prices. The adverse implications of tied credits extend, however, beyond the question of prices. Tied credits also limit the ability of the recipient country to choose an appropriate technology or international consultants of its own choice. In many cases, the domestic projects are over-capitalized and considerable difficulty is experienced in marketing their products, in the domestic or in the international market, unless their costs are written down. This paper does not deal with the wider implications of tied credits but confines itself only to the quantification of higher prices under tied credits and the concrete measures to overcome them.

II. THE EVIDENCE

Some of the information collected on the implications of tied credits for higher prices paid by Pakistan has been summarized in Tables 1 to 3. The detailed information has been reproduced in the Statistical Appendix where the limitations, to which the study is subject, are also brought out.

Table 1 is based on a sample of 20 development projects. The total cost of these development projects is fairly large but the specific items of equipment, where a comparison has been made between the lowest quotation from the tied source and the lowest quotation on international bidding, amount to about $15 million. Care has been taken to compare only such items of equipment as have similar specifications, capacity and quality. In some cases, the comparison is based on price quotations for a complete project ; in others, on the unit cost of each selected item. The overall result is that the weighted average price for these 20 projects comes out to be 51 per cent higher from the tied source compared to the international bids. The worst offenders appear to be Japan, France, Italy and the Netherlands. It is also clear from the table that if more credits had been available from West Germany and the United Kingdom, it would have considerably facilitated the task of switching over projects to the cheapest source of procurement.

Table 2 gives certain illustrations of higher prices for various commodities procured from tied sources. The comparison in this case is easier because the specifications of various commodities can

TABLE 1

INSTANCES OF HIGHER PRICES UNDER TIED CREDITS IN CASE OF PROJECT ASSISTANCE

Serial No. (1)	Name of the Project (2)	Lowest Quotation from Tied Source (Country) (3)	Lowest Quotation in International Bidding (Country) (4)	Percentage Difference between Tied Source and International Bid $(3)-(4)\div(4)$ (5)	Nature of Equipment (6)
1.	Baluchistan collieries	France	Germany, Japan, U.K., Czechoslovakia, Denmark	87	Centrifugal pumps, shovel loaders, underground locomotives, haulage engines, rails, ventilation tubes, air compressors
2.	Chittagong sulphuric acid and superphosphate plant	France	U.S.	45	Complete plant
3.	Table salt manufacture plant	France	Germany, U.K.	71	Complete plant
4.	Khanpur sugar mill	France	U.K.	61	Complete plant
5.	Village electrification and power distribution	Italy	Belgium, Germany, Yugoslavia, Japan, Sweden	63	Steel poles, aluminium conductors, wire, insulators, hydraulic compressors, grid stations
6.	Eastern chemical plant	Japan	U.K.	73	Urea formaldehyde package boiler
7.	Telegraph and telephone dept.	Japan	Formosa, Greece	39	Insulated and sheathed cable, self-supporting aerial cable
8.	Hard-board industries	Japan	Germany	123	Complete plant
9.	Khulna rice mill	Japan	Germany	120	Rice milling machinery
10.	MAKK beverages	Japan	U.K.	25	Complete plant
11.	Karachi Port Trust	Japan	Netherlands	39	60-ton self-propelled floating crane
12.	Nawab Brothers Steel Plant	Japan	Germany	39	Plant for manufacturing steel hose
13.	Atlas Plastic and Rubber Industries	Japan	Germany	25	90 mm. plastic extender
14.	Bengal steel works	Netherlands	Germany	25	Wire-drawing plant (2,000-ton capacity)
15.	Jessore and Dinajpur sugar mills	Czechoslovakia	U.K.	32	Complete plant
16.	Rajshahi and Kushtia sugar mills	Czechoslovakia	U.K.	26	Complete plant
17.	Karachi Port Trust	Netherlands	U.K.	33	Twin-screw bucket dredgers
18.	Karachi Shipyard and Engineering Works	U.K.	Germany	57	Propeller plant, pipeline fittings, engine lubricating pump
19.	Nylon twine plant	U.S.A.	Germany	61	Complete plant
20.	Dacca beverage plant	U.S.A.	Germany	15	Complete plant
	Weighted average for the above projects			51	

TABLE 2

INSTANCES OF HIGHER PRICES UNDER TIED CREDITS IN CASE OF NON-PROJECT ASSISTANCE

Serial No. (1)	Description of Items (2)	Lowest Quotation from Tied Source (U.S.) (3)	Lowest Quotation from Other Sources (indicating Country) (4)	Percentage Difference (3) − (4) ÷ (4) (5)
1.	Channels	$172.60	$106.73 (Japan)	62
2.	Angles (equal)	$171.51	$96.06 (Japan)	79
3.	Angles (unequal)	$164.70	$119.42 (U.K.)	38
4.	Plates	$154.71	$102.34 (Japan)	51
5.	Tees	$207.35	$121.15 (U.K.)	71
6.	Sheets	$161.99	$113.50 (Japan)	43
7.	Billets	$172.22	$91.98 (Sweden)	87
8.	Wheel and axle assemblies (per assembly)	$794.10	$308.70 (Japan)	157
9.	Galvanized iron pipes (1½″ diameter per 100 running feet)	Rs. 147.28	Rs.94.91 (Germany)	55
10.	Corrugated iron sheets	Rs1132.88	Rs868.49 (Japan)	30

TABLE 3

INSTANCES OF HIGHER FREIGHT CHARGES UNDER TIED CREDITS

Serial No. (1)	Procuring Agency (2)	Source of Credit (Loan Number and Date) (3)	Description of Items Procured (4)	Whether International Bids Invited (5)	Lowest Quotation from Tied Source (6)	Lowest Quotation on International Bidding (7)	Percentage Difference $(6)-(7)$ $\div(7)$ (8)	Remarks (9)
1.	Pakistan Western Railway	AID-45 9 Sept. 1962	Freight on 18 locomotives (large)	Yes	$14,500 per locomotive	$6,800 per locomotive (Norway)	113	Higher freight paid
2.	,,	,,	Freight on 20 locomotives (small)	Yes	$9,500 per locomotive	$5,850 per locomotive (Norway)	62	,, ,,
3.	,,	EXIM-Bank 1984-A-Pak 16 Nov. 1962	Freight on 22 locomotives (large)	Yes	$14,500 per locomotive	$6,800 per locomotive (Norway)	113	,, ,,
4.	,,	,,	Freight on 22 locomotives (small)	Yes	$9,500 per locomotive	$5,850 per locomotive (Norway)	62	,, ,,
5.	,,	DLF-105 1 Jan. 1960	Freight on 30 broad gauge, diesel engine locomotives	Yes	$8,380 per locomotive	$5,850 per locomotive (Norway)	43	Waiver obtained in favour of non-U.S. flag ships; cost met partly by cash and partly by IBRD loan
6.	Pakistan Eastern Railway	EXIM-Bank 1984-A-Pak 16 Nov. 1962	Meter gauge locomotives	Yes	$11,500 per locomotive	$7,500 per locomotive (Norway)	53	Waiver obtained; cost met from cash

be more easily equated. Since the bulk of non-project assistance received by Pakistan comes from the U.S., the comparison has been made only between the U.S. prices and the international prices for certain commodities in large use. As can be seen from the table, the U.S. prices are generally 40–50 per cent higher than the international prices in the case of most items of iron and steel procured from the U.S. It also appears that Japan could have been a much cheaper source of supply in the case of many items but, unfortunately, Japan offers negligible non-project assistance to Pakistan at present.

Table 3 brings out some instances of higher freight charges under tied credits. These instances apply to U.S. flag ships. In some cases, the higher freight charges were paid by Pakistan, while in others it was possible to obtain a waiver in favour of non-U.S. flag ships and to meet the cost from Pakistan's own cash resources or from other loans.

III. AN ESTIMATE OF THE COST OF TYING

It is difficult to arrive at an overall quantitative judgment as to the amount Pakistan could have saved by buying on the international market against all the tied foreign credits that it obtained. Complete information is not available regarding all credits nor is it always possible to overcome the difficulty of comparing equipment having different specifications and capacities. A rough estimate made by the author indicates that, if the entire $500 million foreign assistance that Pakistan is likely to receive during the current year is completely untied, Pakistan should be able to save roughly $60 million by procuring supplies in the international market. In other words, the tying up of foreign credits raises the average price of procurement for Pakistan by about 12 per cent. This estimate may appear to be too low. However, it has to be remembered that the instances where the prices in the tied market are much higher than the international bids, cover only a small proportion of the total credits.

In the case of Pakistan, the credits advanced by the World Bank, IDA, West Germany, U.K. and Canada, generally do not suffer from any serious drawbacks, partly because some of these credits are untied and partly because there are a large number of items that Pakistan can obtain from these countries at the most competitive prices. In many other cases also, the recipient country has the option of shifting the source of procurement and thereby minimizing the impact of tied credits on prices. For example, when the French prices were found to be 61 per cent higher than the U.K. prices in the case of Khanpur Sugar Mill, the project was transferred to the U.K. Similarly, when Japanese prices in the case of a hard-board project and a rice milling plant were found to be over 120 per cent higher than the German bids, both the projects were reallocated against the German credit. In the case of equipment for Karachi Shipyard and Engineering Works, the high price quotations under the U.K. credit led the Government to use its own cash resources to procure these supplies from the German market.

Again, it is possible to obtain a lower price even in the tied market by threatening to withdraw the project to another source as was discovered by Pakistan in the case of a village electrification and power distribution project. The prices quoted by the Italian supplier for this project were about 63 per cent higher than the quotations received on international bids. The government decided to place the project on international tenders. Subsequently, some other Italian suppliers offered quotations about 50 to 55 per cent lower than the original Italian quotations. Accordingly, some of the Italian quotations were accepted by the government, whereas in certain cases the source of procurement was shifted to other countries. But there are definite limits to the flexibility that a country enjoys in shifting projects back and forth, from one source to another, as is discussed a little later in this paper.

Despite the fact that the overall average increase in prices on account of tied credits does not appear to be too frightening, it should be noted that the total amounts involved are fairly substantial in the case of Pakistan. To say the least, it is unfair to expect a poor country to give away $60 million each year as a subsidy to the exporters of certain developed countries and then to have to repay this amount *with interest* in later years. This has naturally led to the demand that 'in such cases where the tied nature of credits raises the price of imported commodities and equipment appreciably above the international price, the donor countries should seriously consider advancing a grant to cover the difference between the international price and the domestic price, and treating this part as a measure of domestic export promotion'.[1] Similarly, there are demands that repayment of tied credits should also be tied in terms of the physical exports of the recipient country. The logic of these demands cannot be denied. They will gain momentum unless

[1] Budget Speech of Pakistan's Finance Minister, 14 June 1965.

some concrete measures are devised to reduce the 'loss' suffered by the developing economies on account of tied credits. These measures can be found only through a joint effort on the part of both donor and recipient countries. Some of the elements of this joint effort are explored below.

IV. LESSONS FROM PAKISTAN'S EXPERIENCE

A careful study of Pakistan's experience reveals that there are many instances where projects have been misplaced in a particular country since the countries were selected before calling international tenders. Ideally, the recipient country should invite international bids for all the projects and commodities that it wishes to finance each year and choose the sources of procurement accordingly. The main limitation, of course, is that the extent of credit given by each donor country may not conform to the extent of demand that the recipient country has from each source. Tied credits hurt only when there are such instances of maladjustment in demand and supply of foreign credits from each source. It should be possible to avoid many of these maladjustments through more intelligent programming so that the country's own cash resources and untied credits can be used flexibly to minimize the effects of tied credits. But there are many institutional difficulties in moving towards this ideal. From the experience of Pakistan, it is clear that many aid-giving countries show a definite preference for certain projects, particularly large, 'public-appeal' projects, and insist on obtaining them even though these countries may be unsuitable and uncompetitive sources for their finance. Similarly, some countries have objected to the practice of placing projects in individual countries on the basis of international tenders. The institutional arrangements adopted by Pakistan also discourage international bids. A tentative list of the countries, in which particular projects are to be placed on the basis of previous experience, is drawn up by the government at the beginning of each year and the executing agencies, who are allocated various projects under tied credits, are normally not allowed to invite tenders on a world-wide basis. It is necessary that some of the existing procedures should be changed and a greater spirit of accommodation displayed, both by donor and recipient countries, so that the worst features of tied credits can be eliminated.

One of the most logical ways to avoid the adverse effects of tied credits is, obviously, to work towards a greater diversification in the sources of credit. Such a diversification can considerably enlarge the area of choice. This is supported by Pakistan's experience in the last five years. As the source of credit became diversified and Pakistan's predominant dependence on the U.S. market diminished, it appears that Pakistan was able to procure supplies at more competitive rates in the international market. A close look at Table 1 would show that if Pakistan could obtain larger credits from West Germany and some of the Eastern European countries, it would enjoy much greater flexibility in obtaining its supplies from the cheapest international source. This is more particularly true in the case of non-project assistance received by Pakistan which comes primarily from the U.S. at present. If, as has been recommended recently by the Aid-to-Pakistan Club, other Consortium countries, and the World Bank, also place a certain proportion of their credits at the disposal of Pakistan in the form of non-project assistance, Pakistan will have far greater manœuvrability in procuring its supplies from the international market. It should be recognized at the same time that political factors often impose severe limits on diversification of sources of credit and what is found economically desirable may not always be politically judicious.

V. FLEXIBILITY THROUGH USE OF OWN CASH RESOURCES

An important element in the intelligent programming of foreign assistance is the use that can be made of a country's own cash resources and untied credits in buying the much-needed flexibility in procurement. Over 30 per cent of the development imports are financed by Pakistan at present from its own cash resources. Another 20 per cent are financed against untied credits obtained from the World Bank, IDA and West Germany. Thus, about 50 per cent of total development imports are untied. This flexibility, if properly used, can considerably reduce the high prices which are paid in certain cases from tied markets. Unfortunately, there has not been full adjustment to the realities of tied foreign credits within the country, so that the traditional pattern of trade on a cash basis continues to operate even when a change in it is called for to adapt to the pattern of tied credits that the country has to live with. This full adjustment can be made only if the country regards the total foreign exchange at its disposal, including its own earnings and foreign credits, as a divisible pool which it can allocate to various uses according to the cheapness of the source of procurement. There is a good deal that can be done by such intelligent programming of the cash resources of the country as well as of foreign assistance, particularly in the case of non-project commodities. There are a number of commodities which Pakistan is importing at present from the American market on a cash basis. Efforts can be made to finance these imports against American credits, so that the cash resources are freed for use elsewhere. Similar adjustments are possible, and needed, all along the line in the export and import trade of Pakistan.

Though the burden of adjustment will largely fall on the recipient countries, it is only fair that the donor countries should also give careful thought to the implications of tying up their credits and take all possible steps to overcome their adverse effects. A number of steps can be considered. The donor countries can allow triangular deals whereby the recipient country can finance its supplies in the third markets against tied credits.

Again, credits may be tied to larger areas, such as the Common Market in the case of European countries, so that the recipient country can take advantage of procurement in the entire region. This can become increasingly feasible as the countries of the world get together in regional arrangements wherein their balance of payment problems are already taken care of.

VI. INSTITUTIONAL ARRANGEMENTS TO MAKE TIED CREDITS COMPETITIVE

Most important, however, are the institutional arrangements that should be developed both in the donor and recipient countries to make tied credits increasingly competitive. As was illustrated by Pakistan's experience, the quotations offered by the suppliers are often higher if the suppliers know that it is a tied credit and come down considerably once it is made clear that the supplies will be financed against cash or untied credits. There is no reason why such large differentials in quotations (sometimes as much as 40 to 50 per cent) should exist from the same source of supply. One of the amusing examples in the recent experience of Pakistan was that of Atlas Capco type compressors under French credit. The French suppliers offered certain quotations which, when checked against the quotations received from the Karachi-based agents for Atlas Capco, were found to be 33 per cent to 47 per cent higher for various items ! These instances can be avoided if suitable administrative agencies are established both in the recipient and donor countries, to keep a continuous watch over the situation and to settle such instances of higher prices on the basis of government to government negotiations.

There is an important role that the World Bank can play in getting recipient and donor countries together to discuss frankly and objectively the implications of tied credits. It is no use shying away from this problem or making it a subject of heated political debate. What is needed is careful quantitative analysis and concrete institutional arrangements. There is a strong case for the World Bank undertaking this work since its own loans are untied and it is in a position to review the entire problem with complete detachment and objectivity.

This paper has not attempted to give a detailed theoretical critique of the tied credits but only to present a limited quantitative analysis for Pakistan and to point out certain concrete measures through which the adverse implications of tied credits can be reduced. The main conclusions of the paper are :

(i) The developing countries will have to live with tied credits for a long time to come and should adjust their thinking accordingly.

(ii) The worst features of tied credits can be eliminated by a more intelligent programming of foreign assistance and cash foreign exchange resources by the recipient countries as well as by a diversification in the sources of foreign credits. The developed countries can help this process by allowing triangular deals, by tying credits to regional markets rather than to individual country markets, and by showing willingness to accept projects on the basis of international tenders rather than ' prestige ' or other reasons.

(iii) Institutional arrangements should be made both in donor countries and in recipient countries to study this problem on a continuous basis and to protect the buyer against avoidable higher prices from tied sources. The World Bank can play an important role in a careful and objective analysis of this problem and in suggesting suitable institutional arrangements to the countries concerned.

STATISTICAL APPENDIX

STATISTICAL APPENDIX

INSTANCES OF HIGH PRICES UNDER TIED CREDITS

THE attached statements list instances of high prices under tied credits. A comparison of price quotations obtained from various sources suffers from a number of limitations :

(a) The differences in designs and specifications make comparisons difficult.

(b) In the case of ' turn-key ' quotations, C. & F. prices of individual items are not available. Under such contracts, it is not possible to determine the extent of higher prices.

(c) The executing agencies, who receive allocations under tied credits, are not normally allowed to invite tenders on a world-wide basis.

(d) It is only in a few cases of large orders, where quotations are invited on the basis of equipment of special specifications, that a straight comparison is possible.

Notwithstanding these limitations, the attached statements bring out a number of instances of high prices under tied credits. These statements have been divided into four parts :

Statement I shows, for each lending country, instances of higher prices which have actually been PAID under tied credits. As stated earlier, it is not a usual practice to call international bids in respect of tied credits. Recourse to this is taken only in a few exceptional cases. Where prices have been found to be inordinately high under a particular tied source, executing agencies have occasionally found it possible to finance their requirements from the alternative cheaper sources either against a line of credit available from that source or through cash allocations.

Statement II lists cases where higher prices have been QUOTED under tied credits. Under this group only such cases have been listed where the project was initially allocated to a particular tied source but, due to higher prices quoted from that particular country, actual purchases were not made from that source but it was found possible either to divert it to the more competitive supplier through cash allocations or re-allocation to a line of credit available from the cheaper source or to withhold purchases altogether.

Statement III shows cases of higher prices as estimated by the executing agencies. In some cases the executing agencies have been able to obtain, on the basis of their old established contacts with suppliers in foreign countries, quotations from sources other than the tied source. In some cases, although the bids were restricted to the particular tied source, quotations were also received from other sources.

As these quotations are not obtained on the basis of world-wide open tenders, the comparison in these cases is not as accurate as is given in the first two statements.

Statement IV lists instances of higher prices paid/quoted under tied credits in respect of commodities. It is not a normal practice in Pakistan to obtain international quotations for procurement of commodities. The comparison is based largely on quotations obtained, at about the time the purchases were made from the higher-priced tied source, from other sources on the basis of cash allocations. In the case of some railway equipment, the comparison is based on imports financed against international bids obtained under World Bank credits.

Project (1)	Source of Credit (2)	Description of Items Procured (3)	Date when Bids were Invited (4)	Whethe Inter-nationa Bids wer Invited (5)
1. Baluchistan Collieries (West Pakistan Industrial Development Corporation)	France	1. Centrifugal pumps	February 1962 *	Yes
		2. Shovel loaders	,,	Yes
		3. Underground loco-motives	,,	Yes
		4. Haulage engine with spares	,,	Yes
		5. Rails	August 1963	Yes
		6. Rail switches	,,	Yes
2. Sulphuric acid and superphosphate plant, Chittagong (East Pakistan Industrial Development Corporation)	France	1. Complete plant	May 1963	Yes
3. Village electrification and power distribution (West Pakistan Water and Power Development Authority)	Italy†	1. Steel tabular 30' poles 600 lbs.	July 1963	Yes
		2. Steel tabular 36' poles 600 lbs.	,,	Yes
		3. 132KV 10 MVA	,,	Yes
		4. 66/11 KV 7·5 MVA	,,	Yes
		5. 66/11 KV 5 MVA	,,	Yes
		6. 66/11 KVA 5 MVA	,,	Yes
4. Eastern Chemical Ltd. (Pakistan Industrial Credit and Investment Corporation)	Japan	1. Urea formaldehyde package boiler	November 1962	No.*
5. Telegraph and Tele-phone Department	Japan	1. Insulated and cable sheathed	July 1962	Yes
		2. Self-supporting aerial cable	August 1963	Yes
		3. Insulated and cable sheathed	November 1963	Yes
6. Rajshahi and Kushtia Sugar Mills (East Pakistan Industrial Development Corporation)	U.K.	Sugar mill machinery	December 1962	Yes

TABLE 1

ces Paid for Projects under Tied Credits

Lowest Quotation from [Ti]ed Source (per unit) (6)	Lowest Quotation on International Bids (indicating Country) (per unit) (7)	Percentage of Higher Prices from Tied Source (8)	Quotation Finally Accepted (indicating Country) (per unit) (9)	Remarks (10)
70/14/8	£3,353 (Germany)	84%	£6,170/14/8 (France)	* French quotations were not received against world-wide tenders but were obtained in October 1962 against tenders limited to French suppliers only
02	£4,457 (Japan)	55%	£6,902 (France)	
349/9/7	£4,660 (Germany)	36%	£6,349/9/7 (France)	
)29/10/10	£4,993/17/4 (Japan)	99%	£9,929/10/10 (France)	
7/6/7	£531/11/10 (Germany)	57%	£837/6/7 (France)	
7/3/4	£309 (Germany)	100%	£617/3/4 (France)	
1,465	£207,937 (U.S.)	45%	£332,164 (France)	Orders placed on the basis of revised prices. In the original quotation SAS plant was not included
00† .94	$43.72 (Belgium)	37%	$46.94* (Italy)	* Prices reduced by negotiation
.30 .81	$59.85 (Belgium)	36%	$63.81* (Italy)	† Tenders were called in July 1963 from the Italian credit suppliers, and are given above the line in column 6. On account of very high prices under the tied credit, international bids were invited in December 1963. The lowest quotations from other suppliers in Italy are given below the line in column 6.
,950 ,240	$42,560 (Germany)	43%	$48,832* (Italy)	
,250 ,600	$26,642 (Germany)	70%	$31,024* (Italy)	
,900 ,200	$21,560 (Germany)	85%	$26,964* (Italy)	
,000 ,200	$22,792 (Germany)	76%	$27,664* (Italy)	
1,81,000	Rs. 1,04,000 (U.K.)	74%	Rs. 1,81,000 (Japan)	* Tender enquiry limited to only selected suppliers. Due to lack of U.K. funds, the quotation from Japan was accepted, although U.K. boiler was of a higher capacity
,705/8/-	£31,164 (Formosa)†	56%	£48,705/8/- (Japan)	† Based on supplies from Formosa (major portion) and a few other sources
,130	£9,963/10/- (Greece)	12%	£11,130 (Japan)	
,160/5/7	£26,794/5/- (Formosa)†	31%	£35,160/5/7	
5,105 per	£632,830 per mill (Czechoslovakia)	26%	£706,630‡ per mill (U.K.)	‡ Negotiated price which is still higher than the lowest international bid by 12%

Project (1)	Source of Credit (2)	Description of Items (3)	Date when Bids were Invited (4)	Wheth Inter nation Bids w Invite (5)
1. Baluchistan Collieries (Degari, West Pakistan Industrial Development Corporation)	France*	1. Ventilation tubes	February 1962*	Yes
		2. Compressed air-driven auxiliary fan	,,	Yes
		3. Air receivers	,,	Yes
		4. Air compressors, capacity 200 c.ft.	,,	Yes
2. Table salt manufacturing plant, Warcha (West Pakistan Industrial Development Corporation)	France	Complete machinery for table salt manufacturing	October 1963	Yes
3. Hyesons Sugar Mill, Khanpur (Pakistan Industrial Credit and Investment Corporation)	France	Sugar mills machinery	December 1962	Yes
4. Village electrification and power distribution (West Pakistan Water and Power Development Authority)	Italy*	1. Aluminium core steel reinforced conductor (Weasel)	July 1963	Yes
		2. Aluminium core steel reinforced conductor (Raccon)	,,	Yes
		3. Aluminium core steel reinforced conductor (Dog)	,,	Yes
		4. All aluminium conductor (Gnat)	,,	Yes
		5. All aluminium conductor (Ant)	,,	Yes
		6. All aluminium conductor (Wasp)	,,	Yes
		7. All aluminium conductor (Chafer)	,,	Yes
		8. Galvanized steel line wire No. 8 SWG	,,	Yes
		9. Galvanized steel line wire No. 6 SWG	,,	Yes
		10. 66 KV pin insulators	,,	Yes
		11. 33 KV pin insulators	,,	Yes

[1] *Note.*—The French suppliers (M/s Sodiem) had offered Atlas Capco type compressors.
A comparison of this quotation with that of M/s Atlas Capco received through their Pakis agents is given on facing page :

TED FOR PROJECTS UNDER TIED CREDITS

Lowest Quotation from l Source er unit (6)	Lowest Quotation on International Bids (indicating Country) (per unit) (7)	Percentage of Higher Prices from Tied Source (8)	Quotation Finally Accepted (indicating Country) (per unit) (9)	Remarks (10)
94	£750 (Japan)	392%	£750 (Japan)	* French quotations were not received against world-wide tenders but were obtained in October 1962, against tenders limited to French suppliers only
10/4/2	£610 (Czechoslovakia)	279%	£610 (Czechoslovakia)	
25/3/9	£560/11/7 (Denmark)	172%	£560/11/7 (Denmark)	
73/8/7	£1,678 (U.K.)	41%	£1,678 (U.K.)	
2,000	$147,000 (Germany)	71%	†	† Orders not placed for lack of funds from cheaper sources
32,000	$2,500,400 (U.K.)	61%	$2,500,400 (U.K.)	Financed from the 6th U.K. credit
4.00 / 5.77	$58.70 (Yugoslavia)	60%	Not accepted	* Italian tenders were called in July 1963 from the credit suppliers and are given above the line in column 6. On account of the very high prices under the tied credit, international bids were invited in December 1963. The lowest quotations from other suppliers in Italy are given below the line in column 6
6.00 / 6.11	$147.69 (Yugoslavia)	53%	,,	
9.00 / 6.29	$183.36 (Yugoslavia)	58%	,,	
5.00 / 5.80	$41.23 (Yugoslavia)	60%	,,	
7.00 / 0.149	$81.16 (Yugoslavia)	56%	,,	
6.00 / 9.48	$161.54 (Yugoslavia)	52%	,,	
6.00 / 5.143	$328.75 (Yugoslavia)	51%	,,	
0.276 / N.Q.	$0.174 (Germany)	59%	,,	N.Q. : Not quoted
0.276 / N.Q.	$0.172 (Germany)	60%	,,	
4.80 / I.Q.	$7.29 (Japan)	240%	,,	
6.30 / I.Q.	$3.86 (Japan)	63%	,,	

	Sodiem (France) Quotation	Atlas Capco (Pakistan) Quotation	Difference in Prices
Atlas Capco PR-600 RD	£7,269/12/8	£4,930	47%
Atlas Capco PR-100 RD	£6,412/8/2	£4,837/10/–	33%
Atlas Capco VT-5-FD	£2,373/8/7	£2,115	12%

Project (1)	Source of Credit (2)	Description of Items (3)	Date when Bids were Invited (4)	Whether International Bids were Invited (5)
	Italy	12. 11 KV pin insulators	July 1963	Ye
		13. 66 KV suspension insulators	,,	Ye
		14. 66 KV strain insulators	,,	Ye
		15. 33 KV strain insulators	,,	Ye
		16. 11 KV strain insulators	,,	Ye
		17. 11 KV tension insulators	,,	Ye
		18. 3 (1 × 0·05 sq. in.) 11 KV cable	,,	Ye
		19. 3 (sq. in.) 11 KV cable	,,	Ye
		20. 3 element KWH MDI and KVARH meters 400 volts 5 amps.	,,	Ye
		21. 2 element KWH MDI meters 110 volts, 5 amps.	,,	Ye
		22. 2 element MDI and KVARH meters 110 volts, 5 amps.	,,	Ye
		23. Power factor meters	,,	Ye
		24. Portable power factor meters	,,	Ye
		25. Low voltage ampere 12 lightning arrestors (11 KV)	,, ,,	Ye Ye
		26. Low voltage ampere 30 lightning arrestors (33 KV)	,,	Ye
		27. Low voltage ampere 60 lightning arrestors (66 KV)	,,	Ye
		28. Low voltage ampere 12 lightning arrestors (11 KV) sub-station type	,,	Yes
		29. 60 ton hydraulic compressor	,,	Yes
		30. 100 ton hydraulic compressor	,,	Yes

TABLE 2 (cont.)

Lowest Quotation from Tied Source (per unit) (6)	Lowest Quotation on International Bids (indicating Country) (per unit) (7)	Percentage of Higher Prices from Tied Source (8)	Quotation Finally Accepted indicating (Country) (per unit) (9)	Remarks (10)
$1.97	$0.83	137%	Not accepted	
N.Q.	(Japan)			
$17.70	$10.55	68%	,,	
N.Q.	(Japan)			
$20.30	$13.25	53%	,,	
N.Q.	(Japan)			
$12.40	$8.49	46%	,,	
N.Q.	(Japan)			
$6.60	$3.45	91%	,,	
N.Q.	(Japan)			
$7.70	$5.05	52%	,,	
N.Q.	(Japan)			
$3.40	$2.31	47%	,,	
N.Q.	(Japan)			
$4.40	$2.70	63%	,,	
N.Q.	(Japan)			
143.50	$65,99	117%	,,	
N.Q.	(Germany)			
$68.10	$39.26	73%	,,	
$57.16	(Germany)			
114.60	$58.75	95%	,,	
N.Q.	(Germany)			
108.00	$33.54	222%	,,	
N.Q.	(Japan)			
156.00	$35.58	338%	,,	
N.Q.	(Hungary)			
$28.00	$10.22	174%	,,	
N.Q.	(U.K.)			
$67.00	$28.07	139%	,,	
N.Q.	(Sweden)			
418,00	$137.44	204%	,,	
N.Q.	(Belgium)			
$28.00	$17.60	59%	,,	
N.Q.	(Germany)			
685.00	$507.50	35%	,,	Comparison is between quotations
507.50	(Italy)			obtained from Italian suppliers
799.00	$412.30	94%	,,	under tied credit and international
584.22	(Austria)			tender respectively

Project (1)	Source of Credit (2)	Description of Items (3)	Date when Bids were Invited (4)	Whethe Inter-nationa Bids we Invitee (5)
	Italy	31. 132 KV equipment grid station	July 1963	Yes
		32. 66 KV equipment	,,	Yes
		33. 33 KV equipment	,,	Yes
5. Pak Hard-board Industries, Karachi (Pakistan Industrial Credit and Investment Corporation)	Japan	Hard-board making plant	August 1963	No
6. Sundar Ban Rice Mills, Khulna (Industrial Development Bank of Pakistan)	Japan	Rice milling machinery	March 1963	Yes
7. MAKK Beverages, Peshawar (Industrial Development Bank of Pakistan)	Japan	Beverage plant	October 1963	Yes
8. Jessore and Dinajpur Sugar Mills (East Pakistan Industrial Development Corporation)	Nether-lands	Sugar mill machinery (2 units)	December 1963	Yes
9. Karachi Shipyard and Engineering Works (West Pakistan Industrial Development Corporation)	U.K.	1. Propeller plant	July 1961	Yes
		2. Stand-by engine lubricating pump	November 1961	Yes
		3. Screw espendle type pump	,,	Yes
		4. Gate valve 8″ pressure line	October 1961	Yes
		5. Gate valve 8″ suction line	,,	Yes
		6. Pipeline fittings	July 1962	Yes
10. Nylon twine project (Pakistan Industrial Credit and Investment Corporation)	U.S.	Nylon twine making machinery	March 1963	Yes
11. Dacca beverage industry (Industrial Development Bank of Pakistan)	U.S.	Beverage plant	n.a.	Yes

TABLE 2 (*cont.*)

Lowest Quotation from Tied Source (per unit) (6)	Lowest Quotation on International Bids (indicating Country) (per unit) (7)	Percentage of Higher Prices from Tied Source (8)	Quotation Finally Accepted (indicating Country (per unit) (9)	Remarks (10)
364.430 N.Q.	$245.207 (Sweden)	49%	Not accepted	
316.090 N.Q.	$189.141 (Sweden)	67%	,,	
114.734 N.Q.	$84.358 (Sweden)	36%	,,	
$1,169,200	$525,000 (Germany)	123%	$525,000 (Germany)	* Quotations were obtained from Japan and Germany only. The Japanese quotations, in spite of being more than double the price for a plant of the same specifications, did not contain some essential components which were offered by the German suppliers
66,462	$30,000 (Germany)	122%	$30,000 (Germany)	
160,000	$128,240 (U.K.)	25%	$128,240 (U.K.)	
837,036	£631,562 (Czecho-slovakia)	33%	—	Under negotiation
6,646	£4,734/11/- (Germany)	40%	£4,734/11/- (Germany)	Imported under cash licences
1,092/10/-	£262/8/- (Germany)	317%	£262/8/- (Germany)	,, ,,
307/15/6	£275/16/- (Germany)	12%	£275/16/- (Germany)	,, ,,
677/19/8	£197 (Germany)	244%	£197 (Germany)	,, ,,
750/19/3	£535 (Germany)	40%	£535 (Germany)	,, ,,
3,436/6/-	£2,350/10/- (Germany)	46%	£2,350/10/- (Germany)	,, ,,
837,000	$520,000 (Germany)	61%	$520,000 (Germany)	Re-allocated to German credit
91,133	$79,471 (Germany)	15%	$79,471 (Germany)	,, ,,

STATISTICAL APPENDIX — TABLE 3

STATEMENT SHOWING INSTANCES OF HIGHER PRICES FOR PROJECTS UNDER TIED CREDITS

(As Estimated by the executing agencies)

Project (1)	Source of Credit (2)	Description of Items (3)	Lowest Quotation from Tied Source (4)	Lowest Quotation from Other Source (indicating Country) (5)	Percentage of Higher Prices from Tied Source (6)	Remarks (7)
1. Karachi Port Trust	Japan	60-ton self-propelled floating crane	Rs. 5,247,606‡	Rs. 3,769,986* (Netherlands)	39%	* The bids were limited to the tied source
2. Nawab Brothers, Karachi (Industrial Development Bank of Pakistan)	Japan	1. Press brake with 10 h.p. motor	Rs. 40,000‡	Rs. 30,000† (Germany)	33%	† Karachi Port Trusts, enquiries from Netherlands got them a much lower quotation which could not be utilized due to the insufficiency of credits from that country
		2. Plant for manufacturing steel hose	Rs. 517,000‡	Rs. 400,000 (Germany)	29%	
3. Atlas Plastic and Rubber Industries, Karachi (Industrial Development Bank of Pakistan)	Japan	90 mm. plastic extruder	Rs. 70,000‡	Rs. 55,000 (Germany)	27%	† Japanese press was for 100 tons capacity while the press from Germany was for higher capacity (175 tons)
4. Bengal Steel Works	Japan	Wire-drawing plant (capacity 2,000 tons p.a.)	Rs. 500,000‡	Rs. 400,000 (Germany)	25%	‡ Orders were placed in Japan to utilize the Japanese credit
5. Karachi Port Trust	U.K.	Twin screw bucket dredgers	Rs. 13,795,380	Rs. 10,421,726§ (Netherlands)	32%	§ The quotation from Netherlands is based on informal inquiry by the Karachi Port Trust

Statistical Appendix — Table 4

Statement Showing Instances of Higher Prices paid/quoted for Commodities under Tied Credits

(As estimated by the executing agencies)

Procuring Agency (1)	Source of Credit (Loan No. and Date) (2)	Description of Items (3)	Lowest Quotation from Tied Source (4)	Lowest Quotation from Other Source (indicating Country) (5)	Percentage of Higher Prices from Tied Source (6)	Remarks (7)
1. Pakistan Western Railways*	U.S. (Jan. 1960)	1. Channels	$172.63	$106.73 (Japan)	62%	* All the equipment was procured from U.S. under tied credit. The comparison is based on quotations obtained on world-wide tender in May 1962 for imports of similar equipment financed under IBRD loan No. 320-PAK
		2. Angles (equal)	$171.51	$96.06 (Japan)	79%	
		3. Angles (unequal)	$164.70	$119.42 (U.K.)	38%	
		4. Plates	$154.71	$102.34 (Japan)	51%	
		5. Tees	$207.35	$121.15 (U.K.)	71%	
		6. Sheets	$161.99	$113.50 (Japan)	43%	
		7. Billets	$172.22	$91.98 (Sweden)	87%	
		8. Wheel and axle assemblies	$794.10 per assembly	$308.70 per assembly	157%	
2. Directorate General of Investment Promotion and Supplies†	U.S. (May 1962)	1. Mild steel billets 2½"	$110.00	$84.00 (Japan)	31%	† All prices are C. & F. per ton, Karachi, based on best estimates of the Supplies Directorate. Lowest quotations under column
		2. Channels 6"	$166.00	$115.00	44%	
		3. Mild steel Plates ⅜"	$170.00	$112.00	52%	
		4. Sheets hot-rolled 0·12"	$190.00	$119.00	60%	

Procuring Agency (1)	Source of Credit (Loan No. and Date) (2)	Description of Items (3)	Lowest Quotation from Tied Source (4)	Lowest Quotation from Other Source (indicating Country) (5)	Percentage of Higher Prices from (6)	Remarks (7)
2. Directorate General (*contd.*)		5. Hot-rolled sheets 0·12″	$195.00	$134.00	46%	5 relate to prices available from the Continent and Japan
		6. Hot-rolled sheets scalp 0·12″	$170.00	$112.00	52%	
		7. Cold-rolled corrugated reinforced concrete asbestos sheets 22-G	$195.00	$154.00	27%	
		8. Corrugated reinforced concrete asbestos strips 22-G	$210.00	$182.00	15%	
		9. Corrugated iron sheets 24-G (1·25 coating)	$227.00	$179.00	27%	
		10. Tin plates 90 lbs. base weight (0·50 coating electrolytic)	$212.00	$207.00	2%	
		11. Channels 3″ × 2″	$165.00	$120.00	37%	
		12. Black sheets 24-G	$187.00	$123.00	52%	
3. Supply Directorate (Government of West Pakistan)	U.S. (May 1962)	Corrugated galvanized iron sheets	$226.70*	$181.44	25%	* Procured from U.S.A. under tied credit
4. Supply Directorate (Government of East Pakistan)†	U.S. (May 1962)	1. Corrugated iron sheets 26 SWG	Rs. 1,132.88*	Rs. 868.49 (Japan)	30%	† All prices are C. & F. per ton, East Pakistani ports unless indicated otherwise. Lowest quotations under column 5 relate to prices available from the Con-
		2. Galvanized iron pipes 1½″ diameter	Rs. 147.28* per 100 RFT	Rs. 94.91 per 100 RFT (Germany)	55%	
		3. Mild steel plates	Rs. 746.64*	Rs. 539.60	38%	

				tinent and Japan on the basis of purchases made by the Supply Directorate under cash licences
4. Steel flat rolled carbon sheet of structural quality	Rs. 801.67*	Rs. 657.55	22%	
5. Zinc coated galvanized steel sheets	Rs. 1,447.5*	Rs. 860.00	68%	* Procured from U.S.A. under tied credit
6. Zinc coated galvanized steel sheets corrugated 10/3"	Rs. 1,042.00*	Rs. 843.00	24%	
7. Pig iron standard foundry	Rs. 383.00*	Rs. 334.00	15%	
8. Mild steel	Rs. 629.00*	Rs. 540.00	16%	
9. Steel spring carbon	Rs. 960.00*	Rs. 745.00	29%	
10. Mild steel flat	Rs. 955.00*	Rs. 665.00	44%	
11. Wire steel carbon round finish	Rs. 1,308.00*	Rs. 1,014.97	29%	
12. Mild steel round	Rs. 875.00*	Rs. 672.00	30%	
13. Mild steel channel	Rs. 862.69*	Rs. 699.50	23%	
14. Mild steel beams	Rs. 844.00*	Rs. 625.00	35%	
15. Mild steel angles	Rs. 859.00*	Rs. 617.00	39%	
16. Mild steel hex.	Rs. 1,257.60*	Rs. 700.00	80%	
17. Steel tool high speed 18% tungsten squares	Rs. 16,984.00*	Rs. 9,900.00	72%	
18. Steel tool high speed 22% tungsten squares	Rs. 23,096.00*	Rs. 12,280.00	88%	
19. Rails 60 lbs. 39' long	Rs. 921.60* per ton	Rs. 573.10 per ton	61%	
U.S. (May 1962)				
1. Steel plates of $\frac{3}{16}$" ×4'×8'	Rs. 797.44* per ton	Rs. 494.69 per ton (Japan)	61%	
2. Steel plates $\frac{5}{16}$"×4' ×20'	Rs. 797.30	Rs. 294.14† per ton (Germany)	170%	† Procured from Germany under cash licence

5. Inland Water Transport Authority (East Pakistan)

COMMENTS ON DR. HAQ'S PAPER

BY

JOHN H. ADLER

Economic Development Institute (World Bank)

DR. HAQ deserves the gratitude of all those concerned with foreign aid and its effective use for the benefit of the developing countries, since his study is the first generally available quantitative appraisal of the effects of tied loans and tied aid. I shall not disguise my satisfaction that it is, in part explicitly and even more so by implication, a strong endorsement of the principle and practice of multilateral development assistance.

Dr. Haq distinguishes between three forms of tying credits : to the lending or aid-giving country, to specific projects, and to specific end uses. He is primarily concerned, however, with the tying of credits and grants to the country of origin and one is left with the impression that tying of aid to projects only aggravates the situation caused in the first instance by the practice of country ties. It follows from my remarks in previous discussions that in my opinion the cost of tying loans and grants to projects can be alleviated further by broadening the concept of projects so as to get away from the notion of fixed investment in plant and equipment only. I am uncertain as to what exactly Dr. Haq has in mind with his third category of foreign credits tied to specific end uses ; I assume he refers to an extension of the project concept to allocation for other than investment project purposes. If that is so, his point — in its practical effects a minor point, I submit — is well taken.

Another minor point with which I would take issue is his assertion that 'all forms of tying result, in one way or another, in higher prices'. This is not necessarily so. Tying may result in a less than optimum allocation of resources without raising prices, but with less growth as a direct and indirect consequence. A more expensive plant may well be competitive in the sense that the prices of the goods it produces are the same as those charged by other producers. But it may have to pay lower wages or earn lower profits ; if wages are lower the level of consumption will be lower ; if profits are lower savings and future growth will be adversely affected.

Since I find myself, however, much in agreement with Dr. Haq's general proposition that tied aid is worth less than untied aid, and since I find the evidence which he presents unassailably convincing, I believe that little would be gained by piecemeal comments endorsing or criticizing his observations. Instead, I should like to pursue further some of his remarks and conclusions.

On an analytic plane, Dr. Haq's introductory assertion that 'tied credits are merely a symptom of the basic maladjustment in the inter-national balance of payments and the lack of any automatic mechanism for the correction of these maladjustments' deserves some elaboration. The statement implies, however faintly, that a creditor or donor country is more justified in tying credits if its balance of payments is 'mal-adjusted', i.e. in deficit, than if it is not. There is validity in this line of reasoning, but the historical record is in the opposite direction. The United States, for some time the deficit country *par excellence*, tied its aid only in the last few years while many other creditor countries insisted on tying credits and grants while increasing their gold and dollar holdings. Moreover, much of the bilateral aid from sources other than the United States is doubly tied — to the country of origin and to specific projects. The tying of U.S. bilateral aid, on the other hand, is somewhat mitigated by the fact that a fairly high proportion of it is not tied to projects ; moreover, some U.S. aid continues to flow untied.

Dr. Haq's reference to the maladjustment in the balance of payments may also be interpreted as implying that credits from countries with a balance of payments surplus should not be tied. This argument is similar to one advanced by Governor Horowitz in his proposal submitted to UNCTAD that loans (for credits under the Horowitz Plan) be raised chiefly in countries with balance of payments surpluses. This argument is technically correct if the balance of payments surplus is measured not by reference to the current account but by reference to movements in the international reserves of the donor country. But in practical terms the argument is incomplete because it fails to take account of the claimed or real difficulties of obtaining funds for development aid in the capital markets of the surplus country or through its fiscal system. Moreover, it may be argued that the state of a country's balance of payments is an inadequate or even an inappropriate measure of a country's ability to assume the economic burden of extending credits or giving grants to developing countries, and that the ' burden sharing ' of development assistance should be based on some other measure of the ability to provide grants or loans.

Whatever the merits of these arguments may be, we are probably much closer to the truth if we consider the tying of loans as being closely related in the case of most countries to the objective of export promotion. It is a fact of life that the political support for development assistance in the form of loans or grants comes in all countries in varying degrees from industries which hope to profit from export contracts under such loans and grants. Efficient industries, which can supply goods and services under foreign loans and grants at competitive prices, do not have to rely on tying aid ; the less competitive industries are, the more essential is tying for them. From the point of view of a rational international division of labour and the long-run structure of production of the creditor or donor countries tied aid is bad since it provides stimulation to the less efficient producers. Dr. Haq's examples indicate that cost differentials are the highest for the least efficient industries, such as U.S. shipping.

With the political support for foreign aid of 'needy' export industries in mind, I am much impressed by Dr. Haq's suggestion that the effect of tying aid on the debt burden of recipient countries and on the capital cost of projects financed by foreign aid be mitigated by eliminating the export subsidy element from foreign aid authorizations and by treating it as a separate budgetary item. A scheme along this line would not only reduce the debt service burden of the recipients of tied aid but also bring into the open the export subsidy element and thus take the first step towards its ultimate elimination.

The examples of cost differentials in Dr. Haq's paper, taken together with his account of the price reductions after the magnitude of these differentials has been revealed, also indicate the existence, at least in some instances, of collusion among suppliers in the same country. This is a phenomenon with which many of us are familiar with regard to bids for domestic works. It is not surprising to find it also in the case of foreign contracts. Although the possibility of international collusion cannot be entirely ruled out, it is probably less effective than collusion in a national framework.

When I saw first Dr. Haq's estimate that the tying of aid has cost Pakistan in one year $60 million, or 12 per cent of all credits and grants received, I found it difficult to reconcile this figure with the cost differentials given in the tables and appendices. On second thought, however, his estimate appears plausible because, as he explains, Pakistan derives considerable benefit from the fact that it obtains aid from a large number of national sources, and from the World Bank and IDA. In the case of the two international agencies aid, though tied to projects, is not tied to any particular creditor or donor countries. Moreover, the existence of the consortium of donor and creditor countries permits at least to some extent the substitution of one source of aid for another.

In order to get the full effect of tying development assistance to a single source, one would have to take a country which obtains assistance from one country only. Furthermore, one would have to take account of the part of the development outlays which the country finances from its own foreign exchange earnings. Thus the $60 million, or 12 per cent, figure estimated by Dr. Haq for Pakistan is not so much a measure of the cost of tied aid as it is of the advantages of having access to multilateral and many bilateral sources of aid and of being able to rely at least to some extent on foreign exchange earnings. The cost of tying aid for countries which cannot rely on their own foreign exchange earnings and which have access to one or two sources of development assistance only is bound to be much higher than in the case of Pakistan.

One last point. As an experienced practitioner of receiving tied credits, Dr. Haq suggests that in order to make the most effective use of tied aid, it would be necessary to ' regard the total foreign exchange at a [country's] disposal, including its own earnings and foreign credits, as a divisible pool which it can allocate to various uses '. This is a perfectly rational proposal, based as it is on considering the tying of credits as a *general* constraint on the use of foreign exchange resources and providing for an optimum allocation under this constraint. But the proposal has one serious and perhaps overwhelming weakness : it neglects to take account of the cost of administering such an overall allocation scheme in terms of scarce manpower resources, delays and the spread of administrative interference in the resources allocation processes.

A large amount of administrative intervention in the process of resource allocation is inevitable. The insistence of an aid agency or an aid consortium on devising a development strategy, and attempts to reach an understanding between creditors and debtors, is on balance presumably to the recipient country's advantage. Some benefits may accrue to borrowers and aid recipients even from the controls which the lenders and donors exercise over the application of funds to specific projects and non-project uses. But creditor and donor countries should realize the high, and sometimes intolerable, burden on the administrative machinery which the cumulation of controls imposes. It may well be that fewer conditions and constraints imposed on the use of aid may lead not only to a better use of total resources by the recipient country but may also help to attain the objectives of the controls which the creditor and donor countries consider essential.

―――――

DISCUSSION OF DR. HAQ'S PAPER

THE main issues raised in the discussion of Dr. Haq's paper concerned the cost of tied credits and the possibility of reducing their cost. Indirect cost to donor and receiving countries as well as the distortion of international specialization were mentioned. Estimates of direct costs were questioned. Relationships between the tying of credits, amount of aid, and repayment terms were also discussed. In addition, the role of balance of payments problems in donor countries as the basis for tying of credits was considered. Finally, several of the discussants noted that the tying of credits creates a conflict between making a virtue of necessity and the necessity for virtue.

Dr. de Beers wondered to what extent tied credit was a consortium problem. He felt that high-cost members of a consortium would be induced to pledge large amounts of tied aid that might prove to be unusable. He also suggested that where tied aid is granted on a soft-loan basis, the extra cost due to tying might be offset by the soft terms. He further noted that the conflict between the interests of borrowers and the donor countries' export promotion goals, if resolved in favour of the borrowing country, might — for the donor country — defeat the purpose of tying the aid.

Professor Andreasyan said that where free currency is scarce the only means of providing aid may be to give tied credits. The problem is then one of repayment. Repayment of tied credits might best be made by tied repayments, i.e. in local currency of the borrowing country as is done with tied credits from the Soviet Union. This has the additional advantage of building up export industries in developing countries. Experience has shown that a large proportion of repayments are made in convertible currencies even under such tying arrangements. Professor Andreasyan mentioned that Soviet goods, though sold under tied credits, were priced on the basis of 'low-level world prices'. He also noted that U.S. aid which generated counterpart funds was another example of tied credit. *Dr. Patel* agreed with Professor Andreasyan that Soviet aid to India had been priced at low-level world prices and that repayments and interest payments were in rupees used to buy Indian goods. *Dr. Adler* wondered why, if Soviet industries were competitive, it was necessary to tie aid at all since procurement then could be made from the U.S.S.R. as the lowest bidder. He realized, of course, that it might be necessary to tie aid because of inflexibilities in the aid system rather than because of cost considerations.

Professor Mundell felt that tied aid coupled with soft credit was really a reversion to a world of barter. Carried to extremes, it could only eliminate international units of account and multilateralism. In the catalogue of sins of developed and developing countries, tied aid and inconvertible currencies would seem to be two of the leaders. Professor Mundell also wondered whether the relative importance of tied aid (i.e. the extra cost due to tying) was as important in magnitude as the increasing softness of repayment terms.

Dr. Singer said that he would play devil's advocate and argue that aid may be greater because it is tied. If so, the increase in the total amount of aid may more than compensate for the loss in value due to tying. In this case private vice becomes a public virtue, especially if it preserves the terms of trade of the developing countries that might otherwise have to increase their exports. The use of food surpluses arising from wrong agricultural policies as aid to developing countries is a case in point. *Dr. Adler* wondered whether we are so used to an undesirable situation that we may not be carrying the virtues of realism too far. He took exception to Dr. Singer's argument here. There is no reason why United States shipments of surplus wheat could not be exported under subsidy, as is now the case with cotton. It should then be possible to separate the subsidy component of PL480 loans and, perhaps, to determine the adverse effects of these loans on agricultural production in third countries.

Dr. Singer continued that he saw no collective balance-of-payments arguments for tied credits because developing countries have a passive role in creating international reserves, and since not all developed countries can have deficits at the same time. It follows that tied credits should not be used by developed countries as a cure for liquidity problems at the expense of the developing countries. Liquidity problems should be settled among the developed countries themselves. He would agree with Dr. Haq that the use of tied credits strengthens the case for programme loans and other forms of untied assistance.

Dr. Patel suggested that the World Bank might study the magnitude of the tied credit problem. He felt that economic arguments against tied credits were ignored because most donor countries tie aid, including countries with comfortable reserve positions. He could not readily accept the proposal to separate the element of export subsidy in calculating the value of tied aid because this requires, in effect, that the donor country admit there is an element of export subsidy. The best remedy would seem to be a moral appeal. A partial solution might be to allow countries receiving tied aid to buy from each other, thus increasing trade among them and promoting further international division of labour among developing countries. Another way to reduce the problem of tied aid would be to grant aid for broad non-project programmes, especially where donor countries were small, since the range of possible exports from these countries tends to be more limited. The problem might also be reduced if aid were granted in sufficiently large amounts that no particular export industry has a vested interest in any appreciable part of it. Dr. Patel did not feel that international bidding was a solution, however. Knowledge that imports for a project must come from a particular country invites collusion among suppliers in that country; by extension, international bidding in similar situations may also lead to collusion. Dr. Patel concluded by emphasizing the pernicious effects of tied credits in distorting the international division of labour and blurring the relationship between costs and benefits arising from the use of the credits.

Dr. Adler regretted that Dr. Patel did not support Dr. Haq's proposal to separate the export-subsidy element from the aid element in tied credits. Given the effects in receiving countries, if the aid and export-subsidy elements were distinguished in the donor countries, knowledge of the export-subsidy element might increase support for larger aid programmes.

Professor Stolper pointed out that the problem of tied aid for recipient countries is not merely one of maximizing total resources for development purposes, but is also a matter of rational allocation. While tying of credits may increase the aid total, it reduces freedom of planners and policy makers. Also, Professor Stolper had noticed that several discussants seemed to feel that demands for repayment of tied credits were somehow wrong. If development is successful, why should the recipient country not pay ? In addition, he thought that the impact of aid could not be fully measured without examining uses of counterpart funds. If it were possible for a developing country to clear debts with other developing countries through exchange of counterpart funds, it might be easier to measure the net impact of aid.

Professor Chenery felt that Dr. Haq's estimate of 12 per cent as the increase in cost of aid due to tying was too low. The true cost is probably higher and should include not only the difference between the actual cost of imports purchased under tied credits and the possible (lower) costs if purchased under untied credits, but also the diversion of administrative talent necessary to undo the effects of tying and the cost in terms of priority distortions. He noted that there might, however, be advantages in tying credits : the preference of politicians and special interest groups for tied aid could raise the total ; the suppliers' interest might be aroused in areas where they had no previous interest. The latter might reduce the monopoly power of former colonial suppliers now supplying a particular developing country. Tying could then be viewed as a type of infant reverse industry protection if tying for the first few years increased the number of firms in export markets and increased competition among suppliers of the developing countries. The ' limited worldwide procurement ' plan of the U.S. Agency for International Development (a means of letting a developing country buy from other developing countries) was a move in this direction. Professor Chenery would also agree with Dr. Singer that tying aid is a very inefficient way of handling balance of payments problems, but noted that the efficient means require international action which has not been achievable so far. *Dr. Adler* added here that the World Bank is moving to allow procurement from local suppliers, even at somewhat higher prices, with an element of subsidy or tariff protection implied.

Dr. Faaland said that the distortion of international trade patterns due to tied credits was worse than generally realized. He pointed out that tying influences resource allocation among developed countries and has adversely affected Norway, for instance. He saw the need for agreement among DAC countries to reduce the importance of tied aid.

Professor Delivanis asserted that tied aid is better than no aid, and that the argument here was like the argument for free trade. He also wondered whether such aid might not be made triangular for balance-of-payments reasons. For instance, a grant from a balance-of-payments surplus donor might be procured from a developed country with a balance-of-payments deficit. He disagreed with Dr. Haq's suggestion that the United States and other donor countries subsidize exports in order to reduce the terms of tied credits to world levels. He felt this was unrealistic. *Professor Leduc* agreed with Professor Delivanis and noted that in some cases aid would not have been given if it had not been tied. France, for example, could have given no aid during the 1950's unless it had been tied. Further, he understood that the difference between 'international prices' (whatever they are) and tied prices was diminishing. *Dr. Adler* disagreed ; he felt the idea that tied aid is better than no aid at all is dangerous. Since effectiveness to recipients and cost to donors are usually indistinguishable in the eyes of the donors, they always look at the larger figure for cost instead of the smaller one when it comes to appraising effectiveness.

Professor Okita called attention to the importance of internal pressure from manufacturers in expanding Japanese aid. He noted that another way to reduce the effects of tying would be for donors to finance the local expenditure portion of projects financed under tied credits. He was not confident, however, that governments would be willing to agree to such arrangements.

Professor Wallich mentioned the United States 'letter of credit' procedure, whereby payments by the United States to importers in the developing country had been substituted for payments by the United States to U.S. exporters. This procedure had been used in Latin America and India. Since it involves substituting existing imports for imports under tied credits, the effect is to untie the aid. He also mentioned a United States proposal to Germany that Germany might attempt ' inverse tying ', i.e. allow recipients to spend credits anywhere but Germany.

Dr. Adler closed the discussion by stating that he was unimpressed by arguments of those who said that historical ties were a reason for tying aid by other countries. He also felt that several of the discussants had carried the virtues of necessity too far in their arguments. The fact remains that the tying of credit represents a real cost to recipient countries.

Chapter 10

CAPITAL MOVEMENTS, THE VOLUME OF TRADE AND THE TERMS OF TRADE

BY

H. M. A. ONITIRI

University of Ibadan, Ibadan, Nigeria

I. INTRODUCTORY

IN the attempt to create an international economic order conducive of speedy economic growth in the developing countries, much emphasis has been placed on the expansion of world trade, the improvement of the terms of trade of developing countries and the increased flow of capital from rich to poor countries. This emphasis was restated at the United Nations Conference on Trade and Development and has featured prominently in the post-conference discussions.

It is almost trivial to stress the connection between capital movements, the volume of trade and the terms of trade. The connection has been amply illustrated by historical experience ; it has featured prominently in theoretical discussions ; and it recurs frequently in current debates on international economic relations.

Historically, capital movements have contributed to the expansion of world trade and their pattern and direction have significantly influenced the terms of exchange between manufacturers and primary commodities in the world market. Theoretical discussions have examined the effect of capital movements on the terms of trade and, generally, on the rate of economic growth of the borrowing countries. In recent years, two aspects of the interrelationship between capital movements, the volume of trade and the terms of trade have been explored. In the first place, it has been suggested that a larger flow of capital from developed to developing countries could compensate for the unfavourable trend in the terms of trade of the latter countries. This suggestion is popular particularly with those who are opposed to the artificial manipulation of the terms of

360

trade as a means of accelerating development in the poorer countries. In the second place, a larger flow of capital to developing countries has been suggested as an alternative to better access for their products in the markets of the developed countries. However, in this connection, emphasis is shifting increasingly from 'trade or aid' to 'trade and aid'.

The Conference on Trade and Development provided a forum for exhaustive discussions of both trade and aid measures and ended with resolutions emphasizing the importance of moving effectively on both fronts if the aims of the United Nations Development Decade were to be realized. The major resolutions on the Conference revolve around these central objectives.

The World Economic Survey 1963 [1] has again drawn attention to the major problems facing the developing countries : their declining share of world trade, the deterioration in their terms of trade and their growing inability to obtain enough foreign exchange through trade and aid to sustain a respectable rate of development. The survey reiterates the view that 'vigorous measures are required on a wide front in order to turn foreign trade into a viable instrument of economic development'. It is the task of the international community to explore new measures for realizing this aim, and to ensure consistency in international economic policies. Measures for increasing capital movements must be consistent with the desire to maintain the terms of trade of developing countries at an ' adequate ' level.

In discussing the particular subject of this paper, it is desirable to keep in view all the possible interrelationships between capital movements, the volume of trade and the terms of trade. Capital movements influence the volume of trade and the terms of trade both directly and indirectly. For example, capital movements which pay for the offshore costs of investment projects have a direct effect on the volume of trade ; similarly, as it sometimes happens in the case of tied aid, willingness to accept less favourable terms of trade may be necessary to induce a given volume of capital investment. However, the more fundamental link between these factors is via the growth and structural changes of national production induced by the inflow of foreign capital.

The effect of changes in national production on trade and the terms of trade depends, of course, on the nature of the changes.

[1] United Nations, World Economic Survey 1963 : *I. Trade and Development: Trends, Needs and Policies.*

Leaving aside the import content of project construction and the imports generated by the resulting increase in incomes, capital movement applied to the production of exports and import substitutes will exert a more fundamental influence on trade and the terms of trade than capital used for other purposes.

II. TRADE AND ECONOMIC STRUCTURE

Foreign investment in traditional exports of the developing countries will increase the volume of their exports but it will most likely turn the terms of trade against them. On the other hand, foreign investment in the production of import substitutes in the developing countries may reduce the volume of imports but it will be unlikely to influence the terms of trade significantly. In other words, the developing countries may turn the terms of trade against themselves by investing in traditional exports but they are not likely to turn the terms of trade in their favour by substituting domestic production of manufactures for imports. This asymmetry in the experience of developing countries is an important phenomenon which is worth bearing in mind in current discussions on international economic relations. It follows from this experience that protection of the domestic market in developed countries against imports of primary commodities from the developing countries will be detrimental to the trade of the developing countries whereas the protection of the domestic market in the developing countries against imports from the developed countries is not likely to be detrimental to the trade of the developed countries.

In short, because structural adjustments are much more difficult to achieve in the developing countries than in the developed countries, changes in demand and supply conditions in the international market are more likely in the long run to turn the terms of trade against the developing countries. This problem of structural adjustment is, of course, only one of the many problems facing the developing countries ; but it is a crucial problem.

The primary purpose of capital movement is to effect economic growth in the developing countries. Growth implies changes in the structure of production. Changes in the structure of production imply corresponding changes in the structure of trade. Unless corresponding changes in the structure of trade can be brought about orderly and effectively, economic growth in the developing countries will inevitably cause a deterioration in their terms of trade. Since export earnings are needed for development, the developing countries will continue to strive to increase the value of their exports. Restrictions on import of manufactures and semi-manufactures in the developed countries will restrict the scope for their production in the developing countries and encourage continued concentration on the export of primary commodities. The result can only be further deterioration in their terms of trade. Other lines of policy which the developing countries might follow are the substitution of domestic production for imports and the subsidization of exports of manufactures and semi-manufactures to the developed countries. The more advanced developing countries have realized the limitations of import substitution and this partly explains the renewed enthusiasm with which plans for economic integration in various developing areas are being discussed. Import substitution is a necessary stage in the process of industrialization, but, in the long run, export possibilities would have to be seriously considered.

III. NEED FOR A NEW POLICY

The objectives of international economic policy should be to ensure that the expansion of capital movement proceeds simultaneously with the expansion of trade and the achievement of better terms of trade for the developing countries. In order to achieve these objectives simultaneously, it is necessary to break down the rigidity in the structure of international trade. Separate measures for improving the terms of trade, increasing capital movements and expanding world trade have been canvassed in recent discussions. What seems to be worth exploring, however, are those arrangements which tend to include several objectives in a package deal. In particular, it is important that foreign investment should go hand in hand with the improvement of market access for the manufactured and semi-manufactured exports of the developing countries.

One specific measure in this connection can be proposed. Since developed countries are so reluctant to admit manufactures and semi-manufactures from the developing countries freely into their markets, the developing countries will continue to experience considerable difficulties in this regard even though it is widely acknowledged that this is one way in which they can effectively increase their export earnings. Although developing countries are still going ahead with establishing processing and manufacturing industries with an eye on the foreign market, the process is bound to be slow and difficult. It is important, therefore, that a renewed attempt should be made to break down the barriers which prevent these desirable changes in the structure of trade of the developing countries. Indeed, it can be suggested that international institutions should be involved in arrangements which in effect enable processing industries to be 'transferred' from the developed to the developing countries. The more multilateral these arrangements are, the better.

The essential features of one possible arrangement can be outlined :

(1) An international institution agrees to lend a given sum of money for developing processing industries in an area which produces a considerable amount of world cocoa, groundnut or similar products.

(2) The developed countries who are the major importers of the raw materials agree to give free access to the processed products in their domestic markets.

(3) In order to make the arrangement in (2) possible, the international institution agrees to finance, if necessary, readjustment of production in the developed countries away from processing in favour of industries corresponding to a higher level of technical advancement.

(4) In case some of the developing countries concerned produce too little of the raw products to justify a processing plant in each country, an arrangement will be reached between such developing countries for distributing processing industries for various commodities among themselves. It is to be noted in any case that this sort of arrangement is essential to the formation of common markets in developing countries each of which is too small to realize the economies of large-scale production by itself.

The most controversial part of the arrangement will be the financing by an international institution of structural readjustment in the developed countries. It will be pointed out that these countries have the requisite capital and technical knowledge to cope with this problem. The real problem, however, is that developing countries have not done all they can to facilitate such structural readjustments in their own economies as would enable them to remove the present barriers against the importation of manufactures and semi-manufactures from the developing countries. It is the task of the international community, working within appropriate institutions, to encourage such structural readjustments. Since mere exhortation has so far had little effect, more direct action may succeed. There are circumstances when it may be argued that a given volume of capital which could be invested by a developed country in a developing country should be used rather for financing readjustment of production in the developed country so as to make room for import of manufactures and semi-manufactures from the developing countries.

Effective action with respect to trade in manufactures and semi-manufactures will facilitate the solution to other problems facing the developing countries. If anything, it will make for a more sensible discussion of the 'international commodity problem'. An important aspect of a lasting solution to this problem must be the ability of the primary producers to gradually take over the processing of their raw material exports. Given the new scientific and technical developments, developed countries have more to do with their labour and capital than to continue to use them for primary processing of imported raw materials.

IV. CONCLUSION

No one now pretends that international prices can perform their functions of resource allocation and income distribution much better than internal prices. In a world of planning, controls, regulations and cartels, both internal and international markets are notoriously imperfect. However, so long as international prices still serve as the major indicators of trends in the world market, it is in the best interest of the international community as a whole to reinforce them wherever this will be consistent with other objectives of international economic policy. Greater attention to problems of structural adjustments in the developed countries will considerably enhance the working of market forces in bringing about desirable changes in the structure of world trade. Indeed if the developed countries can be persuaded by this arrangement to allow market forces to work with respect to their imports of manufactures and semi-manufactures, the structure of their production and consequently the structure of their exports to the developing countries may change significantly in favour of more complex products

365

which the developing countries will not be able to produce for a very long time. It is within the frame of such structural changes that capital investment can contribute most significantly to the advancement of the poor countries.

COMMENTS ON DR. ONITIRI'S PAPER

BY

H. W. SINGER

United Nations

LET me start off by saying that in putting forward his proposal, Dr. Onitiri has shown the right instinct for what is important and what is less important. In our attempts to integrate the underdeveloped countries more fully into the world economy, to contribute to their development, and to try to restore trade to its traditional function as an engine of growth, there are obviously four or five possible approaches that we could follow.

One of them, of course, is the aid approach; aid versus trade. But even when we limit ourselves to trade there are several possible approaches. The first approach is import substitution. As Professor Chenery's studies have shown, this is still, quantitatively speaking, the most important single approach in the history of industrialization of underdeveloped countries in the last 10 or 15 years.

Secondly, there is a possibility of developing the trade of underdeveloped countries with each other. This is potentially of tremendous importance when we consider that the underdeveloped countries contain two-thirds of mankind and, although they tend to be concentrated in tropical areas, still they cover an immense variety of different natural resource conditions, different mixes of labour and capital, and different developments of skills and human characteristics. It would be very surprising if, within this two-thirds of mankind, there would not be tremendous opportunities for a fruitful international division of labour. And certainly one can say that only the surface has been scratched so far in developing these possibilities, so that this more long-term approach is also of immense importance.

There is, of course, a third and also largely unexplored item in the possibility of developing the trade of the underdeveloped countries with the so-called centrally planned economies. The imports of the Eastern countries from the underdeveloped countries, on whatever basis you measure them, whether in relation to their GNP, or on *per capita* basis or any other basis, are still very small, and if we could picture a world in which the Eastern countries import from underdeveloped countries roughly on the same basis as the Western industrial countries, again tremendous progress would have been made.

Then, fourthly, there is the building up of new export industries in the underdeveloped countries which export their products to the developed countries. Mr. Prebisch has nailed the UNCTAD flag to this mast in his proposal for preference schemes for the products of manufacturing industries of underdeveloped countries in the markets of the developed countries.

Fifthly, there is the possibility of exporting the primary products of the underdeveloped countries in more highly processed or manufactured form. This is the mast to which Dr. Onitiri has nailed his flag and I believe he has selected a sound and strong mast.

And finally we could, of course, have a strategy opposite to Dr. Onitiri's. Instead of starting from the raw materials end and moving forward into the processing matrix, you could think in terms of importing your manufactured commodities gradually in less and less finished form, moving into the processing matrix from the other end.

Obviously, all these suggestions are in different ways useful and important. It would be silly to present them as alternatives. Practically no underdeveloped country does not travel, or tentatively travel, or plan to travel, one of these different roads to increasing its product. But I do want to say that Dr. Onitiri, by selecting the question of processing of primary products, has picked one of the areas which, to my mind, has been neglected both in discussion and policy.

The second point I want to make is that economists, or anybody interested in promoting the development of underdeveloped countries, have a special reason to pay attention to this particular subject matter because, as Dr. Onitiri has shown, this can gradually penetrate into the minds of policymakers everywhere. This is one of the areas where, contrary to the situation that we found several times before in our discussion, private sins are not converted into public virtue but where private sins lead to public sins also. The sectional vested interests in advanced countries, as Dr. Onitiri has broadly hinted, are by no means identical with the true overall national interests of the industrial countries, even taken in isolation. Yet the vested interests have influenced public policy very much. This is, of course, evident in the tariff schedules of the industrial countries which are very heavily weighted against processing being done in the underdeveloped countries.

These tariff schedules, unless analysed properly, do not tell the whole story, because the tariff schedules of countries are, of course, usually their *ad valorem* tariffs expressed as percentages on the total product that is being imported, or, in the case of specific tariffs, expressing the duty on the total value of the imported product. But to study the true incidence of these tariffs you must relate them to value added at each stage of production. If you recalculate the tariffs imposed by nearly all industrial countries, including those that are very liberal in admitting primary commodities from underdeveloped countries on this basis, you will find that the incidence of the implied tariff on the processing stage is very high — much higher than the tariff schedule on the total value would indicate.

But having said all this in support of Dr. Onitiri's basic approach, let me say also that I have very serious doubts about his specific proposal. My doubt arises because it looks to me that this is not a proper place to spend international money. He presumably wants the International Bank to lend money to industrial countries to enable them to lubricate the wheels of economic adjustment so that they can get out of primary product processing and simple manufacturing and make room for the products of underdeveloped countries. By exhortation or by trying to get an agreed policy we must certainly encourage this in the more enlightened governments of industrial countries. Some industrial governments have already seen, at least in principle, the necessity and value of such policies of lubrication.

But I do not believe that Dr. Onitiri is right in considering this a proper subject for spending money by the International Bank or other international institutions, because, as he very rightly points out, this adjustment is in the interests of the industrial countries themselves. We are not asking them to make some kind of sacrifice for the sake of the world community. We are asking them only to do what in any case is good for them. Of course, we assume that the industrial countries have a reasonably full employment policy, and, above all, we assume that they accept the principle of internal burden sharing.

In the specific case of the U.K., I would certainly say that it is a duty of the U.K. Government to assist underdeveloped countries like India, Pakistan, Hong Kong and Singapore, but I would also agree that it is not the duty of the individual textile manufacturer in Lancashire, or the individual textile worker, the individual cotton spinner or cotton weaver to carry the burden. The burden of this duty, in the U.K. as in any other industrial country, ought to be equally spread over the community as a whole. The people sectionally or individually affected have a right to expect either compensation or help with adjustments. But, this burden of lubricating the wheels of adjustment is a duty of the national governments of the industrial countries themselves, because it is part of their own progress. In any case, the principle that the burden of progress should rightly be spread out in the industrial countries has already been recognized for decades.

It looks to me that what Dr. Onitiri proposes is retrogressive in this respect. He has shifted back to the international community, including the underdeveloped countries, the price which should clearly be paid by the governments of the industrial countries themselves. I am basing this on the assumption that the international institutions which he expects to finance this have limited funds, like the International Bank, where the funds available are determined (*a*) by the governments' contributions, and (*b*) by the possibilities of issuing bonds in the capital markets of the industrial countries. And if you take that as a given quantity, then any use of resources for the purposes which Dr. Onitiri suggests would, of course, reduce the funds available to underdeveloped countries.

In that case, the underdeveloped countries would have paid for this adjustment, and it is here I believe that Dr. Onitiri's case is very weak. I cannot even remotely conceive any reason why the underdeveloped countries should share in this particular burden. However, I do think that this burden should be shared by the industrial countries amongst each other. If Italy wants to help England to share this burden or vice versa, then a special fund might be set up for financing the transitional development in industrial countries or compensating vested interests which have been injured by concessions to underdeveloped countries.

We are moving in the field of intellectual ideas now, not of organization. It is very unpopular to suggest that a new organization should be set up, but intellectually I would say, following through on Dr. Onitiri's proposal in the sense of international institutions, that financing should not be done by an existing international institution which has funds already earmarked for developing countries. It should rather be done by new institutions, in which contributions are limited to the industrial countries and additional to ordinary aid. Dr. Onitiri's idea should be very carefully pondered by people in advanced countries.

One formulation of his idea would be that very often the best aid given to underdeveloped countries is not that appearing in aid budgets or appropriations, but the speeding up of internal transition out of certain lines of production in which the underdeveloped countries might have export production and export possibilities. We need a broader outlook among the governments and the public of the industrial countries regarding aid problems. We need discussions of aid to underdeveloped countries, not only in terms of money actually transferred to them, but also in terms of policies. If the policies of the industrial countries are being governed all the time with an eye to helping the underdeveloped countries, then I think that the spirit of Dr. Onitiri's proposal is tremendously important.

I would apply here the same reasoning that I would apply to another subject that is now very much discussed — the question of international liquidity and world monetary reform. It is very important when the various ideas for monetary reform are being discussed to remember the interest of the underdeveloped countries all the time, even when measures are discussed which directly and ostensibly affect only the industrial countries. I completely accept the idea that the underdeveloped countries have very little of a direct role in the picture of international liquidity because what they want is not liquidity. They are, however, interested and involved in liquidity in the sense that international liquidity considerations have prevented many industrial countries from giving all the aid to underdeveloped countries which otherwise they might have given, or from making the trade concessions to underdeveloped countries which otherwise they might have made. Because of this the underdeveloped countries have a vital interest in what is being done in this field and their interest ought not to be forgotten.

Dr. Onitiri links his proposal for increased processing in the developing countries with another strategy which I have discussed, namely, the co-operation of underdeveloped countries with each other — the establishment of common markets. He said it is to be noted that this sort of arrangement is essential to the formation of reasonable markets in developing countries, each of which is too small to realize the economies of large-scale production by itself.

I am absolutely convinced that Dr. Onitiri is right in suggesting that the present distribution of processing facilities between underdeveloped countries and industrial countries cannot be satisfactorily explained by reference to comparative advantage, weight-losing characteristics of primary commodities, or resource-oriented versus market-oriented production. I do not believe the theory of comparative advantage, either statically or dynamically interpreted, is a full explanation. There has been in world policy a tendency by industrial countries to shift the processing stages out of the underdeveloped countries and into the industrial countries, to some extent contrary to the principle of comparative advantage. And when Dr. Onitiri said that it is time that we reverse this process and shift processing back to the underdeveloped countries as much as we can, I quite agree.

But when he says it makes a great contribution to common markets among underdeveloped countries, I must maintain that this is only true to a limited extent, because of the traditional structure of world trade — of which the location of processing facilities at the present time is only one expression. For instance, all the trade links and transport links go from underdeveloped countries to developed countries. Usually, in fact, they go from one underdeveloped country to *a specific* developed country, and therefore the development of a common market to expand intra-trade among African countries involves a lot more than the implementation of Dr. Onitiri's scheme. It would involve a powerful financial integration and harmonization of policies which we have already discussed. It would certainly involve the complete reshaping of transport networks within Africa. So, in spite of what Dr. Onitiri says, the contribution that his proposal would make to the formation of common markets is, I think, rather limited. Thus I would make the suggestion that we should continue to explore the question of co-operation among underdeveloped countries as a major step towards development, not develop it as an afterthought in a discussion of the location of processing facilities.

A second point that I would make is that I do not believe that what Dr. Onitiri says on import substitution in the earlier part of his paper is entirely correct. I think he has a tendency to underrate the potential of import substitution as a historical engine of growth, because he has the picture that import substitution is a self-terminating process. If you take the import list of an underdeveloped country, pick the imports off one by one and say, 'Now we can produce this domestically', then obviously when you look at it that way, one day you have exhausted your list and you produce everything domestically. Therefore, import substitution is a dead end.

But that, of course, is wrong; that is not what actually happens in life, because the underdeveloped countries do not *de facto* reduce their imports, since they do not accumulate foreign exchange reserves. Because they spend all their export proceeds, they reduce their imports only if they reduce their exports. Of course, if import substitution eats into the supply of exportable goods and commodities that were previously exported — if these are now no longer available for export because they have to be domestically used and consumed — or if the higher incomes from import substituting industrialization result in domestic consumption of things that were previously exported, then of course import substitution is a self-terminating process. But unless we make such assumptions, import substitution simply means that underdeveloped countries shift their imports from one category of goods to another; from manufactured consumption goods they shift more towards capital goods, or whatever it may be. Then in the next stage you can apply import substitution to that new class of goods. At any given point of time, there will be an import list, and if export proceeds are not affected or changed then the import list will always be more or less equally long and equally large and at any given point of time you can study the possibility of domestic import substitution.

Therefore, I think it is wrong to think of import substitution as something that is tremendously important only in the initial stage of industrialization. I believe import substitution is an approach that can be important at all stages of industrialization, and I think it is fallacious to think of it as having a self-terminating character.

DISCUSSION OF DR. ONITIRI'S PAPER

DR. ONITIRI's proposals for encouraging the further processing of primary-product exports in the developing countries, and for international financing of structural readjustment in developed countries (to overcome the reluctance of such countries to admit imports of manufactures, semi-manufactures, and more highly processed primary products from the developing countries) were both considered in the discussion. His views on the role of capital movements in expanding world trade were questioned, as was his point that protection by developed and developing countries had asymmetrical effects on terms of trade. The impact of import substitution and regional arrangements on trade and domestic economic structure were also considered in the discussion.

I. CAPITAL MOVEMENTS AND TERMS OF TRADE

Dr. Ferrer felt that major changes in commercial and financial flows were needed — especially diversification of exports and regional integration among the developing countries — to achieve an integrated world economy. He agreed with Dr. Onitiri that capital flows should effect the needed changes in economic structure of the developed countries, and noted that this had happened up to 1913 when capital flows were a main instrument of change in the world economic structure.

Dr. Faaland said that the World Bank had organized consortia to export capital to underdeveloped countries, but that no similar arrangements had been made to increase exports of the developing countries. He thought that what was being done on the capital side could also be done on the trade side. GATT and OECD were trying to do something, but their discussions were still far from complete. He wondered why the rich countries did not get together on this issue and examine their own policies as well as the needs of the poor countries. He felt that such joint action was more appropriate for achieving his goal than the methods proposed by Dr. Onitiri.

Dr. Onitiri had noted in his paper that capital movements contributed to the expansion of world trade. *Professor Mundell* questioned whether there was any evidence to this effect. While capital exports will, in theory, increase the exports of the capital-exporting country (the transfer effected in real terms) and increase the imports of the capital-importing country, both imports of the capital-exporting country and exports of the capital-importing country will decrease in the short run. There is no obvious reason why, therefore, world trade should increase or decrease as a result of capital movements. If the capital exports are used to establish import-replacing industries, they might well reduce trade in the long run. Capital movements stimulated by tariff barriers (e.g. U.S. plants established in Canada or Europe) are an example of a type of capital movement which really reduces trade. *Dr. Onitiri* agreed with Professor Mundell that capital movements might replace imports through domestic production, but added that capital movements had contributed to the expansion of world trade over the long run.

Professor Mundell also questioned the asymmetry in terms of trade noted by Dr. Onitiri. Why should a small expansion in exports of a developing country differ in its effect on the terms of trade from an equivalent small contraction of its imports ? There is no logical reason why a 10 per cent replacement of imports would not have the same effect on the terms of trade (with opposite sign) that a 10 per cent investment in exports would have.

Professor Brown noted at this point that Dr. Onitiri's conclusion is possible if development is financed by an advanced country at the expense of expanding its own manufactures. The development of primary-producing facilities in the developing country will then change the world ratio of manufacturing to primary production, whereas the development of import-substituting industry in the developing country will not shift this ratio. *Professor Mundell* added that if this were the case, Dr. Onitiri ought to note the reason for what appears to be a categorical statement. *Dr. Onitiri* replied that the terms-of-trade asymmetry results from the inflexibility of resource allocation in the developing countries. If they continue investment in traditional exports, they can sell more only at the expense of a deterioration in their terms of trade, whereas if imports are reduced by developing domestic import-substitution industries, the terms of trade are still not likely to turn in their favour.

Professor Mundell also questioned Dr. Onitiri's statement that 'the primary purpose of capital movements is to effect economic growth in the developing countries'. He did not feel that this was generally true, especially if the capital movements were private. He felt it more correct to say that the purpose of capital movements is to increase world income. *Dr. Onitiri* accepted this point and agreed that the primary purpose 'should be' rather than 'is' to effect economic growth in the developing countries.

Professor Wallich added that the problem of improving terms of trade raises the question of the form that increased revenue from exports should take. Should increases in export earnings go to export producers, as increased income, or to the government in the form of taxes ? It is interesting to see what can be done to convert the increment into investible resources. One possibility is an export tax. Another (once actually proposed) might be to use import quotas in the importing (developed) country to raise prices there, then siphon off the increment by means of a tax and turn the proceeds back to the developing country for investment purposes. This proposal has never got very far. Another possibility would be for the developed countries, when primary-product prices fall to low levels, to engage in compensatory schemes to increase available investment funds. The mechanics of this might be quite difficult, however.

II. IMPORT SUBSTITUTION AND REGIONAL ARRANGEMENTS

Dr. Singer said that import substitution may require new imports, and that import substitution is therefore not necessarily self-terminating. *Dr. Marshall* agreed with Dr. Singer that import substitution might be a continuing process. He noted, however, that to reach higher stages

— such as capital-goods industries — technological skills and quantities of capital are required that are not often available in developing countries. Argentina, Chile and Colombia have found after ten or fifteen years of import substitution that they have reached a point where further substitution is extremely difficult. Import substitution has other handicaps since it has (*a*) been concentrated in high cost industries ; (*b*) exacerbated balance-of-payments problems when imports do not drop ; and (*c*) reduced flexibility of import demand because curtailing imports of raw materials for local factories now causes unemployment and affects the level of activity. Curtailing imports before only imposed austerity on consumers.

Dr. Singer felt that import substitution is a good strategy because it eases the job of industrialization which, in turn, requires the building of industry and the development of markets. If you cater to an existing market, the job becomes easier and this alone justifies import substitution as a serious strategy. He admitted certain implied disadvantages : the built-in tendency to inefficiency, and lower levels of cost-consciousness. These must be overcome. In reply to Dr. Marshall's views on import substitution he remarked that the distinction between easy import substitution (textiles, shoes) and complicated import substitution (electronic equipment, machine tools) depends upon a country's level of development. If you start with easy things and succeed in raising income, providing domestic markets, and industrializing, what is considered hard or impossible import substitution today will become feasible tomorrow. In this sense, where import substitution is effective, it is self-continuing.

Professor Stolper indicated that 'import substitution' had become a dangerous term because it is often not, in fact, import substitution. He found, for instance, in deriving an input-output table for East Germany that import substitutes — taking account of indirect as well as direct effects — raised rather than lowered import requirements. His major objection to the comments on import substitution, however, was that the discussion was about a concept which is only in part operational. Since no country in the world has enough resources to be completely self-sufficient, there is the problem of choice. It is not that import substitution should not take place, but rather that the ease of raising tariffs and using economic theory to defend tariff protection has led to a misallocation of world resources and to an attempt by countries to undo the fact that they are part of the world. Developing countries should pay more attention to productivity than to protection. Professor Stolper approved of Lewis's idea of making a list of imports and deciding which, on the basis of location theory, engineering, etc., might be best produced domestically. The basis of selection here would be the prospective rate of return. A country cannot develop unless it earns profits.

Professor Stolper agreed with the other speakers that regional integration is a worthy goal, but also agreed with Dr. Singer that the value of regional integration — as distinguished from world integration — tends to be overestimated. If it can be achieved only by raising costs and protection, regional integration will run into diminishing returns and will not develop into a self-propagating process.

Dr. Onitiri agreed with Professor Stolper that more attention should be paid to productivity. He pointed out, however, that productivity in producing exports is not unconnected with productivity in import substitution. In the case of Indian textiles, for example, textiles which were formerly imported are now exported. This would indicate that developing countries can shift from inward-looking to outward-looking development as soon as export possibilities are realized.

Dr. Okita mentioned that developing countries are not only developing import-substitute industries, but also labour-intensive types of exports for markets in advanced countries as a result of lower wages. He cited the experience of Japan, which is losing markets in traditional exports to developing countries such as Korea and Hong Kong where wage rates are lower. This is seen in the changing pattern of Japan's export trade and manufactures. A decline in exports of light-industry products to developing countries has been coupled with an increase of capital-goods exports to these countries. Competition from the labour-intensive products of newly industrializing countries has increased in third markets. Finally, more imports of labour-intensive manufactures from these countries are seen in the Japanese home market.

III. Further Processing and Financing Structural Change

Dr. Onitiri, in his discussion of the difficulties faced by developing countries in expanding exports or reducing imports, argued that structural changes in the pattern of trade between advanced and developing countries were needed. In particular, he advocated that advanced countries adopt new policies both to encourage further processing of traditional primary-product exports in the developing countries, and to give freer market access to manufactures and semi-manufactures of the developing countries. Since this might require structural readjustment among domestic industries in the advanced countries that were competitive with the new exports, Dr. Onitiri also proposed that an international institution be established to finance such readjustment.

Dr. Rhomberg suggested that, in addition to changes in the structure of production in the developed countries to accommodate more imports from the developing countries, it is also necessary to make sure that increased production in the developing countries did not result in these countries producing too much of the same export product with a consequent decline in the terms of trade. Any serious efforts to alleviate problems of developing countries must rely to a considerable extent, therefore, upon joint action of the developing countries. Also, while

Dr. Rhomberg agreed with Dr. Onitiri that the self-interest of developed countries lies in changing the structure of their own production, since developed countries are not generally subject to foreign exchange shortages of the sort faced by developing countries, they cannot always be induced — like the developing countries — to adopt the desired projects because foreign loans cannot be used as inducements. Even when developed countries have balance-of-payments deficits, the deficits would make them reluctant to undertake measures that resulted in higher imports unless the proposed structural change also raised their exports. Therefore, developed countries could be expected to adopt such proposals for structural change only under special circumstances.

In reply, *Dr. Onitiri* said that his idea for implementing the scheme through an international institution was suggested by lending consortia of developed countries now sponsored by the World Bank. Since many developing countries subsidize exports to developed countries in order to get around restrictions placed on their products, why not use a more direct method of increasing exports to developed countries through the financing of structural changes in such countries ?

Dr. Kamarck noted, in support of Dr. Onitiri's proposal, that Rhodesian chrome represents an outstanding example of the maldistribution of processing industries. Hundreds of thousands of tons are transported by rail and ship to be processed in the United States even though only three or four per cent of the rock is chrome and the rest is waste. The reason for this is that the U.S. tariff system discourages the importation of chrome and encourages the importation of chrome rock.

Dr. Marshall felt that present rules and standards of international organizations and treaties which treat all countries as equals are unfair to the developing countries, for whom some special treatment is warranted. The problem of adopting Dr. Onitiri's proposal to concentrate processing industries in developing countries lies in this tradition of nondiscriminatory treatment as well as in the resistance of developed countries to giving processed imports free access to their domestic markets.

Dr. Andreasyan asked whether the discussants thought that the developing countries could raise their *per capita* incomes to levels already achieved in the developed countries. If so, how much time would this take ? And did the discussants think that present international and external policies were suitable for achieving this goal ? *Dr. Onitiri* replied that if the developed countries were not interested in changing their economic structures, it would probably take a very long time for the developing countries to attain a decent living standard. Development requires a change in the economic structure of developing countries, which in turn requires a change in the structure of their foreign trade, and this in turn requires a change in the economic structure of the developed countries. If present policies were continued, it would take two centuries or more for developing countries to attain an even moderately decent standard of living, let alone achieve standards already reached in the developed countries. The international community must adopt measures — even unorthodox ones — to insure that developing countries can pursue the comparative advantage (mainly processing) available to them. The level of technology has reached a point now where this can be done.

PART III

THE MONETARY ASPECTS

Chapter 11

CAPITAL MOVEMENTS AND INFLATION

BY

A. J. BROWN
Leeds University

THE rather pedestrian approach to this subject which I propose to adopt is to look first at the probable effects of inflation on international capital movements, and the evidence for their having existed, and then to do the same for the probable effects of international capital movements on the course of inflation in various kinds of national economy. Let me, therefore, plunge straight away into the first of these tasks.

I. THE EFFECT OF INFLATION ON INTERNATIONAL INVESTMENT

There is no absolutely clear *a priori* presumption as to the net effect of inflation on international capital movements. On the one hand, there may be thought to be a presumption that inflationary periods provide high profits and thus both plenty of investible funds and plenty of incentive to invest in real assets and equities — internationally as well as domestically — and an incentive to borrow for the acquisition of real assets. It may also be argued that, since the prices of primary products are normally more volatile than those of manufactures, inflationary periods will tend to increase the attractiveness of investment in primary producing countries relatively to that in manufacturing countries, which, since the latter are usually the net exporters of capital, will tend to increase international investment at the expense of domestic.

On the other hand, so far as we are concerned with fixed interest portfolio investment (which has constituted the greater part of international investment for most of its history), inflationary trends are clearly inimical to such lending, at any rate if they are expected to continue. Moreover, inflationary times, in so far as they disturb international balances of current payments, give rise to fears of exchange instability or restriction which militate against long-term capital movements, though they produce, of course, sharp movements of short-term capital. All that I have so far said applies, obviously, primarily to private capital movements; official ones are a different matter altogether.

How does the historical record look in the light of these conflicting *a priori* considerations? The great periods of international investment, from the middle of last century to the Second World War, were the late 1850's, the decade centred on 1870, the 1880's, the decade before the First World War, and the 1920's. Of these five periods, only one (1905–14) showed a definitely rising trend in world prices; two showed decisively falling trends and the other two little trend of any kind. The four respectively preceding periods of relatively low investment (excluding the First World War, when very special factors were, of course, predominant) were in two cases periods of rising price-trend and in two periods of falling trend. There is singularly little indication here of any systematic association of price-inflation with either particularly high or particularly low international capital movements.

I am aware that this ground has been considerably fought over. Professor Cairncross [1] has suggested that British foreign investment before 1914 (when it was a very large part of all international investment) varied positively with the terms of trade of the borrowing, primary producing, countries. Apart from the unassailable proposition that foreign investment and these terms of trade were both low for a decade beginning in the early 'nineties (as later on in the early 1930's), the perception of this connection seems to me to require the eye of faith. Mr. Maynard [2] thinks that the connection before 1914 is rather between foreign investment and the price-level of primary products, as exemplified in British imports, but this, too, is a very loose connection. The activities for which most lending of this period took place — railway building, municipal development, the extension in general of the 'infra-structure' in overseas countries — responded to extreme movements in terms of trade or in product prices, but was subject to other influences also; to variations in public enterprise and to special factors such as gold discoveries, the arrears of development after the American Civil War, and the settlement after the South African War. They were also

---

[1] *Home and Foreign Investment, 1870–1914*, Cambridge, 1953.
[2] *Economic Development and the Price Level*, London, 1962.

connected (as Professor Cairncross and others have shown) with immigration, which itself responded to product prices and the other factors just mentioned, but also, negatively, to the level of prosperity in Europe.

It may be objected that the century before 1939 provided no experience of inflation on the scale on which we have learnt to live with it more recently, except for the First World War and its brief aftermath, when, as I have already remarked, so many other special factors were at work. For what it is worth, the rate of private long-term foreign lending by the United States market was much lower in the inflationary year 1919 than in the subsequent years when prices first collapsed, then were stable or moderately falling. In the boom, savings went mainly into domestic stock flotations, in the slump into bonds — mainly domestic, but to a smaller extent overseas also. It is tempting to connect the shift with anticipations based upon the projection into the future of the general price-trend of the moment, but this is a connection at which we ought to look more closely.

Any really large increase in the number of investors who expect that prices will continue to rise would be likely to shift the preference for holding equities as opposed to bonds by much more than could be accommodated by the small change in the ratio between the total quantities of the two which a year's new issues could bring about. Relative yields (or the difference between the yields of the two) would have to change. In fact, the excess of the dividend-yield of common stocks over the yield of bonds remained fairly constant from 1910 to 1928, apart from the temporary increase due to the high level of equity yields in 1917 and 1918. The extinction or reversal of the normal excess of the dividend-yield of equities over the yield of bonds has been a rather rare phenomenon, occurring, in the United States, only in 1871–72, 1879, 1886, 1899, 1905, 1929, and, with unprecedented decisiveness and duration, since 1959. Perhaps it is only of this most recent episode that one can confidently say that it seems to be associated with a predominant expectation of continuing price-inflation — and it took twenty years of inflationary experience to bring it about.

In the United Kingdom, for which I have been able to find comparable data running only from 1926, the dividend-yield of equities seems always (since that date) to have been well above that of bonds until 1959. In the years 1946–58, the excess was at least as high as it had been on average in the mainly deflationary years

1926 to 1933, despite the fact that in the 'fifties, there were unprecedentedly high retained profits which like a widespread expectation of inflation, might have been expected to keep the dividend-yield down. The sudden plunge to a negative value — an excess of bond yield over equity yield — in 1959 is again striking.

But this reference to more recent experience brings us to the post-1945 period, which we think of as having been inflationary as no peace-time period of comparable length in the preceding century was. Up to a point, it is true, the postwar inflation, like that of wartime, could be regarded as due to specific causes which were essentially temporary — the boom connected with immediate post-war shortages and the easing of price control, for most non-dollar countries the devaluation of 1949, for everyone the Korean war. Postwar normality, in so far as we may be said to have attained it, begins somewhere about 1953.

Since then, up to mid-1964 consumer prices had risen some 36 per cent in the United Kingdom and 17 per cent in the United States ; annual rates of increase of about 2·8 and 1·4 per cent, respectively. This British increase certainly ranks as a large one in the light of previous peace-time experience ; I do not think we have registered more than half that average rate of net increase over any period of about the same length during peace-time in the last hundred years. The American rate of increase, however, is not so extraordinary ; it is, for instance, apparently less than the average annual rate of increase between the middle 'nineties and the eve of the First World War. Yet, in both countries, little more than half-way through this period since 1953, as I have already reminded you, the dividend-yield of equities fell below the yield of bonds, a strong indication of a rather drastic change in expectations. This change is presumably related, not simply to experience of price-changes in the preceding half-dozen years, but to judgments based upon the total situation of the time.

By 1959, a general rise in price-levels in most advanced countries had been seen to continue with relatively little check in spite of downward movements in primary commodity prices after the Korean boom, and in spite of periods of considerable excess capacity in the British and American economies. With the onset of substantial recovery from the recession of 1958, therefore, it probably seemed reasonable to judge, not so much that there was any special short-run risk of accelerated inflation, but that the pattern into which economic and political forces had settled after the temporary disturbances associated with post-war reconstruction and the Korean crisis, was one which favoured long-term inflationary tendencies. Subsequent events have given no adequate reason for that judgment to be revised. The average rate of annual increase in the consumer price index has fallen a little in the United Kingdom (from 3·1 per cent in 1953–59 to 2·5 per cent in 1959–64), but in the United States it has continued virtually unchanged at about 1·4 per cent. It is therefore not surprising that the judgment has apparently not been revised, and that the 'yield-gap', for the first time on record, has persisted in both countries for a number of years.

This discussion of the reasons for the emergence of the 'yield-gap' must not be prolonged, though there are many things that could no doubt be said about it (some relating, for instance, to the relative rates of effective taxation on income and on capital gains). The essential point is that if one wishes to seek empirical evidence on the effect of expectation of inflation upon international investment, it would seem proper to compare experience since 1959 with that of earlier periods.

In view of this, one is tempted to lay stress upon the fact that net private international lending by the capital-exporting countries seems to have increased fairly steadily from the end of the war until 1958, and then to have fallen off — or at least levelled off. The temptation should be resisted, however, partly because the period for which post-1958 data are available is still short, partly because the levelling off is less marked if one looks at total *gross* capital outflows from either those countries which are net lenders, or the main developed countries altogether. This gross outflow [1] in 1960 (the last year for which such full information is available at the time of writing) was some $5·9 billion — the largest, about equal in real terms to the annual gross flow of international long-term lending in the later 1920's, which together with the pre-1914 decade, constituted the golden age of this activity. Thus, whatever inflation and the expectation of it may have done to aggregate private long-term capital flows, they have permitted them to reach a large absolute total, though one which bears a considerably lower ratio to world income (or the income of the lenders) than did the corresponding figures in the two previous peak periods just mentioned.

What has unquestionably happened to private international investment since its previous heydays is a great change in its form.

[1] From Germany, Japan, Sweden, the U.K., the U.S.A., Australia, Austria, Canada, Denmark, Finland, Italy, Netherlands, New Zealand and Norway.

Before 1914, probably the greater part of the total consisted of investment at fixed interest. In 1930, this was probably still true; the greatly expanded American investment, despite its greater tendency to be 'direct' as compared with British, was probably half or more at fixed interest, and the proportion of total British investment of which this was true seems to have risen, perhaps to something approaching two-thirds. This was still an epoch in which Irving Fisher's contention that equities were safer in real value than bonds was a novelty (indeed, it was a novelty in some quarters much more recently than that).

But all this is now very much changed. I cannot find precisely the classification of external assets that is required to distinguish between fixed interest and equity holdings, but it does not seem that more than 35 per cent of long-term external assets privately held in the United Kingdom can be fixed interest, and the proportion may be much less; for the United States we know that some 70 per cent of long-term private investments abroad are direct, and it may be that the proportion of the total which is not at fixed interest is considerably higher than that. So far as the flow of new investment is concerned, we have the data on the year 1960 from the UN-IMF Questionnaire. These show that 81 per cent of United States and 73 per cent of British long-term capital outflows were direct investment. For some other lending countries the proportion was lower, but presumably some part of the portfolio investment consisted of acquisition of equities. One writer has stated that: 'only about one-twentieth of international investment today is of the kind which predominated a half-century ago: namely the purchase of foreign government, municipal or corporate securities by individual investors'.[1]

How far is this change a product of inflation? To some extent, of course, it is, but there have been other factors working in the same direction. First, as compared with the classic situation before 1914 or that of the 1920's, a much higher proportion of total private saving in the developed countries is corporate rather than personal, so that a greater part of foreign investment is undertaken by enterprises seeking to extend their business rather than by individuals seeking a return on their capital from whatever is the most promising quarter. Secondly, the memory of defaults on bond interest obligations in the 1930's has left some permanent effect, which no

---

[1] J. H. Dunning, p. 27, 'Capital Movements in the 20th Century', *Lloyds Bank Review*, April 1964.

doubt supplements that of inflation. Thirdly, the decline of colonialism has greatly diminished the number of governmental or quasi-governmental borrowers whose standing in the main capital markets of the world is enhanced by the backing, formal or informal, of a metropolitan government. Finally, in place, to a large extent, of old-style fixed-interest lending mainly for governmental and public utility purposes, there has grown up at the present a very large flow of donations and long-term loans from official sources — a total which has in recent years been greater than that of long-term private lending. The total international movement of funds by way of gifts and long-term loans of all kinds, indeed, is almost certainly substantially greater in relation to world income than it was in the 1920's; even more than with the narrower category of private long-term lending, the change in form has been combined with impressive growth in the aggregate.

This great development of official sources of finance is no doubt partly due to inflation; it is partly a response to a need which inflation, by rendering private fixed-interest borrowing more difficult, has helped to create. But I do not think this can be regarded as a very large factor in its development. Certainly there are other factors likely to be more important — increased awareness of the needs of developing countries, political rivalries for their good will, and institutions and habits left over from the international aid programmes of the war and the reconstruction period.

To sum up, therefore, I would not deny considerable importance to inflation as a factor affecting the present form of the international flow of long-term funds, nor a smaller importance to it as a factor limiting the total size of that flow. But I do not think it is by any means the dominant factor in either of these matters. If it had been, one would have expected dramatic changes in both the form and the size of foreign lending to coincide, more or less, with the British and American yield-changes in 1959, which are our only clear indications of the point of time at which expectations of inflation really became widely established among investors. The main change in the form of foreign investment greatly antedates this point of time; it is not clear that any major change in the growth-trend of foreign investment has been associated with it.

II. THE EFFECT OF INTERNATIONAL CAPITAL-
MOVEMENTS ON INFLATION — SHORT-TERM EFFECTS

I now pass to the effects of international capital movements upon inflation, and here I propose to bring grants, as well as loans, into the picture. There are two main groups of such effects to be distinguished; the short-term effects connected with the actual flow of capital, and the longer-term effects of real capital accumulation in the borrowing countries. Alongside the latter there is the accumulation of their current liabilities for interest and amortization with which, however, I do not propose to deal. Let us look first at the short-term effects.

The short-term effects of international capital movements turn, of course, upon the solution of the famous transfer problem. Following Professor Johnson,[1] we may distinguish between 'classical' and 'Keynesian' cases. In the former, we suppose that factors of production are fully employed in both the lending and the borrowing countries throughout, so that there are no short-run level-of-activity effects of the lending in either group of countries. Expenditure by the lending country falls by the amount of the loan and that by the borrowing country rises by the same amount. It is well known that, in a two-country world where this is true, the balance of trade changes by exactly the rate of lending if the marginal propensities of the two countries to spend on foreign goods add up to unity, or rather to a critical value which, because of tariffs and transport costs, is likely to be somewhat less than unity. In these circumstances, too, the total expenditures both on the lending country's goods and on the borrowing country's goods will be unchanged by the lending, and there is no reason why prices should alter.

Generally, of course, the marginal propensities to spend on foreign goods will not add up to this critical value. If they add up to less, then the tendency is for expenditure to be transferred by the loan from the goods of the lending country to those of the borrowing one. With flexible prices, or a flexible exchange rate, the terms of trade turn against the lender, and unless the price-elasticities of demand for imports are so low as to produce a perverse result, the trade-balance is brought into equality with the rate of lending and the transfer of the loan is, at last, fully effected. If, on the other hand, the marginal propensities to spend on foreign goods add up to more

[1] *International Trade and Economic Growth*, London, 1958, chapter 7.

than the critical value, the same machinery is set to work in the opposite sense, but to the same final result — the exact transfer of the loan.

So far, and in so far as this grossly simplified model is relevant, the question is whether the inflationary influence is exerted in the lending or the borrowing countries, which turns on whether the tendency, without price-changes, would be for the transfer of the loan to be over- or under-effected. Professor Johnson quotes the extremely high marginal propensities to import in some small countries as suggesting that the over-effecting of the transfer may be a serious practical possibility, despite the presumption to the contrary which has generally been accepted. I doubt the strength of this particular piece of evidence. In so far as marginal propensities to import of well over one-half occur only in small countries, it seems to follow that the other marginal propensity in the case — the rest of the world's marginal propensity to import from the small country in question — is likely to be very small, and the two together are still not particularly likely to add up to more than unity, or even to a critical value which tariffs and transport cost bring down to somewhat less than one. If this is so, then the general presumption is still that loans and gifts have a net tendency to raise prices in the receiving countries. This is still more likely if we are speaking of the borrowing and aid-receiving countries as a single entity.

But we are not really concerned with what I may call 'ordinary' marginal propensities to import. For the lending country in the present context of constant outlay, it is perhaps most reasonable to assume that the loan or gift in question is diverted from the providing country's expenditure on capital goods and is spent upon capital goods by the receiving country. The relevant marginal propensities are therefore the marginal propensities to import per unit of additional expenditure on domestic capital formation. For the United Kingdom, the corresponding *average* propensity seems to be about 12 per cent. For the United States it must be very much smaller, and for the main lender or donor countries taken collectively it must also be very small — since large parts of the import-contents of their separate totals of domestic capital formation consist of goods which they import from each other. For these countries together, therefore, I should guess that the relevant marginal propensity to import is less than 5 per cent.

What about the receiving countries ? A point of great importance here is that some of the gifts they receive are in kind and some of the gifts and loans which come to them in money are expendable only upon the products (sometimes specified products) of the lending or giving countries. To the extent that this is so, the effect of the transfer upon prices will depend entirely upon whether the goods given, or bought with the money given or lent, have a higher or lower import-content than those capital goods which the givers and lenders might have bought with the funds they in fact devote to foreign aid. It is reasonable to assume that, in most cases, these import-contents are not very different, and that gifts in kind and tied money gifts or loans therefore (on our present assumption that they are diverted from domestic capital formation) have no effect on prices.

I do not know what proportion of total current aid and lending is tied in this sense. For United Kingdom Government aid (including grants, loans and technical assistance) the proportion seems to be rather over a half. If this is representative of the providing countries taken together, then the greater part of official loans and grants can presumably be disregarded as movers of pressure on resources from one country to another. We are left with the remainder of official grants and loans, and with private long-term investment — a net annual transfer from the capital-exporting countries, taken together, of perhaps five or seven billion dollars a year.

Still assuming that the receipts are spent on capital formation, we get some light on the extent to which this is expenditure outside the receiving countries from a table (Table 2-5) in the *United Nations World Economic Survey for 1959*. There, for a number of countries in the two years 1950–51 and 1957–58 the ratios are given of their imports of capital goods to their domestic capital formation. The average value for the two years varies from under 20 per cent (for Argentina and Israel) to over 60 per cent (for Chile and Mexico), the modal value being apparently between 40 and 50 per cent. These ratios would be raised somewhat if certain invisibles were included ; payments to contractors, in particular, may well amount to five per cent or more of gross domestic capital formation in some countries. Extending the list with rough estimates for Australia and Canada (representing the big, highly developed, net capital importers), and making some allowance for invisibles, one may reach the conclusion that an average of these ratios, weighted by amounts of capital and aid received, would probably be in the region of 35 per cent. For all the net capital importers taken as a unit, the figure would no doubt be rather less than this, but not much less, since the extent to which these countries import from each other for the purpose of domestic capital formation is fairly small. The marginal propensity of the receiving countries to spend in the capital-exporting countries untied funds received from them seems likely to be somewhere in the region of one-third. At all events, it seems that, when it is added to the corresponding marginal propensity for the capital-providing countries, which we have already discussed, the sum will be nowhere near the critical value of somewhat under unity — indeed, it will probably be under a half.

On our assumptions, therefore, this points to the conclusion that recent *untied* loans and gifts have had some inflationary effects in the receiving and deflationary effects in the lending or granting countries, while *tied* loans and gifts have had no such effects. But the assumptions are probably unrealistic. If we introduce instead the 'Keynesian' assumption that income and expenditure in each group of countries is affected by changes in their balances of payments consequent upon the transfers, then as Professor Johnson has shown, the previous criteria governing the net shift of demand-pressure from one group to the other still stand, so long as saving is not affected by the financing or disposal of the transfer — that is to say, so long as the transfer is wholly financed by a shift from expenditure of some sort on the part of the providers, and wholly spent (not saved) by the receivers. On these new assumptions, the income of the providing countries will be reduced and that of the receivers increased so long as the proportions of the transfer by which imports are immediately affected in the two groups of countries add up to a critical number which, ignoring transport costs and tariffs, would be unity. But should we modify these new assumptions in turn ?

At first sight, it seems to me reasonable to assume that the proceeds of loans and gifts are wholly spent and not saved, but that some of the increase in loans and gifts involves an increase in total outlay — not merely a diversion from expenditure on goods and services for their own use — by the countries of origin. In so far as this is so, the effect is, of course, to increase expenditure on goods and services in the world as a whole. It becomes still less likely than under our previous assumptions that the transfer is fully effected without changes in relative prices, because import-demand in the donor and lender countries, arising from their own consumption and domestic capital formation, is not cut back by the transfers as much as before — the critical sum for the marginal propensities to spend the transferred funds on imports becomes greater than unity. Inflationary effects are likely in the receiving countries without a corresponding decrease in the probability of deflationary tendencies at the other end of the line.

This is reinforced by another consideration, which is clearest when savings are not affected by the financing and disposal of the transfer in either group of countries, but continues to hold even if they are so affected. In so far as the balance of payments turns in favour of the receivers, equal and opposite multiplicands are applied to the income-levels in both groups of countries. But in so far as the receivers have lower marginal propensities to save, and thus higher closed-economy multipliers than the wealthier lenders and donors, this will tend to raise incomes more at the receiving end than it reduces them at the paying end. For more than one reason, therefore, one may conclude that the short-run effects of international *untied* loans and aid is somewhat inflationary in aggregate, but more so in the receiving countries than with the donors and lenders — with whom, indeed, it may have a net deflationary tendency.

Where the gifts or loans are *tied* (or, for that matter, where they are transferred in kind) our assumption that they are provided partly by drawing on savings and not wholly by an expenditure-switch results in the conclusion that, while they are still (like untied loans) inflationary for the world as a whole, their inflationary tendency is likely to be concentrated mainly in the providing countries. Indeed, on assumptions which are quite plausible, it is wholly concentrated there and there is no change in the balance of payments. One may say, therefore, that where, as in recent times, international transfers have been partly tied and partly free, the resulting inflationary tendencies are likely to have been widely distributed, the tied transfers increasing the pressure mainly at their points of origin and the untied mainly at their points of destination.

In these last few remarks, referring to the effects of transfers if we make 'Keynesian' assumptions, I am afraid I have been using the words 'inflationary' and 'deflationary' to refer simply to the multiplier effects upon levels of demand. But we must not suppose matters to stop there. If the net result of the transfers, plus these multiplier effects, is to change the balance of payments in favour of the receiving countries — as it will be if the untied transfers work in that direction, while the tied ones have little effect either way — we must consider how, in the slightly longer run, adjustment is effected. It must, of course, be effected either by a change in the receiving countries' prices (reckoned at current rates of exchange) in relation to those of the transferring countries, or by a relative increase, not brought about directly through the multiplier mechanism, in the receiving countries' expenditures on goods and services. In so far as the receiving countries have not, as a group, been substantial net accumulators of gold and foreign exchange, and the transferring countries, as a group, have not been substantial net losers of reserves (though some of them individually certainly have), it seems that the adjustment has, indeed, been taking place, presumably by one or both of these mechanisms.

The terms of trade have, notoriously, moved against the receiving countries and in favour of the lending and aid-giving countries as a whole during the last decade. It is plain, therefore, that relative prices have not been shifted in the direction that one would expect to help in the effecting of the transfers — except on the assumption that transferring and receiving countries, considered as two blocs, have very low price-elasticities of demand for each other's goods and services. I do not think it likely that these elasticities are in fact perverse, especially as there has been so much evidence of substitution in the main transferring countries between imports from the receivers of aid and home-grown or home-synthesized substitutes. My guess is that the explanation of what at first sight may appear a paradox lies with pressure of demand in the receiving countries, not directly arising from the expenditure of the loans and grants they have received.

When we discuss the transfer problem, we may deceive ourselves by taking the assumption of *ceteris paribus* a little too far. Demand in the receiving countries for imports from the lenders and donors depends not only on the loans and gifts received, but on their general levels of demand — largely on their total domestic capital formation, less than a quarter of which has recently been financed from outside. Moreover, there is a presumption that external finance will be drawn in most strongly when domestically financed investment is also running most strongly. Private external capital, in particular, is likely to be drawn to a country where there is a boom already.

This consideration seems to me to make a big contribution towards explaining the smoothness of the transfer mechanism in the golden age of untied international capital movements before 1914. It has long been understood that the migration of labour to the developing countries of that day helped to increase their demand for capital and goods from the rest of the world simultaneously. Whale [1] pointed out also, a long time ago, that borrowers of sterling, in the gold standard period, might simply treat their borrowings, in whole or in part, as additional bank reserves, permitting a multiple expansion of domestic credit and thus of demand. It deserves to be stressed, however, that internally financed expansion would draw in imports whether accompanied by externally financed expansion or not, but that the two tend to go together. Of many of the developing countries of fifty to a hundred years ago — especially of the United States — it could be said that they enjoyed largely internally financed booms which also drew in external capital and additional imports in various proportions. We could say the same of recent events, except that we should perhaps say 'development-programmes' instead of 'booms'. In these circumstances, what actually happens to the balance of payments and to the terms of trade between borrowers and lenders depends largely on the incremental ratio of internal to external financing of domestic capital formation in the borrowing countries — a parameter which is not usually considered (or is tacitly assumed to be zero) in theoretical discussions of the effects of foreign lending. The developing countries have, in fact, tended to push their expansion ahead as fast as their foreign exchange supplies allowed, so that the loans and aid they received have been fully transferred to them in goods and services. The widely varying degrees of internal inflationary pressure they have experienced have depended upon their various internal inflationary mechanisms and policies.

If one plots the increases of cost of living indices in these countries for the period 1958–63 against the ratio, for roughly the same period, of aid and long-term loans received to their gross national products, there is some tendency for a positive correlation to emerge. It is far from being a close one; some countries (Peru, Colombia, Brazil) have experienced very rapid inflation without being, in relation to their own resources, among the larger receivers of external funds. Two or three of the recipients of rather large external funds (Tunisia, Malaya, the U.A.R.) seem to have avoided overt price-inflation. The general suggestion, however, is at least as much that external loans and aid have enabled vigorous (and often inflationary) internal development policies to be pursued as that they have eased the pressure on prices of development programmes which were being pursued in any case.

[1] 'The Working of the Pre-War Gold Standard', *Economica*, 1937.

III. CAPACITY-CREATING EFFECTS

It is, however, difficult to isolate the immediate demand effects of international flows of funds from their rather longer-term capacity effects. To some extent, international aid or investment may involve a net increase in the total amount invested in the world. To some extent also, it may involve a greater creation of capacity to produce for a given amount of capital formation (valued at cost), since capital may migrate in search of the highest returns — though especially in the case of official aid the effect may be the opposite, at least in the not very long run. In any case, however, it involves the creation of capacity in places other than those in which it would have been created in the absence of international transfers. What are the effects of this on price-levels ?

The coming into existence of productive capacity has, in itself, no necessary price-effect. If there were a development in a closed economy, or in the world as a whole, in which no new techniques were employed, and increases in capacity for producing the various kinds of goods and services were kept in line with the increases in demand for them consequent upon the increase in income from the working of the new capacity, then there would be no necessary change in absolute or relative prices. An inadequate or an excessive expansion in monetary facilities would, of course, produce such changes.[1] I do not think, however, that it would be realistic to suppose that money-supply has been prevented by any constraints from keeping in line with changes in physical output in the last decade or so. We can, therefore, retain our proposition that a balanced expansion of productive capacity should not, by itself, have either inflationary or deflationary effects.

In a world in which all prices were equally flexible, we could go further to say that an unbalanced expansion of productive capacity — one which, with constant prices, would lead to over-supply of

[1] We cannot in all circumstances dismiss a change in productive capacity, and in production, to which the money supply fails to adjust itself, as a cause of change in the price-level. The pre-Rostow doctrine that prices fell from 1815 to 1850 because of inadequate increases of the supply of money in the face of dramatic increases in the supply of goods and services in general is not to be dismissed out of hand. The objection that money supply is not rigidly tied to gold, and that gold-shortage is therefore not an adequate reason for price-deflation, is not entirely valid ; there may be — indeed, there clearly are at any time — institutional limits to the speed with which the machinery of credit can be developed, and this, together with a slowly expanding gold-stock, is a perfectly possible source of price-deflation, though I admit that the evidence of interest-rates is against it in that particular case.

some goods, shortage of others — need not have any general inflationary or deflationary effect, either. It would simply alter relative prices, and could well produce local inflation in some parts of the world, local deflation in others. But the key fact, of course, is that not all prices are equally flexible. An expansion of capacity biased towards primary products will tend to lower their prices, which are flexible, without correspondingly raising those of manufactures, which are much less so. Similarly, an expansion of capacity biased towards manufactures does little to lower their prices, but it does raise those of primary products. Superimposed upon these relationships we have now the tendency for factor-prices in the manufacturing and service industries to drift upwards in any case, though at rates which show some positive sensitivity to changes in primary product prices, and for the price of manufactures to follow this drift except in so far as it is offset by the increase of the physical productivity of factors of production.

This very simple analysis — which is all I intend to attempt for the present — does not, unfortunately, lead to any firm conclusion about the effects of creating capacity in one place rather than in another, but it perhaps suggests the directions in which one should look for an answer. If international investment means, as it certainly did half a century and more ago, that capacity is created overseas in primary producing or in means of bringing primary products to market, instead of in the increase of manufacturing facilities in the industrial (and capital-providing) parts of the world, then it tends to impart a primary product bias. This is likely to be deflationary for the world as a whole, since primary product prices will fairly certainly be lowered and the pressure of food-prices on wage and salary rates in the industrial countries will be relaxed. There will be some counter-effect, because the diversion of funds for investment from industrial to primary producing areas will also, presumably, have some tendency to slow down the growth of physical productivity in the lending countries — as it did in the United Kingdom in the decade before 1914 — and this will be to some extent anti-deflationary. But this effect is unlikely to prevail so far as the general world price-level is concerned.

One can no longer be so sure as one could before 1914 that the net effect of international lending and aid is to divert funds from investment in manufacturing industry into the development of primary production. Much private international investment is connected with the establishment or expansion of manufacturing industry inside other countries' tariff walls, including those of the countries which are net receivers of loans and aid. A good deal of the development in the receiving countries which is financed by public international lending or aid is at least as conducive to the establishment of manufacturing industry (including that aimed at import-substitution) as to the expansion of primary production. It would be interesting (though difficult) to quantify these statements more precisely. I have not attempted this : nevertheless, it is clear that world developments of the last decade, taken as a whole, have moved the terms of trade against primary producers, which means that their general capacity-creating effects have probably been deflationary on balance, and my guess — it is only a guess — is that, if one could separate out the developments which are due to international loans and aid, their effect would not be seen to have run contrary to this general tendency. I doubt whether international capital has been directed more towards manufacturing, less towards the encouragement of primary production, than capital as a whole. At all events, it would be interesting if someone were moved to try to establish a firm presumption to the contrary. Until this is done, it seems likely that the capacity-creating effects of international investment and aid in the last decade or so have been mildly on the side of keeping world price-levels down.

Looking back over this paper, I cannot feel that I have been able to establish anything very definitely. The fact is that the two entities whose mutual relations I have been discussing are rather an unnatural pair. There is no strong reason why inflation should have a particular bearing upon international investment as such, though plenty of prima facie reasons why it might be expected to have particular (and different) bearings on other sub-divisions of domestic and international investment taken as a whole. My argument in this connection has really been first, that relative yields of bonds and equities show that the historical fact of inflation is not as closely connected with the expectation of inflation — which is what matters for behaviour — as one might think ; and secondly, that much of the change that the expectation of inflation seems likely to establish in international investment habits has in fact happened apparently from other causes.

In the same way, the effects of investment on the occurrence and course of inflation depend mainly upon the total amounts of investment in the various national or regional economies (and in all of them together), and upon the balance between the amounts of capital formation directed, in the world as a whole, towards increasing capacities to produce goods of flexible and of rigid price respectively. The bearing of specifically international investment upon these matters is not without importance, but it is rather oblique. Nevertheless, I hope that the discussion will be thought to have been worth while.

COMMENTS ON PROFESSOR BROWN'S PAPER

BY

JORGE MARSHALL
Bank of Chile

I

PROFESSOR BROWN'S paper is easy to read, stimulating in ideas and, even when we disagree with the author, constitutes in general a plausible effort on a rather difficult subject, especially if one considers that perhaps it is not feasible to obtain a greater amount of empirical data than what he has been able to collect. This leads him to a qualification of some conclusions in such a way that in many cases the opposite proposition may be equally valid. He is thus protected from criticism which a stronger position could have brought about.

The analysis is conducted on the assumptions of a growth model of a capitalist type economy prevailing in the world until the First World War, and only partially afterwards. It is my feeling that this kind of approach, even when valid in those cases where the assumptions match the real world, is not so in those cases where the developing countries do not follow a capitalistic pattern or do so only partially. This argument is developed in the lines that follow.

II

Professor Brown starts his paper with the idea that there should be a 'presumption that inflationary periods account for high revenues, an abundance of incentives and funds to invest in real assets (internal and external) as well as incentives to borrow for the acquisition of real assets'.

This statement may correspond to reality in those cases where there is demand inflation. Unfortunately, in most cases among countries in the process of development which have had long periods of inflation, the demand inflation is quickly transformed into a cost inflation, or a combination of both, and investment revenues not only do not grow but

398

remain stable or even may decline. In those circumstances, the incentives to borrow in a currency of constant purchasing power to carry out direct investments are greatly reduced.

A study prepared in 1963 by the UN Economic Commission for Latin America on *External Financing in the Economic Development of Latin America*,[1] shows some comparisons between the rates of industrial profits of American enterprises and their subsidiaries or branches operating the same lines in Latin America. Taking all industries, the yield is less in the United States than in Latin America, although the difference was small for 1958 ; returns were larger in the United States for 1959. The main element of difference was in the petroleum industries, where profits were bigger in Latin America than in the United States. On the other hand, the manufacturing sector shows greater profitability in American industries than in their affiliates in Latin America. One has to bear in mind that the revenues of U.S. firms are shown as after American taxes, which is not true for their subsidiaries and affiliates in Latin America. Here, only local taxes are deducted. All of which indicates that rapid inflation rates in Latin America did not lead to the higher profits or for a higher propensity to invest. In effect, as Professor Kaldor has pointed out,[2] the profit rate from investments depends on the rate of growth and the proportion of net income saved. That is to say, only when inflation can accelerate the rate of growth will it lead to a higher level of investment.

III

Professor Brown analyses the way in which the inflationary process could have influenced international loans, shifting them to investments in real assets or stocks rather than in bonds or money claims.

His statement refers to the preference for real assets or investment in bonds or fixed-return assets expressed in hard currencies, such as the dollar and the sterling pound, which is made available through capital flows to the developing countries. Nevertheless, it is hard to believe that the composition of foreign investment may have changed in favour of real investment due to inflationary expectations, instead of other factors which are obviously more important.

Even Professor Brown seems to have some doubts himself, adding that the change in composition of the investments came about before the yield rate on bonds surpassed the rate on securities in the industrial countries. Loans on securities with a fixed return disappeared for the developing world — or were at any rate substantially eliminated — during the depression of the 1930's, for well-known reasons. The growing

---

[1] Table IV–8, p. 225.
[2] 'Essay on Economic Development', Center for Latin American Monetary Studies (CEMLA), Mexico, 1961, p. 66.

volume of private direct investment can be attributed, at least for Latin America, to such factors as :

(*a*) The growing demand for certain primary commodities in the investing countries ;

(*b*) Exceptional profits in some specific branches of the economy ; and

(*c*) Eagerness to take advantage of markets protected against the competition of finished imported goods.

Those credits which in the past were offered on securities with a fixed rate of return have nowadays been replaced by loans of governments or international lending institutions, or by credit from producers trying to stimulate their sales abroad, in most cases with government guarantees. All these changes seem remotely associated with the inflationary pressures that have emerged in the various regions of the world after the last war, and even less with inflation in the industrial nations.

IV

A large part of Professor Brown's paper deals with the effects of capital movements on prices and the possibility of their contributing to inflation. The discussion runs in neoclassical and Keynesian terms, following the general pattern of Professor Johnson's *International Trade and Economic Growth*. An effect on prices is brought about where the capital receiving country has to generate income to effect the transfer. But in many cases — as Professor Brown himself asserts — the transfer is directly effected in real terms either because loans are tied to purchases of commodities or capital equipment, or because the demand already existed.

If we take the case of Latin America, the amounts of capital inflows are so small when compared to total income that, if they have had some impact on prices, the impact must have been negligible in comparison with the other casual factors of the inflation prevailing in the region.

Between 1951 and 1960, the annual rate of net capital inflows was around US$900 million, from which we have to deduct the compensatory financing of balance of payments deficits since demand for this type of capital preceded the capital inflow.

Consequently, net capital inflows — after deducting compensatory financing — was only US$670 million annually. Of this, a large proportion entered in the shape of machinery and equipment, that is, in loans or investments tied to additional imports and therefore unable to have any effect on domestic prices. Part of the remaining capital inflows, in the form of foreign exchange loans, was used to meet shortages of imported goods, the demand for which already existed.

The amount of foreign exchange receipts realized from loans untied to specific imports, in any case not greater than US$300 million annually, could hardly have made a great impact on prices in a region with a national income around US$80,000 million yearly.

Brown — Capital Movements and Inflation

Inflows of capital may have had a deflationary effect in some developing countries, especially where investments, loans and aid have come in larger quantities.

In the Chilean case, on which I have more accurate data for 1959–63, capital inflows and amortization payments were as follows :

INFLOW OF CAPITAL INTO CHILE, 1959–63
(In millions of dollars)

	Annual Average 1959–63
I. AUTONOMOUS CAPITAL (long term)	
A. *Gross capital inflows*	*182*
(1) Machinery and equipment	99
(2) Foreign currency	83
B. *Amortizations*	*70*
(1) Loans	41
(2) Direct investments	29
C. *Net capital inflows* (A-B)	*112*
(1) Equipment	99
(2) Foreign currency	13
II. AUTONOMOUS CAPITAL (short term)	
(1) Inflows	61
(2) Amortizations	52
(3) Net inflows	*9*
III. FINANCING OF THE BALANCE OF PAYMENTS (deficit)	51
IV. NET CAPITAL INFLOWS (totals)	
Equipment	99
Foreign currency	73
Compensatory	(51)
Official in foreign currency	(36)
In foreign currency (not compensatory non-official)	(– 14)

See the table in the Annex.

Thus, Chile appears to have had during that period a net capital inflow of US$172 million annually. This is quite a substantial figure when related to exports and the country's national income. Its net effect has been deflationary. Of the total of US$172 million, US$99 million annually came as machinery and equipment, and US$73 million as foreign currency. Of this last amount, US$51 million was used to cover the balance of payments deficit, and another US$36 million yearly were official loans in foreign currency which had the same effect as if they had been compensatory loans. Therefore, the overall result of capital movement was a negative net figure in foreign currency, equivalent to an outflow of capital at a yearly rate of US$14 million. In other words, inflows of capital into Chile have been deflationary. And with variations, the experience might be very similar in the rest of Latin America.

V

In his paper, Professor Brown specifically considers the inflationary and deflationary effects that may result from changes in productive capacity caused by capital movements. Whenever productivity increases in the production of primary goods, and not in manufacturing industries, the result for the world as a whole tends to be deflationary. This is so because prices of primary commodities are more flexible — i.e. are likely to decline — and because low prices of raw materials and crude foodstuffs provide support to rising real wages in industrial countries. As a matter of fact, a good share of private investment, at least of the kind which has flowed into Latin America during the 1950's, has gone into the production of primary goods. Approximately 50 per cent of United States investments — the greatest part of foreign investment during the period — went into petroleum or mining production.

The effect of price fluctuations in primary products is not the same for countries where investments take place, as it is for industrial countries where the increased supply of primary products at lower prices tends to keep down the cost of industrial production.

In the first place, the deflationary bias of investments in primary products has an unfavourable effect on the terms of trade of developing countries — reducing the direct income from foreign trade as well as the fiscal revenues accruing directly or indirectly from exports of primary products. A low rate of increase in the value of their exports is in itself a deterrent to growth and may be responsible for changes and policies from which inflationary forces may develop.[1]

Besides, the cyclical slowdown of foreign currency receipts is conducive to expansionary policies of a compensatory nature, to keep the level of employment from falling. And these policies tend to create inflation or to accelerate an inflationary process already under way.

VI

A point which Professor Brown's paper does not mention is the effect that servicing previous investments and foreign loans, i.e. amortization and interest payments, has on an economy.

This matter deserves a great deal of attention in view of the volume

[1] Dudley Seers, *A Theory of Inflation and Growth in Underdeveloped Economies based on the experience of Latin America*, Yale University, New Haven, 1962.

which these services recently have reached. In Latin America, the amount of these services went from US$1,187·9 million in 1951 to US$2,527 million in 1961,[1] i.e. they more than doubled. In the same period, total credits in the balance of payments for exports of goods, services and private donations varied within 12 per cent. During the years 1951–55, debt service payments on long-term capital for all countries of Latin America were 12·1 per cent of their receipts on current account. They were 17·7 per cent for the period between 1956–60 and reached 24 per cent in 1961. For the entire period, service payments on foreign long-term capital accounted for more than 20 per cent of gross saving.

The greater inflow of capital between 1956 and 1960, in comparison to 1951–55, was not enough even to compensate for the deterioration in the terms of trade for the region and, in addition, helped very little to increase the export capacity of Latin America — although it helped to avoid a decrease. The decrease of savings available to finance investment tends to slow down economic development and it may create or accelerate inflationary pressures in countries which have committed a sizeable portion of their resources to investment.

VII

Professor Brown relegates public capital to a rather secondary place. This fits in with his growth model, in which capital movements are mainly private and determined mainly by market forces. Public capital movements appear in his paper as somehow unrelated to economic forces, and determined rather by political or security reasons or by motives outside the framework of his paper.

We believe that for countries or regions which do not want to follow an entirely capitalist model of development, or which do not think it possible or desirable to adjust to such a model, the analysis of public capital movements is extremely important. And one should not lose sight of the fact that these movements are determined largely by economic factors. Possibilities for development of the less developed nations are indispensable for the security and prosperity of the industrial countries.

Public capital is in an advantageous position to satisfy the financial needs of development programmes without generating inflationary pressures. At the same time, conditions regarding amortization and interest can be such as to alleviate pressure on the balance of payments. Of course, the acceptance of this type of capital by developing countries presupposes that no conditions limiting national sovereignty of receiving countries are imposed.

[1] Table IV–7 of the ECLA study.

Capital Movements and Economic Development

VIII

From the point of view of the developing countries, the degree of regularity in the flow of foreign capital is important. If the flows are irregular, as they have been in the past, the inflationary effect of this irregularity is equivalent to the effect produced by fluctuations in export revenues. The situation becomes worse when the inflow from capital increases when export revenues are high and decreases when they are low.

IX

As Professor Brown says at the end of his paper, the phenomena between which a causal relation is to be established (capital movements and inflation) are a very 'unnatural pair'. Thus he cannot avoid feeling he has been unable to really prove anything in a definite way. I believe that there is much truth in what Professor Brown says. It is quite possible that other forces could have had an impact on inflation as well as on capital movements. Thus, even when one may be inclined to think of a possible correlation between inflation and capital movements, it nevertheless is true that they have been determined by fundamentally different forces.

I have the impression that, all through Professor Brown's paper, inflation is treated as if it were a unique and identical phenomenon through the world. It is fair to say at this point that postwar conditions became definitely inflationary in the industrial countries due to their full employment policies. But this is not necessarily the case for the less developed countries. For example, in Latin America, there are countries with open economies — in Central America, the Caribbean, Ecuador and Venezuela — which have shown rates of inflation as moderate as those prevailing in the United States or in Western Europe. And in the rest of Latin America, even in those cases where inflation has not been excessive, as in Mexico or Peru, the rates are much higher than the ones in the industrial countries, and the reasons behind both types of inflations are quite different. For the former countries, the inflationary process is closely related to their desire to promote a higher rate of growth and at the same time a more egalitarian income distribution in the face of fast increasing populations. These objectives coincide with a sense of national consciousness and an attitude which is partially or totally hostile to purely capitalist forms, as well as to foreign investments of the kind that have prevailed until now. Economic policies formulated and carried out within this framework of ideas have naturally affected the magnitude of inflation as well as the size of capital movements. This is why, in many cases, there appears to be some relationship between both phenomena, even when they cannot be explained by one another in a significant way.

404

NET RECEIPTS* OF U.S. ENTERPRISES AS A PER CENT OF THE BOOK VALUE OF INVESTMENT, BY SECTOR

Year	All Industries		Mining and Smelting		Petroleum		Manufacturing		Other	
	Subsidiaries and Affiliates in Latin America	Principal Enterprises in the U.S.	Subsidiaries and Affiliates in Latin America	Principal Enterprises in the U.S.	Subsidiaries and Affiliates in Latin America	Principal Enterprises in the U.S.	Subsidiaries and Affiliates in Latin America	Principal Enterprises in the U.S.	Subsidiaries and Affiliates in Latin America	Principal Enterprises in the U.S.
1951	18·7	..	14·3	..	33·6	..	17·1	..	11·6	..
1952	16·8	..	11·4	..	31·8	..	13·7	..	10·6	..
1953	12·9	10·6	4·3	8·8	26·6	14·7	10·4	12·7	8·4	..
1954	12·4	10·3	5·3	10·0	25·5	13·8	10·1	12·3	7·9	..
1955	14·4	12·0	10·8	13·7	30·1	14·2	8·9	15·0	8·3	..
1956	15·4	11·3	13·5	15·3	30·8	14·7	8·2	13·9	8·1	..
1957	14·9	10·6	8·7	7·9	23·1	13·6	11·8	12·8	10·2	..
1958	9·8	9·0	7·5	6·5	13·4	10·2	7·4	9·8	8·1	..
1959	9·5	9·8	11·3	7·4	11·2	10·0	8·6	11·6	7·3	..
1960	9·9	..	14·2	..	12·0	..	9·1	..	6·3	..
1961	11·1	..	12·8	..	13·4	..	9·2	..	8·4	..

* Net income from subsidiaries and affiliates in Latin America are computed after Latin America taxes, not U.S. taxes. Net income from principal enterprises in the U.S. are computed after American taxes.

Sources : U.S. Department of Commerce, *Balance of Payments Statistical Supplement*, 1948 ; U.S. Department of Commerce, 'United States Business Investment in Foreign Countries', by S. Pizer and Cutler (*Supplement, Survey of Current Business*), 1960 ; and *Survey of Current Business*, various issues from 1958–62 ; First National City Bank of New York, *Monthly Letter*, several issues from 1955–60, quoted by Raymond Mikesell in *United States Private and Government Investment Abroad*, Eugene, Oregon, 1962, Table 111-11, p. 67.

Capital Movements and Economic Development

ANNEX 2

CHILE: AUTONOMOUS CAPITAL MOVEMENTS, 1959–63

(Millions of Dollars)

Item	1959	1960	1961	1962	1963
I. LONG AND MEDIUM TERM					
A. *Public sector*	*− 11·1*	*− 5·2*	*49·8*	*107·2*	*143·8*
(1) Inflows	15·1	12·5	67·8	121·4	168·9
(a) Foreign currency	(—)	(—)	(30·3)	(56·0)	(92·6)
(b) Equipment	(15·1)	(12·5)	(37·5)	(65·4)	(76·3)
(2) Amortization of credit	26·2	17·7	18·0	14·2	25·1
B. *Private sector*	*80·9*	*91·8*	*96·1*	*103·5*	*48·2*
(1) Inflows	98·5	106·1	113·4	125·7	81·3
(a) Foreign currency	(57·7)	(48·8)	(61·6)	(41·7)	(26·1)
(b) Equipment	(40·8)	(57·3)	(51·8)	(84·0)	(55·2)
(2) Amortization of credits	17·6	14·3	17·3	22·2	33·1
C. *Totals*	*69·8*	*86·6*	*145·9*	*210·7*	*192·0*
(1) Inflows	113·6	118·6	181·2	247·1	250·2
(a) Foreign currency returns	(57·7)	(48·8)	(91·9)	(97·7)	(118·7)
(b) Equipment	(55·9)	(69·8)	(89·3)	(149·4)	(131·5)
(2) Amortization of credits	43·8	32·0	35·3	36·4	58·2
II. SHORT TERM	*− 18·2*	*5·5*	*42·2*	*7·5*	*10·2*
(1) Inflows	24·6	25·7	82·2	137·0	37·1
(2) Amortization	42·8	20·2	40·0	129·5	26·9

CHILE: COMPENSATORY CAPITAL MOVEMENTS, 1959–63

(Millions of dollars)

Item	1959	1960	1961	1962	1963
Changes in Assets	64·3	− 12·6	− 36·0	− 2·1	6·6
Changes in Liabilities	45·2	31·8	96·1	66·4	35·2
Total International Net Reserves	19·1	− 44·4	− 132·1	− 68·5	− 28·6
Capital Depreciation	31·0	32·1	21·2	26·6	34·1

DISCUSSION OF PROFESSOR BROWN'S PAPER

THE discussion centred on the relevance of Professor Brown's analysis of inflation in developing countries, on his use of the tools of classical analysis in handling the transfer problem and on the nature of counterpart funds.

In his discussion of Professor Brown's paper, *Dr. Marshall* suggested that Professor Brown's assertion that inflationary periods raise profits and provide incentive for investment in real assets applies only in cases of demand inflation, and then mainly in the short run. Demand inflation ultimately gives rise to cost pressures and inflation becomes a combination of demand and cost elements. With cost inflation it is not at all clear that higher profits and better opportunities to invest will exist. *Professor Brown* agreed that the positive influence of inflation on investment depends on the source of inflationary pressure, and that this was the reason for his agnosticism about the incidence of inflation on international investment.

Dr. Marshall noted that much of Professor Brown's discussion of the effects of inflation on foreign investments runs in terms of preferences between equities and bonds. He felt this distinction to be of little relevance for the amount and types of investment and lending in developing countries since these are largely a function of needs for raw materials (by the investing country) and protective policies in these countries. Dr. Marshall also said that capital inflow in many developing countries is quite small relative to gross national product. The small amount of untied capital inflow in regions like Latin America has no discernible influence on price movements. He also questioned the conclusion that private foreign investment directed towards primary products would be deflationary in a developing country. Deterioration of barter terms of trade associated with decreasing prices of primary products results in stagnation of export proceeds, which in many cases leads to inflationary pressure. Dr. Marshall added that cyclical swings in international investment can also influence inflationary pressures. He felt that Professor Brown should have dealt with such swings in his paper.

In general, *Dr. Marshall* felt that Professor Brown's analysis was inadequate because he did not consider problems relevant for developing countries. *Professor Brown* replied that he regretted having given the impression of thinking in terms of the pre-World-War-I world. If he did, it was only because it made sense to consider inflation in connection with private international lending, and private international lending was a rather old-fashioned topic.

Professor Mundell agreed with Dr. Marshall. He found a certain incompatibility between the classical analysis of the transfer problem and the sense of reality always present in Professor Brown's paper. He felt that the influence of aid on terms of trade in the real world is minimal. Other factors, such as war or development policies, have much more influence in determining the terms of trade of the developing countries. He added that it is not price or income elasticities which are relevant here, but marginal propensities. That is, what matters is not the amount of aid given but changes in the rate at which it is given.

Professor Borts commented upon Professor Brown's suggestion that international capital movements could have a deflationary impact from a world point of view if they were responsible for productivity increases through technological change in primary producing countries. This might explain the simultaneous increase in profitability of investment in agricultural countries with the long run decline in world market prices for agricultural products.

Dr. Kafka was puzzled by Professor Brown's conclusion that since a capital inflow increases domestic expenditure, it is inflationary. This seemed to him to assume fixed exchange rates ; if allowance is made for flexible exchange rates the consequences might be the opposite. He noted also that Professor Brown suggests that loans in kind or tied loans will have no price effects. This would be so only if the loan covered 100 per cent of project costs. If the loans cover only the foreign component, for instance, the need to obtain complementary goods in the domestic market might very well be inflationary. *Dr. Adler* objected that loans which finance only the foreign currency component of a project need not be inflationary if the local resources used are obtained in a non-inflationary way. He said that the World Bank now insists on this method of financing.

Professor Delivanis pointed out that it is commonly argued (even in Professor Brown's paper) that foreign investment and untied foreign loans reduce investment within the lending or donor country. But this is true only if the loan is made by reducing gold and foreign exchange reserves. Lending is usually followed by an increase in exports of capital goods which, in turn, most probably would increase domestic investment. Professor Delivanis also remarked on Professor Brown's point that the decrease in prices of agricultural commodities can be associated with international capital movements. He could not understand this, considering that prices of industrial commodities did not fall. *Professor Brown* replied that developments during the last decade, including the direction of total investment, had been sufficiently biased towards primary production to worsen the terms of trade of primary producers. The net effect of the international investment has been to lower the general upward pressure on price levels by a more than proportional expansion in the production of goods with the most flexible prices.

Professor Brown noted in his paper that the post–1959 experience, in which equity yields are below bond yields, has been relatively rare. He suggests that the reversal of the normal excess of equity yields over the yield of bonds seems to be associated with a predominant expectation of continuing price inflation, and that it took twenty years of inflationary experience to bring this about. *Dr. Singer* said that if we now assume that the International Monetary Fund is successful in stopping inflation in the developing countries, it would most likely take another twenty years for investors to realize the new situation ; but after twenty years when the perverse yields of bonds and equity capital have disappeared, unless the present institutional position can be reversed and private bond lending revived, private lending to developing countries may come to a standstill.

Dr. Singer also questioned another point raised by Professor Brown, that tied aid is inflationary at the point of origin. Since tied aid is mainly food, and what is given to underdeveloped countries is usually a surplus, this is not necessarily so. To determine the inflationary impact of tied aid, it is necessary to know what would happen in the absence of tied aid in the donor country.

Dr. Andreasyan stated that inflation in developed countries continually decreases the material content of Western aid. On the other hand, the developing countries have to repay their debts in hard currency and the volume of the debts, expressed in hard currency, has not decreased as has the material content of the Western aid. According to United Nations estimates of capital flows from developed to developing countries, and Soviet estimates of debt service payments and other return flows from the developing to the developed countries, there is little difference in the magnitude of the two flows. The result is increased indebtedness of developing countries, reduction in their economic independence and inability to achieve self-sustained growth.

Professor Stolper warned of the pitfalls that may be encountered when dealing with global estimates such as those cited by Dr. Andreasyan. While it is true, for instance, that the United States is now making proportionally more loans and fewer grants, an increasing portion of the loans are made against local currency and nobody really expects this portion to be repaid. Data on aid should be adjusted to take this into account. *Dr. Patel* added that the problem of measuring capital inflows and outflows from the developing countries raised by Dr. Andreasyan is a three-part problem. First, much of the reverse capital flow from developing countries is in the form of private foreign capital remittances. Second, if we look at official loans, the reverse flow so far has been much smaller than the inflow. Third, if we look at local currency loans, the net effect tends to be deflationary. For instance, in the case of PL480 food loans, the government absorbs payment for the food.

Professor Stolper's remarks on counterpart loans or loans made against local currency stimulated an extensive discussion of such loans.

Dr. deBeers pointed out that some of the loans extended by the Inter-American Development Bank were repayable either in dollars or in local currency. *Dr. Onitiri* remarked that expenditure of counterpart funds is not a substitute for the inflow of foreign exchange. When counterpart funds are spent, the expenditure will be inflationary. *Dr. Marshall* added that counterpart funds can also be used to finance exports to a third country. This also implies a transfer of resources. *Dr. Singer* cited a study he had made of the uses of local counterpart funds generated by United States PL 480 loans in India, Pakistan, the United Arab Republic and Israel. He found that roughly 20 to 25 per cent of the funds were used in ways that constituted a loss of foreign exchange to the country that received the aid. It follows that loans repayable in domestic currency combine both grant and loan elements, but the grant element predominates. *Dr. Patel* agreed, with reference to Professor Stolper's point, that this 20 to 25 per cent is a substitute for possible dollar earnings and constitutes a true repayment on the loan element of the local currency loan.

Chapter 12

PRIVATE CAPITAL MOVEMENTS AND EXCHANGE RATES IN DEVELOPING COUNTRIES

BY

RUDOLPH R. RHOMBERG
International Monetary Fund

I. INTRODUCTORY

THE economic and financial literature of recent years has contained a considerable amount of discussion of the relationship between exchange rates and international differences in interest rates, on the one hand, and capital movements between the major industrial countries, on the other. Much less attention has been paid to the question of the effect of variations in exchange rates, or of the choice among alternative exchange rate systems, on private capital flows from industrial to developing countries. The present paper deals primarily with this relatively neglected topic. The principal question that will be considered is the following : how are private capital movements in any one country likely to respond to changes, or expected changes, in foreign exchange rates and in the country's prices and costs, given the other factors which influence the incentive to invest in that country ? Although the paper is chiefly concerned with flows of private capital to developing countries, the general analysis of the influence of changes in prices, costs and exchange rates on movements of various types of capital applies also to international investment in industrial countries. The concluding section elaborates some implications of the analysis with regard to the broader question of the effect of alternative exchange rate systems (fixed or fluctuating exchange rates, unitary or multiple exchange rates) on capital flows.

These questions must be approached mainly through *a priori* reasoning. Countries that differ in so far as their exchange rate systems are concerned ordinarily differ also with respect to a number of other factors influencing the attractiveness of their economies to foreign investors. Many of these factors cannot easily be quantified. Moreover, investment responds not to the actual changes in the determinants of returns on capital assets but rather to the changes which potential investors expect; the historical record reveals the former but not the latter. For these reasons, the scope for statistical testing of theoretical propositions concerning the determination of the extent, timing, direction and composition of foreign investment is very limited. The empirical material presented in this paper is intended only for illustrative purposes.

II. EXCHANGE RATES, INFLATION AND CAPITAL MOVEMENTS

If a country in which investment is contemplated is plagued by rapid domestic inflation, the exchange rate must be expected to depreciate sooner or later. It is generally agreed that the expectation of the depreciation of a currency tends to discourage foreign investment in assets with given prices and yields denominated in that currency. This is so because of the exchange loss which a potential investor has to expect whenever the proceeds of some of the earnings and of the ultimate liquidation of an asset have to be converted into the investor's currency at a less favourable exchange rate than that at which the asset was originally purchased. These considerations, which concern a particular type of foreign investment, are sometimes applied to foreign investment in general. This leads to the view that inflation and exchange instability (i.e. repeated devaluations or a continuously depreciating exchange rate) in the investee country reduce earnings on foreign investments and thus discourage capital inflows and encourage capital outflows.[1]

It is, however, difficult to reconcile the presumed deterrent effect of inflation and exchange depreciation with the continued large inflows of private capital into some of the countries whose currencies show very rapid rates of loss of internal and external purchasing

---

[1] This view finds expression, e.g., in the following statement: ' Balance-of-payments problems, inflation, and consequent currency depreciation have for many years been a way of life in most Latin American nations, with a resulting adverse effect on earnings in terms of U.S. dollars, as well as an erosion of U.S. dollar investments in Latin American enterprises, particularly manufacturing.' (' Proposal to Improve the Flow of U.S. Private Investment to Latin America : Report of the Commerce Committee for the Alliance for Progress ', *Private Investment in Latin America*, Hearings Before the Subcommittee on Inter-American Economic Relationships of the Joint Economic Committee, 88th Congress, Second Session, p. 79).

power. Net inflows of private capital into four less developed countries — Argentina, Brazil, Chile and Colombia — during the period 1951–63 are shown in Table 1. These countries experienced rapid inflation (measured by the cost of living index) and exchange depreciation (measured both by the exchange rates mainly applicable to capital transactions and by those mainly applicable to general commercial transactions). They were, in fact, selected because, among the countries for which the relevant data could be compiled, they had the highest rate of inflation. During the 13-year period 1951–63, the net inflow of private long-term capital to the four countries totalled $4·6 billion. This inflow contributed to the foreign exchange earnings of these countries an amount equal to 10 per cent of their earnings from merchandise exports. They experienced a net outflow of short-term capital (including errors and omissions) [1] of about $1·3 billion ; however, the net inflow of private capital of all types was quite large ($3·3 billion), amounting to 7 per cent of their combined exports.

A comparison between two subperiods shows no consistent evidence — country by country — that long-term capital inflows were smaller in more inflationary periods than in less inflationary ones. In three of the four countries, prices rose much more rapidly from 1958 to 1963 than from 1951 to 1957. Yet during the 6-year period 1958–63, the net private long-term capital inflow into the four countries amounted to the equivalent of $3 billion (15 per cent of export earnings), almost one-fifth of the net private long-term capital flow (including long-term private export credits) from the member countries of the Organization for Economic Co-operation and Development (OECD) to all less developed countries.[2] This

---

[1] Net short-term capital flows can be obtained in Table 1 by subtracting long-term from total capital inflows. It is here assumed that errors and omissions reflect mainly unrecorded capital flows of a short-term character. This item does, however, also contain the net amount of any unrecorded current account transactions. Furthermore, some clandestine capital transactions may fail to be reflected in the entry for errors and omissions.

[2] See Organization for Economic Co-operation and Development, *The Flow of Financial Resources to Less-Developed Countries, 1956–1963* (Paris, 1964), Table IV-4, p. 134. Lack of data for the years before 1956 prevents a comparison of the ratios for the two subperiods of private investment in four selected countries to total OECD private investment in all less developed countries. However, annual U.S. private long-term investment in Latin America was less in 1958–63 than in 1951–57. Even if 1957, a year of extremely high U.S. foreign investment in Latin America (mainly in the petroleum industry), is omitted, it turns out that U.S. investment was slightly more in 1951–56 than in 1958–63. The increase in private long term investment in the four countries, from $1·6 billion in 1951–57 to $3 billion in 1958–63, is thus very likely to represent a rise relative to the supply of private long-term capital available to Latin American countries in general.

TABLE 1

SELECTED DEVELOPING COUNTRIES WITH HIGH RATES OF INFLATION: NET PRIVATE CAPITAL INFLOW AND CHANGES IN COST OF LIVING AND EXCHANGE RATES, 1951–63

	Net Private Capital Inflow				Increase in Cost of Living Index ‡	Increase in Price of Foreign Exchange	
	Amount		Proportion of Exports				
	Total *	Long-Term †	Total	Long-Term		Capital §	Commercial ‖
	(Millions of U.S. dollars)				(Per Cent)		
Argentina							
1951–63	882	1,583	7	12	1,848	846	1,665
1951–57	398	253	6	4	214	164	140
1958–63	484	1,330	7	20	520	258	636
Brazil							
1951–63	1,901	2,146	10	12	3,518	3,052	3,265
1951–57	1,118	1,057	11	10	246	360	264
1958–63	783	1,089	10	14	945	585	825
Chile							
1951–63	535	540	8	9	4,166	4,075	3,502
1951–57	101	178	3	5	1,033	961	1,058
1958–63	434	362	15	12	276	293	211
Colombia							
1951–63	11	351	—	5	194	225	299
1951–57	−181	103	—	3	54	102	112
1958–63	192	248	7	9	90	61	88

* Including net errors and omissions. A minus sign indicates a net capital outflow.
† Direct and other long-term investment.
‡ Annual averages; computed changes are from the average of 1950–51 to that of 1963–64, from the average of 1950–51 to that of 1957–58, and from the average of 1957–58 to that of 1963–64.
§ Exchange rates applicable to capital movements at the end of the year; computed changes are from year-end 1950 to year-end 1963, from year-end 1950 to year-end 1957, and from year-end 1957 to year-end 1963.
‖ Exchange rates applicable to most commercial transactions (excluding principal export commodities) at the end of the year; see also footnote § above.

Sources: Capital movements: International Monetary Fund, *Balance of Payments Yearbooks*; cost of living index, exchange rates, exports: International Monetary Fund, *International Financial Statistics*, monthly issues and Supplement 1964/65.

more inflationary period was also characterized by a substantial outflow of short-term capital from these four countries; it amounted to $1·1 billion, compared with only $150 million for the 7-year period 1951–57. This short-term capital outflow constitutes a loss of foreign exchange resources which these countries can ill afford. Nevertheless, what is surprising — in view of the financial instability of the four selected countries — is not the size of the net short-term capital outflow but rather the large magnitude of the net long-term capital inflow.

In attempting to explain why financial instability was not more of a deterrent to private foreign investment in these countries, the following section draws attention to the manner in which domestic prices and foreign exchange rates enter into the calculation of expected yeilds on foreign investment. To be sure, capital movements respond to a large number of factors which affect the yields expected by investors. Some of these, such as changes in the structure of the economy of the investee country, discoveries of mineral deposits, changes in exchange control or tax systems, the passage of investment laws, the amount of — and experience with — previous investments in the country, and, not least, the country's potential for economic growth,[1] are very likely to play a more dominant role in the investment decision than expectations of changes in prices or exchange rates. But where these changes are large, they must, after all other elements have been taken into consideration, exercise an important influence on the decisions of potential investors.

III. THE RETURN ON FOREIGN INVESTMENTS

The expectation of changes in the foreign exchange rate and in domestic prices and costs influences private capital movements, other things being equal, by altering the expected rate of return on assets which foreign investors may hold in the investee country. The next section will deal with the formation of expectations; the present section sets forth the relation between changes in prices and exchange rates, on the one hand, and the rates of return on different types of foreign investment, on the other.

In some instances, depreciation of the investee currency will

[1] See Graeme S. Dorrance, ' Inflation and Growth : The Statistical Evidence ', IMF, *Staff Papers*, vol. xiii, no. 1, March 1966.

reduce, in proportion to the depreciation, the net revenues obtained from an asset, computed in terms of the investor's currency, while domestic price increases in the investee country will not affect these net revenues. This is true in the special case of investment in a fixed-interest asset, such as a bond, denominated in the investee country's currency. This special case has often served as a starting point for the discussion of the effect on capital movements of expected changes in the exchange rate. However, in so far as capital flows from industrial to developing countries are concerned, investment in local-currency bonds is relatively unimportant. In the quantitatively much more important case of direct investment, the relation between the return on capital and the exchange rate is more complicated. Depending on the circumstances of particular industries, the returns on direct investment capital may be either raised or lowered by a depreciation of the investee currency; similarly, they may be either raised or lowered by a rise in domestic prices in the country where the investment is made.

The analysis of the effects of price changes and changes in the exchange rate may be set out in general terms for any kind of foreign investment and with allowance made for different exchange rates for various classes of transaction (multiple exchange rates). In the following discussion, the effects of exchange control provisions are left out of account; in particular, it will be assumed that earnings and capital can be freely repatriated at exchange rates applicable to these transactions. It will also be assumed that prices in the investor's country of residence remain unchanged and that the currency of that country is freely convertible at a constant par value. For simplicity's sake, the investor's currency will be called ' dollar ' and the currency of the investee country ' peso '.

The rate of return, or yield, y, of an asset is the rate of discount which makes the sum of expected future net revenues, N, equal to the present price (or cost of construction), A, of the asset.[1] The yield can be computed from the formula

$$A = \Sigma \frac{N_t}{t(1+y)^t}. \tag{1}$$

For a given present price, A, the yield will become larger or smaller when future net revenues become larger or smaller. In order to

---

[1] By 'net revenue' is meant the sum of gross receipts from the asset minus the costs incurred in realizing these receipts, such as labour and material costs and taxes; depreciation allowances are not deducted, and the initial outlay on the asset is thus assumed to be realized over the life of the asset.

416

determine the influence of changes in prices and exchange rates on the yield of the asset, it is necessary to ascertain the effects of these changes on net revenues or on the present price of the asset or on both.

As mentioned above, in the special case of a bond denominated in pesos, the net revenue expressed in dollars is simply the amount of the annual coupon earnings of the bond, and in the year in which it matures also the face value, divided by the exchange rate (defined as the price of one dollar in terms of pesos). In the general case, however, various components of the net revenue from a foreign asset may be differently affected by changes in prices and exchange rates. For instance, gross receipts from sales of an industrial or commercial enterprise may accrue partly in pesos and partly in dollars. Many companies will incur certain costs in pesos and others in dollars.

Consider, for instance, the following elements affecting the net revenue of a production enterprise (the peso values are separated into 'real' and price components):

S = gross receipts from local sales in pesos of constant purchasing power ;

p_s = index of local price of products sold (base year = 1) ;

C = cost of locally obtained labour and materials in pesos of constant purchasing power ;

p_c = index of wages and local material prices (base year = 1) ;

T = taxes paid in the investee country in pesos, assuming a constant price level ;

p_t = index indicating the increase in tax payments as a result of inflation (base year = 1) ;

$S_\$$ = gross receipts from export sales in dollars ;

r_x = exchange rate applicable to company's exports (pesos per \$1);

$C_\$$ = cost of imports for current production (not on capital account) and other current payments abroad in dollars ;

r_m = exchange rate applicable to imports and other current payments abroad (pesos per \$1) ;

$V_\$$ = valuation adjustment necessary to maintain the dollar value of the net working capital owned by the investor, expressed in dollars ; [1]

---

[1] $V_\$$ equals exchange loss, resulting from a depreciation of the peso, on net assets denominated in pesos, such as bank deposits in the investee country, or accounts receivable minus accounts payable ; where conditions permit it, such exchange losses can be avoided by raising working capital, or that part of it which is tied up in assets denominated in pesos, in the local market.

r_c = exchange rate applicable to transfers of capital and repatriation of earnings (pesos per \$1).

Net revenues in dollars, N, for a particular year of operation can be expressed as

$$N = \frac{(Sp_s - Cp_c - Tp_t) + (S_\$r_x - C_\$r_m)}{r_c} - V_\$. \tag{2}$$

In general, domestic inflation or exchange depreciation will tend to affect in two ways net revenues expressed in dollars : (1) it will alter the valuation of given 'real' transactions, such as S, C, $S_\$$, and (2) it will induce changes in these real transactions in response to the changed price or cost relationships. The argument set forth in this paper relies on the effects under (1) and leaves out of account those under (2).

In regard to changes in valuation, inflation in the host country will — if exchange rates are assumed to remain constant — tend to increase the dollar equivalent of receipts from local sales (Sp_s), of local costs (Cp_c), and probably also of local taxes (Tp_t). If, on the other hand, constant peso prices are assumed, depreciation of a unitary exchange rate ($r = r_x = r_m = r_c$) will tend to reduce the dollar equivalent of local sales, costs and taxes.[1] Under a unitary exchange rate (or under multiple exchange rates which change in the same proportion) a depreciation of the peso will not affect the dollar equivalent of given transactions which are inherently denominated in dollars, namely, proceeds from exports or costs of imported materials or services.

The effects of changes in the price and cost relations on the real transactions, whose analysis would considerably complicate the presentation, can be left out of account for two reasons. First, the present paper aims only at an identification of the direction, and not of the magnitude, of the influence on asset yields of changes in prices, costs and exchange rates. Except under unusual assumptions, the adjustments which a firm may make in its transactions in response to price changes [2] are unlikely to alter the direction of changes in asset yields which would have resulted from such price changes in the absence of these adjustments. For instance, a rise in the price of materials produced in the investee country will, other things being equal, directly lower the net revenue of manufacturing

---

[1] In addition, there may be an exchange valuation loss, i.e. $V_\$$ may be positive.
[2] The term 'price' is here used in the general sense, including prices of cost items and of foreign exchange.

enterprises that use these materials as inputs. To the extent that similar materials can be obtained from abroad, production costs may rise less than they would have in the absence of such substitution possibilities, but they will neither decline nor ordinarily remain constant.[1] In general, the ' impact effect ' of a price change on the net revenue of a company will indicate the direction, though not necessarily the magnitude, of the ultimate effect after the company has adjusted its transactions to the altered relative prices.

Second, under conditions prevailing in many less developed countries, the error introduced by judging the magnitude of the ultimate effect of a price change from its impact effect may not be very large. Substitution of foreign for domestic materials, inter-mediate products, or services in the production process is in some instances not possible at all ; in others, it is limited to a narrow range of cost items. Moreover, companies producing for the local market are often sheltered from foreign competition by quantitative import controls and are not, themselves, competitive in international markets. As a result, changes in the relation between the exchange rate and domestic prices will not ordinarily induce such substitution of competing imports for the products of local foreign investment enterprises or *vice versa*, nor large shifts of their sales between home and foreign markets, at any rate not in the short run.[2]

For these reasons, the following discussion will consider the effects of changes in prices, costs and exchange rates on the net revenue of an asset (enterprise) under the simplifying assumption that the real transactions, the volume of sales, the employment of labour, the purchase of domestic or foreign materials, etc., remain unchanged. It may also be assumed for the moment (an assumption made only for expository convenience and relaxed presently) that domestic inflation raises all relevant peso price and cost indices in the same proportion $(p=p_s=p_c=p_t)$. Under a unitary exchange rate, formula (2) can then be simplified to

$$N = N_p \frac{p}{r} + N_\$ - V_\$, \tag{3}$$

---

[1] With an unchanged exchange rate, production costs would remain constant only if (1) the supply of foreign materials were perfectly elastic with respect to price and (2) the elasticity of substitution between domestic and foreign materials were perfect. But if these conditions were met, the price of domestic materials would presumably not have risen in the first instance.

[2] To be sure, in the long run, adaptation to altered price and cost relationships may be possible through changes in the capital stock. The extent to which such long-run adaptation can occur will vary from industry to industry in accordance with technological characteristics.

where N_p represents the local net revenue in pesos $(S - C - T)$, $N_\$$ stands for the net revenue earned in dollars $(S_\$ - C_\$)$, and $V_\$$ is, as before, the working capital valuation adjustment.

Whether inflation or exchange depreciation will tend to raise or lower net revenues will depend, under the simplifying assumptions of equation (3), on the difference, N_p, between peso revenues and costs (including taxes) and on the working capital valuation adjustment. Companies producing chiefly for the local market will ordinarily have positive net peso revenues, while enterprises whose output is mainly exported will tend to have negative net peso revenues, i.e. their peso costs and taxes will exceed any peso revenues which they may derive from a small volume of local sales. An illustration of the relative magnitudes of net revenues accruing in local currency and in dollars — N_p and $N_\$$, respectively, in equation (3) — is given in Table 2 for all U.S. direct investment enterprises in the Latin American Republics in 1957, the most recent year for which these survey data are available. In that year, net revenues accruing in local currency were positive in manufacturing and in public utilities, but negative in the petroleum industry, mining and agriculture,[1] and for all industries taken together.

In the absence of exchange rate changes, inflation will raise the net revenue — and thus the rate of return on the invested capital — of enterprises selling mainly in the local market (for instance, manufacturing companies), provided that their selling prices rise at least in step with their wage and other costs and their tax payments. This effect will be particularly pronounced if an appreciable portion of their current cost items is imported from areas in which stable prices prevail. Net revenues of export-oriented firms, on the other hand, will tend to be reduced by inflation. Their local costs will rise, but their sales prices will remain constant.

The effects of exchange depreciation are just the reverse of those resulting from inflation. The dollar equivalent of the net revenue accruing in pesos will be reduced. If this net revenue is positive, for instance in a manufacturing subsidiary, the return on capital will decline, but if it is negative, e.g. in a mining company selling its output at a given world market price, the return on capital will be increased. Moreover, the portion of the working capital subject to exchange valuation adjustment of an export-oriented enterprise will ordinarily be smaller than that of a company selling in the local

---

[1] U.S. investment in Latin American agriculture is in heavily export-oriented enterprise.

U.S. Direct Investment Enterprises in Latin America: *

Sales Receipts, Costs, and Net Income in Local Currency and in Foreign Exchange, 1957 †

(In billions of U.S. dollars)

	All Industries	Petroleum	Mining	Agriculture	Manufacturing	Public Utilities
Local currency						
Revenues	4·35	1·25	0·12	0·13	2·35	0·49
Less						
Costs	4·12	1·03	0·43	0·45	1·82	0·36
Taxes	1·02	0·63	0·16	0·05	0·16	0·03
Net revenues	−0·80	−0·44	−0·46	−0·36	0·37	0·10
Foreign exchange						
Revenues	3·03	1·75	0·70	0·47	0·10	0·01
Less						
Costs	0·84	0·47	0·08	0·01	0·27	0·03
Net revenues ‡ (before depreciation and depletion allowances)	2·19	1·28	0·63	0·46	−0·17	−0·02
Depreciation and depletion allowances §	0·41	0·21	0·07	0·03	0·06	0·04
Total net revenues after depreciation and depletion allowances ‖	0·98	0·63	0·10	0·07	0·15	0·04
Memorandum items						
Revenue paid to the United States	0·81	0·57	0·09	0·05	0·06	0·03
Book value of investment	7·43	2·70	1·11	0·56	1·27	1·00

* Twenty republics.

† Items may not add to totals because of rounding.

‡ Imports other than capital equipment and fees paid abroad. The import data are incomplete; costs in foreign exchange may therefore be understated, and costs in local currency overstated.

§ In the report from which the data for this table have been taken, depreciation and depletion allowances are shown as U.S. dollar equivalents of amounts reported by companies in local currency. To the extent that proper allowance for price increases of equipment or exchange devaluation is not made in the reported figures, total net revenues after depreciation and depletion allowances may be overstated.

‖ No separate allowance is made in this table for the working capital valuation adjustment, V $, except to the extent that this item may be included under another heading in the reported accounts of the individual companies summarized in this table.

Source : Department of Commerce, *U.S. Business Investments in Foreign Countries* (Supplement to the *Survey of Current Business*) (Washington, 1960), pp. 90 and 147.

market. Its accounts receivable are presumably denominated in dollars, and its inventories consist of products awaiting sale for dollars or of materials to be used in production which will be sold for dollars ; in fact, if the company has accounts payable in pesos (e.g. tax liabilities), the valuation adjustment resulting from exchange depreciation may well be negative (indicating a valuation gain) rather than positive.

Regardless of whether a company is oriented towards exports or local sales, inflation accompanied by an exchange depreciation in the same proportion as the increases in those domestic prices and wages which are relevant for the operations of the enterprise will tend to leave net revenues expressed in dollars, and rates of return on capital, unaffected.[1] If prices rise faster than exchange rates, so that the peso becomes increasingly overvalued, yields on investment in companies selling in the local market will tend to increase ; if the opposite trend prevails, export-oriented enterprises will be favoured.

The assumption that all relevant domestic prices and costs change in the same proportion was made merely for expository convenience. Equation (2), or an even more detailed formula that could easily be set out, permits the relaxation of this assumption. For instance, public utilities are oriented towards the local market, but their net revenues are not so likely to rise during inflationary periods as those of manufacturing enterprises, since price regulation prevents their prices or service charges from being increased in step with their costs in local currency.

The assumption of a unitary exchange rate can also be relaxed in the framework of equation (2). Under a system of multiple exchange rates, the investor's dollar earnings resulting from net revenues which accrue directly in dollars may be affected by differential rate changes. A depreciation in the exchange rate applicable to the company's exports, other rates remaining unchanged, would raise net revenues, while a depreciation of the exchange rate applicable to imports of goods and services or of that governing the repatriation of earnings and capital would lower it. To the extent that, as is usually the case, exchange rates for imports and the repatriation of earnings are higher (i.e. more depreciated) than those for a country's principal exports, returns in export industries will be

---

[1] This statement must be qualified with respect to the working capital valuation adjustment : there may be an exchange loss on net financial assets denominated in pesos (though not on inventories, since the inventory valuation gain resulting from inflation offsets the exchange loss on the capital tied up in inventories).

lower than they would be under a unitary exchange rate. As a result, foreign investment in these industries will be discouraged.

In order to give an indication of the magnitude of changes in the rate of return on foreign investments brought about by changes in prices and exchange rates, the results of a few calculations based on data from Tables 1 and 2 are shown in Table 3. These calculations refer to entirely hypothetical cases: they indicate the changes in

TABLE 3

SELECTED COUNTRIES AND INDUSTRIES:
PROPORTIONATE INCREASE OR DECREASE (−) IN NET EARNINGS IN DOLLARS
OR HYPOTHETICAL FOREIGN INVESTMENT ENTERPRISES AS A RESULT
OF CHANGES IN DOMESTIC PRICES AND FOREIGN EXCHANGE RATES *

(In per cent)

	Argentina, Manufacturing	Brazil, Manufacturing	Chile, Mining	Colombia, Petroleum
1950 to 1963	260	30	†	110
1950 to 1957	130	− 30	†	120
1957 to 1963	50	90	− 100	no change

* Calculated in accordance with equation (2), page 418, assuming a (constant) distribution of revenues and costs like that given for corresponding industries in Table 2. It is assumed that local revenues, costs and taxes rise in proportion to the cost of living. For Argentina and Brazil, dollar revenues and costs are converted into pesos by the index of exchange rates applicable to commercial transactions, and total earnings in pesos are then converted into dollars by the index of exchange rates for transfers of capital and earnings (see Table 1). For Chile and Colombia, a somewhat modified version of equation (2) was employed which reflects exchange regulations with respect to mining and petroleum companies, respectively, and makes use of the special exchange rates effective for the purchase of local currency by foreign companies in these industries in the early 1950's.

Changes are based on data for 31 December of the first and last years of each period.

† Chiefly owing to the very unfavourable exchange rate in 1950, at which foreign mining companies in Chile had to convert those portions of their export proceeds which are needed to meet local expenses, application of the price index and exchange rate for 1950 to the assumed cost and revenue distribution of 1957 results in a negative net revenue for 1950. The proportionate increase in the net revenue from 1950 to 1957 and to 1963 can, therefore, not be shown. (The exchange rate for conversion into local currency of the export proceeds of large mining companies increased — i.e. depreciated — by 3,500 per cent between the end of 1950 and the end of 1957, while the cost of living index rose by somewhat more than 1,000 per cent over the same period.)

returns from direct investments in selected industries in the four countries shown in Table 1 under the assumptions (1) that the distribution of revenues and costs accruing in dollars and pesos in these industries corresponds to that found in Table 2 for U.S. direct investment enterprises in the 20 Latin American Republics in 1957 and (2) that this distribution was not affected by the relative changes in prices and exchange rates between the dates shown. As indicated above (p. 418), the assumption under (2) is not likely to correspond fully to reality. To the extent that foreign investment companies can improve their position by adjusting their transactions in view of altered price relations, their net earnings will rise more, or decline less, than is indicated by the computation in Table 3.

In the comparison of hypothetical earnings at the end of 1963 with those at the end of 1950, the joint effect of changes in prices and exchange rates is positive in each of the selected cases. For instance, in 1963 the dollar equivalent of the earnings of a manufacturing company in Brazil would be 30 per cent larger than it would have been if — with its transactions in real terms remaining unchanged — domestic prices and exchange rates had remained at their 1950 (year-end) level. The earnings of a mining company in Chile at the end of 1950, calculated on the basis of the revenue and cost distribution given in Table 2, would have been negative ; between 1950 and 1957 the position of foreign mining companies would have improved considerably, chiefly as a result of the discontinuation in 1956 of the particularly unfavourable exchange rate at which foreign mining companies had to obtain Chilean pesos to meet local operating expenses. In Argentina, the earnings of a foreign-owned manufacturing company would have increased both from 1950 to 1957 and from 1957 to 1963. In two of the other three countries, the direction of the net effect of changes in prices and exchange rates on earnings differs between the two subperiods. For instance, earnings of the export-oriented mining industry in Chile declined between 1957 and 1963 because domestic prices increased more rapidly than the exchange rate for commercial transactions, whereas this industry had been favoured by a reverse development between 1950 and 1957. The dollar equivalent of earnings of a manufacturing company in Brazil decreased from 1950 to 1957 by virtue of an excess of the rate of exchange depreciation over the rate of inflation, and increased from 1957 to 1963 because of the reverse relationship between these rates of change. While these results indicate general tendencies in earnings on foreign investment in the cases examined, the hypothetical character of the calculations should be borne in mind.

In the preceding discussion of the expected rate of return on a capital asset, it was assumed that the price or construction cost of the asset, in terms of dollars, was constant. But the cost in dollars, A, of a given investment programme will, itself, depend on the price level in the investee country and on the exchange rate. Suppose that $A_\$$ represents the cost of the equipment to be imported into the investee country plus any working capital to be supplied by the investor, and that A_p stands for the estimate in a base period of the local construction costs and other local expenses connected with the investment $(A_\$ + A_p = A)$. Some time after this base period, the expected dollar cost of the entire investment project will be

$$A_\$ + A_p \frac{p_c}{r_c}$$

where p_c and r_c are the expected index figures, relative to the base period, of local costs and of the exchange rate applicable to capital transfers.

The expectation of exchange depreciation may, by lowering the expected dollar cost, lead to a postponement of the capital expenditure until after the anticipated depreciation materializes (or until the expectation is revised).[1] On the other hand, the expectation of a constant exchange rate and rising construction costs in the investee country may cause the investor to advance expansion programmes which would otherwise have been undertaken at a later date. The extent to which such changes in timing are induced will, of course, also depend on the effect of the expected changes in local costs and exchange rates on the net operating revenue from the completed production facility.

The discussion of this section is summarized in Table 4. Non-equity investments can be treated, in the calculation of rates of return, as special cases of formula (2) above by setting the appropriate items equal to zero. The expectation of exchange depreciation brings about changes in expected yields which are likely to result in a reduction of the inflow of foreign fixed-interest capital and in an increase of the outflow of domestic capital from the country whose

---

[1] Postponement of an investment project will be advantageous if the reduction of the cost of the investment achieved thereby exceeds the difference between the net revenue which the asset would have earned and the return earned on an alternative short-term investment of the funds set aside for the project. Let the peso cost of an investment be a fraction q of the total cost, A, of the project; let its expected yield (after proper allowance for expected changes in prices and exchange rates) be y and the yield on an alternative short-term investment, e.g. Treasury bills in the investor's country, i. Other things being equal, it will be worth while to postpone the investment for one year if $p_c/r_c < 1 - (y\text{-}i)/q$. For example, if the project yields 12 per cent per annum, the Treasury bill rate is 4 per cent, and 25 per cent of the outlay for the project is in pesos, a 50 per cent expected increase (i.e. depreciation) of the exchange rate in the course of the next year will, assuming unchanged peso costs, just warrant postponement of the investment ($p_c/r_c = 0.67$; $1 - (y\text{-}i)/q = 0.68$).

exchange rate is expected to depreciate. The net effect on equity investment is not certain and will depend on the distribution of suitable projects between export-oriented and local sales-oriented industries. There is a similar uncertainty with respect to the influence on foreign equity investment of the expectation of inflation

TABLE 4

EFFECTS OF INFLATION AND EXCHANGE DEPRECIATION ON RATES OF RETURN ON FOREIGN INVESTMENT AND RESIDENTS' INVESTMENT ABROAD

	Expected Direction of Effect on Rates of Return of	
	Inflation	Exchange Depreciation *
Equity investment (direct investment and purchase of shares)		
Export-oriented industries	downward	upward
Local sales-oriented industries	upward †	downward
Fixed-interest investment (bonds and loans)		
Denominated in local currency	no effect	downward
Denominated in other currency	no effect	no effect
Residents' investment abroad	‡	upward

* Assuming a uniform exchange rate or a multiple rate system in which the relevant rates change in the same proportion.
† It is assumed that companies are able to raise local sales prices approximately in proportion to increases in costs resulting from inflation.
‡ Inflation will not affect domestic residents' returns on foreign investment, but it will raise the (nominal) returns on alternative domestic equity investments.

— abstracting from the effect of inflationary expectations on expected exchange rates — but the net outflow of domestic capital of the inflating country is likely to be reduced.

Two points should be re-emphasized. First, the effects of inflation and of exchange rate changes on yields of various assets were separately stated without regard to the likelihood that inflation would induce the expectation of exchange depreciation and *vice versa*. The interdependence of expectations with respect to a currency's internal and external purchasing power is briefly discussed in the following section. Second, the analysis was based on the assumption that exchange control is absent or, at any rate, that it does not impinge in a material way on the transactions dealt with in this paper except by prescribing the exchange rates applicable to various transactions.

IV. PRICE AND EXCHANGE RATE EXPECTATIONS

Contrary to the assumption made in the preceding section, expectations with respect to the price level and those regarding exchange rates are not mutually independent. Moreover, expectations with respect to changes in particular prices or costs, such as labour costs, materials costs, or competitors' prices, are closely related to expectations with respect to the general price level and the exchange rate. It is not intended in this section to elaborate on the factors which influence businessmen's expectations of changes in the general price level or of the future strength or weakness of the investee country's balance of payments and its exchange rate policy. But something must be said about the interdependence of expectations.

In countries where inflation has persisted for many years, foreign investors would, in the absence of good reasons to the contrary, expect a continuation of inflationary trends. Balance of payments deficits caused by moderate domestic price increases can be financed, for a more or less limited period of time, through a reduction of external reserves. In some cases, the effect of inflation on the balance of payments can be counteracted by exchange control measures. But it is neither desirable nor possible to maintain the exchange rate at a constant level in the face of rapid and prolonged inflation. Over the long run, potential investors must therefore expect that the exchange rate will be depreciated more or less in correspondence with the rise in domestic prices.

For short-run periods, however, the investor cannot safely base his forecast of exchange rate changes on this necessary longer-run correspondence between exchange rates and price levels. For one thing, the balance of payments is affected by factors other than relative prices. Grants of aid from abroad, private capital inflows, favourable crops of export products, or changes in the exchange control system may make it possible for the authorities of a country — even if external reserves are not large — to maintain the exchange rate constant for some time while domestic prices increase. In countries experiencing rapid inflation, exchange rate adjustments are generally made at considerable time intervals even though

domestic prices increase continuously. As a result, the currencies
of these countries may at times be overvalued for several years;
and after adjustment of the exchange rate, they may for some time
be undervalued. The extent of variation in the relation of domestic
prices to the foreign exchange rate in the four countries selected for
this study is shown in Table 5.

TABLE 5

SELECTED DEVELOPING COUNTRIES:

RATIOS OF COST OF LIVING INDEX TO EXCHANGE RATE INDEX,*
LOWEST AND HIGHEST ANNUAL VALUES IN INDICATED PERIOD
(1958 = 1)

	1951–57		1958–63	
	Lowest	Highest	Lowest	Highest
Argentina	1·0	2·4	1·0	2·6
Brazil	0·9	2·4	0·9	1·5
Chile	0·7	1·2	0·9	1·8
Colombia	0·9	1·7	0·9	1·4

* Exchange rate applicable to most capital movements.

Source: Based on data from International Monetary Fund, *International
Financial Statistics*.

While rapid and persistent domestic price increases make it
likely that the exchange rate will sooner or later be depreciated, the
reverse line of causation must also be considered. Exchange
depreciation results in a rise of prices, in terms of local currency, of
imported commodities and services. An exchange depreciation by
x per cent will therefore have the direct result of increasing domestic
prices by a proportion of *x* per cent which corresponds to the weight
of imported goods and services in the total national expenditure on
all goods and services. Experience has shown that, beyond this
direct effect, there will be further induced price and cost increases
resulting from the depreciation of the exchange rate, as well as wage
adjustments made necessary by the induced rise in the cost of living
index. For instance, if imports of goods and services amount to
20 per cent of the gross national product, one should ordinarily
expect domestic prices to rise by more than one-fifth, and perhaps
by as much as two-fifths, of the increase in the price of foreign
exchange.

Beyond these considerations concerning the relation between the exchange rate and the general price level, expectations with respect to changes of particular prices or costs, such as competitors' prices and labour or material costs, play an important role in the decision of the potential foreign investor. For instance, he must consider the relation between changes in the general price level, on the one hand, and changes in wage and other costs and the prices at which the company's products can be sold, on the other. During an inflationary period, wage costs often lag behind changes in prices, though in rapid and persistent inflation this lag is likely to be reduced, and it may disappear almost completely. To the extent that such a lag appears or is lengthened, real wages, and the producers' wage costs in terms of dollars, would be reduced. The real purchasing power of tax payments may also decline in the course of accelerated inflation, unless the applicable tax structure is, on balance, progressive. Reductions in real costs resulting from such lags are likely to be more important when inflation begins or when it is accelerated ; where prices rise at a nearly constant and predictable rate, these lags will tend to diminish and real costs will catch up with their long-run normal level.

The price of the product or service sold by the foreign investment enterprise in the local market can often, though not always, be raised in proportion to the company's costs. It is particularly difficult for companies in regulated industries, such as public utilities, to maintain satisfactory real earnings during inflationary periods.

Under multiple exchange rate systems, it is necessary for the investor to form a view not only of the future strength or weakness of the balance of payments but also of the probable relative changes of exchange rates applicable to various transactions. For instance, in some circumstances experience may lead investors to expect that, whereas the basic export rate would remain unchanged for some time, the rate applicable to capital transactions and the repatriation of earnings would tend to depreciate. This is likely to occur particularly when, during an inflationary period, foreign exchange for capital and earnings transactions is bought and sold at a free or relatively uncontrolled exchange rate while the export rate is maintained constant or is depreciated by less than the free rate.

Expectations are rarely held with complete certainty. An increase in the degree of uncertainty with which a particular outcome is expected ordinarily reduces the response that it evokes. Price and exchange rate instability as such may, therefore, discourage the inflow of foreign capital. This deterrent effect will be most pronounced if the relevant prices are expected to fluctuate widely and in an unpredictable manner. The instability of certain commodity prices in world markets may give rise to greater uncertainty on the part of potential investors about future yields than does the more or less steady increase in domestic prices and costs in some countries with a long history of inflation. However, as has been outlined in the preceding section, the foreign investor is concerned primarily with the ratio of the investee country's prices and costs to its exchange rate. Even in countries where domestic prices have risen steadily, this ratio has often shown wide fluctuations in the short run. The data may not permit conclusive demonstration of the deterrent effect of uncertainty on the total amount of private capital inflow into these countries over a longer time period, but fluctuations of the magnitude indicated in Table 5 in this relative-price factor, which is basic to the profit calculations of foreign investors, must be presumed to constitute an important obstacle to foreign investment, particularly where investors rely on a relatively short pay-out period.

V. SUMMARY AND CONCLUSIONS

The expectation of changes in exchange rates and in domestic prices and costs is only one of a number of elements affecting the decision to invest in a foreign country. Some of the other factors that investors must consider when deciding upon the amount and timing of foreign investments are probably given a greater weight in the decision than the price elements to which attention has been drawn in this paper.

It is, however, sometimes maintained that, other things being equal, inflation and exchange depreciation tend to discourage capital inflows and encourage capital outflows. If this argument were generally valid, countries that have experienced very rapid rates of inflation and exchange depreciation should be found to have had a net capital outflow or, at any rate, only a small capital inflow compared with more stable countries, unless they were unusually attractive to private investors on other grounds. The data for the four countries studied here — i.e. countries where the rate of inflation exceeded that in other countries for which the necessary data could be compiled — raise some doubts about this proposition.

It is argued in this paper that, with respect to the quantitatively most important component of the capital flow from industrial to developing countries, namely, direct and other equity investment, expected domestic price changes and expected changes in the exchange rate do not enter separately into the decision to invest. It is rather the ratio of domestic prices or costs to the exchange rate which determines whether a contemplated investment will be more or less profitable. In the longer run, investors have reason to expect movements in the exchange rate which follow more or less closely the changes in domestic prices in the investee country relative to prices in the industrial countries. Where the investor can take a long view of the profit potential of an investment, changes in the ratio of prices to exchange rates which are expected to be transitory will not affect the investment decision to any appreciable extent, though they may induce the investor to make particular outlays earlier or later than he would have done if stable prices and exchange rates had prevailed.

Investment projects which are undertaken with the expectation of a short pay-out period will tend to be affected to a much greater extent by the relation between expected changes in domestic prices and exchange rates. During a relatively short period (e.g. a few years), investors will not find it possible to rely on the expectation of parallel movements of prices and exchange rates. Their decisions to invest will, therefore, have to be made under some uncertainty, particularly in countries which have a history of rapid inflation and periodic exchange depreciation. This uncertainty may tend to reduce the total volume of investments of this relatively short-term kind. In addition, periods in which the ratio of prices to the exchange rate in the investee country is expected to rise will favour investment in industries supplying mainly the local market, whereas in periods when this ratio is expected to fall investment in export-oriented industries will be stimulated. If opportunities for foreign investment of both types are present in a particular country, the expectation of changes in this ratio may alter the composition of the capital inflow but, apart from the deterrent effect of the uncertainty with which the expectations are held, it will not necessarily reduce the total amount invested in the country.

These considerations may help to explain the continued large inflow of long-term capital into some countries with rapid inflation and exchange depreciation. Although the exchange rates in those countries were not always kept in line with domestic prices, investors appear to have expected that a rough correspondence between relevant domestic prices and costs and the price of foreign exchange would obtain in the long run. Moreover, in countries — for example, Argentina and Brazil — where exchange rates did not depreciate in proportion to domestic price increases in recent years, a change in the industrial composition of new foreign equity investment toward industries producing chiefly for the local market may have occurred.

Residents of the investee country, too, are likely to consider the relation between domestic prices and the exchange rate an important element in their investment decisions. Especially under conditions of rapid inflation, the expected ratio of prices of domestic assets to the price of foreign exchange will indicate whether the purchasing power of their investment will be best maintained by investing at home or abroad. When domestic prices have risen for some time relative to the exchange rate, residents may expect devaluation in the not too distant future and will, therefore, tend to shift funds abroad. Shortly after a devaluation, residents may expect an increase in domestic prices and, for a considerable period, a constant exchange rate, and will tend to repatriate their funds in order to invest them in domestic real assets. Similar considerations apply to foreigners with respect to some of the short-term funds which they employ in the country in connection with their principal business enterprises. Here again, however, numerous other factors determine the movements of short-term funds, and the mechanism just described merely causes a general tendency for short-term capital movements which may be offset by other influences.

The considerations advanced in this paper give rise to some conclusions with respect to exchange rate policy, though these are by no means novel. In comparison with the effect of exchange rate policy on the balance of payments as a whole, its impact on private capital movements is, in the long run, likely to be small. Exchange rate policy should, therefore, be determined primarily with a view toward its effect on the current account balance. Countries that, on the whole, maintain domestic price stability but have to depreciate their exchange rate at a particular juncture to correct a fundamental disequilibrium which has arisen over the years need not fear that the exchange rate alteration will have an adverse effect on investment from abroad. Provided that investors expect the new exchange rate and existing price relationships to be maintained for an indefinite period, such investment is unlikely to decline permanently, though it may shift to some extent from industries supplying the local market to export-oriented industries.

Where the exchange rate is allowed to fluctuate in response to market forces in a general environment of domestic price stability, as in Canada between 1950 and 1962, the rate is likely to remain within fairly narrow limits. Such fluctuations as do occur in these circumstances do not give rise to a large revision of the expectation of exchange rates ruling in the more distant future. Nor do they necessarily make these expectations more uncertain than they would have been under a fixed exchange rate (which is, of course, subject to possible alteration). Private long-term capital movements are in this case not likely to differ very much in amount or composition from the pattern which would have been observed under a fixed exchange rate. Short-term capital will move in and out of the economy in response to short-term expectations with respect to exchange rates, but these movements will tend to be offsetting over a longer period.

Where domestic prices are not stable, the considerations worked out earlier in this paper come into play. A policy of maintaining an overvalued exchange rate through trade and exchange restrictions for as long as it is feasible, and of changing the rate periodically whenever the pressure on the control system and the distortions in the allocation of resources become unbearable, will not only be detrimental to the efficiency of the economy but may also, by increasing the degree of uncertainty as to future exchange rates, tend to reduce the net inflow of foreign capital. While the best solution would be to eliminate the causes of domestic instability, the persistence of inflation in many developing countries makes it necessary to consider also the ' second best ' solution of minimizing the harm done by domestic instability. The exchange rate policy which is indicated from the viewpoint of maintaining reasonably orderly payments conditions on current account, and of permitting the inflationary economy to partake as much as possible of the gains from international trade and specialization, will also assure the least damage to the flow of private foreign capital into the economy. This policy is one of adjusting the exchange rate with as much continuity as possible to its long-run equilibrium level, which will, under conditions of rapid inflation, move in close correspondence with domestic prices and costs. As far as the effect on capital movements is concerned, this policy will leave the relation between various domestic prices and costs, on the one hand, and the exchange rate, on the other, as free of disturbance as is feasible under the circumstances. As a result, incentives to foreign investors will not be impaired as much as they would be under an exchange rate policy which permits substantial, and widely fluctuating, discrepancies between the internal and external purchasing power of the currency.

It is true that maintenance of an overvalued exchange rate under inflationary conditions may for some time lessen pressures for wage adjustments, since the (official) local prices of imported commodities will fail to rise in step with prices of domestic goods and services. However, since imports cannot be allowed to enter freely under these circumstances, shortages of imported goods tend to add to inflationary pressures on the demand side and to undo the mitigating effect of the overvalued exchange rate — via the official consumer price index — on wage demands. Moreover, regarded in this way an overvalued exchange rate is not an anti-inflationary device but merely an instrument for the repression of certain symptoms of inflation. Its use for this purpose adds to the inflationary tendencies by distorting the allocation of resources and diminishing the efficiency of the economy. Therefore, not much weight should be given to this particular argument against adjusting the exchange rate in accordance with changes in domestic prices.

It could be argued that, in principle, persistent overvaluation of the exchange rate would encourage foreign investment in industries oriented toward the local market — a tendency which, as such, may be considered desirable. In practice, however, it is not possible to maintain a significantly overvalued unitary exchange rate for a sufficiently long period to induce the expectation that it will continue to the time horizon of investors, because of the adverse effect of an overvalued rate on other balance of payments components. In order to attract in each period enough foreign investment to offset a *given* deficit in other balance of payments transactions, the degree of overvaluation would have to increase in successive periods so as to provide an additional incentive to foreign investors, and progressive overvaluation would result in a *rising* deficit on other balance of payments accounts.

Foreign investment could also be attracted by maintaining an overvalued exchange rate applicable to the repatriation of earnings in a multiple exchange rate system, while other rates were set so as to produce balance in the country's external transactions. Such a system of multiple exchange rates is a form of differential taxation (or subsidization) of various industries or activities. Multiple exchange rates are, however, easily altered by administrative decision. This adds to the uncertainty with which expectations regarding the relationship between the relevant domestic prices and various exchange rates are held. For this reason, it would be preferable — provided that it is feasible — to introduce any differential taxation which is thought to be desirable through tax legislation and to eschew the administrative flexibility which a multiple exchange rate system may seem to promise. Shifts in resource allocation are time consuming and costly ; they must be permitted to take place, and even encouraged, when necessary. But it should not be supposed that a multiple exchange rate system furnishes the authorities with an instrument for rapid and frequent alterations of income distribution and resource allocation, whose flexibility is not purchased at a price.

An exchange rate policy which, under inflationary conditions, ensures a reasonably close correspondence between the internal and external purchasing power of the currency will not, by itself, be able to provide for an economy all the advantages of growth in a stable environment ; but it will remove at least one source of maladjustments involving the relations between export industries and industries producing for the local market (including import-competing industries) — maladjustments which are particularly difficult to rectify once they have been allowed to persist for some time. Furthermore, such a foreign exchange policy will provide the basis for — though, of course, no assurance of — an uninterrupted flow of imported capital goods and materials necessary for continued development. Finally, it will ensure that access of the economy to private foreign resources obtained through foreign investment will not be needlessly abridged.

COMMENTS ON DR. RHOMBERG'S PAPER

BY

PROFESSOR WOLFGANG F. STOLPER
University of Michigan

DR. RHOMBERG has given us an excellent discussion of the effect of various price changes, including changes in an exchange rate, on the profitability of investments. He comes properly to the conclusion that, depending on the nature of the investment, the type of its market, and the kind of price adjustments that take place, inflation in the capital receiving country may or may not raise the profitability of private investments, and therefore may or may not stimulate the inflow of private capital. He presents two tables to show (*a*) that, in fact, high rates of inflation have been consistent with substantial net private capital inflows ; and (*b*) that total net revenues of certain U.S. investments in Latin America remained positive, in most cases because net revenue in terms of dollars exceeded net losses in terms of local currencies ; in a few cases because local currency revenues exceeded foreign currency losses.

Formula (2) which Dr. Rhomberg has developed breaks total net revenue into its components and it has the advantage that it can be further subdivided, for example, to allow for multiple exchange rates.

So far, so good. I should like to suggest a number of additional points for possible further investigation. As Dr. Rhomberg points out, in any real situation, capital movements are determined by many factors not allowed for in the formula determining net revenues ; and, as he points out, he is reduced to *a priori* reasoning. This does not reduce the value of his paper ; it does, however, reduce the value of the statistical evidence.

Thus — and this is my first point — while I am struck by Table 2 which shows that the profitability of American investments as a whole was in 1957 the resultant of an excess in terms of local currencies of cost over revenues more than offset by an excess of revenues over cost in terms of foreign currencies, and while I find the variations by type of industry shown by the data suggestive, I also find it difficult to relate this Table 2 to Table 1. The latter refers to four countries with high inflation, the former to 20 countries with varying monetary experiences. While Table 2 indicates that US investments in Latin America did all right, it is not clear what conclusions we can draw from it for the question of how inflation has in fact affected net revenues.

Secondly, Dr. Rhomberg assumes free convertibility. However, I should like to suggest for further analysis that in most cases in which we have rapid inflation we also have exchange controls, although it is true that in recent years, Latin American countries have been replacing controls with floating rates.

Exchange control adds a dimension of arbitrariness which it is not easy to discuss in a general manner. When capital flows into a country under a system of controls, there are usually guarantees about the transfer of profits and capital which affect the profitability of the investments, particularly as the exchange rate of the controlling country is likely to be overvalued. This could be subsumed under Dr. Rhomberg's formula 2, by pointing out that inflation is likely to attract foreign capital since it leads normally to high profits in terms of local currency which can be transferred at an artificially favourable rate.

Exchange control adds, however, also other rather undesirable dimensions. In the course of our meetings, it has frequently been mentioned that untied aid is better than tied aid, not only because it is cheaper but because it does not detract from the freedom of domestic policy makers. Like tied aid, exchange controls add to the difficulties of the jig-saw puzzle planners and policy makers have to solve. In addition, I suspect that the private capital that will be attracted will be slightly more shady than otherwise would be the case, while more honest investors will stay away; that it will play a game of its own to beat the regulations and to use them to increase its profits; and that indeed will hardly have any choice but to do so.

My third additional point relates to the fact that most lending countries give investment guarantees. The substantial flow of private capital which Dr. Rhomberg observes in Table 1 must surely be explained in part by the fact that the lending country stands ready to minimize losses while private capital is free to maximize profits. It would be interesting to determine the quantitative importance of this point.

Related to this is my fourth additional point: the large-scale American aid which has flowed over the years into countries like Chile or Brazil in the fifties. This has probably allowed countries like Brazil to continue with inflation while maintaining deteriorating but probably nevertheless continuously overvalued exchange rates. It also has probably assured private investors that aid will continue and that therefore risks to them are minimized.

A fifth additional point in this connection is that Mr. Rhomberg assumes that the local cost of an investment is purchased with dollars, quite properly so from the standpoint of his analysis. But suppose that the local costs are borrowed or supplied by a local partner. In this case inflation would add to profitability, particularly if the transfer at overvalued rates is guaranteed. Professor Rosenstein-Rodan has touched upon this point in another context.

Sixth, I would suggest to add to the discussion the effects of the existence or absence of foreign exchange reserves, a point related to the inflow of aid. The size of reserves must be expected to influence substantially the expectations of investors as to the future course of an exchange rate, the chances of exchange control being more or less drastically applied, and the possibility of maintaining any particular system of multiple exchange rates. Reserves also have a bearing on the ability of a country to control certain prices through possible imports.

Finally, Dr. Rhomberg concludes that, although investors will often be swayed more by considerations other than that of price (which he discusses), his analysis and such data as we have, suggest that inflation itself need not discourage capital flows — a conclusion which Professor Brown's paper also appears to sustain. Perhaps the real answer is that private investors are hopelessly optimistic people willing to take risks which more rational people would not shoulder, but sheltered from their own folly by investment guarantees and large-scale foreign aid.

DISCUSSION OF DR. RHOMBERG'S PAPER

THE principal question considered by Dr. Rhomberg is how private capital movements respond to changes or expected changes in foreign exchange rates and in domestic prices and costs. The paper also considers the effects of alternative exchange rate systems on capital flows. Dr. Rhomberg questions the usual assumption that rapid domestic inflation in developing countries, by causing expectations of exchange-rate depreciation and reduced earnings in their own currency, tends to discourage foreign investors. He found it hard to reconcile this view with continued large private capital inflow into countries experiencing rapid inflation, and suggests that factors other than exchange-rate depreciation affect expected yields. It is not inflation or exchange depreciation, but rather the expected change in domestic prices relative to expected change in the exchange rate — especially for short-term projects — that determines the decisions of foreign investors.

Professor Mundell commented that Dr. Rhomberg's paper can be considered heretical since he presents evidence that inflation has not prevented substantial capital inflows to some of the Latin American countries. But, Professor Mundell pointed out, Table 1 shows that there have also been considerable capital outflows from these countries — especially during the period 1958–63. Although it is not possible to specify the relationship between inflation and capital flows, both existed during this period in Latin America and the capital outflow was probably due to inflation. If so, it is possible that net capital inflow into these Latin American countries would have been greater without inflation.

Dr. Singer doubted the generality of Dr. Rhomberg's conclusion. The countries used as examples, he noted, are all semi-developed ; that there should be continued foreign investment in these countries despite inflation should not be surprising. Inflation and over-valuation of the exchange rate cause a shift in the internal terms of trade. Exporters are penalized, manufacturers for the domestic market subsidized. Private investments in export industries will be discouraged, import substitution encouraged. The four semi-developed countries used in the example are at the import-substitution stage. It should not be surprising, therefore, that they received large capital inflows despite inflation. *Professor Rosenstein-Rodan* added that the term 'inflation' should not be used here without qualification. The word is currently being applied to situations which diverge substantially in respect to the internal terms of trade. For instance, both Brazil and Chile had established price controls in the 1950's. Brazilian administration was inefficient and the price controls were never successfully enforced. Chile, on the other hand, enforced the controls quite effectively. As a consequence, though there was inflation in both countries,

438

price controls seriously affected the direction of investment in Chile while they did not in Brazil.

Professor Stolper observed that Table 1 shows substantial net private capital inflows have occurred despite high rates of inflation in certain Latin American countries. Table 2 indicates that the total net revenue of United States investments in certain Latin American countries remained positive since the excess of revenue over cost in terms of foreign currency was greater than the deficit in terms of local currency. Professor Stolper found it hard to relate the first Table, based on experience in four countries, with the findings presented in the second Table, detailing events in twenty countries — not all of which had undergone major inflation. *Dr. Rhomberg* replied that Table 1 was intended to show the nature of the problem. It was not intended that Table 1 and Table 2 should be related.

Dr. Faaland mentioned another point made by Dr. Rhomberg in his paper, that short-term capital movements depended on domestic prices and that in the long run these changes tend to compensate. Dr. Faaland thought that short-term capital movements quite often become long-term capital movements, and that as such they might be related to inflation and to exchange-rate policies.

Dr. Ferrer felt Dr. Rhomberg's observation that shifts in foreign investment between domestic-market and export-oriented industries are based on expectations of relative change in domestic prices and exchange rates (ratio of cost-of-living indexes to exchange-rate indexes) was valid in theory but not in practice. In both export industries and manufacturing destined for the domestic market, investment decisions are usually made by large corporations that are more likely to decide on the basis of some global strategy than on the basis of relative changes in exchange rates and domestic prices. Changes in the ratio of the domestic price index to the exchange-rate index probably affect domestic investment behaviour more than foreign investment behaviour.

Dr. Ferrer also questioned Dr. Rhomberg's use of exchange rates for financial transactions rather than exchange rates for commercial transactions in constructing his exchange-rate index for Argentina. He argued that the exchange rate for commercial transactions would have been more appropriate, and said that if it had been used the results would have been quite different. *Dr. Rhomberg* agreed that for many purposes the commercial rate would be preferable to the financial rate, but said the financial rate was used because he was concerned primarily with capital movements and this was the relevant rate from the viewpoint of profit repatriation.

While Dr. Rhomberg was careful in his paper to point out that some economies were attractive to foreign investors for reasons other than their particular exchange-rate situation, several of the discussants were concerned about a number of variables omitted in his analysis. *Professor Stolper* commented that capital movements are determined by many more factors than can be included in formulas used by Dr. Rhomberg to determine net revenues. This tends to reduce the value of statistical evidence relating to such formulas. *Professor Mundell* suggested that if there are too many variables, one ends up with no theory. *Professor Rosenstein-Rodan* preferred to reinterpret the problem. The problem for him was not one of too many variables, but of too many independent variables. He suggested that other aspects of the relationship between inflation and capital inflows should be analysed : first, the relationship between inflation and the distribution of income between profits and wages ; second, the incidence of inflation on the relative prices of capital goods and consumer goods. *Dr. Faaland* pointed out here that the figures given in Table 1 are on a net basis. He felt that something more could be learned of the influence of inflation on capital movements if such figures could be obtained on a gross basis.

Dr. Rhomberg's conclusions for exchange-rate policy were another topic of discussion. *Professor Mundell* questioned the conclusion that a country is better off in an inflationary environment with flexible exchange rates than with fixed exchange rates if distortions of the price system are to be avoided. Professor Mundell stated that this conclusion does not follow unless other economic relationships remain undistorted. In Latin America, for example, exchange rates, the prices of utilities, and interest rates all tend to be rigid under inflationary circumstances.

Dr. Ferrer questioned Dr. Rhomberg's view that exchange-rate policies should be designed to equilibrate the current account balance of payments. This may be so, but exchange-rate policy should also take into account internal reactions in the price structure and in the distribution of income that are caused by devaluation.

Professor Stolper had a more fundamental objection. He felt that the assumption of free convertibility in Dr. Rhomberg's analysis was unrealistic because rapid inflation usually brings exchange controls. While effects of exchange controls can be subsumed under Dr. Rhomberg's rate-of-return analysis, exchange controls add new dimensions of arbitrariness, increase the importance of investment guarantees and in general create new considerations which make conventional rate-of-return analysis insufficient. To the extent that investment depends upon guarantees governing the transfer of profits and capital — as in Brazil or Chile during the 1950's — inflation, overvalued exchange rates and continued inflow of foreign capital can coexist. *Dr. Rhomberg* replied that it is precisely because these guarantees exist that investors are able to concentrate more on relative rates of return in making their investment decisions.

Chapter 13

INTERNATIONAL DISEQUILIBRIUM AND THE ADJUSTMENT PROCESS

BY

PROFESSOR R. A. MUNDELL

Brookings Institution

A Cup of Tea

Nan-in, a Japanese master during the Meiji era (1868–1912), received a university professor who came to inquire about Zen. Nan-in served tea. He poured his visitor's cup full, and then kept on pouring.

The professor watched the overflow until he no longer could restrain himself. ' It is overfull. No more will go in!'

' Like this cup,' Nan-in said, ' you are full of your own opinions and speculations. How can I show you Zen unless you first empty your cup?' [1]

International monetary economics needs to follow Nan-in's advice. We have an abundance of theories, mechanisms and techniques for understanding it, but many of them seem to be no better rooted in theoretical understanding than the opinions and speculations of Nan-in's guest. Too many theories are almost as debilitating as too few. The subject has become so cluttered that it does seem necessary to empty our cups.

It would be a mistake, however, to empty out two hundred years of international trade theory and forget about it. We need instead to sift it of its extraneous elements, and to add a little of what appears to be missing. In un-Zen-like fashion, then, we can begin by taking a brief look at what has occurred since Hume, and in particular at the effects on the development of international monetary economics of the classical distinction between the monetary mechanism and the theory of barter.

[1] Paul Reps, *Zen Flesh, Zen Bones* (New York : Doubleday, 1961).

I. BARTER THEORY AND MONETARY THEORY IN INTERNATIONAL TRADE

The distinction between the short-run mechanism of balance-of-payments adjustment and the static theory of barter was an important dimension of the classical dichotomy between monetary theory and value theory. This dichotomy was a powerful tool of analytical abstraction which enabled a clear separation of long-run static analysis from short-run dynamics. In dynamical, short-run, disequilibrium theory monetary elements assume a role of first-order importance in the adjustment process. But after the adjustment process was completed money turned out to be a mere veil, with no influence upon the nature of position of long-run equilibrium. The task of exposition in classical theory, therefore, was to demonstrate the automaticity of equilibrium through examination of the adjustment process, and through this demonstration, the unimportance, in the long run, of monetary phenomena.

The demonstration of the automaticity of balance-of-payments adjustment in the field of international trade theory was a companion to, although it anteceded, the demonstration of a different kind of automaticity in value theory. In a closed economy the system tended automatically towards a full-employment equilibrium, on the premise that money wages were flexible, and it was an equilibrium not affected, in any fundamental way, by the amount of money in the system. Whatever the temporary effects of a change in central bank policy, the money supply had no influence upon the equilibrium rate of interest or the real wage. Instead, money exerted its influence merely upon the price level and the level of *money* wages. Since money could not alter either the level of real wages or the rate of interest, it could not affect the equilibrium level of any real magnitudes in the economic system, and the path was cleared for long-run analysis that could ignore monetary phenomena.

In an open economy linked to the rest of the world by international trade and the gold standard, on the other hand, the central bank could not even affect the quantity of money in the system unless the country was large enough to influence, by itself, the world price level. Whereas in a closed economy the central bank could determine the *nominal* quantity of money, and the public, through spending or hoarding it, could determine its *real* value, in an open economy any excess of new money creation over desired hoarding would escape down the foreign drain. An over-issue of money by the banking system would quickly bring its own corrective, as specie flowed out and forced the banks to take back the redundant currency, or else suffer a depreciation of the gold value of bank-notes. The nominal quantity of money was thus determined in a single economy by international considerations and the barter terms of trade could not be affected permanently by purely monetary disturbances.

To have perceived the essential truth of these propositions, which even today exhibit a fundamental truth, was a supreme intellectual achievement of classical economic analysis. Through this theory mercantilist fallacies could be refuted and the way paved for the emphasis on the doctrine of free trade and other real phenomena, the only considerations that mattered in the long run. Ricardo's love was not the short-run dynamic mechanism which he exposited so brilliantly but the long-run theory of international barter.

The success of the dichotomy proved too overwhelming—epistemologically. In the hands of the successors of Ricardo — Mill, Marshall, Taussig, Viner, Meade, Johnson, etc. — the long-run barter theory of trade developed into a carefully tooled and highly sophisticated engine of analysis. But there was no comparable theoretical development of the short-run monetary theory of the adjustment process. Whereas the barter theory of trade exploited the powerful geometric and algebraic tools that became prominent in value theory, permitting analytical developments surpassing the possible achievements of unaided intuition, international monetary economics analysis never received precise mathematical formulation. Restricted to the raw logic of verbal analysis, it could not and did not develop the rigorous base necessary for ordered progressive scientific accumulation.

This has meant that even today we have a double standard: we demand rigorous logic from practitioners of the fine art of offer curve analysis, in striking contrast to much looser standards exacted in international monetary economics. Attacking the real world from a lower level of abstraction, international monetary economics offers more of an appearance of realism than barter theory, but it is achieved at the sacrifice of precision and rigour.

This is not intended to disparage the important developments in international monetary economics in the last two decades, but only to emphasize that these developments have not succeeded in integrating, or even co-ordinating, classical monetary theory with classical barter theory. Innovations since the 1930's have concentrated on the application of Keynesian economic concepts to the international sphere, rather than on the integration of Keynesian international economics with either classical barter theory or classical international monetary economics.

To a certain extent this characteristic of the discipline has been a natural one. The 1930's witnessed simultaneously two important revolutions ; one in macro-economics, led by writers like Keynes, Hayek and Myrdal, and one in technique led by Tinbergen, Frisch, Leontief and Samuelson. What used to be called the 'new economics' took over the tools of the mathematicians, so that Keynesian economics applied to international trade inevitably assumed a mathematical flavour. In this respect the sophistication of the Keynesian theory in international monetary economics far surpassed the theoretical accomplishments of writers brought up on the older classical tradition, while the original dichotomy between monetary and barter models yet enabled the mathematicians to explore further implications of the barter model.

That bridges are necessary between the barter and the monetary models, on the one hand, and between the classical and Keynesian traditions in international economics, on the other, is as self-evident as the fact that they do not yet exist. How should money be 'added' to barter models of trade, and how can classical analysis be united with Keynesian concepts ?

The general purpose of this paper is to build a part of each bridge : specifically, to build connecting links between classical international monetary economics and the theory of barter, and between classical and Keynesian concepts and methods of analysis. The first bridge requires the development of an explicit theoretical model of the classical balance-of-payments adjustment process which can be shown to be reducible, under not implausible assumptions, to a barter model ; the second requires that the model can be stated either in the classical language of the Quantity Theory of Money, or in the Keynesian language emphasizing expenditure and income effects.

For two reasons, however, this paper does not complete either bridge. This is because of two assumptions it seems convenient to make : one is the emphasis placed on a small single economy looking outward on a large world, rather than a complete two-country model of the world economy ; the other is the assumption that the economy in question lacks a credit market. These simplifications are not damaging to the logical structure of the model, though they do limit the direct applicability of the conclusions to a small country that is underdeveloped in the sense that it lacks an important capital market.

Nevertheless, despite the pristine simplicity of the model, I would maintain that it is of direct use in analysing simple open economies, and in that spirit I have discussed the effects of devaluation, income transfers, budget deficits and reserve accumulation, and not made any attempt to conceal what I believe to be its implications for economic policy purposes.

II. A MODEL

The model owes its origin to David Hume. Based on a very simple open economy, it assumes that wealth is held primarily in the form of money and goods. The key assumption that greatly simplifies the analysis is that there is no market for securities. This assumption is a useful simplification for many of the poorer countries with undeveloped capital markets. For the richer countries we would need to take explicit account of capital markets, but for the bulk of the underdeveloped world this would be an unnecessary complication in an analysis the prime goal of which is to elucidate the balance-of-payments adjustment process.

Consider such a simple economy. The demand for money depends on money income or, assuming output is given, the price level, in accordance with the Quantity Theory of Money. The supply of money is determined by the balance of payments, either because international reserves and domestic money are the same, as under a gold specie standard, or because domestic money is rigidly linked to the stock of international reserves through the banking system.

Three conditions must be met before the system can be said to be in equilibrium. First, the supply of money must be equal to the demand for money; second, the balance of payments must be in equilibrium; and third, the demand for domestic output must equal the supply of domestic output. If the first condition were not met there would be a tendency for spending to exceed or fall short of income; if the second were not met the money supply would be increasing or decreasing; and if the third were not met the domestic price level would be rising or falling.

The significance of the equilibrium conditions can be seen diagrammatically. First let us represent the Quantity Theory of Money

by placing on one axis the quantity of money, M, and on the other
axis, the domestic price level, P.   The line LL portrays the amount
of money that would be demanded at each price level.   Thus at a
price level equal to OP_1,the demand for money is OM_1 ; and at a
price level equal to OP_2, the demand for money is OM_2.   Normally
LL will have an elasticity exceeding unity on the assumption of the
'homogeneity postulate' of economic theory, because a proportionate change in the price level implies a less than proportionate
increase in the demand for money when the price of all imported
goods remains constant ; for this reason LL should point above
rather than directly towards the origin.

Every point in Figure 1 corresponds to a particular combination
of money and price level.   For example, at the point G, the price

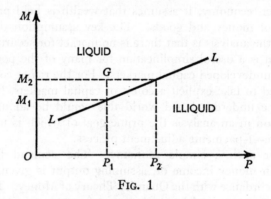

FIG. 1

level is OP_1, and the actual quantity of money is OM_2. G is not
equilibrium point, for it implies inequality between the demand for
money and the supply of money.   At G there is an excess supply of
money equal to M_1M_2.   Only if the supply of money were reduced
to OM_1 would the demand for money be equal to the supply of
money at the price level OP_1 ; or only if the price level were at OP_2
would the demand for money be equal to the supply of money OM_2.

Only points on LL are equilibrium points.   Above and to the left
of LL the supply of money is greater than the demand for money,
and below and to the right of LL the demand for money is greater
than the supply of money.   The area above and left of LL is an
area of excess liquidity, and the area below and right of LL is a zone
of liquidity scarcity.   I shall refer to the first zone as 'liquid' and
to the second zone as 'illiquid'.

From the characterization of the two zones we may now ask what happens when there is an excess or deficient level of liquidity. This is a question in economic dynamics, and can only be answered by reference to observable behaviour. But some progress can be made by noting what an excess demand or supply of liquidity means. The community holds money and goods, so that if they have an excess demand for money they must also have an excess supply of goods, just as an excess supply of money means that they have an excess demand for goods ; this follows because an excess demand for something, on the part of an individual or firm or the community as a whole, must have its counterpart in an excess supply of something else, since a *quid pro quo* has to be offered for any demand made effective on the market. This proposition follows from Walras' Law, which states that the sum of the excess demands for every economic object including money is zero for any individual economic agent.

We have not yet stated what happens in a position of excess or deficient liquidity, although we have found a clue. When there is an excess supply of money there is an excess demand for goods, and this will mean that if increased supplies are not forthcoming prices will rise. And similarly, when there is an excess demand for money there also is an excess supply of goods so prices will tend to fall if no additional supplies are available.

It is important to notice at this point, however, that it would not be valid to assert that the price level tends to rise depending on whether there is excess or deficient liquidity. However valid this dynamic postulate would be in a closed economy, it is incorrect in an open economy. An excess supply of money implies an excess demand for goods *in general* and an excess of expenditure over income, but the *domestic* price level would only be pushed up in so far as the excess of expenditure reflected an excess demand for *domestic* goods. In so far as an excess demand for goods can be reflected in an excess demand for imports the price level will have no tendency to rise. Indeed, as will become clear in the subsequent analysis, an excess of liquidity is entirely consistent with deflationary pressure in the market for home goods and services.[1]

---

[1] In what follows I assume that any excess demand for foreign goods (imports) is automatically satisfied in order to avoid complicating the analysis with the otherwise necessary distinction between the *ex ante* and *ex post* balance of payments ; this assumption would be realistic enough if importers kept sufficient stocks on hand to satisfy any incipient excess demand, and were willing to accumulate stocks (and reduce orders correspondingly) in the event of any excess supply.

Domestic expenditure (expenditure by domestic residents on both home and foreign-produced goods) is assumed to depend on income (defined as domestic output times its price) and the state of liquidity. Specifically, I assume that expenditure equals income if the community is satisfied to hold the existing stock of money, and that any excess of expenditure [1] over income is proportionate to the excess supply of money. Thus, an excess supply of money means that expenditure exceeds income, as the community tries to rid itself of excess cash holdings ; and similarly, an excess demand for money means that expenditure falls short of income, as the community tries to build up its cash holdings.

According to this assumption, expenditure equals income only when the demand for money is equal to the supply of money, so we can describe the condition of balance between the two by the *LL* line in Figure 1, except that we now have an additional interpretation of it. Not only is *LL* the line along which the demand for money is equal to the supply of money, it is also the line along which money expenditure is equal to money income.

We next place in the diagram (Figure 2) a line *BB* expressing the locus of combinations of the price level and the balance of payments, which, assuming for now no capital imports, is equivalent to the balance of trade. I assume that the balance of trade depends both on domestic expenditure and the price level. As we shall see this means that the slope of *BB* will normally be negative.

To see why the slope is negative consider the point *Q*, where income equals expenditure (because *Q* is on *LL*) and where the balance of payments is in equilibrium (because *Q* is on *BB*) ; and suppose from *Q* the money supply is increased by *QW*. At *W* there is an excess supply of money so that expenditure increases and exceeds income. Part of the increase in expenditure falls on imports so that at *W* there is a balance-of-payments deficit.

To correct the deficit the domestic price level can be lowered to shift both domestic and foreign demand away from foreign products on to domestic products. There must be some lower price level at which the balance of trade will again be in equilibrium if the system is stable. In the diagram this point is taken to be the point *Z*.

We now have two schedules which intersect at an equilibrium

---

[1] Expenditure in this sense of course is defined in the sense of a schedule rather than as an actual realized magnitude. An expenditure function of this sort was used by S. J. Prais in ' Some Mathematical Notes on the Quantity Theory of Money in an Open Economy ', IMF *Staff Papers*, vol. viii, no. 2 (May 1961), and is a novelty that deserves wider application.

point, Q, at which the system will rest if it is stable. We could now proceed to an examination of the dynamics. However, we lack one of the basic ingredients for it. We know that the money supply will increase or decrease according to whether the balance of payments is positive or negative, but we do not yet know the conditions under

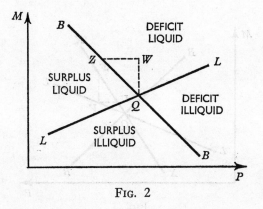

Fig. 2

which the price level will rise or fall. We need also to find the locus of combinations of money and prices at which there is no excess demand for domestic goods.

Can we derive this additional line independently of the LL and BB lines? Definitely not, for there can be only one point in the diagram that is an equilibrium point. Q is already established as the equilibrium so that the line along which there is no excess demand for domestic goods (which we shall denote as the XX line) must pass through the point Q. The XX line is not independent of the other two lines and can in fact be derived from them.

The excess demand for domestic goods is the difference between the sum of foreign and domestic demands for domestic goods and the level of output, and this is equivalent to domestic expenditure minus imports plus exports minus income, when these variables are all expressed in real terms. In other words the excess demand for domestic goods is equal to the difference between the sum of domestic expenditure plus the balance of trade, and income. Thus, by 'adding' the BB and LL curves we get the XX curve, the locus of money and price levels along which there is no excess demand for domestic goods.

It is easy to determine the position of XX in Figure 3. It must

449

have a positive slope that is steeper than *LL*. To demonstrate this fact let *E* = expenditure, *Y* = income and *B* = the balance of trade.

Now consider, in Figure 3, the point *V* on *LL*. At *V*, *E* = *Y*, so the excess demand for domestic goods ($X = E + B - Y$) is equal to the balance of trade surplus (*B*). But *B* is negative since *V* is in the deficit zone above and right of *BB*. Hence, there is excess supply

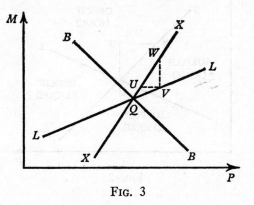

Fig. 3

of domestic goods which can be corrected only by a decrease in the domestic price level or a liquidity-induced increase in expenditure. Thus in Figure 3, an increase in the money supply of *VW* would eliminate the excess demand for domestic goods as would a decrease in the price level by the amount UV.

III. THE ANATOMY OF DISEQUILIBRIUM AND DYNAMICS

Having established the new line *XX*, as derived from the *BB* and *LL* lines, we can note that we could have begun with any two of the lines in order to get the third line. Knowing *XX* and *BB* we can deduce *LL*; knowing *LL* and *XX* we can deduce *BB*; and knowing *BB* and *LL* we can deduce *XX* (as we did in fact). No one of the lines has any priority over the other.

The interdependence of the three curves does not mean, however, that it is not useful to keep all three of the curves in mind. For instead of the four zones of Figure 2 we now have six zones in Figure 3 — repeated in Figure 4. The elaboration of the meaning of these zones can help us to anatomize exactly the nature of the disequilibrium. The six zones are characterized by the state of

EXCESS LIQUIDITY	(*L*)
THE BALANCE OF PAYMENTS	(*B*)
INFLATIONARY PRESSURE	(*X*)

which are denoted positive or negative by the inequality signs in Figure 4.

The zones are useful for policy purposes because they help to determine the direction in which the money supply or price level

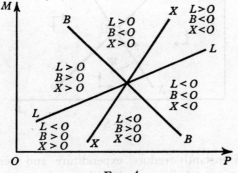

FIG. 4

should be adjusted to reach equilibrium. Thus, if we observe a situation in which *B*<*O* and *X*>*O*, we know that the money supply must be reduced; if *B*<*O* and *X*<*O*, the price level must be reduced; if *B*>*O* and *X*<*O* the money supply must be increased; and if *B*>*O* and *X*>*O* the price level must be increased. We can observe the disequilibrium situation, and, even though we be ignorant of the exact shapes of the curves, deduce the direction in which the money supply and the domestic price level have to move to restore equilibrium.

The development of the *XX* line along with the anatomy of disequilibrium zones allow greater precision in formulating the dynamics of the system. It can be postulated that the money supply increases or decreases according to whether the balance of payments is in surplus or deficit, and that the price level rises or falls according to whether there is inflationary or deflationary pressure (excess demand or supply of domestic goods). In other words the line demarcating price level increases from price level decreases over time is the *XX* line and that distinguishing increases from decreases in the money supply is the *BB* line. The dynamic forces are indicated by the arrows in Figure 5.

From a disequilibrium point like *W*, which could ensue from an 'annihilation' of part of the money supply, following the famous experiment first considered by Hume, the reduction in the money

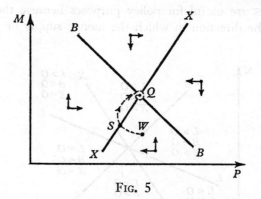

FIG. 5

supply would instantly reduce expenditure and hence imports. This would immediately improve the balance of payments and induce a replenishment of the money supply. (Unlike Hume's analysis, the present model shows that money can have a direct effect on the balance of payments through its immediate impact on expenditure, part of which inevitably falls on imported goods.[1]) From *W* deflationary pressure forces the price level down and the balance of payments surplus stimulates a monetary expansion, both forces moving the path of money and prices to a point like *S* on the *XX* line. After *S* the system travels to the equilibrium *Q* either directly or in a spiral, as indicated in the diagram.[2]

[1] I consider this immediate effect of a reduction in the money supply on the balance of payments as of the utmost importance in the adjustment mechanism, the empirical significance of which was amply illustrated by credit restraint in Italy in 1964.
[2] Strictly speaking *Q* would no longer be the equilibrium if (*a*) the initial disturbance implied a change in the real wealth position of the country (as it would if foreign exchange reserves were 'annihilated' with no *quid pro quo*); (*b*) the process of restoring equilibrium itself influenced capital formation and real wealth (so-called 'hysteresis' effects); or (*c*) the domestic disequilibrium caused a permanent change in foreign wealth positions. In this paper, where emphasis is placed on elementary mechanisms alone, it seems entirely legitimate to abstract from these considerations.

IV. THE CLASSICAL CASE AND DEVALUATION

In developing the model we began with the Quantity Theory of Money; but in the dynamic computation it was shunted into the background. To be sure, it is implicit in the XX and BB schedules, since these curves depend on expenditure which in turn depends on the excess demand or supply of money. But does it not deserve more explicit prominence? Does LL not have direct relevance?

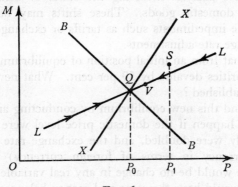

Fig. 6

Its importance asserts itself in another form than in stability analysis: in the solution of all those comparative statics questions that involve shifts of demand between domestic and foreign goods without any alteration in the demand for money, and it preserves its importance even for dynamic analysis in the special case where the community maintains equality of expenditure and income, a case which can be identified most closely with classical analysis.

To investigate this interesting dynamic phenomenon first, consider Figure 6, where it is assumed that spending is always equal to income. Equality of E and Y automatically implies that the excess demand for domestic goods (the degree of inflationary pressure) equals the balance of payments surplus. The dynamic path therefore always remains on the LL line and adjustment consists solely of moving up or down the LL line. Under these conditions we should observe a strict conformity of money and the price level (or money income if allowance is made for output charges) to the quantity theory equation.

The special case in which spending is always equal to income, and in which the demand for money is always equal to the supply of money, may properly be designated the classical case : it amounts to the assumption of Say's Law and is the case in which the separation of real from monetary phenomenon is exact. An excess demand for domestic goods is equal to the balance of trade deficit, the one case in which direct one-to-one correspondence between monetary analysis and pure barter analysis can be established.

The Quantity Theory and the *LL* line has further uses in comparative statics analysis involving the shifts of demand between foreign and domestic goods. These shifts may be induced by artificial trade impediments such as tariffs or exchange restrictions, or by exchange rate adjustments.

Suppose that from an initial position of equilibrium at Q (Figure 5), the authorities devalue by 50 per cent. What new equilibrium would be established ?

We may find this new equilibrium by conducting an experiment. What would happen if the domestic price level were doubled, the money supply were doubled, and the exchange rate (the price of domestic currency in terms of foreign currency) were halved. Clearly there would be no change in any real variable since market participants would have the same real money balances and incomes as before, and there would have been no change in relative prices.

Devaluation from a position of equilibrium will in fact *induce* a proportionate increase in the price level and the money supply. Again the relation between money and prices will be unaltered as predicted by the Quantity Theory. For example, a devaluation, in Figure 6, in the proportion of $\dfrac{P_0 P_1}{OP_0}$ would induce a rise in the price level and the money supply to the levels indicated by S, a point above *LL* along a ray from the origin, OQ extended.

It is hardly necessary to point out, of course, that no country would need to devalue if it were already in equilibrium (unless it needed to accumulate exchange reserves). The usefulness of the analysis is rather in showing what *disequilibria* can be corrected by changes in the exchange rate. We may reverse the procedure and suppose that equilibrium levels of money and prices are at Q, but that the price level and the money supply are actually at levels indicated by S. Obviously a deflationary process would reduce the price level and the money supply to Q under the automatic fixed exchange rate adjustment process. But the deflation involved may be a painful process, and certainly would be if rigidity of factor prices meant that deflation would imply unemployment. This can be avoided by a devaluation of the proportion P_0P_1/OP_0 (without any accompanying change in the money supply or the price level). Instead of bringing Mahomet to the mountain, we bring the mountain to Mahomet.

V. APPLICATION TO BUDGETARY POLICY

Still another reason why the LL line is of great importance is in the analysis of *disequilibrium policies*. Suppose the government runs a budget deficit annually, which it finances by money creation. What new ' equilibrium ' will be established ?

To analyse this question we have to go back to the basic equilibrium conditions implicit in the system and introduce government spending, supposing this to be financed solely by money creation ; [1] and a central bank equation determining the money supply. First we have the condition of equilibrium in the home goods market, namely :

$$Y = E + B + G \qquad (1)$$

where E (domestic expenditure) is defined exclusive of G (government expenditure). Next we have a definition of the relation between exchange reserves and the balance of trade, namely,

$$B = \frac{dR}{dt} \qquad (2)$$

where R represents international reserves. And finally we have the banking condition stating that the increase in banking assets is equal to the increase in banking liabilities (the money supply), noting that in this system of no lending and, for simplicity assuming no taxes, the banking authorities, merged with the government, can only hold goods or foreign reserves. Thus

$$G + \frac{dR}{dt} = \frac{dM}{dt} \qquad (3)$$

remembering that G represents both government spending and the budget deficit. Now if the domestic goods market is in balance (i.e.

[1] Government spending may be partially financed by taxes, but there is no need to introduce even this minor complication to establish the theoretical conclusion.

if equation (1) is satisfied), the price level must be constant, which in turn implies from the quantity theory and the condition that total expenditure equals income, that the money supply must be constant. Hence.

$$\frac{dM}{dt}=0 \quad \text{(4) and therefore} \quad G+\frac{dR}{dt}=0. \quad (5)$$

This in turn implies, taking account of equation (2) that $G+B=0$ so that the balance of payments deficit is exactly equal to the deficit in the government budget.

Consider the point V in Figure 6. This precisely describes the quasi-equilibrium that results from a budget deficit financed by money creation. The money supply is constant, but this is because the increase in domestic assets of the banking and government sector is exactly matched by a decrease in the private assets of that sector. The government, which may initially try to finance its deficit by creating more money, finds that its deficit is really being financed out of foreign exchange reserves ; in every other respect the system is in equilibrium. Of course the process cannot go on forever, because exchange reserves are not inexhaustible, and in that sense the position V is only a quasi-equilibrium.

By a similar analysis it is easy to see that by means of a budget surplus a country can attract reserves at a rate equal to a budget surplus of the government, after all other markets and sectors have adjusted.

VI. ANALYSIS OF THE TRANSFER PROBLEM

We may consider next how analysis of the transfer problem fits into the model. When there are international transfers the equations of equilibrium have to be supplemented. Instead of the equations

$$Y-E=B$$

establishing equilibrium in the market for goods and services ;

$$Y-E=O \quad \text{or} \quad M-L=O$$

establishing equality of expenditure and income or equality of demand for money (L) and supply of money (M); and

$$B=O$$

specifying balance of payments equilibrium ; we must have

$$Y - E = B \qquad (6)$$

as before, for the market for domestic goods and services, but then

$$Y - E = T \qquad (7)$$

for equality of income and expenditure plus transfers abroad (Y being defined as before exclusive of transfers), where T represents net outward transfers ; and

$$B - T = O \qquad (8)$$

establishing balance of payments equilibrium, i.e. equality of the balance of trade surplus and outward transfers (or net capital exports).

To illustrate the transfer process let us consider the effect of an inward transfer so that T is negative ; the country receives foreign aid or borrows. Following the traditional transfer analysis, expenditure in the rest of the world falls, and expenditure at home rises, by the full amount of the transfer directly affecting the balance of trade. Part of the decrease in expenditure abroad reduces exports, and part of the increased expenditure at home increases imports. The financial transfer gets at least partly effected in real terms by the direct impact of the expenditure changes before any effects have been felt on the balance of payments.

Whether the financial transfer is over-effected or under-effected depends on the size of the marginal propensities to spend on imports, as compared to home goods, out of domestic expenditure inclusive of the transfer. If the marginal propensity to consume domestic goods in the receiving country exceeds the foreign marginal propensity to import, the result of the transfer will be an excess demand for domestic goods and a surplus in the balance of payments, which will induce an increase in the domestic price level as money flows in. In other words, a position on the LL line up and to the right of Q will be the new equilibrium.

If, on the other hand, the marginal propensity to consume domestic goods in the receiving country is less than the foreign marginal propensity to import, the primary effect of the transfer is to shift demand away from domestic goods, worsen the balance of payments, and induce a fall in domestic prices as the money supply declines.

In the intermediate case where the domestic marginal propensity to consume domestic goods is equal to the foreign marginal propensity to import there is no change in the price level or the terms of trade. The expenditure changes ensuing directly from the transfer are the same as the final effects ; the receiving country buys, as a result of the transfer, just those goods which the rest of the world gives up.

Thus, even in the case where monetary elements are explicitly introduced into the transfer analysis, the effect of the transfer on the terms of trade is ambiguous. Nothing *a priori* can be asserted. There is no reason to suppose, unless aid is 'tied' or without specific empirical information, that the receiving country gains by more or less than the normal amount of the transfer.[1]

VII. GROWTH AND LIQUIDITY

In a growing economy the money supply will be rising over time and with it probably the willingness of the monetary authorities to acquire reserves. In this case we can relate the budget deficit or surplus to the rate of growth.

First note that if the non-government sector of the community wants to accumulate money, it must spend less than it earns so that

$$Y - E = \frac{dL}{dt} \tag{9}$$

where L is the willingness to hold money and $\frac{dL}{dt}$ is the increase of L over time.

Next recall that a balance of trade surplus results in an increase in reserves so that

$$B = \frac{dR}{dt}. \tag{10}$$

Finally, note the condition that increases in official foreign and domestic assets (net public spending) equal increases in monetary liabilities (the money supply) so that, as before,

[1] This conclusion would have to be altered if it were assumed that the demand for the stock of money in each country were itself dependent, not only on the value of domestic production, but national income, inclusive of the transfer from abroad ; the correct assumption is likely to depend on the particular case, and past nature of the transfer, and in particular whether working balances arising from the use to which the capital import is put are held in foreign currency or in domestic currency.

$$\frac{dR}{dt} + G = \frac{dM}{dt}. \tag{11}$$

Then it follows that when $\frac{dM}{dt} = \frac{dL}{dt}$, i.e. when the community's desires for additional money are satiated at existing prices, there is also equilibrium in the market for goods and services, since

$$Y - E - B - G = \frac{dL}{dt} - \frac{dM}{dt}. \tag{12}$$

Now suppose as before that $L = kY$, the demand for money according to the Quantity Theory, so that

$$\frac{dL}{dt} = k\frac{dY}{dt}. \tag{13}$$

We also have from (10) and (11) that

$$\frac{dM}{dt} = B + G \tag{14}$$

so that growth equilibrium requires

$$B + G = k\frac{dY}{dt} = k\left(\frac{1}{Y}\frac{dY}{dt}\right)Y = k\lambda Y \tag{15}$$

where λ is the rate of growth of output. If the rate of growth is positive the budget deficit will no longer equal the balance of trade surplus. The sum, $B + G$, must equal the resources sacrificed by the private sector to build up its cash balances over time.

Now assume that the authorities want to keep a fixed proportion of reserves to back domestic money creation so that

$$R = aM \tag{16}$$

where a is a fraction. Then, by differentiation with respect to time,

$$\frac{dR}{dt} = a\frac{dM}{dt} \tag{17}$$

so that, if we substitute for $\frac{dR}{dt}$ making use of (11) we get

$$G = (1 - a)\frac{dM}{dt} \tag{18}$$

or $\qquad\qquad\qquad\qquad G = (1 - a)k\lambda Y \tag{19}$

459

after making use of (14) and (15). If (19) is now put in (15) we get

$$B = ak\lambda Y \quad \text{or} \quad \frac{B}{Y} = ak\lambda. \tag{20}$$

In other words the balance of trade surplus, as a proportion of income, that is required to satisfy both the community's appetite for money and the authorities' appetite for reserves, is proportionate to the rate of growth, the factor of proportionality being ak, the ratio of foreign reserves to national income.

But we must take account of the fact that interest may be paid on the foreign reserves held by the monetary authorities; let us assume it is paid at the rate r. Then interest becomes a foreign exchange receipt and the balance of payments equation, instead of (10), becomes

$$B + rR = \frac{dR}{dt}. \tag{21}$$

The increase in the money supply is then determined by the equation

$$G + \frac{dR}{dt} = rR + \frac{dM}{dt} \tag{22}$$

since the interest payments now represent a source of government finance additional to money creation. In this case the required balance of trade, as a proportion of national income, turns out to be

$$\frac{B}{Y} = (\lambda - r)ak \tag{23}$$

while the budget deficit is

$$\frac{G}{Y} = -(\lambda - r)ak. \tag{24}$$

To summarize, the balance of trade must be positive or negative, for monetary growth equilibrium, including growth of exchange reserves, depending on whether the domestic rate of growth exceeds or falls short of the rate of interest paid on foreign exchange reserves. By leaving its reserves on deposit, in a foreign centre such as New York or London, a country may well finance the bulk of its additional reserves needs.

VIII. CONCLUSION

In this paper I have attempted to clothe some of the theoretical conclusions of international trade theory in a formal monetary garb by means of a simple model simultaneously classical and Keynesian in spirit. The basic assumption, that there are no securities, means that monetary and fiscal policies are not distinct from one another and that balance of payments problems persist because of the failure of the authorities to balance the budget. While this assumption does not correspond to reality in a country with a highly developed capital market, I do believe that it fits fairly accurately the position of many of the less developed countries.

Devaluation is a means by which a country, whose prices and costs have got out of line internationally, can restore equilibrium without the less attractive alternatives of deflation or exchange controls. Bygones have to be accepted as bygones. However, looking prospectively rather than retrospectively, incipient deficits can be prevented by a momentary policy which is directed at preserving equilibrium in the balance of payments rather than at financing budget deficits.

International capital movements or foreign aid need not present balance of payments difficulties for either the receiving or transferring country. The bulk of the transfer may be effected in real terms by direct expenditure effects except when propensities to import are low and may even be over-effected when marginal propensities are high. This leaves only a residual gap to be corrected by the adjustment process.

A growing country should make some provision for increasing its international reserves over time to provide the extra safety, convenience, choice of adjustment measures and cushioning desirable. But a secular growth of reserves does not require a balance of trade surplus if reserves are held in the liquid assets of a deposit centre and interest is paid on them. In this connection, it should be remarked that the attachment to a major currency area such as the dollar area or a sterling area presents, for a smaller country, an opportunity that many current plans for international monetary reform do not provide.

As a rule of thumb for a growing country, provision should be made for an increase in the money supply every year. But the proper rule is not to fix attention on a constant rate of growth of the money supply. Instead, the authorities should keep in mind a rate of central bank *credit expansion* more or less equal to the rate of growth after making due allowance for income elasticities of credit demand differing from unity. This leaves room for the adjustment process to operate under fixed exchange rates since it implies that the money supply will grow at a slower or faster rate than central bank credit expansion, depending on whether there is a deficit or surplus in the balance of payments.

Fixed exchange rates, coupled with an absence of controls and a monetary policy that pays close attention to the balance of payments, can be a powerful instrument for generating the confidence needed to attract foreign capital. For the smaller countries there is no alternative system better adapted for generating a climate in which rapid growth can take place. It is difficult to see how the policies currently adopted by many of the smaller less developed countries, with the proliferation of controls, inflated budgets and excessive inflation,[1] can be conducive to attracting needed capital imports or encouraging private investment to proceed in a stable environment of confidence. A restoration of freer markets fewer controls over the private sector of the economy, and greater automaticity in the balance of payments adjustment process could become symbols of a properly run, efficiently managed country.

COMMENTS ON PROFESSOR MUNDELL'S PAPER

BY

Dr. J. MARCUS FLEMING
International Monetary Fund

PROFESSOR MUNDELL begins, with the self-confidence of a true Zen master, by telling us to empty our cups of all we thought we knew about international monetary economics in order to receive the milk — or rather the green tea — of the true doctrine. Before accepting this somewhat Messianic claim, however, and bending our heads meekly to receive the thwacks of his mathematical 'hossu', we ought, I think, to ask ourselves the question, 'What is so special about Mundell's Zen?'

---

[1] I have discussed the growth argument for inflationary finance in 'Growth, Stability and Inflationary Finance', *Journal of Political Economy*, lxxiii, no. 2 (April 1965), 97–109.

The paper before us, like the body of the Buddha, manifests itself at three levels — the level of disequilibrium analysis, or Sambhogakaya, the level of comparative equilibrium analysis, or Dharmakaya, and the level of policy prescription, or Nirmanakaya. (The meaning I attach to these terms will be explained anon.)

Now, in the world of disequilibrium analysis, things are not exactly what they seem. It is a strange world, composed partly of *ex post* realities, like Imports, Exports, Prices, and Incomes, and partly of visionary entities of an *ex ante* character such as Expenditure, which is really a piece of wishful thinking, but nevertheless has magnitude and mixes happily with the real entities in Mundell's equations and diagrams.

The crucial relationship to which I would direct your attention is equation (3). This equation says that Excess Demand, which is a phantom, is equal to the Balance of Trade, *less* Income, both of which would appear to be real, *plus* Expenditure. Now, of course, Expenditure cannot be a reality, otherwise, with the ordinary macro-economic definitions, the phantom on the left-hand side of the equation would have to disappear and become zero. So Expenditure has to be a phantom too. And that is what it is, both in equation (3) and in equation (2). Now I must admit to being rather allergic to this kind of disequilibrium analysis, though I admit it has a respectable ancestry in economic thought. In Buddhist lore, this realm is called the Body of Enjoyment, or the Body of Enlightenment, but while I enjoy it I don't feel entirely enlightened.

In particular, I want to know how this X, the visionary entity on the left-hand side of equation (3), manifests itself. Because it is something which is supposed to *be* there, if only in the mind, at a moment of time. And the precise *manner* of its being there might influence, for example, its effect on Prices, or the effect of Expenditure on the Balance of Payments. Now, though Mundell is never quite precise on the point, a positive X, a state of Excess Demand, presumably means a state of shortage or scarcity when people can't get all the goods they want to buy, and prices are, therefore, rising. Even in this case I have difficulties with the concept of E, or *ex ante* Expenditure as an aggregate. Is it the aggregate of the amounts people would like to spend on each good, assuming other goods to remain scarce, or is it the total amount people would like to spend if there were no scarcities? In the latter case it is not certain that the presence of shortages would necessarily involve such a discrepancy between Expenditure *ex ante* and Expenditure *ex post*; so long as a substantial sector of supply, namely the import sector, is free from shortages, it is quite possible that aggregate Expenditure will not be curtailed, but merely diverted from its preferred objects. In that event, X in equation (3) would equal zero. Nevertheless, there would be shortages and rising prices in the home market.

Similar ambiguities arise when one considers a negative X, a state of Excess Supply. It could mean a state in which demand for and supply of home-produced goods was less than the potential supply of such goods. There is, however, only one casual reference (on p. 450) to the possibility of quantity declines. In general, Mundell appears to assume a full employment economy in which the only meaning that can be given to Excess Supply is that there is an involuntary accumulation of inventories that is excluded from the concept of *ex ante* Expenditure but not from Income. One could wish that Professor Mundell had ventured a little more deeply into what he calls 'the cluttered clouds of verbal analysis'. If he had, however, it might have raised doubts as to the realism, even in developing countries, of a model in which there is full employment but in which prices are sufficiently sticky over a sufficiently wide range to permit significant discrepancies between demand and supply for goods and services — discrepancies sufficiently great to have significant effects on the balance of payments.

There are other aspects of equation (2) that make me uneasy. That equation says that *ex ante* Expenditure will exceed or fall short of Income only if the Supply of Money exceeds, or falls short of, the Demand for it. But in the equilibrium equations (8) and (12) we are told that in a growth situation Expenditure — which is here both *ex ante* and *ex post* — will fall short of Income by an amount corresponding to the rate of increase in the Demand for Money, L, which, in turn, is proportionate to the rate of growth of Income. Should this not also apply in disequilibrium situations even in the absence of growth? That is, in equation (2) should not the excess of Expenditure over Income depend on the *rate of change* of the Demand for Money as well as on the absolute difference between the Supply of Money and the Demand for it? Precisely because it is a disequilibrium situation, Income and hence the Demand for Money may well be rising or falling.

At this point I would like to make an allusion to the diagrams illustrating the adjustment process. What I would like to call 'Mundell's mandalas' are always worthy objects of contemplation, and Figure 5, which illustrates the adjustment process, is no exception. However, the enlightenment they produce may be deceptive. Lines such as the BB line, representing external equilibrium, and the XX line, representing internal equilibrium, are derived from a combination of several equations so that before you can understand their slope you have to understand a substantial part of the system whose operation they are meant to illustrate. For my part, I fear I do not understand the system well enough to know whether the slopes of the XX and BB lines, together with the rightward veering of the path of adjustment, are necessarily such that the system, when disturbed, is bound to reach equilibrium, whether through a process of damped oscillation or otherwise. Suppose, for example, that the BB line were practically vertical, because the balance of payments was not influenced to any significant extent by Money or Expenditure directly but only by Prices or Incomes ; but that the XX line were positively sloped because Money did influence the desire to spend and the pressure of demand on supply in the home market. The situation is illustrated in Chart 1 below, which is a variant of Mundell's Figure 5. In this case, would it not be possible to have widening oscillations despite the inward-curling tendency of the path of adjustment? I just don't know. On these matters even Zen masters sometimes nod. For example, I shall argue in a moment that the *BB* curves need not, as argued in page 448, have a negative slope at all.

Professor Mundell raises the interesting question of how his Zen compares with that of the early patriarchs, particularly the first patriarch who came from the West, David Hume. He rightly observes that in Hume's system Money Supply does not act directly, independently of

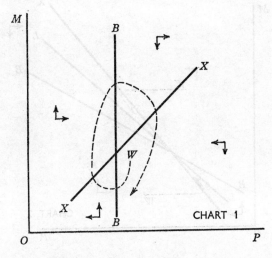

CHART 1

Prices or Income, on the balance of payments. I doubt, however, whether he gives the right explanation for this non-action.

'The classical case', according to Mundell (p. 454), is one in which 'spending is always equal to income', and this in turn arises when the community reacts instantaneously to the excess supply or demand for Money, or at least very quickly relative to the speed of adaptation in the market for goods and services.

There seems to me to be a deep confusion here. Intolerance of excess demand or supply for Money does not lead to an equality of Expenditure and Income but, on the contrary, tends to create a wide discrepancy between the two. For example, any incipient excess supply of Money would lead to a big excess of Expenditure over Income and hence — if domestic prices are slow to react — to a big deficit in the balance of payments. This is certainly not the Humean case. Expressed in terms of

Mundell's diagram, a refusal to tolerate excess demand or supply for Money would mean that both the *XX* and the *BB* curves would tend to approximate the *LL* curve. (See Chart 2 below.) The *BB* curve would be positive with a slope slightly less steep than that of the *LL* curve, while the slope of the *XX* curve would also be positive and slightly steeper than that of the *LL* curve. The positive *BB* slope is explained by the fact that in the circumstances assumed any rise in prices, though it would tend to worsen the balance of payments through its substitution effects, would tend to improve it even more through its effects on the demand for money, and hence on domestic expenditure. However, the slope could not be as steep as that of the *LL* curve, since a proportionate expansion

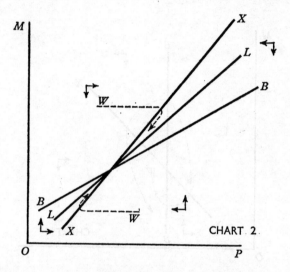

CHART 2.

of Money and Prices from the equilibrium point would involve a deterioration in the Balance of Payments which could only be corrected by a contraction in the Supply of Money. The closeness of the *BB* and *XX* curves to the *LL* curve expresses the intolerance of the system for any substantial divergence from proportionality between *M* and *P*. This system could not possibly be unstable ; as is shown on the attached chart, the path of adjustment from any disequilibrium point would always be a swift, predominantly vertical, movement to between the *BB* and the *XX* lines and thence a slow movement close to the *BB* line towards the equilibrium point.

The true classical case, I submit, is rather different. A feature in the classical model even more crucial than its intolerance of excess demand or supply for Money is its intolerance of excess demand or supply for goods and services. The shape of the curves would be much the same as in the case just examined, since that, as we have seen, depends on the intolerance of excess demand and supply for Money. But the path of adjustment would be different. Starting from a disequilibrium position, it would proceed almost instantaneously and horizontally to the XX line and then travel along that line to the point of equilibrium. (See Chart 3 below.) It is precisely the assumed flexibility of prices that led the patriarchs to attribute balance of payments adjustments to price movements alone, ignoring any separate influence of the money supply. The approximate preservation of proportionality between M and P throughout the process is assured by the fact that the XX curve closely approximates the LL curve.

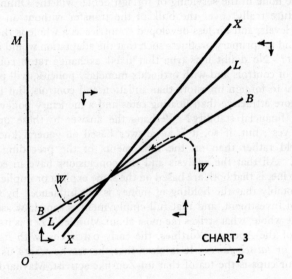

CHART 3

We are now in a position to climb out of the ambiguous half-lights of the disequilibrium process into the sunlit uplands of equilibrium analysis, the realm of the Dharmakaya, or Heavenly Void. I am sure that our Zen master would admit that this blissful realm could be attained by a number of different paths. In other words, different systems of dynamic adjustment, including that followed by the ancient worthies of the classical tradition, are compatible with the same set of equilibrium relationships. It is, therefore, not surprising that the conclusions of this part of Professor Mundell's paper, from p. 450 to p. 453, are relatively uncontroversial, within the limitations imposed by their basic assumptions, of which perhaps the most crucial is the full employment assumption. I particularly liked the growth model in Section VII with the ingenious practical twist at the end.

However, when in the concluding section we descend from the rarefied

atmosphere of equilibrium analysis to the terrestrial world of Nirmanakaya where policies have to be applied by human beings, controversial
propositions come thick and fast.   Most of these propositions are so
impeccably conservative that it would be churlish of me, as an IMF man,
to quarrel with them ; but I am afraid that they would not carry conviction with all economists.   Thus, while no one would advocate monetary
policies aimed at financing budget deficits, does it necessarily follow that
the 'correct' monetary policy is always aimed at preserving balance of
payments equilibrium?   Are prices and wages really so flexible in less
developed countries that we can ignore employment considerations?
While there may be no transfer problems in the provision of foreign aid,
are there none in the servicing of foreign debt; will the Ohlin effects on
expenditure really cover the bulk of the transfer without an adaptation
of price levels, and for less developed countries as a whole is the elasticity
of demand for primary products such that the adaptation would necessarily
be slight?   No doubt it is true that fixed exchange rates, coupled with
absence of controls and with orthodox monetary policies, will prove more
attractive to foreign investors than inflation and controls, but is it necessarily more attractive than floating rates and a monetary policy aiming at
internal financial stability?   Perhaps the answer to these questions is
always 'yes', but, if so, it is an answer based on general knowledge of
the world rather than on the refinements of the preceding economic
analysis.   All that the analysis and the conclusions have in common, it
seems to me, is that both are based on the same explicit or implicit assumptions, notably that the holding of money is not influenced by the profitability of investment, and that full employment is somehow assumed.

On the whole, what strikes me most about Mundell's Zen is its similarity
to that of the Ancient Worthies, the early patriarchs, with its lesson of
wu-wei, or *laissez faire*.   It is clear that the tea he wants us to empty
out of our cups is the tea of that un-Zen-like activist, Maynard Keynes.

DISCUSSION OF PROFESSOR MUNDELL'S PAPER

DISCUSSION of Professor Mundell's paper was concerned mainly with
the stability conditions and adjustment properties of the balance-of-
payments relationship specified in his model.   Also, the policy implications
of the analysis for the transfer problems of the developing countries and
their use of international reserves were examined by several of the discussants.

Professor Borts was concerned with the independence of the liquidity

(*LL* curve) and the foreign-balance (*BB* curve) schedules, and the possibility that the system might degenerate into a single liquidity schedule. He noted that if one assumes the absence of savings in a full-employment income model, the system degenerates into one in which income equals consumption and the balance of payments is automatically in equilibrium. If the *LL* and *BB* schedules are to be independent, he felt that savings would have to be introduced. To do so, however, would be inconsistent with Professor Mundell's assumption that securities markets could be ruled out. *Professor Mundell* replied that even in a non-monetary model, savings could be introduced without having to introduce securities markets.

Dr. Rhomberg would have preferred Professor Mundell to have treated explicitly shifts in the functions discussed in his paper. For instance, what would devaluation — mentioned by Professor Mundell — do to the *BB* curve? How would the *XX* curve (demand schedule for domestic goods) shift as a consequence of devaluation and the resultant change in the relationship between price of domestic and foreign goods? Dr. Rhomberg also questioned Professor Mundell's point that balance-of-payments deficits can be cured through devaluation and proportional increase in the money supply, rather than through the more painful reduction in money supply and corrective deflation. Would not the increase in money supply offset the effects of devaluation? *Professor Mundell* agreed with Dr. Rhomberg. He noted that the starting point for devaluation would be one like point *S* on the *LL* curve in Figure 6, where an increase in the money supply originates the disequilibrium, and where it is necessary only to devalue before reattaining equilibrium.

Professor Brown would have preferred that *ex ante* and *ex post* magnitudes be explicitly identified in the model. *Professor Mundell* agreed that this should have been done.

Professor Delivanis indicated that while an excess supply of money leads to price increases of locally produced goods, as noted by Professor Mundell, there will also be a complementary increase in the price of imports until the supply of imports rises. *Professor Mundell* answered by noting that since the model was intended to apply to a small country, demand changes in its domestic market should have little influence on prices in other, larger countries.

Professor Wallich referred to the negative slope of the foreign balance schedule (*BB* curve) in Figure 2, and suggested that there was another reason — in addition to that suggested by Dr. Fleming — why the balance-of-payments schedule might have a positive slope and why, consequently, the model might be unstable. If the demand for a country's exports were inelastic, the slope would be positive since rising prices would then be associated with the surplus rather than a deficit in the balance of payments. He admitted that this was implausible for a small country. *Professor Mundell* replied that this would be possible only if the sum of demand elasticities for imports of this country and the rest of the world is less than unity. That is, the exchange market would have to be unstable. If it is assumed that increases in prices are proportional to excess expenditures, and that the balance of payments is proportional to the money supply, the system is stable. The system would be stable even if, as Dr. Fleming suggested, the *BB* line were vertical. Further, he noted that this is unlikely since it would imply that prices would have no impact on the balance of trade via changes in the real value of cash balances. The Italian stabilization experience at the end of 1963 and beginning of 1964 was cited by Professor Mundell as a case which approximated his model. Though everyone thought that Italy had to devalue, exchange reserves recovered rapidly without the aid of devaluation when the central bank deflated the money supply.

Professor Wallich and *Dr. Marshall* also questioned the implication of a constant-income velocity of money in the model, which appeared to follow from the straight-line characteristic of the *LL* (liquidity) schedule. Although the shape of the *LL* schedule may not affect the analysis, they thought that it is still of interest in itself. *Professor Mundell* replied that velocity is not constant in the model, nor is the demand for money simply a function of money income. In the Keynesian model, for example, the demand for money is a function of both money income and the rate of interest. While the interest rate could not be introduced into the model after ruling out securities markets, there is an implicit interest rate in the form of the return to capital.

Dr. Onitiri agreed with Professor Mundell's point that a developing country should make provision for increasing its foreign-currency reserves, if only because international investors tend to look at reserve positions and ignore the other side of a country's international-balance sheet. Though high reserve levels may be desirable, Dr. Onitiri would not view present arrangements as better than those which might exist if the international monetary system were reformed, as Professor Mundell seemed to do. *Professor Mundell* said that when he had suggested that developing countries attach themselves to major currency areas to avail themselves of opportunities (to earn interest on liquid assets) that many current plans for international monetary reform failed to provide, he was not referring to all reform proposals but only to those which had a serious chance of acceptance.

Professor Delivanis thought that the dollar area offered fewer advantages to member countries than did the sterling area. *Professor Mundell* replied that in so far as the sterling area is a reserve pool while the dollar area is not, he would agree.

Dr. Onitiri also felt that Professor Mundell's emphasis on the importance of stabilization policy resulted in his neglecting the need for growth, and that he paid too much attention to the balance of payments and to monetary influences on the balance of payments. Dr. Onitiri felt that real forces often require monetary policies with adverse balance-of-payments effects. *Professor Mundell* replied that he did not intend to imply that stability was a substitute for development. Rather, stability seemed more conducive to development than instability. For this reason, while he might find flexible exchange rates attractive in theory, he would not advocate their adoption since they tended in practice to generate instability.

Dr. Marshall agreed that stability was preferable to inflation, more reserves preferable to less reserves, etc., but wondered how meaningful these conclusions were for countries now experiencing inflation and reserve drains. He felt it was necessary to analyse the causes of inflation, the relationship between inflation and development, and the economic and other impacts of stabilization policies to derive meaningful conclusions. He admitted, though, that such analysis went beyond the scope of the paper and the conference.

Chapter 14

FINANCIAL INTEGRATION AND THE FLOW OF RESOURCES IN LATIN AMERICA

BY

Dr. JAVIER MÁRQUEZ

Center for Latin American Monetary Studies (CEMLA) Mexico

I. THE INTEGRATION EFFORT

INTERNATIONAL financial integration may be said to be the inter-connection and/or co-ordination of national financial systems with a view to channelling available financial resources towards the place, within the integrated area, in which they can be put to best use from the long-run point of view of the financially integrated area as a whole.

The argument in favour of financial integration in Latin America is thus as strong as the argument in favour of avoiding waste in underdeveloped countries. Consequently, it is a very strong argument. Its strength derives not only from the abundance of the flow of resources (of uncertain magnitude) among the Latin American countries which can be expected as a result of financial integration, but also from the fact that the necessary effort is not different from the one that countries should make on their own accord in order to improve their national financial systems.

One aspect of financial integration is the harmonization of monetary policies in order to have a reasonable degree of stability within the integrated area. In regard to this, we all know the difficulties which some Latin American countries are going through in order to stop inflation. However, the co-ordination of monetary policies is only one aspect of financial integration, although, no doubt, a basic one when countries agree to free their mutual trade. There are also other aspects of this problem that are important for the channelling of financial resources to their best location. These problems are easier to solve than those raised by a stabilization effort after a prolonged period of inflation. In particular, I do not think that most aspects of financial integration should raise problems as complex as those presented by the freeing of trade in the countries such as those in Latin America that have led separate lives for generations, that have very different cost structures, that may have inefficient production sheltered behind tariff walls of several hundred per cent. Agreeing to free trade in Latin America in those circumstances assumes that countries are prepared to go through an 'integration crisis' or a series of integration crises which in some cases might be profound. Many steps towards financial integration that would be of great benefit to the integrating countries would not require a comparable effort nor an equivalent sacrifice.

So far, Latin American countries have seldom looked at financial integration from the angle of the definition which has been given. In most cases they have been content with discussing ideas and plans which imply *co-operation* to facilitate and increase the financial transactions derived from trade, as well as to achieve other financial aims. They have also established some mechanisms for specific purposes. No doubt, the end result of those plans and mechanisms may contribute to channelling available resources towards their best location, and to that extent they are financial integration mechanisms in their own right. Moreover, a co-operative mechanism gives the opportunity of contact, which is the most expedient way to take steps towards integration.[1] For these reasons, I will consider that a co-operative mechanism is also an integration mechanism when it channels financial resources to the right place, or facilitates the flow of these resources in that direction, or prevents them from going to the wrong place, or when they offer the opportunity to co-ordinate financial policies, or to harmonize the financial systems of the countries with the purpose of finding the best place for the use of financial resources.

It is advisable for the purpose of this paper to give a bird's-eye view of the plans and actual accomplishments in the fields of financial integration in Latin America as well as of the evolution of ideas in this field, for it may help to appraise which road to travel in the future.[2]

With regard to accomplishments, and at the official level, we have the Central American Clearing House (which Mexico has joined)

---

[1] The Central American Clearing House, which is a typical co-operative mechanism, is the origin of the Central American Monetary Union, which is an integration mechanism.

[2] For the next few pages I have borrowed extensively from : CEMLA, *Un programa de integración financiera para América Latina* (mimeo.), March 1963.

and the Central American Monetary Union, while the Latin American Free Trade Area (LAFTA) recently created two co-ordinating bodies : the Advisory Commission on Monetary Affairs and the Financial and Monetary Policy Council. There is also the export financing system, established and run by the Inter-American Development Bank. The most recent addition has been the Meetings of Governors of Latin American Central Banks for the purpose of discussing problems of mutual interest.

The financial mechanisms proposed for Latin America include Latin American central banks, organizations of the Bank for International Settlement (BIS) type, clearing houses, payments unions, a regional credit system, a Latin American stock exchange, and mechanisms with more limited objectives, which have been conceived either as separate units or under one roof. Monetary co-ordination mechanisms have also been suggested, at times with no function beyond that of co-ordination, and on other occasions as a part of concrete or general financial mechanisms. Furthermore, all these plans were conceived at the general Latin American level and at subregional levels, coinciding or not with the two existing subregional groups, LAFTA and the Central American Common Market.

There has been an evolution of the ideas. The main change is to be found in the objectives sought, that is, in the broadening of those aspects of financial integration considered worthy of attention. During the first stage, which could be placed between 1956 and the end of 1962, the purpose was to facilitate the expansion of intra-regional trade, and the Economic Commission for Latin America (ECLA) prepared several plans to enable intra-Latin American financial relations to get out of the bilateralism in which they had been trapped since the end of the war. Within the same objective, and overlapping it, thinking subsequently moved ahead to payments unions and regional credit systems (the two ECLA plans, of 1958 and 1960, and the plan of the Organization of American States (OAS), also of 1960). At the beginning of this stage, payments unions were conceived of as regional in scope, but later they were devised for Latin American countries linked by integration agreements, and their ultimate, if not exclusive, goal was to encourage the growth of intrazonal trade, but not in an indiscriminate fashion: in the ECLA plan for LAFTA, the purpose of the payments mechanism was to guarantee the application of the 'principle of reciprocity', which was understood as an exact corollary of the trade advantages obtained by the countries of the free trade zone. ECLA, as well as the OAS, wanted also to absorb or reduce, in some way or other, the short-run balance of payments effects (deficits) which were foreseen as a result of the elimination of tariffs, that is to say, those plans were partly defensive or precautionary. Furthermore, the ideas upon which the ECLA plans were based, closely followed the features of the European Payments Union and the European Monetary Agreement. As is well known, nothing happened as a result of these plans: the opposition of the International Monetary Fund, mainly on account of their automatism and several discriminatory features, gave strength to the misgivings of some of the LAFTA countries and the plans were abandoned.

The next Payments Union plan (prepared by Professor Robert Triffin for CEMLA in 1962) was no longer defensive; the credit mechanism appears as an *incentive* for the freeing of trade and is linked to agreements in order to follow stabilization policies. Its perspective is, thus, more dynamic and in the realm of regional co-operation. Besides, in this plan automatism is practically non-existent, and the criterion that the granting of credits should be related mainly to the overall balance of payments position of each country and not to the regional one has already arisen. The 'principle of reciprocity' disappears.

The saving of foreign exchange (less need for reserves) which may be secured through a more intensive use of Latin American currencies and the clearing of balances, has likewise become a primary goal; so have the benefits that would be obtained from closer financial relations between the (domestic) banks of the Latin American countries. The last stage of the evolution is that in which interest shifts somewhat from direct or indirect short-term benefits obtained from financial mechanisms towards the value of these mechanisms in relation to the opportunities they present for the co-ordination of financial policies, co-ordination which is considered a *sine qua non* condition for economic integration.

Another outstanding aspect of the change that has occurred is found in the geographical scope of the plans. Initially they were designed to cover all of Latin America, but soon they were directed to the two subregional areas: LAFTA and the Central American Common Market. Nevertheless, later on, the Central American Clearing House, which dates from 1963, took Mexico in (through a special agreement) and considered the membership of Venezuela and Colombia; a *regional* credit mechanism for exports has been set up, and there have been suggestions of financial groupings that are independent of the existing subregional structures; these new proposed groupings include countries which participate in the various organized groups or that may belong to none. Financial integration is thus no longer linked only to trade liberalization agreements. Even though during this last stage we still have arrangements and ideas which concern the two existing subregional groups (for example, the agreement for the establishment of the Central American Monetary Union, and the Financial and Monetary Policy Council in LAFTA), it is easy to see the increasing importance of the regional approach. The newly planned subregional mechanisms are conceived as a point of departure which permits things to get moving without having to wait for the agreement of everybody concerned. The new subregional mechanisms suggested are sometimes conceived as open to those who may eventually wish to join, or they are considered merely as one more among many other similar mechanisms (perhaps in other subregions), which would eventually join together under the same roof, a single agency, or would fuse into a regional agency when circumstances allow. The goal to be pursued would then be the establishment of a common organization, a Latin American central bank or Latin American financial centre. This entity would fulfil, among others, the function of centralizing reserves, or to be, in addition, or exclusively, the managing body of the various mechanisms it might be desirable to establish. In it the Latin American countries would come together through their participation in one or more of those mechanisms and thus have the opportunity of co-ordinating their financial behaviour in the fields in which this may be considered desirable or to their mutual economic advantage, and to increase the influence of the members *vis-à-vis* third parties.

To separate co-ordination from financing, to treat it as a subject in itself, and to consider it as important and urgent, or more, than financing as a factor in integration, is a new attitude, a change, which appears to be winning supporters.

When the main problem was international liquidity (as a result of the difficulty of obtaining access to the Monetary Fund and of the possible increase in balance of payments deficits due to the freeing of intra-Latin American trade), interest centred on credit. The clearing systems devised had as their main purpose the measuring of the amount of credit to be received and to be extended; their clearing functions were quite secondary. However, those same clearing systems have once more entered the scene with force and for their own sake, undoubtedly under the influence of the example of the Central American Clearing House. The clearing opportunities which they offer are considered more important than before, although they still maintain the character of an initial step, or first stage, towards payments unions. Consequently, these two financial integration mechanisms aroused interest since the very beginning of Latin American economic integration efforts and they still arise; but from our point of view, emphasis has shifted from payments unions to clearing houses at least tactically as a means of getting started.

Other mechanisms have been proposed, together with these two (not in place of them), which seek to improve specific aspects of the international financial life of Latin America. It has been proposed that the network of bank correspondent relations be extended throughout Latin America and that such relations include the opening of reciprocal credit lines. Also, that central monetary authorities should guarantee the convertibility and transferability of debts arising from intra-zonal transactions. Along the same lines, it has been suggested that such a guarantee be complemented with mechanisms established within the central banks for rediscounting, at preferential rates, the credits granted by commercial banks to exporters and importers and with systems of exchange insurance and preferential forward sales of foreign exchange for intra-regional trade. Also suggested, were funds for guaranteeing documents arising out of intra-Latin American trade, and for the purchase and negotiation of a prompt remittances system, a reserve pool to derive larger yields from their investment, a regional reinsurance organization, a mechanism for issuing Latin American securities in the main capital markets, Latin American mutual funds, and the establishment of a Latin American stock exchange and/or the linking of the stock exchanges of various countries.

Ever since ECLA began to deal with these topics, it had been foreseen that the application of plans would proceed by stages. For example, clearing houses would begin with, say, weekly or monthly clearings, and the term would be gradually extended; then the clearing system would be transformed progressively into a payments union with increasingly ambitious functions; reserve pools, beginning with the simple task of placing limited resources at interest rates slightly above those that might be obtained by the central banks themselves, would subsequently enter other fields and diversify their services. This has always been the form, both explicit and implicit, in which plans have been presented, but it seems to me that while the final goal of the plans is increasingly ambitious the planners suggest an increasingly gradual approach.

The explanation may be found in the resistance with which the first projects met. Many considered them too revolutionary in their financial aspirations and too complex. The authors of the new plans probably wished to present them as easy to handle and with no more risk than the central banks would be willing to assume, and both purposes are better satisfied with a step-by-step approach. Other factors may have been a growing interest in the co-ordination opportunities that any plan might offer (and which are obtainable at any level of financing) and the greater liberality of the International Monetary Fund, together with the tight reserve position of the majority of the countries of the region, which creates a strong resistance to parting from them, however secure, or to risk them in transactions with the countries of the region that have greater balance of payments difficulties.

Over the eight or nine years of financial integration efforts and in the course of the often heated debates over the different mechanisms, many ideas have been discarded, others have been bolstered up, and changes in attitude have taken place. The fear of clearing systems has gone by the board and its machinery no longer seems as complex, if it does at all, as it did before. The thesis that a clearing house requires exchange restrictions in the participating countries in order to function effectively has been abandoned. The same is true of the thesis that financial integration mechanisms should seek to balance payments (or trade) within the region, to say nothing of the idea that they should force this balance. Almost no supporters of automatic credits remain, except during clearing periods (perhaps longer than had been foreseen at the beginning) and this within pre-agreed margins. But the most important aspect of the change in attitude is the growing interest in financial integration in sectors of the community that, when the movement started, were indifferent or hostile to it.

But the movement towards financial integration has been a piecemeal affair ; the problem has not been approached as one co-ordinated whole. I have no quarrel with the contention that the step by step, or gradual, approach is the only possible, expedient, or politically acceptable one, but there are grounds for believing that, so far, the approach has not been as organized as it could conveniently be. Particularly, some of the more important aspects of financial integration, such as agreement on a common monetary policy, including exchange policy and mutual help in devising the most conducive means, in each country, to sustained financial stability, have not been touched. Although their importance is increasingly recognized, this recognition has not yet led to any action (except in Central America). These aspects of financial integration should have been part and parcel of any agreement to free mutual trade. In fact, they should be considered a prerequisite of free trade, for free trade between inflationary and stable countries cannot last if the stable ones have substantial export capacity. Even among stable countries, there should be ways of guaranteeing that stability will be maintained.

In addition to this part of financial integration, which in an orderly economic integration process should have precedence over the devising of some of the financial gadgets which are being currently discussed, there are all the legal and policy harmonization changes in the financial field that are a part of an integration policy and would maximize their beneficial effects. Again, we have here practically a vacuum.

In fact, Latin America has barely started to scratch the surface of the field of financial integration, and some of the basic aspects of this subject have been deliberately and systematically dodged.

There are 'reasons' for this. One is that, however sincere the desire to integrate may be today, it must be accepted that, probably everywhere, short-run national interests, as interpreted by each country, tend to have precedence over most other things, and this is all the more so when countries do not have much financial leeway. Integration steps are taken *provided* they do not affect short-run national preferences. When the present is pressing, the future never seems clear or important enough to make an effort or a temporary sacrifice.

This human and, accordingly, understandable attitude, feeds on the pressures of vested and not too respectable interests, that magnify their short-run sacrifices, which they identify with long-run national interests. Moreover, the economists, and technicians generally, are not free from guilt, for in their efforts to work out the technical beauties of their conflicting, parallel or overlapping plans, they may have created some confusion.[1]

---

[1] When the authorities do not want to do something, for whatever reason, they have an easy way out by asking technicians (preferably more than one) to prepare another paper on the subject, 'in order to make sure'.

Be this as it may, there are deep-rooted, and other, obstacles to taking financial integration steps. However, the fact seems to be that economic integration is here to stay, and that the process of trade liberalization in the LAFTA countries has reached the stage in which it has become compulsory in some trade sectors, while at the same time development plans may be co-ordinated. Moreover, there is increasing emphasis on economic integration of the *region*, as different from the regional groups, subgroups and the 'independent' countries. To the extent that the desire to integrate is sincere, the absence of supporting financial integration could only be interpreted as a case of economic schizophrenia, for it does not make sense to take a commitment in one field and not support it in the other, or to decide the best location of investments and not the best location of savings. One should hope, accordingly, to see progress in financial integration in Latin America at least commensurate to the progress of integration in trade and planning.

II. LOOKING TO THE FUTURE

I have argued in favour of an organized financial integration effort, and I have indicated that, in my opinion, co-ordination of financial policies should have precedence over other aspects of financial integration, when there is a commitment to free mutual trade. From there on, I confess that I do not have anything that could be termed a plan, but just considerable confusion on what should be the next step. This is probably the subconscious reason for arguing in favour of the establishment of a body that would co-ordinate and push the financial integration efforts of the region as a whole. However, I suppose that one should be content with a pragmatic approach, provided the overall situation is taken permanently into account. That is, personally, I would probably proceed — in no particular order, but as circumstances permitted, and depending on the progress of economic integration and the willingness of countries — to link various money and capital markets. All the time, whether there is linking or not, or whatever the progress made in those fields, I would try to harmonize, again in no particular order that I can think of at the moment, the financial legislations and practices of countries, their banking structures, etc., so that, as all of these things improved, the linking, and the consequent flow of resources, is made easier when circumstances permit.

I would constantly bear in mind, 'dynamically' (i.e. taking into account the many changes that accompany the passage of time), a great number of circumstances, their consequences (sometimes conflicting ones) and the opportunities they may offer.

I obviously cannot list them all, but will mention very briefly a few of them, although perhaps not in any logical order, as a reminder, among other things, of some of the more down to earth situations, complexities and opportunities of financial integration which might confront a financial integration planner in Latin America, besides those mentioned previously in this paper.

(1) Given a certain structure of the investment preference or investment decisions in the countries, there is, at each moment of time, an optimum possible distribution of the available financial resources between short and long term. This should be a good reason for linking the money and capital markets, nationally and internationally, to get as close as possible to the best proportions.

(2) To the extent that these two financial markets are kept separate — because the countries, or some of the countries, so decide — the best geographical distribution of the resources available in each one could be sought through the establishment of close relations between each of the two markets in the different countries. This, in turn, would be facilitated by the harmonization of the rules and practices that govern their operations.

(3) Due to market imperfections, however, a free financial market in which savers, or the institutions that handle savings, are allowed to use their liquid resources in whatever way they please, would not result in the best possible long-run allocation of savings. Nevertheless, in *laissez-faire* economies, the interconnection of national financial markets and the diversification of saving instruments should, to some extent, reduce market imperfections.

(4) Although financing is expected to follow, and not lead, investment decisions, when savings are relatively scarce as they are in underdeveloped countries, the availability of financial resources for specific investments may be a decisive factor in investment decisions. The consequences for development of redirecting savings may be as important as the increase of savings, or more.

(5) In Latin America, as elsewhere, the growing importance of corporate savings leads to a certain specialization of savings ; that is, savings made in one trade may tend to become investments in the same trade, whether or not such investments are justified. A second best means of redirecting these savings would be to direct

them to other countries of the region in which there is a shortage of the corresponding production. Although not abundant, there is no lack of such direct intra-Latin American investments at this moment, and there are ways of promoting them.

(6) To the extent that financial markets are interconnected, there will be a tendency toward the equalization of interest rates. Countries with relatively low rates of interest that open their market to other countries with higher rates should be prepared to accept an increase in theirs, or to use some device to keep down their rates to residents. The expediency of financial integration would be greater between countries in which the interest rate structure is similar or less dissimilar.

(7) The Latin American countries have, of their own accord or because of special incentives, accepted planning, and a plan should, no doubt, include the capacity of the financial systems to provide the necessary flow of resources. However, a plan which is not more ambitious than the total available financial resources would permit, may still find an obstacle in the structure of the available resources compared to the requirements of the plan. This possibility is more likely to occur when there is no connection between the money and the capital markets. While it should be accepted that the existence of ambitious and independent national development plans would tend to separate countries financially, for they would try to retain whatever savings are generated in each one, it is conceivable that the relatively scarce financial resources under the plan of one country may be the relatively abundant one under that of another country because of differences in the investment preferences of the savers. This suggests the desirability of comparing the financial side of the independent national plans, for it might be possible to favour them all on the basis of the complementarity of financial resources.

(8) However, in Latin America no plan is all-embracing. There is always a sector of investments, the size of which varies from country to country, that is left to market forces. The complementarity argument for the interconnection of financial systems which has just been given applies also to this sector.

(9) The Central American countries have decided to co-ordinate their national development plans, while the Inter-American Committee for the Alliance for Progress (CIAP) tries to co-ordinate those of the region as a whole. To the extent that there is such a coordination, in order to avoid duplication, overlapping and waste

generally, financial integration seems a natural accompaniment to it. The extent and nature of the co-ordination of plans should be a guide to the extent and nature of the possibilities of beneficial financial integration. No doubt, here, as in many other respects, integration should affect the flows of both domestic (i.e. regional) and foreign resources.

(10) The LAFTA countries have decided to give special treatment to its relatively less developed members, or those of smaller 'economic magnitude'. Three subgroups have been established, each having to give the others, and receiving from them, special tariff concessions of a compensatory nature, in order to allow them to catch up in their development. One aspect of the co-ordination of national development plans would be to extend to investments the principles behind the differential tariff treatment. This possibility is being increasingly discussed and is gaining supporters. Probably, a 'differential location of investments treatment' would be more conducive to the desired levelling of relative development and/or dynamism than the (tariff) system which is being followed at present. For financial integration the proposal might mean that the favoured countries should be financially less open to the others and *vice versa*. It would not be consistent to decide that investments, in general or specific ones, should increase or be made in certain countries and at the same time closing the financial markets of other member countries to the countries where the investments are to be made especially if these are considered of importance to the rest of the countries.

(11) If two countries agree that a third one is the best location for a certain investment from which they will benefit, and if there is foreign financing for such investment, there is a good case for those countries, in addition to the country of investment, incurring the foreign debt.

(12) Protection of relatively less developed countries, as well as co-ordination of development plans with a view to the best long-run location of investments, seems a good argument in favour of co-ordination of foreign (non-regional) investment policies.

(13) So far, co-ordinated investment planning in Latin America has referred to industries serving several countries. However, countries benefit from investment in other countries not only to the extent that these investments are in industries (activities) that export to them, but also to the extent that such investments increase incomes in the country where the investment takes place and this

has a positive income elasticity of demand for the exports of the others. Accordingly, the case for financial integration to promote investments that increase income in one country is stronger in the measure in which the income elasticity of demand of the country of investment for the exports of the other integrating countries is high.

(14) If the final goal is regional integration, a Latin American common market, investment planning, however loose, should refer to all countries, independently of the group in which they may be today or whether they belong to none. This is all the more so if we are after the best long-run location of investments, and not merely after the best one today. Financial integration becomes then, to that extent, independent of integration in other areas at the present time.

(15) There may be asymmetry between economic and financial development. The less developed countries do not always have the more imperfect financial systems. Such countries may also have available more liquid savings than the more developed ones. To the extent that financial integration involves improvement of financial systems, the changes needed may be greater, or more difficult to make, in the more developed countries. Moreover, since finance is a complex of things, what is easy for one country, whatever its development, may be difficult in another.

(16) The balance of payments problems of one country affect its relations with the countries with which it has integrated or tries to integrate. Such problems may present themselves in spite of policy co-ordination and the efforts of the country with balance of payments problems. Consequently, it would be in the interest of the other countries to help it — with their own resources and/or through their joint efforts in international agencies — to overcome those problems.

(17) Countries and/or exporters are not, or should not be, interested in increasing their exports to those that have payment difficulties. Conversely, countries and/or importers should not make more commitments than they can afford. Consequently, one should reject gadgets that lure countries into over-importing.

(18) Many aspects of financial integration require, almost by definition, a mechanism in order to come to something, while others might be left to the market. However, the pace of development which the Latin American countries are aiming at is faster than the market would provide and, whenever financial markets are too slow to keep pace with development aspirations, it is more than legitimate to try to devise mechanisms which would make up for

the deficiencies of the market. To create financial machinery ahead of a foreseen need, anticipating the known slowness of market forces, is not putting the horse before the cart.

I suggested that this list was meant as a reminder of some of the things that a financial integration planner in Latin America might want to bear in mind. I would readily agree that such a planner would probably not need to be reminded of any of the points made and that he would already know them, together with many others (and may very well object to many of the implicit suggestions). In fact, the list was also meant as an argument for financial integration *per se*, because of the benefits it can bring to economic development, independently of any process of economic integration (in trade or planning), and also to strengthen the argument in favour of financial integration, when such a process is in motion. Several of the points also suggest the direction of the flow of resources which might be expected from financial integration in Latin America. However, the main purpose of the list was to strengthen my case for a subregional approach to regional financial integration. If taken in conjunction with the description of the evolution of ideas on financial integration in Latin America given at the beginning of this paper, I think that the list does serve that purpose.

Let me hasten to say that I am aware that some of the points, problems and opportunities mentioned in my very incomplete and spotty list are far-fetched if applied to many, or most, Latin American countries at this moment; I also realize that their importance is not the same for the development of all the Latin American countries or for the flow of financial resources within Latin America, and that I have no illusions concerning the short- or medium-run viability of some of them, or even concerning the need to apply many of the suggestions in many cases.

I mentioned already that one obstacle to financial integration was the pressure of short-run problems. These affect the establishment of mechanisms that involve making foreign credit, postponing exchange receipts, taking commitments to make prompt payments, forgoing the direct control or use of reserves, permitting the outflow of resources, etc. Several Latin American countries, including some of the larger ones, have such pressing balance of payments problems. They are the ones that stand in the worst position to take more than token steps towards financial integration. This, however, is not the situation of other Latin American countries, for some have a relatively easy reserve position and/or considerable stability.

The attempt to have all countries agreeing to join in one common financial mechanism on the same basis and with commitments which bear some proportion to their relative development and economic magnitude is doomed to failure. Even within LAFTA, the situations, reserve and stability-wise, are so different that the common denominator in which the countries may be expected to agree will be so low that it will not amount to much. I can see no reason why countries in better relative reserve position and the stable ones, in whatever group or in no group, should not join among themselves in more ambitious financial integration plans than are possible with the less stable ones, while the latter join them when their situation improves. The same countries may also join temporarily with the less stable and these among themselves in other plans which, although not as important, would nevertheless be favourable to their relations and set the ground for their joining the preferable ones.

Moreover, one can conceive that even within these two 'sectors', of the more and less stable countries, there may be differences both in relative balance of payments problems and in willingness to take risks. I do not see why there should not be more than two groups, so that the more conservative countries (within those in a better position) do not put a brake on the less conservative ones, while the experience of the latter stimulates the conservative ones to join them.

Generally, *if the whole programme is co-ordinated*, so that the arrangements between the different groups do not create situations which impair the regional approach at some future date, the subregional approach should, in my opinion, speed the rate of regional integration, while the regional or the 'large subregional' approach is likely to slow it up.

The above concerns mainly, but not exclusively, those financial mechanisms referred to at the beginning of this paper which are being currently discussed at the official level in LAFTA and Central America. As was stated, there are signs of interest in forming, for specific purposes, groups which are independent of them, but I believe that this movement is too slow and that the attempts to reach overall agreements within the existing subregional groups is slowing the regional process in fields in which there are negotiations and blinding countries to other possibilities.

The list which I have given contains several of them. I do not conceive that any of the pertinent ones could be tackled at the regional level, but I do think that there is *something* in each one at *some* international level, be it pairs of countries or small groups, and that as the countries develop and their economic relations increase and diversify, perhaps as a result of free trade, the groups that can benefit from their relations in each of those points would be larger. No doubt, it would be difficult to conceive that some of the countries will have, for very many years to come or ever, much use for some of the linkages suggested, and it would be futile to try to link them in those respects.

This does not disturb me. The problem is the same; that is to say, to the extent that a country has those links with other countries and these latter have similar links with different ones, they would all still have to travel the same road. The important thing is that when, say, Argentina and Paraguay link in some way their financial systems, they remember that Argentina may want to link her own system also in the same manner with Chile and Brazil and Paraguay, perhaps, with Brazil and Bolivia, Chile with Brazil and Peru, Brazil with Mexico, Mexico with Guatemala, etc. It would be most complicated if the financial systems of each country were linked differently with different countries to solve the same problem.

COMMENTS ON THE PAPER BY DR. MÁRQUEZ

BY

Professor ROBERT A. MUNDELL

McGill University

DR. MÁRQUEZ's paper is a well-balanced mixture of candid cynicism and constructive advice; I greatly enjoyed reading it. He described the evolution of ideas and plans (which have been at best fragmentary), discussed the obstacles to financial integration (which seem deep-rooted), listed eighteen points representing casual thoughts, dangers and suggestions, and finally made a plea for a unified attack on the subject of integration, yet one that would still permit a subregional approach as a beginning, paying due attention to need for eventual co-ordination of various subregional plans.

Dr. Márquez is surely right that financial integration should not raise problems more complex than those presented by the freeing of trade. This is not because financial integration will be easy in Latin America but rather because the freeing of trade will be extremely difficult if it means an eventual movement toward a high common tariff wall. The major obstacles to be overcome will be the need to prevent the less developed — and less developable — subregions of Latin America from going the way of the Mezzogiorno after the Italian Risorgimento, the southern United States after the middle of the nineteenth century, the Canadian Maritimes after 1900, and countless other depressed regions sacrificed on the altar of high tariffs benefiting politically-associated regions.

Financial integration is usually easier to achieve than free trade, yet historically it follows rather than precedes it. This is probably because financial integration implies a greater political commitment; in the extreme instance of a common currency it implies a far-reaching surrender of sovereignty, and perhaps political union.

It is necessary to distinguish between 'monetary' integration and 'capital' integration. If we then assume that monetary activities are centred around 'national central banks', and capital market activities around 'national development banks', we can conceive of the different stages of integration as different degrees of collaboration between central banks and development banks.

The first stage of integration is simply periodic meetings between central bankers (much like the monthly BIS meetings) and development bankers. Monthly meetings, consultations, mutual criticism and praise constitute the first valuable step toward financial integration, a step that can be short but which should on no account be by-passed.

The second stage of integration may involve either a co-ordination of monetary policies or a reserve pool, in the case of monetary integration, a co-ordination of lending policies or a capital pool, in the case of capital integration. In Europe policy co-ordination came first, but in Latin America, with countries subject to widely disparate rates of inflation, reserve and capital pools may be more initially feasible. The reserve pool would help the area to economize on foreign exchange reserves, acting in a regional context as the IMF acts in a world context; a capital pool would, similarly, improve the allocation of scarce capital resources especially in smoothing out the phasing of national development projects.

Assuming the second stage of integration involves the pooling of monetary and capital resources, decisions with respect to location of the central institutions (which we might conveniently call the 'Latin American Monetary Fund' and the 'Latin American Development Bank'), and the conditions of access to the pooled resources, would be important, tangible ones involving considerable commitment. Perhaps equally important would be the learning process involved in disciplining one another, and imposing conditions on access much like the IMF or the IBRD has to do today.

In this connection I find it a pity that the U.S. has not taken the Marshall Plan as their model for the Alliance for Progress. The Marshall Plan owed its success and popularity not only to U.S. generosity, but also to the fact that the Europeans themselves had to divide up the available funds, and therefore take the blame for any mistakes ; self-discipline is better than imposed discipline, and OEEC became the nursery in which European integration was hatched.

Even today part of foreign aid funds could be allocated to the external reserve of a Latin American Monetary Fund, beginning with a reserve pool, and the security for a Latin American Development Bank, beginning with a capital pool. If one accepts (as I do) the principle of a regional approach to world development, the sooner Latin America begins to allocate external funds on a Continental basis through their own institutions, the more quickly will they be able to sort out the mistakes of aid-giving countries from their own limitations.

In the further stage of integration that involves policy co-ordination (it seems unduly speculative to go further now) the big problem will be linking inflationary countries with stable countries, if this is possible at all. I agree here with Dr. Márquez that the first step will probably have to be subregional, taking care that the structure recognizes the possible interests of unstable countries that should join later on.

As a final thought, is it not appropriate to take the world economy as the model for the beginnings of Latin American integration? The postwar world economy was underpinned by the triumvirate of the IMF, the IBRD and GATT. The counterpart of GATT exists in the Montevideo treaty. How long will it take to get a Latin American Monetary Fund and a Latin American Development Bank?

DISCUSSION OF DR. MÁRQUEZ'S PAPER

ONE of the main topics considered in the discussion of Dr. Márquez's paper was the experience with financial integration in various parts of the world. The need for financial integration was also considered. The most intensive discussion, however, centred on the difficulties faced in planning for financial integration and on the means that might be used to overcome such difficulties.

I. EXPERIENCE WITH FINANCIAL INTEGRATION

In discussing the meaning of 'financial integration', it was recognized that the term includes such varying degrees of integration as consultation and reserve pools all the way up to unified central banks and common currencies. *Dr. Kamarck* mentioned the varied experience with financial integration in Africa after the African states achieved independence during the postwar period. He cited the experience in East Africa where a former monetary and economic union is now breaking down. He saw this as a by-product of planning which gave evidence of inequality in the distribution of benefits to the different countries. The breakdown is also a result of another aspect of planning, which is that one cannot plan for other countries. The breakdown of integration in East Africa is in sharp contrast with the sucess of French-speaking West Africa in maintaining monetary integration. Dr. Kamarck felt this success was due in part to an abundant supply of administrative officials. *Professor Leduc* agreed and said that financial aid from France is probably the main basis for monetary integration among the French-speaking African countries (with the exception of Guinea) south of the Sahara.

Professor Wallich said that he saw the combination of monetary co-ordination and an industrial bank, the Central American Bank for Economic Integration, as being very hopeful in Central America. Monetary stability and stable exchange rates have been achieved, and there is also co-ordination of investment plans since member countries are anxious to place investment projects with the Central American Bank for Economic Integration to benefit from outside financing. In effect, the Central American Bank for Economic Integration is a substitute for private foreign capital. Of particular interest is the rapid rise in intra-regional trade that has followed the reduction in tariffs. This tends to disprove the common notion that since primary exporting countries produce more or less the same goods and export them to the rest of the world, they have nothing to sell to each other. *Dr. Márquez* noted, however, that the Central American Bank for Economic Integration Bank, as an official agency, is used by entrepreneurs only if private capital is unavailable.

Dr. de Beers pointed out that the Inter-American Development Bank is in reality a Latin American regional bank. He also mentioned the role of the Inter-American Committee for the Alliance for Progress, which reviews national plans of the different countries and serves as a regional co-ordinating institution. *Dr. Singer* added that the United Nations has a number of activities which serve as a basis for regional co-operation, including the Colombo Plan in Asia, the ECA, ECAFE, and various development institutes set up under the United Nations Special Fund. *Dr. Onitiri*, however, said that if we are to judge according to concrete achievement rather than on the basis of conferences, reports, plans and similar developments cited by Dr. Singer, the trend — in Africa at least — is towards disintegration rather than integration.

II. The Need for Financial Integration

There was general agreement in principle among the discussants of the need for financial integration. *Professor Mundell* argued, for instance, that despite all objections and problems expected to arise in Latin America, there is need to develop Latin American resources on a continental basis.

There was, though, a question of whether trade integration or financial integration had precedence. *Dr. Márquez* said that financial integration had precedence because integration of trade cannot be maintained unless it is based on relatively stable financial arrangements. *Professor Mundell* replied that while this may be so, historically financial integration requires greater political commitment. *Dr. Okita* observed here that the prospect for financial integration seems better than that for integration of trade and economic planning because less violation of national sovereignty is involved.

Dr. Singer asked to what extent financial means could be used to redress trade imbalances of the less developed countries in the region after trade is freed or finances are integrated. *Dr. Márquez* answered that he believed financial compensation would be better for compensating the less developed countries than more rapid trade liberalization on the part of the more advanced countries in the region. *Dr. Ferrer* noted that while integration proceeds largely through trade liberalization in more developed areas, there is also need for new, regionally oriented production projects as well as trade liberalization in less developed areas to take advantage of the economies of scale allowed by integration. *Dr. Márquez* agreed. *Dr. Ferrer* remarked that regionally integrated production makes the integration of capital markets most important, but to date regional financing needs had largely been ignored. *Professor Wallich* questioned the need for further development of regional capital markets. He observed, in discussing Central American arrangements, that industrial banks would suffice for financing purposes. He saw as a next step the possibility of a common tax, perhaps a customs surcharge, to raise funds for the industrial bank.

Dr. de Beers viewed financial integration as a means for handling multinational projects. While such projects are not necessarily good, he felt that such projects tend to be ignored. *Professor Singer* said there were reasons for this. He thought that multinational projects should be subject to the conventional cost benefit analysis. Since there are usually extra costs involved in such projects, it is necessary to show that they are clearly better than national projects. *Dr. Ferrer* felt that national projects may be more relevant for integration purposes than multinational projects if they serve demand in other countries.

Dr. Faaland asked how beneficial regional integration really was. While financial integration may benefit Latin America, he did not see that financial integration in French Africa had been beneficial because the financial arrangements discriminated against other African countries. Whether financial integration is beneficial or not should be judged by its external effects.

III. PROBLEMS OF FINANCIAL INTEGRATION

Several major conclusions were reached in the discussion of problems of financial integration. The first was that an economic motive stronger than goodwill was necessary for integration to work. *Professor Brown* noted, for instance, that Dr. Márquez's case for countries obtaining foreign financing for investments in a third country if they agree that the third country is the best location for the particular investment is unrealistic. The Marshall Plan is instructive on this point in that it teaches that some sort of bribe is necessary to achieve a co-ordinated plan of investment. *Professor Singer* added that if a programme or multiproject approach is employed, it is much easier to reach agreement on location of new industry. *Dr. Faaland* agreed that some sort of economic inducement of the Marshall-Plan type is needed for integration to succeed. He noted that the Marshall Plan's success was aided by similarities in the levels of development of the European countries and by the obvious need for common reforms. While it is best to have clear economic advantage for each country in regional arrangements, failing this, other common interests and feelings of political solidarity may benefit regional plans.

Several others also mentioned the need for external assistance — as extended in the Marshall Plan — to attain financial integration. In addition, *Dr. Kamarck* drew attention to the need for additional economists. Otherwise, there are too few economists available to work on regional plans. He saw the success of financial integration in French West Africa, for example, to stem from French aid and administrators. *Professor Mundell* disagreed. He felt that the use of foreign advisors has been overdone. Also, if the developing countries must depend upon foreign planners, then shortcomings and mistakes in the plans will always be blamed on foreign planners. This defeats the purpose of imposing self-discipline and other virtues necessary for regional economic development.

A second conclusion reached in the discussion was that different levels of development and different rates of inflation in the same region are likely to inhibit integration. *Dr. Marshall* stated that in Latin America different rates of inflation tend to limit integration. *Professor Borts* wondered whether it might be necessary in Latin America to impose currency restrictions to avoid capital flight. *Dr. Márquez* felt that the problem of capital flight is in fact a major problem in the integration process, but noted that integration should be started only after stability is first established. The process of financial integration involves the opening of capital markets in the more advanced countries of the region to the less advanced countries, rather than the use of exchange controls to prevent outflow of capital from the less developed countries within the region. *Dr. de Beers* also saw the danger of capital flight with currency unions, and in addition pointed out that stability is a necessary but not a sufficient condition for integration. Proper exchange rate valuation is also needed.

Dr. Faaland observed that regional integration was easier in Europe than in Latin America and other areas because the level of development of the different countries was more equal. *Dr. Márquez* replied that this is more valid with regard to trade liberalization and investment than with regard to financing. It is less difficult to initiate financial integration than commercial integration among countries with unequal levels of development. The Central American countries, for example, are integrated commercially and trade freely among themselves despite differences in levels of development.

Dr. Onitiri felt that there were basically three problems in the integration process : (1) general economic problems, such as the lack of foreign exchange, which lead to differences in monetary policies ; (2) the divisive effects of competition among power blocs, seen in the break-up of Africa into French and British spheres of influence after the independence movements ; and (3) the pressure in new countries to establish their own monetary and planning institutions. This last follows from a desire to enjoy new freedom and the failure to realize its limitations in the area of monetary policies. To overcome these problems, Dr. Onitiri called for an integration fund to ease the process of integration and — in the case of Africa — urged that Britain and the Common Market countries avoid rivalry in their relations with African nations. *Professor Mundell* commented that Latin American countries already have experienced the joys and problems of monetary freedom. Perhaps the time has come when loss of this aspect of sovereignty might be to their benefit.

INDEX

Entries in the Index in Black Type under the Names of Participants in the Conference indicate their Papers or Discussions of
their Papers. Entries in Italics indicate Contributions by Participants to the Discussions

PRINTED BY R. & R. CLARK, LTD., EDINBURGH